Praise for Joe Nick Patoski's

The Dallas Cowboys

"It's hard to match the thoroughness of the account presented by Mr. Patoski.... *The Dallas Cowboys* adroitly traces the ascendancy of the team while shedding light on its unique position today as an athletic, commercial, and cultural powerhouse."
—Charles Dameron, *Wall Street Journal*

"That the book is a feast for Cowboys fans should come as no surprise—every big game from the famous 'Ice Bowl' with the Green Bay Packers in 1967 to the Super Bowl triumphs of the 1990s are recounted in loving detail. The surprise, perhaps, is how invigorating a read it is for those—such as myself—who usually root for the team not wearing a blue star on their silver helmets.... *The Dallas Cowboys* stands as the definitive biography of a city and a football team."
—Allen Barra, *Dallas Morning News*

"Patoski's a natural storyteller. This book couldn't have been written by anyone else."   —Michael Corcoran, *Austin American-Statesman*

"Thoughtful and well researched."
—Christopher Kelly, *New York Times*

"Patoski's in-depth study gives readers everything they want to know about 'The Boys' and much more, from the field to the front office, the media, and, of course, the famous Dallas Cowboys Cheerleaders. The author also tracks the parallel development of the city of Dallas, with a focus on business and politics.... A fittingly exhaustive history of a larger-than-life franchise."   —*Kirkus Reviews*

"Monumental."   —Steve Bennett, *San Antonio Express-News*

"Those looking for just the football facts have to wash them down with a lot of civic history along the way, and the book is better for it. Patoski must be fascinated by the Cowboys to have devoted himself to this herculean task. Luckily for those fans whose curiosity extends beyond the sidelines, he's also taken with the complicated region that the team calls home."

— John Williams, *New York Times Book Review*

"If you like football, and particularly the Cowboys, you'll be hard-pressed to find a better storyteller than Patoski."

— Glenn Dromgoole, *San Angelo Standard-Times*

"If you think you know the remarkable story of Dallas and its pro football team, think again. Joe Nick Patoski's extraordinary book adds greatly to the colorful history of Big D and America's Team. Whether recalling stories on the field or off, he's at the top of his game with *The Dallas Cowboys*."

— Carlton Stowers, author of *Dallas Cowboys:*
The First 25 Years and *Staubach: Portrait*
of the Brightest Star

"Immense.... Patoski provides a comprehensive record of everything to do with the iconic franchise of America's Team."

— John Maxymuk, *Library Journal*

"Love 'em or hate 'em, the wild, woolly and sometimes scandalous story of the Dallas Cowboys explains the explosion and evolution of professional sports into the multiplatform entertainment and merchandise phenomenon it is today. Patoski's clear-eyed outsider's perspective provides context to the America's Team mythology whose roots predate the JFK years of Camelot."

— Hector Saldaña, *San Antonio Express-News*

THE DALLAS COWBOYS

ALSO BY JOE NICK PATOSKI

Willie Nelson: An Epic Life
Selena: Como la Flor
Stevie Ray Vaughan: Caught in the Crossfire
(coauthor Bill Crawford)

THE DALLAS COWBOYS

THE OUTRAGEOUS HISTORY OF THE BIGGEST, LOUDEST, MOST HATED, BEST LOVED FOOTBALL TEAM IN AMERICA

JOE NICK PATOSKI

BACK BAY BOOKS
LITTLE, BROWN AND COMPANY
New York   Boston   London

To all the good people of Dallas and Texas,
and to football fans everywhere

Back Bay Books / Little, Brown and Company
Hachette Book Group
237 Park Avenue, New York, NY 10017
littlebrown.com

Originally published in hardcover by Little, Brown and Company, October 2012
First Back Bay paperback edition, September 2013

Back Bay Books is an imprint of Little, Brown and Company, a division of Hachette Book Group, Inc. The Back Bay Books name and logo are trademarks of Hachette Book Group, Inc.

The publisher is not responsible for websites (or their content) that are not owned by the publisher.

The Hachette Speakers Bureau provides a wide range of authors for speaking events. To find out more, go to hachettespeakersbureau.com or call (866) 376-6591.

Library of Congress Cataloging-in-Publication Data
Patoski, Joe Nick.
 The Dallas Cowboys : the outrageous history of the biggest, loudest, most hated, best loved football team in America / Joe Nick Patoski.
  p. cm.
 ISBN 978-0-316-07755-2 (hc) / 978-0-316-07754-5 (pb)
 1. Dallas Cowboys (Football team)—History. I. Title.
 GV956.D3P35 2012
 796.332'64097642812—dc23   2012019443

10 9 8 7 6 5 4 3 2 1

RRD-C

Printed in the United States of America

Contents

Contents

THE DALLAS
COWBOYS

Introduction

Everything's Bigger in Texas

OURS IS BIGGER screamed the message across the front of the navy-blue-and-gray T-shirts draped on mannequins at the entrance of the Cowboys pro shop. The fifteen-thousand-square-foot bazaar was neither souvenir stand nor gift store exactly but another element of what was becoming known as the Cowboys Experience — as was the newest, most modern football stadium in the entire universe. In Cowboys tradition, the shop set new standards for swag, extending the brand to a logo-adorned tailgating rig with an official Dallas Cowboys grill and official Dallas Cowboys charcoal briquettes and official Dallas Cowboys barbecue sauce.

Two sections over, two babes in designer jeans and matching caps with matching blond ponytails stylishly bobbing out the backs admired pink designer tops and thongs with the Cowboys star attached. The Dallas Cowboys logo adorned sleeping bags, soft monkeys, draft-day caps, stadium shot glasses, hitch covers for trailer hitches, a five-foot-high inflatable helmet, and miniature cheerleader uniforms. Premium items, such as framed photographs of Aikman or Irvin or Smith in action, fetched $99 each, while $299 bought an old-timer a Don Meredith–autographed helmet. A jersey signed by current QB Tony Romo was priced at $1,199.

The pro shop was but one segment of the spanking-new Cowboys Stadium, where everything was bigger, better, and state-of-the-art,

3

which explained why thousands of visitors were paying sixteen dollars and up to peep at a building still under construction.

The giant dome sat, bloated and squat like a chrome Transformer bulldog, in the middle of a 140-acre asphalt field, a long spit from the part of Interstate Highway 30 that's identified by green signs bearing the profile of a fedora as the Tom Landry Highway. The guys on the Ticket, a sports-talk radio station, referred to the stadium as the Death Star, citing how it dwarfed all other neighborhood landmarks, including the Texas Rangers baseball stadium; the thrill rides and roller coasters at Six Flags Over Texas; the high-rise chain hotel, slides, and tubes of the Six Flags Hurricane Harbor water park; a slew of chain restaurants and bars; and a fairly humongous Walmart.

"Look what Jerry did," said the sprightly blond tour guide with the little Cowboys star painted on her right cheekbone. She pointed toward the east from the end-zone standing-room section. "See?" She beckoned to the thirty fans in her tour group. Straight ahead was Rangers Ballpark, home of the Texas Rangers major-league baseball club. Off to the left in the distance was the white dome of Texas Stadium, the former home of the Dallas Cowboys, months away from its date with a demolition crew. Off to the right in the far distance loomed the gleaming skyline of downtown Dallas.

Jerry planned it like that, the guide said. He wanted fans who bought party passes, the twenty-nine-dollar standing-room-only tickets with access to the open end-zone areas, to have that sweeping panorama. The guide went on to demonstrate how much Jerry cared, pointing out that the television, radio, and press midlevel seating areas were close to the goal lines. Prime 50-yard viewing was reserved for the fans—the people—or at least those people who had the wherewithal to pay hundreds of thousands of dollars to lease private skyboxes, game tickets extra. Getting a box would be a popular write-off for any of the twenty-three Fortune 500 companies clustered around Dallas and Fort Worth and the airport in between, a real middle-management-employee pleaser.

The outstanding attribute of Cowboys Stadium was size: sixteen hundred toilets, three thousand flat-screen televisions, and 100,000-spectator capacity. Its centerpiece, the Mitsubishi Diamond Vision four-sided LED video display hanging above the field, was the world's biggest scoreboard: a pair of high-definition video screens seventy-three feet tall and a hundred and sixty feet long that hovered almost a hundred feet above the ground from 20-yard line to 20-yard line (most of the field) and two smaller screens, one facing each end zone. Each large screen was the equivalent of two thousand fifty-two-inch televisions. The translucent cover above the video screen and the field was the fastest retractable roof in the business; it could close in twelve minutes, enabling eleven thousand tons of air-conditioning to kick in and keep fans in 72-degree comfort no matter how blazing hot the outside temperature was. The three hundred private suites, leased for $175,000 a year and up, were the most luxurious ever built.

The Statue of Liberty could fit inside Cowboys Stadium standing up. Laid down on its side, the Empire State Building could too. The two 1,292-foot-long curved steel arches that bore the weight of the building and the roof, eliminating the need for support columns, were each bigger than the Gateway Arch in St. Louis, creating the world's largest column-free room, 104 million cubic feet. The slanted glass exterior walls on both ends made the venue glow warmly at night.

Cowboys wide receiver Roy Williams declared the facility "the greatest thing on Earth" before he'd even run a skinny post on the field. It made the retired Cowboys Hall of Famer Drew Pearson wistful. "I wish I could turn the clock back a little bit, lace up the cleats and strap on the hat," he said when he first saw the stadium.

Football was merely one of the amusements that Cowboys owner Jerry Jones envisioned for the facility. Rock legends, the king of country music, basketball, and soccer were all fair game to sell out the house and generate the kind of gross and net receipts that could lead a promoter to early retirement. No Final Four, no tournament, no world championship, including the Super Bowl, was too big for this stadium's glass-concrete-and-steel britches.

A fairly broad mix of entertainment and sporting events during August and early September of 2009 introduced the stadium to the public. But the concerts by George Strait, the Jonas Brothers, and Paul McCartney; the international soccer matches (one of which set an all-time attendance record for the sport in the state of Texas); the college and high school football games; even a Cowboys preseason exhibition game were all merely dry runs.

The exhibition against the Tennessee Titans stirred up the stadium's first controversy by revealing one glaring flaw. The forty-million-dollar high-def scoreboard, which was unofficially dubbed the JerryTron, extended to below a hundred feet over the field, low enough for Tennessee's punters to hit the bottom of the screen during warm-ups, pissing off stadium officials with each kick. Then, in the third quarter of the game, A. J. Trapasso, the second-string Titan punter, booted one from his own 37-yard line that was high enough to bounce off the metal grating of one of the end-zone boards and deflect the ball backward (in the replays, the ball looks like it is entering a Star Wars mother ship). Tennessee coach Jeff Fisher threw his red challenge flag to point out the interference to game officials, who declared the punt a dead ball.

Fox network announcer Joe Buck observed, "Good thing [Trapasso] wasn't a Cowboy." The remark gained gravity after the game when Dallas Cowboys owner, president, and general manager Jerry Jones (the Jerry behind JerryWorld, as the stadium was becoming known), was asked about the kick. He didn't think his JerryTron was too low. He thought the Titans' kickers were trying to hit it.

"That's not the point. How high is high if somebody just wants to sit there and kick straight up?" he snapped during a postgame press conference. "If you look at how you punt the football, unless you're trying to hit the scoreboard, you punt the ball to get downfield. You certainly want to get some hang time, but you punt the ball to get downfield, and you sure don't punt the ball down the middle. You punt it off to the side."

He knew what he was talking about. Jones took pride in being the only National Football League franchise owner who'd excelled as a player on the college level.

Punter Trapasso admitted to aiming for the board and nailing it three times before the game but claimed he'd tried to avoid it during the game. "We were peppering that thing during warm-ups," he said. "Mind you, they're good kicks that are going up there and hitting it. It's nothing that is going to happen every time, but it's got to be addressed. I don't know how much further up it can go, but it's in the way."

The Titans' regular punter, Craig Hentrich, agreed. "I hit it probably a dozen times in pregame. Probably somewhere around a five-second punt is going to hit it and some of the guys in the league wouldn't be able to punt here if it's not raised, they'd just be nonstop hitting it. I don't know what the people were thinking. I guess they should have tested things out before they put that thing in place."

The JerryTron was so massive, the Fox TV announcers admitted to being distracted from the field of play—a common reaction, judging from camera shots of Titans QB Kerry Collins, Coach Jeff Fisher, and other players glancing skyward.

The screen marked the triumph of televised sports. The video of the event out-wowed the event in real time—and at the event.

For years, rock concerts in large venues had utilized huge video screens to satisfy fans in the nosebleed seats, far from the stage. With the JerryTron, which *Fort Worth Star-Telegram* sportswriter Randy Galloway immediately inflated into the JumboJerryTron, spectator-sports events could apply the technology to achieve the same effect. As Ed Fiducia, a Dallas salesman, marveled, "You feel like you're at home watching the big screen when you're at the game. It's brilliant."

A network camera caught Jerry standing alone in his private suite during the game, a diagonal shadow crossing his face, one side of it bathed in warm light, the other in a dusky shadow, which drew attention to his watery, surgically enhanced almond-shaped eyes. For a brief moment, he appeared beatific, almost angelic.

So it went for the man behind the Show Palace of America's Team, or whatever the stadium would come to be known as. There was plenty of hype and anticipation, little of it spontaneous and much of it magnified by the local mass media, whom the Cowboys ruled. No other subject generated as many column inches in the *Dallas Morning News* and the *Fort Worth Star-Telegram* or hogged as much airtime on the six television stations with local news programming.

Some aspects of the stadium deserved criticism, such as the acoustics that amplified echoes to the point that "fans needed a decoder to interpret the most basic messages," wrote the *Morning News*'s Tim Cowlishaw.

But acoustics were not the issue. What mattered was Ours Is Bigger.

Ever since there was a Texas, going back to 1836, Texans have enjoyed expressing their zeal for bigness. The pride was rooted in Texas's once-upon-a-time status as the largest state in the Union and in the astounding amount of wealth that the discovery of oil brought to some of its people. Then Alaska was admitted to the United States, in 1959, a year before the Dallas Cowboys came into being, relegating Texas to number two. That was about the same time that Texas's dominance as the world's greatest oil producer began to wane, the state giving way to Saudi Arabia, Iran, Iraq, and the whole Middle East as oil's newest and biggest play. But those technicalities didn't stop Texas or Texans.

One of the sincerest forms of expressing large love was through the game of football, a team sport that has been the national pastime in Texas since the early twentieth century. For all the ways its various parts were refined and finessed, the game was built on brute strength, physical power, and strategy — as close to war as most folks could get (or cared to get, at least), a grudge-settler and rivalry decider. The

Dallas Cowboys, the home state's professional team of choice, were the pinnacle of Texas's infatuation with football, the one true thing that brought together fat cats and yardmen, painters and politicians.

It took one big sumbitch to build this stunning pleasure dome. And Jerry Jones was the sumbitch to do it. After playing football, he'd proven to be exceptionally gifted when it came to buying and selling oil and gas leases in his native Arkansas, Texas's poorer hill-billy relative to the northeast. Energy ownership, a gambler's instinct, and a surplus of good luck blessed him with enough money to buy the Dallas Cowboys in 1989 and then proceed to fire the only coach the Cowboys ever had, something that a significant number of long-time Cowboy fans had not forgiven him for. But now this outra-geous, over-the-top building was making everyone forget the fallow post–Super Bowl era of the Cowboys, one marked by too few wins, too many dramas, and too much meddling from the owner.

For a brief period that autumn of 2009 when the stadium opened, all was forgiven and forgotten, for Jones had championed one last hurrah of the Texas brag with something that was the largest and grandest. Jones had become enough of a Texan as the Cowboys owner to know the other part of the Texas brag equation: it ain't bragging if it's true.

Cowboys Stadium (aka JerryWorld; aka the Death Star) was all about superlatives — a $1.2 billion jewel, constructed with the help of the good citizens of Arlington, who kicked in $325 million, and the spectators paying from $2,000 to $1 million for licenses to dib seats that were each priced from $59 to $340 per game. With standing-room-only tickets going for $29, a $60 fee for a tailgating space, $75 for a close-in parking space, $10 for popcorn, $12 for Cowboyritas, and $40 for a pizza, the revenue streams flowed.

Jones compared the look of the stadium's exterior to "a really con-temporary cell phone," then to a tractor. "As beautiful and as proud of it as I am, it's a tool to entertain a lot of people," he said.

Dallas had long ago shed its stereotype of being an oil baron's playground full of women with fake boobs and cotton-candy hair, a city that was once the divorce capital of the world. Twenty-first-century Dallas was a gay hotbed, according to *Time* magazine. Its officeholders included the country's only big-city African American district attorney, a gay county judge, and a lesbian Latina sheriff.

Dallas had the largest rail construction program in the country (DART), with several new lines joining the existing lines, including a genuine subway that would eventually connect Fair Park, an area with the largest collection of art deco exhibition buildings in the world, with Dallas–Fort Worth International Airport, one of the world's busiest. The Dallas Museum of Art, the Nasher Sculpture Center, the Meyerson Symphony Center, and the Crow Collection of Asian Art would soon be joined by four new buildings, including a theater and an opera hall, designed by Pritzker Prize–winning architects — a $300 million add-on.

The city could brag that it had the top high school in the United States, according to *Newsweek* magazine (the School of Science and Engineering Magnet), and that four other high schools in the Dallas Independent School District had made the top half of the magazine's list.

It was only fitting, then, that football's finest showcase was the home of the Dallas Cowboys.

"This to me is what football can be for the future," Jerry Jones proclaimed when Cowboys Stadium officially opened on September 20 with a game against the New York Giants. His image on national television was followed by a video roll call of the Seven Man-Made Wonders of the World, concluding with the Roman Colosseum before the shot dissolved into the new stadium with announcer Al Michaels's declaration, "What the Roman Colosseum was to the first century is what Cowboys Stadium is to the twenty-first century!" Former president of the United States and Dallas resident George W. Bush, wearing a coat and tie, conducted the coin toss midfield to start the game. Flames erupted from cannons on the field as a hundred-yard-long flag was unfurled for the national anthem. Randy White, Bob Lilly, Rayfield Wright, the Triplets (Aikman, Smith, and Irvin), Roger Staubach, and other legendary Cowboy players were on hand.

Paid attendance for the first official game was 105,121 — an all-time record for an NFL game in the United States. The arena's record is unlikely to be broken; Arlington officials complained that Jones sold close to thirty thousand party passes to access standing areas behind the end zones, prompting police to erect barricades and turn ticket holders away and inspiring some fans to chant curse words at Jones. Thirty-seven arrests were made, including thirty on suspicion of public intoxication; two for public intoxication and assault; and one each for public intoxication and marijuana, public intoxication and resisting arrest, and public intoxication and evading arrest. "There [were] beer bottles flying around and a lot of pushing and shoving," Arlington mayor Robert Cluck told the *Fort Worth Star-Telegram*. "I don't think we want to see a repeat of that."

The televised game attracted 24.8 million viewers and a 15.1 final national rating, the largest audience in the three-plus seasons of *Sunday Night Football* for the NBC network. Locally, NBC's *Sunday Night Football* telecast drew 1,700,608 Dallas-area viewers, while the Emmy Awards on CBS drew just 166,075 viewers, and ABC's showing of *King Kong* counted 86,359 pairs of eyeballs.

The Giants' Lawrence Tynes kicked a field goal as time ran out, earning the visitors a 33–31 victory. At that point, it had been thirteen years since the Cowboys had won a playoff game; the first home game played in their new house did not suggest that this status would change come December.

Jerry Jones may have built something even bigger than the football team he owned. But Jerry Jones couldn't be happy with that; he admitted a week later that he would love nothing more than to coach the team he owned. He wanted to be George Halas, the owner-coach of the Chicago Bears, a founder of the National Football League, and one of the key reasons the Dallas Cowboys even existed.

The prevailing sentiment was that by building the stadium, Jerry Jones had done something no one before him had. But somewhere on the other side, Clint W. Murchison Jr. was enjoying a hearty laugh. Poor Jones. All the hype, all the gripes, all the hoo-haw about this stadium was a rerun of what Clint experienced in 1971 when Texas Stadium opened as the home field of the Dallas Cowboys. Exactly what section of the other side Clint was on depended on whether his embrace of Christianity late in life had resolved the dilemma posed in Matthew 19:24: Was it easier for a camel to go through the eye of a needle than for a rich man to enter the Kingdom of God?

In other words, JerryWorld was hardly the first state-of-the-football-art stadium in that metropolitan area. Clint Murchison (pronounced "Murkison") built his palace expressly for football, designed the grandstands to be closer to the action than any comparable stadium's before it, incorporated luxury suites into it like no stadium before it, and protected the seating area with a roof so the game could be played in the elements while the spectators stayed dry.

That's where the similarities ended. Murchison was the one who created the mystique and prestige out of nothing. Jones just bought it.

To the old guard who remembered his backstory, Jones was still an uncouth, reptilian Arkie, no matter how fairylike his visage had been rendered. Until all the old farts were dead and gone, Jones's past would not be forgotten.

The team before Jones was a whole other organization, led by a brain trust that designed the blueprint upon which professional football franchises were subsequently built. Dallas too was very different then, an adolescent city just beginning to flex its muscles as a powerhouse.

This is the story of that team, those people, and the city that made them.

1841–1960

The Boy Who Loved Football

THE TWENTY-NINE-YEAR-OLD GENTLEMAN watching the football game at the Cotton Bowl, the storied stadium on the grounds of the State Fair of Texas, would have been called a nerd if the word had been in general use in 1952. His close-cropped hair was a modified crew cut, sensible if not particularly dashing. Above his bulbous nose and small mouth were black horn-rim glasses. He favored short-sleeved white shirts with ties, a realistic compromise between minimalist formality and the blazing extended summer heat that defined the climate of the North Central Texas prairie.

The one feature that didn't match the rest of his bookish appearance was his icy-blue, beady eyes. They radiated intelligence and dominance, although they didn't necessarily reveal the deep mind behind the face. He could have been an engineer at the new Texas Instruments company in Richardson, just over the Dallas line, a spin-off of an oil-industry and military electronics contractor that was hiring engineers from all over.

The man had been a Phi Beta Kappa at Duke University and was at the top of his class at the Massachusetts Institute of Technology, where he had indeed received his master's in mathematics. He did regard himself as the smartest man in the room or in the state, depending on the situation. But he was neither an engineer nor a TI rising star. He was one of the richest men on Earth. More significant,

13

he was a full-blown football nut, watching the Dallas Texans and the New York Giants do battle in the first official professional football game played in his hometown, and in its most storied stadium.

Clinton W. Murchison Jr. was a son of one of the Big Four of Texas oil. A storied wildcatter and the ultimate Texas wheeler-dealer, the elder Clint grew up in Athens, Texas, eighty miles east of Dallas, where he and his best friend, Sid Richardson, shared a fondness for cattle- and horse-trading as boys, a game of skill that was all about getting the better end of a deal.

The gift served the elder Murchison well as a wildcatter, lease hound, and driller capitalizing on some well-placed bets on where oil deposits were located under the surface of East Texas. His success led to an audacious construction project: the first major pipeline to transport oil from the East Texas field, the biggest oil discovery ever, to refineries. Despite the well-intentioned good breeding that went with being grandson of the founder of the Athens bank, there was a touch of outlaw in old Clint. The wealth created when some of his wells struck oil grew considerably larger when he ran what was called hot oil through that pipe during the Great Depression.

Throughout his life, the elder Murchison was constantly railing against state and federal regulation of private industry, especially the industries he was involved with. But Murchison also curried favor with powerful politicians, especially during and after World War II, when the oil reserves of the Big Four of Texas gave Allied forces a decided edge over both Germany and Japan. It wasn't a coincidence that President Franklin D. Roosevelt's hunting and fishing trip to Clint's very own Matagorda Island off the Texas coast in 1940 occurred around the same time that the government decided to maintain the 27½ percent tax deduction known as the oil depletion allowance, a tax break for oilmen created in 1926 that had been unprecedented in American business. It was old Clint's kind of government welfare.

—

CLINT SR. MOVED TO Dallas in 1928 because that's where the banks were and it was a good place to raise his sons, John Dabney, Clint Jr., and Burk Yarbrough. They had lost their mother, Anne, when Junior was only two. The boys slept in their father's bedroom on the farm they lived on that sprawled across several hundred acres of what is today prime North Dallas real estate and they were looked after by nannies.

Clint Murchison Jr. developed a love for football at an early age. The five-foot-seven, 130-pound teen was a fair halfback at the Lawrenceville School prep academy in New Jersey, a boarding school for the privileged that was not particularly noted for its football program. After graduating from Duke, joining the Marines in World War II, and marrying his Dallas sweetheart, Jane Coleman, Clint Jr. played club football at the Massachusetts Institute of Technology, where despite his small size, he earned a reputation for being someone who liked to hit.

In 1950, Clint Jr. and John Dabney joined their father in his unpretentious office at 1201 Main in downtown Dallas and began doing business as Murchison Brothers, an enterprise created by their father that included Murchison Brothers Oil, and they separately launched ventures such as Clint's Tecon Construction Company (pronounced "take on," as in "We'll take on any project"). They took their cues from the old man, who had diversified and expanded his holdings to satisfy the trader in his soul.

The Texas to which the Murchison boys had returned after college and military service was in dramatic transition; the rural population was moving to the city as prosperity ran rampant in business sectors far beyond oil. Trammell Crow was constructing and operating warehouses in a dozen states. Carr P. Collins and his sons made millions selling insurance. Texas Instruments chairman Erik Jonsson built up a multimillion-dollar fortune through electronics, while

Leo Corrigan used his acquisition of small shopping centers in Dallas to create a far-flung empire of office buildings, shopping malls, more than four thousand apartment units, the Emerald Beach Hotel in the Bahamas, the Biltmore Hotel in Los Angeles, the Hong Kong Hilton, and the Adolphus in Dallas.

The Murchison brothers built their own impressive portfolio: Centex Construction company; Tecon general construction; the company that made Daisy BB guns in Arkansas; housing projects and land development from coast to coast; the Royal Gorge Bridge in Colorado; a motel chain; a chain of drive-in movie theaters; Henry Holt publishers in New York; and an array of other entities.

The brothers embraced their father's method of finding good people to run operations and then stepping aside. They were about making deals and borrowing as much as bankers would bet on their deals, which was a lot. Tecon Construction, Clint Jr.'s baby, started up with little more than a bulldozer, a concrete mixer, and a load of cement and went on to tackle such massive projects as a sixty-million-dollar joint venture on a dam in Iraq, the Eisenhower Lock of the St. Lawrence Seaway, the Barkley Lock Project on the Cumberland River near Paducah, Kentucky, and the removal of a hill that was threatening to slide into the Panama Canal.

Not every venture panned out. John lost millions in a timber investment in the Pacific Northwest and in uranium mining. And early on, Clint and his business associate Robert Thompson bungled an opportunity when Clint Sr. gave them a new subdivision of affordable concrete homes in North Dallas and the directive to sell them to veterans returning from World War II. But the two ex-Marines were having too good a time chasing skirts and traveling around (thanks to Clint Jr.'s unlimited funds) and failed to sell a single home over the course of several months. So Clint Sr. handed the task to a woman who had once sold hats at Neiman-Marcus and now ran her own millinery shop. Ebby Halliday sold all of the homes, launching her career as the top residential real estate agent in Dallas. Clint's company Centex Homes expanded to build residential communities, apartments, military housing, office buildings, shopping centers, and industrial plants across Texas and throughout the United States.

Clint Jr. was a red ass, brusque and acerbic to one and all. "You have all the qualities of a dog except loyalty," he once informed a business competitor. He often walked past acquaintances without acknowledging them. "Why should I? I saw them yesterday," he said more than once. He was abrupt and curt on the telephone. Clint Jr. had no use for social niceties. His business was business. Friends attributed the harsh facade to his introverted shyness. His comportment also spoke to a greater truth: with his kind of wealth, Clint didn't have to make nice.

But there was one subject where Clint showed another side of his personality. Talk about the game of football, and he perked up. Like many Texans, he was completely hooked on the sport.

THE GAME WAS a good fit for Texans. From the time of its inception as a popular team sport, in the late nineteenth century, it had spoken to Texas's legacy as a republic that had won its independence from Mexico by fighting hard and using whatever means necessary, the rebels ultimately surprising the enemy during their traditional siesta and taking them in a rout. Thoroughly modern in its warlike representations, football appealed to a population of optimists, boosters, and true believers who considered themselves the chosen people, befitting their fresh arrival on a frontier only newly established. "Texas is a rough land, and Texans are a rough people," Texas high school football coach Sonny Detmer observed, and no other sport was as rough and physical as football.

By 1900, thousands of small towns had been established across the state, most lacking amusements and diversions but brimming with citizens hungry for something to get excited about. Football delivered. Since then, the two most popular sports in Texas have been football and spring football.

A team formed at Dallas High School in 1900 by George Sergeant and Marion F. Brinker was the first high school team in North Texas. The same Dallas team played through the 1901 season as North Dallas, and the high school version of the game grew quickly, becoming a state religion in the fall. For many smaller communities, especially, high school football was the biggest entertainment around.

College football was the Southwest Conference, which ultimately included the University of Texas Longhorns, the Texas A&M Aggies, the Texas Christian University Horned Frogs, the Baylor Bears, the Rice Owls, the Arkansas Razorbacks, the Texas Tech Red Raiders, and the hometown Southern Methodist University Mustangs.

SMU's trip to the Rose Bowl on New Year's Day 1936 sparked the beginning of three decades of football greatness at the local college, highlighted by running back Doak Walker, a product of Highland Park High, just down the street.

Walker's play earned him the Heisman Trophy in 1948 and attracted such huge crowds that for Walker's last year, Southern Methodist moved its home games from the 23,700-seat Ownby Stadium on campus to the Cotton Bowl at Fair Park, home of the postseason classic of the same name, where the SWC champion played a worthy national competitor on New Year's Day. The Cotton Bowl subsequently expanded capacity from 46,000 to 75,504 and became known as the House That Doak Built.

At the time, professional football didn't have much of a following in Dallas or elsewhere in Texas. Pro teams were clustered in the Northeast, the Midwest, and on the West Coast. The closest franchises—the Chicago Bears, the Chicago Cardinals, and the Washington Redskins—were more than eight hundred miles away.

The hugely popular high school and college versions of football were often cited as the two greatest obstacles to professional football's gaining a foothold in Texas. Sunday blue laws, which restricted commercial enterprise in deference to churches, didn't help. Good Christians were supposed to be home with their families after church, not sporting around.

Professional sporting events in Dallas were pretty much limited to golf with the standout players Byron Nelson and Mickey Wright; baseball with the minor-league Dallas Rangers; and rassling at the Sportatorium, a rickety, sheet-metal glorified gospel tent down in the Trinity River bottoms on Industrial Boulevard.

Dallas's growing population was primed for bigger sports entertainment to rally around, but pro football wasn't quite as much of a civic plum as a big-league baseball team. And compared to the Southwest Conference, the National Football League appeared rather pissant.

THE GAME OF PRO FOOTBALL, its roots extending back to 1895, when the Latrobe, Pennsylvania, team beat the Jeanette team 12–0, was a risky financial enterprise and, at best, a rich man's toy. Founded in Canton, Ohio, in 1920, the American Professional Football Association awarded franchises for $100 to the Canton Bull Dogs; the Cleveland Indians; the Dayton Triangles; the Akron Professionals; the Massillon Tigers; the Decatur Staleys; the Chicago Cardinals; and teams in Rochester, New York; Rock Island, Illinois; and Muncie and Hammond, Indiana. Two years later, the National Football League was born, and owner-coach George Halas of the Chicago Bears, the former Decatur Staleys, took his team on a seventeen-city tour. By 1933, the year the forward pass was legalized, franchises cost $10,000 each, and the championship game between the Bears and Giants took in a gate of $23,000.

A rival league called the All-America Football Conference popped up following the end of World War II, adding additional drag to the National Football League's efforts to make professional football more than a rich man's toy. The rival league was merged into the NFL in

1951, prompting the Boston Yanks to move to New York. One season later, though, Ted Collins, the owner of the Yanks franchise, now the New York Yankees, returned the franchise to the league after losing $1 million. Pro football fans in New York preferred the city's established team, in residence since 1925: the New York Giants.

Dallas radio-station owner and sports broadcaster Gordon McLendon first championed the idea of bringing professional football to Texas in 1951, believing that the professional version of Texas's favorite spectator sport was a viable concept despite the state's football-saturated Fridays and Saturdays. Bert Bell, the commissioner of the National Football League, wanted nothing to do with McLendon, whom he regarded as an outlaw.

Unlike most broadcasts of sporting events, McLendon's Liberty radio network's baseball games were called by way of delayed re-creations assembled using ticker-tape information provided by a Western Union operator, accompanied by sound effects to make the broadcasts more authentic. McLendon himself announced, greeting listeners in his booming baritone—"Hello, everybody, everywhere, this is the Old Scotchman from high atop the press box way up in the azure skies"—and he was so good at taking advantage of radio as theater of the mind that his re-creations on the Liberty network often attracted larger audiences than the actual real-time broadcasts of the same games.

"We would be about one batter behind the actual play," Wes Wise, McLendon's protégé (and Dallas's future mayor), explained years later. "The telegrapher was right here next to us, and he would give us a signal, okay, this is going to be a triple. And so then we'd hit that baseball bat [dangling from a cord] so it would sound like a triple. We'd hit the baseball bat harder if it was a triple, and harder still if it was a homerun. If it was a single it would just be click. When people began to find out that it was recreated, instead of resenting it, they liked it better."

The Old Scotchman's Game of the Day calls were so good, the

Liberty network grew to 458 affiliates at its peak; Major League Base-ball tried to shut down his broadcasts, which led to a flurry of lawsuits and countersuits and ultimately intimidated owners of all professional sports teams as well as the NFL's commissioner, Bert Bell.

MCLENDON MAY HAVE BEEN considered unworthy of a pro foot-ball franchise in the eyes of the National Football League com-missioner, but McLendon knew there were others with the wherewithal—namely, Giles Miller, a thirty-two-year-old Dallas millionaire who was an ardent fan of the Southern Methodist Mus-tangs. Miller, who also followed the University of Texas Longhorns in Austin and attended high school games weekly, had been promot-ing a new postseason college game in Houston called the Lone Star Bowl in 1951 when McLendon told him the New York Yanks were up for sale.

In January of 1952, Giles Miller and his brother Connell, sons of the founder of Texas Textile Mills, bought the team with the help of several oilmen; the head of the 7-Eleven convenience stores; the president of the Mercantile Bank; sundry relatives and associates; and J. Curtis Sanford, the founder and initial underwriter of the Cotton Bowl Classic. The Miller group paid $300,000 for the Yanks, a princely sum that was largely the assumption of a $200,000 eight-year lease at Yankee Stadium for the departed team. The relocated team was chartered as the Texas Rangers; by September, when they played their first National Football League game in the Cotton Bowl, they were the Dallas Texans.

The Texans games aired on Gordon McLendon's KLIF, but instead of the Old Scotchman doing the play-by-play, Jerry Doggett and Charlie Boland called the games.

The Dallas Texans roster included a local SMU grad named Jack Adkisson, who would later achieve notoriety as the professional wrestler Fritz Von Erich; two future Hall of Famers, defensive end

Gino Marchetti and defensive tackle Art Donovan; and two African American players: halfback Buddy Young, the five-foot-four onetime track star known as the Bronze Bullet and the Fastest Human in Pro Football, and halfback George Taliaferro, the first black player to be drafted by an NFL team.

Black fans had been turned off after an August preseason exhibition against the Detroit Lions at the Cotton Bowl because they weren't allowed to purchase the good seats, which sold for $3.60, only the $1.80 end-zone tickets. The roped-off colored seating area was overflowing, moving *Dallas Express* columnist C. H. Gentry to comment, "Someone has made a sad underestimation of the buying potential of the colored citizen relative to better seating capacity at sports events, and that they should be made to realize that black or white, the average fan wants the best seat available, regardless to prices." Attendance at the exhibition game was 34,035. Half as many turned out to see the first game that counted.

C. W. Murchison Jr. was among the 17,499 fans on hand on September 28 to witness the first official Dallas Texans game, a National Division match against the New York Giants. Clint had purchased twenty season tickets in advance. Texas governor Allen Shivers, also on hand, thought he had seen the future, declaring, "This is a new era in sports in Texas."

One of the few opportunities for the crowd to get worked up came when the Texans drew first blood: after Giants defensive back Tom Landry fumbled a punt return on the Giants 22-yard line, halfback George Taliaferro took a pitchout and threw a pass to Buddy Young for a touchdown. The Giants took control from there, emerging victorious, 24–6.

Clint Murchison Jr., along with a few thousand others, showed up for three more Texans games — all of which the home team lost. The enterprise that Giles Miller and his investment group funded was drowning in red ink. As attendance declined, Washington Redskins owner George P. Marshall dismissed the Texans' dire financial straits by quipping, "They'll just dig another oil well if they need more money."

But Giles Miller became desperate, and he proposed making the team civically owned, like the Green Bay Packers. He sent co-owner D. Harold Byrd to the all-powerful Dallas Citizens Council to ask for a loan of $250,000 so the Texans could finish the season. The Dallas Citizens Council rejected the request. Their financial support was for the Dallas Symphony, Fair Park, and fine art—entities that enriched Dallas—not for football. Rejected, Byrd told the others in the owners group, "It is time to call in the dogs, piss on the fire, and go home."

The Millers returned the franchise to the league in early November. The final two games on the original home schedule were played on the road, with the team practicing in Hershey, Pennsylvania. Its final game was at the Rubber Bowl in Akron, Ohio, where they beat the second-stringers of George Halas's Chicago Bears 27–23 on Thanksgiving Day, part of a Turkey Day doubleheader. Seeing the three thousand spectators there for the game, far fewer than the number who had watched the earlier game between local high school teams, Texans coach Jim Phelan told his players they should "go into the stands and shake hands with each fan" rather than be introduced by the PA announcer.

The Texans' failure could be blamed on Bert Bell's oversell on the joys of ownership, on Bell's failure to warn the Miller group about the hidden costs of operations, and on Bell's meddling in selecting front-office personnel. Texans management had no selling strategy, in spite of team publicity director Tex Maule, who had given up the same position with the Los Angeles Rams to come to Texas. And competition was brutal. The Cotton Bowl hosted high school games on Friday nights and sometimes Thursdays, and Saturday day and night games for SMU and other colleges. It wasn't just because of low turnout, but the season proved so demoralizing that almost half the team retired from pro football when it was over.

———

As THE DALLAS TEXANS were going down, disappointed season-ticket holder Clint Murchison approached the NFL commissioner, Bert Bell. It was Murchison's business to know what kind of deals were being done around Dallas, and he knew most of the owners in the syndicate well enough and had read Bill Rives in the *Dallas Morning News* closely enough to glean the team's financial situation. Murchison proposed to Bell that he buy the team, on the condition that his accountants had sufficient time to examine the team's books, due diligence and all.

Bell turned down Murchison. He'd already set it up for the defunct Texans to be sold to Carroll Rosenbloom, who would move the team to Baltimore and have them play as the Colts. Bell had been sued for breach of contract when he moved another franchise out of Baltimore two years before, and this move would render the lawsuit moot.

Bell carried a high opinion of himself and' may not have taken the twenty-nine-year-old Murchison seriously. Bell clearly didn't realize he was dealing with the smartest man in the room, as well as the richest, nor did he realize how badly Clint Murchison wanted a football team.

Clint Jr. sincerely believed a professional football franchise *could* be a wise investment, a classic low-buy, high-sell proposition. He showed his doubting father how much the value of franchises had increased since World War II and talked about the potential that television presented in broadening its appeal. Clint continued to sniff around the league and was a frequent visitor with Bert Bell and with George Halas, the Chicago Bears owner-coach who headed up the NFL's expansion committee—even though the committee's position was there would be no expansion. Bell advised Murchison he'd have a better chance buying an existing team and moving it.

Murchison later said, "I wanted the fun of being able to see professional football in my hometown." He approached the struggling San Francisco 49ers football club, one of two NFL franchises on the West Coast. He was told the team wasn't for sale. Bert Bell then persuaded him to talk with Violet Bidwell Wolfner and her husband, Walter, the owners of the Chicago Cardinals. But the Wolfners wouldn't go in more than half and half and wouldn't move the team from Chicago, even though the Cards consistently lagged behind their crosstown rival Bears in attendance.

Murchison came close when he turned his sights on the Washington Redskins. He knew DC well from frequent trips to lobby the federal government, and he had watched games at Griffith Stadium. The Redskins owner, George Preston Marshall, was in enough of a financial bind when Murchison came calling that he agreed to sell the team for $600,000 as long as he could continue to manage the franchise for five years. At the last minute, Marshall demanded that his management contract be extended to ten years. That was enough to throw cold water on the deal. Murchison never forgot, nor would he let Marshall forget. Soon enough, Bert Bell and George Preston Marshall would have their days of reckoning, and the immovable George Halas would be moved.

The Other Son of an Oil Baron
Who Loved Football

THERE MUST HAVE BEEN something about the game of pigskin that affected geeky sons of filthy rich oilmen who resided at latitude N 32°85', longitude W 96°85'. Blocks away from where Clint Murchison Jr.'s mind raced like a computer, bouncing from projects for his Centex Construction to land deals and oil-lease swaps to million-dollar bank loans and 100-yard-line fantasies, was Lamar Hunt.

It was no secret that many rich men wanted to buy NFL franchises, so many that in 1958, talk began to float around about developing a rival league. One of the disappointed suitors, the mild-mannered Hunt, was behind the talk, and it was no rumor.

Hunt was an even younger version of Clint Murchison, an affably meek young man with soft facial features and eyes that were framed by larger, darker horn-rim glasses than Murchison's. He too had excelled playing football at prep school, quarterbacking the squad at the Hill School in Pottstown, Pennsylvania, and suiting up at Southern Methodist University as an offensive end, although rarely playing.

If Clint Murchison Sr. was a character, Lamar Hunt's daddy was flat-out gonzo.

Haroldson Lafayette Hunt had been an Arkansas gambler, bookie, and professional poker player known as Arizona Slim who would bet

26

on two guys throwing a stick, as someone who knew him once said. That was before he started betting on plots of ground that might contain oil below the surface. His guesswork, gambles, and hunches paid off in spades and H. L. Hunt became the biggest of the Big Four of Texas oil. His biggest win came from besting Columbus Marion "Dad" Joiner, a seventy-year-old geologist and pioneer oilman whose well on Daisy Bradford's farm in Rusk County had begun producing three hundred barrels of oil a day after four years of failed attempts. The two men holed up in suite 1553 in the Baker Hotel in downtown Dallas for thirty-six hours, deep in negotiations. No one, other than the two parties, knows exactly what went on, but at the end, a deal was struck. Joiner would escape the considerable debt that had built up in his speculative venture, avoid lawsuits for overselling shares of his leases, and walk away with $1.25 million. Hunt got the well, the Daisy Bradford No. 3, and four hundred acres, making several hundred million dollars by pulling oil out of the ground. A month after he bought Joiner's leases, Hunt built his first pipeline, and his wealth increased exponentially until it was one of the largest fortunes in the world.

H. L. Hunt, pale-faced with prominent jowls and a white tuft of hair on top of his head, moved to Dallas after striking it rich and lived in a replica of George Washington's Mount Vernon on White Rock Lake in Dallas, where the Stars and Stripes flew day and night. He was a religious man who neither smoked nor drank. He brought his own sack lunch to work and liked to exercise by crawling around his office on his hands and knees—a key to a long life, he believed. His charm, persuasive power, and ability to bullshit afforded him the luxury of setting up three separate families, all of them unknown to one another.

In the April 5, 1948, issue of *Life* magazine, Hunt appeared on the cover along with a headline that asked "Is This the Richest Man in Dallas?" That same month, *Fortune* magazine reckoned Hunt was the richest individual in the United States.

H. L. Hunt eschewed civic organizations and was not one for philanthropy or high society despite the prominence his money brought. He fancied himself a writer and published a science fiction book titled *Alpaca*, about a futuristic society where citizens were given votes according to their wealth. He also composed a song titled "We're Just Plain Folks." Hunt quietly underwrote the Facts Forum, a foundation that published political tracts and books written by Senator Joseph McCarthy and that evolved into the Life Line foundation, which produced a daily fifteen-minute radio program carried by more than four hundred radio stations across the United States. Mixing right-wing ultraconservative politics with Christian fundamentalism, the program featured spiritual hymns and diatribes against communists, socialists, liberals, the Fourteenth Amendment to the U.S. Constitution, and big government. Hunt owned a food company, HLH, and personally handed out food samples at the State Fair of Texas every October.

Lamar, the youngest of H. L. Hunt's four sons from his first family, with Lyda Bunker, wanted nothing so much as to be an athlete. Perhaps it was in his genes, because his father had once tried out for a professional baseball team. After college, Lamar used his business clout to feed his passion for competition. He looked like Clark Kent, but his ambitions were more like Superman's with the same gambler's instinct as Arizona Slim.

Like Clint Murchison Jr., Lamar Hunt was a chip off the old block only to a point, a little more buttoned-down and a little less wheeler-dealer than his daddy, perhaps, but eschewing the pomp and refined preening of many of his second-generation big oil peers. Like Clint, Lamar saw potential in the entertainment value of professional football and tried to buy in early. In 1958, he approached the National Football League commissioner, Bert Bell, about buying an expansion franchise, but he, like Clint, was urged to buy an existing franchise, such as the Chicago Cardinals, instead.

Hunt made the obligatory run at Violet and Walter Wolfner but once again they didn't budge. Hunt could have 20 percent, tops. Young Lamar graciously bowed out and started reviewing who else had been to Chicago. Clint Murchison Jr., whom Hunt knew of but did not know, had made a bid. So had fellow Texan K. S. "Bud" Adams of the Ada Oil Company in Houston. There were several people of means who wanted to be football owners: Barron Hilton of Los Angeles and the Hilton Hotels chain; minor-league baseball owner Bob Howsam in Denver; William Sullivan of Metropolitan Coal and Oil in Boston; Max Winter, a Minneapolis restaurateur who owned a piece of the Minneapolis Lakers of the National Basketball Association; and sports broadcaster Harry Wismer of New York, who'd once owned a piece of the Washington Redskins and the Detroit Lions.

National Football League teams rarely filled stadiums, and exposure on television was limited since each team cut its own broadcast deal. Its audience was nowhere near the size of baseball's, and college and high school games still dominated fan interest. But Hunt and the other suitors saw potential, especially in Texas, and in early June of 1959, Lamar Hunt paid a visit to Bert Bell to ask again about expansion. Bell reaffirmed what George Halas had been saying. Expansion was off the table. If Hunt wanted in, he should buy an existing team.

Hunt then asked Bell another question: Would he consider being commissioner of both the NFL and the new league Hunt was thinking about starting? ("I told myself I didn't want to go into this if it meant some kind of battle," Hunt later said. "This was one of the more naive thoughts in the history of pro sports.") Bell appeared startled before he demurred, but he gave Hunt his blessing to pursue his new league. In fact, he asked Hunt if it would be all right if Bell revealed plans for the new league when he testified in front of the U.S. Congress on July 29.

Bell's testimony worked in his favor; it gave the impression that Lamar Hunt's league was under the auspices of the National Football

League, which would provide the NFL with immunity in case the rival league went out of business and antitrust charges came up. Lamar Hunt didn't care. By Bert Bell's saying so, "we were in business," he reasoned.

But by Bell's saying so, the previously intransigent George Halas and the NFL expansion committee suddenly had a change of heart. The league would expand after all, Halas announced in August, standing alongside Pittsburgh Steelers owner Art Rooney at the commissioner's behest. The committee recommended that two new franchises be awarded to Dallas and Houston to compete in the 1961 season, although other cities were under consideration. And the owner of the Dallas franchise would be Clint Murchison Jr. Murchison's persistence and known interest to Halas would finally be rewarded while at the same time conveniently providing the start-up league some direct competition.

Lamar Hunt did not mince words when he heard the announcement. "The American Football League has tried from its inception to operate its relationship with the National Football League from the highest plane and with an amicable attitude on all matters," he said. "It is now apparent that Mr. Halas and the National Football League are not interested in this type of relationship but are interested in continuing the stalling and sabotaging efforts which have kept pro football out of Denver, Seattle, Minneapolis, Louisville, Buffalo, Dallas, Houston, and Miami despite repeated efforts from those cities to expand the National Football League."

After Commissioner Bell died suddenly of a heart attack in October, Halas met with Murchison to convey the league's support for a Dallas franchise to play in 1960, although the owners would have to approve the move at their annual meeting in January.

Neighbors and rivals, two of the richest men in the world living in the same part of the same city, both football hounds — only in Dallas. Pro football was coming to town.

The Great Dallas Football Pissing Match

THE FIRST HARD EVIDENCE that Clint Murchison was actually getting a National Football League team came on November 24, 1959. The loquacious Bedford Wynne, the well-connected socialite, political fund-raiser, and high-profile college football booster who was Murchison's minority partner and the face of the franchise, had called a press conference. Though few knew much about Murchison, everyone knew Bedford, and Bedford couldn't wait to get the radio, television, and newspaper reporters together and tell them the news.

There was going to be a team, and the team had a name—the Rangers, thought up by Murchison, who said it had come to him "like a bolt from the blue." Rangers were "historical, proud, tough. My grandfather, who was one [a law enforcement Texas Ranger, that is], would have loved it." It was also the name of the American Association AAA baseball team playing down on the river bottom in dilapidated old Burnett Field; up until that point, they had been the biggest professional sports team representing the city.

And there was a man hired to run it all. Tex Schramm was introduced as the general manager of the Dallas Rangers football club, contingent on the approval of the National Football League owners.

The cherubic big-boned Schramm could have passed for a native son of the state, and not just because his name was Tex. Outgoing and effusive, backslapping and loud, he gave the impression of being a classic good ol' boy, a born salesman with a confidence-winning smile.

The small gaggle of reporters had been informed that the designated general manager would be keeping his day job as second in command at CBS Sports until February in order to oversee the broadcast of the 1960 Winter Olympics in Squaw Valley, California, a personal project that Murchison's new hire had championed over the objections of just about every other executive at the television network. For the first time, an Olympics would air on TV.

His name attached to the title of general manager at the press conference sounded sweet to the ears of Texas Earnest Schramm Jr. He was a football man to the core. His colleagues and friends would've sworn that he had been put on this earth to create the ideal National Football League franchise. He was one of those rare birds who were all about bigger and better, and he had the ability to promote any idea that popped into his head, convincing everyone within range what a great idea it was.

Tex Schramm had grown up in San Gabriel, California, born to parents with obvious Texas roots. His daddy, Texas Sr., had been a basketball player at the University of Texas. His job at a Los Angeles stock brokerage provided the means for his offspring, an irrepressible bundle of energy who was always thinking, always animated, always on the move, to pursue his own interests, which were mainly sports.

As a boy, young Tex, or Tec, as he was known around the house, did poorly at school as far as grades were concerned. But he was a popular boy. He sold more tickets to the school play in elementary school and to a puppet show in high school than had ever been sold at the schools before. In high school, he organized an elementary school all-star football game between rivals Alhambra and San

Gabriel. A B-team high school football player, he raised money for letter sweaters from local merchants, then became manager of the track team and sports editor of the Alhambra High School newspaper, the *Moor*. While attending junior college, he worked as an usher at the Santa Anita racetrack, where he developed skills betting on the ponies. He then enrolled at the University of Texas, where he joined the Phi Kappa Psi fraternity (one of his frat brothers was Bedford Wynne), wrote for the *Daily Texan*, and eventually earned his degree in journalism after serving as one of the youngest captains ever in the U.S. Army Air Forces during World War II. There, he refined his skills in running organizations and learned to surf with a longboard while stationed in Hawaii. After the war, Big Mama, as his young wife, Marty, the former Martha Anne Snowden, was known, read his required books so she could help him graduate.

The summer before graduation, Schramm interned at the sports department of the *Los Angeles Times* and impressed the staff with his personality and hustle. After Schramm graduated from college, *Austin Statesman* sports editor Wilbur Evans, who'd taught Tex at UT, hired him as a thirty-five-dollar-a-week reporter. Schramm was covering the Kansas Relays, one of the most popular spectator sporting events in the Midwest, when he got a telephone call asking if he would be interested in becoming the publicist for the Los Angeles Rams, a professional football club in the National Football League that had recently relocated from Cleveland. The *Los Angeles Times*' Paul Zimmerman had recommended Schramm to Rams majority owner Dan Reeves after getting to know Schramm over his summer breaks from UT. Schramm jumped at the hundred-dollar-a-week position. The Rams were drawing large crowds, including Hollywood movie stars, to the Los Angeles Coliseum, in part because football was the only major-league sport in town. But the Los Angeles Dons, of the upstart All-America Football Conference, which was competing against the National Football League, were drawing even bigger crowds.

Alhambra High School graduate Texas Schramm was announced as the new head of publicity for the Los Angeles Rams on April 24, 1947. He was determined to outpromote the competition. To win the hearts of the LA fans, Schramm cranked out five customized stories a day, full of florid copy for sportswriters at the newspapers in the city. More often than not, what Schramm wrote was printed verbatim with the sportswriter's byline.

The aggressive promotion contributed to the folding of the Dons and the All-America Football Conference at the end of the 1949 season, and the Rams kept on innovating.

They distinguished themselves as the first club to utilize a scouting system to evaluate college prospects; the first to hire a full-time scout, Eddie Kotal; and the first pro team to allow Negroes to play with whites, beginning with Kenny Washington in 1946. And in 1950, the Rams and the Washington Redskins became the first pro football teams to broadcast all their home and away games on television, the new entertainment medium that threatened to render radio and movies obsolete.

The Rams registered a precipitous drop in attendance when their home games were televised. Schramm, who was moving up in the front-office ranks to become majority owner Dan Reeves's right-hand man, anticipated the impact and had worked out a deal with the NBC affiliate and sponsor Admiral Television to guarantee the Rams revenues equal to a 15 percent increase in attendance, which came to about $250,000, a significant sum, to compensate the club for lost ticket sales. The Rams subsequently became the first club to black out home games in order to draw bigger home crowds, although they had to contest their right to do so in federal court.

As part of his promotional juggernaut, Schramm came up with Tom Harmon's Little All-American Team, a selection of small-college all-stars chosen by small-college coaches. By recognizing the best players, the Rams were effectively tipped off to small-college prospects who otherwise might have been overlooked.

Schramm attracted other talented people who knew how to promote. When his right-hand publicist, Tex Maule, a former sportswriter, resigned in 1952 to return to his native Texas and work for the new Dallas Texans team in the NFL, Schramm replaced him with an ambitious kid who had been doing publicity for the University of San Francisco and who had eyes almost as sparkling as his own pale baby blues, Pete Rozelle.

Schramm took full control of the team in 1954, when he was officially knighted as the Rams general manager. He held the position for three years until Reeves's alcoholism and feuds with others in the ownership group convinced Tex to bail out and head for greener pastures.

With his jumped-up personality and knowledge of pro football and television, Schramm landed a job in New York with CBS Sports, a division of the most popular of the three national networks. Along with his wife and three daughters, who cried and yelled all the way about not wanting to leave Los Angeles, he moved east. Tex reported directly to new CBS vice president for sports Bill MacPhail, who had been hired from the Kansas City Athletics baseball club, where he had been publicist; MacPhail's father had run both the New York Yankees and the Brooklyn Dodgers. CBS started broadcasting National Football League games in 1956, working out separate deals with several teams.

The rival network NBC aired the Baltimore Colts versus New York Giants NFL championship game from Yankee Stadium in 1958. The game was tied at the end of regular play at 17–17, and fans watched the drama unfold on flickering black-and-white screens across the nation in the first overtime pro football game ever played. Finally, quarterback Johnny Unitas marched the Colts down the field, and Alan "the Horse" Ameche bulled his way into the end zone from the one-yard line to give Baltimore a 23–17 victory. The contest proved to be such riveting television, it became part of sports mythology as "the greatest game ever."

"College football was the thing then," Bill MacPhail explained. "Until [CBS] got the NFL, people in Texas and Nebraska had never seen it."

Schramm's greatest achievement at CBS had nothing to do with football. CBS already had rights to broadcast the 1960 Summer Olympics in Rome, but no one planned to air the 1960 Winter Olympics, which would be staged in Squaw Valley, California, six months prior. No Winter Games had ever been broadcast live, largely due to geographic and technological limitations. In fact, no Olympic Games at all had been broadcast on television in any form other than short film clips shown on newscasts.

Schramm lobbied his superiors at CBS and then the Olympic Committee. His CBS bosses were wary, but the Olympic Committee thought it would be such good publicity, they awarded CBS broadcast rights for $50,000. Schramm made over twenty trips to California to measure the terrain and even laid cable himself on the slopes above Lake Tahoe. The first live telecast of an Olympics aired on February 18, 1960, hosted by CBS News broadcaster Walter Cronkite, with skating legend Dick Button and ski jumper Art Devlin providing commentary. For ten days, the Winter Olympics was the talk of television viewers across America, climaxing with the U.S. men's hockey team's 9–4 upset of Czechoslovakia for the U.S.'s first gold medal in hockey.

Schramm managed to pull off the broadcasts, and by doing so, he helped the network tap into a potentially huge new pool of advertisers, which is the lifeblood of network television. The NBC network reached out to offer Schramm the title of director of sports; CBS wanted to give him the responsibility of broadcasting the Summer Olympics in Rome. But by the time the Olympics flame was extinguished on the ski mountain in northern California, the man who made the first televised Olympics possible was already hunkered down in his namesake state conjuring a professional football team out of thin air.

TEX SCHRAMM FULLY UNDERSTOOD that Clint Murchison was the kind of owner whom front-office types like himself fantasized about working for. He carried an apparently unlimited cache of cash and had the good sense to delegate, step back, and let his people run the operation. All Tex had to do was win.

But first, he needed to get paying fans into the seats, and fan interest was still tepid for pro football in Dallas. The local populace had better things to do, like making money, building companies, and creating empires. Tractor-trailer trucks painted with the message "Thanks to all of you for helping O. L. Nelms make another million" captured the feeling.

Egging that mood on was the mobility made possible by the automobile; the advent of air-conditioning, which made the torrid Texas climate tolerable; and the general feeling of prosperity in the economic boom following the end of World War II. Slowly but surely, outsiders became not only tolerated in Dallas but recruited—and welcomed to occupy all the new homes being built on the prairie and to work the jobs being created by businesses and corporations based in the city.

Growth was a constant. The city population according to the 1960 census was 679,684, up from 434,462 in 1950, while the metropolitan area had bulged to 1,083,601.

Inventing new businesses was practically a local tradition. In September of 1921, the Pig Stand, the nation's first drive-in restaurant, opened at the intersection of Chalk Hill Road and the Fort Worth Highway. Seven years later, the first convenience store was created when Joe Thompson, an employee of the Southland Ice Company, started selling milk, bread, and eggs from an ice dock to customers who drove up in their cars. From that came the 7-Eleven convenience store.

Dallas was the home of the Frito corn chip, the number-one

snack food in America. The company that produced the simple Texas variation on a fried tortilla chip was on the verge of joining forces with the Lay potato chip company in Big D, which would create the largest food distribution network in the nation. Dallas was also the national headquarters of Dr Pepper, a prune juice–based concoction invented in Waco that was the most popular carbonated soda after Coca-Cola, Pepsi-Cola, and 7-Up.

Snack foods and soft drinks complemented another Dallas first — the first employer-sponsored hospitalization plan in the United States, created in Dallas by Justin Ford Kimball in 1929. Kimball sold twenty-one days of hospital care for six dollars to schoolteachers, marking the beginnings of Blue Cross Blue Shield and the private health-insurance market.

In 1956, an executive secretary at the Texas Bank and Trust named Bette Nesmith Graham invented Liquid Paper, a product that allowed typists to correct typing errors flawlessly. Two years later, an engineer at Texas Instruments named Jack Kilby invented the integrated circuit, which effectively ushered in the computer age and which would eventually lead to replacing the typewriter with the computer word processor. Kilby went on to invent the handheld calculator and the thermal printer and was awarded the Nobel Prize for physics.

Real estate had become Dallas's oil (there were 35 counties out of the 254 in Texas where oil had not been discovered; Dallas County was one of them). Residential real estate agents and commercial developers, including Trammel Crow and Ray Nasher, were focusing on new concepts like shopping malls and wholesale market centers. Highland Park Village, the nation's first self-contained shopping center, opened in 1931 in North Dallas. Wynnewood, the first planned community in Texas, with homes, apartments, and a shopping center clustered together, was platted out on 820 acres in the Oak Cliff part of South Dallas in 1946.

Dallas had style, too, in marked contrast to other cities in Texas, the South, and the southwestern United States, an attribute directly linked to Neiman-Marcus, the department store established in 1907 that defined luxury on an international scale through its exclusive high-end merchandise and renowned customer service.

The store's public face, the debonair Stanley Marcus, was known as the city's merchant prince. It was because of Marcus and Neiman's that "everybody got a fur coat on graduation if they were going somewhere north [to college], or even if not," explained Anne Peterson, a well-heeled Dallasite.

Neiman's reputation grew large in 1927 when the store became the first in the United States to stage a weekly retail fashion show. In 1952, Mr. Stanley, as Marcus was known, took the store to the next level by embellishing its annual Christmas catalog with over-the-top luxury gifts, beginning with a live Black Angus bull along with a sterling silver barbecue cart, priced at $1,925. He later introduced His-and-Hers Christmas Gifts for the catalog, trotting out the most expensive, outrageous gifts imaginable, starting with his-and-hers Beechcraft airplanes, priced at $176,000 for the two, and followed by a pair of camels, all of which generated reams of free publicity.

Big D's big growth spurt really began in 1907, when the business establishment took control of the city government and promoted the idea that businessmen were best equipped to lead because they could run the government like a business. The leadership wasn't always right. Banker and civic leader R. L. Thornton supported the brief resurgence of the Ku Klux Klan as a political force in the early 1920s, and the electric company even dimmed the downtown streetlights for the KKK's first nighttime parade there. But the Klan soon faded, and in 1930 a civic-minded cabal of bankers, utility- and insurance-company executives, railroad presidents, and owners of major retailers put their heads together and formed an invitation-only business club of leaders called the Citizens Charter

Association. After achieving their initial goal of persuading the citizens of Dallas to change the form of city government from the commission plan to the council-manager plan, they began endorsing city council candidates.

Business was Dallas's business, and the oligarchs made sure the city was run like one, which meant efficiently if not always democratically.

By 1959, Dallas could claim the tallest skyscraper west of the Mississippi, the symbol of its self-generated prosperity. The five-hundred-fifty-foot, forty-two-story Southland Life building, a blocky, cool steel-and-turquoise porcelain enamel panel structure, was slightly taller than the spiky Mercantile Bank building, the smaller no-frills Republic National Bank tower with the arty spire, and the distinctive Magnolia building topped by the rotating neon Pegasus, advertising Dallas as much as Mobil gasoline. It was on the twenty-eighth floor of the Southland Life building in the offices of the Wynne law firm where the principals first came together to make an NFL franchise.

THE DRIVEN PART OF the zeitgeist, that determined something extra, came from Dallas's being a city with no reason to exist, as it lacked a port or a navigable river. Its leaders had to will its success.

Dallas was actually founded by John Neely Bryan in 1841 on the east bank of the Trinity River for what seemed like good reason: it was near a limestone-bottom ford that was the only reliable river crossing for miles, a place where three forks of the river and two Indian traces converged (the area is right by the present-day Dealey Plaza and the Triple Overpass). The Tennessee-born Bryan had come from Arkansas to Texas to seek his fortune. He had been a farmer, lawyer, and land man, but most of all he was a trader.

Bryan started out with one hand tied behind his back. After he surveyed the land and returned to Arkansas to get his affairs in order, the Native Americans in the area—more than half of his pro-spective trading-post customers—signed treaties with the white man and left, while three major Indian settlements about fifteen miles west were destroyed by military forces in the Battle of Village Creek, which opened the territory to Anglos and their slaves arriv-ing from the south and the east.

Though Bryan thought steamboats would soon be able to chug up from the Gulf and increase commerce, the river was not navigable.

So instead of opening a trading post, he started a town and wore many hats, including postmaster and ferry operator transporting customers across the Trinity River. His cabin served as the court-house. Bryan endured for eight years before he left the community he'd established to join the California gold rush in 1849. He returned to Dallas the following year and stayed until 1855, when he fled to join the Creek Nation after shooting a man who had insulted his wife.

In 1852, Bryan sold the town site of Dallas and the ferry conces-sion for seven thousand dollars to Alexander Cockrell, described by historian A. C. Greene as "Dallas' first capitalist." Cockrell built a toll bridge over the Trinity in 1855 to replace Bryan's ferry, and he started a lumber business with a sawmill. After Cockrell was shot dead in 1858 by the Dallas marshal in a personal matter, Cockrell's widow, Sarah, established a flour mill and built a fancy three-story hotel.

Three years earlier, Victor Prosper Considerant had brought a group of two hundred Belgian, French, German, Swiss, and Polish colonists to establish a socialist utopian community three miles west of Dallas on the chalk bluffs above the forks of the Trinity. The peo-ple of La Réunion followed the teachings of French philosopher François-Marie-Charles Fourier and introduced art, music, dance, fine cuisine, beer, and science to the primitive Dallas settlement. Idealism met the hard reality of the North Central Texas prairie within a year. A late-spring blizzard and the low productivity of the limestone soil that the commune was built upon spelled disaster. By

1860, the community was absorbed into Dallas, infusing the Cockrells' settlement with refined elements including Dallas's first piano, first brewery, first barbershop, first butcher shop, first photographer, and its second mayor, Ben Long.

John Neely Bryan returned to Dallas in 1861 to serve in the Confederacy in the War Between the States after Dallas County citizens voted 741–237 to secede from the Union. He served as a trustee in the Dallas Academy for Men and Women and played an instrumental role in lobbying the Houston and Texas Central Railway to reroute their east–west tracks through Dallas rather than Corsicana to the south—Dallas's first communitywide effort to attract business.

In 1871, Bryan was one of the directors of the Dallas Bridge Company, which erected the first iron bridge across the Trinity, and Dallas welcomed the arrival of the Houston and Texas Central Railway and the first passenger train the following year. The Texas and Pacific Railroad came the year after that, the trains more than doubling Dallas's population in a year, to seven thousand citizens.

John Neely Bryan's last years were marked by a downward spiral leading to his admission to the Texas State Lunatic Asylum in Austin, where he died in 1877 and was buried in a pauper's grave. As one denizen of the Capital City liked to point out, "The man who founded Dallas went crazy when he realized what he had done and did the only sensible thing to do by winding up in Austin."

The next forty years were marked by growth (which attracted outlaws such as Doc Holliday and Sam Bass): East Dallas and Oak Cliff were annexed; levees were constructed along the Trinity River to prevent flooding; and in 1911, Southern Methodist University, the city's first institute of higher learning, was established.

In 1914, civic promoters spearheaded by *Dallas Morning News* publisher George Dealey successfully lobbied for a Federal Reserve bank in Dallas as headquarters for the Eleventh Federal Reserve District, beating out other Texas cities and New Orleans, which was considerably larger and regarded as far more influential.

By 1960, Dallas's identity was a bundle of contradictions. It claimed one of the highest church-attending populations in the country but also ranked high in divorces. You couldn't buy mixed drinks in a bar or restaurant, but you could buy them in private clubs, which were a dime a dozen in the city. Gambling was considered sporting, and whoring was tolerated as long as it was discreet.

Outsiders regarded Dallas as a superficial place where a person's net worth and ability to make more money were the only measures by which he or she was judged. Just as true then as now, if not for money, Dallas would not be Dallas. The Texas political pundit Molly Ivins wrote that Houston was degenerate, but Dallas was perverse.

The *Morning News*, established in 1885, represented proper Dallas. So did insurance companies, which started appearing in 1898, the Federal Reserve System bank, Neiman-Marcus, and the twenty-five-thousand-member (including Billy Graham) First Baptist Church, a megachurch before megachurches were cool, with the largest Southern Baptist congregation in the nation; its sanctuary was the centerpiece of a chunk of downtown Dallas real estate worth several hundred million dollars.

Low-down Dallas operated in close proximity. Several generations of freedmen gathered east of downtown along Elm Street in an area known as Deep Ellum, a maze of cafés, bars, dives, and brothels. Historically a mecca for undesirables, in the 1860s it had attracted the outlaw Belle Starr, who settled in nearby Scyene; in the 1920s, the blues singer Blind Lemon Jefferson; in the 1930s, the bank robbers known as Bonnie and Clyde; and in the 1940s and 1950s, the gambler and hoodlum Benny Binion, who would go on to fame as one of the founders of Las Vegas after he was run out of Dallas.

Dallas's modern era began in 1934, jump-started by R. L. Thornton. Thornton, the president of the Dallas Chamber of Commerce and head of the Mercantile National Bank, colluded with Nathan Adams of the First National Bank of Dallas and Fred Florence of the Republic National Bank to lead the civic push to stage the Texas Centennial Exposition in Dallas in 1936. They succeeded by promising to invest $10 million in the Fair Park grounds and despite the fact that Houston, San Antonio, and Austin had closer historical and geographical ties to the founding of the state. More than fifty buildings were constructed, and more than ten million visitors came to see the $25 million extravaganza.

Part of the centennial deal was the tacit understanding between the county sheriff and local hoodlums that gambling, prostitution, and other vices would be restricted to a specific area downtown referred to as the Zone. As long as the vice didn't get out of hand and the tourists went home happy, no one would go to jail. "It was against the law but let's just ease up—that was the attitude," explained Eddie Stone, who ran numbers for Benny Binion as a young boy. "A lot of things are against the law. Going a mile over the speed limit is against the law, but everyone does it. They all bet. There wasn't much other recreation, you know. Dallas was the center of the Baptist church, so they had to appease them and keep the law what it was. I never saw [First Baptist Church pastor] Dr. Criswell in those places but I bet he pulled a slot machine from time to time."

The art deco buildings of Fair Park that had been erected for the centennial remained occupied through the next year after Thornton and his group of influential Dallas civic leaders offered incentives to the Pan American Exposition to stage its fair in Dallas. Millions more discovered the city, including *Fortune* magazine, a new publication devoted to business and finance as imagined by Henry Luce. It profiled the Marcus family and Dallas's Neiman-Marcus department store, praising it as the greatest shopping experience between New York and San Francisco. Four years later, the *Atlantic Monthly* followed suit, describing Dallas in glowing terms as an ideal cross between east and west.

After the Pan Am Expo closed, the State Fair of Texas became the permanent occupant of Fair Park every October, attracting more than one million visitors annually.

R. L. Thornton had pushed for the creation of the Dallas Citizens Council months after the Pan Am fair closed, in 1937. He was tired of rounding up his business friends every time there was a reason for the city to chase greatness for the good of Dallas. Professional men, educators, artists, historians to cite lessons from the past, women, blacks, and Mexican Americans were excluded from the organization.

Besides successfully lobbying for the council form of local government, the Dallas Citizens Council bailed out the chronically underfunded Dallas Symphony, and through its political arm, the Citizens Charter Association, it endorsed mayor and city council candidates. Bond issues were won or lost on the CCA's endorsement.

But for all the emphasis on and evidence of business as a model for greater good, a mean streak ran through Dallas, one that was common to the Protestant South: whites held tight control of the levers of power, and the Bible was regarded as sacred text to be read literally; thus did the Dallas Independent School District create a course for the Old Testament in 1952 in which Judaism was portrayed "as a half-baked religion awaiting Christ's arrival for its completion," one author wrote.

Segregation was historic and so was the hostility whites exhibited toward blacks.

In the 1920s, a city ordinance went so far as to designate specific whites-only and blacks-only streets. In 1950 and 1951, several South Dallas residences in the Exline Park neighborhood that were occupied by Negroes were bombed, an indirect result of a hate speech by Pastor John G. Moore of Colonial Baptist Church in Dallas; he headed a homeowner association and proposed an eight-foot-high concrete-block wall to separate black parts of town from white parts. The bombers included a labor leader and two Hispanics, and they were assisted by the Dallas police.

The Dallas Citizens Council was instrumental in calling for a special grand jury to investigate the incidents, which were defused without revealing names. Some South Dallas folks blamed the discretionary omission on the "white" Dallas Citizens Council, likening the business-leaders group to the Ku Klux Klan in coats and ties. But this citizens council was not associated with the White Citizens Councils in the South that were formed in the 1950s to fight desegregation; it had actually been working to improve race relations since the 1930s.

Dallas mayor Wallace Savage reckoned of the first bombing, "Actually neither the man who threw the bomb nor the Negro who moved into a white neighborhood is primarily responsible. The incident was a symptom of a serious condition in Dallas that must be remedied." The real problem, the mayor recognized, was a black housing shortage. Negroes weren't satisfied being clustered in the West Dallas floodplain, the traditional colored quarter. One of the few existing middle-class colored neighborhoods in North Dallas disappeared with the expansion of Love Field, Dallas's municipal airport.

Progress came slowly. Negro Achievement Day at the state fair was abolished in 1953 when a fair official declared that all citizens were welcome on all days, and blacks were allowed entry to the state fair during its entire run. Although they couldn't eat in restaurants or ride midway rides, they could pay to see the four-legged girl in the freak show. Mayor Thornton had been pressured to open rides and restaurants, but he wouldn't budge on rides where there was the possibility that black skin might touch white skin.

Thornton, it was said, kept a statue of a Klansman in his home, which was not unusual considering the attitudes of the local white leadership. *Dallas Morning News* editor Dick West, writing an opinion piece headlined "Mixing Races in Schooling," implied Negro students were inferior and all Negroes were immoral. The state of Texas attempted to outlaw the NAACP in 1956 for "drumming up lawsuits." And in the summer of 1960, U.S. district judge T. Whitfield Davidson Jr. issued an opinion that justified slavery and demeaned blacks and tried to implement a system of voluntary desegregation.

Race problems were often swept under the rug and forgotten in the barrage of impressive numbers that city officials were continually touting. The Republic National Bank, with over $102 million in reserves, was the largest bank in the South in 1960. The Southland Life Insurance Company, with over $250 million in assets, was "prepared to meet the Challenge of the 60s."

The city fancied itself an educational center with distinguished institutions scattered throughout, among them Southern Methodist University, the University of Dallas, the Hockaday School for girls and St. Mark's for boys, the Southwestern Medical School of the University of Texas, and the Baylor University School of Dentistry. Culture and fine arts were represented by the Dallas Symphony, the Dallas Opera, the museums of art and natural history, and the Dallas historical museum.

In the northern part of the city were two self-contained, landlocked communities — Highland Park and University Park — where the wealthiest residents lived. Jews as well as people of color were banned from Highland Park.

If the state fair was not enough entertainment, every Sunday in October locals could take a three-hour trip on the Houston highway to Huntsville to witness the Texas Prison Rodeo "featuring Top TV Stars and Daring Inmate Riders."

By adding Fort Worth's 356,268 residents and another 245,270 in Tarrant County beyond the city limits, the expanded metropolitan population of North Central Texas swelled to well over 1.6 million, one of the ten most populous regions in the United States.

And with everything else it had going on, Dallas would soon be able to say that it had once been the largest metropolitan area in the United States without a major-league professional sports franchise.

1960–1969

Two Teams, One Town

Tex Schramm's biggest task was to sell the pro game to the locals while simultaneously distinguishing his club from their cross-town rival Dallas Texans of the upstart American Football League. Just as the Los Angeles Dons and the entire All-America Football Conference had folded, so too would the Dallas Texans and the American Football League, Schramm believed. He knew he had the better product to sell in the form of the National Football League. But all was contingent on the NFL owners approving Dallas's announced expansion franchise and fast-tracking the club for play in 1960 at their January meetings.

That did not stop the thirty-nine-year-old Schramm from taking care of the first two matters of business: securing a coach and players. Clint Murchison had already been in talks with two graduating college players, Don Meredith of the SMU Mustangs and Don Perkins of the University of New Mexico Lobos. Three days after Tex Schramm had signed on the dotted line, it was announced that Murchison had signed Don Meredith to a personal-services contract worth $150,000 over five years. If his new boss's quest to snag an NFL team for Dallas failed, Meredith made clear his intent: "I'm going to law school," he quipped; he'd already been accepted at SMU law school. Perkins was signed as a favor to Murchison's friend Clinton Anderson, a U.S. senator from New Mexico, a member of the board of directors of the Dallas football club, and perhaps Perkins's most ardent advocate after the Negro running back had broken rushing records at UNM. Baltimore had drafted Perkins in the ninth round in late 1959 and received a future draft pick in exchange for Dallas's getting him.

Dandy Don Meredith was an even smarter signing than Schramm. He was a hometown hero who had quarterbacked the SMU Mustangs for the past three seasons and he drew huge crowds to the Cotton Bowl, where "Meredith to [Henry] Christopher TD" was the biggest playmaking combination in town.

As far as football in Dallas went, "that's all there was," as one longtime fan put it. That would be conveniently ignoring the Cotton Bowl Classic on New Year's Day and the annual Texas-Oklahoma college clash at the Cotton Bowl that filled the stadium during the state fair every October and also filled the Dallas jail the night before the game with drunk and rowdy fans from both schools equally eager to settle the Red River Shootout on Dallas's downtown streets.

Despite the Mustangs' tepid record during Meredith's three years at quarterback—their best season was his senior year, in 1959, when the team went 5-4-1—his passing set school, conference, and national records and put butts on the wooden bench seats.

Meredith wasn't just football. The handsome kid with the eagle's beak, known as Joe Don and as Jeff and Hazel's kid back in his hometown of Mount Vernon, a hundred miles northeast of Dallas, oozed charm and charisma like a movie star with skills or a silver-tongued politician, not like some good ol' boy football player.

His outgoing personality was honed at Meredith Dry Goods, the mercantile store on the town square that his father and mother ran. When Don was six, his father positioned him at the entrance of the store and told him, "Son, when you see someone come in that door, you greet 'em by their name. Even a dog likes to hear his name."

At Mount Vernon High School, Meredith was elected senior class president; he won Mr. MVHS, was chosen by his classmates as most talented, and received best-actor recognition for his lead role in the school's one-act play (which went to the state competition). He was active in 4-H, the FFA, and the Methodist Youth Church Fellowship.

An All-State quarterback for the Mount Vernon Tigers, Meredith turned down other colleges' offers and went to SMU because, he said, "it was close to home and easy to spell." He was better at basketball than football—his mother had been a high school hoops star in East Texas—and he even won a metal ice chest for scoring 52 points in a single game at the Dr Pepper Invitational Tournament in Dallas during his junior season in 1954.

MEREDITH HAD BEEN PICKED by the Chicago Bears in the third round of the NFL draft in November of 1959 and by the Dallas Texans in the first round of the upstart American Football League's draft. Lamar Hunt pursued Meredith aggressively but to no avail because George Halas of the Bears immediately dealt rights to Meredith to the pending Dallas NFL franchise.

Subsequently engaged to Alma Lynne Shamburger, a striking blond SMU cheerleader and campus queen from Wichita Falls, and assured a handsome wage by Dallas, Meredith was anointed as the star who would play well and sell the football club to local sports fans. Having at least one player who talked like them, enjoyed the same things they did, and was already a fixture on the Dallas football scene could only help.

MURCHISON HAD MEREDITH, but he wasn't stopping at players. In December, at the recommendation of Tex Schramm, Clint Murchison Jr. signed the greatest coach in football. At least, that's how Jim Lee Howell, the head coach of the New York Giants, described his defensive assistant, Tom Landry. The accolade, as well as the interest in Landry expressed by Lamar Hunt and his Dallas Texans and by the AFL's Houston Oilers, merited a personal-services contract from Murchison.

Landry had almost signed an agreement to coach Houston when Wellington Mara, the owner of the Giants, told him Dallas was going to get a franchise. So on his way to Houston, Tom Landry flew to Dallas, his offseason hometown, for an interview. He was picked up at the airport by Edwin "Bud" Shrake of the *Dallas Times Herald*, and when Landry returned to Dallas a few days later to sign a five-year deal at $34,500 per year, he was accompanied by that other University of Texas graduate Tex Schramm.

Though Charles Burton of the *Dallas Morning News* wrote that Murchison "expects to be awarded an NFL franchise at a January 20 session of the pro circuit," George Halas still wasn't sure if the votes were there. Ten of the twelve clubs had to approve the idea. Because of the uncertainty, Landry's deal was similar to Don Meredith's. If Murchison didn't get a team, Landry's contract would be null and void, and Landry could then either shift his focus to the insurance business he had established in Dallas or coach somewhere else. But Landry was born to have this job.

Tom Landry had grown up during the Great Depression in the small farming town of Mission in the Rio Grande Valley of far South Texas, a region whose culture was more Mexican than American. He was a son of Ruth and Ray Landry, an Illinois couple who had moved to the valley to relieve Ray's chronic rheumatism. Ray worked as an auto mechanic in his shop behind the family's house and he served as chief of the volunteer fire department as well as the Sunday-school superintendent at the Methodist church. Ruth was a hands-on homemaker known for her chocolate pies.

Tommy, the younger brother of Robert and the older brother of Ruthie and Jack, sold newspapers and caddied at the local golf course, spending his earnings watching Westerns at the local movie house, where he fantasized about being a cowboy. By junior high, when he started wearing shoes to school, football had captured his imagination; he organized a sandlot team and called the plays.

"I learned something playing in the sandlots, something that today's youngsters aren't able to experience," Landry later related in an oral history. "Here is where you learn to cry and to fight, to overcome all situations according to your own abilities and initiative without some supervisor always looking over your shoulder."

When the shy, soft-spoken Tommy entered high school, he fell under the influence of twenty-two-year-old Bob Martin, the newly hired junior varsity coach of the Mission High School Eagles. Martin had come from the storied football town of Breckenridge and lived in a garage apartment two doors down from the Landrys. He got Tommy to focus and practice by throwing footballs through a tire swing. In high school, Tommy became Tom, was elected president of his sophomore and then senior class, and was chosen as Cutest Boy twice. He started on the basketball team, ran track, and played softball. But football was where he excelled. Bob Martin was promoted to head coach and he switched Landry from center to quarterback. During study hall, Landry would learn defensive theory from Martin, who preached the importance of playing your position.

Coach Martin instituted tough rules during Landry's senior year, banning soft drinks, imposing a curfew, and discouraging team members from dating—rules that young Tom dare not ignore, lest his neighbor find out. Martin challenged players to tackle him and to box with him. Martin's discipline and his prize student's exceptional passing, running, and punting helped lead the Eagles to an undefeated season in 1941, outscoring opponents 268–7. In the regional championship game, the farthest a Class A school in Texas could advance at the time, Landry threw two touchdown passes and ran 64 yards for another as the Eagles trampled the Hondo Owls, 33–0. Landry was voted onto the all-Valley team and rewarded with an athletic scholarship from the University of Texas.

He played freshman football at UT for D. X. Bible as a

quarterback, defensive back, and punter while his brother Robert joined the U.S. Army Air Forces to fight Germany in World War II. After Robert lost his life while ferrying bombers to England, Tom enlisted in the U.S. Army Air Forces, where he trained in the Eighth Air Force and became a copilot and gunner on B-17 Flying Fortress heavy-bomber missions. Landry's crew flew thirty missions and survived a plane crash behind enemy lines.

Resuming his studies and football at UT in 1946, Tom majored in business engineering, worked on oil rigs in the summer, and competed with future All-American Bobby Layne at quarterback before Landry broke the thumb on his passing hand. Texas's new coach, Blair Cherry, had already decided to switch his offense from the single wing to the T formation and had been working with Layne, so Landry changed to fullback on the offense and became team cocaptain. The Longhorns won the Sugar Bowl against Alabama in 1947 and beat number-one Georgia in the Orange Bowl in 1949. That was the same year Landry married a fellow student, a dazzling redhead named Alicia Wiggs, a Highland Park High School graduate from the nicest part of Dallas and a Bluebonnet Belle finalist at UT. The two had met on a blind date outing to Hamilton Pool, a scenic cave and waterfall west of Austin.

Landry's college experience convinced him to give professional football a try. Tom and Alicia moved to New York, where Tom joined the New York Yankees of the All-America Football Conference as a punter and defensive back. After the AAC merged into the National Football League in 1950, Landry moved to the New York Giants, receiving a seven-hundred-dollar bonus on top of his seven-thousand-dollar annual salary.

"He probably was the best defensive back in the business," Giants running back Frank Gifford said of Landry. "He approached the game with a zeal none of us could match. He was cool and calculating about football. Emotion had no place in his makeup. He always appeared to be looking beyond the game itself, searching for an unknown key. He had to know why things happened. While most of us played the game, he studied it."

It was almost natural, then, that in 1955, Landry became a player-coach, driven by economics as much as his critical thinking. "I didn't have any money and the opportunity was there," he explained in an interview. "Every team needed four or five coaches." He retired as a player in 1956 after earning All-Pro honors as a defensive back two years in a row.

Coaching full-time, Landry developed the 4-3 defense formation for the Giants, which became the standard defense around the league: four defenders on the line backed by three linebackers, two cornerbacks, and two safeties. The relationship of the linebacker to the width of the playing field was redefined, establishing what Wellington Mara called "the inside-out theory of defensive football"— protecting the middle while trusting the flanks to pursue the ball.

Defensive back Dick Nolan was in awe of Landry's work ethic. "The offense would go home, and we'd be sitting there going over the next opponent," he said.

> I remember one time Tom was at the blackboard, showing me that if their flanker came out on the strong side on a third-down play, and the fullback flared to the weak side, I was to follow the fullback out a few steps and then race back quickly because they would be bringing the wingback inside me to take a pass. "But Tom," I said, "what if I commit myself that completely and the wingback isn't there?" And Tom just looked at me without any change of expression and said, "He will be." I had seven interceptions that year and Tom got me five of them.

Giants publicist Don Smith joked, "Once one of Tom's defensive men lost a page from his playbook. We found it at a Chinese laundry. Someone had exchanged it for a dozen shirts."

Another high-profile assistant coach, Vince Lombardi, directed the Giants offense.

Landry did not look at assistant coaching for a pro football team as a career mainly because the pay, though a help, was minuscule. "I figured I would coach for a while and then go home and earn some money in the off-season," Landry said. Every year, he returned to Texas, first to resume studies at the University of Houston, where he received an industrial engineering degree in 1952, then to work for Cameron Iron Works. But in 1957, Tom and Alicia moved their off-season home to Dallas, where Tom intended to start a small insurance business.

The next year, he went to a men's Bible-study breakfast at the Melrose Hotel in Dallas at the invitation of his friend Frank Phillips. "We probe into the Scriptures and have some good fellowship together," Phillips told him. Landry was not disappointed. One passage, Matthew 6:25, grabbed his attention: "Therefore I tell you, do not be anxious about your life, what you shall eat or what you shall drink, nor about your body, what you shall put on. Is not life more than food, and the body more than clothing?"

"Not a very dramatic story, is it?" Landry later said about the conversion that led him to dedicate his life to Jesus Christ. But it was true. "These informal sessions of probing, questioning and searching the Gospels together began a whole new era of my life," he said. A devout churchgoer, he became a member of Highland Park Methodist, the church Alicia had attended as a child.

A year later, Tom Landry accepted Clint Murchison's offer to coach the new Dallas franchise, even though he didn't think the NFL team had much going for it. "This won't last two years," he confided to his wife after signing the contract. "You can't build from the ground up." Expansion clubs failed more often than they survived; at least, that had been his experience. "Certainly it's a little bit of a gamble," admitted Landry at the time. "Everything is. A major factor is that I want to stay in Dallas. And I believe Texas will develop into one of the nation's major sports centers, along with California."

Getting Tom Landry as coach was another step forward for the team. Tex Schramm was thrilled. "All we've got is a coach and a pitcher, but that's a start," he crowed. "Now we've got to get some more players."

ONE OF THE FIRST CALLS Tex Schramm made after being offered the GM job was to his old team the Los Angeles Rams. The club was known for having the best scouts in pro football. Their people actually attended games and spring practices to size up talent instead of perusing the *Street and Smith's Sports Annual* or calling coaches, as was the usual custom. If there were free agents to be signed, the Rams scouts would know, Schramm believed. So he phoned former Rams coach Hamp Pool, and Pool recommended Gil Brandt, a baby photographer in Milwaukee, Wisconsin, and one of the most astute scouts Pool knew. Brandt was a persuasive talker with a prominent boxer's nose, but he had never been a full-time scout, nor had he played college or pro football or coached, although he had been a quarterback and defensive back in high school. Still, he knew how to analyze and evaluate players like few others did and he carried stats in his head with a photographic memory.

Brandt laughed when Schramm called.

"Tex, I don't know anything about television."

"No, we're going to have a team in Dallas and I'm going to be the general manager," Schramm told him. "Steal all the information you can from the Rams so we know who to go after."

It didn't take much to persuade the twenty-nine-year-old to join his football club. Brandt's photography business was built on contracts with three hospitals. He'd bought the fourteen-hundred-dollar camera and arranged for nurses to take the pictures. Hospitals added three dollars to each patient's bill and kept 25 percent. Brandt developed the pictures and took 75 percent of the action.

"That job left me free weekends for my hobby...football," he explained.

Brandt developed his scouting skills in college at the University of Wisconsin and then, after being encouraged by former Wisconsin receiver Elroy "Crazy Legs" Hirsch, he started feeding information to Eddie Kotal of the Rams.

After Schramm left the Rams, Brandt scouted for the San Francisco 49ers. When Brandt arrived in Dallas, he immediately put to good use the blank standard contracts that Bedford Wynne had filched from an existing team and mimeographed with the addition of a new letterhead identifying the Dallas Rangers. Dallas was still awaiting approval by league owners when the 1960 NFL draft was held on November 28, 1959, so after the draft, Schramm instructed Brandt to get busy and find potential talent among the undrafted. "This will be easy," Schramm told Brandt. ("Of course to Tex, everything was easy," Brandt would later say.) Brandt rounded up twenty-eight players who signed the bottom lines with the understanding that the contracts were null and void if Dallas didn't get a franchise.

Brandt's first signing was a Dartmouth player named Jake Crouthamel. "The Dartmouth coach was a guy named Bob Blackman who had been a coach at Pasadena City College," Brandt said. "So we knew him from Rams training camp. Tex said, 'That'll be easy, you'll just go up there and Blackman will help you get the guy.'"

Unfortunately, the Los Angeles Chargers of the fledgling American Football League had drafted Crouthamel, so a bidding war ensued. The protocol, Brandt explained, was to send a contract through the mail to a draft pick. "If it was a first-round choice, it might have been for $5,500," Brandt said. "If it was less than that it was for $4,500." Brandt ended up signing Crouthamel for $7,500. He couldn't wait to get out of Crouthamel's residence and go to the

White Bear Inn in Hanover, New Hampshire, to call Schramm and inform him the club had its first signing.

"How much did we pay?" Schramm asked.

"You have to understand why we paid him..." Brandt started to explain but Schramm cut him off.

"How much did we pay?" he asked again. As soon as he heard the number, Schramm heaved a sigh audible over the phone and then said, "We'll go broke if we pay this kind of money."

BACK HOME, detractors were already referring to the Dallas Rangers as the Halas Strangers in honor of their roster of discards and George Halas's influential role in establishing an NFL franchise in Dallas.

Lamar Hunt's Texans weren't having that problem. "It's a good name for a team in our area and people will associate it with pro football because it was used here before," Hunt reasoned. "I'm not concerned because those Texans failed."

Hunt played to the home folks by signing all–Southwest Conference fullback Jack Spikes from Texas Christian University in nearby Fort Worth; Cotton Davidson, the quarterback from Baylor; and an exciting halfback named Abner Haynes from North Texas State College in Denton, twenty-five miles north of Dallas.

Building a team that hadn't even been officially approved appeared to be a giant challenge to almost everyone but Clint Murchison, who viewed the undertaking as just another deal to seal. Simultaneously selling that same team to football fans while fending off a competing entity in the same city whose pockets were just as deep as his turned out to be the hard part.

If the Dallas Rangers were going to put a team on the field for the 1960 National Football League season, they would have to overcome the objections of George Preston Marshall, the owner of the

Washington Redskins. Marshall and Murchison did not like each other, going back to the time Murchison had tried to buy the Redskins. For his part, Marshall considered Murchison "personally obnoxious."

Marshall threatened to go to court if Dallas was awarded an NFL franchise for the 1960 season. "I will go into the meeting with plenty of legal counsel," he vowed. "The only reason for expansion I've heard from the other owners is that we could destroy the new [American] league. If that is the only reason, then we are guilty of monopolistic practices. No one can give me an intelligent reason for adding a couple more franchises." Marshall called the signings of Landry, Schramm, Meredith, and Perkins "premature, without sanction, and against the constitution of the NFL." He backed expansion, he said, if "the purpose was to improve conditions. I am against it so long as it involves anti-trust action and where it would hurt the colleges. I am unalterably opposed to expansion this year."

Lamar Hunt agreed wholeheartedly. If Murchison was awarded a team in Dallas after years of George Halas's saying there would be no expansion, it would be a direct response to Hunt's American Football League. The newly appointed AFL commissioner, Joe Foss, chimed in. "They put a team in Dallas just to make things tough for us. Their actions have been aimed at destroying us rather than competing with us."

"Ridiculous," harrumphed Murchison's man in charge, Tex Schramm. "The fact that we decided to enter this market at the same time as our competitors is just free enterprise in action."

Schramm and Murchison had bigger fish to fry, anyway: convincing the National Football League owners to vote them in. It helped that Clint Jr. knew his way around the District of Columbia. He and the other half of Murchison Brothers, John Dabney Murchison, had several key operatives in place to grease the wheels of government, including the lobbyist Bobby Baker, a highly effective fixer known as the 101st senator; attorney-lobbyist Irv Davidson, whose clients included Caribbean dictators; and Tom Webb, a former football player for the University of Maryland Terrapins who had been a special assistant to FBI director J. Edgar Hoover, a friend of Clint Sr., before he started lobbying and working for the Murchison family in 1952.

Baker, who was then secretary to the Senate majority leader, Lyndon Johnson, would later get caught up in a corruption scandal linked to Johnson. After the fact, he explained the Murchison-Hoover dynamic: "Murchison owned a piece of Hoover. Rich people always try to put their money with the sheriff, because they're looking for protection. Hoover was the personification of law and order and officially against gangsters and everything, so it was a plus for a rich man to be identified with him. That's why men like Murchison made it their business to let everyone know Hoover was their friend. You can do a lot of illegal things if the head lawman is your buddy."

Baker's and Davidson's official role in the latest Murchison Brothers deal was to reassure Congress. A Dallas NFL franchise would not threaten the league's antitrust status, the lobbyists promised. The political contributions made on Murchison's behalf, including $25,000 to Senator Estes Kefauver, calmed many doubters, especially after Kefauver raised red flags about George Preston Marshall's Redskins television network being a monopoly.

THE NFL OWNERS HAD other matters to tend to first when they gathered at the Breakers in Palm Beach in 1960 for their annual January winter meeting. The league needed a new commissioner, since Bert Bell had died; the front-runners were interim commissioner Austin Gunsel, a former FBI agent, and San Francisco attorney Marshall Leahy. After twenty-three ballots cast over seven days, a surprise candidate was elected: thirty-three-year-old Pete Rozelle, the general manager of the Los Angeles Rams and former team publicist who had been hired eight years earlier by Tex Schramm.

Expansion came up for a vote once Rozelle was approved. First, Max Winter was awarded a franchise for Minnesota to start play in

1961, ending the American Football League's incursion into the upper Midwest. The subject of Dallas came second, due to the expected objections of George Preston Marshall. However, Marshall voted yes. He had started to change his mind a few weeks earlier when Clint Murchison made a not-so-innocuous proposal to the Redskins owner over the telephone: Did Marshall want to buy the rights to "Hail to the Redskins," the second-oldest fight song in professional football? Clint asked.

"Why would I want to do that?" Marshall asked. "I don't need permission." His ex-wife had written the popular anthem. "Yeah, you do," Clint informed him. "I own it."

CLINT'S LOBBYIST FRIEND Tom Webb had purchased the rights to the song from its composer, Barnee Breeskin, the orchestra director at the Shoreham Hotel in Washington and leader of the Redskins Wigwam band. Marshall's ex, Corrine Griffith, was just the lyricist. Breeskin, who went to high school with Webb, worried that Marshall was going to try to obtain the rights for free, and he willingly transferred his rights, anticipating a handsome payment in exchange.

Murchison then had a face-to-face meeting with Marshall in his hotel room, and he reiterated his proposal. "No one else would introduce us, so here I am," Murchison announced when Marshall opened the door. After a ten-minute chat, Marshall relented and got the rights to his beloved song. Murchison paid Breeskin two thousand dollars, and Dallas had a National Football League franchise.

As Tex Schramm would later observe, "People that are successful in this league have a little larceny in their hearts."

TWO DAYS BEFORE the Dallas Rangers were given the green light to field a team for the 1960 season, the owners of franchises in the new American Football League elected Lamar Hunt president.

Less than six weeks later, the previously intractable Wolfners moved the Chicago Cardinals to St. Louis. Three months after that, the American Football League announced a five-year multimillion deal with the ABC network to broadcast league games, guaranteeing exposure and income to the franchises. The war was on.

Six hundred thousand dollars bought the newest National Football League club access to five players from each of the thirty-six-man rosters of the twelve existing NFL clubs. The league had created a player pool, allowing each team to freeze twenty-five players, leaving the rest of their roster up for grabs. Dallas was given the list of eligible veterans the day before the special expansion draft was held, on March 13, from which a thirty-six-man roster for the Dallas Rangers was filled out. "We didn't have any chance to find out medicals or anything," Gil Brandt later said. "You had to roll the dice."

Several players were homesick Texans, such as running back L. G. Dupre, a Baylor star who played for the Baltimore Colts, and linebacker Jerry Tubbs, who signed after leaving San Francisco. "I had told the 49ers that if they could get me a good permanent job in Dallas for the offseason periods I might play with them again," Tubbs said. "They tried but they couldn't find one that was satisfactory to me. I don't like to mix the two. I don't like to have a job which may be dependent on how well I play football." At the same time, he wasn't thrilled to be coming back to Texas under those circumstances. "I don't like the idea of losing," said Tubbs, who never lost a game with the Breckenridge Buckaroos in high school or with the Oklahoma Sooners in college.

"The only reason that Tubbs was on the list is that he had convinced San Francisco that he was going to retire," Gil Brandt said. "So he was on the list. But we had guys like Charlie Oney, who was really a good player but he lived in Hawaii and his father-in-law had some big company and Oney was making twenty-two thousand dollars a year, which was unheard-of at that time. He decided he could do better by staying in Hawaii and working."

Don McIlhenny, the former SMU running back, came from the Green Bay Packers. And Gene Babb from Odessa and Austin College signed with the Dallas club after signing with the Houston Oilers of the start-up AFL.

Eddie LeBaron was obtained in a trade with Washington for future draft picks. Landry needed an experienced quarterback, and the former All-Pro known as the Little General (for his five-foot-seven, 165-pound frame) was the perfect fit, the kind of leader who could teach Meredith. It was a career move for the smallest quarterback in professional football. LeBaron had turned thirty and was contemplating practicing petroleum law in Midland, Texas, after spending the last three years with the Redskins and going to law school at George Washington University in the offseason. LeBaron's incentive with Dallas would be his hiring on with minority owner Bedford Wynne's law firm.

Meanwhile, college and high school officials complained about the entry of two professional teams in Dallas and the likelihood that Friday and Saturday pro games would infringe on their turf, especially if the games were televised. That, said Howard Grubbs, the executive secretary of the Southwest Conference, would be "ruinous to college and high school athletics."

In June, Tex Schramm's wife and daughters arrived in Dallas, stepping off the airplane at Love Field into a furnace blast of summer heat like nothing they had ever experienced in Southern California or Connecticut. They were not amused.

"We just looked at each other and said, 'Oh my God!'" said one of Tex's daughters, Christi. That night, Tex took his brood to the Rib on Lover's Lane for their first taste of Texas barbecue, which the girls liked. He then drove his family to Sunnybrook Lane on the northern fringe of Dallas to inspect the site of their new home. When completed, it would be Tex's vision of a Southern California–style ranch home, with lots of trees, a creek running through it, and plenty of privacy. A faux Tudor or French Provincial manse in more prestigious Highland Park with its snooty traditions and high-achieving schools was not Tex. His Dallas was wide open, shiny and new, and growing by leaps and bounds—just like LA, only without the mountains and the beach.

"You're gonna love it, you're gonna love it," Tex promised his daughters.

To his girls, the two-acre tangle of vegetation on Sunnybrook Lane looked like an impenetrable thicket. "We got out to look it over, it's hot, and we're walking around looking at all the brush," Christi said. "Of course, we hated it."

"You have to have a vision, you have to see what we're going to do," Tex insisted. "We're going to put the house down here, we're going to have a long drive. It's going to be private, it's just going to be beautiful."

"We thought, there's just no way this could be beautiful," Christi said. After the tour of their home-to-be, the Schramm family returned to the temporary living quarters with red bites and ferocious itches all over their bodies. It was their introduction to Texas chiggers, which had burrowed into their skin. "We'd never been exposed to chiggers before," Christi said. "So once again we all screamed and yelled and cried, 'We hate Dallas!'"

Little by little, they adjusted. A professional golfer named Lee Trevino moved in next door. A neighbor across the creek, Ray Nasher, collected and displayed giant fine-art sculptures in his backyard. Tom Landry and Gil Brandt lived five minutes away. Clint Murchison's home was a ten-minute drive. Tex and his wife, Marty, sent their girls to public schools. The family's phone number was listed in the local directory. If someone wanted to call and talk about the team, Tex was easy to find. He was an open book. He knew his target audience, showed his enthusiasm by buying into the market, and wanted nothing so much as to hear from the customers.

CLINT MURCHISON delegated operational control to Tex Schramm, who delegated to Tom Landry and to Gil Brandt. Landry enjoyed absolute authority over the day-to-day running of the team. Brandt was unhindered in the area of drafting and scouting players. Schramm orchestrated it all.

Clear lines were established between the owners, the front office, the coaches, and the players. Like the military, they had a policy of no fraternizing among the troops (although it did not necessarily apply to owners and certain women). This both acknowledged and eased the arrangement between Tex, a man who enjoyed a Bullshot, his beloved vodka-and-beef-bouillon concoction, every afternoon and was not easily shocked by human behavior, and Tom, man of faith whose ability to look the other way when necessary underscored the respect he had for the other man's capabilities.

The only time all the characters gathered on the same stage was Sundays. Even then, Clint and his sidekick Bedford Wynne, his party pal and crony, stayed in the background, preferring to work hard at having fun.

The Wynnes and the Murchisons were part of the same East Texas story, going back to when Toddie Lee Wynne of Wills Point was the attorney and business partner of Clint Murchison Sr. of Athens. Toddie Lee's brother, Angus Sr., was known as the king of the boomtown lawyers. Clint Sr.'s grandfather had founded the Athens bank and was a recognized trader, a trait that still held two generations later. Clint and Toddie Lee's partnership unraveled in 1944 when Murchison discovered Wynne had done an outside oil deal behind his back. They split the proceeds and went their separate ways. Clint took the ranches in Mexico. Toddie Lee took Matagorda Island off the Texas coast. Wynne kept American Liberty Oil and American Home Realty, among other holdings, putting his nephew Angus Jr. in charge of the realty company. Their building of the

Wynnewood housing development project helped trigger the real estate boom that drove Dallas's economy following World War II. Toddie Lee and his wife famously lived in a pink mansion on Lakeside Drive in Highland Park.

Clint Jr. and Bedford rekindled the old Murchison-Wynne partnership through football. Family members thought Bedford's involvement was predicated on his knowledge and passion for the game. But Clint liked Bedford just as much for his garrulous manner and considerable wild streak. He was the popular guy that Clint wasn't. As a friend and business partner, Bedford kept an eye out for potential female companions for Clint and himself.

Bedford was the rainmaker at the family law firm. A first-class trial lawyer, he was also general manager of the firm, charged with bringing in new clients. "He was always on the golf course and getting into all these deals," his nephew David Wynne explained.

In early 1960, the venture Murchison had put together with Wynne as front man moved from the Wynne and Wynne law firm's high-rise digs to a single rented office at 4425 North Central Expressway, where Schramm, Landry, and Brandt worked with hardly any elbow room to set up their respective operations.

Tex Schramm enlisted Kay Lang, a onetime Ice Follies chorus girl who had worked with Tex for the Los Angeles Rams, to help arrange ticket sales. The temp gig turned permanent in a matter of weeks, with Tex bragging, "I don't believe there is any other woman holding such an important office in major league sports." Jimmie Parker, the assistant athletic director for the Dallas Independent School District, was hired as business manager. Larry Karl, Tulane University's sports publicist, became the team's director of public relations.

The team practiced at Burnett Field, the derelict home of the Dallas Rangers baseball club on the levee banks of the Trinity River just south of downtown. The dark and dingy facility was "like a dungeon," said lineman Jerry Norton. Players were advised to hang their equipment over rails rather than put it in the locker because the rats would eat the leather at night. The ladies' restroom doubled as the training room.

In June, the team name changed from the Rangers to the Cowboys. Sports fans had been confused over which Rangers were being talked about, the minor-league baseball club or the NFL expansion franchise. Bedford Wynne lobbied for the Steers in honor of his favorite college football team, the University of Texas Longhorns, but Clint Murchison settled on Cowboys, which projected a western flavor similar to Rangers. Dallas Cowboys had a ring to it, he thought.

The new name did not go down well among the relatives of owners. "We didn't like that, none of my friends," complained David Wynne, Bedford Wynne's nephew. "Even though I was on a ranch every weekend riding my horse, we weren't cowboys. We didn't think of ourselves like that. That was totally Fort Worth. It didn't have anything to do with Dallas."

FOOTBALL, THOUGH, was about to have everything to do with Dallas. In July, the first Dallas Cowboys training camp was organized in Forest Grove, Oregon, on the campus of Pacific University, a site that had been recommended to Gil Brandt. Landry was partial to Oregon because the New York Giants had trained at Willamette, about forty miles from Forest Grove. But the dorms at Pacific University were mold-ridden and overrun with rats, and the weather damp and drizzly, hardly ideal training conditions.

And it wasn't just the weather. Don Perkins, one of the first two players signed to Dallas, could not finish the Landry Mile, a mile-long endurance run up and down a hillside that the coach wanted all his players to finish. But rather than booting him off the squad, Landry made an exception for Perkins. "It was not because he wasn't in shape," Gil Brandt said. "He just couldn't run a mile."

With frustration settling in, training camp was moved to St. John's Northwestern Military Academy in Delafield, Wisconsin, for the last two weeks of preparations, but that proved even worse — a leaky, dank castle with bats flying in the dorms and mosquitoes everywhere. The motley crew of has-beens, castoffs, and never-weres rebelled, hanging Brandt in effigy in the form of two stuffed burlap bags in front of the academy's entrance.

While the Cowboys battled the elements, the American Football League was battling the Cowboys and the NFL. Seeking to stop the inevitable, the AFL filed a $10 million antitrust lawsuit against the National Football League and requested the Dallas Cowboys facilities be padlocked in the name of unfair competition and violation of antitrust laws. Tex Schramm belittled the suit. "In the final analysis this decision as to what Dallas wants in the way of professional football will rest solely in the hands of the people," he said. "Apparently, Lamar Hunt and his league are unwilling to risk a decision on this basis. We don't think they will find sympathy either in the court or with the people of Dallas."

New NFL commissioner Pete Rozelle chimed in. "They moved into our territory in New York, Los Angeles, and San Francisco. Why shouldn't we be allowed to move into Dallas?"

Behind the scenes, Clint Murchison reached out to Hunt and proposed sharing the Dallas NFL franchise. Hunt declined, telling Murchison, "I feel obligated to remain with the league I helped form."

Some people, including those in charge of the Cotton Bowl, the only stadium suitable for both teams, sympathized with Hunt and the Texans, mainly because Hunt approached them first. The Dallas Texans got first pick of open dates from the landlord, the State Fair of Texas. Hunt dibbed most Sundays in September and October, reasoning fan interest would be highest at the start of the season regardless of how either home team played. But the Cowboys got a leg up by scoring the Salesmanship Club game in mid-August. The popular annual exhibition had always featured two NFL teams. For 1960, the Dallas NFL franchise would play the 1959 NFL champion Baltimore Colts—the former original Dallas Texans.

The Salesmanship Club game always drew a good crowd, no matter who was playing, a testament to civic leaders in the business community who belonged to the club and to the general respect sales and salesmen were accorded in Dallas. The August 19 exhibition, advertised in newspapers as the one "with the real pros," drew almost 40,000 fans to watch Johnny Unitas pass the Colts to a 14–10 win over the Dallas Cowboys.

A couple weeks later, the Dallas Texans concluded a perfect 6-0 exhibition season by trouncing instant intrastate rivals the Houston Oilers 24–3 in front of an estimated 55,000 fans at the Cotton Bowl, the largest crowd to watch either Dallas pro team.

The Cowboys were going full speed ahead, and Bedford Wynne, the team's secretary-treasurer, showed the team's appreciation for getting admitted to the senior league by hosting a party for Pete Rozelle at the Four Wynnes Ranch near Kaufman. The dapper Rozelle, wearing a stylish plaid suit and alligator shoes, was happy to hear accolades after all the time he'd been spending hurling accusations at the upstart league.

Most of the ownership group turned up at the party: Toddie Lee Wynne Jr., the executive vice president of American Liberty Oil; W. R. "Fritz" Hawn, another running buddy of Clint Jr.; Fort Worth publisher and oilman Amon G. Carter Jr.; New Mexico senator Clinton P. Anderson; Leo F. Corrigan of Texas Bank and Trust; J. Howard Edmonson; defense contractor James L. Ling; Paul Middleton; football insider Field Scovell; oilman Max Thomas; and Robert F. Thompson, Clint Murchison's occasional business partner.

Bedford Wynne was happy to be the front man. "Bedford wanted to do the talking," Gil Brandt said. "He never met somebody that he didn't like. He and Clint were very good friends. The difference was that Bedford's pockets were a lot shorter than Clint's. He had that champagne attitude. He just didn't have the money. Clint liked him because Clint lived in a shell.

"When we brought a player to town and wanted to show off, we brought 'em up to the Wynne and Wynne law firm on the twenty-eighth floor of the Southland Life building. They had the whole floor with a big lobby, a battery of lawyers, and an impressive view of the city."

Bedford's office served to woo players, but Bedford's days as spokesman for the team had pretty much ended when Tex Schramm signed on. Tex made clear he was in charge. His charitable way of elbowing Wynne aside came in the form of a dismissive remark Tex made about Bedford now and then, good-naturedly referring to him as "that cocksucker" and smiling when he said it. "You know I love Bedford, but I'd walk into my office after lunch and he'd be sitting in my chair," he privately bitched to a confidant.

As September neared, the Cowboys and the Texans launched advertising campaigns, taking advantage of the emerging advertising and marketing community's abundant talent pool. To rising radio and television broadcasters, Dallas was comparable to playing in AAA minor-league baseball: the last stop before arriving in the big-market cities of New York, Chicago, and Los Angeles.

But Gordon McLendon, one of the greatest programming talents in the history of radio and a master showman himself, made Dallas more than just another AAA media market. After his dramatic re-creations of baseball and football as well as his live play-by-play talents went national on the Liberty network, McLendon became one of the founding fathers of Top 40 radio via his Dallas station, KLIF, attracting the largest radio audience in the area with a format that featured the most popular music of the week along with exciting presentations of the news and constant promotions. One giveaway involved throwing dollar bills off the top of a downtown skyscraper, which created a riot and generated reams of free publicity.

In the McLendon tradition, Lamar Hunt hired thirty pretty Dallas women to drive around the city in bright red sports cars to work prospective ticket buyers. The Texans were promoted as the Zing Team of Pro Football, which sounded as if they were a soft drink rather than a group of grown men paid to play a very physical game. The Cowboys countermarketed by inviting fans to "Follow the GO team of the Senior Pros...the only NFL team boasting two unanimous All-Americans at quarterback," and they one-upped the Texans with a catchy theme song, a marching tune with clarion trumpets and stirring, strident lyrics: "Go! Dallas! Cowboys! Stand up! Stampede!"

Hunt wasn't impressed. "I thought they took a very blasé approach. They almost told the public, 'Well, we're the NFL. Our ticket offices are open. Come see us.' In contrast, we took the hard-sell approach." Hard sell indeed. One of the women in the red sports cars promoting the Texans, Norma Knobel, was so persuasive in her sales skills she ended up marrying Hunt.

"Lamar believed in spending the money for advertising," Gil Brandt said. "We spent our money on player development."

Cowboys reserved tickets were priced at $4.60. The Texans charged $4 flat. And the competition didn't stop there.

The Texans led the way in freely discounting and giving away tickets. Members of the Spur Club who sold one hundred season tickets to Texans games were given a red blazer. Tickets attached to balloons were released by the Texans, and two hundred thousand Texans tickets were inserted into packages of Fritos, though few were used.

Both teams reached out to younger fans. For a dollar, a kid could join the Texans Huddle Club and gain free end-zone admission all season and attend football clinics. High-schoolers were admitted to games for ninety cents. The Cowboys countered with Knothole Gang tickets, priced at a dollar or less for end-zone seats, and with their five-for-one deal, where five kids could get in free to Cowboys games if they were accompanied by an adult buying a $2.75 general-admission ticket.

A LOT OF MONEY was at stake. Economists guessed the two pro teams would bring four million dollars into the community. The more interesting inside play was guessing which owner was most able to afford to lose money. "The key financial battle is shaping up here in Dallas," the *Wall Street Journal* reported. AFL franchises, including the Dallas Texans, were projected to lose between two and four million dollars the first year. Tex Schramm insisted money was not an issue for his club, saying, "We're financed for the long pull."

The battle for fans heated up. By September, the Texans claimed they'd sold more than 5,000 season tickets and the Cowboys had sold 3,000, less than the 1952 NFL Texans, who sold almost 5,000 season tickets, according to owner Giles Miller. By contrast, the new Los Angeles Chargers of the AFL had sold 10,000 season tickets, half what their crosstown rivals, the NFL Rams, had. St. Louis, the new home of the Chicago Cardinals of the NFL, counted 10,000 season-ticket holders.

Both Dallas teams' games were carried on radio and television. KBOX, the Top 40 competitor of KLIF, carried the Cowboys games on the radio, sports broadcaster Frank Glieber doing the play-by-play alongside Bud Sherman, the sports director at WBAP TV Channel 5.

Texans games were broadcast on city-owned WRR radio with Charlie Jones doing play-by-play and assisted by Bill Mercer, a KRLD news and sports reporter. "Charlie and I worked by ourselves," Mercer said. "There was no money for spotters or an engineer. I did stats and did color."

KRLD TV Channel 4 televised the Texans and Cowboys both. A

rotating cast of play-by-play announcers called the Cowboys' TV games, including national broadcasters Gil Stratton and Tom Harmon, and, ultimately, Wes Wise, the sports director at WFAA Channel 8.

The Cowboys announcer gig complicated Wise's sports-director job because Channel 8 and Channel 4 were rivals. "I bent over backwards to be fair to both the Texans and the Cowboys," Wise said. "I'd go to the practices of both, the ones that they'd allow you to go to. I was with the Cowboys at training camp at Forest Grove, Oregon. It was tough to do double duty but you felt like you had to do it."

Providing color for Wise was Davey O'Brien, the Heisman Trophy–winning quarterback from TCU whose drawl was so distinctive, his line "Yes, Wes," would be repeated by the few fans tuning in.

THE DALLAS COWBOYS made their official debut at home on Saturday night, September 24, 1960, in front of a crowd of 30,000 who watched them lose to the Pittsburgh Steelers and local hero Bobby Layne, 35–28. The Blond Bomber, a notorious party boy fond of drink and dames, was one of the few players on the field to forgo a face mask, which Layne considered an obstruction.

Featured special guest entertainers were Roy Rogers, King of the Movie and Television Cowboys, and his wife, Dale Evans, who rode around the stadium in a convertible waving to the crowd. But not all in the crowd waved back. Roy and Dale found themselves being pelted by paper cups, programs, and ice before they were hustled out of the stadium while police hauled sixty-five rowdy troublemakers off to the pokey.

The crowd count appeared to be inflated. Steelers owner Art Rooney later reported he was paid for 13,000 tickets sold, not 30,000.

The next day, the Dallas Texans attracted a crowd of around 42,000 who watched the other home team beat the Los Angeles

Chargers, 17–0. That crowd was smaller than the one that had turned out on September 2 to watch the Texans play the Houston Oilers in an exhibition match, but it was still impressive enough to answer the question of whether God-fearing fans would turn out to watch football on the Lord's Day.

The Texans' second home game, against the New York Titans on October 2, was billed as Texans Teen Salute. Students with ticket stubs from high school football games the previous Friday night were admitted free. That was the same night the Cowboys played their second home game, drawing an estimated crowd of 18,500. The second Texans game was also Barbers Appreciation Day. All barbers wearing their white jackets were admitted free. By game time, so were any and all fans wearing white.

Tex Schramm was not amused. The crosstown rivals were papering the house with freebies, and those fans who did show up to watch his team's debut were not the kind of crowd he had anticipated. "I'm surprised Lamar Hunt didn't have a day where ice throwers at our games got in free to see the Texans," he complained. "About the only thing left for them to do is open the gates and forget about tickets."

The Cowboys were taking the high road. "We think that when the product is worth having, it should be paid for."

While the Cowboys could have learned a few promotional tricks from the Texans, there were some things the Cowboys did better, Schramm liked to point out, such as playing pro teams fans had actually heard of.

But when it came to football and sports in general, Lamar out-innovated Clint. He had started not only a team from scratch but an entire league. Backing up his motivation was the five-year agreement the new league had with the ABC television network. Unlike the NFL, which allowed teams to cut their own broadcasting deals, the ABC arrangement was for the whole league, guaranteeing each franchise $200,000 and helping the bottom line.

On the field, the AFL brought color to a black-and-white game, introducing the two-point conversion after touchdown and free substitution; "the most exciting rules in the game — pro, college, or high school," according to the *Dallas Morning News*'s Charles Burton.

Player name identification on uniforms, shared gate receipts and television rights, and ABC's utilization of moving cameras on the field for televised games, as well as fixed cameras positioned at midfield, like the NFL, gave the AFL a whole other look. Team rosters featuring far more African Americans, who played in many different positions, achieved the same effect internally.

But no matter what Lamar Hunt and his new league did, it was never enough, not with two teams competing for fans in a one-team market. After Hunt wooed sportswriters assigned to cover the Texans with a trip to Las Vegas, Clint Jr. responded by flying all the scribes covering the Cowboys to Spanish Cay, his private island in the Bahamas, where he plied them with Coca-Congas, a concoction of coconut milk, rum, and lime juice.

Despite his competitive nature, Hunt wasn't entirely comfortable about the split in Dallas that the two teams had created. The Lions Club backed the Texans. The more powerful Salesmanship Club was behind the Cowboys. When Hunt threw a party for his first wife's dentist at Lamar's brick, middle-class home, one of the invited guests was Don McIlhenny, who had played with Lamar at SMU and then with the Green Bay Packers before being added to the Cowboys roster. Lamar cornered McIlhenny as he was leaving the party.

"Don, I hope you're not mad at me," he said.

"For what?" McIlhenny inquired.

"For starting this new league," Hunt replied.

"I'm not mad at you. I think it's great," McIlhenny told him.

"Swell!" Lamar said, brightening visibly. "Then come over again sometime and we'll shoot some baskets."

DURING THE OCTOBER 9 game against the Redskins at Griffith Stadium in Washington, Eddie LeBaron, the Cowboys' diminutive quarterback, who was known to his teammates as the Squirrel, threw the shortest touchdown pass ever, a *two-inch* pass to Dick Bielski to cut the 'Skins lead to 19–14 before Washington went on to a 26–14 win, their first of the season. Two weeks later, after passing his bar exam, LeBaron was admitted to the bar in the state of Texas and proceeded to join the prestigious Wynne, McKenzie, Jaffe, and Tinsley law firm.

LeBaron was clearly a leader, no matter his physical stature. A Marine and a Korean War hero, as well as a Pro Bowl quarterback, he was just small, that's all. "The team had a play called the Poor Little Bastard play, when all the team would dog pile on him," marveled the sportswriter Gary Cartwright. But from a receiver's or a defender's perspective, he was the one who accurately tossed the ball above and beyond the mash-up of big men pushing and shoving, more often than not hitting his target.

Despite the talents of the Little General and veterans such as Jerry Tubbs and Frank Clarke, the team had little to sell. The Cowboys lost every game at home. They looked horrible and played worse. The only good news was that precious few witnessed the debacles. Twelve thousand tickets had been sold for the San Francisco 49ers game at the Cotton Bowl, but a cold November rain kept most of the crowd away. Those who did show completely disappeared from the view of the press box when they took shelter under the upper deck during a downpour.

The season's one highlight came on a cold December day at New York's Yankee Stadium in the next to the last game. L. G. (Long Gone) Dupre caught two LeBaron touchdown passes and ran for another, leading the Cowboys to a 31–31 tie with Tom Landry's old team. University of Texas Coach Darrell Royal compared tie games to "kissing your sister," but this one felt like a victory to the Cowboys and to New York fans, who responded by showering the field with whiskey and beer bottles.

When the Cowboys arrived back in Dallas, two fans were waiting at Love Field holding a sign that read NICE GOING, COWBOYS.

The coach was perhaps the most valuable player of that first season, simply for organizing the team and recruiting three assistants — Babe Dimancheff, Brad Ecklund, and Tom Dahms — to oversee the backfield, offensive line, and defensive line, respectively. At the very least, Landry cut a dashing figure on the sidelines, dressed impeccably in coat, tie, and a snazzy fedora that his wife had picked out for him. His sartorial splendor, in marked contrast to most coaches' outfits, was a tip of the hat to Landry's college coach Blair Cherry, who believed coaches should appear businesslike and professional in public.

THE PRO FOOTBALL PLAYERS themselves weren't celebrities around Dallas. Singer Trini Lopez was a star, not players with stars on their helmets. TV kiddie-show hosts Mr. Peppermint, Officer Friendly, and Icky Twerp, and disc jockeys Jimmy Rabbit and the Weird Beard, were better known. But the quarterbacks carried just enough name recognition to get involved in the presidential campaign of Republican Richard M. Nixon, who was running against John F. Kennedy. Don Meredith, the more familiar face owing to his career at SMU, chaired the Dallas County Athletes for Nixon. Eddie LeBaron, a well-connected former resident of DC, was part of Nixon's national committee.

Dallas fans took sides, save for a few who were so smitten with football of any sort that they attended home games of both teams. Affluent North Dallas tended to go with Clint's team because of his family connections. South Dallas tilted toward the Texans, who featured Lincoln High running back Abner Haynes.

Mike Rhyner's father chose the Texans for his family in blue-collar Oak Cliff. "The first thing I remember really being grabbed by [on television] was the '58 [National Football League] championship game between the Colts and the Giants," Mike said.

"[My father's] explanation why we were going to be Texans fans and not Cowboys fans had more to do with the entrepreneurial spirit of Lamar Hunt: 'Look, this guy has been trying to get into the NFL for years and years and they never would let him and so finally he had enough and went out and started his own league. When he did that the NFL said no, no, no, wait, wait, wait and tried to talk him into coming on board with them. But by then he had his thing up and running so they said okay you're going to do that, we're going to put a team there of our own.' All that kind of went over the head of a ten-year-old kid. I didn't care. All I knew is that we had two football teams and that if my dad said we were going to support the Dallas Texans, that was fine with me."

The teams had fans—the Texans estimated average attendance of 24,500 led the AFL—but they lost about what the Cowboys did that first year: $700,000. H. L. Hunt was asked about his son Lamar dropping a million dollars a year on his football team. He replied, "At that rate, the boy only has 123 years to go."

Blackie Sherrod, the most prosaic of Dallas's sportswriters, wishfully envisioned a silver lining in the two Dallas teams if they'd only quit feuding. "Should the Doves of Peace suddenly descend upon us and olive branches flutter all around and Peace and Goodwill might become the uniform of the day, then us tenderfeet might have a right dandy pro football team in the city limits," he wrote after that first season. "That is, if you could lump the Cowboys and the Texans in the same pot and pick out the choicest chunks."

Curtis Sanford, the Dallas sports promoter who founded the Cotton Bowl Classic, proposed something equally tasty: a showdown between the two local pro teams with Texas-death-match wrestling rules—$100,000 to the winner; the loser leaves town. Lamar Hunt was all for it. "It doesn't sound like a bad idea at all. It would solve a lot of problems," he said. "Utterly preposterous, it's simply impossible," Bedford Wynne protested. Clint Murchison wisecracked that the winner should be able to leave town and the loser had to stay.

Tex Schramm preferred looking at the bigger competition. "The real problem is to put on an attraction of sufficient interest to cause people to go to the inconvenience of attending in person," he wisely observed. "Our competition comes from air-conditioning, swimming pools, television, barbecue pits, and other attractions that might keep fans at home."

Reality Bites, the Greek Chorus
Wails, and a Star Is Born

When the season ended, most of the players returned to the cities they'd come from and to their main jobs. Playing pro football for a living was a marginal proposition for all but a handful of players: salaries averaged well under ten thousand dollars.

Tom Landry went back to the drawing board: watching film, studying playbooks, developing more schematics with his assistants. Tex Schramm gave the sportswriters at the newspapers plenty to write about and kept the radio and television broadcasters talking about the Cowboys. Gil Brandt worked his network of scouts across the nation to figure out whom to draft.

Meanwhile, Clint Murchison Jr., along with his older sibling, John Dabney, was making deals and redefining the Texas millionaire as "more Brooks Brothers than illiterate millionaires in ten gallon hats," according to *Time* magazine. The brothers were featured on the cover of the June 16, 1961, issue for a story headlined "Making Money Work: A Texas Technique." The coverage focused on their hostile takeover of the Allegheny Corporation, a prominent New York holding company whose businesses included New York Central, the Baltimore and Ohio Railroad, and Investors Diversified Services, one of the world's largest mutual funds. The Murchisons had been kicked off the board of IDS the previous year, and, offended, they took on noted Wall Street financier Allan Kirby in a proxy fight over the acquisition, ultimately ousting Kirby.

The Murchison brothers were portrayed as wheeler-dealers who flew their own planes, used telephones with scrambling devices to prevent their conversations from being wiretapped, and borrowed money to grow their enterprises, which consisted of more than a hundred companies.

They had taken to heart Clint Sr.'s advice: "Money is like manure. If you spread it around, it does a lot of good. But if you pile it up in one place, it stinks like hell."

After Clint purchased Spanish Cay, an island in the Bahamas (emulating his father, who had once owned Matagorda Island, off the Texas coast), sidekick Bob Thompson mentioned Junior's island purchase to Senior, who groused, "Next thing the sumbitch will want is a string of racehorses and mistresses." When Thompson related the old man's reaction to Clint Jr., the son called the father on the telephone and asked, "Do you know where I can get a string of racehorses?"

It was not a wholly facetious question. The Murchison brothers counted a Vail Mountain ski lodge, the Palm Springs Racquet Club, and the Daytona Speedway among their numerous holdings.

John Dabney was the more conservative and cautious of the two and tended to investigate potential deals with a thoroughness that bordered on nitpicking. Clint worked more impulsively and enjoyed taking on projects that would be fun as well as profitable. One of C.W. Jr.'s more storied enterprises was an experimental methane-gas processing plant in Oklahoma, which was lovingly hyped as the Caloric Reclamation Anaerobic Process, or CRAP.

Clint even invested in a venture with Dallas broadcasting entrepreneur Gordon McLendon. McLendon consistently exceeded his own exploits, hatching outrageous promotions that included arranging treasure hunts, having a girl in a bikini perch on a billboard along

Central Expressway, and putting a man atop a flagpole to draw attention to his station. Now McLendon created a floating commercial radio station off the coast of Sweden called Radio Nord to thwart the restrictive broadcast laws of Sweden and bring to Europe the popular Top 40 sound that McLendon had developed in Dallas.

Radio Nord's studios were on board the *Bon Jour*, a trawler anchored in the Stockholm archipelago, which was beyond the jurisdiction of Swedish broadcasting regulators. Clint's associate Bob Thompson fronted the venture, and Jack S. Kotschack, a Finnish-Swedish entrepreneur, managed the station. Murchison and McLendon remained silent partners.

Radio Nord went on the air on March 8, 1961, broadcasting in Swedish and presenting a McLendon-inspired mix of music, news, contests, and disc jockey banter with commercials peppered in between. McLendon's formula proved so appealing, several nations, including Sweden, passed laws to ban it. The new laws cramped the station's broadcasts effectively enough that Radio Nord had to go off the air sixteen months later.

The *Bon Jour* was later renamed *Mi Amigo* and was anchored off the coast of southern England, where the onboard radio station became Radio Atlanta, named for McLendon's home town of Atlanta, Texas. The offshore station eventually became the southern station of Radio Caroline, the most popular pirate radio station ever.

In 1964 McLendon shared his offshore broadcasting experience with Eastland, Texas, oilman Don Pierce, who created a mirror of McLendon's radio station on a pirate ship off the coast of England that was going to be called Radio KLIF London but that went on the air instead as Radio London.

Murk (as C.W. Jr. was known) didn't make much on the Radio Nord deal, and profit was always his first priority, but he did help give birth to pirate radio. Tweaking the noses of the powerful was almost as much fun as making money. Besides, his friendship with McLendon earned invitations to wild parties at McLendon's Cielo

Ranch, near Lake Dallas, where guests included movie star and Western icon John Wayne and a bevy of pretty women.

Like McLendon, Clint was an outsider in Dallas, although not as much as the Hunts were. All three families had accumulated immense wealth, moved in similar circles, and attended the same debutante balls and society fund-raisers as the rest of the Dallas elite, but neither the Murchisons nor the Hunts nor the McLendons were regarded as civic-minded enough to be invited to join the powerful Dallas Citizens Council.

For all his wheeling and dealing, C.W. Jr. had most of his fun being around the football team and running with his Rover Boys, as sportswriter Blackie Sherrod called Clint's associates Bedford Wynne, Bob Thompson, Fritz Hawn, George Owen, Mitch Lewis, Steve Schneider, and other assorted friends. Sherrod would have known. One night, he came home to find a goat tied to the stair railing of his apartment with an attached note from Clint: *You got my goat with what you wrote, so am delivering the same.*

Sherrod was hardly the only one surprised by an animal. When J. Edgar Hoover, the director of the Federal Bureau of Investigation, came to Dallas for a quiet stay at Bob Thompson's, he was greeted by a jackass tied to the stairwell inside Thompson's front door.

Thompson, who referred to Clint as Little Murchison, and Mitch Lewis loved to barhop with Clint in New York, jumping from Toots Shor's to the 21 Club and back over the course of a well-spent evening. In Dallas, the whole city was fair game.

"The Rover Boys would all show up at Bud [Shrake]'s apartment whenever he threw a party," Gary Cartwright said. More often than not, Clint arrived with a woman who was not his wife. The press guys did not report his indiscretions. They knew Clint liked Bud and his girlfriend at the time, a stripper named Jada who worked for Jack Ruby.

Bob Thompson was Clint's pranking target as well as his collaborator. After Bob sent Clint numerous postcards from Hawaii, where he was relaxing on a friend's yacht during one particularly torrid Texas summer, Clint hired workers to tear down the wall in Thompson's garden, bring in a twenty-four-foot cabin cruiser, and place it in Thompson's swimming pool; Clint attached a sign that read JUST SO YOU WON'T MISS YOUR BOAT.

Clint sent the bills for the workers and the wall's teardown and restoration to Thompson.

Turnabout was fair play; Clint's friends hatched a plan. A few days before Christmas, while the Murchisons were entertaining at home, the friends had a large gift-wrapped box delivered. The box was so big it took two people to carry it in. When it was plopped down in front of Clint, a small voice inside the box pleaded, "Just don't give him a knife." Clint pulled the ribbon and out popped Lamar Hunt. Hunt may have been a pain in the ass as well as the pocketbook, as far as Clint Murchison was concerned, but theirs was a friendly sparring.

Murk was not quite so magnanimous toward George Preston Marshall. Clint and his Washington buddies set their sights on the Redskins owner, coming up with the Chicken Club, a conspiracy hatched among Murchison, Thompson, Tom Webb, and Dr. Joe Bailey, who was Clint Murchison Sr.'s heart surgeon and the Cowboys' cardiologist. They all took pleasure in one-upping one another, doing whatever they could to get laughs.

The night before the Redskins' December 1961 home game against Dallas, the Chicken Clubbers snuck into the stadium and spread ten pounds of chicken feed on the field. The plan was to disrupt George Preston Marshall's annual halftime Christmas extravaganza featuring Santa Claus in a wheeled sled towed by Alaskan huskies. When Santa arrived, seventy-six crated chickens that Murchison's Chicken Clubbers had smuggled into the bowels of the stadium would be released onto the field. As "Jingle Bells" played, the chickens would eat the feed and hopefully attract the attention of the huskies, who would go after them. All the chickens were white save for one black one, a subtle dig at Marshall, whose team was the only one in the league without black players.

The scheme was foiled when Redskins general manager Dick McCann discovered the chickens in the dugout before they could be released and refused the hundred-dollar bribe offered him by the two young men with Dallas field passes who were guarding the chickens.

Marshall complained to the commissioner's office about the "childish and immature" stunt, telling Rozelle, "I don't know anyone that can stop it but you." The tomfoolery ceased, except for anonymous calls to Marshall at all hours for the next several months. Whenever Marshall answered, the only sound he heard on the other end of the line was a clucking chicken.

Chastened but defiant, the Chicken Club returned for another appearance in DC the following season: while "Hail to the Redskins" played, four banners that each read CHICKENS were simultaneously unfurled from the upper decks, and two men dressed in chicken suits ran onto the field, released a live chicken, and threw plastic eggs until they were apprehended by security.

Murk's horsing around didn't stop at the stadium. Tom Webb and company arranged for Bob Thompson's prize Tennessee walker to be led through Duke Zeibert's restaurant to win a bet with Murchison.

Murchison enjoyed pranking other teams too. For the Cowboys' first game in Chicago, Murchison staged a photo shoot with a live bear being "shot" by a cowboy. Afterward, Clint's crew took the bear to his penthouse suite and fed the animal alcohol. At an official function in New York, Clint placed a Cowboys sticker on Mayor Wagner's portrait, right on the mayor's lapel. New York restaurateur Toots Shor managed to score Murchison a few extra tickets to a Giants-Cowboys game at Yankee Stadium, and Murchison returned the favor when Shor asked for box seats to a Giants-Cowboys game in Dallas: he mailed him two entire sections' worth of tickets for the game at the Cotton Bowl, where there was always plenty of room, since the team was averaging 21,000 spectators per game at home in 1961.

Murchison wasn't the only one in on the joke. "A guy come in one day at the dealership and asked if I'd seen the car parked downtown with two Cowboys tickets laying on top of the dash," said Eddie Stone, who worked for auto dealer W. O. Bankston. "He said somebody broke the windshield and left two more Cowboys tickets on the dash."

OF COURSE, the real game was on the field, and the highlights of an otherwise expectedly miserable 4-9-1 season in 1961 were the play of Don Perkins, the other original Cowboy besides Don Meredith, and first-round draft pick Bob Lilly from TCU, who had been installed at defensive end for his pass-rushing skills and his speed, despite his six-foot-five, 260-pound interior-lineman size. Lilly had been wooed by both leagues but was swayed by the Cowboys' Gil Brandt. On one of his first meetings with the draft pick, Brandt pulled out a hundred-dollar bill and stuck it in Lilly's pocket, telling him, "Go have some fun." After Lilly signed with Dallas, Brandt sidled up to Lilly. He wanted his hundred dollars back. Lilly told him to go to hell.

Don Perkins, an African American, had grown up in Waterloo, Iowa, where he was student-body president and where he led his high school football team to an undefeated season and the state's eleven-man championship his final year. He excelled at the University of New Mexico, where he set several rushing records over the course of the 1957, 1958, and 1959 seasons and led the nation in kickoff returns his senior year.

Perkins had signed a personal-services contract with Clint Murchison in 1959 for $10,000 a year with a $1,500 signing bonus. But he broke his fifth metatarsal during training camp and sat out the 1960 season. Once he finally did take the field for the Cowboys, he recorded the first 100-yard rushing game for the team, averaged 4.1 yards per carry, and earned NFL Rookie of the Year honors.

Don Perkins received less than a hero's welcome when he first arrived in Dallas. He landed at Love Field and hailed a cab to take him to his temporary residence. The cabdriver informed him he'd flagged down the wrong cab. It was against the law for a white cab-driver to drive a black fare from the airport. So Perkins waited for a colored cab, which took him to his new home in South Dallas — Oak Cliff, to be exact, one part of Dallas where African Americans could live, according to the segregation laws.

After the 1960 college all-star game, which Perkins had been planning to play in until he broke his foot, Gil Brandt took Meredith and Perkins back to Dallas and offered to treat them to dinner at the Highland Park Cafeteria. But while standing in line, Perkins was informed by management that he couldn't eat at the cafeteria. It was for white people only.

Perkins was no stranger to the segregated South. His father had eventually settled in Waterloo, Iowa, after leaving his hometown of Sterrett, twenty-five miles south of Dallas. He'd gotten into a fight with a white boy, and, fearing jail or even lynching, the elder Perkins had escaped to Canada; he drifted down to Iowa in search of work once he felt it was safe to return to the United States.

COMING TO DALLAS WAS like going home in many ways. Perkins had fond memories of summer trips to Texas to see kinfolk when he was growing up. But despite the familiarity, he was entering a place like none he'd known before. Dallas itself was the most racially divided city he'd ever lived in, with laws to back that up.

It was not easy that first season, the second season, or in subsequent years. At the end of every season, Perkins inevitably high-tailed it back to Albuquerque, where his football stardom at UNM guaranteed him a job better than driving trucks, which was the best offer he could get in Dallas.

When Perkins joined the Cowboys, the league's unspoken policy of stacking limited the number of blacks on a team's roster, and certain positions, such as middle linebacker and quarterback, were considered off-limits for black players. The Cowboys would be different. When Tex Schramm was GM of the LA Rams, the football club had more players of color than any NFL franchise, and he prided himself on remaining color-blind with the Cowboys.

The Cowboys were one of the first nongovernment organizations in Dallas in which blacks and whites worked alongside each other, in concert with each other, toward a common goal. Blacks roomed with blacks, and whites roomed with whites, but when it came to the game, race vanished. They were all Cowboys.

Schramm quietly arranged for the Ramada Inn by Love Field to drop its all-white policy for visiting NFL teams, which had been bussing their black players to a run-down colored hotel in Fort Worth.

SINCE THE TWO DALLAS teams refused to play each other, one of the few competitions beyond ticket sales was in the broadcast booth. Charles Boland, who had called the NFL Dallas Texans games in 1952, did the play-by-play for the Cowboys on their new flagship radio station, KLIF, assisted by former SMU coach Bill Meek.

Frank Glieber became the voice of the Cowboys on television, replacing Lindsey Nelson, on CBS, which for the first time secured a contract with the entire NFL rather than individual teams. Glieber also hosted four different Cowboys shows on radio and television for KRLD.

In an interview with the *Dallas Times Herald*, Murchison was asked how long two pro teams could survive in Dallas. "As long as the Texans are here, there will be two teams," he replied. He wisecracked through the Q and A, and in response to a question about whether he would retain ownership of the team *if* the team moved, he answered, "Have you stopped beating your wife?"

Lamar Strikes Back

ONE WAY TO ATTRACT fans and beat the competition was to put a better product on the field. The Cowboys continued trying to improve their roster by drafting Guy "Sonny" Gibbs, the six-foot-seven quarterback from the TCU Horned Frogs in Fort Worth, in the first round and defensive end George Andrie in the sixth round, although Andrie's school, Marquette University, had dropped football in his senior year.

Gil Brandt and company scoured college and pro rosters for free agents and potential trades, and they obtained kicker Sam Baker from Cleveland, tight end Lee Folkins from Green Bay, and Dick Nolan from the New York Giants, with the idea Nolan would be a defensive assistant to Landry, who had coached him in New York. But Nolan was activated as a player and started at safety for several games before he was hurt.

Tex Schramm found Jerry Norton, a journeyman on the line who'd retired from the St. Louis Cardinals, working construction in Dallas. "Tex called and wanted to know if I would come out," Norton said. He went to his boss, Eddie Garland, and told him the situation. "Yeah, go ahead and play, you don't do a damn thing anyway. Do what you've got to do." So Norton quit construction and suited up for the Cowboys, a team unlike any Norton had played for. "They had every troublemaker, everybody over the hill," he said. "That was the trouble with an expansion team. It was either that, or guys that were young and had never started before."

Free-agent signees were an unconventional bunch: receiver Pettis Norman from Johnson C. Smith, a historically black small college in Charlotte, North Carolina; Mike Gaechter, a defensive back who also excelled in track and field at the University of Oregon; and Cornell Green, a basketball player from Utah State who was also the number-one pick of the Chicago Zephyrs franchise in the National Basketball Association.

Those efforts paid off with five wins and a handful of individual highlights for the 1962 season, while Landry institutionalized the quarterback shuffle, with Eddie LeBaron and Don Meredith alternating every other play.

Eddie LeBaron's stellar passing qualified him as one of the league's top-ranked quarterbacks, which earned him a trip to the Pro Bowl; Billy Howton's team-leading 49 catches complemented Frank Clarke's 47 pass receptions (averaging 22 yards per reception) and 14 touchdowns, which earned Clarke All-Pro status; a stellar ground game earned All-Pro honors for Don Perkins; Perkins's backfield counterpart Amos Marsh averaged 25 yards on kickoff returns. Two individual achievements in a game against the Philadelphia Eagles were most memorable: Mike Gaechter's record-setting 100-yard interception for a touchdown and Amos Marsh's 101-yard kickoff return, the combination of which led the Cowboys to a 41–19 win in the Cotton Bowl.

The offense even finished second in the league, averaging 350 yards per game, and in points scored. But the team finished fifth in the Eastern Conference at 5-8-1, nowhere near close enough to back up Schramm's boasts that his Cowboys were superior to Lamar Hunt's Texans.

"The NFL was very traditional—two back offense, you run the ball, you throw on third down and every once in a while you throw on first down," said young quarterback Jerry Rhome, who grew up playing and watching football in Dallas. "Shoot, the American Football League had them all over the field. They were doing all kinds of things. They were running reverses and fake punts. They had to."

Slowly but surely, AFL attendance increased from barely half-full stadiums to near sellouts. Network viewer numbers were on an upward curve, giving hope to team owners, who were emptying their pocketbooks to offer competitive contracts to graduating college players and to any NFL player willing to jump leagues. Despite the considerable odds, the new league was surviving.

While the Cowboys were getting kicked up and down the field, the Texans were winning big, posting an 11-3 record for 1962. The major breakthrough came on December 23, at rickety Jeppesen Stadium on the campus of the University of Houston, where the Texans played the Oilers for the AFL championship.

The Oilers provided formidable opposition, aided by blustery winter weather, which evened the playing field. At the final gun, the teams were tied 17–17, and the game went into two overtimes before being resolved, a first for a pro football championship. The Texans' Abner Haynes won the coin toss at the start of OT and announced to officials and a national television audience, "We'll kick to the clock," meaning his team would kick into the gusting wind. Haynes, who had torched the Oiler defense with a running touchdown and a pass-reception TD, meant to say the Texans wanted the wind at their backs, but when he prefaced that remark with *kick*, he put his team in a deep hole. Despite the gaffe and the pounding the Texans D Line took from fullback Charlie "the Human Cannonball" Tolar, the Texans prevailed, winning 20–17 with Tommy Brooker's field goal after 77:54 of football, the longest game ever played.

The wild finish captivated a national television audience of 56 million, who had no other football to watch that afternoon.

The Texans would enter the 1963 season as the American Football League's champions, while the ABC television network increased its renewal offer to the AFL. The Texans' quarterback, Len Dawson, was the AFL Player of the Year, running back Curtis McClinton won AFL Rookie of the Year honors, and Hank Stram, not Tom Landry, won the Knute Rockne Professional Football Coach of the Year award.

Despite the Cowboys' poorer record, NFL partisans were unyielding. "We hated [the Texans]. No one would ever consider the Dallas Texans," said David Wynne before acknowledging the other side of the coin. "You have no idea the number of times we sat there with ten thousand, fifteen thousand people in the Cotton Bowl. They might as well have been playing checkers in there."

Loser Leaves Town

With everything looking to be in the Texans' favor, the good people of Dallas were somewhat puzzled when rumors began to fly that Lamar Hunt wanted to move the team. The biggest sports topic around Dallas (besides the desire for major-league baseball) had been which Dallas franchise would fold first. The standoff between two men who could each afford to drop several million dollars more to win the argument had turned into a high-risk poker game of Mexican Sweat. Both had survived three seasons, and the upstarts appeared to have the edge with an average announced attendance of 22,201 a game for the 1962 season, slightly higher than the Cowboys average of 21,417 fans. More significant, the Texans were winning.

In fact, actual attendance for both teams was closer to 10,000, Hunt admitted years later. "The Cowboys drew only 9,800, but we had a championship team and they were losing, so beating them [in attendance] was nothing to be proud of."

As much as Lamar Hunt loved football, it was his nature to watch the bottom line. His team was losing money, and in addition, he, along with other AFL owners, had had to pump cash into the New York Titans to keep the franchise from folding after the league took it over from owner Harry Wismer. Even before the Texans won the AFL title, Hunt had started looking at Atlanta, New Orleans, and Miami as places to move his team, although officially he was making exploratory trips for league expansion. Hunt considered New Orleans to be the most attractive, but Tulane University, which owned the big stadium in the city, balked, fearing the pro game would hurt attendance at Tulane games.

Kansas City mayor H. Roe "Chief" Bartle caught wind of Lamar's stated reasons for his travels, and he launched a campaign to secure an AFL franchise for his city. The offer Bartle made was so loaded with incentives that Hunt was convinced it would be better, for him and for the league, to move the Texans to Kansas City instead of awarding Kansas City an expansion franchise. If Hunt came north, he was guaranteed free rent at Kansas City Municipal Stadium, the downtown baseball park where the American League Athletics played; in addition, another fourteen thousand seats would be added to the venue; he'd be guaranteed sales of three times as many season tickets as were sold in Dallas; he'd have TV and radio rights; and in the future, a stadium would be built just for football. All Hunt had to do was call the moving vans, and profits were assured.

Lamar Hunt may have been Dallas proud, but he was no fool. Kansas City was close enough to Dallas that the owner could commute by plane, and the market appeared ripe for pro football.

Before announcing the team's move, Hunt met again with Clint Murchison and Tex Schramm. "We came to the conclusion that the Cowboys were not really interested in leaving," Hunt said. What he didn't say was that Texans general manager Jack Steadman had asked Schramm what it would take for the Texans to leave town. Schramm, after consulting with Clint Murchison, had come up with a number: $150,000, to be paid under the table. Hunt took the offer, and in exchange provided the Cowboys with his mailing list and his practice facilities.

Hunt had already signed an agreement to move to Kansas City anyway, but he pocketed the loose change from Murchison before he went public about the move.

Hunt called a press conference in Kansas City on February 9 to tell the world the Dallas Texans were moving to Kansas City, contingent on Kansas City's fulfilling the promise of selling 25,000 season tickets. After the Cowboys had been created, Hunt said, "I thought we could win the attendance war if I had a winning team. I was wrong. Two teams cannot operate successfully here, especially with the territory being saturated with television. If we could black out TV, two clubs might be successful, but that cannot be done. Dallas is the sorest spot. It is the only one having two clubs where the potential is not large enough to indicate that either can be successful in the competition. If we move to Kansas City, it probably will relieve the tension between the two leagues."

H. Roe Bartle took to the podium and graciously stated, "The mayor of Kansas City wants a team here even if he has to steal under the shades of night from a great city like Dallas." Kids holding a banner that read WELCOME HOME, K.C. SOMETHINGS stood behind the men as Hunt adjusted his tie.

Kansas City business and civic leaders got busy selling season tickets even as a Keep Our Champs at Home movement was started by the Spur Club, and on May 22, Hunt called another press conference making the move six hundred miles north official, even though only 13,025 season tickets had been sold in Kansas City. Even if the demand was less than anticipated, he had $600,000 banked before the season had started, more than any other AFL team had generated in season tickets.

"Kansas City has earned the right to be represented in pro football and I am flattered that Kansas City has chosen the Dallas Texans as the team they want," Hunt said, keeping his game face on. Four days later, he demonstrated his geographic sensitivity and proved his ability to grease a pol and buy influence when he announced the team would change its name to the Chiefs.

"We flipped a coin, and I lost," C. W. Murchison Jr. joked.

But Tex Schramm was hardly magnanimous in his farewell. "We think we've made big strides in the past three years in building a team that can uphold the football tradition of the Southwest. We're quite optimistic about the coming season. We think we're definitely in position to bid for a championship a year ahead of schedule," he said, referring to Landry's original five-year plan.

Blackie Sherrod regarded the Texans' departure as a jab to the entire city. "Regardless of motives or strategy, the image of Dallas as an enthusiastic, progressive metropolis was damaged," he wrote in the *Times Herald*.

Instead, the puny attendance figures of the warring pro teams became a black eye to the city itself.... The city must take a new look at its sports picture, make immediate plans to repair the damage. Slick up the Cotton Bowl, make badly needed repairs to the stadium and its surroundings, do a little enthusiastic sprinting instead of cautious, reluctant steps in the dark. The Cowboys themselves have much work to do. They must promote in surrounding areas, something that's been sadly neglected. They must stimulate, encourage, sell, merchandise, bang the drum and cymbal. The city's climb back into a progressive sports reputation is a must. And it won't be an overnight thing. Recovery will be slow, but it's much better than none at all.

After having quietly paid the $150,000, the Cowboys moved into the Texans field house and practice field on Yale Boulevard by Central Expressway, forever abandoning the rats and other charms of the not-so-friendly confines of Burnett Field; the deal included a clause giving Lamar Hunt the option to purchase 25 percent of the Cowboys if the Kansas City franchise folded. The Cowboys also relocated team offices a few blocks north to 5738 North Central Expressway. Before home games, the team would stay at the new Holiday Inn Central instead of their old pregame headquarters, the Ramada Inn at Love Field.

The Dallas Cowboys Football Club of the National Football League had the Cotton Bowl to itself on Sundays. If Landry's plan was all that Schramm, Murchison, and Brandt believed it was, the dividends were about to pay off. The quarterback shuffle was history. Landry was going to let LeBaron and Meredith duke it out in camp for the starting job.

Tex Schramm moved the 1963 season's training camp to Thousand Oaks, California, an hour north of Los Angeles, as part of an arrangement with Glenn Davis, a former LA Ram star who was in charge of the *Los Angeles Times* annual summer charity exhibition game. Davis had suggested to Tex that if the Cowboys were at Thousand Oaks, the team could provide the competition for the Rams in the preseason game, which attracted crowds in excess of 50,000.

Summer home was the campus of California Lutheran College. CLC's facilities were as ideal as the area's weather. Unlike at the first three training camps, in Oregon, Wisconsin, and Michigan, it hardly ever rained in this part of Southern California. The constant Pacific breezes kept daytime high temperatures well below 90 degrees, and nights were cool and pleasant enough that you could sleep with the windows open.

The NFL's league-wide television deal with CBS for just under five million dollars a year was renegotiated to three times that amount as the nation's sports fans began to embrace the pro game on TV.

Locally, Frank Glieber returned to call games on television, paired with Davey O'Brien, while KLIF became the flagship station of the Cowboys as the Texas State Network obtained the rights to broadcast Cowboys games on the radio statewide. Rick Weaver, an announcer from the West Coast by way of Wichita, Kansas, was paired up with KLIF newsman Gary DeLaune in the radio booth.

Tex Maule, the *Sports Illustrated* writer who covered the NFL, set the bar high in a preseason article headlined "Dallas Defense Can Win in the East." Maule boldly predicted the franchise would finish atop the Eastern Division in its fourth year of existence. His optimism was understandable. He wanted to see the Dallas franchise succeed as much as any local did, since he'd covered sports for the *Morning News* before he reached the big time.

The team offered reasons to be optimistic. Tom Landry felt Don Meredith had matured enough as a quarterback to take the reins. He showed his stuff in a November game against San Francisco, ginning up 460 yards passing. The D end Lilly had two seasons far beyond anyone's expectations under his belt. Perk's ability to pound out yardage produced numbers that ranked him just behind the legendary Jim Brown. Billy Howton, in his twelfth season of professional football, was on the verge of setting the all-time league record for receptions. And captain Jerry Tubbs, the seasoned pro and defensive captain and the team's new player-coach, was mentoring the Cowboys' number-one draft pick, Lee Roy Jordan, at linebacker. An All-American at Bear Bryant's Alabama for three years, including one in which the team won the national championship, Jordan, at six foot one and 215 pounds, was considered small for his position but oversized in his effort, drive, and dedication. He grew up on a farm in Excel, Alabama, where every family member was a work hand, chopping cotton, clearing weeds, picking cotton. He'd been to Miami and Atlanta with the football team, "but Dallas was a step up," Jordan admitted. "It was so spread out. Flying in, you'd start seeing homes for a long time before you landed."

His first Cowboys contact was with Gil Brandt, a man he judged to be "full of it," but in a good way. "He was a salesman selling the Cowboys. He had a lot of information. Whether you could understand it or not, he was putting that information out."

Likewise, most players had been intimidated by the Cowboys playbook, which required critical thinking rather than gut reaction. But Jordan understood where Landry was coming from. The coach was specific: if a play started out a certain way, you had a particular response.

"It was quite extensive, starting from the front and going through every defense that we would have on there and what every player did on every play, what his responsibility was," Jordan said. "He gave you keys that would get you to the point of attack, where the ball or the runner intended to go. You had a primary responsibility. The secondary response was move to the ball. He was an engineer, so he drew these defenses so that if everybody took his responsibility the way it was designed, there would be no place for a runner to run, there wouldn't be any open holes. That was the deal—everybody take care of their responsibility down the line and keep spacing between you and your team."

Understanding that plan was one thing. Executing it was a whole other proposition, but Jordan was up to the task, and Tubbs told Jordan he was going to be the leader of the defense, since all the action went through the middle linebacker. Jordan had been a leader at Alabama and didn't mind challenging others to play their best, advising Bob Lilly on ways to make the defensive line stronger and urging him to motivate George Andrie to play at his level.

And it wasn't just the pro football team that was coming together in Dallas.

The city had grown into the nation's third-largest technology center, with Texas Instruments and defense contractor Ling-Temco-Vought leading the way. Trammell Crow and John Stemmons's Home Furnishing Mart had grown into the Dallas Market Center, the world's largest wholesale trade complex. In response, former Neiman-Marcus model Kim Dawson started up her own modeling agency in Dallas to provide talent for Crow's Apparel Mart, which was under construction to service the burgeoning fashion trade that Neiman-Marcus had inspired. And in September, Mary Kay Rogers, a successful marketing and direct sales trainer for Stanley Home Products who'd been passed over for promotion several times in favor of men she had trained, struck out on her own, investing five thousand dollars to launch her new business, Beauty by Mary Kay.

In Dallas, success seemed to be a matter of simply wanting it badly enough and being willing to work hard enough to get it. That all-things-are-possible attitude appeared to be infecting the local professional football club too.

Then the season started.

The boos that were mixed in with the cheers that greeted Don Meredith during pregame introductions at the first home game were a portent of what was to come. The Cowboys dropped their first four games, including the September 22 home game against the defending NFL champions, the Cleveland Browns, a game in which running back Jim Brown broke down Dallas's defense to set a single-game rushing record of 232 yards. "He was bigger than any of the linebackers and could run as fast as he wanted to," Lee Roy Jordan said. "He just ran fast enough to outrun whoever he needed to and was very elusive. You could never really get a good shot on him."

At the season's halfway mark, the Cowboys were 1-6. Fans and sportswriters howled that the wrong team had left Dallas. One of the few positives was Meredith, who, despite suffering early boos, had finally earned the right to start at quarterback.

He demonstrated his leadership through humor. Coach Landry had been sending in plays through receivers Buddy Dial and Pettis Norman, and one game, Norman had come in with a play called by Landry that Meredith ignored, instead diagramming a simple play in the grass that resulted in a touchdown. When Meredith returned to the sidelines, Landry began to chew him out for disregarding his called play. With Norman and several other black receivers standing behind Landry, Meredith told the coach with a straight face, "You know I can't understand what those niggers are saying." Landry's jaw clenched while Norman and the other players behind Landry tried to keep from laughing.

Whatever good the wisecracking Meredith did for the team on or off the field was negated by a flimsy offensive line that could not protect him against hard-charging defenses—so Dandy got used to taking physical hits from the opposition as well as verbal hits from the hometown fans.

Still, the Cowboys' performance did not detract from Dallas's reputation as a football hotbed. The second weekend of October, during the extended run of the State Fair of Texas, 55,000 witnessed the hometown SMU Mustangs' Friday-night upset of Heisman Trophy nominee Roger Staubach and the Naval Academy, the number-four-ranked college team in the nation, 32–28, when SMU's Billy Gannon scored from the one-yard line with 47 seconds left to play. The next day, number-one Texas punished number-two Oklahoma, winning 28–7 in the annual Texas-OU game in front of a sold-out house of 75,504. The Cowboys game the next day against Detroit was almost an afterthought, with less than a half-capacity crowd on hand to watch the home team's 17–14 victory over the Lions.

Pro ball had a ways to go if it was going to capture the hearts and minds of Texas football fans to the extent that the Southwest Conference or high school football did. But average attendance for Cowboys games had ticked up to nearly 27,000 because of growing expectations and the absence of the Dallas Texans.

For all the optimism exuded in the growing city, Dallas's ugly side reared its head in late October. The *Dallas Morning News*, through editorial-page editor Dick West, had been relentless in attacking President John F. Kennedy and his policies since his election in 1960, and in 1962 Kennedy became the convenient symbol of big bad federal government after he persuaded Congress to remove the distinction between repatriated profits and profits reinvested abroad, a decision that reduced the earnings wealthy oilmen enjoyed on foreign investments. Then, early in 1963, Kennedy announced he wanted to remove special privileges and loopholes, including the oil depletion allowance, in order to lower the tax burden on the poor. Texas oilmen would have to pony up another $300 million in taxes annually if Kennedy's plan went through.

Into this heated atmosphere, Adlai Stevenson, the U.S. ambassador to the United Nations, came to deliver a speech at the Dallas Memorial Auditorium on United Nations Day, October 24. Although the majority of the audience supported the United Nations and wanted to hear what Stevenson had to say, a noisy minority booed him, heckled him, and frequently interrupted his speech.

"The people who were jeering him were people of the extreme far right," said Wes Wise, the sportscaster and newsman who covered the event for KRLD. "At one time Stevenson stopped in the middle of his speech and said to this one particular man who was the worst, 'Sir, I don't have to come all the way from Illinois to teach Texans good manners, do I?' He got a big cheer for having said that."

After the speech, the protesters followed Stevenson to his car. One woman hit Stevenson on the head with a DOWN WITH THE UN sign while a man spat on him. "I just followed him out [of the building] with the camera and I could tell in the little tiny opening of the Bell & Howell camera that something had come over his head," Wes Wise said. "I didn't know it was quite as bad of an attack as it turned out to be. We didn't even edit the film. We got it on the air that night. The next day, [Walter] Cronkite put it on CBS and played it back over and over. The woman who hit him over the head claimed quote unquote 'a Negro pushed me from behind and forced me to hit him with the placard.' There wasn't a black face in the crowd and Cronkite told viewers that they'd see by the film there was no black face in the crowd."

The announcement that President Kennedy was coming to Dallas in late November as part of a brief political swing through Texas put official Dallas on edge again. "After the Stevenson incident, the city was terrified," Dallas historian Darwin Payne said. "The leaders did not want to have an embarrassing incident when the president came." Mayor Earle Cabell and police chief Jesse Curry made speeches encouraging citizens to give the president a good reception on his visit.

"Welcome Mr. President" read a black-bordered full-page ad in the *Dallas Morning News* attacking Kennedy for being a communist sympathizer. It ran on November 22, two days after Alabama governor and strident segregationist George Wallace came to Dallas to announce his candidacy for president of the United States as a Democrat. Among those who paid for the newspaper ad were Nelson Bunker Hunt, Lamar Hunt's brother, and oil magnate Bum Bright. "Wanted for Treason" leaflets with Kennedy's face were found in some newspaper racks around the city.

When Air Force One landed at Love Field that Friday morning, a large crowd welcomed the president and the First Lady. Vice President Johnson and his wife, Lady Bird, and Governor Connally and his wife, Nellie, joined the parade through downtown Dallas, where thousands of cheering people lined the streets. As the procession wound along Elm Street toward Stemmons Freeway and the Market Center, where local leaders were waiting with a luncheon to honor him, President Kennedy was gunned down and killed.

"We were on the practice field and Bedford Wynne came out and was talking to Tom," defensive captain Jerry Tubbs said.

I came out off of defense and was standing back there with Tom and said, "Coach, what's going on?" Bedford come up and he never did that. Coach said, "Some nut shot Kennedy," and we just kept right on. I went back to the huddle and somebody asked me, "What's going on, why is Bedford out there?" I said, "Somebody shot Kennedy." We didn't know if he was alive or dead. We had a player, I won't say who it was because he probably didn't really mean it, but he said, "I hope they kill the son of a bitch." That was kind of the attitude about Kennedy in Dallas.

Jerry Norton, the lineman from Texarkana who had been traded from the Cowboys to the Green Bay Packers, was driving back to his home from practice in Green Bay when fellow lineman Bill Forrester pulled alongside him. "It was cold as hell, and he was honking and honking and I rolled down the window," Norton recalled. "He said, 'They just shot Kennedy.' We'd been talking about Kennedy going to Dallas and thinking you better not go to Dallas cause you'll get shot. I said, 'How about that?' and rolled up the window. I thought he was kidding. Then I turned on the radio and heard the news."

The next day, Stanley Marcus called Erik Jonsson, the president of the Dallas Citizens Council, with a suggestion. "You ought to have a sunrise service for the president out at the Cotton Bowl, show that Dallas is grieving just as they are all over the country."

"Try again, Stanley," Jonsson replied. "We'll not have any meetings of any size anywhere if we can help it."

A day later, KRLD news director Eddie Barker persuaded members of the Dallas Citizens Council, including Jonsson, to go on camera and talk about the assassination for a segment that would be watched on CBS by viewers nationwide. "We made the tape and then that damn Barker cut us to pieces," Jonsson complained. "He added two black preachers to his piece of film, and one of them said, 'We got to put an end to the hate in this town.' Well, we were not a town of hate. That was a stupid thing for him to say, even if it'd been true. But he said it, and it was on the tape."

The Dallas Cowboys Football Club, along with everything and everyone else associated with the city, was considered complicit. On Sunday, two days after the shooting, the Cowboys played the Browns in Cleveland. The American Football League had canceled their games out of respect to the fallen president, but the National Football League would play their games as scheduled, commissioner Pete Rozelle announced, though televised games were being preempted by news coverage.

The Browns-Cowboys game at Municipal Stadium started as a solemn affair—"like a funeral," one eyewitness said—and grew more so after pregame warm-ups. Players in both dressing rooms in the bowels of the ancient stadium watched portable black-and-white televisions as Jack Ruby emerged from a gaggle of police and reporters in the basement of the Dallas police headquarters brandishing a Colt Cobra .38 pistol and then fired into the gut of Lee Harvey Oswald, the accused murderer of President Kennedy.

Cars with Texas license plates in the parking lots around Municipal Stadium were fair game for window smashing, key marking, and trashing.

Jerry Norton, the Texan who played for the Green Bay Packers, was in the lobby of a Milwaukee hotel when he heard about Oswald's being shot. "I asked our team doctor if the shot was going to kill him. He said, 'It's according to where they shot him.' Three of us from Texas were there and this lady came in and said, 'Well, I hope they kick them out the Union, get rid of them.' I turned around to her and said, 'Lady, I hope to hell they do. We're getting tired of supporting all you damn Yankees.' She just took off."

A week later, Stanley Marcus called a friend in Dallas to relate what he was hearing in New York about the Giants-Cowboys game. New York fans were describing the score as Giants, 34; Assassins, 27.

The Cowboys were a convenient target.

"The people of Dallas didn't have anything to do with it, so a lot of people kind of threw that at us," rookie Lee Roy Jordan said. "In Philadelphia and New York we got booed and hazed, called murderers and everything. *We* were the ones who killed President Kennedy. It was way off beat for people to think that, but they just identified us with Dallas and Dallas had killed the president."

Except for a brief mention in Gary Cartwright's wrap of the Cleveland game, the sports pages of the Dallas and Fort Worth newspapers did not say much about that dark day and the shadow it cast over the city. There was no need to dwell on that negativity. The Cowboys had raised expectations high enough that when they revealed their shortcomings, which they seemed to do whenever the going was getting good, they provided plenty of negativity.

Losing was taking its toll. "I was kind of dirty at times because I would get frustrated that we weren't winning," linebacker and coach Jerry Tubbs said, admitting, "I did some things; I'd clothesline receivers."

And when a season that had begun with high expectations ended with a three-game losing streak and a 4-10 record, Gary Cartwright led an increasingly vocal chorus calling for Tom Landry's head. How many years was it going to take for the Cowboys to field a decent team?

The city might have suffered a black eye publicity-wise, but its reputation as a football town remained stellar when the Cotton Bowl Classic hosted for the first time in its history the nation's two top-ranked college teams: number-one Texas against number-two Navy, the second game of the year in the stadium for both teams. For the Naval Academy, returning to Dallas was a mixed blessing, since the team had been embraced and adopted by former U.S. Navy commander President John F. Kennedy. Navy quarterback Roger Staubach dazzled the sellout crowd by completing 21 of 31 passes for 228 yards. But Texas's bulldog defense harassed the scrambling Staubach constantly and sacked him for 47 yards in losses as the Longhorns rolled to a 28–6 stomping.

"Dallas wasn't looked at too fondly," Staubach said. "There was still a stigma. But we stayed for a week at the Holiday Inn on Central and people were nice as could be to us. I could see it was a growing city, but we lost to Texas, so I wasn't really crazy about Dallas. I'd lost two football games here."

At the end of December, Stanley Marcus took out a print advertisement in both Dallas papers headlined "What's Right with Dallas?" Underneath the vertical-script Neiman-Marcus logo, he noted, in part:

> We think there's a lot right with Dallas. We think the dynamic growth of this city in the past thirty years has been no accident; that the factors that motivated this growth are still

present and can continue to contribute to the development of Dallas as one of the major centers of distribution, banking, specialized manufacturing, insurance in the country. We think Dallas' leadership which has devoted itself unselfishly to community problems and needs is unique in the country. We think our local government has been distinguished among all American cities by the integrity and honesty of its elected and appointed officials. We think that our citizens are friendly and kindhearted human beings who extend genuinely warm welcomes to newcomers in our city.

Marcus went on to recognize the truth in an observation that Dallas needed to address "an absolutism of political temper which is fundamentally hostile to our principles." He described "the man who thinks that he alone possesses wisdom, patriotism and virtue, who recognizes no obligation to accept community decisions with which he disagrees, who regards any means as justified by the end, who views the political process as a power struggle to impose conformity rather than a means of reconciling differences."

Nowhere in his paid advertisement did Marcus bring up the Cowboys.

From the Darkness, Light

DALLAS MAYOR EARLE CABELL resigned his position in early February of 1964 to successfully challenge right-wing congressman Bruce Alger. The move had been orchestrated by the Dallas Citizens Council, whose members realized Alger's zealotry was bad for the city's image, even though most of them agreed with Alger's politics. It was not in the city's best interests to be defined by the congressman and his ultraconservative followers, so it pleased the Dallas Citizens Council greatly when the popular Cabell bested Alger in the congressional race.

J. Erik Jonsson was drafted by the Citizens Charter Association arm of the Dallas Citizens Council to fill the rest of Cabell's term on the city council. The city council then voted Jonsson mayor, and by their doing so, the city gained a leader who was a local but didn't sound like one and who didn't come from the traditional leadership sectors of banking and retail. Unlike Cabell's pronounced Texas drawl, the Brooklyn-born Jonsson's accent was worldly and urbane — he was the kind of Dallasite the rest of the world needed to see and hear.

Before he announced his candidacy for mayor, Jonsson traveled to cities around the world with urban planner Vincent Ponte, whom he'd hired as a consultant. Great cities, Jonsson learned on these journeys, all had ports. Dallas was three hundred miles from the Gulf of Mexico, and a navigable Trinity River remained a pipe dream. But rail transportation had transformed both the nation and Dallas a century earlier, and aviation was doing the same thing now. With the advent of the 707 jet, airplane passengers could travel coast to coast in six hours. From Dallas, though, just about any American city was accessible in three hours or fewer, due to its central location.

Shortly after he took office, Jonsson declared the need for a new airport between Dallas and Fort Worth, despite considerable opposition from city and county leaders. The Federal Aviation Administration agreed with Jonsson and sent a letter to the mayors of Dallas and Fort Worth advising them that if they didn't take steps toward building a joint airport within six months, the FAA would select a site for them and mandate the airport's construction.

Not that there was anything wrong with Love Field, which was considered a modern state-of-the-art airport convenient to most of Dallas's residents. But Love Field had no room for future expansion, and if the two cities couldn't get together on a future airport, the FAA would do it for them.

Dallas leaders were nothing if not consistent. Why should Dallas accommodate Fort Worth? was their almost universal response. Love Field worked great. Fort Worth should go build its own airport.

Jonsson changed that kind of thinking. He leaned on business and civic leaders, forcing them to recognize that air travel was growing at a breakneck pace and that airports weren't keeping up. If Dallas honestly aspired to urban greatness, its leadership needed to think bigger and build bigger, utilizing all that open space Texas was known for. Dallas's competition wasn't Fort Worth, Jonsson complained. It wasn't Houston either. The competition was Chicago, home of O'Hare, the busiest airport in the world.

Jonsson had plans for the city beyond the airport and he was prepared to move it toward the twenty-first century with his Goals for Dallas initiative, a major makeover underwritten by bonds approved by voters.

The goals would improve the government of the city; the design of the city; its health, welfare, transportation, communication, and public safety; its elementary and secondary education; its higher education and continuing education; its cultural activities, recreation, entertainment; and the local economy.

Erik Jonsson had a vision for the city, but that vision did not include the Dallas Cowboys. "He really did not want Dallas to be identified as a sports city," said *Dallas Morning News* reporter Hank Tatum. "He wanted Dallas to be the city on the hill, the Emerald City that was bigger than a sports franchise."

Clint Murchison Jr. had a vision too, as evidenced by his new home at 6200 Forest Lane, which was finally fit to be occupied. The eight-bedroom, twelve-thousand-square-foot modern ranch house on twenty-five acres of prime North Dallas real estate in the Brook Hollow subdivision had taken more than eight years to finish. Clint himself dreamed up the place, which mixed elements of the architecture of Mies van der Rohe and Frank Lloyd Wright and featured lots of glass and steel and Italian travertine marble walls. He imagined the electronic bar that mixed drinks to order ("I don't care for tending bar," he told *Time* magazine), designed the home theater complete with a commercial movie projector, and installed such custom features as hand-finished panels that hid television sets, a lighting system without switches, a climate-controlled wine cellar, a room exclusively for Christmas presents and wrapping, a state-of-the-art sound system, and an underwater viewing room built into the side of the massive swimming pool.

Stanley Marcus proposed a collection of expensive Venetian glassware for the new home's dining room, but that was one area where Clint flinched. "The Venetian glassware is extremely handsome," he wrote to Marcus. "But I must admit the Italians have finally reached my choke price. I have too many unruly friends who insist upon throwing their goblets into the fireplace."

Clint was involved with the intricacies of furnishing his home, but he continued to stay out of the operations end of the football club. The one exception was coaching the Town North YMCA pee-wee football teams that his sons Burk and Robert played on on Saturday mornings during their elementary school days. Murchison eschewed the Tom Landry method of rotating guards to send in plays for the Cowboys offense in favor of flashing hand signals to his charges, a violation of YMCA football rules. After the games, he would call Landry to needle him, telling him that Murchison-coached teams never finished below second place.

But Landry already had a leg up on Coach Murk in the form of Salam Qureishi, the Cowboys' own Indian. Salam Qureishi had arrived at the Case Institute of Technology in Cleveland, Ohio, on a teaching fellowship the same month Tex Schramm had been hired by the Dallas Cowboys. A quiet man from the village of Singahi in Uttar Pradesh, India, Qureishi was a gifted statistician exceptionally knowledgeable about computers, something the IBM corporation was developing. IBM's truck-size metal contraptions could do mathematics faster than any human being and functioned like human brains, only quicker. At least, they did when they were properly programmed by humans, which was where Qureishi came in. He understood how computers worked. Because of that knowledge, he was hired by IBM straight out of college in July of 1961.

Tex Schramm had been introduced to the computer when he worked on the first televised Olympics for CBS. "IBM was doing all the scoreboards and the statistics, and they had computers—massive computers," he later said. Knowing he was to take the reins of the Cowboys after the Olympics, Schramm kept peppering the staff running the IBM computers with questions about what computers could do for a football team.

The Cowboys placed considerable emphasis on building a team for the future through the draft, not through trades. But scouts could reveal only so much about players, and though word of mouth was valuable, even the most trusted scouts in Gil Brandt's vast network could be helpful only to a point. The same went for film as an evaluation tool, when you could find film. The Cowboys would build a better system with the Indian.

"Our thought was that we could eliminate a lot of mistakes by finding out how fast a guy was," explained Brandt. "Paul Brown [of the Cleveland Browns] was really the first person that started timing people, but he timed them after they got to training camp, and he timed them for the purposes of cutting or keeping. But they were already saddled with them. We wanted to know before we got there. We changed from timing them for 50 yards and 100 yards to 40 yards. That's how the forties began. We set perimeters. We weren't going to draft a wide receiver who ran slower than four-point-seven [seconds in the 40-yard dash], we don't care what his background is. We're not going to draft a lineman that's shorter than six two. We had these parameters, so the players that we drafted were either going to wash out or going to be somebody that was going to turn out pretty good.

"We weren't going to trade for veterans that were over the hill to save your job for a year," Brandt said. "We were going to build our team with our players and our specifications. We were going to get smart guys with good character, tall guys, fast guys."

Shortly after the 1962 draft, Tex Schramm called the Dallas office of IBM. Taking note of the use of computers in the emerging space race between the United States and the Soviet Union, Schramm posited that if the company could help send a man to the moon, they could help the Cowboys win the NFL championship. "I want IBM to help me pick our new players from the draft," he said.

IBM's Dallas office referred Schramm's query up the chain of command until it reached the Statistical and Operations Analysis Group in San Jose, California—a one-person operation headed by Salam Qureishi. His adviser at IBM, Bob Togasaki, asked Qureishi if he knew anything about football. He replied that in India he had played the kind of football that Americans called soccer, and his knowledge of American football was limited to the names of Lou Groza and Johnny Unitas and to what he had seen on television.

Qureishi nonetheless flew to Dallas to meet Tex Schramm. Schramm told him he wanted a computer program that could evaluate and select college football players eligible for the NFL draft more efficiently than humans. Money was no object.

"With my heavy Indian accent and his Texan accent, we understood each other poorly at first," admitted Qureishi. "Somehow, we hit it off after a few initial missteps. To a statistician, the task was a selection-and-ranking problem: select the best set of players from a given universe of college players with known, measured characteristics."

After the Indian explained his approach, the Cowboy said, "Salam, don't you know football is played by only one sex—male?" When Qureishi said *set,* Schramm had heard *sex.*

Despite the occasional miscommunications, Qureishi sold Schramm on his solution. On his way back to the airport, Qureishi asked the local IBM salesman where he could get bacon.

"Why do you want bacon from Dallas when you can buy bacon in San Jose?" the salesman asked.

Qureishi answered that as he'd left San Jose to go to Dallas, his IBM sales manager had told him to "bring home the bacon."

The Dallas sales rep howled with laughter. "You probably already have," he told the Indian.

"We had an Indian who knew absolutely nothing about football and coaches who knew nothing about computers and less about Indians," Schramm said. "Luckily, Landry is always looking for a better way to do things. If he had not wanted to cooperate, we never could have succeeded."

A week later, Schramm called the IBM branch manager in San Jose and told him he was ready for the Indian to come back. Qureishi was provided mounds of statistical data gleaned from films and scouting reports. Analyzing the data was the hard part. Scouts relied on opinion and judgment. Qureishi wanted to rely on stats. The San Francisco 49ers and the Los Angeles Rams—Tex Schramm's old team—joined the experiment, which lowered the Cowboys' investment while increasing their database.

Qureishi needed a profile of what a great player should look like. Once he knew those criteria, Qureishi would develop a questionnaire that scouts could use to evaluate prospects.

Coaches and scouts offered three hundred variables for what made a player great. "At that time, the most sophisticated computer system could work with something like only eighty variables," explained Qureishi. "It was immediately evident that we would have to cut down. We reduced everything to five dimensions. But there was a problem of semantics. We had to make sure that the scouts and coaches all meant the same thing when they analyzed a player."

"We used to ask how quick a player was," Schramm said. "One coach said he was quick as a cat; another said he was quick as two cats." Later, Schramm said, "It was a long, painful process. It took us four years to find the elements that made successful football players. We finally got down to five things. One: character. Two: quickness and body control. Three: competitiveness [scouts had to evaluate to what extent the statement "He would hate his mother if she were on the other side" described a player]. Four: mental alertness [statement: "He finally catches on after much repetition"]. Five: strength and explosion [statement: "He is strong as a bull"].

In a trial run, just before the 1964 draft, all the scouting information that the Cowboys had collected on players was fed into the computer programmed by Qureishi with additional help from statisticians Ben Epstein and Shanti Gupta. Two hours later, it produced a list of the one hundred best prospects that year, starting with O. J. Simpson, ranked as the best college player in America, and followed by Joe Namath, Dick Butkus, Gale Sayers, and Fred Biletnikoff. (The computer didn't lie. Eighty-seven players on that list eventually turned pro.)

Qureishi stayed up for seventy hours straight to make sure his system really worked.

The experiment went so well, the system was implemented in the 1965 draft, which was held in Washington, DC. Qureishi flew to Washington from Dallas on the team charter, sitting next to Clint Murchison Jr., though neither talked to the other on the flight. Qureishi helped make choices in rounds sixteen through twenty, the traditional bottom of the barrel.

SALAM QUREISHI ARMED Gil Brandt and company with the numbers they craved most at a speed previously unimaginable. "Everybody could do what you were able to do, but because they were doing it manually versus a machine, we were able to get it done so much quicker," Brandt said. "A coach could say, 'I want to know all of the wide receivers that are 5'11", 185 pounds, and run 4.6 or better.' Within minutes you had that list." The computer radicalized game analysis. "At the end of the season, coaches could look at the data and see we ran 49 EGO 45 times in a game, 1.2 per carry to the left, and on 2080 EGO to the right, we gained 7 yards a carry," explained Brandt. "You found out that stuff more quickly. So when you were facing teams that you had to make a play on third down to keep a drive alive or you had to stop a play on third down, those are things that give you just a little bit of an advantage. It wasn't one dominant thing—the playbooks, the scouting, the game management. It's all of these things rolled into one, and all of a sudden it becomes a huge thing."

WHILE SCHRAMM AND BRANDT were working on the team, Clint Jr. lent a hand. In February of 1964 Murchison publicly tore up Landry's five-year contract, which had another year to go. Instead, he signed him to a new ten-year contract—the lengthiest agreement ever offered to a professional football coach. "Tom has been with us for four years and this will round it out to an even fifteen," Murchison said in announcing the extension. "This is in line with my philosophy that once you get a good man, hold on to him."

It was the right thing to do. "We were having our third bad season," Murchison later said. "The press was on him, the fans were on him, and the players were starting to complain. Tex called me and said he was concerned about it and asked what I thought we should do about it. I said I thought we should hold a press conference and announce that we were giving Tom a ten-year contract. It was an innovation in sports at that time, but the purpose was to let the players and everybody else know that Landry had the confidence of Tex and myself, and that there wouldn't be any point in further complaining."

Landry was also given the opportunity to buy 5 percent of the team. Tex Schramm had already bought 10 percent of the ownership at 1960 prices from Murchison.

The year before, Landry had turned down a ten-year extension. "Even though I had great confidence in the future of the Cowboys, I felt we first had to get over the building program," he said. "I refused for the benefit of both myself and the club.... From a coach's view, up to this point we've done about half of what's necessary to put a team in the right frame of mind and give it sufficient knowledge to win championships. Our defense is a prime example. When I was with the Giants we could make changes and the defense would react immediately. We've never approached that point here. I hope we will in the near future."

THEN LANDRY PRAISED his team's owner. "He recognized the pressure on me even before I thought about it."

With Landry set and the coaches at work, Gary Cartwright and the rest of the sports scribes moved on to other subjects, such as the team's new uniforms. Back when Dallas had two pro football teams, the Texans were regarded as having the more appealing helmet logo—an outline of the state of Texas, like a farm-to-market highway sign, against a bright red background—and snazzier uniforms. The Cowboys' oversize star was as silly as the team logo, which showed a cartoon football player riding an undersize cartoon pony.

Tex Schramm unveiled a new look for the 1964 season. The blue-star logo on the helmet was slightly downsized and highlighted with a silver border against a newly designed pearl-metallic-silver-blue backdrop that matched the new pearl-metallic-silver-blue pants. Individual numbers replaced stars on the shoulders of jerseys to make players easier to identify by television viewers. Schramm bucked tradition and suited up the Cowboys at home in their white jerseys and metallic-silver-blue pants uniforms. Most teams wore their whites on the road, donning colored jerseys for home games. Schramm's decision had a double benefit. It allowed fans to see visiting NFL teams wearing their at-home colors, adding value to the fan experience, especially when the Cowboys were getting clobbered, as was often the case. It also gave the Cowboys a consistent look, no matter where they were playing. The day would come, Schramm predicted, when "everyone has a color television set. Then maybe we'll get away from white altogether."

THE NEW IMAGE had been spurred on by local sportswriters, a collection of journalists with increasing clout and influence due in some part to their talent turning a phrase. In early January of 1964, Edwin "Bud" Shrake, the *Dallas Morning News* columnist, wrote about a petition he'd received from a group called the Greater North Texas Loyal Fans, Boosters, and Season Ticket Holders Committee for Providing the Dallas Cowboys with Sartorial Splendor. Shrake agreed with the petitioners, who compared the Cowboys uniform to that of a high school football squad. Days later, Gary Cartwright weighed in, calling the distinctive features of the old uniforms "little stars and junk." Coach Landry remarked he'd never seen a uniform win a game. But Tex did the deed.

Three weeks after the uniform change, Shrake presciently described the new uniforms as made for national broadcast, noting "TV numbers on the shoulders, large numbers front and back, and three stripes on each sleeve. The pants are metallic silver, and the socks royal blue with three stripes. The new helmet is to be metallic silver, with either a boot, a TV number, a star, a D, or the CBS-TV eye as the emblem."

The boot-and-spur logo designed by assistant public relations director Bill Morgan was tested, but the star prevailed.

"Unfortunately, the new finery will be filled with the same old football players, and so the Cowboys are 7 point underdogs," Cartwright wrote before the 1964 season opener.

CBS Sports had ponied up $28.2 million for the right to broadcast NFL games in 1964. In response to ABC's more exciting coverage of AFL games, CBS had added a second isolation camera so that viewers could watch replays, and a fifteen-minute pregame and postgame program for each game. The number of commercials was bumped up from sixteen to eighteen per game. Ad time for the Dallas network of twenty-seven stations broadcasting the team's games sold out for the first time in history. There was enough anticipation to justify Don Meredith and Buddy Dial hosting their own weekly television show.

Jay Randolph, a West Virginia sportscaster, had been called in toward the end of the 1963 season by Gordon McLendon to do color for Cowboys games on the radio, and he became the radio voice of the team. He replaced Rick Weaver, who had called a Wichita State football game and then hired a plane to get to a Cowboys away game, at considerable expense to the team. Gordon McLendon was not pleased and fired him. Joining Randolph in the radio booth was the familiar Dallas sports and news broadcaster Bill Mercer.

The exhibition season generated more excitement than usual. Meredith went out with a knee injury at the Salesmanship Club game against Green Bay, which the Packers won 35–3 in front of 60,000 at the Cotton Bowl. But Clint Murchison reported only one significant injury at training camp: "Tom Landry smiled and pulled a muscle."

Stranded in Billings, Montana, for the final exhibition game, Murchison bought three hours of time on KOOK to hear his team play on the radio, much like Bob Thompson had done the previous week while vacationing in Santa Fe.

Focus on the coming season was distracted a bit by another entertainment phenomenon: the Beatles, four young men from Liverpool, England, who played rock-and-roll music and wore their hair long in front. Their appearance at Memorial Auditorium on September 18 pushed all other news back until the Cowboys took the field.

The start of the Beatles concert was delayed because a bomb threat had been phoned in. At their Dallas press conference, for which bassist and lead singer Paul McCartney wore a black cowboy hat, they were asked how they liked Texas. "Well, really, fahn," McCartney said in a bad imitation of a Texas drawl. Drummer Ringo Starr was asked if he was going to run for president. "You gotta watch yourself down here," he said, indirectly referencing the Kennedy assassination and getting a big laugh from the assembled press. Asked if the band members were scared, John Lennon said, "More so here, perhaps." Lennon referred to a reporter as "cousin," trying to sound like a Texan. Before the press conference ended, Starr and McCartney yodeled and held their hands up as if they were riding horses.

The real Cowboys in Dallas unveiled their fifth edition at the Cotton Bowl, and the defense, Tom Landry's calling card, was actually the team's weak point. The offseason acquisitions of star wide receivers Tommy McDonald, from the Eagles, and Buddy Dial, from the Steelers; the signings of free-agent tight end Peter Gent, a basketball star at Michigan State, and Bob Hayes, the Olympic gold medal–winning track star who had been a future draft pick in 1963; and the presence of veteran running backs Don Perkins and Amos Marsh made the offense look like an unstoppable juggernaut, at least on paper.

But the Cowboys started the regular season as bad as ever, recording a 1-4-1 record near the halfway point of the season. At the end of the tie game against the Giants at the Cotton Bowl, some fans unfurled a banner that read ANOTHER FIVE YEARS?

Still, they managed to win a few. "Like men finely tuned to a single destiny, the Dallas Cowboys fought savagely to blow another football game on this damp, muggy, uncomfortable afternoon in the Cotton Bowl," Gary Cartwright wrote. "The Washington Redskins would not hear of it.... Meredith and Roach helped the intrigue in that you were never certain to which colored jersey either was going to throw.

"Not since Gen. Custer said, 'No sweat, baby, I happen to KNOW they're faking!' has history had more fun with a prophecy," Cartwright continued, burying the knife deeper.

Dandy Don, number 17, whose image adorned the team office and billboards, was so beaten up with his bad left knee, bum right ankle, and right shoulder separation that he said, "I've been real pleased with the crowds' reaction the last three or four weeks. I believe they must belong to some sort of humane society."

The Cowboys beat Chicago on the road for their second consecutive win, and three hundred fans were waiting when the team arrived at Love Field. After three wins in a row, historic for the club, more than 55,000 gathered at the Cotton Bowl and watched the Philadelphia Eagles upset the Cowboys 17–14. And the soap opera played on. "It is permissible to say the Cowboy offense was flat, like Lake Michigan laced with a finger of Bourbon," wrote Cartwright.

After one sack, Meredith complained to one of his linemen. "You didn't try to block him," he said, picking himself up.

"Don...I hurt." The lineman moaned.

"What the hell do you think I do?" Meredith snapped. "I'd like to go to bed and stay till Easter but I'm at least trying to play football."

In a matter of weeks, the lineman was an ex-Cowboy.

The *Dallas Morning News* editorial cartoonist Bill Callahan introduced a new character: the Cotton Bowl Jinx, a sleazy, snake-like devil who always arrived just when the Cowboys had apparently turned a corner and drawn a crowd to the Cotton Bowl, at which point they would get whomped, stomped, whipped, and just plain beat.

It was these games, typically preceded by a two- or three-game winning streak away from Dallas or a huge upset on the road, where there was a prospect of hosting a worthy opponent in front of the home folks, that brought out the most florid prose, particularly from Cartwright. After a loss in DC against the Redskins, he wrote, "This only seemed like the week that was. Actually it was much worse."

"You did a real fine job," Landry told Meredith after the final game of a 5-8-1 year. "We'll get you more protection next year."

"Promise?" Meredith called over to him.

Meredith had played the entire season with torn cartilage in one knee, and Landry praised his performance as "perhaps the most courageous and gutsy season any professional quarterback ever played." But Meredith was not Landry's kind of quarterback, the kind who could execute his plan. Dandy was too impulsive and instinctive.

ALTHOUGH THE TEAM didn't live up to expectations, the average attendance of 38,000 for each of seven home games exceeded them, setting a record for a Dallas pro football team.

New Look, New Reasons to Hope

THE CITY OF DALLAS was becoming newer and shinier by the day. The Republic Center II tower, the city's tallest when it opened in 1964, was surpassed the following year by the fifty-story First National Bank building, later renamed Elm Place, the tallest building west of the Mississippi River.

Dallas growth was defined by H. Ross Perot's Electronic Data Systems, which had grown into a Fortune 500 company in the 1960s and was guided by Dallas historian A. C. Greene's Dallas string of E's: "exuberance, expectation, expansion, entrepreneurship."

And Dallas style was defined by its local airline Braniff, whose End of the Plain Plane advertising campaign, cooked up by Mary Wells at the New York ad agency Jack Tinker Associates, was all about fashion. The new Braniff featured jelly-bean-color seats, by designer Alexander Girard with Henry Miller fabrics, and stewardesses attired in designer wear by Emilio Pucci.

The Cowboys mirrored the End of the Plain Plane in one way. "They had the coolest uniforms," said Ned Rifkin, who grew up in New York State and later became undersecretary of art at the Smithsonian Institution.

They also had the power to make things change.

For all the city's progress, elements of Dallas still remained classically Southern: white folks lived on high ground north of the

Trinity River; colored folks clustered in the river bottoms along the Trinity, which frequently flooded. Since World War II, blacks had been migrating to Oak Cliff and elsewhere in South Dallas, triggering the first significant wave of white flight in Dallas.

The residences of the Dallas Cowboys reflected that. White players lived mostly in North Dallas. Most black players lived in South Dallas. Players gravitated to apartments because they never knew for sure whether they'd last an entire season with the Cowboys. Some players who had started families bought homes near one another and put down roots.

One group of white players and their families clustered in a five-block area of Lake Highlands: the Manderses, the Howleys, the Jordans, the Reeveses, the Liscios, the Lillys, the Andries, the Tubbses, along with the family of assistant coach Gene Stallings. Many had lived in the Connecticut Village apartment complex when they first came to Dallas, which Bitty Jordan had found. They moved together as they started families.

Black players had fewer options, although several resided in the upscale Wedgwood Tower high-rise apartments in Oak Cliff, the black version of the Preston Tower high-rise in North Dallas.

Once the team members were on the field, though, the black/white divide disappeared. Players traveled together, went out to dinner together, and hung together, despite the lingering effects of segregation laws. And the community noticed. They weren't black Cowboys and white Cowboys, just Cowboys, especially when they started winning.

"The Dallas Cowboys are, possibly, the only Texas institution in existence that united Anglo, black, and Latin loyalties throughout the state," A. C. Greene observed some years later.

Fueling the optimism already generated, the Cowboys gave Don Meredith a three-year extension on his contract along with a slight raise after his initial five-year deal expired and before the 1965 season began. "I got what I wanted and I hope the club gets what it wants next year," he said, ignoring the hard truth that he was being paid less than top draft picks Craig Morton and Jerry Rhome, whose quarterbacking services were being sought by rival American Football League teams as well as by the Cowboys.

Tex Schramm downplayed the obvious by denigrating Meredith's sketchy history. "In evaluating his new contract we completely disregarded his 1964 record," the general manager said. "His performance was poor because of the circumstances...he was injured before the season started and got worse with each game...but he continued to play when most players would have quit. He has the deepest respect and admiration from our entire organization."

Dandy Don was feeling his oats despite the nitpicking. He was well compensated and could make up for whatever he wasn't getting paid with his offseason job at Clint Murchison's Centex Construction company, which allowed him to work in New Orleans or spend the winter in Hawaii. He had married again, this time to an outgoing honey from the west side of Fort Worth named Cheryl King, better known as Chigger. A University of Texas grad and a Tri Delt in the same sorority pledge class as another knockout babe, named Farrah Fawcett, Chigger was an accomplished horsewoman and painter. She could also keep up with Don, no matter how much he roared.

Meredith's off-the-field reputation and his freewheeling persona concerned Coach Landry enough for him to ask Lee Roy Jordan to be Meredith's roommate and chaperone for out-of-town games.

"We had a great rapport," Jordan said. "He respected me and we had the little routine down. The night before a game, Don would pick out where we were going to have dinner and I would handle the cab and getting back on time before curfew. He would have a cocktail and an after dinner drink and if it was time, I'd have the cab ready. That was the best babysitting job I ever had, Goddog, it was. And it was entertaining too, for a country boy like me to be out there with Don Meredith, the quarterback, and be responsible for him."

In exchange, Meredith turned Jordan on to his favorite country singer-songwriter, Willie Nelson, taking Jordan to a Greenville Avenue club to watch the smiling, clean-shaven performer dressed in a coat and tie.

New muscle had been added to the team in the form of Ralph Neely, the hulking, speedy University of Oklahoma All-American tackle, and Jethro Pugh, a massive six-six, 248-pound defensive lineman who was the first draftee ever signed from North Carolina's Elizabeth City State University.

And joining backup quarterback John Roach, who'd been obtained in a trade with the Green Bay Packers, were Craig Morton from California and Jerry Rhome from Tulsa. The strong-armed Morton, an All-American, was Dallas's first pick and considered so valuable he was shadowed by Murchison Rover Boy George Owen until he signed. Rhome, a future pick from 1964, was Meredith Jr., an All-American quarterback at Sunset High School in Dallas, where he was coached by his father, Byron, who also broke down game film for Gil Brandt and the Cowboys. Jerry had seen every home game Don Meredith ever played at SMU and enrolled at the college to follow in his footsteps, leading the Southwest Conference in total yards and passing as a sophomore. But when SMU coach Bill Meek was fired, Rhome transferred to Tulsa University, where he could continue passing the ball.

Rhome had also been drafted by the AFL's Houston Oilers; he had been mentored by Oilers coach Sammy Baugh when both were at Tulsa. "He taught me how to operate flare control, how to build pass patterns, how to read coverages, and how to key on where to throw," Rhome said. But the opportunity to compete with his idol Meredith in his hometown was a far greater incentive than Baugh, despite Dallas's offense being nowhere near as sophisticated as the Spread that Tulsa employed.

Dan Reeves, another quarterback, from South Carolina, had signed as a free agent, although not as a quarterback. "I got calls from Dallas and San Diego wanting to sign me after the draft was over," Reeves said. "I didn't know whether I would get a chance or not. Being from the South, the team that I had always watched was the Washington Redskins. I didn't know a lot about Dallas or San Diego, but the guy from Dallas was the nicest gentleman. My wife and I just liked him 'cause he was so honest and took us out to eat. We signed with Dallas even though it was for less money. I had been a quarterback in high school and college and they said they would try me on defense — I played safety in college — and try me at running back and wide receiver."

The rookie class of 1965 focused on speed. The sporting public thought the Cowboys' IBM computer had gone haywire when it told the Cowboys to draft an Olympic track star as a future pick in the 1964 draft. What the sporting public didn't know was that Bob Hayes had been a star receiver for the Florida A&M football team, and he was a steal in the seventh round. Schramm recalled that Landry had gone home, since there were no choice players left, and Brandt had departed to sign the number-one pick, Mel Renfro, so Schramm selected Hayes and another wild card as the tenth-round choice, quarterback from the Naval Academy Roger Staubach. Staubach had won the Heisman Trophy as a junior but he was looking at a four-year commitment to the U.S. Navy before he could play pro ball, too long a layoff to maintain skills, most coaches and scouts believed.

Gil Brandt had tried to sign Staubach after his junior year, paying a visit to Betty Staubach in Cincinnati to suggest her son consider quitting the Naval Academy a year early. She threw him out of the house. The Kansas City Chiefs had also drafted Staubach, and Lamar Hunt went to Annapolis and offered Staubach an open-ended contract if he chose to leave the service early, or five hundred dollars a month while he remained in the service, along with a ten-thousand-dollar bonus. Captain Paul Borden, a U.S. Navy legal officer looking out for Staubach, informed Tex Schramm of the offer, and Tex matched it. So Staubach signed with Dallas and the established league, receiving more money every month from the Cowboys than from his Navy salary, along with a bonus, which went to his wife's family and his mother. From the Cowboys' point of view, a forty-thousand-dollar bet on a former Heisman winner with the kind of discipline that only a service academy could instill was a smart gamble.

Bob Hayes made more sense, in a twisted kind of way. If Dallas wanted speed, an Olympic gold medalist who'd run 100 meters in ten seconds flat at the 1964 Olympics in Tokyo and came from behind to win another gold medal in the 440 relay, clocking 8.6 seconds over the final 100 meters, filled the bill. The team already sported several stars—Meredith, Perkins, Lilly, Jordan, Tubbs, Frank Clarke. The World's Fastest Human, as Hayes was billed, came from a whole other galaxy. At Florida A&M, a historically black college, Hayes played halfback, wingback, and receiver, and scored a team-high eleven touchdowns as a junior, leading the team in punt returns two years running and kickoff returns for four years.

The Cowboys were gaining notoriety for their draft picks and for their scouts' ability to find and sign free agents, some of whom played for small colleges under the radar and some of whom excelled in basketball instead of football, as was the case of Cornell Green and Pete Gent. "They'd sign everybody because you could bring as many as you wanted to training camp," explained starting offensive tackle Tony Liscio. "They'd have a crowd of people out there. By the time we got there most of them were gone."

"There was a hundred and something rookies there, so you were just one of many," confirmed one of the training-camp survivors, Dan Reeves. "My roommate Obert Logan, a free agent from Trinity, and I were kind of tackling dummies. By the first week, every time coaches said the linebackers need somebody over here to tackle, it was 'Logan, you and Reeves go over there and let the linebackers tackle y'all.' 'Defensive backs need somebody to tackle, you and

Logan go.' The two-a-days were just as hard as you could go, full pads, hitting, tackling, being tackled, scrimmaging, which was all good because it gave me an opportunity. They had a lot of running backs...but I got some opportunities because some people started getting hurt." Reeves made the cut largely because he played every position he could at camp. "Coach Landry called exotic plays and liked the fact I could throw the football and open up the halfback pass," Reeves said. "Little things like that kept me around."

Once the veterans arrived, Landry showed another side of his coaching to Reeves. "We had our first meeting and he got up and starting talking about goals. I was thinking, 'Goals? What in the world is he talking about?' He had goals of things that he wanted to achieve and plans how we were going to achieve those goals. I was impressed he was that organized and knew how to accomplish those things, what we were going to have to do, what we were going to have to work on. I never had football coached that way. I don't know why from the first time I started playing football, I could tell you what everybody did, what everybody's assignment was on every play. So, that was impressive that Landry was that organized in what he wanted to accomplish. Our practices were very well organized. If we were going to be out there for two hours and fifteen minutes you knew exactly what you were doing because they had the practice schedule posted up there. You could prepare mentally for what you were getting ready to go through."

Among the exotics who made the squad was Colin Ridgway, the Cowboys' new punter, who had never played American-style football before. His experience was limited to Australian-rules football, and that showed at an exhibition game against San Francisco at Kezar Stadium when he booted one high into a stiff bay wind for a net five yards.

Six of the eleven starting offensive players in the lineup had never started a pro game for the Cowboys. Seven of the top twenty-two offensive players hadn't even been on the team the year before. But the Cowboys were loaded. "It all smacks of the old familiar alibi," warned Gary Cartwright before the start of the 1965 season. "But for the first time in club history the alibis are enforced with great talent."

On opening day, the track star Bob Hayes showed what he could do with his blazing speed, catching two passes for a touchdown and 81 receiving yards. The team was clicking.

The scribes who had been skewering the team relentlessly began to change their tune. It wasn't just that the Cowboys were winning. People were reading about the team in unprecedented numbers. Covering the pro teams in Dallas was initially a booby prize to aspiring sports reporters, a sop if you couldn't swing the Southwest Conference beat or cover enough high school games. The first full-time pro football writer was Sam Blair of the *Dallas Morning News*, a Dallas native and graduate of Woodrow Wilson High School who'd started covering the AFL Texans in 1959 and then the Cowboys when they were still a pipe dream known as the Dallas Rangers. His coverage played it straight and set the bar against which all other reporting was compared.

The best and brightest of the bunch were from the gang who had worked together at the *Fort Worth Press* in the 1950s under the tutelage of Blackie Sherrod. "Blackie kind of gave us our head and let us write," Bud Shrake said of his coming-of-age with the *Fort Worth Press*. "If we got too far off base, he would yank us back. But he let us make all these literary allusions in the first paragraph. You'd read one of our stories you might not even know what it was about because it had so many references to F. Scott Fitzgerald. The readers didn't know what the hell it was. Some days we didn't either. But he encouraged us to use our imaginations and write as well as we could.

"Since we were an afternoon newspaper most of what we wrote had already been out in the morning in the *Star-Telegram*. So we had to come up with a new angle on every story. And the new angles were pretty wild sometimes. Mostly, they were literary invention. As a police reporter I learned how to report. Under Blackie, I learned how to write."

A distant mentor was Tex Maule, the lead NFL writer at *Sports Illustrated*, who had been a sportswriter for the *Morning News* after working for Tex Schramm and the Los Angeles Rams in the early 1950s. "We knew him but he didn't know us," Gary Cartwright said of Maule, the first writer Cartwright read who used the phrase *soft hands* to describe the way a receiver cradled the ball without bouncing it on the catch.

The competition between newspapers was fierce, and reporters hustled to score a scoop, grab eyeballs, and dominate the football talk around the watercooler at work. The Monday morning following the Cowboys' deflating 24–17 loss to the defending champion Cleveland Browns in front of an overflow Cotton Bowl crowd—the Dallas Cowboys' first official sellout at home—Cartwright wrote this classic lead paragraph:

"Outlined against a gray November sky, the Four Horsemen rode again. You know them: Pestilence, Death, Famine, and Meredith."

Don Perkins's eyes would widen at the mention of Cartwright's name. Pettis Norman believed Cartwright "was there just to tear people down." Buddy Dial called him "poison-pen Cartwright" and "a wormy little old devil. I mean, he breathed an ill wind." Lee Roy Jordan considered him unworthy of acknowledgment. "We didn't read Gary. He was very negative on everything, every subject, every time, every article. Everybody was an open target for him. It was like his duty to criticize everybody on the team."

Cartwright's friend Pete Gent admitted, "I've never known that kind of fury against any reporters. . . . He doesn't know how close he came to guys dragging him to the back of the plane and just beating the shit out of him. Guys were still on speed, man. They were half-drunk. They wanted to kill him."

Meredith tried to defuse the situation by telling his teammates the reporter was doing his job, just like the players were doing theirs.

Rumors of threats on Cartwright's life made by certain players and fans were greatly exaggerated, the reporter insisted. "They never got on me for criticizing sloppy play by a player, but if you got something wrong that hurt the team itself, Schramm would come at you," Cartwright said. "Landry even defended me. The Cowboy Club fan base had weekly luncheons, the Cowboys were still losing and I was coming down hard on them. One fan stood up and asked Landry, 'When are y'all gonna fire Gary Cartwright?'"

Landry calmly explained, "What you've got to realize is, after the game is over, he's the one with a typewriter."

Cartwright actually admired the members of the organization, especially Schramm. "He loved sports, loved to talk football, and would argue with you about anything," Cartwright said. "During training camp, the coaches, team officials, and sportswriters would gather after practice at the 5:30 Club, where we'd talk and drink. He liked sportswriters (because he had been one), liked to talk about football, and he liked to drink scotch."

Tex's open-door policy at camp paid off in spades, as the *Fort Worth Star-Telegram*'s Frank Luksa observed. "We flew with them, we ate with them, hell, we'd go to their rooms," he said. "You got to know them as people as well as players."

The press and the broadcasters were Tex's best salespeople and he tried to shoot square with them. "Blackie would phone and say, 'Hey, I've got this, Is this correct?'" Tex said. "I'd tell him the truth. Sometimes he'd say, 'Well, you just blew my story.'"

Another piece of evidence of the press's growing influence was the opening of Bud Shrake West at 4744 Maple in November of 1965. Its name honored the sportswriter who'd graduated to the big time at *Sports Illustrated*. Bob Thompson, Clint and Jane Murchison, Lamar and Norma Hunt, *Sports Illustrated* staffer Dan Jenkins, Tex Schramm, Frank Clarke, Don Meredith, Peter Gent, Jim Boeke, Tony Liscio, Don Talbert, Bob Lilly, Clint Youmans, Dave Edwards, and Colin Ridgway were among the distinguished guests at the opening of the ramshackle establishment. Clint contributed a selection of photographs of himself, one of him smiling while holding a Cowboys helmet, another of him dressed in full team uniform, including a number 17 jersey, with an expression of shock, perhaps because he was posing as the quarterback while wearing his distinctive horn-rim glasses.

"When he left Dallas to write for *SI*, he and a couple friends started this bar," Gary Cartwright said. Shrake had written a series of letters to friends describing his New York adventures and his entrée into literary society, including stories about parties at Norman Mailer's, meals and drinks at Elaine's, and being stoned most of the time. In his own hepcat, scaled-down manner, he tried to capture that zeitgeist in his broke-down club in Oak Lawn.

"For six months, it was the hottest club in Dallas," Cartwright said. "I'd get players to talk to the crowd — Lilly, Meredith, Neely. It was a funky little bar and it would be packed for these talks. On other nights, the two college guys who ran it wouldn't show, or forget to pay the electric bill. It self-destructed."

The corps of photographers was as illustrious as the writers, beginning with Jim Laughead. The longtime Dallas resident, who favored shapeless hats, overalls, and bright red vests on shoots, had already established his credentials photographing college players leaping, scowling, and diving, which Laughead encouraged by shouting "a-huckin' and a-buckin'." Along with his son-in-law James (Brad) Bradley, he created the football action pose, which became a photographic cliché. The Cowboys designated Laughead as the team's official photographer from the beginning. Local papers' photographers, such as Al Panzera, Linda Kaye, and John Mazziotta, were given plenty of pages for their multiple sequence shots that diagrammed plays.

Russ Russell, a photographer who worked for the *Fort Worth Press* and then the *Dallas Times Herald,* was so prolific and spot-on, the Cowboys started buying his work directly. Russell shot with a

Honeywell 500 mm lens. "Everybody was using 4x5 Speed Graphic with a roll-film back, which gave you a slightly telephoto lens," he said. "You had eight shots that way on a roll of 120 film. The Honeywell was a single lens. It was real slow, like f8, and you had to prefocus it. You had to open it up, focus it, shut it down and then shoot. The telephoto lens compresses everything, so a guy coming in at the quarterback looks like he's ten feet tall. He may be four or five feet away but he looks like he's about to crush him. I got the running backs coming through the line, so my pictures were a lot better than Jim Laughead." Once Curt Mosher, the Cowboys publicist, started buying Russell's photos, Dave Boss of NFL Properties was not far behind.

SCHRAMM DID NOT RELY solely on the media to hype his team. Before the Cowboys took the field, he approached Dee Brock, a high-profile model married to *Times Herald* columnist Bob Brock. He told Brock about his vision of a cheerleader squad composed of professional models and even showed her kid-leather costumes that had been designed for the squad. But a football field was not a modeling runway, Brock informed him. Most models did not have the athleticism required of cheerleaders. How much was the pay? Brock asked. Schramm told her he thought the women would want to perform for free. Brock told Schramm if he wanted to have professional models, they would have to be professionally compensated.

A onetime cheerleader for New London High in East Texas who was partial to wearing her blond tresses in a beehive, Mrs. Brock convinced Schramm of a better way: she advised him to have countywide Dallas high school cheerleading tryouts and select twelve of those cheerleaders. The kids would not require any compensation other than free tickets; they all attended the National Cheerleaders Association summer camp at Southern Methodist University, so they all knew the same cheers. "We'd be halfway there on the cheers already," Brock told him.

In lieu of leather costumes, they wore traditional cheerleader uniforms. But traditional cheerleading and the focus on showing spirit with organized cheers fell flat with the pro football crowd, which was hardly surprising since only one team, the Baltimore Colts, boasted cheerleaders at the time.

"It seems to bother the new cheerleaders that the fans who come out to the Cotton Bowl to see the Cowboys don't necessarily cheer," Brock said of her high schoolers. "They are so used to enthusiastic and partisan high school crowds that it makes them work even harder to get a spark started among the fans. The lack of cheering really threw me for a loss the first year. Then I called the manager of the Baltimore Colts cheerleaders and she explained that the same thing had happened in Baltimore in the early years. Now, Baltimore has some of the most vocal fans in the country, and cheering seems to be catching on here in Dallas."

In 1965, the squad was expanded to include high school boys, who could help the girls do stunts. Dubbed the CowBelles and Beaux, the fourteen cheerleaders (plus four alternates) entered the field before the start of games in a Model T, cheering, flipping, leaping, and flying. Their stunts got the fans' attention. Their cheers did not.

Halftime entertainment usually came courtesy of the Tyler Junior College Apache Belles or the Kilgore Junior College Rangerettes, both high-kicking female dance teams in short skirts, boots, and cowgirl hats; or the marching bands from Grambling or Prairie View A&M, traditional black colleges known for their drum lines. The Greater Fort Worth Lions Club band played in the stands during time-outs.

The pageantry helped Mike Rhyner, the Oak Cliff teenager who had been a Dallas Texans fan, to come around on 1965's Cowboys when he took a job bussing tables at the private Cowboys Club inside the old roller rink by the Cotton Bowl. "The guy that ran that...was just a real hard ass," Rhyner said. "But part of the job was you got to go to the Cotton Bowl and watch the games, for a while anyway. That's what I would do. I would go out there and watch the game and then report to my appointed station and bus tables and make about five bucks for it."

His timing was impeccable.

"It didn't look good at first. I believe they started 2-5 that year. Then they won like five of their last seven, and the only two teams that they lost to were two teams that were clearly better than they were." That would be the Cleveland Browns, who beat the 'Boys by a touchdown and an extra point, and the Washington Redskins, whose margin of victory was a field goal.

The final game of the season, against the football New York Giants at Yankee Stadium, ended the year on a high note. Meredith threw two touchdown passes to Bullet Bob Hayes, including a 65-yard bomb, and the Cowboys went home with a 38–20 victory. Their 7-7 record was good for a second-place tie in the Eastern Conference and a slot in the Playoff Bowl, pitting the second-place teams of both conferences in a postseason match.

The flight home from New York provided rookie Bobby Hayes the opportunity to have his first taste of champagne (followed by many more), which inspired him to grab the intercom and serenade the passengers with an impromptu version of "Darktown Strutters' Ball."

Ten thousand crazy Dallas Cowboys fans were in the same mood as Hayes and waited at Love Field to greet their conquering heroes. Once the team landed, fans knocked down the chain-link fence and surrounded the plane. Broadcaster Bill Mercer descended the stairway at the back of the plane flanked by two linemen, who told him, "Stay with us, Bill, or you may get killed."

"It was a mob," said Dave Manders's wife, Betty. "I ended up under the wing of the plane, people were pushing and shoving so much. I was wearing a white coat and they pushed so hard, all the buttons of my coat came off."

The Playoff Bowl experience would be a new one for Dallas, off the field and on. Lee Roy Jordan had been to the Orange Bowl before as part of the Alabama Crimson Tide, so he called his old coach Bear Bryant to ask about recommendations for the team. "He told me who to call to get into the dog tracks, what restaurants and places to go to that would be fun." Don Meredith was buying drinks for all comers at the team's hotel, charging the bar tabs to Tex Schramm's room.

The partying atmosphere and the newness of it all might have been factors in their rout by the Colts, 35–3, but no one was complaining too much because the Playoff Bowl, also known as the Runners-Up Bowl, the Leftover Bowl, and the Losers Bowl, was not that big of a deal. The Green Bay Packers' Vince Lombardi derided the postseason game as "the 'Shit Bowl,' a losers' bowl for losers." At least the game provided national television exposure for the Tyler Junior College Apache Belles' precision high kicks during halftime.

The Playoff Bowl appearance also exposed the football team to the nation. Rookie Pete Gent, the tight end who'd played basketball at Michigan State and who was the first Cowboy to grow his hair long, much to the displeasure of his coach, told a friend that after the game, management had instituted a no-tattoos policy for the following season. The Cowboys were too stylish and too telegenic to show tats on TV. Image mattered. And the bottom line was on the line. For the first time since its inception, the Dallas Cowboys Football Club had recorded a profit.

Peace and War

IN APRIL OF 1966, the American Football League owners elected a new commissioner to replace Joe Foss, voting in Al Davis, the street-smart Brooklyn-bred owner of the Oakland Raiders. Davis immediately orchestrated raids to sign NFL players in retaliation for the New York Giants' signing kicker Pete Gogolak from the AFL's Buffalo Bills. Fuck a merger, Al Davis sneered. His league could stand on its own and didn't need to pay bribe money to the NFL to settle the feud. They'd simply sign up the best talent.

Tex Schramm, who had been promoted to the position of president as well as general manager of the Dallas Cowboys Football Club the year before, and his "nephew" Pete Rozelle had already taken the threat on.

When Davis declared war, Tex Schramm and Lamar Hunt had already been secretly talking. It started during the first week of April, when Lamar flew into Love Field from Kansas City and sat in Schramm's car in the parking lot. Both feared being seen in the terminal lobby near the bronze statue of a Texas Ranger, a popular meeting place. No one should know about the conversation, especially Al Davis. Their discussions continued for two months with the men meeting at Hunt's home, at Schramm's place, or in Schramm's car at Love Field.

The conversations led to a flurry of behind-the-scenes negotiations with owners of both leagues. On June 8, Pete Rozelle, flanked by Tex Schramm and Lamar Hunt, announced the merger of the two professional football leagues.

Under the agreement, the NFL and the AFL would expand to twenty-four teams, to be increased to twenty-six in 1968 and to twenty-eight by 1970 or soon thereafter. The two leagues would officially merge to form one league with two conferences in 1970. All existing franchises would be retained, and no franchises would be transferred outside their metropolitan areas. AFL owners would pay $18 million in reparations over twenty years to seal the deal.

The leagues agreed to play an annual AFL-NFL world championship game beginning at the end of the upcoming season and to hold a combined draft, also beginning in 1967.

Preseason games would be held between teams of each league. Official regular-season play would start in 1970. Pete Rozelle was commissioner of the expanded league. In protest, Al Davis resigned as AFL commissioner, observing that "generals win the wars, politicians make the peace."

New York Jets owner Sonny Werblin showed up for the celebration at Toots Shor's after Rozelle's press conference, along with Ralph Wilson of the Buffalo Bills, Barron Hilton of the San Diego Chargers, and Billy Sullivan of the Boston Patriots. Werblin had aligned himself with Al Davis by vocally balking at the merger, even though he was selling his team for $17.5 million despite having paid $1 million for it two years earlier, and Werblin was still complaining, calling the announcement "another Munich."

Al Davis bitched that the AFL "gave it away."

Tex said the merger would result in "better football and a great thing for fans." Lamar Hunt simply chalked it up to "basic economics." No longer would rookies get disproportionately better deals than veterans, or so it was hoped. The Jets' Joe Namath, one of the first bonus-baby beneficiaries of the league wars, signed in 1965 to a record-setting contract worth $427,000—money that new owner Sonny Werblin couldn't have offered without the start-up league's new television deal with NBC. Namath remarked, "I graduated just in time." The NFL minimum salary was immediately raised to $7,500 a year.

Hunt and Schramm both flew back to Dallas after the official announcement. Hunt, who normally traveled coach, couldn't get a cheap seat, so he bought a first-class ticket and rode next to Tex, who was in a celebratory mood. When the stewardess informed Schramm there was a two-drink limit on the flight, Hunt, who eschewed alcohol, offered Tex his drinks while observing, "Gee, Tex, you're going to get bombed."

Schramm wobbled off the flight with a shit-eating grin plastered across his face.

The U.S. Congress would approve the merger and pass legislation exempting the agreement from antitrust action, and New Orleans would be awarded an NFL franchise and begin play in 1967. Houston oilman John Mecom Jr. was designated the Louisiana team's president and its majority stockholder. One of the minority owners was none other than Bedford Wynne, who gave up his stake in the Cowboys.

The championship, which would eventually be named the Super Bowl by Lamar Hunt after he saw television ads for Super Balls, was underwritten by the $9.5 million that CBS and NBC paid for permission to televise the game for the next four years.

Before the merger was made public, both leagues had spent a combined seven million dollars to sign their 1966 draft choices. The Cowboys beat Kansas City to sign their fifth-round pick, Walt Garrison, a running back from Oklahoma State who led the Big Eight Conference in rushing yards his junior year. Brandt thought he had all the right qualities to succeed Don Perkins when Perk eventually retired.

A few days before that year's draft, a dapper older man from the Chiefs had shown up, bought Garrison a pair of boots, taken him and his friends to dinner, and stayed close. He was a babysitter, much like George Owen was for the Cowboys, put in place to make sure a representative from the other league couldn't get to the player.

"Rozelle with the help of Tex was a very forward-thinking person," Gil Brandt said of babysitting. "In the old days they used to have a person in Brownwood that recruited for [the University of] Texas and another one that recruited for Baylor and another one who recruited for whoever. And they'd say we want Joe Smith and then it would be their job to try to get Joe Smith. We got businessmen. In fact the governor of Oregon was one of the babysitters. They had the latitude to do anything they wanted with these kids. Leading up to the last game of the season, they couldn't offer them money or anything like that, but form a relationship with them. Then as soon as the last game of the season was over, the players were no longer under NCAA rules, they took care of the player."

In Walt Garrison's case, on the morning of the draft, while the two men were sitting in the coffee shop of the student union, the babysitter from the Chiefs got a phone call. He left to take it, came back, smiled, and extended his hand to Garrison. "Walt, been nice visiting with you, I gotta go." Garrison was stunned. The man from KC said, "Dallas drafted you in the fifth round. Kansas City was going to take you in the seventh round. I'm out of here." Garrison never saw him again.

He did see Gil Brandt, who promised him the world, as Brandt was prone to do. "I didn't like Gil," Garrison said after he'd made the team. "His job was to lie."

In Garrison, Dallas had roped in a real cowboy—the first true cowboy on the Cowboys, as it were. Garrison had grown up in Lewisville, a small town half an hour north of Dallas, where he'd played all sports for the Fightin' Farmers, earned district honors in basketball and honorable mention in football, and rodeoed during his off time. The team's PR flacks exploited it to the max, telling anyone who would listen about Garrison's signing bonus: a two-horse in-line trailer.

Garrison had watched Abner Haynes play for the Dallas Texans in the Cotton Bowl a few times, but he'd never been to a Cowboys game. And though he had kinfolk in Oak Cliff, "I didn't think of it as a city," Garrison said. "It seemed like it took a week to get there." There were also kinfolk in Fort Worth, which was more his style. "I wouldn't go to Dallas for nothing," he said. "I hate Dallas. People over there are so snobby. The people over in Fort Worth got more money than anybody in Dallas. They just don't act like it, they still wear blue jeans and boots."

Garrison was introduced to his teammates in San Francisco at a mid-August preseason exhibition following the college all-star game, which number-one draft pick John Niland had also played in. "I've got a locker and a uniform and shit and I don't know anyone and I'm in a meeting before the game with Bob Lilly and Meredith and Dan Reeves and Haley and all these guys. I'm thinking, 'What the hell am I doing?' I didn't play of course, because I didn't know nothing.

"It was the first time I ever met Coach Landry. He was bigger than I thought he was, number one. And very standoffish. Coach Landry introduced us to the other players—Willie Townes, Dickie Daniels, Mike Johnson, and the other draft choices who had been in training camp. I'm kind of embarrassed because I'm out of my element totally. So then we go back to training camp and start training."

Garrison had a job to do and that was to make the team, which he did, moving up to number two behind Don Perkins. The quiet, articulate, and very black Perkins took to the gregarious white-boy yahoo.

"Perk and Dan Reeves are probably the reason I made the club," Garrison said. "Perk would show me stuff that took him seven, eight, nine years to learn. Keys and stuff like that. Dan Reeves picked me for a roommate. Back then veterans picked who they wanted. So why Dan picked me, I have no idea. But he was [like] a coach back then. He was a smart guy and he would study. In college, hell, I never studied plays. Hell, we didn't have that many. Playbook up there was thin, playbook at Dallas was thick. Holy shit, Dan spent a lot of time teaching me how to study, but more importantly what to study."

Coach Landry had something to do with Reeves's becoming Garrison's roomie. "He asked if I would room with a rookie; you didn't room with rookies back then," Dan Reeves said. "Coach Landry thought that would be good to get him ready to play. He was going to miss a lot of training camp because he was in the college all-star game. I was looking forward to rooming with somebody who played the same position, running back. So it worked out great. We became tremendous friends."

Teaching felt natural to Reeves, who was learning from Ermal Allen, the offensive-backfield coach for the Cowboys. "Coach Allen was very thorough and that helped me a great deal and prepared me to play. He always covered the little details that really made a difference. That fit right in with what I had been doing my whole life. With a coach like that I could help Walt get his assignments down, pick up the offense and everything."

The Cowboys' loss in the Losers' Bowl was a faded memory by the start of the seventh season. Their previous 7-7 record merely hinted at the pent-up firepower the team began to brandish. Landry finally had a razzle-dazzle offense that was loaded with speed, and a futuristic-looking double set that linemen used getting into position before the ball was snapped. Not only did it look cool, the repositioning covered up running-back shifts and often drew opposing D-lines offside.

"Landry just wanted to cause a little confusion because those linebackers calling the defenses couldn't see," lineman Tony Liscio said. "He had timing plays, flea flickers, reverses, these screen plays that were fake screen this way, screen this way, middle screen, side screen, so many timing plays. Most teams would have drop back pocket protection and they'd have fake running plays — two types of pass protection. We had nine different types — roll, a half roll, fake protection, fire protection, drop back protection, we had all these different schemes and then he ran all those damned formations, too."

For its part, the defense, bolstered by the return of linebackers coach Jerry Tubbs backing up Lee Roy Jordan, had finally mastered the Flex that Landry had designed so they could adapt to whatever offense was thrown their way, earning them the sobriquet Dooms-day Defense from Gary Cartwright. The team was that good.

The Cowboys were hot and a hot ticket. For the first time ever, kids started showing up three hours before kickoff to grab dollar end-zone seats at the Cotton Bowl. Wealthier out-of-town fans jammed private airports flying in for Cowboys home games.

The Cowboys opened at home, utterly destroying the New York Giants 52–7, which inspired Gary Cartwright to write, "It was as though Lewis Carroll was locked in overnight with the Cowboys' record book: Dallas in Wonderland. In smashing the Giants, the Cowboys did everything in epic proportion."

In October, the team traveled to St. Louis for the Cowboys' first game at the new Civic Center Busch Memorial Stadium. The stadium was a jewel as far as the seating went, but the field was a mess, mainly due to the turf that had been laid down to cover up the dirt portion of the field used during baseball games. The day before the game, Tom Landry was walking past the offensive line as they practiced on the field when clumps of grass flew at him. He picked up a handful of sod and wryly remarked, "This is really Busch." The 10–10 tie there snapped Dallas's unbeaten record.

The away game against Philadelphia literally slipped from the Cowboys' grasp. With 1:30 left on the game clock and the Cowboys one point behind, Dan Reeves caught a Meredith pass and carried it to the Eagles 13-yard line for a 23-yard gain, setting up an easy field goal for the Cowboys to overcome Philadelphia's 24–23 lead. But after the whistle blew, Philly free safety Joe Scarpati swiped the ball from Reeves's arm. The officials ruled it a fumble. The ball went to the Eagles. Reeves was so enraged, he began chasing an official to complain and accidentally knocked him down. He was ejected from the game. During practice the following week, Reeves found a wrapped box in his locker. Inside was a football with part of its cover torn off, a gift from Clint Murchison.

In the season-defining November 13 victory against the Red-skins, *Star-Telegram* beat writer Frank Luksa led with "[The Cow-boys] beat Washington 31–30 on a 20-yard field goal by Danny Villanueva in the final 15 seconds, but that scarcely tells the story. The Don Meredith–led drive began at the Dallas 3 with 1:13 on the clock. Meredith (21 of 29, 406 yards) outdueled Sonny Jurgensen (26 of 46, 347 yards) and Hayes caught nine passes for 246 yards, including a third-quarter TD that broke for 95 yards."

The win started a four-game streak. Kicker Danny Villanueva, who had put his foot into 889 total kicks (field goals, points after touchdowns, and punts combined), recalled the final minute of the Washington game: "Nobody thought much [about staging a come-back] when Pat Richter of the Redskins punted the ball inside the 5," Villanueva said. "Suddenly Meredith completes a few passes, then takes a late hit from linebacker John Reger. The ref throws his rag [15-yard penalty to the Redskins' 12] . . . and now I'm like a leper. Everybody moves away.

"Meredith comes to the sideline. He stands there with a stem of grass in his mouth. He's chewing on it, then he starts singing, 'Yes-terday's dead and tomorrow's blind, and I just live one day at a time.' I'd never heard that song before — or since," Villanueva said of Mer-edith's impromptu rendition of Willie Nelson's "One Day at a Time." Villanueva ran onto the field with his holder Danny Reeves. Reeves took a low snap and put the ball in place. Villanueva's life flashed in front of him as the kick sailed through the uprights.

One week later, the night before the Cowboys disposed of the Steelers at Pitt Stadium, the starting quarterback prepared his rookie fullback Walt Garrison by taking him out on the town, as was traditional with rookies. He gave him the order: "Meet me in the lobby in ten minutes."

Reeves, Meredith, Buddy Dial, Lee Roy Jordan, and Obert Logan were waiting downstairs in a limo.

At dinner Meredith asked what Garrison was drinking. Beer was not an acceptable answer, so Garrison went with a bourbon and Coke. Meredith ordered scotch. "Tell you what, you drink a drink every time I do," the quarterback instructed the rook.

So he drank. One. Two. Three. Four—more than he'd ever drunk before in his life.

Garrison spent the next afternoon returning punts and kicks and covering kickoffs with a massive headache. The Cowboys were firmly in the lead in the fourth quarter when Landry sought him out. "Thirty-two," he said. "Go in there for Perkins."

Garrison arrived in the huddle feeling like homemade shit. His quarterback took notice. "Lookee here," Meredith said to the other nine players crouched together. "We've got one Lewisville Farmer, a great guy, an All-American. We'll see how he can carry the ball."

Meredith called a trap up the middle and Garrison ran the ball into the defensive line, gaining a yard. Garrison returned to the huddle on the verge of puking. Meredith wasn't letting up.

"Oh yeah, Walt, I've read all your clippings. Evidently the Pittsburgh defense forgot to read them. Let's try that play again."

The Cowboys ran the same play, only Garrison gained nine yards for a first down. Garrison returned to the huddle and threw up a little bit. The quarterback was grinning through his face mask.

"You know what you are? You're a little pussy. You ain't got any guts. Now I can't call you a pussy...let me see, I'm going to call you Puddin'. When I call you Puddin' you'll know you're a little pussy."

Meredith called the same play. Again and again, without a huddle, to run the clock out. "We don't need to huddle," Meredith told his men. "Get up to the line." On one of the repeated plays, Meredith walked up and talked across the line to middle linebacker Bill Saul, nodding back toward Garrison as he said, "Bill, he's getting it."

The next week, on Thanksgiving night, a full Cotton Bowl and a national television audience watched the Cowboys battle longtime nemesis Cleveland. CBS had wanted another game after the traditional Thanksgiving game at Detroit, and Tex Schramm was the only owner representative to volunteer. In anticipation of the holiday game that would have a captive television audience of tens of millions, he orchestrated a makeover of the Cotton Bowl. The grass on the field was painted green to look more appealing on television than the faded fall straw of other Texas football fields. A big *D* with a circle around it was painted on the 50-yard line in the center of the field. Each end zone was filled with twenty-foot-high letters that spelled out C-O-W-B-O-Y-S. Yard-line numbers were colored blue and ocher. The home team's benches were painted bright baby blue.

The State Fair of Texas had spent $75,000 on lighting improvements in anticipation of the nationwide color telecast of the game. The Cowboys and CBS pitched in another $90,000. The Cotton Bowl was already targeted for either a $17 million makeover, including a partial roof and the expansion of its existing capacity to 81,000, or a $3 million remodel. The short-term cash infusion was merely a cosmetic Band-Aid for CBS.

The spectacle began with the national anthem. Dixieland jazz trumpeter Tommy Loy, the balding bandleader from the Levee nightclub that Clint Murchison frequented, played it straight and soloed without accompaniment. His rendition stirred the entire crowd. (Loy was invited back again and again to play "The Star-Spangled Banner" at home games.)

Maybe it was the improved lighting, but the team responded to the TV razzle-dazzle to put down the Browns, 26–14, deftly removing from around their necks another jinx that had hounded the team.

Clint Murchison was no fan of glitter when it came to what he believed was the greatest game ever invented. He had written league offices to complain about the quick-cutaway camera work being employed by cameramen at NFL games, a technique already standard in American Football League broadcasts. Nor did Murchison much care for the splashy video montages at the start of game broadcasts, especially when they made his team or his coach look less than noble, such as the shot of Tom Landry wincing.

But as an owner, Clint Murchison appreciated television's clout. Player salaries may have been climbing, but not as fast or as high as television revenues. If his franchise stayed in long enough, it would be worth tens of millions, making good on his investment.

Murchison's front man, Texas E. Schramm, managed to hold the line in negotiating contracts with his players too. The word *cheap* put too fine a point on his skills. If Tex couldn't reach an agreement with a player, he would drop the hammer and threaten to cut the player from the roster altogether if that's what it took to get a contract done. Both parties went into negotiations fully aware of the clause in every NFL contract that restricted a player from going to another team unless management traded him. If a player didn't like the team he was working for, he could either play in Canada or retire.

It was smart business on Clint Murchison's part to let Schramm do the talking. Murchison might have been the wealthiest owner in professional football, but he didn't like paying any more than was necessary. Schramm took the heat gladly. That was part of his job.

For all his public shyness, Murk didn't hide his pride in the Cowboys. After beating the New York Giants again, 17–7 in New York in the final game of the regular season, the Cowboys flew home with a 10-3-1 record, clinching the home-field advantage for the championship game against the Green Bay Packers, which was two weeks away. As the Braniff charter flight made its final approach, the pilot informed passengers that more than ten thousand fans were waiting at Love Field. On the final approach, Clint Murchison grabbed the flight attendant's intercom and spoke: "Welcome to Dallas, former home of the Kansas City Chiefs."

Thousands of fans were indeed waiting at Love Field to greet the flight, so many that normal airport operations had been shut down. Airport fences were knocked over and a throng swarmed around the bottom of the stairs as the team deplaned. "Somebody said the whole runway is full of people, what's happened?" said backup quarterback Jerry Rhome. "We thought maybe there'd been a wreck or something."

A ten-year-old boy lay crying after he'd lost his footing and been trampled. Fans carried COWBOYS ÜBER ALLES and LANDRY FOR PRESIDENT signs. Two bands were on hand, with the Brimstones playing a cover version of the Rascals' "Good Lovin'" and the Social Mariachi playing "Cuando Calienta el Sol," a Dandy fave, although Meredith had skipped the flight home to hang in New York. The team owner stepped off the plane unrecognized.

Longtime football observers said they hadn't seen Dallas like this since Doak Walker ran wild at SMU. The *Dallas Morning News* expanded its coverage by adding a young pup sportswriter named Randy Galloway to write sidebars at Sunday home games. For a newspaper or television reporter, getting the Cowboys beat was now a plum. "It was like being in Rome and being told to cover the Vatican," Galloway said. "You were covering something that was quickly becoming a religion. They were going to own Texas."

Newspapers mattered and it wasn't just Tex's journalism roots. It's that the print stayed there, as Schramm made clear to young Galloway from the start. "With Tex, it was that bleepitty-bleep paper is just hanging around all day, maybe hanging around in the men's restroom, it's in the dentist's office, it's sitting there on the chair, it changes hands. On TV, Verne Lundquist's got two damn minutes, he says something, it comes and goes, but Verne and those guys have got two minutes and that's it. Tex was much more concerned about what went on in a newspaper than anything else."

"'Cowboy,' a fine old word in the Texian Lexicon, is a money word in Dallas these days, both positive and negative," Steve Perkins wrote in the *Dallas Times Herald*. "The proprietor of Hubbard's Cafeteria in Richardson told neighbor Jerry Tubbs, the Dallas linebacker coach, that he has had to figure the Cowboy TV games in his budget. Every Sunday that Dandy Don Meredith and his group are on the tube, Hubbard's business falls off by 35 percent. It's an old story that the hardest hit trade on any Sunday afternoon is the golf driving range business. The manager of a North Dallas golfing gallery complained to Cowboys general manager Tex Schramm that he has zero business on Sunday afternoons, though he does catch some action from the going-home crowd. He asked Schramm if the pros might consider some other time, like midnight, or even Saturday. Schramm said, 'Would you believe, Monday?'"

Real estate salesmen learned to bring along portable TVs whenever there were homes to show on Sundays. Meredith, defensive captain Chuck Howley, Pete Gent, Cornell Green, and Frank Clarke could also be seen and heard outside of the games—all had TV or radio shows. Speaking-engagement rates for players had climbed from $25 to $150 in two years. Meredith commanded $300. Players signed autographs for $100 an hour. Landry had a TV pregame show. Schramm had a weekly radio program.

And there were other perks to excelling as a Dallas Cowboy. The Oak Farms Big Play winner—awarded to the outstanding player of the week—received all the milk his family could drink for a month, a hundred-dollar bond from W. O. Bankston, and the Golden Helmet award from Titche's. Zales gave out the Unsung Hero award and provided winners with heavy discounts on jewelry.

"We're lined up to be 'rat-there' for a long, long time," Meredith promised, liking how the pieces were falling into place. "It's showtime."

All season, RadioShack and Crabtree's Electronics had been advertising Cowboy antennas, priced from $4.95 to $8.95, to "beat the blackout" that was mandated for home games. Users of the antennas could pick up television stations in Sherman-Denison, Tyler, Abilene, or Waco that were televising the game. On December 28, Maynard Weitzel, manager of the Sherman Chamber of Commerce, announced that twenty-five cable-fed color television sets would be installed in the six-hundred-person-capacity ballroom of the Sherman Municipal Building at no charge, since all the motel and hotel rooms in Sherman had already been booked. The December 30 edition of the *Dallas Morning News* reported that the Irving Jaycees planned to file an injunction against the NFL and its seventy-five-mile blackout rule.

Cowboys mania was for real in 1966, and there was no better opponent for the Cowboys to prove themselves against than the Green Bay Packers. Vince Lombardi needed no more motivation than Jim Lee Howell's exaltation of Landry as the best coach in football back when Lombardi and Landry were both assistants for the Giants. His team was the opposite of the Cowboys, with a down-and-dirty, grind-it-out offense led by quarterback Bart Starr, and a brutal, never-give-an-inch defense. Few questioned their renown as the league's elite team. But the Cowboys' multiple offense, Landry's now near impenetrable 4-3 defense, and Meredith's leadership suggested Dallas was in position to eclipse them.

The Cowboys had personality and personalities, beginning with Pete Gent, arguably the most intelligent player on the team and Don Meredith's running buddy, who was quoted as saying, "What I lack in speed I make up for with cowardice," in a *Life* magazine article about the Cowboys headlined "High in Spirits and Knee Deep in Talent."

"The only way I kept up with Landry," Gent had said, "I read a lot of psychology—abnormal psych. I had just gotten through reading how you could send out supposedly anonymous questionnaires, but they could find out who was actually answering by coding the return address in pinholes, and not two weeks later here comes this questionnaire from the Cowboys. I held that son of a bitch up to the light, and there are the fucking pinholes."

"In Landry's offense, we had Pettis Norman who was a vicious blocker, we had Billy Truax," offensive tackle Tony Liscio said. "Then you have a guy who didn't even play football in college and you make him your tight end. He took a beating. The guy took a lot of pain." The physical abuse didn't stop Gent from developing a rep as a man about town, running with the Talbert brothers—Don, who played for the Cowboys, and Diron, who played for the Redskins—aka the Varmint Brothers, who were so wild in their college days at the University of Texas in Austin that signs reading NO SHIRT, NO SHOES, NO SERVICE, NO TALBERTS still remained in watering holes around campus.

Don Meredith, the team's go-to guy for hillbilly songs, kept himself front and center, releasing a forty-five record with "Travelin' Man" on one side and "Them That Ain't Got It Can't Lose" on the other on Reveller Records, a label owned by Ray Winkler, the cowriter of Jim Reeves's country classic "Welcome to My World" and owner of the Reveller Club on Greenville Avenue, a straight-up-country-music nightclub that Meredith frequented. The record was picked up by Dot Records for national distribution.

Meredith was a marked man, in a good way. Five players were having dinner at Toots Shor's in New York one night before a game against the Giants. A looker at the next table who had a date kept eyeing Meredith. Dandy returned the favor. He asked Toots if Toots might be able to persuade the young lady's date away from the table for a couple minutes. "Sure," Shor told him. The restaurant owner informed the man he had a telephone call. As soon as he got up and walked off, Meredith leaned in and within earshot of his dining partners said with a confidence-winning smile, "Darlin', if you've got a shower, you won't need no towels because I'll lick you dry." The lady wrote down her phone number and passed it to the Cowboys quarterback.

The nation's football fans tuned in to CBS for the thirty-fourth annual National Football League Championship game on the first day of 1967, the second half of a TV doubleheader that began with the Kansas City Chiefs besting the Bills in the AFL Championship game in Buffalo. The winner of the NFL clash would play the Chiefs in the first NFL-AFL world championship game.

The Cowboys believed they had the upper hand. Meredith and Bob Hayes were expected to join together for an unstoppable passing combination. But Lombardi gambled and assigned only one defensive player to cover Hayes. Alternating defenders Herb Adderley and Bob Jeter held the Bullet to a single pass reception for one yard. Whether it was nerves and jitters or a bruising defense, it took a while for the Cowboys offense to get in the groove. Frank Clarke scored on a fourth-quarter touchdown bomb for 62 yards, while Don Perkins and Dan Reeves rushed for two TDs that were augmented by two Danny Villanueva field goals.

The performance was admirable, almost heroic, but not quite enough. A Dallas touchdown had been called back when left tackle Jim Boeke was penalized for illegal motion for moving his left foot before the snap. Then the Packers' Tom Brown intercepted a Don Meredith pass in the end zone on the following play as time expired, ending the game with the Cowboys two yards shy of the goal line and one touchdown short, 34–27. A Cotton Bowl full of broken hearts couldn't believe their silver-and-blue 'Boys. They had come closer than ever before, which made coming up short harder than ever to take.

What wasn't obvious was that the Cowboys were redefining how professional football was played. The Packers may have beaten them strength for strength, but Dallas had introduced finesse and quickness into the equation for a winning team. The title of the Cowboys highlight reel that NFL Films put together was "Speed, Inc." Bob Hayes was a game changer, a team changer, and a league changer.

Hayes had already inspired Clint Murchison to break his own rules about meddling. The owner approached the coach during the 1965 season to recommend that instead of running a reverse with receiver Frank Clarke, Landry call a reverse with Bob Hayes.

The coach accommodated the owner and the team lost 17 yards on the play. "We lost yardage and I haven't heard from Clint since," quipped Landry, who won the Associated Press Coach of the Year recognition. Don Meredith received the Bert Bell award from the Maxwell Club of Philadelphia, given to the league's best player.

The Packers went on to play the Kansas City Chiefs in the first NFL-AFL championship, at the Coliseum in Los Angeles in front of 61,946 spectators. No matter what had transpired since Clint Murchison and Lamar Hunt got simultaneous hard-ons for football, Lamar's plan for fielding a championship game-worthy team had worked faster than Clint's, and in front of an almost as rabid fan base.

Green Bay's 35–10 trouncing of the Chiefs provided small satisfaction to Clint, much less to Tex or Tom, despite proving the established league's superiority. All of them knew full well that there but for fortune, occasional odd incidents, luck, and one very perplexing brain fart, the Dallas Cowboys would have been accepting that first world championship trophy.

And as far as fortune went, the business ledger had been as good as the team's 10-3-1 record. The NFL championship at the Cotton Bowl attracted 74,152 fans, generating $2,773,861 in gross receipts. Winning and losing players earned the largest shares in the history of the league championship, with each Packer taking home $9,813.63 and each Cowboy getting $6,527.85. Each Packer earned an additional $15,000 for beating the Chiefs.

The Cowboys had generated close to 60 percent of the Cotton Bowl's total receipts in 1966. Their draw and Clint Murchison's threats to pull up stakes justified a $2.6 million upgrade of the stadium written into an upcoming bond election, promising aluminum-back grandstand seats, bigger locker rooms with air-conditioning, more restrooms and drinking fountains, and new grass. But these changes were merely cosmetic. If the Cowboys were the embodiment of a new kind of pro football, the place they played should be just as future-leaning, or so Clint Murchison believed.

Cowboys Matter

THE WHOLE CITY WAS behind them now. The Cowboys were the most important topic of conversation on Ken Dowe and Granny Emma's morning drive show on KLIF; they generated more column inches in the newspapers than any other team; and they filled up the news segments of the ten o'clock broadcasts as well as the sports segments. The team's fortunes were Dallas's fortunes.

Which made losing hard. "The front office would come in on Sundays," Tex Schramm's daughter Christi said. "They'd come in after Christmas. They worked because they wanted to. I think everybody realized they were creating something really special, even the secretaries. I'd work in the summers with them and you heard very little bitching. If they had to stay late, they did it because that was what was required of them. As they got closer and closer to becoming a winning team, the pressure increased. With my dad, if we'd lose a game, well, that night we'd just make sure we were in our rooms. We didn't come out of the room much. Monday was a bad day, Tuesday was a bad day. By Wednesday you're looking forward to the next game and you're hyped up. But for the couple of days afterwards, it's mourning a loss. It was a personal loss to my dad, I know."

Days after the Cowboys' 1966 season concluded one game too early, Clint Murchison unveiled his plans for the football palace of the future. If the city of Irving could arrange financing for a new stadium at a top price of thirteen million dollars, seven million less than a city of Irving spokesman had estimated it would cost, the Dallas Cowboys Football Club would relocate, Murchison promised. Neither the State Fair of Texas nor the city of Dallas was going to help build a new stadium. Improvements to the Cotton Bowl were "pouring money into a hopeless situation," Murchison contended. The old guard that dominated the State Fair of Texas board so cherished the glory days of the Texas Centennial Exposition in 1936 that they were loath to change or modernize anything, including where the Cowboys played.

Downtown Dallas had been Murchison's preferred site, but a downtown stadium wasn't part of Mayor Jonsson's Goals for Dallas plan. To Jonsson, a stadium would be an empty vessel most of the year, hardly a magnet of dynamism. Murchison tried to sweeten the offer and bought ten more acres of derelict downtown property adjacent to his proposed stadium to build an art museum and a music hall. Jonsson dismissed it as a pipe dream, as opposed to Jonsson's thoroughly researched, well-articulated, and citizen-tested vision for a new Dallas.

"Merchants liked it; hotel operators liked it; restaurateurs liked it; convention promoters liked it; the president of the Dallas Citizens Council liked it so much he even proposed expanding the concept; both newspapers loved it," Clint parried. "Erik Jonsson hated it." And when Erik made up his mind, Murchison concluded, "He, like Caesar, did not deviate."

So an eighty-six-acre teardrop-shape lot bordered by Highway 183 to the south, Loop 12 to the west, and Carpenter Freeway to the east became the preferred future home of the Dallas Cowboys, even though it wasn't much more than a glorified freeway intersection.

"As I see the situation, Irving would like to build the stadium and the City of Dallas wouldn't," Murchison reasoned before shifting into pig-lipstick-salesman mode. "Irving is an excellent location. The [location] is actually closer to the population center of Dallas than the Cotton Bowl. It's what, 10 minutes from the middle of Oak Cliff? Eight minutes from downtown Dallas?"

Murk called a press conference to describe his ideal football venue. "The main emphasis should be on the number of seats on the sidelines," he said. "It will be the finest football stadium to date in the world...and be constructed so that all but one end zone will be in the shade." His vision left out air-conditioning, a surprising omission, considering its transition from amenity to necessity throughout the southern United States. Murchison stuck to the high road. "I have concluded that a dome is impractical and esthetically undesirable for football in this area," he said, not mentioning the considerable savings realized by leaving the facility open-air.

"The question arises, why am I doing this?" Murchison posited rhetorically. "Do I have some selfish motive? I want to make one point clear: I can make just as much money at the present stadium. But I think I owe the efforts that I have made and am making to the thousands of Cowboy fans who don't have parking passes, who don't have comfortable box seats, but who are the real reason it is possible for the Cowboys to remain in Dallas. Inadvertently, I have become a spokesman for Cowboy fans. They are my customers and I am going to try to do my best for them — at least I am going to try."

By doing so, he would also make his team the best-looking on television, an attribute that mattered to the tens of millions of fans who couldn't afford tickets.

The Murchisons had an odd history with the city. No building or institution bore the Murchison name, despite the family's astronomical wealth. Nor did Clint maintain high visibility at the Cotton Bowl. More than once, he was refused admission to the locker room after a game because security guards did not recognize him. "Who is this guy?" the guard would ask a team official, only to hear back, "He owns the team."

Clint Jr. said he tuned out local politics after he was kicked off a Dallas Chamber of Commerce subcommittee in 1950 for advocating for a regional airport shared with Fort Worth. Accumulating wealth was more fun than participating in fuddy-duddy civic affairs.

Few witnessed Murchison's playful side. Like his father and like his occasional business partner Gordon McLendon, Clint Jr. had a small circle of unusual Fellini-esque friends, cronies, and syco-phants. He enjoyed consorting with so-called lowlifes as much as rubbing elbows with the landed gentry. He could move about a dark anonymous private club on Industrial Boulevard as easily as he did at the 21 Club, Danny's Hideaway, or Jilly's in New York.

Murchison was flip and sarcastic when he wanted to be. If some-one left a message for him that was billed as very important, he'd begin the subsequent conversation by asking, "Is this important to you or to me?"

Clint was on a first-name basis with President Lyndon B. Johnson. But he was not Dallas society. Civic duties were limited to advocating on behalf of the Boys Club. "He was the most boring human being that ever came down the pike," one family friend said. "Which was weird because his father wasn't that way and his brother wasn't like that. John Murchison was a pretty regular guy."

John Dabney Murchison was the other half of Murchison Broth-ers, which technically meant that he owned half of the Dallas Cow-boys Football Club. He sometimes attended games, but that was about it for his involvement with the team. He and his vivacious wife, Lupe, rode the charity circuit like no Murchison had before and thoroughly enjoyed living in New York, their residence during the long Allegheny takeover fight. They developed a refined taste for modern art and acquired significant pieces, a pursuit they brought back to Dallas. If Clint Jr. was the shy retiring owner who needed an extrovert such as Bedford Wynne or Tex Schramm to front for him, John Dabney was invisible.

Which was fine for Erik Jonsson, who had bigger fish to fry than the Murchisons in his attempt to sell the city on a regional airport. Dallas and Fort Worth held simultaneous elections to create the new airport authority. Fort Worth voters approved the measure. Dal-las voters rejected it. That did not stop Jonsson. The airport was going to be built, damn it, and voters were going to approve bonds to buy eighteen thousand acres of land for the airport, damn it. And eventually, they did, damn it.

First, Dallas voters bought into Jonsson's other vision — the $175 million Crossroads bond election, which included $13 million in additional improvements to the Cotton Bowl and Fair Park and surrounding land for parking.

Irving voters had already committed to issuing $20 million in bonds for a new stadium to be paid for by Cowboys fans. Anyone desiring season tickets would first have to pay for a personal seat license to dib a seat. The license functioned like a bond. The creative method of payment was a portent of full-blown corporate welfare in stadium financing. But while some stadiums were expected to experience operating deficits from the outset, Murchison was determined his facility would pay dividends.

Murchison had a soapbox to campaign for his stadium because the Dallas Cowboys were the hottest ticket in town, evidenced in ways big and small, including the Athletic House in Highland Park Village advertising an authentic NFL uniform for boys (helmet, jersey, shoulder pads, and pants for $10.95), while Cullum and Boren sporting goods sold Official Don Meredith footballs for $9.95 — the first inkling of Cowboys merch.

Would 1967 finally be the year? Tom and Tex and Clint believed it would. So did the cabbies working Love Field, the bankers working the downtown towers, and the dice players working the back of bars on the wrong side of town. Dave Campbell, who published *Texas Football* magazine, the bible of the sport in Texas, showed he too was a believer by publishing the first annual Dallas Cowboys yearbook, ninety-six pages thick.

All the preparation and future-thinking were about to pay off. Really. Finally. One of the clearest signs was Don Perkins, the Cowboys' most dependable running back, who had retired after the 1966 season to become director of information for the state of New Mexico, only to be pulled back to the team with a handsome raise. Perk's ability to grind out extra yards nearly every carry was irreplaceable.

Gil Brandt was crowing about tight end Rayfield Wright, the six-six, 255-pound seventh-round pick from Fort Valley State, an obscure institute of higher education in Georgia that happened to field a football team. It was the kind of program that Dick Mansberger knew every which way. One of Brandt's most potent field reps, Mansberger scouted historically black colleges and universities, many of which were still getting players that white-majority universities (and pro scouts) tended to overlook.

Brandt himself was accumulating more air miles than Mansberger and the other scouts, flying DC-3s and driving rented cars to remote college outposts such as Eugene, Oregon; Spokane, Washington; and Boise, Idaho, over the course of four days, returning to Dallas for three, then heading back out to another region the following week.

Prospects and college trainers were sent copies of *Life with the Dallas Cowboys*, a special annual magazine that touted the Murchison ownership, the first-class organization, and Dallas itself as a great place for families and for singles. Frank Clarke addressed the lingering aura of segregation, and the odds of making the team were clearly laid out. The magazine made the Cowboys look like the finest team in sports. If it was sent to college trainers, Brandt reasoned, players going into the training room would have something to read.

And even the man bankrolling the sales job, alleged shy guy Clint Murchison Jr., showed his true colors and dry humor in a guest column for Blackie Sherrod of the *Dallas Times Herald* before the season started:

"I'd like to scattershoot, but I used my last load arguing for that downtown stadium. I consider myself an authoritative Cowboy fan since I have seen more Cowboy games than anybody except Tom Landry, Frank Clarke, and Don Meredith.... The other day, I was asking Landry his opinion of our prospects for the year. As a coach, he naturally expressed certain reservations and pointed out several weaknesses in our lineup and depth. I can recall asking Tom this same question before our league opener in 1960; I believe he gave me a similar answer then. To refresh my memory of that year's team, I searched through my desk for the battered checkbook on which I had scratched down the list of starters for that first game.... This team missed by three points defeating the 1960 champions of the NFL; coaches are never satisfied."

CLINT WAS CLEARLY SATISFIED by the overcapacity Cotton Bowl turnout of 78,807 on a hot Monday night for the Salesmanship Club game against Green Bay. But the torrid heat and the huge crowd provided the ingredients for an evening of wilding, courtesy of criminals from the surrounding neighborhood. The football game became an afterthought amid reports of assaults, robberies, and break-ins.

"Young hoodlums running in small packs terrorized football fans leaving the Fair Park grounds Monday night," reported the *Dallas Morning News*. The six robberies, one assault case, eleven car-prowling cases, and minor acts of destruction were "the worst I can remember," said police chief Charles Batchelor. One fan was shot in the heel, and his wife was beaten. All the reported assailants, according to the newspapers, were Negroes.

There were also numerous reports of gate-crashers. A fire department official said, "There were violations at the Cotton Bowl last night, and those in charge will be put on notice." The implication was the Cowboys had sold more tickets than the stadium had capacity. Tex Schramm insisted, "We were not oversold."

It wasn't the worst development for Clint Murchison, who could have been accused of hiring the street thugs to make his point with the State Fair board, Mayor Jonsson, and the city council over the condition of the Cotton Bowl. "The amount of discomfort that people will put up with is decreasing as the quality of television is increasing," Murchison warned, acknowledging the growing clout of the game as television programming.

The approved Cotton Bowl fix-up plan, which called for tearing down the same African American neighborhood of low- and middle-income homes around Fair Park where the wilding had occurred through the use of eminent domain, did not go down well. A series of protests broke out, led by young black activists and future leaders such as Al Lipscomb, J. B. Jackson, the Reverend Peter Johnson, and Elsie Faye Higgins—the kind of organized civil unrest the Dallas Citizens Council and the Dallas leadership had striven so hard to avoid. And stadium improvements were scaled down.

Meanwhile, the football club's swank new offices at 6116 North Central Expressway—the site of the old Dallas Texans practice field—provided a marked contrast to the Cotton Bowl, setting a new standard for football clubs everywhere. A twenty-four-year-old New York woman fresh out of the Parsons School of Design named Carol Hermanovski and her husband, Dell, were the designers responsible for the cool modern look. Dallas's money and urban newness had prompted the couple to move to Texas to do interior design projects in what she considered a very progressive environment. "Dallas was so ready for modernism and my husband and I were modernist designers," she said.

Hermanovski was unfamiliar with Dallas before she moved. "I thought it would be a backwater, all desert and cactus," she admitted. "I was worried I wouldn't be able to find my favorite cosmetics." She found instead a "new and clean and crisp" city full of garden apartments "with your own patch of green" and streets lined with fern bars, young singles, and exceptional wealth and surprising taste.

The Hermanovskis' portfolio impressed architect Bob Oglesby, who had been hired to design the Cowboys' new offices in the Expressway Tower. He liked their portfolio enough to contact Carol (Dell Hermanovski had been called into the Army) and introduce her to Tex Schramm.

"I wanted to evoke the image of football and the feel and the excitement of the game in this interior," she said. "I didn't want to do anything cliché but to somehow evoke the spirit and the excitement of the game."

Hermanovski was nervous about her interview. But Tex was easy. "He understood it, he got excited about it. I showed him a desk for his office that was made by Knoll. It had stainless steel legs and inlays and a rosewood desk. It was more like a table desk, it wasn't one of these heavy honkers, and Tex asked, 'Is that what people are using now?' I told him not everybody is using this, but this desk is you, this desk is progressive and timeless and modernist and forward-thinking."

She had Tom Landry draw a play diagram for her so the first thing visitors would see upon entering the Expressway Tower offices — before receptionist Doretha Gray, even — was a three-dimensional diagram of a running play on the wall, with Xs and Os in wood and lines of movement in stainless steel, along with the words *The Dallas Cowboys Football Club* spelled out in masculine Euro-style typeface.

Hermanovski contacted Dave Boss, the creative director for the NFL, to posterize Cowboys photographs and blow them up larger than life; they would be hung along the entryway as a sequence of images that culminated with a player scoring a touchdown. The images "evoked the excitement, the energy and the power of the game," she said.

Tex could be intimidating, Hermanovski admitted. "He had a deep booming voice and he always wanted to know why. 'Why do you think it should be this? Give me some reasons.' I could always back up my design with reasonable justification, why it should be this way, and he loved that. That's what made him have confidence in me."

Tex frequently consulted with Hermanovski about the perfect color for the leggings for the pants of the Cowboys uniform. "He was obsessing constantly about that silver-blue color," she said. "He was so concerned about how that color looked on TV, and of course that was something you couldn't control because each person's TV was set differently. There were too many variables. But he was always trying to get that perfect silver-blue. At times he got it a little much like a pale turquoise and I would tell him it's got too much green in it."

After the new offices opened, Carol Hermanovski convinced Schramm to let her redesign the team logo, which was still the cartoonish football player on an undersize pony. "Tex, on a bumper sticker that logo doesn't read well at all," she told him. She proposed a clean silhouette of the Cowboys helmet with the blue star as the focus, which Schramm agreed to. "As a result," Tex wrote in a letter of recommendation, "we have one of the most unique and attractive suite of offices in the professional sports."

The organization was sleek, classy, and computerized. And Tex Schramm fretted that other teams would follow suit with IBM, which owned the software that Salam Qureishi, the Cowboys' Indian, had developed. So in September of 1966, Tex proposed a new company that would own the player-selection system and be financed by NFL clubs using it. In early winter of 1967 Salam Qureishi and his wife, Naheed, visited Tex and Marty Schramm in Dallas for three days. That summer, Tex called and asked for another visit. This time, he introduced Qureishi to Murchison to talk about the new company. Murchison told Qureishi he was a great believer in debt. The company he envisioned would be equally owned by the Cowboys, the 49ers, and the Rams as well as the New Orleans Saints and A. Salam Qureishi, with each entity contributing $30,000. Qureishi's stake came from a loan offered by the Cowboys' bank, to be paid off in five years.

Qureishi observed that Murchison was so unassuming, the only hint he was a wealthy man was his monogrammed shirt. Yet he recognized Murchison's intelligence. They would visit every couple of weeks, talking about how to develop the new company, which Murchison wanted to rival Electronic Data Systems, the North Texas–based computer-data company founded by H. Ross Perot.

Optimum Systems Incorporated launched in July of 1967 and IBM awarded the new company rights to the player selection system that Qureishi had developed. Applications of the system were plentiful, including selecting the best cadets for Lackland Air Force Base's academy in San Antonio; the best administrative management system for the city of Sunnyvale, California; and an information system for the San Francisco Police Department. Scouting for the NFL was just another set of stats.

The scouting combine split the country up and assigned a grading system so that a player couldn't be drafted without a grade, assuring an even playing field among the participating clubs while minimizing travel expenses. The technical aspects of pro football moved Salam Qureishi to declare it "easily the most scientific game ever invented."

"It was just another weapon that we had to do the job that had to be done," Coach Tom Landry said dryly. Landry's lack of agitation was rooted in his deep faith. "I'm a great believer in my own convictions," he said in a magazine profile. "But I pray a great deal that I'll make the right decision. I have no doubt that there is something other than man himself that leads man."

Some players referred to him as Pope Landry I. He wasn't the easiest man to communicate with, and there were times it took a two-by-four over the head to get his attention. "He would never pat you on the behind and tell you 'good job,'" complained an ex–defensive back. "And if you intercepted a pass, Landry would look at you like that's what you're supposed to do!"

The coach was progressive in his strategy but conservative in his insistence that it took many years for a player to adapt to his system. Dan Reeves slowly but surely became a true believer. "He tells you what's going to happen and on Sunday it happens," he said. Even Meredith had come around. "I thought I knew a little about football," he said. "But Landry would be up at the blackboard saying, 'Okay, we'll do this, then they'll do that and then we'll…' You'd interrupt him and say, 'Coach, what if they don't do that?' Landry would just look at you and say, 'They will.'" And they did.

Meredith's habit of ignoring Landry's play-calling infuriated the coach. "Sometimes we'd be out there in the huddle and [Landry would] send a play in on a real crucial down," lineman Tony Liscio said. "The guy would say, 'Landry said to run this play.' Meredith said, 'No, that won't work, let's run this other play.' And he'd go over to the sideline after that and Landry would chew him out: 'Don, I sent this play in, you didn't run it.' Meredith would say, 'I didn't think that would work, Coach, so I tried something else.'"

Early on, Meredith chunked a pass that wasn't caught and muttered "I'll be a son of a bitch" when he returned to the sidelines. Landry gave him the eagle eye and said, "That wouldn't help your passing a bit."

"Don was always very cool," Liscio said. "He was at ease with everything. One time, we had practiced all week, and Landry told us, 'They're going to be in this defense in this situation, they're going to do this in this situation.' He'd tell you exactly what they were going to do and most times the teams would do it. So we're out there in the middle of the field and there was that defense Landry told us about where the outside linebacker had shifted to come inside. Everybody shifted except that linebacker didn't move. Don came up to the line and looked at the situation and said, 'Hey, you're supposed to be in here' and the guy moved in there. The linebacker couldn't help but laugh."

Another time, when a referee named Tommy Bell, who knew Meredith from East Texas, was working a game at the Cotton Bowl, Meredith spotted a good-looking gal walking down the grandstands. "Hey, guys, check this side over here," Meredith told his teammates in the huddle, inviting them to take a gander at the pretty young thing coming down the aisle. Then he raised his head and signaled Bell, who called an official time-out so the whole offense could take a look. "He was loose, man," marveled Tony Liscio.

WHETHER USING COMPUTERS or not, the Cowboys followed the draft with the Kicking Karavan, a promotion in which scouts covered ten thousand miles and offered tryouts to all comers in twenty-nine cities, ultimately attracting thirteen hundred candidates and inspiring Danny Villanueva to train like he never had before. "I want to prove a personal thing," he said. "I'm going to get rid of every one of those kids and then the Cowboys are going to pay for what they've done to me. If they wanted to make a point to me, they've succeeded. Now I want to make a point with them." Villanueva ranked thirteenth among NFL punters, with a 39.2-yard average—not great but so far sufficient to fill the Cowboys' needs.

Twenty-seven finalists were brought to Dallas, and three were signed: Mac Percival, a basketball star at Texas Tech who was teaching in nearby Garland and who was later traded to the Chicago Bears; Harold Deters, who wanted to leave when he got to Dallas because he missed his dog (Brandt let Deters have the dog brought to Dallas); and Terry Swanson, a University of Massachusetts punter.

"WHAT WE REALLY SIGNED were great legs," Gil Brandt said. "Whether the coaches can teach them the rest, we don't know." Deters made the Cowboys squad and nailed one of four field goal attempts and an extra point before he was cut.

And then it was game time. The eighth season of the Dallas Cowboys started with a bang: they dispensed with Cleveland at Municipal Stadium in Ohio, 21–14, and then took the Giants to the woodshed at home, 38–24.

The team dropped what should have been a close game with the Rams, losing 35–13 at the Cotton Bowl as LA rushed for four times as much yardage as Dallas did. The game was noteworthy as the first game that Verne Lundquist sat in the Cowboys broadcast booth.

The previous season marked the start of Bill Mercer's run as the play-by-play announcer on the Cowboys radio network, a position Mercer got after Jay Randolph resigned to take a job with the St. Louis Cardinals baseball club. Mercer proved to be such a steady, stand-up voice that fans watching the televised game began turning down the TV announcer's play-by-play to hear Mercer's more excited, more specific radio version. He was also the accommodating host of the *Tom Landry Show.*

Oddly enough, Mercer was one of the few media people who didn't get along with Texas Schramm, a man who made cultivation of the media corps a personal mission. "Tex and I were a little strained," Mercer said. "He had decided—and I wouldn't admit it—that I liked baseball more than football because I was doing the [minor-league] Spurs' broadcasts.

"[Assistant general manager] Al Ward gave me five things he wanted me to go out and get done for them. I did all five. One of them was to see if I could get Tex Schramm on the radio. I got Tex Schramm his own show on KRLD and I was his MC. Then Al called me in. It was the late summer of 1967. 'Bill, we want you to go down to WFAA Channel 8 and take the job as the sports anchor.' I said, 'You want me to take the job?' He said, 'Well, you have to go down and talk to them. It's already set up.'" Mercer hesitated. He was teaching at North Texas State, doing baseball, calling basketball, and calling the Cowboys.

Ward did not hide his disappointment. "Okay, we'll never help you on anything else," he informed him. When Mercer showed up at Love Field to fly to the next game, Ward told him, "Bill, you sit in the back with the players from now on." Mercer no longer rated flying up front with the management.

Mercer understood the rules. "Tex was very progressive," he said. "His guy was the commissioner. He brought him along. He was hard to work for because you had to be on his side and I wasn't. He protected the Cowboy image. I respect that. Some of the writers got irritated with him sometimes. That's why he wanted me to go to Channel 8—so I could keep the image of the Cowboys alive."

Verne Lundquist took the job that Bill Mercer did not pursue. For three years, he had been the sports guy at KTBC in Austin, the largest one-television-station market in the United States, thanks to station owner Lady Bird Johnson, who happened to be married to the president of the United States. Now a San Antonio TV news anchor, Lundquist flew to Dallas, where he was driven to North Park Shopping Mall, the first enclosed shopping mall in the Southwest, and into Channel 8's studio there. He passed the live audition and was hired, taking a cut in pay from his news-anchor gig but taking a leap into the big time in a big city with big sports, where the buzz was all about the Dallas Cowboys.

"I got an apartment on Northwest Highway which was full of young people in their twenties and thirties, a lot of stewardesses and singles, and all anyone talked about was the Cowboys," Lundquist said. He started as the WFAA Channel 8 sportscaster on September 27, 1967.

The first game Lundquist covered pitted the Cowboys against the Rams in the Cotton Bowl in early October. Expectations were sky-high for the team that had come within one minute and two yards of winning the NFL championship the year before. But the LA Rams creamed the Cowboys, with defensive back Eddie Meador intercepting Meredith three times. Lundquist had to use word pictures in his sports report. "As the new hire, I'd asked, who was going to film the game? The answer was, nobody. Channel 8 didn't film the games because it was too expensive."

Local stations regarded film as a luxury for Cowboys reports. Lundquist asked news director Bert Shipp for sixteen hundred feet of film to cover a game; Shipp offered eight hundred feet. And that was how Channel 8 became the first in the market to use its own game film, taken by Lundquist and by Jack Murray.

"Jack and I would go to home games and sit on the roof of the Cotton Bowl," Lundquist said. "He was up on a little platform and if I thought we should shoot the play, I'd tug on his pants leg and he'd start the camera. The minute that the play hadn't gone anywhere, I'd tug on his pant leg and he'd shut it down. We went through an entire season and never missed a touchdown, including a 90-yard return by Bob Hayes against Pittsburgh. The film ran out just as he crossed the end zone. Nobody else [among local sportscasters] was doing it — it was a leg up."

After the Rams debacle, the Cowboys' Al Ward called. "We don't normally do this, but we'd like to get to know you," he told Lundquist. "We'd like to have you as a guest on the charter to Washington so you can see who we are and what we do." On the flight up, Ward came to the back of the plane to visit with Lundquist, telling him, "Our normal process for the radio network on the road is to hire a local guy, but since you're with us, would you like to do the postgame radio show?"

Lundquist demurred. KLIF was carrying the broadcast and Verne was working for the ABC affiliate that also owned another radio station.

"Aw, nobody'll ever hear it," Ward assured him and Lundquist agreed to give it a shot.

The Cowboys beat the Redskins on a touchdown pass from Meredith to Dan Reeves in the last minute of the game. Lundquist interviewed linebackers Dave Edwards and Harold Hays and receiver Lance Rentzel for the postgame show. "I don't think we ever got to either Meredith or Reeves that day, but I did the thing and they were happy with it," Lundquist said. "The next morning I got a call at home from Jack Hauser, the assistant GM from Channel 8. He said, 'I was driving home yesterday afternoon. Tell me I'm wrong, but did I hear you on KLIF?'"

Lundquist's new radio gig was tolerated by station management, mainly because Cowboys listeners associated him with Channel 8.

ON SATURDAYS before Sunday home games, the players' kids were welcomed to play ball with their dads after practice, the team's version of Cub Scouts. Then the players would head off to the Holiday Inn on

Central Expressway, a couple exits toward downtown, near the team offices. After a late-afternoon meeting, married players went home and ate dinner with their families while the single players catted around, but they were all back in their hotel beds by eleven p.m.

In his free time, fullback Walt Garrison drove over to Mansfield, near Fort Worth, where his rodeo partner Bill Robinson had their horses ready at the Kowbell Indoor Rodeo, so he could go bulldogging.

That worked fine for a few weeks, until a caller reached Tex Schramm and told him, "We think it is so good that y'all let Walt come over here and bulldog the night before a game." The next morning, Coach Landry and Garrison had a heart-to-heart talk. "We don't do that, Walt," he told Garrison. "You can't do that anymore."

Garrison took heed, saving cowboying for the offseason, when he and Bill Robinson would load up the pickup truck and the in-line trailer and ride rodeos across the nation.

Other players preferred hunting, fishing, or photography. Some pursued theology, science, or math. Some sought careers as bankers, real estate agents, printers, writers, or entertainers. And a few were men-about-town with reputations as connoisseurs of the striptease. As such, they couldn't help but discover Bubbles Cash.

Bubbles Cash had been following the Dallas Cowboys since their very first year, when she was a teenager working as a carhop at the Sivils in Oak Cliff, the world's largest drive-in restaurant, according to *Life* magazine.

Sivils girls were known for their beauty and their distinctive majorette outfits and white boots, uniforms conceived of when Mr. and Mrs. Sivils were watching cheerleaders at a football game on television.

Young Bubbles, who grew up in the nearby town of Grand Prairie and for whom "Dallas may as well been New York City," was a Sivils star. "I had my uniform altered and had it cut down to show my top and I had my pants taken in, they were white satin, just real sexy," she said. "I had people coming out there to see me walk and calling on me to wait on them. I had people waiting in line for me to wait on them."

Owner J. D. Sivils introduced the fourteen-year-old Bubbles to the other side of Dallas in a back room where he played poker with his friends. "I met some people out there that I ended up knowing later in life, including one guy who I went into business with," she said. The job gave her confidence to become the stripper she'd aspired to be.

"I had an ambition from when I was a child that I was going to be a star stripper in downtown Dallas," she said. She had seen Candy Barr sing with the Goree Girls at the Texas Prison Rodeo, where the men and women incarcerated in the Texas penal system had the opportunity to ride horses or bulls or perform on four Sundays every October in Huntsville. "I made my plans accordingly," Bubbles said. "I wasn't going to do the things that [Candy] did to get in trouble [five years in prison for possessing two marijuana cigarettes]. I was going to play it safe, play it on the square, not do things that people wouldn't like or that I could get in trouble for."

Bubbles quit Sivils in 1962, married, and started dancing at age seventeen. "I had my baby first, started my diet and my practicing, and [her husband] sold his boat, the *White Trash,* and paid for my boob operation. I told him before we got married that I wanted out of Grand Prairie and that I wanted to be a dancer in downtown Dallas. I told him what I wanted and he gave it all to me."

She showed up for amateur night at the Theater Lounge, one of two strip clubs operated by brothers Abe and Barney Weinstein, won, and was soon working for $125 a week plus tips, playing both the Theater Lounge and the Colony Club.

In the fall of 1967, she was working a small joint called the Calves Bar near the Dallas Cowboys practice field when a bunch of players, led by Meredith and Niland, showed up for a round of beers. On a break, she sat down with the players and asked, "Who's gonna ever get me tickets to a Cowboys game?" Jerry Rhome, the backup quarterback, volunteered some tickets to the Falcons game in early November.

Bubbles and her husband, Mack, and their friends Cotton and Judy Moore attended the game at the Cotton Bowl together. "I dressed conservatively," she said. "High top, little suit, long sleeves, not a revealing top, except for the fact I had a short skirt." *Short* was an understatement.

It was little wonder that Bubbles attracted attention walking up the aisle toward the concession stand. When she descended the same steps holding a large pink swirl of cotton candy, applause broke out. "So I did a little dance on the steps, did a little complete turnaround, a little bumping of my hips while holding the cotton candy," she said. She liked the attention. She just didn't realize how much she was getting. "I saw the cameras from across the football field on me," she said. "I could tell all the eyes were on me. It just broke out all over the stands. The guys that started the applause were just tickled to death, and the women were happy and laughing, and it was happening. I never had a grand stage like that before."

She did the concession-stand walk only once that game. Afterward, she said, "Cotton and Judy walked out in front of us; [Judy] was embarrassed by the whole thing. She didn't sign on for that."

Bubbles was featured on the television news reports that night. Steve Perkins wrote her up in his *Dallas Times Herald* column the next day. No one knew her name until strip-club owner Barney Weinstein saw the coverage and started calling all the Dallas newspapers and television stations to inform them the mystery lady in the short skirt was none other than Miss Bubbles Cash.

A crowd was lined up around the block to witness her next performance at the Weinstein brothers' Theater Lounge, drawn by this advertisement:

She upset the Cotton Bowl, now see her in person at the Theater Lounge, Bubbles Cash.

"Barney was a real showman," Bubbles said. Weinstein got on the phone to Tex Schramm, and Tex, sensing a promotional opportunity, made sure Bubbles got tickets to all home games and to New Orleans, where the Cowboys were playing the following Sunday at Tulane Stadium. "Al Hirt was playing, it was very festive," Bubbles said. "I got a lot of attention. I started getting press from all over the country." She also represented the Cowboys at out-of-town games in Miami, in Green Bay, and in Baltimore, where a club offered her a job on the spot.

Players started acknowledging Bubbles from the sidelines and began showing up wherever she danced. The front office took an interest in her too. "Tex was my guy," she said. "Brother Landry," as she called the coach, not so much. "What a square," she said with a giggle. Abe and Barney Weinstein hired a skywriter to circle the Cotton Bowl on Sundays with the message *Hello Bubbles Cash.*

"It was a happy deal. Everybody needed a good laugh and good-hearted fun," she said. "Barney thought the world of me, he and his wife, May, and he wanted me to play this thing out and enjoy it and have all the fun and publicity. Money can't buy that kind of publicity. I thought I was at the top already, but that was the happening of my life, living out my dream."

All of Dallas took note. "When Bubbles walked, it set the bar for everybody who was dressing to go to the game," Judy Stone, the daughter of car dealer Eddie Stone, said. "Dressing to go to the games was as big a deal as dressing to go out. It wasn't 'Let's get warm' or 'Let's just throw on some comfortable jeans and a T-shirt.' One of the last games I remember going to before I got sober, I had on a black T-shirt with red light bulbs on it that spelled out *Expensive.* There was a tiny nine-volt battery that fit in the cleavage that flashed off and on."

Bubbles Cash was one of the first well-known women in Dallas who publicly acknowledged having augmented breasts. The silicone-breast-implant technique had been developed in the early 1960s by two Houston plastic surgeons, Doctors Frank Gerow and Thomas

Cronin. Word about the new procedure traveled fast up Highway 75, so Dallas soon rivaled Houston as the boob-job capital of America.

On top of that, Bubbles stayed in the public eye by running for governor. "Mack, he was a sign man and he made me some bumper stickers — Vote Bubbles Cash for Peace," she said of her husband. "I was selling them at the club for a dollar. I announced my candidacy saying I wanted to end the war in Vietnam and bring the troops home. I didn't want to see another brother come home in a box. 'Peace at any price is no peace at all.'"

SIDESHOWS LIKE Bubbles helped the Cowboys turn the cavernous Cotton Bowl into the team's twelfth man. "The Cotton Bowl was rowdy," sportswriter Randy Galloway said. "They didn't even sell beer, you had to smuggle shit in, which everybody did, in flasks and whatever. And you drank as much as you could drink before the game and ran out at halftime for the quick beer. It was not an alcohol-driven crowd, but the Cotton Bowl had become one hell of a home-field advantage."

A line formed at Fair Park for tickets to the Christmas Eve play-off game against Cleveland a full day before they went on sale. Some fans played dominoes while they waited. "The Cowboys' unofficial mascot, stripper Bubbles Cash, early Wednesday wandered up and down the line of ticket seekers handing out autographs and building up morale," noted reporter Bill Sloan. Bubbles had become so popular that Blackie Sherrod interviewed her in the KLIF booth. She became so tied to the team that when she found her father, who had abandoned the family when she was a little girl, the first thing he said to her was "Are you still with the Cowboys?"

One measure of her impact was the flurry of exotic dancers who started running onto the field to kiss players. If one didn't know any better, one would think they were part of the pageantry of a Cowboys game.

Meanwhile, the team Bubbles was cheering on won games against New Orleans, Pittsburgh, Atlanta, St. Louis, and Philadelphia while dropping three games for a 9-5 record and a playoff slot.

TWO DAYS BEFORE CHRISTMAS, Clint Murchison formally announced his plans for Texas Stadium in Irving. It would be ready for occupancy by the 1970 season. Financing would be through a bond-option plan. Season-ticket buyers would be required to purchase $250, $500, and $1,000 bonds, depending on where they wanted to sit. A $50,000 bond entitled the holder to buy an inner-circle luxury box, "the ultimate in spectator comfort." Season tickets for the twelve seats inside each box were another $576 per seat per year.

Some fans immediately complained. That kind of up-front money priced them out of the stadium. Don Griffin formed the Committee for Free Support of the Cowboys. Less than 1 percent of the five thousand fans who answered his mail survey, including three thousand who claimed to hold six thousand season tickets at the Cotton Bowl, were in favor of the bond option. Griffin gave the survey to Clint Murchison but received no reply other than the owner's comment, "I think they've got a point. I'd like everything to be free too. Unfortunately, life is not that way."

Murchison assured one disgruntled fan who wrote him a letter that plenty of individual game-day tickets would be available, and all seats "will be protected from sun and rain, will have backs and arm rests, and will have adequate parking available for their occupants. I hope to see you there."

To another not-so-pleasant complainer, he wrote: "If I had any guts I would tell you that you are stupid. However, since I don't, I will merely thank you for your comment."

But for now, the 'Boys were in the Cotton Bowl, where they destroyed the Cleveland Browns, 52–14, for the Eastern Division championship and once again earned a shot at the National Football

League championship, which was once again against the Green Bay Packers. The only difference from the 1966 season was that this deciding match would be played in the cold winter climes of Wisconsin.

The Packers may have beaten the Cowboys the year before in the big game, but Meredith and the rest of the team believed they were the superior team, despite the underperforming 9-5 record. The winner would represent the league in the second NFL-AFL world championship game.

Thousands of fans gathered in sweater weather at Love Field to send off the team with good-luck messages and to watch the football club board a Braniff jet with its sleek *BI* on the tail.

The day before the big game, the Dallas press met with Vince Lombardi, the coach and general manager of the Packers, who showed off the eighty-thousand-dollar heating system the team installed underneath Lambeau Field to maintain playing conditions in case temperatures dropped below freezing. Lombardi told Channel 8's Verne Lundquist that the system guaranteed a playable environment.

That was a good thing because Cy Elsberger, the U.S. Weather Bureau weatherman for Green Bay, had forecast a high of 12 degrees Fahrenheit for game day. He missed by 25 degrees.

"No sporting event, with the possible exception of the Winter Olympics, ever had been contested in such brutal coldness," wrote Sam Blair of the *Dallas Morning News*. It was so cold, the halftime show was canceled.

"The field was not too cold if you win," Clint Murchison said, spiking all excuses.

The day of the championship game dawned ominously.

"Good morning. It is eight a.m., and the temperature is sixteen below zero," chirped the hotel operator on her round of wake-up calls.

"I said, 'Come on, lady, you're joking!' Then I opened the blinds, saw the ice caked on the windows, and decided maybe she wasn't,"

Bob Lilly said. "George [Andrie] had gone to early Mass when I woke up. I looked out the window and I couldn't believe how sunny and clear it was. Then George came in the room. He didn't say anything about the temperature outside. He simply got a glass of water, pulled back the curtain and threw the water on the window. The water froze before it ran down the windowsill. And it was seventy degrees in that room."

The electric-grid system meant to keep the field warm in any condition had failed. Its pipes had frozen in the wind-chill temperature of 41 below.

The game was played as scheduled on the last day of 1967 in front of a sellout crowd of 50,861. The entire stadium breathed steam. The cold was so severe that Clint Murchison, who always sat in the stands rather than in the press box, retreated to the relatively warmer confines of the radio booth with Bill Mercer and Blackie Sherrod.

"Frank [Luksa, writing for the *Dallas Times Herald*] had a light coat, like a raincoat, and was carrying his portable typewriter when he got off the bus and slipped and fell into a ditch," Verne Lundquist recalled. "I spent most of the day in the radio booth with Blackie and Bill. But I also walked next door and saw the [CBS network] group with [Pat] Summerall, [Frank] Gifford, Ray Scott, and Jack Buck. Frank put a cup of coffee on the ledge and it froze. They had the window cracked just a little bit to let the ambient noise in. I went down on the front end of the writers' press box one level below and they had given all of the guys ice chippers. They were clearing the windows so they could see, but also to give a clearer view to those poor guys sitting behind them from papers like the *Appleton Post-Crescent*."

The broadcasters and sportswriters who endured the epic game came away with war stories.

It was so cold that: "A guy went to get us coffee and by the time he came back, the coffee had frozen," said Bill Mercer. "Ice was building up on the inside of the booth. Our spotter went to a service station to get us some windshield de-icer. He came in, gasping for breath, and we used all three cans of de-icer during the game to see through the window."

What Mercer and his radio sidekick Blackie Sherrod saw wasn't pretty.

It was so cold that Bullet Bob Hayes, the Cowboys' most potent offensive weapon, was frozen out of the game. The Florida native's hands were so swollen and cracked by the second quarter, he stuffed them in his pockets whenever he wasn't the intended receiver, an inadvertent tip-off that was exploited by the Packers. He caught three passes.

It was so cold that officials' lips froze to metal when they tried to blow their whistles. They shouted calls instead.

It was so cold that icicles formed below Tom Landry's nostrils. Three linemen came home with frostbite. Even the locals were brutalized by the wind-chill temperature of 30 below: four suffered heart attacks; fourteen were treated for exposure.

Unfortunately, northern Michigan native Pete Gent, one of the few Cowboys conditioned to stand the weather, watched the game from his hospital room, nursing a broken leg suffered in the Cleveland game the week before.

After George Andrie grabbed a Bart Starr fumble and ran it in for a touchdown, Dan Reeves threw a halfback touchdown pass to Lance Rentzel, the only finesse play of the day, and it put Dallas ahead, 17–14. But with 13 seconds on the clock and no time-outs left, the Packers were third-and-goal on the Cowboys' two-foot line. In true Lombardi-coached fashion, Bart Starr pushed straight ahead behind center Ken Bowman and right guard Jerry Kramer, who double-teamed Jethro Pugh, the Cowboys' stellar defensive tackle, allowing the quarterback to fall across the goal line for the Packers' third consecutive NFL title.

"It was just like someone beat you to pieces," Bill Mercer said. "The flight on the way home was awful. Meredith was sitting in front of me, crying. 'It's my fault, it's my fault.' I sat up and put my hands on his shoulders. 'Don, Don, Don. It wasn't your fault, it was the weather.'"

Dan Reeves, one of the Cowboys' few standouts, thought the elements neutralized any Cowboys edge. "Being an old Southern boy, I thought 32 degrees was freezing, but I learned that that ain't true," Reeves said. "The difference between 15 degrees above and 17 below is like going from 70 degrees to 102 degrees."

Five hundred fans greeted the team at Love Field, some bearing signs such as NEXT YEAR!, THIRD TIME'S THE CHARM, and WE THINK YOU'RE STILL GREAT. "Weeping openly was Mrs. Chris Wetzel, 38," the *Dallas Morning News* reported. "Follow them to Irving?" she was quoted as saying. "I'd even follow them to Fort Worth."

"In Green Bay, the temperature was between Spitsbergen and Archangel," wrote Kent Biffle in his page-1 wrap. "In Dallas, people curled up with TV sets and old grudges to watch the replay of the greatest tragedy since *Hamlet*. The final minute should have been mercifully blacked out in Dallas. That's when a monumental groan went up in Dallas and a monumental cheer went up in Green Bay. They'd done it again."

"We had their number," said the Packers' Max McGee. "Lombardi had the hex on Landry."

The loss and his obsession with a new stadium moved Clint Murchison to speak out. "If I owned Green Bay, I'd dome it."

After the Ice Bowl, as the coldest game ever played was dubbed, the Packers went on to defeat the Oakland Raiders 33–14 at the Orange Bowl in Miami in Super Bowl II for their second straight NFL-AFL championship. A full house of 75,546 watched the game, which was blacked out in Miami per the rules of both leagues. Still, close to thirty-nine million viewers watched the national broadcast of the game that established Vince Lombardi's team as the premier squad in pro football.

Dandy Flambé, or Next Year's Champions Again

A PSYCHIC WOUND FESTERED. The unthinkable had happened. Green Bay had Big D's number. "I see the quarterback sneak in TV replays all the time but it isn't a strong memory," a haunted Jethro Pugh said with a moan. "Maybe I've blocked it out of my mind. I had a tough time with it. Something like that can create doubt." Doubt was the kind of negative not allowed on the Cowboys. Winning was now what it was all about. Next year would be the year. Honest.

Despite the Cowboys' crushing loss, after two consecutive appearances in the NFL championship game, the team's appeal had spread far beyond Dallas. Players started noticing. "We had as many fans on the road as the other team did most of the time," running back Dan Reeves said.

"If You've Got It, Flaunt It!" declared the advertisement for Braniff International, the Dallas-based airline formerly known as Braniff Airways. The ads continued the advertising campaign that Mary Wells (who had become Mary Wells Lawrence, having married Braniff president Harding Lawrence in Paris) created for television and print, and Braniff's goal, intoned the debonair mellow-voiced announcer in one TV commercial, was to create "the most beautiful airline in the world. We won't get you where you're going any faster, but it'll seem that way."

The First National Bank of Dallas went for a more direct approach in capturing the Dallas zeitgeist with the cheery jingle sung in sweet harmonizing voices: "Give us an opportunity to say Yes! An opportunity to say Yes! Give the First in Dallas an opportunity to say Yes!—to *you*."

With opportunity, style, and prosperity bubbling up all around, the Cowboys became the kind of beautiful people who were escorted to the best tables at Old Warsaw, Mario's, Trader Vic's, and Ports O' Call atop the Southland Life building.

The diversity of jobs the players held down in the offseason reflected their star power. Linebacker Chuck Howley, the roster's elder statesman, took the sensible path, opening Chuck Howley's Cleaning Center, a dry-cleaning operation specializing in uniforms. "You have to have something ready for you when you're through with pro football," Howley reasoned. "It's not too smart to wait until then to get started." Mike Gaechter followed in Howley's footsteps, opening a janitorial-supply store.

Others let name recognition do the heavy lifting. John Niland stood to give Howley plenty of business by opening the Kings of Bar-B-Que restaurant across from the Inwood Theater on Lover's Lane. Mel Renfro opened a record store called Mel's House of Sound in Wynnewood Village. Pete Gent worked at TracyLocke ad agency, showing up at work wearing a top hat, and partnered with Bob Hayes in the National Graphics printing service, selling posters of players such as Meredith, Neely, Garrison, and Hayes; customers included an Oklahoma oil company that ordered twelve thousand posters at a dollar a pop. Hayes was also doing PR for RC Cola and the Harlem Globetrotters and ran track for pay in Australia. Dan Reeves did public relations for Gifford-Hill Concrete, while Buddy Dial did PR for Allied Chemical and managed a farm in the Rio Grande Valley. Willie Townes was a disc jockey on KCLE-FM in Cleburne. Dave Edwards booked the Cowboys charity basketball team.

Some used their high profiles to score more traditional employment in the public, financial, real estate, and automotive sectors. Frank Clarke was an equal-opportunity specialist with the federal Housing and Urban Development program. Jerry Tubbs worked as a loan officer at Dallas Federal Savings and Loan. Mike Connelly was a stockbroker for Eppler, Guerin, and Turner. Craig Baynham worked on the staff of Campus Crusade for Christ. George Andrie and Dave Manders sold properties for Phil Ross Real Estate. Tony Liscio sold cars at Garland Chrysler-Plymouth. Ralph Neely invested in real estate and became an independent oil operator. Jethro Pugh was a substitute teacher for the Dallas Independent School District.

Pettis Norman, a loan officer at the South Oak Cliff State Bank, was urged by African American community and business leaders to run for the Texas Legislature as a representative from Oak Cliff. He staked out a centrist position, offering the opinion that the Student Nonviolent Coordinating Committee, one of the leading civil rights organizations, was inspired by communists. "I don't think there is any doubt that orders come from Cuba and China. And these people sometimes infiltrate peaceful gatherings and marches to incite otherwise peaceful demonstrators. They need to be stopped. We must consolidate our gains and find common ground with all our neighbors, regardless of color or ethnic origin. We do it on the Cowboys and we get along at the bank. There are enough reasonable people on all sides to work out mutual problems."

Six Cowboys made personal appearances at Sears department stores, and they moved so much merchandise, the stores ran out of stock. And the players' rising profiles in the community became even more obvious when three thousand fans welcomed the team home at Love Field after an August exhibition game in Los Angeles, their first win over the Rams after ten consecutive exhibition-game defeats.

Kay Lang reported season-ticket sales (forty-eight dollars per season ticket) had almost doubled before the start of the 1968 campaign. Still, the Cowboys remained last in the league in that department, in no small part due to the Cotton Bowl's large capacity and the fact that fewer than forty thousand seats were between the goal lines. Tex Schramm put a positive spin on the obvious. "I've never been that concerned with season ticket sales," he said. "I think we too often use that as a badge of success. Of course, you live danger-ously with a big stadium, but then you have the excitement of the big crowd when your team is going good."

The Cowboys juggernaut and the influence of the print medium led to the start-up of a weekly newspaper devoted solely to the team, called the *Cowboy Insiders Newsletter,* while daily newspaper cover-age expanded regionally. For a couple of years, Carlton Stowers of the *Amarillo Globe-News* had been the only out-of-town sportswriter to consistently show up, but he was now joined by reporters from newspapers in San Angelo, Lubbock, Abilene, Odessa, Midland, Tyler, and other smaller Texas cities.

Relentless promotion was a significant factor in the broadening appeal. The Kicking Karavan went on another expedition, this time crossing borders and going to Toronto and to Mexico City (where los Vaqueros had a huge fan base) with snapper Dave Manders and bringing fourteen finalists back to Dallas. Two were good enough to sign to contracts: Al McFarlane and Bill McWilliams, who was a hammer thrower from Bowdoin. But the new kicker was Mike Clark, the team's first Texas Aggie and a six-year pro obtained from Pittsburgh.

The trade for Clark was the last straw for Danny Villanueva, who had punted and kicked for three seasons. His promotion to vice president at KMEX television in Los Angeles prompted him to retire from the team.

But the Round Mound of Sound, Frank Glieber, returned as the television voice of the Cowboys for 1968. Glieber had left Dallas for a job in Cleveland in 1965 and then came back to become the sports director at KRLD radio and television and to call games for the Cow-boys, much to the relief of fans and players, who'd never taken to Jack Buck. No one called a Cowboys game on TV better than Glieber.

———

Burgeoning fan interest prompted Clint Murchison to up the capacity of the stadium he planned to build, from fifty-five thousand to sixty-five thousand. The stadium, Murchison crowed, would not be the eighth wonder of the world, like the Astrodome, but rather the world's finest football facility. "The front rows are seven and one half to twelve feet above ground level too so you can see over Jethro Pugh," he said.

Tex Schramm also improved the views of fans in the stadium and those watching on television by persuading the rules committee of the NFL to paint the out-of-bounds area white to provide contrast to the green field of play.

It's a surprise he had a moment to do it; training camp was Tex Schramm's favorite time of the year. Like Tom Landry spending quality time with his players, Schramm enjoyed his captive media audience at Thousand Oaks and wined and dined them to win them over. "Tex would take the writers out to dinner every night at training camp on Clint Murchison's tab," photographer Russ Russell said. "We ate at the finest restaurants. [Publicists] Doug Todd and Curt Mosher were taking these guys somewhere every night."

Schramm got to know the reporters and broadcasters well enough to be able to weigh in when it was called for. "Tex might not like something that you wrote and he'd call you at home," said writer Carlton Stowers. "It was just pure Tex—'That's the most chickenshit article I ever read blah, blah,' and the next day everything is fine."

Steve Perkins got a call from Tex at the crack of dawn one Sunday, Tex pointing out that a story Perkins had written was "wrong, wrong, wrong." A groggy Perkins was unable to get in a word edgewise until Tex paused to catch his breath.

"Other than that, how did you like the story?" Perkins asked.

Tex broke out laughing. "I'll see you at the game," he said, and hung up.

"I don't think Tex ever held a grudge against anybody, that was just his nature," Carlton Stowers said. "But, boy, he could be Mount Vesuvius for about ten minutes. We all got a dose of it."

The writers and broadcasters focused on the team, not the players' extracurricular activities. Salaries were of little interest. Exploits off the field were considered newsworthy only if a police report was filed. A player could skate if he'd gotten involved in a fender bender and happened to slug the other motorist, unless the authorities were summoned. That understanding gave reporters access. They could call any player on the team at home any time of the day. The Cowboys playbook included a page on media relations stating what a player was expected to do, including the mandate that if a reporter called, the player should call back.

The press could walk into any coaches' meeting and take notes and listen and talk to the players. "As long as they adhered to unspoken rules," Russ Russell said. "Private lives and derogatory comments were off-limits. Violate the code, and reporters would no longer be privy to conversations with players in the locker room."

Beat reporters weren't out to change society or uncover a scandal. They were reporting on a football team everyone was crazy about. And it went both ways. After Blackie Sherrod wrote about the love beads, peace medallions, Nehru jackets, and Maharishi gear some players were wearing when traveling as a team, Coach Landry banned necklaces and medallions on road trips.

At the beginning of training camp, Don Meredith and Chuck Howley met with Tom Landry to carve up Thousand Oaks bars and restaurants. Coaches had their places; players had theirs. Once that was settled, everyone got down to business. Almost everyone. Receiver Lance Rentzel, acquired the year before from Minnesota, was profiled as being a bachelor Hollywood swinger and regular at LA's the Factory club who willingly paid a record eight-hundred-dollar fine when he was nailed by assistant coach Ernie Stautner for missing curfew at camp. Rentzel projected such star power, Columbia

Records recruited him to make a single, "Looking Like Somethin' That Ain't," backed with "Beyond Love."

Besides providing a bored press with a surplus of glitter and glam, training camp at Thousand Oaks produced a new addition to the offense, the Flip formation, lifted from San Francisco, in which both wide receivers, Hayes and Rentzel, split to the same side. Training camp also inspired Walt Garrison to develop a new obsession to keep him from walking the halls of the players' dorm late at night: whittling. He remained a backup to Don Perkins and held him in high regard as a mentor. During camp, he asked his role model, "Perk, why are you helping me? I'm trying to beat you out."

Perkins gave his protégé a paternal smile and said, "Walt, I want to go to the Super Bowl. If you're better than me, you ought to be playing."

Meredith, the last of the original Class of 1960 after Mike Connelly was traded to Pittsburgh, was joined at 1968's training camp by Lieutenant Roger Staubach, USN. The 1963 Heisman Trophy winner voluntarily showed up on leave from the Naval Air Station in Pensacola, Florida, although he would return to active duty once football season started. He wanted to learn the system and size up the competition of Meredith, Craig Morton, and Jerry Rhome before he took the leap into professional football.

Roger the Dodger, the scrambling quarterback, was one of a kind. The only child of Bob, a wholesale shoe salesman, and Betty, a homemaker, he excelled at football, basketball, and baseball for the Purcell High School Cavaliers in Cincinnati. Early in life, he demonstrated a keen competitive streak and the leadership skills he would display in the Navy, qualities he said he developed "because I wanted my parents to be proud of me."

His father noticed that when he played baseball, he never seemed nervous at crunch time. His third-grade teacher, Sister Aloysius, saw similar traits. "It seems like you're the center of attention on the playground," she told young Roger. "But you better do your homework or you're not going out there." He switched from receiver to quarterback in high school. His coach said, "The other players listen to you and you're really competitive. I see you out there playing basketball and baseball, and that's what I want my quarterback to be." He was all-city quarterback his senior year, although he considered himself more skilled at the other sports. At the U.S. Naval Academy, he was recognized with the Heisman Trophy and the Maxwell Award for football, and he lettered in basketball and baseball. A devout Catholic, he attended Mass every morning without fail.

Staubach was a standout at Thousand Oaks, keeping up with the rigid training regimen and showing a fierce competitive streak, running harder, testing defenses, playing all out. Tex Schramm thought Staubach looked like a million bucks. If he didn't work out at quarterback, Schramm thought, he had the toughness to excel as a running back. Landry told a reporter Staubach would not be subject to the five-year learning curve Landry claimed was necessary for a pro quarterback to fully develop.

"Part of a quarterback's progress is in his maturity as a man," the coach said. "Roger will be 27 next year when he comes to us." A Rams official visiting camp as part of a scrimmage cut to the chase, predicting, "When he gets here next year, it's goodbye Rhome... Hell, it's goodbye Meredith."

Roger Staubach oozed confidence. Before camp, he was dubious. "I didn't know for sure I was going to get out [of the Navy]. I was thinking about maybe staying in, but down deep in my heart I wanted to play again." After camp, he knew he could. "I should have a good ten, 11 years to play," he said. "I'm in better shape now than I've ever been in, and I'm going to make sure the same is true next summer." Compared to his Navy hitch and the time served in Vietnam, pro ball was practically relaxing.

Among the few not impressed was the number-one quarterback. "I thought he was really such a nice guy, but when I saw him come out here on his vacation I thought... well, in East Texas I guess we'd call it empathy," Don Meredith later said, his competitive streak having mellowed not at all. "He couldn't throw very well. I was almost embarrassed for him," Meredith reported. "We were throwing at one of those big boards and Roger's first throw, I think, missed the whole board."

Meredith sized up Staubach as a good athlete, but with one caveat. "Everything he did was a learned thing instead of natural. He was good and strong and all that. I'd be inclined to think he wouldn't make the team. At least it was good publicity. We get Roger Staubach and the Heisman Trophy in camp."

Backup quarterback Jerry Rhome was watching Staubach too, and he didn't sign his own contract until he was assured he'd get equal playing time with Morton in exhibition games. Rhome understood Landry and his complicated offense but was unable to convince Landry to put him to good use in the Shotgun, the pass-friendly offense where the quarterback took the snap three to five yards behind the center. Rhome was a great short passer but had one of the weaker arms in the league. He knew that shortcoming trumped his knowledge of the game. Rhome complained to a reporter that he'd get into a game "when [boxer] Floyd Patterson wins a decision." After training camp and getting an eyeful of Roger Staubach, he knew a trade was in his future.

BEFORE TRAINING CAMP OPENED that summer, Don Perkins went public about difficulties he had finding a nice place to rent in North Dallas, and he voiced the opinion that black Cowboys "do not feel a part of the team or a part of the city." The race issues the team was dealing with were largely external, beyond the team and the organization. But they were there, and now the lid was off.

"Do you know my wife, Virginia, and I would be embarrassed to have you visit our home in Dallas?" Don Perkins asked a reporter. "We'd have to take you to a nice restaurant. . . . Why? The Negroes on the Cowboys can only find roach-infested houses."

Steve Perkins of the *Times Herald* took an informal survey of

African American players on the team that showed "none believes there is a racial problem on the Cowboys. They are nevertheless bitter about many aspects of their off-the-field life in Dallas and are 100 percent in agreement with Perkins bringing matters into the open. One facet of team arrangements irks them plenty. This is the practice, on the road, of using separate rooms for Negro and white athletes who wind up without roommates. (Last season Sims Stokes was often booked into a single and another white player was too.)

"Most of the Cowboy Negro veterans were surprised to learn that a new policy in rooming was instituted two months ago by Tex Schramm, whereby this year's rookie crop was grouped alphabetically," Steve Perkins wrote.

Team harmony was not in question. "I never thought about not being a part of the team," Pettis Norman said. "There's not a feeling among the Cowboy players they're exploited in any way. I've never been excluded from anything because I was colored. And it wouldn't matter to me who I roomed with as long as it's a teammate of mine."

Jethro Pugh saw no prejudice. "When Lilly hits a quarterback and just wipes him out, I get the same charge as if Willie [Townes] hit him. On defense, we're just out there to crack heads."

Finding somewhere to live was another matter. Renting a place in North Dallas was almost impossible for a black man. Home ownership was the only sure path to the nice part of town as Norman, Pugh, Mel Renfro, Mike Johnson, and Bob Hayes learned.

"Perk called me to help find him housing for this season," said Pettis Norman, who lived in South Dallas. "So far I haven't found him anything. The sad part about it is everybody shakes your hand and pats you on the back, and yet when you come to look for an apartment they say, 'Why did you have to pick my place?'"

The disconnect puzzled Bobby Hayes. "It's tough after a game when the white players head north and the colored players head south," he said. "We play together and love one another. Why not live together?"

Mel Renfro said, "I could write a book about what I've been through."

Cornell Green, who was, like Perkins, one of a handful of Negro players who did not live year-round in Dallas, said it took him two months to find a place before the start of every season. In the locker room, Green was best buddies with Dan Reeves and Walt Garrison. "His locker was there with Walt and I," Dan Reeves said. "He was thirty-four, we were thirty, thirty-two. Whichever one of us got to the dressing room first would light the other one a cigarette and hand it to 'em when we got there. We were just close, close friends."

Don Perkins's public complaint got results. A newspaper reader and Cowboys fan helped the Perkins family find what they were looking for, location included. Then Tex Schramm reached out to real estate agents and movers and shakers on behalf of other black players who wanted to live closer to where they practiced. "It's a problem in all cities and it is difficult on our players," Schramm admitted. "If the problem is as acute as Don indicates, then we will do more."

The housing crisis was resolved, but the Green Bay jinx remained.

A late-August rematch of the NFL championship was staged at the Cotton Bowl for the annual Salesmanship Club game, with two major differences: Game-time temperature was 104 degrees warmer than it had been at the previous meeting in Green Bay, on the last day of December. And the results wouldn't count, since the regular season was still a month away.

That didn't stop Dallas and the entire Great Southwest from getting all het up. "If you don't already have a pair of these Cowboy-Packer reserved seats for August 24, you have two choices," advised Bob St. John of the *Dallas Morning News*. "Trade your car or wife, or settle for general admission."

A rabid crowd of 72,014 in the remodeled Cotton Bowl, featuring folding aluminum seats with backs, witnessed the return of the dark cloud of doubt as the Cowboys dropped the exhibition to the Packers, 31–27. The pain of defeat and the acknowledgment of frailties did not bode well. After the game, Don Meredith smoked a cigarette in front of his locker and contemplated events quietly without offering a single wiseass comment to the press. Landry chased everyone, including scouts and equipment people, out of his coach's quarters.

Gloom settled under the high-pressure bubble of late summer for a few days. But all was pretty much forgotten when the Cowboys beat the Oilers, 33–19, in a sold-out Astrodome, partially redeeming the NFL, whose preseason record against the AFL in the second year of interleague exhibitions was 10-13, after beating AFL teams thirteen games to three the year before. A Dallas bookie claimed he lost $18,000 on the preseason game but would win it back sooner or later. "As long as Dandy sticks in there, I'll get rich."

Dandy was sticking in there. He graced the cover of the September 16, 1968, issue of *Sports Illustrated* with the caption *Dallas on Top*. He was calling the plays as often as not, even though Landry still sent them all in. More than once, Meredith sent the guard or tackle shuttling in a play back to the sidelines to show up Landry.

Gil Brandt mailed a hundred copies of the *SI* Cowboys issue to his top college prospects, just to let them know who they were dealing with. The magazine picked the Cowboys to go all the way, as did *Pro Football Weekly*.

And the team believed. "Meredith has so much confidence now, it's scary," said Danny Reeves, who called him the quarterback everyone knew he could be.

Meredith's cool was certainly without peer. When their Braniff charter headed home after a game in snowy New York, a chunk of ice slid off the wing and was sucked into one of the jet engines. The passengers heard a loud *ka-whump*, and the jet lost altitude briefly before rocking side to side. The pilot stabilized the jet and regained altitude, only to be jolted again with another *ka-whump* and another loss in altitude. A stewardess ran down the aisle and began lifting up floor mats amid shouts and screams. "Aren't you scared?" rookie DD Lewis asked Meredith, who was sitting next to him in the back of the plane. Meredith calmly held on to his scotch, took a long drag off his cigarette, smiled, and said, "Naw, DD, it's been a good 'un."

That wasn't the first time his wit took the edge off. After getting knocked out on a play, Meredith came to, twisting and writhing, and mumbled, "Oh, why did I ever do it?" The trainer looking at him asked, "Why what?"

"Why did I ever leave Mount Vernon?"

A few years earlier, Sam Huff, the New York Giants linebacker, put a hit on Meredith that broke a protective pad filled with red liquid Meredith was wearing around his bruised waist. The liquid spilled all over Meredith's jersey, prompting Huff to apologize profusely, thinking he'd torn open Meredith's stomach. "It's all right, Sam." Meredith groaned as he lifted himself up, surrounded by trainers. "Just do me a favor. Write my mother." The trainers and the quarterback all broke out laughing.

But in 1968, after stomping Detroit 59–13 to open the regular season at home, Meredith was more circumspect in the locker room. "I'm not trying to be more subdued or snobby," he told the reporters clustered around him. "Your job is to ask questions. My job is to answer them. It's not my obligation to elaborate, though. Most of the in-depth quotes should come from the coach. I think I've done too much of it in the past. I've gone overboard. Maybe this is more natural to me. Maybe I've figured out I don't need to be like I was before."

The *Dallas Times Herald*'s Dick Hitt devoted a column to what he called a "Pick-Hitt with Apologies to KLIF." The words to a song had been mailed to the newspaper, he wrote, with an anonymous note attached to the lyrics: "I wish I could take credit for writing these words. But I cannot. They were written by Dandy and Landry and many others, coaches, players, office personnel. Names we don't even know. Names we have known and may have forgotten. They were not written on paper with ink. They were written on the floor of the Cotton Bowl. They were written in blood, guts and pride. It took nine years to write them. Not written by me, but by you and thousands like you. But most important of all, they were written by the Boo-Birds. And you know what I think? I think they deserve it." A Cowboy fan.

The song, "Bye-Bye Boo-Birds," was catchy, with the opening lines:

Pack up all your boos and jeers
Let Dandy hear lots of cheers.
Bye-bye boo-birds.

"Obviously, this stirring anthem was written in blood, guts and pride on the floor of the Cotton Bowl, but it'll probably never be another 'Ballad of the Green Berets,'" Hitt commented.

Still, a forty-five was released and played on local radio stations and at games, spurring the Unknown Cowboy Fan to scribble two more songs: "Doomsday Defense" and "Danny Get Well" for Dan Reeves.

The latter was inspired by the fact that Reeves was getting banged up consistently. One night after practice, he hobbled into the press room, where the team physician, Marvin Knight, and some players and trainers were playing cards and drinking. "Doc, my knee is swelling up again," Reeves told Knight.

"Well, goddamn it, of course it's swollen up," the bald-headed doctor drawled in his Walter Brennan voice. "I told you we've got to get them chips out of there, Danny."

"When can we do it?" Reeves asked.

"Fuck, let's do it right now," Dr. Knight said, folding his hand. "Let's go to the hospital. Nobody is using the surgery room this time of night."

"Can I be your assistant?" Cornell Green grinned at Dr. Knight.

The next morning, Reeves showed up at practice on crutches and with a bandage on his knee.

"How'd that go?" Dr. Knight was asked.

"How do you think it went?" he cracked. "We took the god-damned chips out."

Dr. Knight was an irreverent hard-ass when he needed to be, telling Gent he wouldn't take him out of his cast until he cut his hair. He was also the go-to guy for everyone, since almost every player got brutalized sooner or later. The embodiment of the bruised-and-battered Cowboys was the quarterback. Meredith was movie-star handsome, now with long sideburns that highlighted his prominent aquiline nose. He was also an easy target for getting roughed up. "The only thing they haven't hurt is my nose, God love it," the quarterback said as he beamed after his team disassembled Detroit.

"So the next game they shattered his nose," wrote Bob St. John, detailing the injury Meredith sustained against the Cleveland Browns.

He wasn't kidding. You couldn't make this stuff up. Every time the team looked invincible in their flawless execution of Tom Landry's tactics, something, or somebody, screwed it all up. More often than not, Meredith was fingered as the culprit, justly or unjustly.

By September's end, just enough fear had seeped back in to get folks to wondering about their team.

"The question for today is: Are the '68 Cowboys great, or are they kidding everybody once again?" asked Steve Perkins.

That wasn't an easy question to answer, although internal and external tweaks were made.

The team switched to the Hilton Inn on Mockingbird on North Central, a couple exits north of their old pregame headquarters for home games, which brought them closer to the action should players be in need of amusement. Lance Rentzel and Craig Morton, the two hunkiest Cowboys, were plotting an ultra in-spot for Dallas, like Los Angeles's the Factory, and they had imported two babes as office employees. They soon settled on the name Pearl Street Warehouse and brought in John Wilbur as a partner. Dapper dresser Bob Hayes became fodder for conversation when he put taps on his tennis shoes.

But on the field there remained an immovable force known as the Green Bay Packers.

The Monday-night game on October 26 had sold out weeks in advance.

"An optimist is someone who comes to Dallas two days before the Cowboy–Green Bay game and expects to find tickets," style columnist Maryln Schwartz wrote. "A dreamer is someone who finds the tickets and expects to get hotel or motel reservations." The Monday-night rematch and Dallas Fashion Week filled up area hotels. A caller from Cleveland phoned the Dallas Chamber of Commerce in search of a room. "You come up with an extra ticket and you can stay at my house," the chamber official said. Even the motels in Sherman and Mineral Wells, more than sixty miles away, were booked solid with Dallas fans who wanted to watch the blacked-out game on TV.

The Packers put the whomp on the home team, 28–17, as Meredith and his injured shoulder were factors in the Cowboys' first loss of the season, making it four in a row, including the Salesmanship Club exhibition, in Green Bay's favor. Lombardi clearly had Landry's number.

"It doesn't mean the quarterback is no good," the coach said about Meredith's shoulder after the game. At 6-1, they were still in the catbird's seat. But opponents knew the catbird had a wounded wing, which made Meredith a target. The following week, the New Orleans defense sacked him five times.

"Our team seems to lack the killer instinct," Tex Schramm told his KRLD audience on the *Ask Tex Schramm* show. "We have the facility to play according to the caliber of the opponent. We need to be like Cassius Clay. No matter whom he fought, he chopped them up, knocked them out, stood over them and glowered and wondered who the next victim would be. That's the way we need to leave the field. We have the potential to be just that. This Washington game is a pivotal game. Not only for this season, but future years. The Cowboys either show they're championship material or perennial runners-up."

The Boo-Birds returned to ride Meredith on Thanksgiving Day after he failed to throw a touchdown pass despite the Cowboys' 29–

20 win over their Capitol Division rival Redskins. Afterward, the quarterback unloaded on Dallas fans. "They're really something else," Meredith said. "They really are. I'm getting tired of it. You know, the fun's about over. I walked off the field with Sonny Jurgensen. He's a good friend. He's had a lot of that happen to him. Sonny said, 'They always seem to like the backup quarterbacks, don't they?' What people fail to realize is, we're human beings. I've got feelings like anybody else. If people think I don't try…they're so wrong. I try harder than anybody because I'm the one that's out there. I don't understand it. I've never booed anybody in my life. I never will."

Landry, for his part, said, "It's a better team than we've ever had before." And for all the fretting, bench-jockeying, and hand-wringing, the team absorbed but one more loss on their way to a stellar 12-2 record, the Cowboys' best yet.

It was only fitting that Gary Cartwright's first novel, *The Hundred Yard War*, was published by Doubleday that fall on the heels of a very high-profile drug bust of Cartwright in Austin. Cartwright had departed the *Dallas Morning News* in 1967 for the *Philadelphia Inquirer* and to freelance for *Sport* magazine. But he quit Philly and moved to Austin while waiting for his book to be published, picking up work by joining the staff of Fagan Dickson, an Austin lawyer who was challenging Congressman J. J. "Jake" Pickle, the protégé of President Lyndon Johnson. The Bring Lyndon Home anti–Vietnam War campaign drew enough blood for Cartwright to be set up for possessing and attempting to distribute marijuana, which could get him life in prison. His legal team of West Texas defense attorney Warren Burnett, Dave Richards of Austin, and state senator Babe Schwartz got him off with probation and a fine.

Cartwright's novel was about a mythical team called the Dallas Troopers who were led by a mythical quarterback, Rylie "Long John" Silver, who could easily be confused with Dandy Don Meredith, given his "brilliant, erratic" nature and his penchant for singing country music songs and chasing women.

The bombastic lead character, Poss Dixon, based on Tex Schramm, was originally intended to be a stand-in for Tom Landry, but as Cartwright explained, "Halfway through the book, I thought, I don't really understand the guy. So I had [Landry's] character fired and replaced by a Vince Lombardi character." He also traded Rylie Silver, got Poss Dixon demoted, and ruined the Lombardi character.

It was his fantasy of how things would have turned out if he, Cartwright, were in charge. Bud Shrake of *Sports Illustrated* called his friend's book "certainly the best novel ever written about pro football."

As far as how things would turn out, "all football signs point to victory for Dallas," Steve Perkins wrote in the *Dallas Times Herald*, predicting a Cowboys win over Cleveland followed by the NFL championship game in Dallas the following week and then Super Bowl III. "It is a case of style vs. style, and the Cowboys clearly, on the record, have the right style to defeat any Cleveland team."

The bar of expectation had been raised after Dallas clobbered the Browns 28–7 earlier in the season. Dandy was having his best year yet, despite numerous injuries. In fact, he prepared for the Cleveland game by leaving the hospital where he had been recovering from a broken rib, a punctured lung, and pneumonia. Landry found little to complain about on his television show and at Cowboys Club luncheons. Occasionally, he even cracked a smile. The ticket office had already printed up league-championship game tickets, and travel agencies were advertising Super Bowl package trips to Miami. Sportswriters were visualizing the AFL's Houston Oilers as the opponent in an all-Texas final.

But it was not to be. The Cowboys started the Cleveland game flat and became flatter from there.

With two minutes left in the game, and the team trailing the Browns 31–13, Landry sent in Craig Morton to quarterback. "Bad passes, bad passes" was all Meredith could mumble. It was one of those dreadful dead-arm days for Dandy, while Doomsday was duped by the Browns' Frank Ryan.

"Dallas streets were virtually deserted from noon to midafternoon Saturday as thousands clustered around TV sets," reported the *Dallas Morning News*. "Turning off the tube and coming out of the shock was a major effort for many."

What was supposed to be a prelude to the ascension to the throne of all pigskin turned into the most deflating loss yet, 31–20.

After the game, Don Meredith told reporters, "Fellas, I just can't talk about it. There's nothing I can say."

Before the plane home took off, Meredith finished a hamburger and then turned to his seatmate Pete Gent and said, "Come on, let's go to New York," and both exited the charter before it left the boarding gate. They stayed with Meredith's pal Frank Gifford, the former New York Giant who had moved to the broadcast booth to call games on television. Three years of losing the championship bid was too much. After this loss, Dandy was ready to accept that standing offer to be a broadcaster.

"The sometimes tumultuous saga of Don Meredith reached its lower valley here Saturday, with the Cowboy quarterback standing mute and alone on the sidelines watching a floundering team he once prodded to peaks," Blackie Sherrod said in his obituary of the game.

"The Dallas Cowboys were reincarnated as the Ancient Mariner here on a cold, bleak Saturday afternoon with 81,496 fans watching in person and the world looking on through the miracle they call television," wrote Bob St. John in the *Dallas Morning News*, mixing his classics. "Dallas was a Greek Tragedy....There is movement underway to have the Playoff Bowl rescheduled for Friday, the 13th. Meredith, it sometimes appears, is destined, as a matter of fact, to play kind of a Hamlet, though this can probably be likened to writing his epitaph."

Disappointment, Heartache, and Another Roll of the Dice

THE CHARTER FLIGHT, an hour and a half late, due to fog, was greeted by hundreds of fans at the new Braniff terminal at Love Field. Twenty-five were still waiting for Meredith to emerge after the rest of the team had deplaned. "I wonder what he's waiting on," one asked. "He's got to still be on the plane," replied another. "He's probably just waiting for the crowd to clear." Then one man interjected, "He's probably afraid somebody's going to boo him, since that's all he's heard all season." "Don't be silly," snapped a woman standing nearby. "Nobody would dare boo Don now."

"Oh, well, at least it means the Cowboys in the trenches will be home for Christmas."

"Were those trenches? I thought they were graves."

More than forty-four thousand tickets had already been sold for the NFL championship game the next week. Braniff canceled its newspaper ads encouraging fans to make Super Bowl reservations early. A twenty-eight-page NFL championship game section for the *Dallas Morning News* the following Saturday was trashed.

"We are not mean enough," concluded Lee Roy Jordan.

"This is by far the most disappointing day I've ever had," Tom Landry said upon arrival. "We felt like this team was ready and able to win the world championship. Now we must decide if this game is significant. I think Meredith can return. I hated to take him out. In my opinion, he wasn't wholly responsible. I don't know what he will do. I can't speak for him. But you can bet he feels worse than anybody right now about this game. Certainly, nobody in the world feels worse than Don Meredith. I would too. I do.

"All I know is Meredith was a better quarterback this season than he ever has been, and this is the best team we've ever had."

Gary Cartwright, freelancing for the *Morning News*, weighed in on the blame game. Meredith, Cartwright wrote, "threw an interception that should have been credited against Landry's disciplined system of play. According to Landry's gospel, the Cleveland defensive back who intercepted Meredith's final pass should have been on the other side of the field. Unfortunately, the Cleveland defensive back was in the wrong place. It wasn't that Landry was wrong; Cleveland just wasn't right."

Cleveland wasn't that good either. They would lose to the Baltimore Colts, who would play the New York Jets in the third NFL-AFL world championship game, in Miami. The Jets' brash quarterback Joe Namath, aka Broadway Joe, the long-haired, hedonistic antihero of pro football, stood in front of a crowd of six hundred people holding a glass of Johnnie Walker Red in his hand as he accepted the Miami Touchdown Club's NFL Player of the Year award and predicted, "We're going to win Sunday. I guarantee you." Namath delivered a Jets win in the Super Bowl, despite his team's being three-touchdown underdogs.

The day after Christmas, the Irving City Council accepted a $17,964,000 bid from the Tecon Corporation, owned by Clint Murchison Jr., to build Texas Stadium. Irving mayor Robert Powell did the legal work as Murchison's title lawyer.

Dallas went on to beat Minnesota 17–13 in the Playoff Bowl in Miami, a postseason game for third place notable mostly for the cognac-colored felt hat the Dallas coach wore instead of his usual gray felt fedora—the new hat had been given to him as part of an ad campaign for the Garland-based Byer-Rolnick hat company. Meredith went 15-24, including a 51-yard TD bomb to Hayes, before Curley Morton took over for the second half. At one point, Meredith completed 13 of 15 passes, a writer informed him after the game. "Well, nobody's perfect," Meredith cracked. He was recognized as the most valuable player, but the head of the running-back figurine on the trophy he was awarded had been knocked off by the time he arrived in Dallas.

The day after the game, the *Times Herald* ran a story by Steve Perkins stating that Meredith was hanging up his cleats, which Meredith promptly denied to Perkins and to other sportswriters. He had been grumbling and was taken out of context, Meredith insisted. He was just down, demoralized, and physically beat up. He'd get over it and so would everyone else.

Steve Perkins then threw gasoline on the smoldering coals with his book *Next Year's Champions*, hyped as "the story of coach Tom Landry, the Vince Lombardi of the Southwest, and how he is tortured by his brilliant but frequently erratic charges." The book was full of behind-the-scenes stories and inside dope that only a beat reporter could have ferreted out, including one tidbit from Bob Lilly, who'd commented that if Landry could coach robots, he'd win every game. Telling stories out of class like that earned Perkins exile to the doghouse. He had violated Tex Schramm's unspoken rule about not repeating things said in confidence that reflected negatively on the team.

"The book is very candid, so much so that hard feelings have already risen from some of the Cowboy people who have seen advance copies of the book and who would rather not have some of their conversations and comments see the light of day," wrote Olin Chism of the *Dallas Morning News*. "He touches many a sensitive nerve."

"You're not going to be in any [coaches'] meetings anymore," Tex Schramm informed Steve Perkins shortly after the book was released.

Lilly and other players wouldn't talk to him. Denied access, Perkins seldom left his room in the dormitory at training camp, where he drank alone. He rarely attended practice, and he approached players and coaches only when he needed to file copy. They'd tell him whatever he needed and he wrote the stories. The sense of friendship and family that once existed, whether it was real or imagined, vaporized.

Steve Perkins remained a thorn in Tex's side, maybe even more so, writing that while Tex was negotiating new contracts with NFL players, he wanted to ban "insider and tell-all books and magazine articles that tell things too much like they are."

Those who kept confidences were rewarded. At Clint Murchison's invitation, Blackie Sherrod, Andy Anderson, and Bob St. John joined Tom Landry, Al Ward, and Curt Mosher at Murchison's private island in the Bahamas, Spanish Cay, to go fishing.

And eventually the media's focus switched from the past to the present and future. Assistant general manager Al Ward denied rumors that the Cowboys were planning a regular-season game in Mexico City. They were far and away the most popular NFL team throughout Mexico, with their games beamed throughout the country. *Ricos* from Mexico City and Monterrey flew in for games in Dallas.

The players kept busy. Lance Rentzel, the team's leading receiver for the past two seasons, married movie star–dancer Joey Heatherton from the *Dean Martin Variety Show* at St. Patrick's Cathedral in New York in April. Rentzel said their engagement was "my best catch of the year." Meredith, Morton, and Neely were among the ushers. The couple appeared on the *Tonight Show* with Johnny Carson.

Bob Lilly, voted Oak Farms Dairy's most popular Cowboy, went to Europe with his wife. Danny Reeves spent seventeen days in Vietnam with American troops.

Some Cowboys hustled off the field as much as they did on the field. Mel Renfro was looking for locations for Ozark Fried Chicken franchises. Mike Johnson was selling Chevys for Earl Hayes; Dave Manders sold ad time for KBOX. Walt Garrison found happiness breaking horses for Dunn Brothers Inc. pipeline suppliers; Bob Hayes endorsed the Bob Hayes Dash N Fashion men's stores franchise, which were renamed Bob Hayes 22 Shops; while John Niland became a vice president at First Security Bank Carrollton. Banker Pettis Norman was appointed to the Dallas Parks board. Recently retired Frank Clarke was doing weekend sports for Channel 8, the first African American in the market to do so, and he auditioned for CBS.

The Silver Helmet Club, owned by Mike Gaechter, Dave Manders, and Dave Edwards, opened its doors, while Lance Rentzel and Ralph Neely finally opened their Pearl Street Warehouse near Casa Dominguez, a popular Cowboys hangout.

Bob Lilly and George Andrie ran a football kids' camp. Draft pick Calvin Hill announced plans to enroll at Perkins Divinity School at SMU and became active in the Fellowship of Christian Athletes.

And Don Meredith led a charmed life. He headed Don Meredith Inc. and was studying to be a stockbroker with First Texas Bank. He posed for Jantzen sportswear as a model. He invested, along with Lance Rentzel, in Trini's Mexican restaurant franchises, named for Trini Lopez, the first of which opened in Dallas. He and his wife, Cheryl (Chigger), were the subject of the On the House column in the *Times Herald Sunday* magazine, showing off their new white stucco Spanish Colonial home. Dandy joined country singer Charley Pride and folk-pop singer Bobby Gentry in a syndicated TV variety special, *The Sound and the Scene,* filmed in Toronto, which moved TV critic Jerry Coffey to enthuse, "Don has more on-camera presence—poise, style, a sense of humor, a sense of timing—than any other sports personality or former sports personality that I can think of. More, indeed, than a lot of long-time show biz professionals I can think of. He's no great shakes as a singer, though I suspect he's better at that than his brief vocal turn on this show ('There's a Little Bit of Everything in Texas') indicated."

THE ATTENTION PAID TO Cowboys players reflected the role of spectator sports as Dallas's top leisure attractions. Campisi's Egyptian Lounge solicited sports fans to "Com'A See Us After the Game" and take advantage of their private club to drink alcohol, eat spaghetti and pizza, talk about boxer Curtis Cokes's latest bout, and maybe find someone to make a bet with over an upcoming game. Continental Trailways beckoned baseball fans with a twenty-dollar package to go to Houston to see major-league baseball. Lamar Hunt's Dallas Tornado soccer team was importing players from Scotland's Dundee United for its United Soccer Association season. Fans of team sports could choose between the new American Basketball Association's Dallas Chaparrals with their red-white-and-blue basketballs, or the Dallas Black Hawks Central Hockey League team at the Fair Park Coliseum, or the Dallas–Fort Worth Spurs minor-league baseball club in Arlington. But area sports fans mostly focused on the Dallas Cowboys, arguing about the football team's fortunes, the high price of season tickets (now up to sixty-three dollars each), and the new stadium they were going to move into.

Irving voters had approved measures to issue bonds for the new stadium in 1968, then again in early 1969, and a week after the second Irving election, Murchison drove up to the construction site in a beat-up Chevy coupe. He joined Tex, Tom, Don Meredith, and Mayor Robert Powers in donning hard hats and breaking ground for the new stadium in front of two thousand onlookers.

"Some people have questioned how Texas Stadium will look when it is completed," Murchison told the gathering. "Some people have questioned its design, as is their right. I got this architect to make this up and I want to present it to the city of Irving. It's the latest, the final plan for Texas Stadium." He handed the microphone to the mayor, then pulled out a photograph of the Roman Colosseum with the Cowboys helmet logo attached. Clint Murchison's eyes twinkled.

Don Meredith was introduced by the mayor as "the man who's going to bring us the Super Bowl."

"I sure hope you are right about the Super Bowl," Meredith told the mayor. "We've had a little trouble bringing the title to Dallas. Maybe we'll do a little better bringing it to Irving."

Then Murchison quoted R. L. "Uncle Bob" Thornton. "As one of the most progressive mayors of the city of Dallas used to say: Let's get the dirt flyin'."

Murchison gigged current mayor J. Erik Jonsson shortly afterward with an acerbic letter, dictated to his longtime secretary, Ruth Woodward:

Dear Erik:

I noted in the morning paper your comment that until the Astrodome was built, everyone thought the Cotton Bowl was pretty good. Of course, until the transistor was developed, people thought the vacuum tube was pretty good.

The transistor happened to be developed by Jonsson's company Texas Instruments.

Thirty-eight thousand sideline seats were offered to bond purchasers. The choice eight thousand seats that were between the 30-yard lines went for $1,000 each, or four $250 bonds. And that was just the dibs. The actual season tickets were additional.

Clint Murchison acted offended when he heard renewed complaints that some fans were being priced out of the new stadium. "We're doing more in this than any sport franchise anywhere in this country has ever been asked to do," he contended. "It seems reasonable to me that the people who have the best seat, who have the best parking, should be the ones who put up the most money for this stadium."

He mentioned the bonds weren't a great investment, financially. "Although when you consider the value of the option—in personal satisfaction; I don't mean money—I think a man will be getting a good deal," he said. "It's better than most."

Murchison admitted many friends had advised him to stay put in the Cotton Bowl. "But I think that occasionally it is incumbent to put yourself out on a limb and do what's good for the community, and I think the majority of people will agree eventually, and I'm willing to put my reputation on the line to that effect," he said. "And I've done it." He paused and added, "That's assuming I've got a reputation."

By late June of 1969, sixteen thousand $250 bonds had been sold. Sixty of one hundred inner-circle boxes were claimed at $50,000 each.

Clint Murchison especially looked forward to the football season after his father, Clint Sr., the king of the wildcatters, passed away that month. Football had taken his mind off the myriad business interests that otherwise occupied his time, and now more than ever he craved a distraction. The lost art of letter writing gave him almost as much pleasure as his Cowboys did, especially after he received a letter from a college student from Tyler named Marsha Spivey asking about his philosophy of life.

He wrote her back to explain he was no navel-gazer:

"Frankly, I am of the opinion that a person should not begin stating his philosophy of life until he is 60 or 70 years old," Murchison said in his letter. "In fact, I believe that most of the successful people I know spend very little time philosophizing and a great deal of time doing. Maybe that's a philosophy, but if it is I don't want to think about it because if I did I would be breaking my own rule."

WITH THE SEASON four months away, the football team appeared to be in top shape. Their number-one draft pick, running back Calvin Hill from Yale, was typically unconventional. The team also acquired tight end Mike Ditka from the Pittsburgh Steelers, while Dave Manders, who had been expected to retire, got in shape to take the center job from Malcolm Walker.

The only questionable was Meredith, who was having a hard time getting it up.

In early July just before training camp, Meredith met with Landry for a heart-to-heart. The previous year, Landry had put his faith in his quarterback until the end, and it had paid off until Cleveland upset their championship plans, leaving Dandy full of doubt.

There were expectations at home that he wasn't meeting, he told the coach. His marriage was falling apart. Chigger and Don were not the same couple who had found happiness on the rebound five years before. Cheryl had given birth to a daughter, Heather, who was blind and had other disabilities. Don did not discourage celebrity. He liked being in the limelight and at the center of attention. Chigger had been fine with it as long as she was involved, but Don more and more frequently rambled and was not one to refuse a flirt and make it into something more.

Meredith had actually gone in for his heart-to-heart with Landry wanting to be talked out of what he was about to say. "You know, Coach, I think it's time for me to retire," he somberly told Landry, hoping Landry would resist and say, *Come on, Don, you're just getting started,* since he'd been playing for only seven years and was just reaching his prime. He was only two seasons removed from NFL Player of the Year honors. But with his knees, his shoulders, his lung, and his nose, he was beat up pretty good, he told his coach. Maybe it was time to get out.

Landry surprised him. "Don, that's the very best thing you can do; if that's the way you feel, it's probably the right decision," he responded, trying to show compassion but coming off cold. "I understand completely. Let's pray."

Landry could no longer wait on Meredith. He was who he was, too much like Bobby Layne and not enough like the man Landry needed to lead with his system. "I tried to talk him out of it," Landry later insisted. "But when you lose your desire in this game, that's it."

When the decision was made public, Meredith put on a smiling face. "I have come to love this man," he said, announcing his retirement at age thirty-one. He would later refer to Landry on *Monday Night Football* as "ol' Stoneface" and made the observation that "in a personality contest between Tom Landry and [Minnesota coach] Bud Grant, there would be no winner." Despite their wide gap in demeanor and approach to the game, the two men's respect for each other was clear. Meredith just wished for more emotion from his coach, and maybe more hand-holding. "I expected him to flip on the light for me but he never did." And for his part, Landry expected a player to do his job to the best of his ability. Period.

Desire was one thing. Being physically pummeled was another. Meredith had suffered fourteen nose breaks, numerous rib breaks and cracks, pneumonia, and a punctured lung. He had no cartilage in his left knee and no feeling in two fingers. But he was hurting inside too. The Boo-Birds nagged him. With a wife and two daughters, Mary Donna and Heather, the latter with many disabilities, and a brand-new baby boy, Michael, the quarterback was switching his focus. "I needed to get out of the public eye and dedicate myself to the situation at home," he said.

He could go out with his head held high. He had been named the National Football League Player of the Year in 1966, had racked up over 17,000 yards passing, and come tantalizingly close to winning the whole shebang. But he was no longer willing to pay the price to be the type of quarterback Coach Landry wanted.

As thanks for his efforts, Tom gave Don a checkbook-size leather-bound copy of the New Testament.

"We were just a little different in our outlook on life," Landry would later say. "I think Don would rather have had a good time and really didn't discipline himself like I believed you have to do to become a top quarterback. But there's no doubt he performed extremely well. He was probably the toughest guy I've ever seen at quarterback. He would be badly hurt and still play. He took an awful beating."

Lee Roy Jordan, the captain of the defense, witnessed that up close and personal. "He took the brunt of the criticism because of the way our whole offense played," he said. "A lot of times it's not always the quarterback's fault. The other team has something to do with it as well as our team's preparation and route running. But it was on Don's shoulders. You're going to get the blame if you're the quarterback."

MEREDITH TOOK THE HITS for the Cowboys to become the team they were destined to be. He kept the city engaged when the relationship between the Cowboys and Dallas citizens was still uncommitted. He spoke the language of the earthy people and moved with ease in Clint Murchison's circles. He defined Dallas in all the best ways.

And he was giving up. Meredith's designated successor would be Craig Morton, the rifle-armed starting-quarterback-in-waiting since he arrived from the University of California in 1965. "This next season will be the first time that Tom has indicated I have a chance to be number one," Morton said. "He told me when I first came to the Cowboys that it would take five years for me to become an NFL quarterback. Of course, I didn't believe him then. But I do now. I just had no idea of the complexity of the pro game. This reading the defenses and being able to switch to the alternate keys is something that just takes time."

Backing up Morton would be the twenty-seven-year-old rookie Roger Staubach. Scouts and coaches remained skeptical that he'd still have skills after five years of active duty following graduation. But Staubach had practiced throwing passes during downtime in Vietnam and had quarterbacked the Pensacola Naval Air Station Goshawks for two years when he showed up to train with Meredith, Morton, and Rhome at Thousand Oaks in the summer of 1968.

During an exhibition game against Baltimore he distinguished himself by scrambling for thirty-one seconds to successfully evade defensive players chasing him.

"Psychologically, mentally I knew I could play, I just didn't know if it would be in Dallas," Staubach said. Then he got a phone call from publicist Curt Mosher. Meredith had retired. Rhome had already been traded. Staubach had two months left at Pensacola and had already moved up to number-two quarterback. He resigned his commission from the Navy. It was time.

Morton was clearly destined to start, but Staubach meant to challenge him. By no means would either be mistaken for Dandy, but Morton had accumulated enough experience to acknowledge the tar pit he was stepping into, stoically vowing to an assembly of sportswriters, "If I can take it as well as Don took it, I'll be a man." He had to give it too.

For his part, Tom Landry wished Don Meredith had told him sooner; if he had, Landry wouldn't have traded away Jerry Rhome.

Meredith's departure forced Dave Campbell to pull four color pages from his *Texas Football* magazine's Dallas Cowboys special issue.

A week later, Don Perkins, thirty-one, followed Meredith into retirement. "You can interpret it as you like, but it *is* official," he said. "It's as final as I can be at this time. I don't want any fanfare. No big splash. No press conference. If a fellow can make a graceful exit without stirring the water, he should. That's what I'm trying to do if you'll let me." Perkins was going to work for CBS covering NFL games and on Governor David Cargo's youth commission in New Mexico, and Dallas was now losing both its face and its fifth all-time NFL leader in rushing yards.

Although Howley, Lilly, Pugh, Jordan, Rentzel, Hayes, and Morton remained, there were no original Dallas Cowboys left. Linebacker DD Lewis was called up by the Army. Pete Gent, Don Meredith's party pal and a rugged tight end, was traded to the New York Giants. No more would he be seen listening to the Beatles on

Craig Morton's portable turntable on the flight home from out-of-town games while smoking a cigar. But Gent continued to live in Dallas. "It's small enough that I feel at ease wherever I go," he said. "The people here are great. Dallas is just 'down home.' There's an atmosphere to this city that I really love."

Following in the footsteps of Don Meredith the year before, Roger Staubach made the cover of *Sports Illustrated* when he was in training camp, while Landry blew off the Landry Mile and instituted a new system called aerobics, articulated by his friend Ken Cooper, who had written a wildly popular book and started the Dallas Aerobic Center, dedicated to physical fitness, the year before.

Training camp was about studying and translating as well as about conditioning and practicing, beginning with the Cowboys playbook:

P 42 Power 47/26 N.O. Pinch

Ram call <u>odd</u>   *Frisco call <u>odd</u>*

Sine qua non: "X" Adjustments on ODD/GAP

OFF T	pull expecting to cut "T"
	no penetration turn up & seal past center
OFF	spring for position
FB	sara upfield, butt or shoulder
	Sara rides in, cut
HB	Do not get ahead of "O"
	Alert for daylight

Some players did not fully appreciate the precision of the instructions.

"They went overboard with all the stats," traded quarterback Jerry Rhome said. "They'd get up there in training camp, they'd put them on the board and start going through it. 'This is our goal, we ran for 4.1 yards last year on first down, and we're trying to reach 4.3.' Who gives a crud about all that? Every player would be asleep by the time the meeting was over. That was the only negative thing about Landry's approach. It's okay to say these are our goals, this year we want to raise our rushing average from 3.4 to 4 yards, four or five things. But, man, they had like fifty. Players would sit there and snicker, like 'Are you kidding me?' It was a little far-fetched. It was good that coaches were looking for those details, but for them to think the players are going to sit there and take all that in, gee."

Landry had huddled with the assistant coaches and Dr. Ray Fletcher to establish goals that were outstanding and goals that were doable. "It gave players more of an incentive to see that even if they didn't reach the exceptional goals, they'd get the makeable goals," explained Gil Brandt. "We did goals for our players after we got them and goals for our scouts. There was x number of dollars available for raises. Scouts were graded on what they'd done. They were graded on the grade they gave a prospect and how that player turned out. If we got a hundred thousand dollars and there were ten scouts, one might get thirty thousand and one might get only three thousand. It was a game within a game."

For the high school cheerleaders, pro football proved to be another animal. Dee Brock, the mother hen of the CowBelles and Beaux, went to Tex Schramm during the offseason with a new plan. The boys and girls from Dallas County high schools were dropped in favor of an all-girl squad of young women at least eighteen years old who didn't cheer but precision-danced in the spirit of the Tyler Apache Belles and the Kilgore Rangerettes.

Because Roger Staubach excelled in preseason play, the quarterback they'd be cheering would have to come out on top in the latest Cowboys-quarterback controversy. Morton had earned the starter's position, but when he was sidelined for injuries, Staubach found himself starting the first game of the regular season at the Cotton Bowl.

The old rookie was nervous. "I'm thinking, 'Man, I'm 0-and-2 here. We better win this game or I'm out of here. They're going to cut me.' We had three kids when I was in the Navy and moved the family here and bought a house even though I told Marianne I didn't know how long I was going to be around." It looked like a while, if going 7 for 15 and one TD while leading his team in a clinical dispatch of the Cardinals, 24–3, was any indication. Still, Morton had healed up by the next game and started, snapping back to form in victories over New Orleans and Philadelphia. Calvin Hill's running prowess prompted Landry to call him "the best runner I've had." Five games into the season, Hill led the league in rushing, Craig Morton was the highest-rated quarterback in the NFL, and the Dallas Cowboys were undefeated.

All was not sweetness and light outside the lines, though.

On October 14, 1969, two days after the Cowboys beat the Falcons by a touchdown in their closest game yet, Mel Renfro petitioned U.S. District Court judge Sarah T. Hughes to order the Executive Duplex Apartments at 6135 Rencon Way in North Dallas to stop discriminating against Negroes, a violation of the Fair Housing Act of 1968. "This has happened to us a few times before in the six years we've been here," Renfro told a reporter. "We got tired of being pushed around and decided to do something about it. In the past, we would talk to real estate people on the phone. Things would look fine until my wife would tell them we were Negro. Then they would say, 'Well, that presents a problem.'"

"You just get sick of it after a while," Pat Renfro said. "'Oh, Mrs. Renfro, I just love to see your husband play football with the Cowboys, but we just don't have anything available for you.'"

Tex Schramm had urged the Renfros to go to court. "I agreed with Mel that he should seek legal recourse," he told the newspapers. "The Cowboys are 100 percent with him in this case, and we're going on notice now to support the right of all our players to enjoy the rights and benefits of all citizens." Seven of twenty-two starters on the Cowboys squad were African American.

Mel Renfro won $1,500 in damages and was offered another duplex. He thought what he and his wife had gone through was a positive. "People who used to have these same problems have told me that our taking a stand helped to change this. I hope so." Schramm's support was invaluable. The incident underscored the growing influence the Dallas Cowboys had on the city, and it lifted the rug up enough for all to see: race remained a divisive subject in Dallas.

"In order to have a team that's a unit, to perform together, to stay together, it's got to be off the field, in your everyday life and in all your activities," Renfro said. "I don't see much of that here. I can't feel it. I hope for better things — better things for myself, my family, the Cowboys."

Jethro Pugh weighed in with his own experience. "When I first came here me and Mitch Johnson rode all over town in his little Volkswagen, and finally we had to settle in a place so bad that it was burglarized three times in two months. When we went on a road trip, we'd have to lock everything in the trunk of a car and drive to a friend's house and leave it there, then move in again when we got back Sunday night."

Housing was only part of the story. "I really tried hard to find a job this year," Pugh said. "I wanted one bad, but I never did find one. I substituted as a teacher — the way that works is you get a call every morning or so to come in and sub. When you accept the first call, the next three schools that call you think you just don't want to work. The calls fall off. So the work is not very consistent after a while."

Bob Hayes saw an ugly side to the fans when he tried to redo his contract. "My wife would go shopping and people would tell her she should be back in Africa picking cotton," the world's fastest human related. "She took it in stride and I'm proud of her. Some small-minded people felt I was asking for a million dollars. Well, I'm not asking for a million dollars. Not anything like that."

Two months earlier, players' and coaches' wives were at the center of another racial controversy. The Cowboys' wives were almost as big a draw as their husbands whenever they modeled furs and clothes at benefits. But they withdrew as models for the benefit show for the Dallas chapter of Children's Asthma Research Institute and Hospital after the wives of several Negro football players said they hadn't been asked to participate. Mrs. Pat Renfro read about it in the newspaper. "Up until then, we hadn't even been invited to attend," she said. "We were upset, hurt, and angry. One of us, Dede Townes, is even a professional model. We would have liked to have been informed." Tex Schramm said it was best that none of the wives participate.

Schramm went the extra mile to back up his players. Meritocracy was the best means to ease racial tensions, he believed. He'd seen how it worked in Southern California, where Jackie Robinson went to high school before he broke the color line in major-league baseball and where Tank Younger starred on the field for the Los Angeles Rams. Tex didn't care if you were black or white, eight or eighty, crippled, sick, or flying. If you could play, you could play. Tom felt that way too. The football field was an oasis of equality where talent, physical strength, and the ability to win were all that mattered.

THE COWBOYS' UNBEATEN STRING snapped when Cleveland burned Dallas 42–10 in early November in their first rematch since the previous December. The Cowboys had an excuse: quarterback Morton was playing with a separated shoulder. But overall play was so poor that Coach Landry ditched the fedora and switched to a ball cap at halftime, to no avail. Afterward, he issued a pearl of wisdom to his team: "What you do about a game like this is forget it." The coach knew what he was up against. "Nothing will satisfy anyone until we're in the Super Bowl and win it," he said.

The second loss came against the Rams in Los Angeles in mid-November, by a single point. The following week, Dallas played San Francisco to a 24–24 tie on Thanksgiving Day. Otherwise, the team appeared to be unstoppable. Despite President Nixon's prediction that the Washington Redskins would skin the Cowboys, the visitors won 41–28 on their way to the Capitol Division title.

The first decade of pro football in Dallas closed out with the Cowboys going to the playoffs and hosting the Cleveland Browns at the Cotton Bowl, the first of three games they would need to win before becoming Super Bowl champs. The 11-2-1 record made many fans forget Don Meredith, as Craig Morton passed with precision and Calvin Hill churned out rushing yards; had not a sore big toe sidelined Hill late in the season, he would have easily rushed for over 1,000 yards. Hill ranked second in league rushing yards, won Rookie of the Year honors, was profiled in *Esquire, Time*, and *Vogue* magazines, and was recognized as the Texas Pro Athlete of the Year. The team appeared to be headed for a Super Bowl showdown with Lamar Hunt's Kansas City Chiefs.

"We'll be ready this time," Craig Morton promised. Victory was practically a foregone conclusion for the Dallas fans who camped out waiting for the ticket booth to open.

The day before the contest, Browns owner Art Modell went over to Clint Murchison's house to watch a college all-star game on television. Murchison and ex–minority owner Bedford Wynne were studying lists and making notes when Modell arrived. The game on television was already in progress.

Modell was taken with the fact that the owner and his sidekick were so interested in the all-star game they were going over the lists of college players they might draft. The names on the list, however, were female. "What they were doing was going over lists of prospective stewardesses to be used for the Cowboys charter flights," Tex Schramm later explained. "[Clint] was so thorough that he even attended stewardess graduation exercises at the school, to check out the rookies to see if any of them might qualify as replacements." Modell was flabbergasted when he realized what Murchison and Wynne were up to. "No wonder everybody thought the Cowboys were so thorough."

Modell had the last laugh, and the Cleveland Browns, the team that ended the Cowboys' stellar 1968 season and Don Meredith's career, ended the Cowboys' stellar 1969 season too.

The Cowboys struggled from the very first series of plays on a rainy December afternoon. A fumbled ball on a punt return gave Cleveland a 7–0 gift seven minutes into the game. At the half, it was Cleveland 17, Dallas *nada*. Boos showered down from the stands. Morton ended up 8-24 in passing with two interceptions. To rub it in, the Browns' Bill Nelson was relieved late in the fourth quarter by Jerry Rhome, the former Dallas Cowboy backup quarterback, who made two completions before time ran out.

The 38–14 loss to Cleveland was the last straw for many fans, especially when the University of Texas Longhorns played on the same field four days later in the Cotton Bowl Classic and beat Notre Dame 21–17 to win the national college championship (the last school with an all-white team to do so).

Ralph Neely was fed up with the Boo-Birds and said so. "I really don't give a damn what they think anymore," he said. "The fan now is secondary." Neely had been ragged once too often. "You try not to let the booing affect you. But when Don Meredith got booed, every-one thought he had a steel shield around him, where he couldn't hurt. But it hurt him. A fan pays his seven bucks for a seat and he's got a right to express his opinion. But when he starts belittling the players he goes too far. I could never sit in a crowd and watch a foot-ball game where I knew the players. I hear these guys calling Landry or Morton a dumb SOB and I want to pop them in the head. They go out there and have a few drinks and they think they own you."

At least Don Meredith realized it wasn't him. And now he was counseling the only coach the Cowboys ever had. "I listened to some of it on the radio," he told a reporter. "It had to be the worst game I ever heard. It was so bad, I couldn't study [for a security business exam]. After it was over I called Tom and went over to his house for the first time. He asked me, 'What can I do?' I told him to hang it up, forget it, get out. Obviously, he didn't follow my advice. He is such a fine man. I hate to see things like that happen to him. It was kind of sad for such a dedicated, disciplined man to wind up in such a situation. We used to be at odds on a lot of things but we learned to respect one another for different reasons. We're not exactly identical personalities. Here was a man who devoted ten years to his team. His philosophy was challenged and all but destroyed. He had taken a torpedo in the hull and was drifting."

Quitting was not in Landry's vocabulary. "I never thought about it," he said. "I'm a football coach. That's my life. If I didn't like it, I wouldn't do it."

The team owner acted inconvenienced. "We've won a conference or division title the last four years," Murchison pointed out. "I like to win football games, but I don't intend to cut my throat if we don't. I intend to go to Miami and have a good time. I'm looking forward to 1970, the decade of the Cowboys. I have absolute, complete, unequivocal confidence that next season will be better than this season. We just have football fans here who are unhappy right now."

The Rams kicked Dallas every which way around Miami and all the way back to Texas in the very last Playoff Bowl ever played, 31–0. Not even the winning team much cared.

But the Cowboys' growing cadre of fans were beginning to believe that if it wasn't Cleveland or Green Bay, some other team was going to rise up to deny the Cowboys their destiny. They had been patient for the first five years while Landry built a team around his sophisticated schemes. But the past five years had turned torturous. The team was championship caliber but couldn't seal the deal. Dallas, the city, was clearly on the rise, bursting with get-'er-done accomplishments. If only the hometown team reflected that. The Cowboys had the best record in professional football for the past five years, 52-14, but they hadn't made it to the big dance yet.

Tex Schramm counseled calm. "When your team runs off the field and they boo you, then it's time to do something," he acknowledged. "I know it and I'm sure the players know it. Our entire organization has to reevaluate our systems, our methods, the way we do everything. The best thing you can do now is *not* base your decisions on emotions. Nobody's smart when they're mad."

The initial plan that Landry, Schramm, and Brandt had devised wasn't as flawless as they'd originally thought. Something wasn't working. Landry sent questionnaires to the players asking what they thought might be wrong. The responses he received included *overly prepared, too much finesse,* and *prima donnas.* Some players blamed Landry's puritanism. Piety was one thing, but shows of religious faith had no more role in pro football than in the ownership of a bar or restaurant. The results on the field were what mattered. Football was about aggression and violence and emotion. Too much emphasis had been placed on finesse rather than brute strength, several players said.

Although frustration had welled up again, just like it had for the previous five years whenever the Cowboys got close and then blew it, there was the knowledge that by the time the next season rolled around, there would be plenty of reasons to look forward.

Linebacker Lee Roy Jordan thought his coach was being too hard on himself after the team fell short. "Landry was a quality person and had a good group of good football players who were good people," Jordan said. "The character was there and that was one thing he always emphasized in people he was going to draft and sign is how they would handle themselves in the public and how they would handle themselves off the field. And he certainly drafted because they were good football players, but he wanted something else to go along with that."

1970–1979

Two Super Bowls, Two Quarterbacks, and Millions of True Believers

TEX SCHRAMM should have been satisfied.

Pro football was the most popular spectator sport in the United States and growing, if television dollars and ratings were any measure. And before the 1970 campaign got under way, the merger between the National Football League and the American Football League was officially completed. The NFL now consisted of two conferences of thirteen teams each: the American Football Conference, which was the ten old AFL teams plus the Cleveland Browns, Pittsburgh Steelers, and Baltimore Colts; and the National Football Conference, aka the old NFL minus Cleveland, Pittsburgh, and Baltimore. Dallas remained in the Eastern Division with the same rivals, just as Schramm wanted, even though the grouping with New York, Philadelphia, and Washington made no geographical sense. "That's where the great media giants of the country were," said sportswriter Frank Luksa, "and Tex knew that." He also knew that the club could walk away from a game at New York against the Giants with a $1 million gate, compared to a $450,000 gate from a game at Green Bay.

What gnawed at Schramm, despite this thing called parity, was what had already been achieved on the playing field. The Kansas City Chiefs—the old Dallas Texans—followed the New York Jets as

Super Bowl champions in the fourth championship game, in January of 1970. For all the odds against him, Lamar Hunt not only beat Clint, Tex, and company to the big game, he waltzed away with the trophy. Guided by Hank Stram, the only coach the Texans and Kansas City had ever had, the Chiefs massacred the Minnesota Vikings, 23–7.

Hank Stram attributed a good deal of the Chiefs' success to the fact that AFL coaches had no choice but to innovate in the early years of the league. NFL coaches played it more conservatively. "Most teams came at you with fairly basic offenses and stuck to the 4-3 defense," he said, referring to the defense that Tom Landry developed. "This was particularly so in the NFL, which was influenced in the early '60s by the success the New York Giants had enjoyed for a number of years. The men who played such a large role in the success, Vince Lombardi with the offense and Tom Landry with the defense, moved on to head coaching jobs and the influence spread. Our league was brand-new, of course, and it was different in that we had head coaches like myself, [Texas native] Sam Baugh at New York, Frank Filchock at Denver, and Eddie Erdelatz at Oakland, who believed in doing it their own way." Stram wasn't putting down the Giants and their system. "I'm just saying mine was not the Giant personality," he said.

Tom Landry was neither offended nor defensive. He knew he shared the same mind-set when it came to multiple offenses, even though he and Stram took very different approaches to their defenses, and he knew how the publicity machine worked. "When you're on top, people listen to you a little more," Landry said.

Lamar Hunt was magnanimous toward his former rivals. "I can sympathize with the Cowboys for what they're going through right now and how some people are questioning Tom Landry's ability," he said. "The people of Dallas have developed a very strong feeling about that team the past few years and I know they're deeply disappointed right now. But I find no pleasure that the Chiefs are here and the Cowboys aren't. I just hope they come back strong. You know, adversity is difficult to live with but you can certainly profit from it. We did."

For all of Tex Schramm's inclination to throw verbal darts at the AFL at any opportunity, he was glad to see the war end, even if an increasing number of pundits were positing that the AFL had the upper hand over the establishment's old boys. With the merger complete, he also hoped the wild escalation of player salaries had finally been tamped down.

But Schramm knew that a few ongoing battles would keep some fires burning. Tex represented the owners' interests across the negotiating table from Ed Garvey, the attorney for the NFL Players Association, and Garvey was asking for privileges that crossed the line, as far as Schramm was concerned. The players wanted more money, more flexibility to change teams, the ability to hire agents in negotiating with their clubs, and for Pete Rozelle to be gone as league commissioner. Schramm and the owners eventually coughed up $19.1 million in financial incentives, accepting agents into the mix while keeping Rozelle in place.

Schramm's negotiations on behalf of the owners reflected the hard line he took with his own players, most recently with Calvin Hill, who wanted his three-year contract renegotiated after he'd won NFL Rookie of the Year honors. If Schramm said yes, the line to renegotiate contracts would be backed up outside his office, he believed.

"Tex was a hard-liner from the standpoint of 'it's our game, they work for us and they've got a lot of advantages being pro football stars and by God we will control that end of it,'" said sportswriter Randy Galloway. "'If they don't like it, the hell with them.'"

The president and general manager of the Dallas Cowboys did remind Hill about the extra pay that came with every Cowboys playoff victory. Tex genuinely enjoyed bargaining and had earned a reputation for getting the better end of the deal. But Ed Garvey's growing demands were forcing his hand.

Accepting the idea of dealing with agents rather than the players themselves was bad enough. Agents were a violation of the special personal relationship between player and management, Schramm felt. Agents were not family, nor did they represent the best interests of the team or league. Their constant demands for more money and a larger slice of the television pie were messing up a good thing. The family feeling had been critical to establishing what Schramm liked to describe as a peak performance organization.

But, as he would note with increasing frequency, "you can't legislate intelligence."

The first agent Tex dealt with willingly was the exception, since Mary Lou Andrie *was* family. "Every year George would come in, we'd work out a contract," Schramm said. "He'd take it home and she'd send him back the next day. After the third year, when George came to me and said he wanted to do next year's contract, I told him to go home, keep the kids, and send Mary Lou over and we'd work it out."

Pat Toomay, the defensive end drafted out of Vanderbilt, pondered hiring an agent but sounded out the wrong advisers. "I was in school when I signed the contract," he said. "I was a middle-round pick and agents were a big thing. I didn't know whether to get one or not. So I asked Gil Brandt, 'Do I need an agent to negotiate this with you?' Confront the snake in his lair."

"Pat, I'm going to call DD Lewis right now and you can talk to him," Brandt told Toomay. Lewis was a fifth-round pick from Mississippi the previous year. "You talk to him and you can ask him if this is a fair deal or not," Brandt said.

A salary survey conducted a year later by the NFL Players Association revealed Lewis was among the lowest-paid linebackers in the league. "So I was right down at the bottom there with him." Toomay laughed.

"I asked my [Vanderbilt] coach about hiring an agent and he told me the same thing—'The Cowboys will treat you right. Tom Landry is a man of God.' Then, as I'm leaving his office, Coach said, 'By the way, ask Gil Brandt where is that suit he's sending me? It's not here yet.'" The Cowboys had a deal with Haggar men's clothing in El Paso to supply suits to college coaches whose players were signed by the Cowboys. It was part of Gil Brandt's incentive system to reward college coaches if they produced a player that made the Cowboys—though other coaches preferred vacation trips.

Pat Toomay started paying enough attention to notice the Vanderbilt trainers' room was stuffed with Cowboys paraphernalia. "I began to see how the flow of information was controlled even outside the realm of the team," he said. "You feel that they're going to be fair, and that wasn't the experience. I had trusted Landry, the image of Landry, that they would be fair, then you find out on the backside that you were the fool."

Schramm was on top of every aspect of the sport, especially television, that powered pro football. Eyeballs focused on the NFL on TV meant a steady string of advertisers ready to spend big bucks to win fans' wallets and assured prosperity for the league.

That did not stop Tex Schramm criticizing the use of bootleg Cowboy antennas to pick up television stations seventy-five miles beyond Dallas in order to watch home games that were blacked out locally. The long-distance receptors were big draws for bars, clubs, and other gathering places across the Metroplex. Apartment complexes even used the long-range antennas as part of sales pitches to prospective renters. Schramm and Murchison viewed public facilities that solicited customers with the signal boosters as thieves stealing money out of their pockets. Murchison was particularly steamed that on a rainy Sunday, five hundred fans gathered to watch the game on a Cowboys antenna at the Petroleum Club (a club he belonged to) when there were over twelve thousand empty seats in the Cotton Bowl.

Average attendance was down to 60,171 from a 1966 high of 67,158, and Schramm proposed that the Federal Communications Commission either extend blackouts to all Texas stations outside the Dallas–Fort Worth area or permit closed-circuit broadcasts—pay

TV—as an extension of seating capacity. "[Pay TV] is preferable to doubling ticket prices," Schramm argued, noting expenses had doubled in the past ten years. "We're faced now with a league operating at more than ninety percent stadium capacity and everyone has agreed that we've reached the top figure on TV revenue. With expenses spiraling, there has to be additional revenue."

If blacking out nearby television stations was necessary, Schramm said, "I'd have no compassion for the people in the Dallas–Fort Worth area." Hometown fans were obliged to show their support by attending games in the Cotton Bowl. "The life blood of the game is home attendance," Schramm said. "You can't exist economically without it, nor do I believe you can exist aesthetically either. I don't think football should or could be played before a studio audience and stay at its present competitive level.... The thing we are more interested in is a full ball park."

Schramm was conveniently ignoring the obvious. The Dallas Cowboys Football Club claimed a profit of $1,940,000 in their first decade because of television. (Claiming any kind of profit was deceptive, since the worth of an NFL franchise was judged by its value, not its profitability.) The admission price for an expansion franchise had skyrocketed from $600,000 in 1960 to $25 million. And after a new four-year deal with CBS and NBC, the twenty-six clubs in the National Football League would now split $130 million, or about $1.25 million per team per season. Extra sugar was sprinkled on top when the ABC network paid $8 million to the NFL to air *Monday Night Football* for thirteen Mondays in the 1970 season, bringing pro football to prime time.

If television was bad for the Cowboys, as Tex Schramm complained publicly, the combination of television and the Cowboys' success on the field had a brutal effect on Southern Methodist University, Don Meredith's alma mater. For the first time, attendance at games played at SMU and the entire Southwest Conference was down, except for the University of Texas and Texas A&M.

TAKING SOME OF COLLEGE football's audience and making as much money as possible, in combination with Tex Schramm showing no mercy negotiating player contracts, allowed the organization to squirrel away money so that Clint Murchison could finish his construction project.

Slowly but surely, the new Dallas Cowboys football stadium was taking shape, rising above the featureless prairie and shapeless mass of functional suburbia known as Irving. Texas Stadium, as Clint Murchison had boldly named it—*not* in honor of the Dallas Texans, he liked to joke—was that rare project that coaxed him from the shadows.

Murk made clear he was in full control, even though this project had a footprint so huge and ambitious even close friends and family wondered if he had finally bitten off more than he could chew. Texas Stadium was his design, built by his construction company, and he was the one who sold it—to the city of Irving, to the residents of Irving (most of whom would never set foot inside), to Cowboys fans, and to the general public.

He sold Texas Stadium on television, on the radio, and in newspaper interviews and advertisements, coached by public relations guru Mitch Lewis, a friend of the Murchison court. On TV, Murchison touted the superiority of his facility as a spectator venue by comparing it to the Cotton Bowl and Rice University Stadium in Houston.

Advertising designer Stan Richards was hired to create a sixteen-page brochure for the suites aimed at the business community, pitching "an opportunity of a lifetime to secure a box in what was going to be a great stadium." A related pitch was tailored to corporations and extremely wealthy individuals through a character named Stanley Mudge, who promised purchasers of self-contained box seats, or suites, there'd be no more sitting with your legs up next to your ears, no more long lines at concession stands, no more this, no more that.

Judge Roy Hofheinz had developed the luxury-suite concept with the skybox, incorporating fifty-three self-contained units into the Houston Astrodome. The Dallas owner aimed to build an entire level of private boxes called the Circle Suites. The members of the upper class who could afford a $50,000 suite or a $300,000 prime-location Golden Circle Suite would be separated from hoi polloi by elevators and security. A corporation could write off the box on its taxes as an entertainment expense.

For the rest of the fans, Murchison set up a display of two standard stadium seats in front of the newly completed One Main Place office complex downtown, advising passersby to buy their bonds now in order to reserve their season tickets.

The stadium's seating capacity was smaller than the Cotton Bowl's by design. The Cowboys never sold more than 31,000 season tickets in the Cotton Bowl and rarely sold out the house, averaging 63,265 fans for home games in 1969. Locals knew seats would likely be there if they walked up at the last minute. Now there would be demand.

Murchison had his fingers in lots of the stadium action. The Irving City Council would award the $20 million insurance policy for the new stadium to the Kenneth Murchison Corporation, in which Clint Murchison had an 8 percent stake. He was also an investor in the Cebe Corporation, which won the food concession contract for Texas Stadium. Murchison's own Texas Stadium Corporation controlled the liquor license for the boxes and was featuring Marlboro cigarettes on the giant billboard topped by a 115-foot tower in front of the stadium. Coach Landry spoke out against raising the billboard "as a citizen, a taxpayer, and a human being," but dollars spoke louder—the TSC received an additional $1,250,000 for a five-year lease on the advertising space.

The team owner may have rubbed civic leaders the wrong way by publicly sparring with State Fair of Texas oligarchs over the Cotton Bowl and city of Dallas oligarchs over a downtown stadium. But what

Clint Murchison was making possible on his own terms would play a critical role in defining Dallas as a place of prosperity and possibility.

Dallas had matured into a commercial center that was separate from both coasts and from Chicago and was swimming in capital, entrepreneurial dreams, and entrepreneurial dream makers. To underscore the sense that this was more than another regional hub, the North Texas Council of Governments hired a Dallas copywriter to come up with a new name for the Dallas–Fort Worth Standard Metropolitan Statistical Area—the Dallas–Fort Worth Metroplex, or Metroplex, for short. The neutral-sounding nickname suggested something big and something that could be anywhere.

Proof that the city was strong in the wake of Kennedy's assassination could be found in the John Fitzgerald Kennedy Memorial, a four-walled open cenotaph (empty tomb) dedicated on June 24, 1970. The fifty-foot-by-fifty-foot concrete walled space enclosing an eight-foot-square black granite block with Kennedy's name engraved was about as inoffensive as a memorial could be. The problem was, tourists headed to Dealey Plaza, where Kennedy was shot, and rarely wandered to the memorial.

A new wave of talented individuals had taken note of the percolation of money and energy in North Texas, including a direct sales specialist named Dick Bartlett. Drawn by a growing community of graphic designers and catalog product managers, Bartlett had resigned from Tupperware to move to Dallas. Dallas was an ad-world hotbed— an ideal place, Bartlett thought, to set up his own shop.

"Graphic arts, catalog production, and industrial film and other ancillary marketing disciplines were beginning to blossom in Dallas, a central location in America," Bartlett said. "That excited me. The people here and their attitude towards business had a 'Get 'er done' kind of mentality."

Less than twenty-four hours after Bartlett arrived and set up operations at Expressway Towers on North Central Expressway, he was negotiating with Clint Murchison about developing a new company;

Murchison wanted to get in on direct sales and hired Bartlett to develop a catalog of fashion jewelry that could be marketed. Bartlett was underwhelmed by the person but knocked out by what he represented. "I knew I was looking at a billionaire, or close to it," Bartlett said. "He had wealth way beyond my comprehension. But he was a really polite, sort of mild-mannered person who didn't strike me as being terrifically dynamic. Yet I knew what he was doing at that time with the Cowboys was about as dynamic as you could be. He drove an ugly brown Buick, and I mean ugly. When we met for lunch, guess who picked up the tab? He never paid for a meal. That was his MO."

It was all part of the same trend among businesses expanding vertically to grow their markets. The Southland Corporation, owners of the 7-Eleven convenience store, started its own broadcast division in 1970 to make commercials in-house, and the Stanford Agency became 7-Eleven's in-house ad agency, coining the now-familiar phrase "Oh, thank heaven for 7-Eleven."

Stanley Marcus's former catalog guru Roger Horchow was redefining mail order, just as Dick Bartlett had redefined direct sales at Tupperware. Bartlett's future boss Mary Kay Ash had redefined independent contractor sales with her female-empowering cosmetics company, guided by a God-first, family-second, career-third belief. Tom Merriman, a musical arranger, refined the concept of the radio jingle, a rhyming song sung by harmonizing singers on behalf of radio stations and commercial advertisers, utilizing Dallas talent.

The go-go business climate complemented Mayor Erik Jonsson's new urbanism. The airport that Jonsson championed was still under construction but was already bringing about its intended effect, persuading corporations to relocate to a central location with good weather and low taxes, to distribute products more efficiently.

The wide-open business environment spilled into the popular culture.

The catalyst was a bill allowing liquor to be sold by the drink that had been passed by the Texas Legislature in 1970 and signed into law by Texas governor Preston Smith the following year, ending the quirky practices of private clubs and brown-bagging liquor into restaurants and beer bars.

The approval of liquor by the drink was instrumental in the rise of a new concept known as the fern bar. "Nice" drinking establishments for young men and women who liked to mix and mingle as well as consume booze sprouted along Greenville Avenue like mushrooms after a long soaking rain, bearing names such as Diamond Jim's, Whiskey River, and T.G.I. Friday's. Elsewhere in town, places like the Scene West, the Swingeroo Club, and Lance Rentzel's Pearl Street Warehouse catered to swinging singles too.

The fern bar's residential companion piece, the garden apartment, which came with a conspicuous pool and sometimes a private club, started appearing above the walls of the new Dallas North Tollway, each complex becoming filled with a bevy of singles as soon as the concrete had cured.

The sixties may have arrived in Dallas a few years behind schedule, but they came with a vengeance, and minus much of the patchouli froufrou. "It was the damnedest thing you ever saw," said David Wynne. "I grew up in a repressed society, just totally repressed, and then all of a sudden somebody's turned a switch and these women are coming out of the woodwork, wanting to assert themselves."

"My girlfriend and I lived with a bunch of flight attendants just off the tollway," said Judy Stone, who learned to love the Cowboys through her father, Eddie, a hard-core Dallas sports fan and bettor who worked for car dealer W. O. Bankston. "We'd hang out by the pool all day long then would put on bikinis and drive our convertible Jeeps up and down the tollway and pick up guys. They'd follow us back to our apartments. It was wide open."

Smack-dab in the middle of this exciting environment were the Dallas Cowboys, who stayed in the news during the six-month lull between seasons. By now, they were almost bulletproof. Russ Russell, the team's game photographer, realized that one night after leaving a party John Niland had thrown following a playoff game. "I was rushing out some pictures to Dave Boss of the NFL and had to get them in the mail and I was drunk as a skunk. The cops pulled me over on the [Dallas North] tollway. I got out and was leaning on the car. The officer asked where I was going. I told him the post office."

"Where have you been?"

"I've been to a party."

"Are you drunk?"

"I've had a couple," Russell said, leaning on the car.

"We thought maybe you might have because you were weaving all over the road; can you explain that?"

"Would you believe me if I said I was trying to run over the rats that were running across the road?"

The cops began to laugh as a black Buick pulled up behind Russell's car. The doors opened and Rayfield Wright, Jethro Pugh, and Cornell Green got out.

"You all right, Russ?" Green asked. "Everything okay?"

The cops turned pale at the sight of three men who were each twice their size.

"Would you ask your friends to please move their car?" a patrolman said to Russell.

"Yeah, guys, I'm fine," Russell told the football players. "Y'all go ahead. Thank you."

After they left, the patrolman asked Russell, "Who the hell were they?"

"That was Rayfield, Jethro, and Cornell," Russell replied. "We've been to a party."

"Oh, you work for the Cowboys?" the cop said, his face lighting up. "Well, you drive careful now 'cause you look like you've had too much to drink."

It wasn't all fun and games. The 1970 player draft in January followed script, producing several intriguing picks. The Cowboys had wanted to arrange a trade with Pittsburgh that would give them the first overall pick so they could sign quarterback Terry Bradshaw, but owner Art Rooney turned them down. Instead, the Cowboys' first-round selection was a running back who grew up in South Dallas and who had excelled in anonymity at West Texas State College, in the small Texas Panhandle town of Canyon, where he played in the backfield alongside the highly touted Eugene "Mercury" Morris. Red Hickey, the Cowboys' lead scout under Gil Brandt, compared the pick, Duane Thomas, to the Cowboys' previous number-one draft pick, Calvin Hill, whose left foot happened to be wrapped in a cast due to an infected big toe. Hamp Pool, the former Rams coach, described Thomas as "the best running back I ever saw in college."

"If there was something we didn't need in the draft it was a half-back," Tex Schramm admitted. "We had Hill, and Walt Garrison had done an outstanding job taking over for Don Perkins at fullback. But our scouts, especially Red Hickey, kept touting Duane Thomas." Hickey had also mentioned Thomas's history of disagreeing with coaches and trainers at West Texas State. Landry focused on his playing potential and kept asking Hickey if Thomas was better than Hill. Every time he did, Hickey would respond, "He'll be your halfback."

"Then I think I'll try to handle him," Landry finally decided.

For his part, Duane Thomas, who stood six foot two, weighed 220 pounds, and ran the forty in 4.6 seconds, promised to deliver. "I can't express how I feel," he said after being selected number one by the Cowboys. "Dallas is my team, yes, even after the Cleveland game," Thomas said. "I have a lot of respect for the Cowboys' running backs, but Dallas must have some respect for my ability. I'll make the team and do the job," he promised. "It just means so much to be selected by the team you like and be able to play in your hometown."

Thomas took the initiative and prepared to live up to his commitment, getting involved with special teams at training camp. "Tom was saying he needed someone to run back kickoffs," he said. "I never ran a kickoff back in my life, so I raised my hand. I got in there and ran it back."

Fellow rookie Pat Toomay quickly learned to keep his distance from Thomas. "He was a number-one pick, I was sixth round and we were alphabetically roomed together at the Hilton for pre–training camp testing," Toomay said. "He makes a bunch of long-distance phone calls under my name. And I didn't have any money. I tried to talk to him about it. I told the staff that my roommate's making long distance phone calls with my name, I can't afford this. So they made Cliff [Harris] and I roommates. They took us out of alphabetical order."

Walt Garrison, the Cowboys' bulldogging real cowboy, was a solid replacement for Don Perkins. Danny Reeves had been promoted to coach the backfield and was young enough at twenty-six to relate to the players in a way that Tom Landry could not, and he could still be activated if needed. Reeves would also serve as the strength coach in the offseason under the direction of Alvin Roy, the Kansas City Chiefs strength coach who had been hired by the Cowboys. Reeves would hopefully function like Jerry Tubbs, who continued playing for three years while coaching linebackers.

Reeves, who'd busted up his knee and then was beaten out by Calvin Hill, was a designated player-coach at Tom Landry's request. It had never crossed Reeves's mind before, but the more he thought about it, the better it sounded. "I'd heard of coaches getting fired, but I never heard of a player getting fired, and I heard of players getting cut, but never heard of a coach getting cut. So, I thought, I've got two chances."

More muscle had been added to the defense too, including linebacker Steve Kiner from Tennessee and two nimble defensive backs: third-round pick out of Clemson, Charlie Waters, and a walk-on from Ouachita Baptist College, Cliff Harris, who beat out Waters to make the starting lineup. Landry was putting the finishing touches on his Flex defense, bringing one defensive tackle nose-to-nose with the offensive guard while the adjacent defensive end lined up in a frog squat three feet off the line of scrimmage. The backside end had an extra split second to read, react, and move laterally to respond to the play, while the nose-up tackle exploded across the line of scrimmage in an attempt to disrupt the offensive play.

Additional speed was added to the receiver corps with second-round pick Margene Adkins, who had played high school ball in Fort Worth and at Henderson County Junior College before going to the Canadian Football League. Thomas and Adkins were the first high-profile local draft picks since Bob Lilly, Sonny Gibbs, and Jerry Rhome.

The only unresolved position was quarterback, where Craig Morton and Roger Staubach vied to be starter. Morton had the edge in experience and seasoning. His accuracy was exceptional. But his rival Staubach seethed with competitiveness.

Even Dandy Don Meredith briefly entered the mix when he contacted Tex Schramm to offer his services. He would come back from retirement, but only if he could start over Morton. His domestic troubles were beginning to clarify. Divorce from Chigger King, the Fort Worth girl who had stolen his heart, was in the works.

But Schramm rebuffed Meredith. Morton and maybe Staubach were the future. "I thought I could come back," Meredith would later say. "I was surprised, but there was little interest in me coming back." And that was that.

At one point in the preseason, the every-other-play quarterback shuffle was reintroduced to howls of displeasure from the QBs, the other players, and the fans. In Landry's analytical head, it was his only choice. The two players were so evenly balanced, he couldn't commit.

The 1970 season began colored by the realization that however loaded with talent the team appeared to be, the quarterback question lingered. Who would start at QB seemed to have become as much a constant as the glamour of the team's players, the class associated with the club's operations, the genius and faith of the coach, and the multiple offenses and basic defense he designed.

Landry was upbeat going in. "I feel better this year than I have ever felt about the potential of this team," he said. Landry's born-again get-tough attitude was based on his four musts to get to the Super Bowl: technical ability, consistency, dedication, and competitiveness. Landry was analytical in breaking down what his team lacked. "There are different types of player motivation—like a fear motivation, an incentive motivation, and an attitude motivation," he said. "I lean toward the attitude motivation. I try to change a boy's attitude or try to give him the proper attitude so that he will be motivated to accomplish the same thing. I've been criticized for not using more fear motivation—a driving type of process. When you lose the big game four years in a row after four first-place seasons, everyone is seeking a reason. Maybe we do need a little more of a motivation mixture, including some fear type. And it is indeed true that some guys aren't as well motivated unless we use a little bit of fear."

That was the knock on Landry: he just didn't breathe fire like Lombardi or Van Brocklin or Shula. "I think Coach Landry feels maybe he has been lax on players in the past," assistant Danny Reeves said.

"I don't think he is going to put up with anything this year," said Roger Staubach, who started at quarterback when the 1970 season kicked off because Craig Morton came off flat in preseason exhibitions while fighting a nagging shoulder injury. Landry benched Ralph Neely and Bob Hayes for not showing enough want-to too.

The defensive play of Herb Adderley, who'd been acquired from Green Bay, and the reintroduction of the guard shuttle system so Landry could call plays for Staubach, led to an opening-day victory over Philadelphia. Bob Lilly saw a difference in the team's general demeanor. "Tom made more noise and showed more emotion today than any time that I've been around him," he said. "That's good. It affected the entire team." Landry affirmed that he'd gotten worked up. "I was especially involved today because I was calling the [defensive] plays," he said. "I was very intent on our getting the job done.

Maybe I was more expressive than before but maybe that was just a result of my feelings coming to the surface."

Rookie free safety Cliff Harris was the major reason for the Giants' 28–10 downfall, swiping two interceptions while receiver Lance Rentzel threw a trick 38-yard TD pass to Bobby Hayes. Roger Staubach was so erratic in the first half that Landry wanted to pull him; Staubach talked him out of it at halftime while walking up the ramp of the Cotton Bowl.

"Hey, Coach, I started this game," Staubach protested. "I want to finish it. I just ask you to do that. If you want him to play next week I respect that, but this is different."

Landry could tell Staubach was agitated and meant what he said. Staubach stayed in and the Cowboys came back to beat the Giants.

The talk of a newly turned leaf and all the right stuff quickly turned to uncertainty again the next game, when Landry pulled Staubach after throwing two interceptions in the first half of a 20–7 loss to St. Louis. A sure touchdown pass that Lance Rentzel dropped in the end zone didn't help. The quarterback from the Navy didn't like Landry's call and complained about the two-quarterback situation, saying, "That's not football."

Landry responded at the press conference after the game: "I'd be happy to have the quarterback situation settled, but it isn't yet." The second-year guy wasn't ready, not in his coach's mind. But Morton proved just as ineffective. He changed his throwing motion to compensate for chronic shoulder pain, only to develop issues with his elbow.

The Cowboys dispatched the Atlanta Falcons, but the following week, the team was totally crushed by Minnesota, 54–13, tying for the worst loss in franchise history.

And so it went. The victory over defending Super Bowl champs Kansas City in an away game at Municipal Stadium, 27–16, on a Morton-to-Hayes touchdown pass and Duane Thomas's rumbling for 134 total yards was particularly sweet. John Niland and Ralph

Neely hoisted Clint Murchison on their shoulders and carried him off the field after the clock wound down. Game balls were awarded to the owner and the coach.

Then, in the team's first appearance on *Monday Night Football,* the new ABC prime-time telecast hosted by Don Meredith, Keith Jackson, and Howard Cosell, everything went south. The Cowboys were thrashed every way imaginable by the St. Louis Cardinals at the Cotton Bowl, 38–0. Cornell Green's interception of a Cardinal pass was the only highlight of the night. During the fourth quarter, what was left of the crowd started making up for the Boo-Birds of old, calling for the man in the TV booth to come back.

"We want Meredith! We want Meredith!"

All was forgiven in that instant. Staubach and Morton weren't working out, the fans were saying. Please come back.

"I had so many funny stories to tell," Meredith admitted to the national audience tuning in as the game wound down. "But I can't tell funny stories with something like this going on. But I tell you one thing, folks, I'm not about to go back down there." Been there. Done that. Still feeling it.

Meredith would better serve the team by calling games on TV. Every time he opened his mouth and showed off his biting wit and distinctive drawl, he reminded viewers at home of the Dallas Cowboys — including during the first *Monday Night Football* game, broadcast on September 21, when Meredith called out the name of Cleveland Browns receiver Fair Hooker and then said, "Fair Hooker — I haven't met one yet." He proceeded to open up a broadcast from Denver by saying on the air, "Welcome to the Mile High City, and I really am."

Meredith's broadcast-booth associate Cosell had a reputation for criticizing players, coaches, anyone. "Gee, Howard, nobody's perfect," Meredith liked to reply.

Even when the microphones weren't on, Cosell and Meredith parried, with play-by-play announcer Keith Jackson as the neutral middleman. During one commercial break, Cosell asked Meredith not to interrupt him when they returned to the air. "I'm sorry, Dr. Cosell," Meredith shot back. "I didn't get a Harvard education. Neither did most of our viewing audience." Following the break, they were all smiles on the air as they tossed insults at each other between their teeth, pure showtime.

"The charm of Meredith is, he comes on like a riverboat gambler with a heart of gold. He seems to have the lifestyle of a guy who expects to be shot any day by a guy he dealt aces to," affirmed Jim Murray of the *Los Angeles Times*. "What Dandy is doing in a broadcasting booth is something for Dallas, Texas, to account for, anyway. He was the best quarterback the Dallas Cowboys ever had and still could be." Ouch.

The drubbing by St. Louis in front of America's football nation appeared to hammer nails in the coffin. The Cowboys' record was 5-4, meaning the playoffs were out of reach unless they ran the table, which moved Bob St. John of the *Morning News* to write off Morton as "too much of an individualist to be a leader." He had already sized up this edition of the Cowboys as the worst since 1965. Bullet Bob Hayes was firing blanks. *Both* quarterbacks were hurting. The U.S. Army called up Cliff Harris, the standout rookie defensive back, for four months of active duty; his replacement was another rookie, Charlie Waters. Calvin Hill went down when he broke his leg.

The only escape from the physical and psychic slump was provided by a costume party that Lee Roy Jordan, Cornell Green, and several other players had organized before Halloween. Bobby Hayes came as a white rabbit and his wife, Altamese, was a Playboy bunny.

Lee Roy Jordan, Dan Reeves, and two other white players from the South came dressed in white hoods and robes with *KKK* on the backs. "I felt I needed some way to show the blacks on the team, especially those from the West Coast, that color meant nothing to this ol' Alabama boy," Jordan said. "All I wanted to do was play winning football. To show you how naive I was, I drove the fourteen-mile trip to the party in my costume and must have caused about eight wrecks along the way."

Blaine Nye, who had been moved from right guard to left guard, came as a big can of deodorant. The Cornell Greens were gypsies. The Mel Renfros arrived as witch doctors. The Jethro Pughs dressed as "Orientals." Larry Cole was the Jolly Green Giant; Ron Widby came as Frankenstein. Mike Clark dressed in drag and his wife dressed like a Cowboy player. Dave and Betty Manders came as a dog and a fire hydrant. Mike Ditka was Dracula and attempted to bite Joey Heatherton Rentzel's neck.

"We got on a roll after that," Jordan said. "That next week we had meetings and got talked out what we needed to talk out, that we needed to play better and we got it going."

"When we ended getting beat by St. Louis, hell, there wasn't anywhere else to go because nobody loved us," Dan Reeves said. "I think my wife didn't like us anymore. We were out of it, three games down with five games to play. That's where the leadership came in. Lee Roy, Bob, they said, if we're going to get it done, it's got to be us. No matter what the game plan is, no matter what happens, we've got to get it done."

The Cowboys went on to win five games in a row, despite the distracting arrest of Lance Rentzel before Thanksgiving. Rentzel, the playboy stud-monkey with the movie-star wife, had exposed himself to a ten-year-old girl while sitting in his car in front of a Catholic girls' school in the exclusive University Park neighborhood. Though he was a tough blocker and agile receiver who led the team in receptions the previous three seasons, his performance on the field had been almost overshadowed from the start by his man-about-town image and his marriage. He may have been one of the team's glamour players — handsome and charismatic — but he clearly had personal issues. He left the team and would be traded at the end of the season.

It turned out Rentzel had had a prior indecency incident in Minnesota. When Rentzel had returned to Minnesota with the Cowboys, a fan unfurled a sign referring to his indecent exposure before the game, but Tex Schramm spotted it and had it pulled down.

The University Park incident couldn't be hushed up, though, because the victim was the daughter of a prominent attorney. When the charges were made public, it became national news.

The team kept its focus. They dispatched the Cleveland Browns, 6–2, in a defensive struggle in Cleveland, removing the Browns jinx, rising to a 9-4 record, and moving Bob Lilly to crow, "This is the first time we've ever had a team. That's the great thing about the way we're playing now." Lee Roy Jordan chimed in. "We had to like each other. Nobody else liked us."

The Cowboys destroyed the Houston Oilers, 52–10, in the final game of the regular season, with Craig Morton lobbing five touchdown passes — four of them to the revived, renewed, and resuscitated Bob Hayes — but he had to totally rely on the Doomsday Defense, Mike Clark's field goal, and Herb Adderley's interception and runback into the red zone with less than a minute to play to beat the Detroit Lions 5–0 in a home playoff game for the champions representing the NFC East.

Asked after the game what impressed him most, Tom Landry managed a smile when he said, "Zero."

In the National Football Conference championship, the Cowboys beat San Francisco, coached by Dick Nolan, one of Landry's most talented assistants in the early years, by a touchdown, 17–10. It was also the final 49ers game played at Kezar Stadium in Golden Gate Park. Duane Thomas burned the 49ers D-line for 143 rushing yards. Walt Garrison broke three ribs in the first quarter and had to be carried off the field, only to return to rush for more than 100 yards. Lee Roy Jordan said the game ball should be sliced into forty pieces because the win was a team effort. Tex Schramm, brandishing a copy of the November 17 edition of the *San Francisco Examiner* with the headline "Cowboys Fold Early This Year," did not disagree.

Ten thousand fans were waiting for their Cowboys at Love Field when the team returned from San Francisco on their Braniff charter. Men cheered. Babies cried. Women fainted. One fan held a sign that read DUANE THOMAS FOR PRESIDENT.

They had finally reached the big game, Super Bowl V, the fifth championship game between the two former rival leagues. In a strange season where all hope had been abandoned in November and where neither Craig Morton nor Roger Staubach asserted himself as the superior quarterback, the Cowboys were heading to Miami's Orange Bowl.

Duane Thomas had stepped in and delivered when Walt Garrison was sidelined earlier in the season, then took over Calvin Hill's spot, rushing for 803 yards that season, averaging 5.3 yards per carry. Thomas's explosive combination of grace with power effectively led the team into the championship game. Walt Garrison proved almost as relentless despite several injuries, racking up 507 yards for the season.

The Cowboys rated. Gil Brandt hosted a big party for college coaches at the NCAA annual meeting in Houston and drew six hundred people, who devoured three hundred pounds of roast beef in less than three hours.

Braniff International added extra Dallas–Miami flights. The Taylor County sheriff's posse rode on horseback 184 miles from Abilene to Dallas, armed with an arrest warrant for Johnny Unitas, the Colts' QB, on their way to Miami.

The whole organization was giddy by the time they arrived in Florida. Clint Murchison sent a note to Tom Landry at the Galt Ocean Mile Hotel in Fort Lauderdale: *I have taught you all I can. From now on, you're on your own. Sincerely, Clint.*

Murchison paid for Salam Qureishi, the IBM computer guy that Clint had installed in his own company, Optimum Systems International, to come to Miami as his guest, putting him in a suite along with a couple other high-profile guests. "There was much drinking and lots of girls," Qureishi recalled.

Ten of the team's cheerleaders were flown in for the game, thanks to the largesse of millionaire bachelor and Dallas mayoral candidate Peter McGuire, who contributed $1,800 to get them to Miami.

Players, coaches, and friends of Clint were holed up at the hotel without their wives, per Landry and Schramm's mandate, unlike the Colts' wives, who were staying with their husbands, all expenses paid, as was noted by many significant others of Cowboys players. "We were not allowed to speak with our husbands," Betty Manders said. Annette Liscio complained directly to assistant general manager Al Ward. Her husband was traded the next season.

Before the game, team members voted to award a player's share for the Super Bowl to Rentzel, who had by now been indicted by a Dallas grand jury. Along with the active players on the roster, he would receive $15,000 if the Cowboys won and $7,500 if they lost.

Miami Herald columnist Edwin Pope depicted the Cowboys as the NFL's Peyton Place, suggesting they were the soap opera of the league with their star-crossed players and unusual coach. But when Pope described the owner as "a 130-pound former halfback at MIT," he went too far. The description moved Clint Murchison to write Pope a Dear Ed letter: "With reference to your recent column about the Dallas Cowboys, you're full of shit. I weigh 142 pounds."

The game needed little buildup. This was Doomsday versus Johnny U.—the Cowboys defense against the most storied quarterback in professional football. Fifteen-dollar tickets were selling on the street for a hundred dollars and more. But Duane Thomas put all the pomp and circumstance in perspective when he was asked how it felt to be in the ultimate game. "If this is the ultimate game," he softly replied to an inquiring reporter, "why are they playing another one next year?"

Tommy Loy was flown in to play his version of the national anthem, like he did before every game at the Cotton Bowl. And despite everyone's high hopes, bringing in Tommy Loy to do his trumpet solo of "The Star-Spangled Banner" was about the only thing the Cowboys did right.

The game became known as the Stupor Bowl and the Blunder Bowl for the sloppy play and poor execution of both teams, with eleven turnovers and penalties galore. The Cowboys defense held the Colts to 69 yards on the ground and 11-25-3 passing, forcing four fumbles. The few passes that were completed needed assists from the zebras. Johnny Unitas threw a 75-yard pass to Ed Hinton, who tipped the ball before it was caught by John Mackey. A field official ruled that Cowboys defender Mel Renfro had touched the ball too, which made Mackey eligible, only Renfro insisted he never got close to the ball. ("I didn't tip it," he would be saying two weeks later. "I was never so upset about a call in my life.") The Dallas D sent Unitas out of the game with cracked ribs. His replacement, the thirty-seven-year-old journeyman Earl Morrell, got plenty of help from game officials too, including a crucial call when Duane Thomas fumbled on the Colts one-yard line in the third quarter. Dave Manders held the ball at the bottom of the big pileup in the end zone, only to get hooked by a Baltimore lineman as he stood up. Baltimore cornerback Jim Duncan shouted, "I have it!," as he was peeled off the pile, and referee Jack Fette called a Baltimore recovery, costing the Cowboys the game. Bubba Smith of the Colts told his hometown paper in Beaumont that Dave Manders recovered it, but Billy Ray Smith screaming "Our ball! Our ball!" got the official's attention.

The Cowboys offense wasn't anything to crow about. Craig Morton went 12 for 26, distinguished by a short touchdown pass to Duane Thomas and tarnished by three interceptions. Danny Reeves dropped a pass that he should have held on to in the Colts end zone. Walt Garrison let a fourth-quarter pass slip through his fingers and be intercepted, which led to the Colts' only touchdown. The Colts went on to win in the final five seconds on Jim O'Brien's 32-yard field goal, 16–13, taking the Lombardi Trophy in the first year it had that name.

Bob Lilly threw his helmet sixty yards across the field in frustration. Duane Thomas sullenly told teammates after the game he was to blame for the fumble and for being held to 35 yards rushing. Dave

Manders fumed that he was robbed. More than one player privately muttered that if Meredith was running the offense, they would've won. Dan Reeves philosophized, "All losses are tough but the last-second field goal was really tough."

They'd lost, but Chuck Howley, who along with Lilly was the only remaining player from the 1961 squad, had been a one-man wrecking crew, intercepting two passes, recovering a fumble, and harassing Colts QB Johnny Unitas out of the lineup. Howley was honored with the most valuable player award, the first time a defensive player was recognized and the only time a member of the losing team had been cited.

Despite the team's disappointment over losing the last and most important game, getting to the Super Bowl brought a measure of satisfaction. Pettis Norman said he had never enjoyed the final weeks of a season like he had the one that had just ended. "It used to be, if you dropped a pass, you'd come back to the bench and thirty heads would turn away from you," he said. "Now you get everybody rushing up to you to tell you it's okay, forget it, don't worry about it. Catch the next one."

Bob Lilly witnessed a sea change after the 38–0 debacle against St. Louis. "The pressure was removed. It wasn't like you would want it to come off, but it was off. And we were written off. The next week we played a loose defensive game against Washington. As we won one or two more, our confidence started back. We weren't concerned about a championship until the Houston game. After the St. Louis game, [Landry] was still in control but let the assistants use more of their ideas. We started dealing with our own coach. To me, that's when Tom became head coach, assistants became assistants, and everyone knew where they stood."

Getting back would not be an issue.

"I wish next season started this week," Roger Staubach said with a sigh days after the Super Bowl. "I feel this way because I didn't get to play in the Super Bowl. I would have given anything to play in that game. Losing that game was just a killer for us. We're still a team that couldn't win the big game." He had asked to be traded but Craig Morton's shoulder surgery convinced Landry and Schramm to keep Staubach whether he started or not. Landry had chosen Craig Morton to start against Baltimore more as a reward for his running the team all season than anything else, even though Staubach seemed to provide the spark when the offense needed it.

Morton knew what it was like to walk in Don Meredith's shoes, exposed to the Boo-Birds. "I have come to realize the deep hurt and frustration that Don once felt and which may have put an early end to a great career," he said. "At first, I felt all the personal things that booing represents. I accepted them and made this rejection a personal challenge." To an extent. "I could never really accept being called the worst quarterback in football and receiving much of the criticism and blame for losses which in my mind weren't all my fault."

One way that Morton tried to deal with the criticism got him in hot water with the coach. Edward J. Pullman of the Southwest Hypnosis Research Center had developed a program for Morton, hypnotizing him over the phone on game days, which drew the ire of Tom Landry when he found out. "Obviously, it has its place or it wouldn't be used in medicine," the coach said. "But when my players start getting into it, that makes a different case. Morton was under tremendous pressure and I could see where something like that could help ease the pressure. But in a game like ours, I can't see that you could rely on it continuously. The way I see it, that may be all right if you have a problem. But once the problem is removed, it's no longer necessary."

The Cowboys' loss to the Colts left "more broken hearts and bitterness than, perhaps, the club has ever experienced," Bob St. John wrote in his wrap for the *Dallas Morning News*. But that didn't stop two hundred thousand fans from lining the streets of downtown Dallas and gathering in front of city hall to celebrate the home team.

And then came the letters. The NFL home office in New York

received more than five hundred complaints about the officiating, and many fans began advocating for instant replay. Videotape could freeze a shot or be rewound to review a play, something the television networks were beginning to do. Why not let officials review plays the same way? Dave Manders being cheated out of his fumble recovery with the world championship on the line did not need to be repeated.

"We had to play against sixteen men," defensive captain Lee Roy Jordan said at a January football banquet in Birmingham where Don Meredith was speaking. "One official made five or six calls against us himself. I was very upset with the officiating. In the second half, every time we broke up a pass or made a long gain on third down, I looked up and saw a flag."

Schramm was pushing for sudden-death overtime to eliminate ties in regular- season games, but he came up short. But Tex opposed using instant replay for officials because "the game would become a farce," he insisted. "You'd never finish a football game." But he was keeping an open mind. "The only practical advantage I see would be to have a set-up with three officials monitoring coverage of the sidelines. If you wanted to question pass interference and holding, things like that, I don't believe it'd be practical to run plays back a bunch of times. Sideline coverage is another matter. There's no judgment call there on whether a man has his feet in bounds. Look at the films and you'll see the officials are right at least 80 percent of the time. Another 10 percent is questionable. I think they do a great job considering they have to make decisions instantaneously and can't go back and look at films."

Technicalities were no excuse for losing the Super Bowl, no matter how much those in the Cowboys organization wished they could've changed the outcome. If the Cowboys wanted another chance, they'd just have to suck it up and win them all next season.

This Year's Champions in the Finest Football Facility in the World

SELF-EXAMINATION ON THE HEELS of defeat at the Super Bowl was quickly overshadowed by the players' increasingly busy social schedules. Duane Thomas appeared on Dick Cavett's television talk show in New York. Roger Staubach was appearing everywhere on behalf of the Fellowship of Christian Athletes, an organization he was already involved with before joining the Cowboys, and he was part of an all-star lineup, including Steeler quarterback Terry Bradshaw, Tom Landry, and Miss America Phyllis George, at Encounter '71 at Fort Worth's Travis Avenue Baptist Church. Similarly, evangelist James Robison featured Lee Roy Jordan at his Irving Crusade. "There is a simple solution to all our problems and that is belief in Jesus Christ," Robison testified. "I just wanted the people of Irving to know here is an athlete, parent, and businessman who makes God the center of his life."

The Rio Grande Valley town of Mission celebrated its native son with Tom Landry Day.

And a new crop of players added to the story lines too, including a lumpy, balding soccer player from Austria named Toni Fritsch, the latest Kicking Karavan acquisition, with whom Cowboys assistant Ernie Stautner communicated in German. Fritsch's sidewinder kickoffs and field-goal attempts would complement the efforts of Ron Widby, the punter from Tennessee who was an All-American basketball and football player and who had played pro hoops before joining the Cowboys.

Tex Schramm was trying to promote Craig Morton as the silent majority's Joe Namath.

Morton ran his own bar and restaurant and enjoyed the nightlife as much as Don Meredith had. In fact, several players now had their names attached to bars or restaurants. "Ditka and Edwards and a guy named the Dobber [Mike Dobber Stevenson] had a little place off of Lemmon Ave. called the Dirt Dobbers," said photographer Russ Russell. "When liquor by the drink and eighteen-year-olds were legalized, they put in a place over by Love Field [at 3121 Inwood Road] called the Sportspage. They were making more money out of that than they were playing football."

Craig Morton raised the ante when, along with two investors, Parks Bell and Billy Bob Harris, he opened Wellington's at 3120 Northwest Highway in the Bachman Lake area of singles apartments. The swinging joint featured the look of a San Francisco pad and became a hot spot overnight, loaded as it was with Dallas Cowboys and their friends. Patrons could watch *Monday Night Football* with Morton when he wasn't playing.

A Cowboy out in public couldn't buy a drink and had no trouble finding female companionship. Illegal substances were readily available. Dealers selling cocaine, which had become an illicit commodity of status, offered free lines of blow. If a Cowboy was snorting your stuff, it must be righteous.

Clint Murchison joined the restaurant game by opening his own restaurant in midtown Manhattan on East Forty-Ninth Street at Park Avenue called the Dallas Cowboys Chili Parlor—his other pet project besides the new football stadium about to open. Murk was inspired by the sudden closing of Toots Shor's, one of his regular New York hangouts, and by the *Dallas Morning News*'s Frank X. Tolbert, who was responsible for the concept of the chili cook-off, elevating the humble bowl of red into the state dish of Texas and a bone of contention.

Murchison one-upped Tolbert by flying in serious chili from El Nido restaurant, near Santa Fe, New Mexico, and having Sam Lobello oversee the barbecue, steaks, tamale pies, and three-dollar bowls. The joint opened with limos lined up around the block and ten thousand pounds of beef on hand. The new place, Murchison crowed, was doing more business than the 21 Club.

Around this time, Lamar Hunt passed along a letter to Murchison from an unhappy patron of the chili parlor, who had mistaken Hunt for that other football-club-owning, geeky-looking oil millionaire from Dallas.

Murchison wrote back: *Lamar, Didn't I tell you? Whenever someone comes into my New York restaurant and complains, I have instructed the maître d' to tell him that you are the owner. This way, I avoid a lot of crank letters.*

Murchison wasn't too far from the football, spearheading the effort to have the soon-to-open Texas Stadium in Irving host the 1972 Super Bowl game. The Dallas Chamber of Commerce and Lieutenant Governor Ben Barnes accompanied him to the NFL's annual winter meeting in Florida to make a presentation.

Bill Wallace of the *New York Times* thought it a terrible idea. He called Dallas "a dull, commercial town without a grain of sand or a palm tree or a temperature assuredly 50 degrees. The Super Bowl is an extravaganza, a joy which relates to a winter resort, no matter how plastic." Murchison's leverage with the other owners would be tested, and Wallace was hoping the other owners would prevail, writing, "Taking the glamour of the Super Bowl to Irving, Texas, is like wearing the Kohinoor diamond to a bowling alley."

Steve Perkins of the *Times Herald* read Wallace's article and wrote that it was clear the New Yorker had never been to the Longhorn Ballroom.

But even with Lamar Hunt letting it be known he favored Dallas, the owners voted to hold the game in New Orleans. The worm turned after Oakland's owner Al Davis stood up beforehand and said, "Wait a minute! What happens to this game if Dallas is the home team?" The New Orleans Saints were no threat to be in that position at the end of the regular season.

In addition to readying the new stadium, the Cowboys had opened a private, members-only facility just before the start of the 1970 season. The Cowboys Club, on the second floor of the Expressway Towers building, featured a lunch-buffet room, a full-service dining room, and a cocktail lounge, all stuffed with memorabilia for fans to better connect to their beloved team. Membership in the "Swinging Spot on Central," with its rich walnut doors and weekly team luncheons during football season, exceeded seven hundred by the end of the year.

IN THE WAKE OF the ultimate game, a former sportscaster broke the Dallas Citizens Charter Association's stranglehold on city politics. Wes Wise, an independent, was the first mayoral candidate to win without the endorsement of the invitation-only Dallas Citizens Council's political arm since the 1930s. Wise's gimmick was the Volkswagen Beetle that he drove. More significant was his willingness to build a coalition without the Dallas oligarchs. But most significant of all, Wise came into the election with a high profile due to his previous jobs as sports anchor on Channels 8 and 4. His election illustrated the rise of sports as part of Dallas culture more than it indicated the validation of outsiders. Sports mattered.

"There were times that I thought it's just not right that Dallas has been controlled by a certain group of very wealthy people for such a long time," explained Wise. "I knew I had the name identification from radio and TV, so I just decided to do it."

Clint Murchison congratulated the new Dallas mayor, writing him a note.

Dear Wes,
What I really like to see is an elected official without any obliga-
tions to the fat cats. Or to the skinny ones, for that matter.
Congratulations!

Wise was a game changer for Dallas, just like Murchison's football club, and neither Wise nor Murk minded saying so. "[My elec-
tion] was good for the city just as the Dallas Cowboys were good for
the city—to change that image," Wise declared.

Wise had already served one term as a city councilman and frequently locked horns with Mayor Erik Jonsson. Wise thought Jonsson's lack of desire to work with Murchison on a new stadium
downtown had been a mistake. "His big argument was [a new
downtown] stadium would be sitting empty for half of the year and
would be of no use during the offseason," Wise said, going on to
point out that stadiums host a variety of events.

"He was basically conservative and I was moderate," Wise said of
Jonsson. "By Dallas standards I would be considered as being too
liberal, although I've always considered myself as a moderate. The
unions would always support me and I always got the black vote
even though I'd have a black opponent."

From that perspective, too, Wise viewed the Cowboys' move to
Texas Stadium as a loss. "If it hadn't been for the blacks in the Cotton
Bowl area I don't think the Cowboys could have made it in those first
few years," observed Wise. "They supported the team tremendously.
But those people are being priced out of the situation now. They were
just not going to be able to afford to go to the Cowboys games."

For all the progress that had been made, race remained a source
of occasional friction for players, and a sore spot, if not a festering
wound, in the greater community. Mark Washington, a Cowboys
cornerback who would return a kickoff for 100 yards his rookie season, and his wife moved to Richardson, which was the edge of North
Dallas sprawl in 1970. The arrival of the only black couple in that

part of Richardson was exciting for kids who thought having a real Dallas Cowboy in the neighborhood was cool. Other residents were not so enthusiastic. Weeks after the Washingtons moved in, someone spray-painted graffiti on Arapaho Road that read: *This area is reserved for future ghetto.* The Washingtons moved out a few weeks later.

Roger Staubach had several sit-downs with black players addressing the subject. "They'd talk about their parents or grandparents, how they were treated, and it was horrendous," he said. "But as a team, we didn't really have conflict because of racial issues." His second year on the team, Staubach asked to room with an African American, Reggie Rucker, a rookie receiver from Boston University, something no white Cowboy player had requested before. "He and I worked out in the offseason together," explained Staubach, whose Christian values extended to "how you treat somebody else."

However Dallas was regarded racially, the team considered itself a model of harmony. The same year Dan Reeves joined the Cowboys, 1965, civil rights leader Dr. Martin Luther King Jr. was jailed in his hometown of Americus, Georgia, triggering race riots. Reeves had never played alongside black athletes before, but he adjusted quickly. "We'd go to team parties together, sit together, eat together, and socialize together. Heck, I'd go to Cleveland and St. Louis and, shoot, you could almost cut the tension in the room [between black and white players] with a knife. It was totally different in Dallas."

One of the surest signs that old hatreds were breaking down occurred during a practice shortly after Jethro Pugh's arrival. Lee Roy Jordan, the white linebacker from Alabama, noted Pugh's presence by shouting from the sidelines, "Hey, ref, throw your flag. His lips are offsides." The deliberate provocation was made in the name of camaraderie and building teamwork. No personal trait was off-limits in a locker room where guys got along, and Jordan's comments reminded older players of the time Don Perkins returned to the huddle after a grinding run with white chalk all over his face. "Well, boys, I guess I made it," he deadpanned.

In the midst of celebrating reaching the Super Bowl and gearing up for a return engagement to win it all, the unlikeliest star in the Cowboy firmament, Duane Thomas, should have been the Cowboys' local hero. He was from Dallas, all right, but he'd grown up on Baldwin Street, the wrong side of the tracks as far as proper Dallasites were concerned, had the wrong kind of habits, and had the wrong color of skin to be a full-blown star.

Actually, Thomas was unlike any other player on the roster, black or white. He was beyond good as a player, but he was not to be confused with Calvin Hill, a Perkins School of Theology divinity student, as a role model. He was a space cowboy in addition to being African American, and that made him dangerous. He smoked pot like Pete Gent and Don Meredith and others had done and sampled his share of coke like Bullet Bob was notorious for doing. He was no stranger to psychedelic drugs and had been sighted at the Armadillo World Headquarters music hall in Austin scoring mescaline. His hair was wild, neither trimmed nor sculpted, and whatever he had to say was stated spontaneously.

When he had something to say, that is.

Before training camp in the summer of 1971, Thomas announced that he wanted to renegotiate his contract with the Cowboys. He had had the best season rushing of any Cowboy running back since Don Perkins and was named Rookie of the Year by the *Sporting News*. He also had a wife and a family and a string of bad debts, along with some lousy investments, that demanded his renegotiating a three-year contract that paid $20,000 a year.

Tex Schramm told Thomas, "I didn't renegotiate Calvin Hill's contract after his rookie year."

"But I'm not Calvin Hill," Thomas replied nonchalantly.

So he retired. "I decided I couldn't stand the strain, the hassle any longer," Thomas said at the time. "I'll get a job, but at least I'll stay sane, I love the game, the playing, but I can't stand the hassle with people who are supposed to be fair to you."

A few days later, Duane Thomas called a press conference back in Dallas, demanding an $80,000 base salary plus incentives. "They never made the Super Bowl until I got there and I don't think they will again if they don't get me," he insisted. "The problem is I'm black," Thomas said. "If I was white it would have been totally different. They would have done me justice. A revolution is coming in pro football. Players like me are tired of being on our knees all the time. I want equality. I've stated my position and they know what I want."

Tex Schramm, Duane Thomas said, was "sick and demented" and "totally dishonest." ("Two out of three ain't bad," Schramm responded.) Landry was worse. "He's a plastic man," Thomas said, before adding, "actually no man at all."

Gil Brandt was a liar in Thomas's eyes. "I thought Gil was trying to help me, but every time Gil went to help me, he curved me, and I wound up worse than before," complained Thomas. "I don't want to go around smiling in the public's face while I carry around the feeling that I've been took. When I smile, I want to mean it. Nobody in the office cares what happens to the players. They look at you not as a person, but as a specimen. It's all business, the dotted line. Then you get in the season and you're supposed to be one big happy family. I'll probably get me a job and go to school."

Brandt was defensive. "He doesn't elaborate on anything," he said of Thomas. "I hope someday he'll enlighten me what he means. I'd like to know more about it." Brandt said he gave Thomas a car to drive around and gas money, and that the team held seminars after the Super Bowl on finances, real estate, investments, and taxes that Duane didn't attend.

"If he had a lot of money, I'd sue him," groused Brandt.

"I really have no comment regarding what he called me," Tom Landry said of Duane Thomas's disrespect. "That's his opinion and the way he feels. I've always gotten along fine with Duane and always thought a lot about him. I know he came up the tough way and in a tough environment and doesn't seem to accept anybody helping him.

255

As far as black players being treated badly, I know what I feel and to me there is no difference...no difference in my eyes. If there is a difference then it's on their side, not mine.

"We've equated Duane with Calvin and [Jim] Brown because they were great runners. Calvin was as a rookie and Brown was throughout his career. We have not done this because he is black, but because Duane, too, is a great runner. Obviously, Duane is angry and that may have something to do with what he's saying."

Bob Hayes defended Landry. "I don't think anyone on the team has had more differences with Tom Landry than me. But I respect him. I don't give a damn, black or white, that cat is a good coach and a good man."

Schramm said Thomas's contract status was unchanged and that "he is in violation of that contract every day he is not in camp."

The resentment inside Thomas built up. "Tex Schramm gonna tell me I ought to be happy to be a Cowboy," Thomas complained privately. "I say I *am* the fucking Cowboys, ain't nobody coming to see your ass. He's sitting up there, pontificating like you have some celestial white light beaming up your ass. And thinking it's all about you, that you put this team together. You ain't done nothing."

Letters to both newspapers ran strongly against Thomas, calling him a prima donna, calling him spoiled for complaining about his salary, saying he was undisciplined and a kook. Pete Rozelle called Thomas's complaint "an unhealthy thing" and invoked the gag rule stating that players couldn't criticize their coaches or the front office.

Still, the huffing and puffing of Schramm and Brandt couldn't cover up what everyone knew. Dallas was the Jack Benny of NFL franchises. "The book on Dallas," wrote Los Angeles sportswriter Mel Durslag, "is that it offers the good Christian life instead of money."

Duane Thomas didn't stop with the press conference. In an interview with Channel 4's Dick Risenhoover, who'd known Duane from his West Texas State college days, the running back unloaded. On Landry, he said, "We were talking and he was saying, 'Duane, I can show you the way of life.' And I say, 'Really?' I look at Tom Landry going around giving overdoses of mis-used Christianity, going around on his football trips, that is what he really believes in, so therefore, to me Tom Landry believes in an idol God, see, because he really believes that, hey, that he'd be doing the right thing. He really believes that, hey, that people want him to act like that, never knowing that, hey, people looking at him like he's crazy, you know, being different, which he is, you know, he's very different. He's very strange, but he doesn't like for people to question him. You see, and he goes around ego-tripping, never realizing that, hey, man, [you're] just like us. Why don't you come down, hey, and be down to earth with us, hey, and stop trying to jive us, hey, or stop trying to get us hung up on all these technical words because like they don't mean nothing, you know, like they don't mean a thing."

When Thomas finally showed up for training camp in Thousand Oaks, he was accompanied by an African dashiki–wearing gentleman named Ali Khabir, the former Melvin Collins. "The only reason I could come back is for my people—the black people," Thomas said after emerging from the limo. Khabir, allegedly the minister of a church in Watts, refused to shake Landry's hand, to which the coach responded, "That's fine with me!"

Thomas, who had been staying at the great running back Jim Brown's house in Los Angeles, where Brown was pursuing an acting career, wanted Khabir to get a tryout with the Cowboys and be his roomie. Tex Schramm, the tightest man in training camp, turned down both requests. "That was one of the most unusual things I've ever experienced," Schramm said. "Nobody had any idea where Duane was and suddenly he's there with this guy in a long robe. The two just stared at me. I wasn't sure whether to bow or run. We refused the tryout and they left again."

Tex Schramm concluded Thomas was messed up. "Duane had a lot of emotional problems," he said. Blackie Sherrod agreed. He wrote that Thomas "marches to his own drum; he hears music nobody else can hear." Many assistant coaches and management types were convinced Thomas was high on some kind of drug they'd never heard of, but drug testing was not required of athletes at the time. "He was just out of control," Schramm said, ignoring Thomas's contention it was all about the contract.

One of Thomas's South Dallas neighbors when Thomas was growing up, the entertainer Bobby Patterson, saw it differently: Duane took on any dare that came his way. "Whatever it was, he'd do it, and do it without fear."

Trying to extinguish what appeared to be a four-alarm fire, Schramm worked out a trade with the newly renamed New England Patriots to send Thomas and two other players in exchange for running back Carl Garrett and a first-round draft pick. The Cowboys had already sent linebacker Steve Kiner, the hippie from Tennessee who had been Duane Thomas's roommate, to New England.

Garrett reported to Thousand Oaks and Thomas reported to the Patriots camp in the Northeast. He lasted one day at camp. He refused to take a physical, and then, during offensive drills, Coach John Mazur told Thomas to get down in a three-point stance with his hand on the ground.

"Well, in Dallas, they taught us how to get down in a stance like this with both hands on the knees," Thomas told the coach. "That way we could see the linebackers better."

"Well, here we do it my way in a three-point stance," Mazur instructed him.

"Maybe so," Thomas replied. "But I'm doing it my way."

"No, you're not," Mazur said, steaming. "You're going to get out of here right now. Get the hell in the locker room!" Thomas said Mazur was "standing there like Hitler."

Thomas's ex-roomie Steve Kiner tried to back him up, saying, "Duane just doesn't know what he wants. He hasn't changed since he was with Dallas. He wanted to do things his own way there. The coaches would tell him something in practice and he wouldn't listen. When Sunday came, though, he was all football player."

He was back on the Dallas roster the next day, anyway. Pete Rozelle nullified the trade, and Thomas resumed his contract holdout.

The contract talk subsided amid the growing buzz about the glittery new palace where the football team was going to perform. Texas Stadium was finally built, and the Greater Southwest Billy Graham Crusade staged ten days of spiritual mass-gatherings to christen it, beginning September 17. The Graham crusade's chairman, Tom Landry, was on hand for the inaugural night, as were former president Lyndon Johnson and Lady Bird Johnson and the singers Johnny and June Cash.

"What a beautiful stadium this is!" Graham declared to the gathering in his dynamic preacher's voice, gushing over the $35 million physical plant and its $1.5 million scoreboard with 9,000 light bulbs operated by an IBM 1130 computer that could display messages, slides, or even animation.

The former president and his wife, the king and queen of country music, and the only coach the Cowboys had ever had were joined by another dignitary recognized by Brother Graham. "Tonight we have on the platform the man that is responsible for this beautiful stadium and responsible for the Cowboys, Mr. Clint Murchison," Graham said under drizzly skies. "I want him to stand and let's welcome him. This is his first night and it happens to rain on his first night. Someday I'm going to get courage enough to ask him why he left that hole up there, and I think I know. Somebody told me that Clint Murchison said that football is supposed to be an outdoor game and so he left that hole up there. And the fellows that are right out in the center are going to be in whatever kind of weather it is, but the other people are going to be comfortable. What a wonderful stadium!"

Graham continued with a weather report. "In fact, to you who are watching by television, it's been raining here in Texas for the last two days. And tonight, in spite of the weather, there are 43,000 people here. I don't know what kind of crowd this would have been, had we had good weather. But this is a tremendous stadium. It is two-thirds filled tonight. The Cowboys will be playing here very soon, and Tom Landry will be walking back and forth as he normally does during a game and we'll be watching."

Over nine hundred attendees came forward to give their lives to Christ that night.

While Billy Graham was saving souls, the Dallas Cowboys were launching their 1971 campaign still mired in quarterback controversy. Coach Landry couldn't split hairs, although he finally admitted his indecision could not continue. "We won't go through this next season," he promised as the current season got under way. "It will be resolved before then." Roger Staubach was antsy, demanding either to start or to be traded, even though he knew the score. "I think we were that evenly matched," he said after the fact. "I think the other coaches told him, you've got to have one quarterback, one starting quarterback. It divides the team."

Even after Staubach threw five bombs against Baltimore and beat them 27–14 to close out the exhibition preseason with a perfect 5 and 0 record, Landry ordered the resumption of shuffling QBs.

Don Meredith, former professional quarterback and now widely known national sports broadcaster, did not hold back when he told Sam Blair, "Landry's responsibility as a head coach is to pick a quarterback and in my opinion, it's his responsibility to go with him. Now, after he has spent this long with them he doesn't have any idea which one is best, then get another goddam coach."

Don Perkins chimed in at a March of Dimes fund-raiser. "I don't like it. It's like ten men working together and a messenger. There is more cohesion with eleven people staying intact. I think the QBs want to call their own plays and as pros they should. The situation with the team is different now than in '62. We had nothing going then and we were willing to try anything to win a football game. Now the situation is reversed. Dallas has good personnel. Tom is very stubborn. If he thinks this is the best way, he will stick to it, no matter what."

Frank Luksa of the *Star-Telegram* found Landry difficult to fathom, gently complaining that "like the Loch Ness monster, his emotions aren't available for public scrutiny." Landry was playing hunches, Luksa speculated, like a poker player who had drawn two pairs.

Tom Landry, impassively cool, always dapper in his hats and formal game wear, and as physically fit and disciplined as any of his charges, was a paragon of the Protestant work ethic both on and off the field. He was also an enigma when it came to communicating. His aloofness could easily have been mistaken for what is today called Asperger's syndrome if he wasn't such a high-profile figure. Off the field, he seemed pleasant enough and comfortable with small talk. But once his coaching hat was on, an impenetrable firewall went up around him.

Landry's assistant coaches, especially the younger ones, like the player-coaches Mike Ditka, Jerry Tubbs, and Dan Reeves, became the conduits for messages. Roger Staubach could go to Dan Reeves, someone closer to his own age and attitude, and ask him to relay information to Landry without subjecting himself to unneeded criticism from Coach.

"You were kind of a sounding block for a lot of people who if they had any frustrations could share them with you, and you could talk to Coach Landry about them, and get things done," Reeves said. "There wasn't a lot of that went on. There weren't a lot of disgruntled players. The biggest thing, I think, was as a player you never make as much money as you think you should."

The assistants, especially a player-coach like Reeves, walked a fine line. "Probably the toughest part was learning to keep things to yourself," Reeves said. "I knew a lot of things that were going on in the coaches' meetings that I couldn't share with players and a lot of things that players were complaining about that I couldn't share with coaches.

I might tell Walt [Garrison], but he'd be the only one. If you told too many people then all of a sudden something that nobody was supposed to know would get out. You had to keep your mouth shut."

"Landry was a great man, a great football player, a great coach, and a great Christian but he was also almost on another plane of thinking," observed team photographer Russ Russell. "I don't know how to say it . . . I never at a game heard Landry say anything except I should have done this at that time, or I should have done that, I think we could have won the game if I had done this. He never said Ditka, or the special teams coach."

"If you ever spent a lot of time listening to him, when he'd start recapping a game he would talk about the quarterback in the first person," observed writer Carlton Stowers. "Every once in a while he'd slip into, 'I threw to Drew going down the sidelines.' I think Landry always felt like if the guy on the field would do it the way he drew it up and the way he told them to do it, every play would be touchdown."

Roger Staubach thought he'd come close enough to Landry's ideal that he was still steamed about not playing in the Super Bowl game with the Colts, and he was more determined than ever to start or be traded to a team where he could start, such as Kansas City.

But off the field, Staubach was the more determined hustler out of necessity, eschewing the celebrity-restaurant route for insurance as a path to additional income. "We had three kids," he said. "If something happened, if I got hurt, I had to have a [another] livelihood. I had an engineering degree, a BS, and that's pretty much what I was." So he joined the Henry S. Miller Company, a real estate firm with an insurance wing, selling insurance on commission. "The commission thing made sense because I wanted to have the freedom to go out and work out every day," Staubach said. "During the season I wasn't going to go down to an office or anything. I was a football player. It was perfect." He moved to real estate management within the year. And found time to become the spokesman for the Hemophilia Foundation. And accepted as many speaking engagements in front of high school football teams, Boy Scouts, church groups, and civic groups as humanly possible.

Morton's investments in a bookstore near the campus of his alma mater, the University of California at Berkeley, and two sporting goods stores in Davis, California, were bleeding money so severely he was forced to declare bankruptcy. Among his debtors was the Dallas Cowboys Football Club, to whom he owed $50,000.

After Staubach separated his shoulder in an exhibition game, it was back to the same old, same old. Morton started the season as the Cowboys' number-one quarterback and told everyone around him he intended to keep the job. Staubach was champing at the bit to heal up and get back to competing.

THE 1971 CAMPAIGN OPENED on the road at Buffalo minus running back Duane Thomas, who still refused to play unless he got a new contract, and with Morton going all the way at the helm, throwing 10 for 14 and two touchdowns to outrun Buffalo, 49–37. The team stayed on the road to roll Philadelphia 42–7, but Morton sputtered the following week against the Redskins in the home opener, which was played in the Cotton Bowl because Texas Stadium wasn't yet ready for football, and was replaced by Staubach, who threw 6 for 9 but fell short in a comeback attempt, losing 20–16. The Cowboys had the *Monday Night Football* slot for the following week but Texas Stadium was still not finished, so the Cotton Bowl again was the home venue, this time for a 20–13 win over the New York Giants.

Before the broadcast, Howard Cosell, the acerbic East Coast–accented wise guy on *Monday Night Football* and Don Meredith's foil, spoke at a special noon luncheon in front of seven hundred Cowboy fans. Cosell was much despised in middle America, but he was directly responsible for Don Meredith's rising star as a television personality.

It had taken two years for Meredith to reach his real TV prime — one year to chill and divorce Chigger King and another to reemerge on ABC's *Monday Night Football*. The role was originally created for Frank Gifford, the handsome former running back for the New York Giants and Meredith's longtime friend, who had already transitioned into broadcasting. But when Gifford couldn't get out of his existing contract with CBS, he recommended Meredith.

Monday Night Football presented Meredith as the likable, drawling good ol' boy who had the advantage of being the one guy in the booth who had actually played the game, knew the pain, and had the nerve to get away with declaring the victor before the final gun whenever he crooned the "turn out the lights" line from Willie Nelson's song "The Party's Over."

Meredith spoke to a lot of the heartland when he verbally sparred with Cosell. For 1971, Keith Jackson was replaced by Frank Gifford, and the pheromones created by the chemistry that the three cooked up grew even more irresistible, with Meredith winning an Emmy Award for excellence in television sportscasting.

Meredith remained the consummate hipster, Mr. Cool Daddy, if ever there had been one on the team. Stoney Burns, the publisher of Dallas's *Notes from the Underground* alternative newspaper, once ran into Meredith on the street in North Dallas and, taking note of the beads around his turtleneck sweater and his hair curling over his collar, approached him to ask, "Are you a hippie?"

"Could be," Meredith said, shooting him a smile and a twinkle of the eyes. Retired, Meredith didn't bother holding back, showing up at the Armadillo in Austin in the company of Bud Shrake. The hall was in the process of being shut down by the liquor control board when the two agents spied Meredith and turned to putty. The Armadillo's Bobby Hedderman quickly grabbed an old Texas School of the Deaf basketball trophy out of the basement, and Eddie Wilson, the Armadillo's trail boss, made an impromptu presentation of the award on the stage of the hall while the band playing took a break. Meredith didn't quite know what to do but played along. When Wilson made the trophy presentation on the stage, Meredith stared blankly at the small audience. "You may not know it," he said to the crowd, breaking into that winning grin, "but this is what I always wanted." The liquor agents left with autographs, and the Armadillo stayed open.

TEXAS STADIUM ITSELF finally officially opened on October 24, 1971. A full house of 65,708 fans braved traffic jams, parked more than a mile from the stadium, and jumped fences and freeway medians to watch the home team do battle with the New England Patriots, consuming seventy-five thousand soft drinks and thirty thousand hot dogs (a state record) along the way.

The hole in the roof, a two-and-a-half-acre void above the field, appeared to be the signature element of the giant facility. But the sports world and general public were busy gossiping about the Circle Suites, the exclusive ring of upper-class seating where the owners of the 176 private boxes had instant replay and closed-circuit television and "256 square feet of personal privacy and prestige," as Blackie Sherrod wrote, with ideal views of what he called "the Hot Pants Parade."

Each suite had two rows of six comfortable seats, three televisions, and a wet bar. Bedford Wynne served crepes in his suite that were heated in a microwave oven. The El Chico restaurant suite doled out pink papaya daiquiris. Caviar was a popular hors d'oeuvre.

A zebra rug adorned the floor of the W. C. Boedecker/Jack Burrell box. Braniff International's suite featured a marble entry. The National Bank of Commerce embraced the look of an English pub. Frederic Wagner and J. L. Williams went for a Louis XIV court style with blue velvet drapes and couch, shag carpet, mirrored walls, and a crystal chandelier. The Miller family went with a Grecian theme along with a chandelier. Bud Shrake, writing for *Sports Illustrated*, described the various suites' décor as Ranch-House Plush, Neiman-Marcus Mod, Las Vegas Traditional, Psychedelic Flash, Molded Plastic Futurama, and Tahitian Fantasy.

Defensive end Pat Toomay dubbed the suites' occupants the Romans.

"The new stadium was surgical," Toomay explained. "It was austere and the concrete made it very cold, and the Romans were up there in their suites. It was like we were an adjunct to whatever they were doing. It was so gladiatorial. The distance and the abstractness of watching these men run around on this billiard table was highly ritualized. You had to see it in a different way because you were so far removed that you couldn't see the piss and blood or smell the fear."

The suites were worlds away from the boisterous heathen crowds formerly associated with the physical game. Men dressed in suits and ties. Women went semiformal, with a disproportionate number of minks, considering the temperate climate. The occupants amused themselves playing bridge, quaffing drinks, and ordering snacks from their private waiters, and eyeing the action in other suites. Each suite's caterer became a matter of name-dropping one-upmanship.

Don Meredith noted the mixed response to the suites and the stadium, which "some people describe as the finest facility in football and others call a vulgar display of wealth," he said. Both were considered attributes in Texas.

Outsiders could have dismissed Clint's description of the stadium as "football's finest facility" as so much bluster. But it was true. Most new stadiums, including the much-ballyhooed Astrodome, were built as multipurpose facilities to accommodate baseball and football both. Clint built his place for football, and as such, it became the first pro football facility that acknowledged the game's ascent to America's favorite pastime.

The home-team bench was moved across the field, opposite the press box. That way, the Cowboys would be facing the overhead cameras instead of showing their backs. And as advertised, the stadium was partly covered, protecting spectators but leaving a hole over the field so weather could still be a factor in the game. At least, that's what Murchison told the press, conveniently ignoring the natural element of grass in favor of his new Tartan Turf carpet as a playing surface, which was so hard and so slick, visiting and home players complained from the get-go.

In truth, Murchison had originally envisioned a breezy facility not unlike the open-air beach resorts he frequented in Mexico or his own Spanish Cay in the Bahamas, because he'd determined the cost of air-conditioning the stadium was prohibitive. But as the facility took shape, more private suites were added, closing off the upper rim and reducing ventilation, while the machinery designed to open and close a roof was discovered to be too heavy for the roof girders to support and too expensive to install. So instead of a breezy stadium, Murchison designed a huge hot plate. Dick Hitt of the *Times Herald* couldn't help himself and called Clint's creation the "Half-Astrodome."

Except that the Astrodome couldn't brag about having eighty-five restrooms, carpeted locker rooms, a hundred and twenty-five blond and brunette usherettes dressed in miniskirts and heels, and parking-lot attendants from charm school.

"We gave up the shoeshine boy for the lawyer when we moved," observed Jethro Pugh. They gained the midlevel manager. "[Cowboys games] became a big corporate, more upscale deal," David Wynne said. "If you had a box at Texas Stadium, you were somebody."

Many of those somebodies were so refined, they didn't know how to cheer, which explained how the atmosphere went back ten years, from electric to staid, in one home game.

ALL THE COLUMN INCHES, quarter-hours, and watercooler talk about Texas Stadium and the football team's owner ignored the bigger news: the football team on its field was jelling into the best in the game.

Three games into the season, Duane Thomas, having no other option and needing money bad, reported to the Dallas Cowboys, just in time to see the starting running back, Calvin Hill, go on the injury list with a strained knee. Thomas started the sixth game for the home team with the 3-2 record—the Texas Stadium inaugural. After opening ceremonies featuring the Tyler Junior College Apache Belles and the Monahans Loboes marching band, the Dallas native ran crazy. Less than three minutes had expired on the clock when Thomas broke out on a 56-yard dash to the end zone, putting up the first Cowboys points on the million-dollar scoreboard.

Witnesses included LBJ and Lady Bird; another former first lady, Mamie Eisenhower; and Lieutenant Governor Ben Barnes, all guests in the owner's suite. Another thousand "Romans," including county judge Lew Sterrett and Dallas mayor Wes Wise, watched from the Circle Suites, along with 64,000 other fans. Roger Staubach went 13 for 21 passing, throwing two TDs to Bobby Hayes and running for another. The performance and the 44–21 victory suggested the quarterback controversy was clarifying. "It was a nice way to break in the new stadium," the coach said.

Duane Thomas did not speak after the game. No matter how well he performed on the field, Thomas had nothing to say. He had decided to do what he'd done when he was at West Texas State and take a vow of silence. That way he could concentrate on the task at hand without distraction; at least, that's how he thought about it. "I had certain resistance about West Texas but once I got out there, I started realizing what I had, and that was the isolation," he later explained. "I could focus. That's what West Texas really provides." His *omertà* proved disruptive, though, mainly because the Cowboys publicity machine required players to accommodate the media. Plus, Dallas wasn't West Texas, and the glare of the lights on Thomas wasn't about to dim. Within weeks of his last statement to a reporter—"Haven't you ever felt like not saying anything?"—sportswriters covering the Cowboys had nicknamed Thomas the Sphinx and were questioning his mental stability.

Duane Thomas excelled on the field but was more determined than ever to be his own man off. He flouted Landry's team rules mandating players wear coats and ties when they traveled, a dress code that spoke to the pride of being a Dallas Cowboy in public. Duane chose to wear his shirt untucked and flipped his tie over his shoulder. He favored a toboggan cap, which he pulled over his eyes. He wouldn't answer during roll call at practices, which frustrated Dan Reeves, the former halfback who had become an assistant coach, and who continued calling out, "Duane... Duane... Duane."

"He sees me," Thomas muttered to another player while continuing to refuse to answer. "He knows I'm here." Coaches got no more than a head shake from the man whose name they were calling.

"He wouldn't say a word, he wouldn't answer questions when you asked him a question," Reeves later said. "It was just miserable, miserable. It's no fun coaching a guy who won't open his mouth. I'd be in the meetings with the running backs and we'd be watching film. 'Okay, Walt, what do you do on this play, now you got this defense, what are you concerned about?' Walt answered. 'Duane. Okay what about this defense right here? They're running a blitz right here, what is your concern?' Nothing."

After Thomas got clocked on a running play against New Orleans and was taken out of the game, Jethro Pugh came up to him to ask, "How's the leg?"

Thomas sent him a mean look and said, "Are you a doctor?"

"Fuck you, man," Pugh shot back, shoving Thomas as he did.

He spared almost no one. When Calvin Hill returned to the active roster, Dan Reeves wanted Thomas to try playing fullback, which Thomas refused to do. Urged by Roger Staubach to reconsider, Thomas replied, "You shut up."

"It was unusual," Staubach said with understatement. "He played extremely well on the field, he was a very smart guy and he knew his job and he knew his formations. It was just off the field he was not communicating."

Thomas made an exception for one of his blocking linemen, Tony Liscio, who returned to the team in November. "For some reason, he respected me for coming out," Liscio said. "He would talk to me. He wouldn't talk to nobody else. I didn't have much to say to him. He would say, 'Nice block,' things like that. He was a thinker. He seemed like a pretty intelligent guy."

Landry had no choice but to tolerate Duane the Insane because every time he got the ball he was Jim Brown reincarnate, wiggling and weaving through a secondary with ballet-like grace that disguised his brute power.

Duane Thomas was clearly a badass, and the man who was handing the ball off to Duane Thomas more and more frequently was his polar opposite. Roger Staubach—Navy grad, Vietnam vet, man of deep and abiding faith—was a straight arrow. He also knew how to win.

He was becoming the kind of player Tom Landry had been looking for to lead his system ever since he'd drawn up his first playbook, although Staubach sometimes gambled and scrambled too much for Landry's liking. "He did not believe quarterbacks should run and he told me that time and time again—'Hey, Staubach, you're going to learn someday. Your job is to throw the football.' So I definitely went against his philosophy of what a quarterback should do," Staubach said.

His coach preferred his going by the playbook. "In the long run, it doesn't pay off," Landry said of Staubach's scrambles. "He has to stop running. We don't want him to run. When he gets more experience, he won't run." A few weeks later, Landry emended his analysis: no one else could scramble like Roger the Dodger. "He's going to run, but he can't tuck his head in against those big linemen."

Before his first shoulder separation, Craig Morton had one of the best arms in football, passing with nearly an 80 percent completion rate over one season. But Coach Landry had started seeing a drop-off in accuracy and a little too much Don Meredith. Craig Morton started the first three games at QB, throwing two interceptions along with two touchdowns in the second win, then failing to score a touchdown the first three quarters of the third game against Washington. Landry finally put in Staubach, who went 6-9 but threw no touchdowns in the Cowboys' 20–16 defeat. "I knew that I could be his starting quarterback," Staubach said. "I was going to get a real chance. That's the first time I felt like I was the Cowboy quarterback."

Landry alternated Morton with Staubach in the next three games, until Morton threw three interceptions in the team's 23–19 loss to Chicago, their third of the season. From there, Staubach started every game.

Tex Schramm couldn't have dreamed up a better representative of the Dallas Cowboys product. Staubach was ruggedly handsome with smoldering eyes and curly hair, as well as a devout Catholic with a tireless work ethic who was married to his childhood sweetheart, Marianne Hoobler. He was the all-American hero, a paragon of virtue, and right behind Landry on the all-star God squad. He took pride in being square. "I have values I believe in," he said. "I believe in Christian principles, being faithful to my wife, caring about people. I don't try to be anything. But if that's square, that's my life. I enjoy my Christian ideals. I believe there's something greater than what we're here for. From what I understand, every pass up there is a touchdown. They don't have any defensive backs up there."

He was fond of saying, "God has given us good field position in the game of life, but you've got to have goals. Not just sports goals or immediate goals but eternal goals."

He enjoyed sex as much as Joe Namath, he publicly confided to former Miss America and born-again Christian Phyllis George in a television interview. "Only I do it with one girl. It's still fun." And he was down on dope. "I can see a situation where [if] somebody is feeling depressed he might try drugs," he acknowledged. "But I've never found drugs necessary. I'm adamant about drugs. I'm against marijuana."

Staubach's embrace of the square was in pointed contrast to Craig Morton and many of his teammates with reputations as party animals on the prowl, ready to boink a pretty gal at any opportunity. Official Dallas may have been straitlaced, but unofficial Dallas was hedonism unleashed, where scenes involving sticking amyl nitrite poppers up the nose, smoking weed, and leaning over a mirror to inhale lines of powdered cocaine at parties made the old-guard playboys like Don Meredith and Pete Gent seem like lightweights.

Meredith was half expecting Staubach to adapt. "There's one thing he's gonna have to learn," he joked. "He needs to know an NFL quarterback is a different breed of cat. He needs to start smoking, drinking, things like that if he's gonna live up to the image."

The jury was still out. Staubach was still trading places week by week with Morton in the Oak Farms Send Your Favorite Cowboy to Hawaii contest.

With a marginal 4-3 record after the Chicago launch, Landry's public decision to go with Staubach resulted in a road win at St. Louis and a 20–7 rout of Philadelphia in the second home game played at Texas Stadium, during which Staubach scrambled and rushed for 90 yards. "Really, I'd much rather stay in the pocket and pass," Staubach said afterward. "That's what I'm supposed to do. But there were times today I felt I had to run. I really don't enjoy getting out there and having people taking shots at me, but Philadelphia is a very physical team and they put a lot of pressure on me." Staubach followed up with another solid outing against the Washington Redskins, completing 11 of 21 attempted passes and scrambling for 49 yards, including a 29-yard improvised run for a touchdown. Blackie Sherrod observed that Staubach's running pleased everyone but the coach, "who wishes very much for a deer rifle and a telescopic sight every time his quarterback runs with the ball." The Washington game had been pumped up by President Nixon, who admitted he was an unabashed 'Skins supporter, which made him a sworn enemy of the Dallas Cowboys. "I hated to go against the President," Tom Landry said after the game, "because he's my man."

Then Duane Thomas and a healed-up Calvin Hill both played halfback in a reconfigured offense that waxed the New York Jets and

Joe Namath, 52–10, along with anyone else that got in their way. Craig Morton even came off the bench to throw a touchdown. Everyone stepped up. Lance Alworth, acquired from the San Diego Chargers, racked up more than 1,000 yards in pass receptions for the season, while Walt Garrison was setting records for receptions among Cowboys backs. Tony Liscio, who had retired the year before, after he'd been traded to San Diego for Lance Alworth, unretired to step in at left tackle. Ralph Neely's season had ended in November when he wrecked his motorcycle and broke his leg, tearing ligaments and dislocating his ankle. Don Talbert had broken a bone in his foot, and Forrest Gregg, the former Packer lineman, had a groin pull, so Landry called Liscio to ask him to return.

Liscio said yes, figuring if he made three games on the injured reserve list, his pension would bump up considerably. Although he hadn't played for a year, Liscio picked up where he'd left off.

Bob Lilly, Rayfield Wright, John Niland, and Chuck Howley were all enjoying outstanding years too, as was Herb Adderley, the All-Pro defensive back from Green Bay—the Cowboys' nemesis—who had been obtained in a trade, with six interceptions to his credit.

Duane Thomas continued to maintain his silence while being advised by Jim Brown, who had been marginalized by the league and front-office officials once he got out of football, largely for his staunch advocacy of black pride for African Americans. Brown himself had talked to Tex Schramm when Thomas returned to the team and had made it clear Thomas would fulfill his contract and "do no more." Schramm delicately opined that Brown's attitude "was certainly not of a constructive nature."

Still, Thomas did not stop running, scoring four touchdowns against St. Louis in the regular-season finale to match Hill's own four-touchdown game earlier in the season; Staubach passed and ran with confidence; and Doomsday held fast.

On Christmas Day at Metropolitan Stadium in Bloomington,

Minnesota, the Cowboys beat the Vikings 20–12 by forcing five turnovers, including a game-killing interception by Cliff Harris. The game-time temperature of 30 degrees was almost balmy compared to the Ice Bowl in Green Bay four years before, warm enough for Duane Thomas to speak publicly, stating the obvious: "We've got two more to go."

The next week, on January 2, the day after the University of Texas put the big whomp on Penn State in the Cotton Bowl Classic, the Cowboys kept their unbeaten streak alive in their house, beating San Francisco 14–3 in a yawner witnessed by a flood of celebrities including former president Johnson. Clint Murchison sent a note to Johnson a couple days after the game, writing, "Best line of the day: 'President Nixon called the Cowboys' locker room and President Johnson answered the phone.'"

It wasn't that warm out, but the Associated Press's Denne Freeman approached Duane Thomas for a comment after the game only to be told, "Man, don't ever try to interview me after a game." At least he was being consistent. Thomas had hung up on *Sports Illustrated*'s Tex Maule when he called. Mike Jones of the *Morning News* got a "Go away, man, leave me alone" after approaching Thomas after the St. Louis game. When a reporter from Chicago inquired about field conditions at the game in Minnesota, Thomas asked, "Were you there?"

Tom Landry was the epitome of tolerance in dealing with Thomas. "We've come to accept him as he is," he said. "I don't know if I can enlighten you. He is a unique person. His sole object is to be prepared to play football. He does it his own way. He doesn't like distractions. At meetings he says maybe two words. He seldom is not ready to play. He listens. He doesn't ask many questions. Thomas acts as if he is not part of the team, but he is part of the team. The team has to understand him and I believe they do. We've never asked him why he doesn't talk to reporters or sign autographs."

Football was on everyone's mind, and as the Cowboys prepared to meet the Miami Dolphins in Super Bowl VI in New Orleans —

Dallas's second consecutive appearance—former president Johnson sent a telegram to Tom Landry that teased Johnson's successor, who had suggested plays to the Redskins' George Allen and was doing so again, telling Miami Dolphins coach Don Shula that a slant pass to Paul Warfield could beat Dallas:

"My prayers and my presence will be with you in New Orleans although I have no plans to send in any plays."

Before the big game, Roger Staubach was recognized with the Bert Bell Award for the Most Valuable Player in the National Football League, a distinction that only one other Cowboy—Don Meredith—had earned before. Staubach won the Oak Farms Dairy My Favorite Cowboy contest too.

The whole team had been on fire all season. "The club was ready mentally since training camp," receiver Lance Alworth said. "To me, it was a team with a mission." At the conclusion of weight-lifting sessions conducted during the offseason, Staubach would say, "Let's lift one more for the Super Bowl; I'm going to take you to the Super Bowl." The Doomsday Defense had given up a single touchdown in the previous twenty-five quarters of football. The Super Bowl was theirs to lose, and the whole world was watching.

The significance of the big game was noted in part by the Vitalis hair tonic commercial that Staubach and Miami quarterback Bob Griese filmed and by the $1,300 raised by the Sunrise Optimist Club and Victory and Company to send the Dallas Cowboys Cheerleaders to New Orleans for the game. One man went to the airport to hand deliver a three-hundred-dollar check to take the girls out for a nice meal in New Orleans. Even in 1971, the cheerleaders still operated as a volunteer organization and depended on fans' largesse to travel.

The National Football League released a poll before the big game. Pro football, respondents said, was more popular than major-league baseball, although a majority of American men admitted they would rather attend a World Series game than a Super Bowl. Still, the sixth Super Bowl would mark a sea change in sports preference. With sixty-five million television viewers witnessing the event, it would be the most watched television program ever.

For the players, the business was the game. To Clint and his wealthy play pals, football was an excuse to go out and have fun. "For all the movers and shakers from Dallas, a road trip was a big party for them," said Dallas Cowboy Pat Toomay. "And none of us could ever go. We're going to work. And it was like, 'Who's having the fun here?'"

Linebacker Dave Edwards nicknamed Clint's Rover Boys the steak eaters—garrulous, fun-loving men of means who always ordered the biggest steak on the menu. "You felt like you were the source of something from which people were drawing a lot of energy," Pat Toomay said. "Half the time, you were exhausted and beat up and being exploited in that deep way. You were getting paid and all that; you just weren't getting paid what you should have been getting paid."

Bob Lilly was pumped on the bus ride to Tulane Stadium. The team photographer asked him how the game would go. "We're winning this game, don't even think about it going any other way, there's no way we can lose this game." No thrown helmet at the final gun. This time, Lilly, Staubach, Hayes, Thomas, Hill, Garrison, Jordan, Ditka, Landry, Stautner, Reeves, Tubbs, the other assistants, Tex—*everyone*—felt sure. The memory of too many close calls remained fresh. This would be the one.

The citizens of Dallas certainly thought so. Downtown streets were deserted. Police, the sheriff's department, and telephone operators reported few calls. The desktop pay TVs at Love Field were all occupied, with rubberneckers looming over users' shoulders. Water pressure across Dallas dropped two to three pounds during commercial breaks because fans were using toilets, and it dropped five pounds at halftime according to city water department officials—a record.

Once the Kilgore Rangerettes completed their pregame high-stepping show and it was game time, the Battle of New Orleans for all the marbles seemed almost like an afterthought. It sure wasn't much of a contest. The Dallas Cowboys soundly beat the Miami Dolphins of the AFC in every facet of the game, including the final score, 24–3. Three times, Miami coach Don Shula sent in the slant-in pass play from Bob Griese to Paul Warfield that had been suggested to Shula by President Nixon. Three times, cornerback Mel Renfro jammed the play. Warfield was limited to four receptions all day, and Bob Lilly pursued the Dolphin quarterback so relentlessly he sacked him for a record 29-yard loss on a single play.

The halftime Louis Armstrong salute with Ella Fitzgerald, Carol Channing, Al Hirt, and the U.S. Marine Corps Drill Team, with the Tyler Apache Belles making a cameo, stirred up more excitement than the game itself.

But a win was a win, and this win counted like no other. No more listening to the commentators or reading the articles about the Cowboys choking. The monkey was off their backs. This was it. Craig Morton turned to Landry when the gun went off and shook his hand, saying, "I'm so happy for you, Coach." The players, led by John Niland, carried the smiling Landry on their shoulders off the field.

Roger Staubach was awarded most valuable player of the Super Bowl for completing 12 of 19 passes and throwing two touchdown passes, to which the quarterback responded, "Holy cow!" He won a sports car for the honor but asked for a station wagon instead.

It was one of the few times that season that Staubach won something he didn't deserve.

Duane Thomas's ground game had made the critical difference; he'd rushed nineteen times for 95 yards and a touchdown, averaging five yards per carry, and catching three passes for 17 yards. "All he did was take the ball and run every time they called his number — which came to be more and more often," wrote Hunter S. Thompson in his book *Fear and Loathing on the Campaign Trail*. "In the Super Bowl, Thomas was the whole show." Perhaps. But *Sport* magazine, the sponsor of the MVP award, effectively disqualified Thomas before giving the citation to Staubach. Magazine personnel feared Thomas would pull the silent treatment at the MVP banquet in New York afterward.

After the game, at Jim Brown's urging, Duane Thomas agreed to speak to broadcaster Tom Brookshier, a former defensive back for the Philadelphia Eagles, while some of Thomas's teammates were trying to pull Clint Murchison into the shower. "Lemme put my pants on," Thomas said. Brown led the way into the interview room, where Bobby Hayes was finishing his remarks, then the two climbed onto the platform with Brookshier, in front of cameras as several million viewers watched at home.

"Are you that fast? Are you that quick?" Brookshier asked, microphone in hand, nervous, knowing this was the first interview the Sphinx had done this year and knowing Thomas was one intimidating dude, especially to a fledgling sportscaster.

"Evidently," Thomas said with a blank face as Brown looked over his shoulder, trying to stifle a laugh. The black/white divide was on full display, and the black performers in this pageant had mastered the mau-mau. Brookshier wilted and tossed the next question, about Thomas's speed, to Brown, who had played against Brookshier.

"Duane Thomas is probably the most gifted runner in football today," Brown replied. "He's big and he has great speed. That's very obvious but he has fantastic moves. He's probably as smart as any football player playing today. So that combination is fantastic.

"Are you nervous, Tom?" Brown asked with a laugh.

Brookshier soldiered on. "You must like the game of football. I'm told in practice you run farther than anyone else. You like football?"

"I do. I do. That's why I went off in pro ball. That's why I am a football player."

Brookshier followed up, noting Duane's weight fluctuated between 205 and 215.

"I weigh what I need to," Thomas replied, again betraying no emotion.

Before Brookshier could sputter out another question, Jim Brown interjected in a calm, authoritative voice, showing off some of the moves he'd learned in his new career as a Hollywood actor:

"Duane says he feels good today. He wanted to win the Super Bowl. He wanted to play football. He wanted to come back and show the American public that he is a good football player. I think that has been accomplished. I think the silence has enabled him to do this. There was no controversy involved. There was no conflict with his teammates or his coaches. I think he should be commended for this, but I don't think he wants to say any more at this particular time. But he wanted to let the American public know that he is a good football player and that he wanted to win the Super Bowl."

Brown told reporters he had advised Thomas to remain silent "because by playing football he'd disprove all those things that were manufactured against him. Didn't you read all that what was said in the papers about his physical and mental condition? It was all manufactured. Now Duane wants to get some money. He should get it. He's one of the greatest backs that ever lived. He's the most gifted runner in football today."

The pair retreated to talk privately in another room, where Duane turned down another interview request, explaining, "I gotta get myself together."

"Are you happy now?" another reporter asked Thomas as he made his way out of the locker room.

This time he beamed.

"I never said I was sad," he said softly.

"You don't look happy," the reporter observed.

"Happiness is inside," Thomas responded, a Buddhist talking point that flew completely over the reporter's head.

Less than two weeks later, Duane Thomas was busted for smoking pot. He and his brother Bertrand had been driving a car loaned to them by a Dallas car dealer when they were pulled over near Greenville, forty-five miles northeast of Dallas, for driving while black. Police said a reported stolen car had matched the description of Duane's luxury ride. Tex intervened, voiced the club's support, and got the Thomas brothers lawyered up. Duane and Bertrand went to trial, drawing quite a crowd to the steps of the Hunt County Courthouse, and received five-year probated sentences, despite the fact Greenville was still notorious for the WELCOME TO GREENVILLE, THE BLACKEST LAND, THE WHITEST PEOPLE banner that had stretched across Main Street as recently as ten years earlier and the reality that an African American convicted of marijuana possession in Texas usually did prison time.

But the big game, the one that counted, belonged to Duane and every other Cowboy. "It's the happiest I've ever been as an athlete," Roger Staubach gushed. He meant it. It was Don Meredith's team that made it to the Super Bowl the year before. These were his guys. The four passes Staubach completed to wide receivers Lance Alworth and Bobby Hayes came at the right time, and the running game and the tight ends did the rest. "I've been a world champion before, but this is one of the greatest feelings I've ever had in athletics," said Bullet Bob Hayes, who was now the only man on earth with an Olympic gold medal and a Super Bowl ring.

Jerry Tubbs enjoyed the win, but admitted, "It was a big relief. It's like you're constipated and the bowel finally goes. We got rid of all that crap. It wasn't fun being next year's champion."

Tex Schramm savored the moment. It had taken twelve years — not five, not ten — and there had been enough distractions along the way. This, he finally could appreciate.

When it was his turn in front of the microphone, Tex couldn't help himself. He beamed in front of the cameras, looking positively cherubic and talking totally Tex, declaring, "They can't say we can't win the big one anymore. And we'll be back. This is just a start. We'll be stronger in the next six years." The architects who designed the team were still in place. The quarterback was an all-American role model. The coach was the kind of upright man that parents wanted their boys to grow up to be. The Cowboys were forces of good, of God, and of style. Even Duane was good for the team, on the field for sure and off the field because when people were talking about him, they were talking about the Dallas Cowboys.

(Schramm's joy would be moderated only a bit once he learned that during the game, his residence at 9355 Sunnybrook Lane was burglarized of a television, one hundred dollars in change, and his car keys. The red-and-white sports sedan that the keys started was slammed into a second car parked in the driveway.)

Clint Murchison backed up Tex's contention that a dynasty had been created. "This is a successful end to our 12-year plan," Murchison said before plugging his New York chili parlor and cryptically informing Tom Brookshier and millions of viewers at home, "We have had plenty of the thick. Now we can enjoy some of the thick." (He already had, evidently.)

A beaming Tom Landry, hatless and in a blue double-breasted blazer, accepted the Lombardi Trophy from Pete Rozelle. "The only thing I can say is I'm delighted we're all still here," he remarked. He was referring to Bob Lilly, standing beside him, about to fire up a cigar, and to Chuck Howley, who was busy whooping it up.

Coach was struggling to emote. "I'm not really conscious of my true personal feelings yet," he said after the game. "I do know I'll just have a restful night and afterwards I'll probably get to feeling just how much it means."

Stars for Sale

THE COWBOYS WERE ASCENDANT. Roger Staubach met the president of the United States at the White House and graciously shook hands, alleviating the sting of the Dallas Bonehead Club's giving President Nixon their annual bonehead award for being "the coach of the Miami Dolphins."

Staubach delivered the keynote address at close to a hundred functions that winter and was recognized with a forty-five novelty record, "Ballad of New Orleans," which described his derring-do at the Super Bowl. And he updated his look, letting his hair grow out into a wavy mane, cultivating sideburns, and slipping on a pair of hip white loafers. Tex Schramm followed suit, growing his own pronounced sideburns and sporting white loafers to go with his not-quite-screaming-loud checked sports coats.

The club president was effusive in praising his quarterback and all he stood for. "I think Staubach is now the football idol of the country," Schramm declared to reporters. "He's more in demand than any football player. The really broad spectrum of American fans still want to look at their sports heroes with the old connotation of an American athlete, you know, clean, wholesome. I don't mean [Joe] Namath himself exactly, for he is a true star, but the image he portrayed. That was coincidental with the hippie period in this country and I think you'll find the hippies are now on the way out. There was a little revolution for a while, but that sort of novelty is over.

"If you're going to attract businessmen, solid companies, whether for investments or endorsements or any sort of commercial connection these people want to be associated with a top clean image," Schramm said. "The auto companies, the toy companies, the soft drink people, they want their product associated with a Roger Staubach."

These players were on everyone's mind, and Don Meredith contemplated what winning the Super Bowl really meant to the Dallas Cowboys, and then to himself personally, while speaking at a sports seminar sponsored by the University of the Pacific titled "Sport: An Existential Inquiry into the Phenomenon of Competition."

"Dynasty is the right word," Meredith said. "For one Dallas victory only creates an insatiable need for another. This is the most regimented organization in football. The Cowboys have goals and itineraries for everything from the Super Bowl to the bus trip from the hotel to the practice field. Coach Landry believes that winning is the thing, the only thing. I once told him that he should get out of the rotten business because he wasn't giving himself a chance to live. He's an unemotional man, yes, but he's so well organized that he really has no need to communicate. I think I've matured a lot over the past three years but it was impossible to mature in that regimented atmosphere. They told me I was a professional and then insulted my intelligence with ridiculous rules that implied I didn't know how to take care of myself."

Dan Reeves had a greater appreciation of Landry's aloofness and regimen. "Coach Landry never talked about the past," he said, citing one exception: "One day we were out at the practice facility on Abrams Rd. and it came a rainstorm and we had to go inside. That's the first time that I ever remember Coach Landry talking about his being in service and what he did and all and talk about his crash in the plane. That was just awesome 'cause you know you won't get Coach Landry to talk about himself."

The coach even had a humorous side, Reeves said. "Coach Landry wasn't a very outgoing person but if you got him in a situation where he felt comfortable he was one of the funniest people and genuinely down to earth people you'll ever meet in your life." He recalled assistant coach Ray Renfro, who would refer to someone whose name he didn't know as podnah. "You always knew whether Ray knew somebody or not if Ray said, 'Hey, Podnah, how are you doing?' My first year coaching, we started an offseason program and brought in the players and their wives. Coach Landry was going to announce we were going to pay them for this offseason program. We had a list of all the players and I called them to see if they could come. I called Blaine Nye and didn't remember his wife's name, which is Annabelle. Sure enough, she answers the phone. 'This is Dan Reeves, is Blaine Nye there?' She said, 'No, he's not.' 'Mrs. Nye, would you have him call me?' She said, 'Why, sure I will, Dan.' At the meeting the next day I said, 'Coach, I think it would be a great idea if we would put the players' wives' names on the list. When I call, I'd like to know what the wife's name is.' Ray Renfro said, 'Oh yeah, Coach, that'd be great. After the game, when we meet outside the locker room, the wives are always there and I never know what their names are.' Coach Landry didn't bat an eye. He said, 'What did you call them, Mrs. Podnah?'"

If players such as Don Meredith needed emotion from their coach, Landry was the wrong mentor. "He was not going to make a rah-rah talk to get you fired up about playing," Dan Reeves observed. "He felt like the greatest motivator was preparation and we never went into a football game that we weren't very well prepared. We weren't going to be surprised by anything the other team did because he covered every detail. His greatest motivator was preparation. And nobody was as organized or as prepared as Coach Landry had his football team."

———

WINNING THE SUPER BOWL was quite an achievement. Coming back and doing it again and again was what Tex Schramm was after. He'd created a system to bring in new players as older ones wore out, and he was doing the same in the front office with young Joe Bailey. Joe had accompanied the team cardiologist, his father, to the second training camp at St. Olaf's College in Northfield, Minnesota, in 1961. Dr. Bailey had operated on members of the Murchison family and was part of the Chicken Club in DC and an honorary Rover Boy, attending summer training camp ostensibly to help Dr. Marvin Knight, the team physician, give physicals.

Young Joe worked four summer training camps as an equipment boy alongside Tommy Landry, the son of the coach, and went on to excel in football and baseball at the University of North Carolina. After graduating, he married, fathered a child, and worked for Merrill Lynch for a year. Then, late in 1969, he ran into Tex Schramm at the Dallas-Washington game at RFK Stadium. The only thing keeping him from entering into a management program at the financial firm was the Dallas Cowboys, Bailey told Schramm. "Then would you be interested in coming down to Dallas and working for us?" Tex asked. The organization needed a shot of youth, and no kid impressed Schramm more than Bailey did.

Bailey took him up on the offer. And he was sold when he entered the Expressway Towers building and took the elevator up to Tex Schramm's office on his first day of work. Eileen Gish, Tex's secretary, had sweetly informed Bailey, "Mr. Schramm is ready to see you," but as he walked into Tex's office, the automatic door closed in his face. Tex was on the phone with Dr. Knight, furious because Calvin Hill had been caught dancing in New Orleans during the Pro Bowl with an infected toe. "That moron!" Tex was yelling into the telephone receiver when he noticed Bailey. Without missing a beat, he swung around in his chair, extended a hand, and broke into a grin.

"So, how are ya? Geez, it's good to see ya!"

Bailey hit the road as a scout, mainly watching basketball games in search of another Pete Gent or Cornell Green. "I was on the road three hundred days the first year," he recalled. "I would hang around with Dick Mansberger, who scouted the historically black colleges. I went on the road with Gil for a little bit, and with some of the other guys. I'd learn as much from observing other scouts. It's a culture unto itself, just like trainers, equipment guys, assistant coaches, and PR guys have their own cultures." At the end of the year, Bailey was called by Brandt to Miami to join the Dallas Cowboys at the Super Bowl.

Bailey stayed on the road scouting for another year before taking a desk job with the club in Dallas and enrolling in graduate school at SMU. When business manager Tom Hardin announced he was leaving the Cowboys, Bailey promptly threw his hat into the ring for the job. Former receiver and broadcaster Irv Cross was Schramm's pick to succeed Hardin among more than two dozen applicants, but when that deal couldn't be consummated, the job fell into Bailey's lap. Schramm recognized his potential and figured he could mentor the twenty-five-year-old himself. The kid had all the makings of a great business manager.

With the right people in place in the organization, the Dallas Cowboys Football Club should have been positioned to outlast them all, including the new competition in town.

Lamar Hunt's Dallas Tornado soccer club didn't count, since they could hardly draw 10,000 fans to a game. Soccer may have been the most popular sport in the world, but it was no threat to the NFL, certainly not in Dallas. And the Dallas Chaparrals of the upstart American Basketball Association were such a bust that they were renamed the Texas Chaparrals for the 1970–1971 season and played home games around the region to no avail. San Antonio car dealer Red McCombs bought the team and moved them south, where they were reborn as the San Antonio Spurs.

But back in September of 1971, a month before Texas Stadium officially opened for football, major-league baseball owners had voted to allow Robert Short to move the team he owned, the Washington Senators, to Texas, just as Short had moved the pro basketball team he once owned, the Minneapolis Lakers, to Los Angeles. Lamar Hunt and Fort Worth businessman Tommy Mercer owned the minor-league Dallas–Fort Worth Spurs and had overseen the construction of Turnpike Stadium in Arlington to house the team in 1965. The ten-thousand-seat facility could expand to fit up to fifty thousand and could host major-league baseball *and* football if needed, and it was ready and waiting for Short's Senators, which were renamed the Texas Rangers.

That nickname might not have been right for the football team, but it fit the relocated baseball club just fine. Still, between the suburban location, the Texas heat, and a legacy of performing miserably, the Rangers didn't immediately capture the imagination of the sporting public. Their manager, Ted Williams, the Boston Red Sox slugger, retired after one season, complaining on his way out the door, "You can keep Dallas."

Schramm wished he could.

"Fuck! Goddamn baseball," he burst out in a front-office meeting.

Public relations assistant Doug Todd had tried to convince the boss that the baseball Rangers would be good for the football Cowboys. Major-league baseball and football could create a critical mass of interest and elevate both franchises.

Tex glared at Todd. "Jesus Christ, what are you talking about?"

"It gets more people out, more people interested in sports, and if it's sports, they'll be talking about us, because those guys aren't any good," Todd reasoned defensively.

"Well, let me tell you something," Tex hissed. "When I was in Los Angeles with the Rams, I saw what happens when a major-league baseball team comes to town. *I saw it happen,* and it did not have a positive effect on the Los Angeles Rams, believe me. There is nothing good about this. Either you're for us or against us. Baseball is an anachronism. Football is a contemporary sport, willing to change rules and bend with the times through innovation.

"They're competition, damn it," Tex said, ending the meeting. The notion of sharing the fan base was not in his DNA.

The real depth of fan interest in the Dallas Cowboys could be measured by the renamed *Cowboys Insiders Football Weekly.* The weekly mag edited and published by Jim Brannan featured a profile of a player and his family, Samantha Stevenson's women's column, the daily Cowboys beat writers and columnists, a business writer named Shad Rowe, and loads of advertisements for hotels, bars, chain saws, car washes, hair replacement for men, the Country Dinner Playhouse ("'Pro' Theater for Dallas"), the Computamatic Football board game, Braniff ("Fly with Braniff. The Cowboys do"), Pepsi (guard John Niland posed holding a can and surrounded by peewee footballers who happened to be coached by Clint Murchison), Marlboro cigarettes, Chuck Howley Uniform Rental, tall men's clothiers, Jones-Blair Paint (endorsed by Bob Lilly), and *The Cowboys Sing Holiday Halftime* record album ("Offense & Defense Together in a Great Christmas Album"). With a print run of 28,000, the *Insider* had plenty of advertising support.

Bob Lilly's Pro Report had joined as print magazine competition in 1971. Its general manager, Russ Russell, had been taking photographs of the team for the *Dallas Times Herald*, the Cowboys, and for the NFL for more than a decade. Russell rounded up the usual suspects—Glieber; Lundquist; Luksa, who moved to the *Dallas Times Herald* in 1972 to replace Steve Perkins; St. John; and Anderson, along with women's writer Patsy Leftwich—to contribute columns, meaning several writers were contributing to both weeklies. Lilly also wrote a weekly column that was carried by five newspapers.

On the daily front, Steve Perkins departed the *Dallas Times Herald* after covering 164 games, including two Super Bowls, to freelance for magazines and write more books like his latest tome,

Winning the Big One, now in its second printing for Grosset and Dunlap publishers.

Frank Glieber's play-by-play of Cowboys games on CBS and, in Dallas, on KDFW, the new expansive call letters for the former KRLD TV, were beamed to eight television stations in Mexico belonging to the Telecadena network. Monterrey broadcaster Fernando Von Rossum provided the Spanish play-by-play over the CBS feed. "The Cowboys are Mexico's home team," Von Rossum told Glieber. "People went wild when they won the Super Bowl, just as they did in Texas. If we ever get them to Mexico City for a preseason, we would sell 100,000 tickets overnight."

Tex Schramm took note. He was also keeping tabs on the U.S. Congress, which was contemplating legislation to lift the TV blackouts of home games if they were advance sellouts. Schramm suggested the Red Menace was taking over American sports. "I think our people have to decide whether this is a country of free enterprise in regards to sports," he declared. "Whether they want it conducted in a Socialistic or Communistic manner is up to them. I personally feel that sports is better served by private enterprise."

Schramm's former boss at CBS, Bill MacPhail, said he thought blackouts would eventually be ruled illegal and that NFL owners "exaggerate the impact on attendance. Only the weak teams need them now."

Still, the FCC allowed the NFL to black out KXII in Sherman, sixty-two miles north of Dallas, as well as any other CBS affiliated stations within a hundred-mile radius of the game. Sherman businessman Charles Everton presented Schramm with a petition bearing eight thousand signatures opposing the blackout. Tex could ignore the signatures but he couldn't ignore the new, more powerful version of the Cowboy antenna known as the All American Sports Amplifier, selling at Preston TV for $109.50 plus another $80 for antenna and installation. The cost was twenty times as expensive as the first Cowboy antenna, but this upgraded model picked up

Channel 6 from Wichita Falls, one hundred twenty-five miles from Texas Stadium, beautifully.

As long as the blackouts continued, radio wielded disproportionate clout. KRLD radio outbid the Texas State Network, whose affiliates included KLIF in Dallas, for radio broadcast rights to the Cowboys. Gordon McLendon had sold off most of his media holdings, including KLIF, to Fairchild Industries for $10.5 million as he moved his investments into precious metals.

For the first time since 1965, Bill Mercer would not be calling the play-by-play on the Cowboys radio network. His replacement, Verne Lundquist, who had been Mercer's sidekick and understudy, was joined by new boy Al Wisk, and Frank Glieber when he wasn't calling games on television.

Tex Schramm had enjoyed giving Bill Mercer a hard time during his tenure with the Cowboys for being a baseball guy, and Mercer's exit to go to work for the new Texas Rangers baseball club proved Schramm's point. As far as Mercer was concerned, there were more games to call over the course of a season compared to football. What Mercer—and even Schramm—didn't realize, though, was how thoroughly the Cowboys were still sucking the oxygen away from all other sports, baseball included, in Dallas and Fort Worth.

Local interest in sports led to a new program on WRR-AM, the small radio station owned by the city of Dallas. The premise of *Sports-Line* was to generate a dialogue between telephone callers and the host, Brad Sham, a twenty-one-year-old Chicago native who was one of the station's reporters. Sham was a brash kid who had aspired to be a play-by-play baseball game broadcaster ever since he first heard Jack Brickhouse call games for his hometown Cubs. He later fell under the influence of Jack Buck, the golden-throated voice of the storied St. Louis Cardinals baseball club, who also did play-by-play radio and television broadcasts of all kinds of major-league and college sports for the CBS television network, including a brief spell for the Cowboys. But more than Buck or Brickhouse, Sham wanted to be Rick Weaver ("in Your Receiver"), a sports guy who hosted a show on WBBM in Chicago (after Weaver called the play-by-play for the Cowboys in the early 1960s). Weaver brought in guests to talk sports while encouraging listeners to call in with their opinions.

Sham's first guests on *SportsLine* were Toby Harrah, the all-star shortstop for the Texas Rangers baseball club, and Dallas Cowboys tight end Mike Ditka. Dallas listeners became smitten with this new concept of sports talk, just as Dallas restaurant-goers were going crazy for a new concept in dining and drinking. The opening of T.G.I. Friday's in the Old Town shopping center on Greenville Avenue—the third T.G.I.F. after New York and Memphis—in the spring of 1972 was greeted by lines of patrons outside the entrance. In its first year, the restaurant netted two million dollars in revenues and was the highest-volume restaurant in Dallas. "That's where all the hot girls were," said David Wynne. "There weren't any bars anywhere. Friday's was the first of everything."

Wynne had witnessed the revolt against old Dallas society up close and personal. "My English wife really opened my eyes to my hypocrisy: the wonderful woman who helped raise me was black, I'd always worked with black folks, and I was 'big brother' to a black youngster—supposed to be setting the right example and all. Brook Hollow Golf Club, where I grew up, wanted around twenty thousand dollars to become a full member. I asked myself, 'Why am I a member of this club? Who do I like here?' The 'ofay' powers there refused to vote my big brother in because he worked with some black entertainers. They were afraid he was going to show up for lunch with Ike and Tina or Little Richard. And bring my little bro to swim in the pool? Ha! There would've been a riot! Sadly, not much has changed in forty years."

At the same time, rookie Jean Fugett, a graduate of Amherst College in Massachusetts, arrived in Dallas naive and oblivious to its racial history and the fact he and other young blacks were integrating North Dallas and its nightlife. "I came with an Afro as big as

Lincoln on *Mod Squad*," he said, referring to a popular television show with a modern black character. "My first day in Dallas, someone yelled at me, 'Hippie, get a haircut.' I wondered why all my older black friends and veterans on the team all lived in Oak Cliff," he admitted. "I finally realized I was one of the black players who was integrating North Dallas." Fugett got an education from Abner Haynes, the native Dallasite and first star for the former Dallas Texans who was representing players as an agent. "He advised me, guided me, and kept me out of trouble," Fugett said.

Jean Fugett gradually learned about Dallas's rarely mentioned black brain drain. "I realized that the only African Americans I knew with a college degree were from somewhere else." Young African Americans with ambition knew enough to leave Texas as soon as they could and seek prosperity elsewhere, as was the case with the new mayor of Los Angeles, Tom Bradley, a Texas expat.

Old society did not adjust well to the changes the 1970s brought to its city. Haute Dallas traditionally did its partying behind closed doors, the better to party harder. "There was no nightlife," recalled David Wynne. "Unless you were at a private club or belonged to a social club there really wasn't much to do. So there were a lot of parties, these huge wild, parties." Especially when a debutante made her society debut at the Idlewild Men's Club, founded in 1884, or the Terpsichorean Men's Club, founded in 1898.

"Men would spend four hundred thousand dollars on their daughters' debutante [parties]," said Wynne, who became president of the Terpsichorean Men's Club. "Troy Post, [an insurance tycoon] who came out of nowhere to run Braniff, took us on that big orange 747 to Acapulco and put us up at a golf club resort. His daughter was making her debut. People were re-creating the Viennese Opera House at the Sheraton Hotel. My uncle Toddie Lee [Wynne] threw one with a big circus motif with elephants and other animals walking through the party. Harding Lawrence [who became president of Braniff International in 1965] and [second wife, New York advertising guru] Mary Wells threw a party where you took your date out to Love Field and they put you on a 727, flew to New York. We were met at the airport with a string of maybe thirty limousines which drove everybody to the Lawrence's three-story apartment where we were entertained with a cocktail party, then taken by limo to some fancy Greek restaurant where we were throwing plates all over the place, then to some nightclub that was all the rave in New York. At six o'clock in the morning they poured you onto the plane for the flight home. This kind of stuff went on all the time."

As wild as the gentry could be, the new Dallas lifestyle trumped all that.

"An apartment complex with a swimming pool was the key," Wynne said. "That's where all the stewardesses were. They were everywhere. There was American Airlines Stewardess College out by the old [Greater Southwest Fort Worth] airport out there off of 183. I had the phone number to the pay phone where the steward-esses were and I always knew when the classes changed. There was a group of us who had the inside info over there. We'd just call up and ask if anybody over there was looking for a date, and we'd go pick them up. Then there was a Braniff [stewardess college] right there on the [North Dallas] toll road. The more daring stewardess students would leave their windows open and stand there in their underwear and freak out the drivers. There were a lot of steward-esses for other airlines living in these apartments too, and they were all young and great-looking."

The creation of Southwest Airlines, a low-fare, post-deregulation start-up that flew between Love Field, Houston Hobby, San Anto-nio, and Austin, threw gasoline on the hedonistic fire, plying passen-gers with free drinks and eye candy in the form of good-looking stewardesses dressed in hot pants. The airline was dreamed up by two businessmen, Herb Kelleher and Lamar Muse, who sketched a triangle on a cocktail napkin while having drinks. Their idea would link Dallas, Houston, and San Antonio with jet service using Love

Field and Hobby Airport and would eschew DFW International, which was under construction, and Houston's new Intercontinental Airport. Using the stock symbol LUV, Southwest operated only 737 commuter jets and utilized nonunion employees to turn around flights in fewer than twenty minutes, far quicker than conventional airlines, while promoting cheap fares and "spreading LUV all over Texas."

In 1973, construction of Reunion Arena, a Hyatt Hotel, and the Reunion Tower landmark would begin in a dilapidated rail yard in the southwestern corner of downtown Dallas. The developer was the Woodbine Development Corporation, a real estate company headed by Ray Hunt, H. L. Hunt's youngest son, part of the elder Hunt's second secret family. The city was desperate to develop the derelict fringes of downtown and offered thirty-eight million dollars in street and infrastructure improvement, as well as a long lease on the city's historic Union Station rail terminal, if Hunt would build there. In exchange for the favors, Hunt donated the land for the city to build Reunion Arena.

Clint Murchison might have been unsuccessful in persuading Dallas leaders to make room for his football stadium downtown, but he wasn't complaining. He was too busy adding income streams to Texas Stadium. In November, a three-screen drive-in movie theater opened in the stadium parking lot, operated by McLendon Theaters. The stadium was a pro football facility first and foremost, but in its first year it managed to also host college and high school football games, evangelical crusades, a black-college battle of the marching bands, a women's football team known as the Dallas Bluebonnets, Dallas Tornado soccer, and professional wrestling. The grudge match between hometown heel Fritz Von Erich and Dory Funk Jr., one of the storied Funk brothers from the Texas Panhandle, drew 28,112 rassling fans.

Those business triumphs came at the expense of domestic tranquillity. Jane Coleman Murchison had grown so tired of her husband's philandering she filed for divorce and moved into the Murchison's four-floor penthouse in New York in 1972. A gorgeous lady from a prominent New Orleans family, Jane, like most Dallas women of social standing, had tolerated her husband's fooling around as long as it was discreet and out of the public eye. But now Clint wasn't being discreet. "With all that stuff he and Bedford were doing, I wondered how long can their marriage last?" a family friend mused. It turned out to be not too long. The divorce became official in January 1973.

The divorce may have exposed Clint Murchison's personal short-comings but made not one whit of difference to fans, who were bumping into a host of issues with their championship team.

The opening of the 1972 edition of training camp should have been celebrated as joyful reaffirmation of the Cowboys. They were picked to return to the Super Bowl and scheduled to appear in ten nationally televised games, more than any other NFL team.

Instead, there was a rash of controversy and injuries clouding camp at Thousand Oaks. Most of the former came courtesy of Duane Thomas, who was talking to the press and had vowed to turn over a new leaf after Landry said the silent treatment could not con-tinue. But he was still pissed he wasn't getting a raise.

Sportswriters had continued to make hay of Thomas's silence. Most were convinced he was either high or a complete weirdo. One woman from Dallas informed a gaggle of sportswriters at the Los Angeles Coliseum before an exhibition game, "He is a sick young man. We all knew that in Dallas. He needs a psychiatrist." Thomas told a reporter from *Black Sports* magazine he had a revelation once he heard he was supposedly zonked on dope when he was traded to New England. "I found out all about the press and its power when that went down," Thomas said. "What chance does a player have when the owners of pro teams control the press?"

After being popped for pot and managing to skate, Thomas kept his head down and his name out of the news while adopting a vegetarian diet. He didn't seem that off when he reported to Thousand Oaks. But Thomas was still playing by his own rules. Twice he told Landry he wanted to quit, and twice he was talked out of it. Then he missed a team meeting and practice. When Coach Landry went to his room to ask why, Thomas told him, "I didn't feel like it." He wasn't paid to practice or attend meetings, only to perform, he said.

Landry walked out of the room looking for Schramm. "That's it. Trade him," Landry said.

Landry was perplexed. He informed reporters, "He just didn't feel like working today. He didn't offer any explanations. He never does offer explanations. I just thought we had to do something, basically because he missed practice. This is based on his failure to comply. That's the big thing. I've been very patient, but I had to make the decision to trade him after I talked to him today. His indifference to practice is what did it."

Much as he hadn't wanted to trade Duane Thomas, Landry arrived at his decision knowing that rookie running back Robert Newhouse had impressed the assistant coaches. The San Diego Chargers took Thomas and initiated negotiations for a three-year contract worth between $275,000 and $300,000. But the contract was never formalized, and although he suited up for the Chargers' game against the Cowboys, Thomas wandered off the field during the national anthem and was traded again to Washington.

"Man, that whole episode is one of the most bizarre sports stories ever in this town," said Mike Rhyner. "It was that rare case where there was a guy on the team that they couldn't win without. They just absolutely had to have him. And you take him away and they weren't going to get where they wanted to go. It was that simple. So if that meant bending the rules or letting him do his own thing, no matter how divisive it may have been, that's what they had to do and they did. And there was not a player on that team that liked it. Here's a guy who jacked around with the whole system, he just essentially did this to everybody and got away with it. For a while he pulled it off."

Once Duane Thomas was gone from the Cowboys, the story lines shifted to that perennial old topic: quarterbacks. Roger Staubach tried to scramble for the fourth time in an exhibition game against the Los Angeles Rams in the Coliseum and separated his shoulder because he crashed into Marlin McKeever rather than stepping out-of-bounds. The rough physical play of the Los Angeles defense violated the unspoken protocol of the exhibition season to go easy on starters. McKeever sent flowers to Staubach, who was expected to be sidelined for three months.

The return of Craig Morton became the new story. Benched and forgotten, Morton had opted to tough it out in 1972 and try to regain his starter's role rather than demand a trade. Staubach's preseason injury sped up the timetable. Backfield coach Danny Reeves was reactivated as the backup QB.

Texas Stadium did not sell out on opening day against Philadelphia. Super Bowl champions or not, the Cowboys found that the stifling September heat "drove the lizards to cover," wrote Blackie Sherrod, and kept at least ten thousand fans away, more than a few of them wondering why Clint Murchison's palace wasn't air-conditioned like that new domed stadium being built in New Orleans. Still, the home team prevailed, 28–6.

The home opener also debuted the Dallas Cowboys Cheerleaders' new, sexy star-spangled look to take the fans' minds off the heat. Dee Brock had sketched out a new costume with a cleavage-revealing, midriff-baring halter top; white hot pants; and thigh-high white boots. Paula van Waggoner of the Lester Melnick women's specialty store designed it, and Leveta Crager stitched the uniforms together. Out of a hundred entrants, a dozen girls had passed muster in front of the panel of judges; the girls included Dixie Smith, Anna Carpenter, Deanovoy Nichols, Vonciel Baker, Rosemary Hall, and Carrie O'Brien, and they met fans' approval with their coordinated dance routines and revealing uniforms.

At one point, Tex Schramm had asked his teenage daughter

Christi to sketch out uniforms. Christi patiently drew what she thought a cheerleader costume should look like: a functional sleeveless top and short pleated skirt. But when she showed it to her daddy, he just smiled and handed it back to her. "No, that's not quite what I'm looking for," Tex said.

He wanted something racier, and he eventually found it with the help of Dee Brock, publicist Mitch Lewis, Joe Bailey, Bedford Wynne, and other consultants who appreciated a well-turned ankle.

Lawrence Herkimer, the founder of the Dallas-based National Cheerleaders Association, and who had judged Cowboys cheerleaders competition in the early years, regarded the new version of the Dallas Cowboys Cheerleaders as beneath his dignity. "They weren't cheerleaders." Herkimer sniffed. "They didn't lead cheers. They were pom girls, dancing girls. They got out there and performed. I told them, 'You don't need me to judge, just turn on the record player and let them start wiggling.' You just say, 'You, you, you, and you.' That's it. They weren't a cheerleader squad. They were a T-and-A squad."

Tex Schramm wouldn't argue the point. Nor would Dee Brock, who said, "This is showbiz; this isn't cheerleading."

Bubbles Cash was flattered. "I think they got the idea off of one of my costumes. I had a white leather hip hugger, white leather miniskirt with a crop top, and it had a turtleneck and I had tight-fitting boots."

It also reflected the popularity of topless bars, like the Pussycat A' Go Go and the Follies Buffet, which were replacing the old burlesque strip clubs that Bubbles Cash, Candy Barr, and Chris Colt and Her 45s once worked.

The task of reconciling these two conflicting images fell to Texie Waterman, whom Dee Brock had sought out after the Cowboys won the Super Bowl early in 1972, feeling that the girls needed more pizzazz to reflect the football team's rising profile. Waterman had danced on Broadway and could teach the cheerleaders all the right chorus-line moves to provide color.

Taking dance lessons from Texie Waterman was as much a rite of passage for Dallas girls of means as going to Hockaday or a faraway boarding school or attending a formal at the Dallas Country Club. If a young lady aspired to be a performer or entertainer, Waterman's demanding classes were ideal launching pads or, as in most cases, reality checks on such dreams.

With her oversight, the cheerleaders created a new hybrid: professional football cheerleaders whose job was not so much to lead cheers (that tradition had never gotten much traction in pro football) as to provide stimulating eye candy for fans in the stadium and those tuning in at home.

The Dallas Cowboys Cheerleaders put the football club's pageantry on equal footing with the Redskins' storied band and half-time activities, maybe even more so. Viewers across the nation grew accustomed to the pretty women waving pom-poms and doing high kicks. They would become as integral a part of the Cowboys brand as the football team, a complement to Tommy Loy's solo trumpet rendition of the national anthem and to Crazy Ray, the black mascot decked out in cowboy gear who waved his toy six-shooters and rode a wooden horse, whooping it up and acting crazy, conveying the impression to viewers at home that the sidelines of Texas Stadium were more happening than those at other NFL stadiums.

Crazy Ray was the Cowboys' first honest mascot. A concessions vendor named Wilford Jones, he shined shoes by day at the Four Seasons Barber Shop at Elm and Akard downtown and sold concessions at DFW sporting events. His sharp attention-getting whistle earned him the nickname Whistling Ray. He raised his profile selling pennants and swag in the stands of the Cotton Bowl dressed in a cowboy hat, a western shirt gaudy with fringe, a vest, jeans, chaps, and a holster holding two toy cap guns.

He was called Crazy Ray by the time he quit selling and started patrolling the sidelines, mugging for the television cameras. He became a staple of NFL television coverage, as much as the ubiquitous, rainbow-wigged Rock 'n' Rollen, whose John 3:16 sign inevitably found its way into camera shots after touchdowns and field goals.

But Crazy Ray and "Up Against the Wall, Redneck Mother" on the sound system were mere embellishments compared to the Dallas Cowboys Cheerleaders' growing renown, a testament to Tex Schramm's keen eye for showmanship and his understanding that it wasn't just about the players on the field but about the image, look, and brand. It was all icing, though. The cake was crossing the goal line more than the other team did. Winning mattered. To everyone. On the field. In business. In life. It had become part of the Dallas zeitgeist.

By mid-October, the Cowboys with Craig Morton at quarterback sat pretty with a 4-1 mark, despite Morton's propensity for misfiring. He tossed three interceptions in one game and was tied for most interceptions thrown for the season. Morton was a conventional QB, taking the sack rather than scrambling, which was easier to defend against, since Morton wouldn't be taking off and running.

The second loss came on the road against the Redskins, coached by George Allen, who were becoming Dallas's number-one nemesis. Allen called the Cowboys "without a doubt the best team in football with experience, speed and depth," which meant that by the Redskins' beating them, 24–20, "we won the Super Bowl," according to Allen's logic. The defeat hurt so bad, Tom Landry told his troops after the game he was removing his Super Bowl ring and wouldn't wear it again until they started playing like champions once more.

Even while injured, Roger Staubach continued to lead all other teammates in the Oak Farms My Favorite Cowboy contest. In early November, he was back on the bench as the number-two quarterback, although he had already been promoted to number one in Tex Schramm's heart.

Dissent within the post–Duane Thomas edition of the Cowboys wasn't remotely tolerated, if Herb Adderley, the former Green Bay All-Pro starting at left cornerback, was any indication. He became a

Landry target at a team film-viewing session, during which Landry ran the projector and called out players' mistakes. Watching Adderley defend on a play, Landry raised his voice in anger and called, "Herb, you're clueing again!," meaning he was guessing on a play.

Adderley challenged Landry, which no player did, and then left the room. The coach didn't forget. Landry benched Adderley after he swatted down a potential touchdown pass, complaining, "Herb, you've got to play the defense like everybody else!"

"You mean I'm supposed to let a guy run by me and catch a touchdown pass?" Adderley protested.

"Yes, if that's what your keys tell you to do!"

"No," Adderley argued, "I don't play that way."

"Then you won't play at all. Stay or leave; I don't care."

Herb Adderley was a victim of Landry's counterintuitive system, which required players to go against their instincts. Landry preferred seeing Adderley as a distraction. "My feeling this year is we must make changes as we see them," he said. "There's no second place for us anymore. Once you've become world champions, you've got to win. You can't wait."

After twelve years in the league and three championship rings, two with Green Bay and one with Dallas, the two dynasties of the modern era, Adderley stood up to the criticism. "I'm a team man, I have to go with the team. I'm a winner." He'd talk to the brass at the end of the season. "I have no doubt about my future here. I'm not in it."

Lance Alworth, Bobby Hayes, Larry Cole, and Billy Truax lost their starter gigs too.

The annual Thanksgiving Day game in Dallas against the San Francisco 49ers, renamed Navy Day, in honor of Secretary of Defense Melvin Laird administering the oath of enlistment to 278 Navy recruits on the field before the game, saw 49er quarterback Steve Spurrier re-creating Pearl Harbor, bombing the home team with devastating accuracy to wipe out Dallas 31–10, as Craig Morton surpassed Don Meredith in Boo-Bird decibels.

The Cowboys finished the regular season with a 10-4 record, good enough to make the playoffs as a wild card, the fourth team from each conference with the best record after the winners of each conference's three divisions had been declared.

Doomsday Defense had held back the opposition when it counted, despite issues at one of the cornerback and safety positions. Walt Garrison ground out more yards than he had over the previous two seasons. Dave Edwards, Mel Renfro, John Niland, Jethro Pugh, and Rayfield Wright all delivered standout performances.

The Cowboys reached their third consecutive NFC championship game after exacting revenge with a 30–28 comeback win against the 49ers at Candlestick Park, a win engineered by Roger Staubach, who came off the bench late in the third quarter with the Cowboys behind 28–13. He sparked the offense to put up 17 points in the fourth quarter, including touchdown passes to Billy Parks and Ron Sellers in the final minute and a half.

Staubach said he became inspired after Craig Morton, who'd been benched, went to Staubach, gave him a hug, and said, "I have confidence in you. You can win it in some way."

"I think that gave me more confidence than anything that happened," Staubach said after the game, which was being called the greatest comeback in the thirteen-year history of the football club by their coach, who was laughing and waving his arms while the stalwarts of Doomsday, Bob Lilly, George Andrie, and Larry Cole, did somersaults.

The National Football Conference championship pitted the Cowboys against their hated division rivals the Redskins again. Dallas had thumped the 'Skins 34–24 in the next-to-last game of the regular season, a win highlighted by Craig Morton bootlegging and running 12 yards for a touchdown as if he were Roger Staubach.

This time around, though, the Redskins ambushed Dallas, 26–3. Coach Landry went with Roger Staubach for the whole game because of his play in the improbable victory against San Francisco the previous week, despite Staubach's limited game experience during the regular season. "I'm not going to second-guess myself," Landry said afterward. He didn't need to. Almost every Cowboy fan in the world was doing it for him.

"They had the wrong man in there," the 'Skins' Diron Talbert said. "Staubach was rusty and couldn't find his secondary receivers."

Craig Morton, who didn't play against Washington in the final game, rallied to win the Oak Farms most popular Cowboy contest ahead of Staubach, although that consolation prize mattered little to either quarterback in a season cut short.

Washington went on to face the undefeated Miami Dolphins in Super Bowl VII, which the Dolphins won by a touchdown, 14–7, to complete a perfect record, never since matched.

The season over, Morton said, "Whatever happens, I have no plans to leave. You need two quarterbacks to win and I think that was proven this season." The season also proved that Tex Schramm had been premature in declaring the start of a dynasty after the Cowboys won the Super Bowl the year before. "Even the Ice Bowl loss to Green Bay didn't affect me like this," he said dejectedly.

Despite falling short, the Cowboys dominated the hometown sports pages so thoroughly that competitors for the local sports dollar were crying uncle. The SMU Mustangs fired their coach, Hayden Fry, after he led his team to a 7-4 record. The win-loss record was not the bone of contention; the problem was the team's declining attendance figures. In 1965, SMU averaged 42,781 fans at home games. In 1972, the Mustangs were last in attendance in the Southwest Conference, with a 25,653 average. The school's board of governors felt something had to be done, and there was no way they could ask the Cowboys to move.

Hayden Fry informed the press that school president Dr. Paul Hardin told him the Cowboys helped evaluate his coaching before he was canned. "That's a ludicrous accusation which I totally resent regardless of who said it," responded Tex Schramm before unleashing a torrent of other words not fit for print or broadcast.

Schramm was the go-to guy to put out fires. It was Schramm who received the cease-and-desist letter in the summer of 1973 from the executive committee of NFL Properties. The use of the name Dallas Cowboy and display of the team logo at Clint Murchison's New York chili restaurant violated league rules. Tex passed the letter along to Clint Murchison, who wrote the three committee members: "Gee, fellows, it's only a game!" He shortened the restaurant's name to the Cowboy and removed all offending logos. When Murchison discovered there was a gay bar with the same name in the city, he changed the name again, to Cowboy and Cowgirl.

The Organization Man

AFTER THE SEASON OF CHALLENGE, as the Cowboys' NFL Films highlight reel for 1972 was titled, three assistant coaches—Reeves, Renfro, and Franklin—left in search of greener pastures, and Chuck Howley and Dave Manders retired, as did Mike Ditka, to coach the ends full-time. Wild-haired receiver Billy Parks asked to be traded to a West Coast team. He wanted off the Cowboys bandwagon. "The way they try to promote [the game] and sell it is out of proportion to its value to society," said Parks, the other half of the Duane Thomas trade to San Diego, who never took to the Cowboys media machine or to Dallas. "The whole purpose is to sell to make a buck, to get the fans. With the electronic media, they can make anything God-like." Parks had thrown a fit during Navy Day at the stadium the year before, complaining that the team was wrapping itself in the American flag.

"I don't think it's as much disliking the Cowboys as it is his feelings towards Dallas," said Mike Ditka, delicately trying to explain Parks. "I don't know where his feelings came from but he doesn't really feel socially that he can adjust to the situation in Dallas. He has that California blood in him and he just thinks that's the only place to live." Roger Kaye, the Beatle-haired beat writer for the *Fort Worth Star-Telegram*, wrote that "Parks is an individual, and Landry says there is no place for complete individuals in football." Parks had hardly endeared himself to his teammates. One unidentified player opined, "You could forcefeed all of 'Harpo's' brains to a humming-bird and he'd still fly backwards."

Billy Parks was traded to Houston instead of the West Coast, along with lineman Tody Smith, a native of nearby Beaumont. Smith tried to reassure Parks about his new home team. "Dallas is twenty years behind the rest of the country in social attitudes. Houston isn't."

Dallas was a special place, the Cowboys were a special team, and their best player, Bob Lilly, was a special player. Even so, if Lilly had played for any other team, he probably would have made twice what he made with the Cowboys. Contract negotiations were becoming rather heated, and no one's contract talk epitomized that better than Lilly's.

A protocol had been established for negotiating with favored players such as Lilly. Schramm's secretary, Eileen Gish, would wel-come players into Tex's office, one at a time. "Bob," Tex would tell Lilly in the early years, "you've got a twelve-thousand-dollar contract, you did real good, we have a year option and I want to tear the con-tract up and I want to give you a two-thousand-dollar raise." Lilly would say, "Hell of a deal, Tex," and they'd shake hands. The next year Schramm would bring him in and say, "Bob, you made All-Pro. I want to tear your contract up and give you a four-thousand-dollar raise." Bob would say, "Hell of a deal, Tex."

Lilly had made All-Pro eight times since he joined the team in 1961. At the most recent Pro Bowl Game, Chicago's Dick Butkus and the Vikings' Alan Page told him they were making $100,000 and $90,000 a year, respectively. Lilly made $40,000. "So he comes back home and he's pissed off," said Russ Russell, who had been doing side projects with Lilly. "He wanted to renegotiate and the front office wouldn't do it. He'd just married Ann [his second wife], got on a plane to go to training camp, landed in Los Angeles after having two or three pops on the flight. Instead of going to Thousand Oaks, he got on another plane to Las Vegas and goes over to Abe

Schiller's at the Flamingo and spends two days. Tex is calling me, everybody he knows, he wants to know where Bob is."

Lilly returned to Dallas after Vegas and called a press conference to announce his retirement. "Money's not so much of a problem as their technique," he told reporters. "One of the things we all face is the overall coldness and impersonal way the club is organized and administered." He was tired of having to wait until he was in camp to renegotiate his contract and tired of being nickel-and-dimed by his boss. "They've led me to believe they're not a high-profit organization." So Lilly was hanging up his cleats.

Schramm, along with Landry and Brandt, who *never* got involved with contract negotiations, flew to Dallas. Tex spent several hours trying to talk Lilly out of retiring and finally succeeded when Lilly's salary was doubled. The atypical response indicated Schramm was adapting to the times. Schramm had never before made an effort like he did with Lilly. When Craig Morton had left camp a few days earlier over contract negotiations, Tex hadn't chased him. He had other quarterbacks. But he'd never had a player like Lilly.

Schramm had never had a coach like Tom Landry either. Pro football's first comic book, titled *Tom Landry and the Dallas Cowboys*, affirmed the broad appeal of the Cowboys. So did a novel about the Dallas Cowboys that promised an insider's look at a pro player's life. Pete Gent was in the first generation of individualists who excelled on the field enough for Landry to want them as players, but Gent didn't always fit into the system that Landry had conjured up. He did turn out to be a skilled writer. His first novel, the semiautobiographical *North Dallas Forty,* published in September of 1973, captured the violence and win-at-any-cost attitude of pro ball. The characters on the North Dallas Bulls were based on real people, including the party-hard quarterback Seth Maxwell (Meredith), his devout Christian backup QB Art Hartman (Staubach), the stone-faced born-again coach B. A. Quinlan (Landry), as well as the hypocritical owner Conrad Hunter (Murchison), his rich pals, and Phil Elliott (Gent himself).

At least, it looked that way to uninformed readers. "The backup quarterback was this guy that was a Christian that messed around," Roger Staubach said of the book. "And I'm the backup quarterback."

The story line peeled back layers of the Athlete as Noble Hero. Dexamyl spansules, marijuana, LSD, mescaline, speed, codeine, Novocain, Demerol, Benzedrine, amyl nitrite, Compazine, and other legal and illegal pharmaceuticals, wrote Blackie Sherrod, were "the cast of the characters from *North Dallas Forty*, the fierce, damned and praised, highly profitable novel from the caustic quill of Mr. Pete Gent, whom you will kindly recognize as ole No. 35 in your Cowboy program. These are the materials that Gent's pro football players sniff and swallow and inject and smoke and stuff up their noses or whatever in pursuit of life's looser strata [and to overcome injuries so they could play, which Sherrod overlooked]. And these drugs are the main objections that Dallas players and coaches and brass make to the book, if they admit having read it at all."

The book was a bestseller, its popularity a slap in the face to Tex and Tom and team officials, as well as a left-handed compliment to the Cowboys brand. Management had striven to project a clean image built on talent, faith, discipline, teamwork, and moral values, even though that struck a whole lot of people as hypocritical and arrogant. The book merely heightened the skepticism.

The organization's reaction was muted at first. No, they hadn't read the book and wouldn't, several players, coaches, front-office personnel, and friends of the team said. But they had heard enough about it to make clear that Gent's tome was sour grapes. "Gent wasn't the greatest receiver we ever had, but he was pretty good," said Russ Russell, the Cowboys photographer with *Pro Football Weekly*. "Well, they [the management] moved on, he went to New York and couldn't make the team. That's when he got vindictive and came back and decided to put all the dirt in the deal. He was disgruntled. He wanted to still play but couldn't."

"It wasn't well-received as a book that we would all be proud of for our friends and neighbors to read," Lee Roy Jordan said diplomatically while seething inside. "He wasn't one of my favorite guys as a player and I think he knows that. He experimented with things that no one else had ever experimented around our football team."

The real Cowboys were just as interesting. Lust and abandon always simmered under the surface, and it was bubbling to the surface more and more in Dallas. Example A was Judy Stone, freshly kicked out of her parents' home at the age of sixteen. So she moved in with Jimmy Bankston, the son of auto dealer W. O. Bankston, who employed Judy's father. Her other roommates in the three-bedroom house were a NASCAR driver named Richard Thorp, and Cliff Harris, number 43 for the Dallas Cowboys, Captain Crash. "Jimmy owned four car dealerships, so we drove anything we wanted," Judy recalled.

Hedonistic would hardly suffice to describe their lifestyles.

"We had a nice Samsonite suitcase that you push the button like in *Get Smart* [the television spy comedy] to pop open," Judy Stone said. Inside were Thai sticks, cocaine, amyl nitrite, Quaaludes, and other illicit substances. "It was kind of like mom's pantry," Stone said. "We had a case of amyl nitrite and good vodka and good tequila in the freezer at all times. We got issued guns when we moved in. I was in charge of reloading, we had a reloader room; I was making pipe bombs before I was eighteen. We all had guns strapped to the end of our headboard. I took a gun to school every day. It was that 'we're Texans' mentality—we carry guns because we can."

The football player was the exception. "Cliff was straighter than the rest of us," Stone said. "Cliff didn't do drugs during the season. He didn't stay out and party during the season. He would go out and drink and stuff during the offseason. But during the season, he was really regimented. I remember sitting around and watching game tapes with him one time and him showing me things that they circled where other players would like jab them in the side and do all this illegal stuff and I was completely flabbergasted that that stuff went on. We didn't have parties or do stuff when he was in game mode."

Everyone hunkered down when it was football season, and those who weren't ready to sacrifice paid a price. Dave Manders, the starting center when the Cowboys won the Super Bowl, didn't report to training camp and threatened to retire if he didn't get a $2,500 raise. It was a bad year to play hardball, not just because Lilly had already tested Schramm, but also because John Fitzgerald was ready to replace Manders. Schramm found no reason to accommodate Manders and let him retire.

"We listened to the second preseason game while we were at Lake Eufala in Oklahoma," Betty Manders, Dave's wife, recalled. "We heard when Fitzgerald snapped the ball over the head of the punter in the end zone. The newspapers started saying he was having trouble with his long snaps."

On Clint Murchison's birthday, September 12, Tex Schramm hatched a plan to get Manders to jump out of a giant wrapped gift box, much like Lamar Hunt had done a decade earlier. Betty Manders hated the idea. "It was a slap in the face," she said. "They were having this lavish party and they wouldn't give Dave $2,500. I rode with Dave to the party and we were greeted by Gil Brandt, who brought me in to hide me so Coach Landry and Clint couldn't see me. Dave was in a huge gift box and they brought him in and I lost it. I started poking Tex: 'You should not do this to my husband. This is downright ugly. You need him.' I went on and on. I used words I've never used before."

"Now, Betty..." Tex tut-tutted.

"Don't call me Betty," she shot back. "I don't ever want to hear from you. This is what you do to people. This is how you treat someone who's been with you for nine years, that's never done a wrong thing, he's done everything you wanted, he's a family man."

Betty Manders was escorted to her car while Dave stayed and entertained Clint and company.

—

When Betty and Dave Manders watched Roger Staubach call his own plays in the opening game against Chicago and eke out a win over the Bears, they also saw John Fitzgerald muff another long snap, and after the game, the return of Dave Manders and Chuck Howley was made official. Manders got his $2,500 raise. Howley, who owned his own cleaning business and counted the Cowboys among his clients, didn't need the money. He returned as a member of the taxi squad because Coach Landry asked him to. "He had a couple of young linebackers and wanted me for insurance."

The home opener of the fourteenth edition of the Dallas Cowboys attracted 52,715 spectators—13,000 short of a full house and the smallest Cowboys crowd yet at Texas Stadium—along with the ABC *Monday Night Football* crew, all on hand to see the coach's one hundredth victory, a complete drubbing of the New Orleans Saints, 40–3. Staubach left the game with a shoulder injury and Morton went 5-7 backing him up.

Most stadiums were less than full for the NFL home openers, thanks to the new law that the Congress passed mandating that the NFL lift television blackouts of home games that had sold out seventy-two hours before kickoff. Thus was born a new statistic whose numbers spoke loudly to every franchise's health: no-shows, fans who bought tickets but stayed home. Kansas City led the league with 16,031 no-shows in Arrowhead Stadium for the Los Angeles game. Tex Schramm responded by speculating road games might no longer be televised and suggesting the league offer the networks one national game of the week. The disappointing turnouts were tempered by the four-year, $214 million contract the league was signing with the networks. TV might be hurting gate receipts but each team's making in excess of $2 million a year for television broadcast rights soothed the anguish.

———

SINCE EVERY TEAM NOW had access to the same tools, the draft was no longer the Cowboys' berry patch to pick from. The rest of the league had caught up with the Cowboys in their analysis methods and whispers began to circulate that Brandt and company were losing their touch. Bill Thomas, the running back from Boston College who was the number-one draft pick in 1972, would not last a season before being traded.

Brandt worked hard to stay ahead of the pack. He went to the University of Colorado to design new tests for players, such as short shuttles and vertical jumps. "The rule of thumb was that you found out that anybody that ran under seven [seconds] in the short shuttle has about a ninety-five percent chance of making it."

A handful of prospects emerged from the 1973 draft — number-one pick Billy Joe DuPree, a tight end from Michigan State; number-two pick Golden Richards, a wide receiver from Hawaii; and number-three pick Harvey Martin, a defensive end from South Oak Cliff by way of East Texas State who immediately went out and bought an orange Mark IV Lincoln as soon as he was drafted. A free-agent wide receiver from Tulsa named Drew Pearson also managed to stick for a season that would be defined by another Dallas-Washington battle for supremacy atop the Eastern Division.

After beating Chicago on the road and pounding New Orleans in the home opener, the Cowboys trounced St. Louis 45–10 at Texas Stadium before heading to RFK Stadium to face Washington. The team was up 7–0 when Landry pulled Staubach for missing a signal. Morton stepped in but was ineffective, throwing the interception that won the game for Washington, 14–7. George Allen, whose mark against Landry as coach of the Rams and the Redskins was an impressive 10-4, gave hope to a rising tide of Cowboy Haters who resented the team's shiny uniforms, gleaming stadium, sterile and efficient organization, and fans so holy and passive their seats were known as pews.

Rooting for Dallas was like rooting for General Motors, and defensive end Pat Toomay and broadcasters Verne Lundquist and Frank Glieber all agreed Dallas fans needed to step up their game.

"There were periods of nothing," Toomay said. "It was like playing in a TV studio. That really helps your momentum. It sure would help to get some support."

"They sit on their hands," Lundquist said. "I think it's because of the living room atmosphere. Cowboy crowds have been less vocal ever since they moved from the Cotton Bowl. The atmosphere is too socially acclimated now."

"You get the impression the Cowboys are playing in a concert hall," Frank Glieber observed. "You get light applause. In the beginning, it may have been due to being in such palatial surroundings. The whole atmosphere is unlike any stadium I've ever been in, mainly due to the luxuriousness. Another factor could be they can't sell beer."

Roger Staubach returned as starter following the Washington loss and remained in charge into December despite constant bangups, a pulled calf muscle, and the slow death of his mother, Betty. "She had pancreatic cancer," Staubach said. "She was in our house so we were taking care of her at the beginning of the season. [Landry] knew we had to put her back in the hospital for just a short time for feeding." Landry took his quarterback aside after the Thanksgiving Day game, a loss to Miami, and said, "Roger, I know what you're going through with your mom. I'm going to take over calling the plays and you just go out there and execute." Landry wanted to return to his system where he called the plays, not the quarterback, and this was a good time to re-implement it.

Meanwhile, Lee Roy Jordan did his part, personally shutting down Cincinnati's offense with *three* interceptions in less than five minutes during the first quarter, one for a touchdown. An improvised sign held up in the stands toward the end of the Cowboys' 38–10 win said it all: THOU SHALT NOT PASS OVER JORDAN. Jordan grabbed another interception the following week against the New York Giants in a 23–10 win at Yankee Stadium.

The lackluster Thanksgiving Day 14–7 loss to Miami left Dallas at 7-4, second best in the East behind the 8-3 'Skins. There had been enough stutter steps and misfires that the Cowboys' only hope for reaching the playoffs was to win the rest of their games. A Mel Renfro interception, a shutdown of the Broncos' running game, and two Staubach-to-Fugett touchdown passes were the decisive factors in the 22–10 win at Mile High Stadium against the Broncos, leading up to the showdown with the Redskins, whom they needed to beat by seven points to stay in playoff contention.

The Cowboys led Washington 3–0 at halftime, despite three missed field-goal attempts by the Redskins and a sputtering offense. Then the Cowboys turned on the afterburners in the second half and charged to a 27–7 win as Doomsday stopped the running game and forced turnovers, while the offensive line held long enough for Staubach to roll out, bootleg, and scramble his way down the field and for Calvin Hill to gin up 110 rushing yards.

Texas Stadium came alive like never before. Although a WE LOVE YOU CHARLIE WATERS banner had been removed shortly after it was unfurled early in the season, management finally relented on the stadium sign ban and the fans responded with a spirited display, including COWBOY BRAND THAR SKIN; EAT YOUR HEART OUT GEORGE; REDSKINS BUG US THE WAY WATERGATE BUGS NIXON; WASHINGTON HAS ITS TROUBLES: FUEL RATION WATERGATE AND COWBOYS; and WILL ROGERS NEVER MET GEO. ALLEN.

With both teams tied at the top of the East, the Cowboys had the edge to advance as division champions. Days after Roger Staubach's mother passed away, the Cowboys smothered the Cardinals 30–3 in the final game of the regular season, in which Drew Pearson caught his first touchdown pass as a pro and Lee Roy Jordan snagged another interception.

"I was up in Cincinnati for the funeral," Staubach said. "I was true portrayal of what pro football is really like," Schramm wrote in his guest column. "What has happened is one person, who in my opinion has a sick approach to life, has indicted the whole NFL and Dallas Cowboy organization. I consider the book offensive and malicious." The book, he said, was "a total lie." Ninety-five percent of the players in the league were decent human beings "who in no way resemble the degenerate characters depicted in Gent's book."

The organization preferred to champion a new nonfiction title, *Staubach: First Down, Lifetime to Go,* cowritten with Sam Blair and Bob St. John and published by Word Press, a religious press. Staubach's personal story offered a whole other view of pro football, one without salacious details. He was not shy about where he stood, just as he hadn't been after winning the Super Bowl two years earlier. "The things I was saying just weren't in vogue then," Staubach said. "Neither was I, especially. I wore my hair short and didn't dress flashily. Apple pie, God, and American patriotism just weren't things people were speaking about in those days. That's changed now. There were anti-God movements then but now it has run the cycle, and people more and more are coming back to religion."

What kind of religion was subject to interpretation. Take the Liles family of Richardson. A God-fearing family who prayed before meals, they had a Sunday ritual of going to Cowboys games, first at the Cotton Bowl, then at Texas Stadium. "Having Cowboys tickets was the one thing that could get you out of going to church," said Jeff Liles, who grew up loving the Cowboys. "Every Sunday, we would drive past churches on our way to take the shuttle buses at Valley View Mall to the game. Our church was Texas Stadium. Our whole family went and we had extra tickets to take along friends."

Area churches knew enough to wrap up services early if the Cowboys were playing at noon. It wasn't just because they were a football team. It was because they presented themselves as clean and wholesome role models too, starting with Coach Tom Landry.

Patti Hunt and Jacque Wynne, wife of Toddie Lee Wynne, new

only at practice one day, but I started. It was an icy day, but I had one of the best games I've ever had. We had to beat the Cardinals to win the division. I remember that season more than any other because of my mother's sickness."

Staubach and company bucked the Rams 27–16 in the first round of the playoffs on two more Drew Pearson touchdown receptions, including an 83-yard bomb that Pearson told Staubach Betty was responsible for.

But a Super Bowl return was abruptly canceled by the Minnesota Vikings, who put the hurt on a flat Cowboys team at home in the NFC championship, 27–10. Bob Lilly sat out his first game ever from a hamstring pull, and Staubach never found the right receivers in the end zone and threw four interceptions. The Vikings' Fearsome Foursome kept Garrison and Newhouse plugged up. "Afterwards, I said I guess Mom was asleep up there," Staubach said.

Tom Landry took the loss like the coach he was—gracious and precisely analytical. "I'm just trying to analyze what happened to us," he said calmly. "I had hoped we'd play better. That's the biggest disappointment…that we didn't play better and we made errors. This was an excellent year for the team. They did such a great job and played so well and won so many key games down the stretch. So, it's just a shame that it ends this way because that's what people tend to remember—the way it ended."

The mastermind was deflated. "I guess I have a sense of history," Tex Schramm said with a moan. "I wanted us to be the first team to make the Super Bowl three times," he said. Close but no cigar. Duane Thomas's prophecy was proving true: the Cowboys couldn't get to or win the Super Bowl without him. Or maybe there was something more to it. The Vikings suffered the ignominy of losing to Miami for a second consecutive Super Bowl, 24–7, giving fuel to the perception that the AFC was indeed superior to the NFC.

How Do You Spell *Cowboys*? M-O-N-E-Y

DESPITE THE COWBOYS' falling short, the season had been remarkable for not being remarkable, ending with pretty much the same cast as it started with. There was no quarterback shuffle or controversy, no big dogs cut down, no fussing and fighting internally. The system prevailed.

Lee Roy Jordan, after enjoying his best year yet at linebacker, won the Oak Farms My Favorite Cowboy contest, edging out Craig Morton and third-place finisher Roger Staubach.

The club realized a profit of $1.57 million in 1973. Tex Schramm, who had exercised his option to buy 20 percent of the team, sold off his piece of the action. Tom Landry, who bought 5 percent of the club at 1966 prices, was in the process of selling his shares back to Clint Murchison too, in order to set up a trust for his wife and children.

The Cowboys fell off the front page in mid-January, subsumed by something bigger, grander, and more outrageous than Texas Stadium. On January 13, the Dallas–Fort Worth Regional Airport, twenty miles from the downtowns of both cities, officially opened to commercial air service. J. Erik Jonsson's dream (and Clint Murchison's long-ago vision) had been realized in a Texas-size way. The island of Manhattan could fit inside the airport's 17,800-acre footprint, boosters liked to brag.

The futuristic concrete construction with automated railcars linking the terminals amid a spaghetti maze of roads worked like a magnet to draw companies that depended on business travel as well as entertainers and sports figures, who moved to Irving, Grapevine, Colleyville, and Las Colinas and other suburbs near the airport.

"The whole conglomerate kind of multi-business model began here along about then," said Dick Bartlett, the head of direct sales for the Mary Kay Corporation. The opening of the 1.4-million-square-foot World Trade Center on Stemmons Expressway, the world's largest wholesale merchandise mart, and completion of the fifty-six-story Renaissance Tower were cherries on top.

They were all part of an unprecedented boom that complemented the football club in raising the region's profile. And there could always be a Cowboys angle to the news. Thomas J. Manton, a Dallas Independent School District teacher at Metropolitan Center East High School, was one of nineteen teachers honored by the Perot Foundation for academic excellence. Manton taught English by reading newspaper accounts of Cowboys games, a subject most students could relate to.

One of the team's first media stars, the player who had made the Cowboys so important in the community, departed ABC's *Monday Night Football* in 1973 to accept a three-year deal with NBC. The Don Meredith would call pro football games alongside Curt Gowdy as well as act in television shows. NBC also promised no one would call him Dandy Don. He quickly scored a gig on a new drama series called *Police Story* and substituted for Johnny Carson on *Tonight Show*.

After one million copies of the paperback edition of *North Forty* flooded bookstores, airports, and newsstands every Blackie Sherrod offered his soapbox to Tex Schramm. "Pe Gent was a member of the Cowboys, his book is given valid

members of the Park Cities branch of the American Cancer Society, threw the first Cattle Baron's Ball at the Wynnes' Star Brand ranch in Kaufman County, inviting the black-tie crowd to dress cowboy and drawing Tom Landry, the Murchisons, various Rockefellers, and country music singer Charley Pride. The event, at which all of Dallas society and their friends and associates played ostentatious cowboys, raised $56,000 and within a few years was the world's largest single-night fund-raiser for cancer research through the American Cancer Society.

Separately, the members of the Cowboys Wives Club got into a tiff about where the money raised went, an argument divided along racial lines. Tom Landry stepped in to split the pot for the wives and then suggested the club disband, which it did.

If only Landry could have been so persuasive with the upstart World Football League. The rival was raiding the NFL for players, signing them to future contracts, which only exacerbated threats by the NFL Players Association to go on strike and cancel the season if demands weren't met. Some players didn't show at training camp; others who did wore No Freedom/No Football/NFLPA T-shirts.

Born-again John Niland, after hosting a midsummer golf tournament for the Fellowship of Christian Athletes, ignored the NFL Players Association and came to training camp because "that's where the Lord wants me to be," he said. "It may not be my will, but as a Christian I feel I belong in camp. I must be submissive to my owner. The Bible is very descriptive about this. It says even if my master isn't fair, I'm a servant to him. I'll be working with a Christian, Tom Landry, and that's even more reason to be there."

What Niland didn't say and wouldn't say until years later was that he had been strung out on amphetamines and alcohol and had physically abused his wife, Iree, before he found Jesus.

The strike ultimately lasted less than a week, although exhibition games were canceled and Rayfield Wright, Jethro Pugh, and DD Lewis left camp after they arrived. Players' rep Ed Garvey was so angered that the players did not stay together that he said he wouldn't have wanted to fight alongside Roger Staubach in World War II because Staubach had crossed the picket line.

Schramm defended his quarterback by going after Garvey. "It's time someone told the fans how the players' union spells freedom," he said bitterly. "It's M-O-N-E-Y."

"I came to that 'don't care' conclusion independently doing research on the team," defensive end Pat Toomay said. "I dug out the 1972 press book after we won the Super Bowl and there on the cover is Tex, Clint, and Tom. I never noticed that before. Not a team picture. Sure, they put together a good organization, but see what I mean? The organization will overcome. They feel there are enough players out there in the woodwork. When you play chess, you have chess pieces. You can always come up with the pieces."

Toomay was unhappy because the selection of defensive lineman Ed "Too Tall" Jones, the six-eight giant from Tennessee State, as the Cowboys' number-one draft pick meant a new defensive strategy for Coach Landry. Toomay, who had led the team in sacks, was being shifted to defend against run situations along with Larry Cole. Jones and second-year vet Harvey Martin would defend in passing situations, leading Toomay to play out his option and request a trade.

Toomay's dissatisfaction and even the strike were still small potatoes compared to the World Football League, which turned out to be real enough to generate rumors that Craig Morton, Otto Stowe, Calvin Hill, Jethro Pugh, Robert Newhouse, Rayfield Wright, DD Lewis, Dave Edwards, Mel Renfro, Charlie Waters, and quarterback Danny White, the Cowboys' number-three draft pick, had all signed future contracts with the WFL. Landry said if the rumors were true, all lame-duck Cowboys would be demoted to backup roles. One signing was no rumor: Calvin Hill inked a contract with the Hawaii franchise to begin play in 1975 for $400,000, more than four times what he was being paid by the Cowboys. And Craig Morton had evidently signed some kind of agreement with the WFL's Houston Texans franchise.

State district judge Charles Long granted the Cowboys a temporary injunction preventing agents or WFL people from talking to players under contract, which pleased Schramm. "I'm very elated," he said. "This is what we had asked for. This was one of the most serious threats to the Cowboys and to the sport we have at the present time. I feel so strongly about it that I brought this action. I felt gratified that the judge saw the gravity of the situation." The league raids threatened the existence of the Cowboys, he said grimly, while making clear to Craig Morton he wasn't being picked on. In a brief talk in a hallway, Schramm said to Morton, "I hope you understand that what we are doing is not aimed at you personally. It's what we think is right for the Cowboys. And we're not mad at you because we know you are doing what you think is right."

"I understand," Morton replied. "I feel the same way."

At the same time, Schramm was sending people undercover to suss out the situation. "I spent five days at State College [Pennsylvania] trying to figure out whether [Heisman Trophy winner John] Cappelletti and all those guys were going to the World Football League," business manager Joe Bailey said. "We had a bunch of espionage going on. It was an enormous drain on resources and created huge hurdles for Tex and the organization."

For all the success of the Dallas Cowboys, the perception of the team's front office as tightfisted and antiunion grew. It was bad enough that players were bitching about Scrooge Schramm behind his back at the team's Christmas party; while the Cowboys organization was considered first class, it was a cheap date when it came to paying the hired help. The numbers did not lie: Dallas was sixteenth among twenty-six teams in player salaries.

Calvin Hill, who was playing out his contract before jumping to the World Football League, thought Schramm and the front office were hypocrites for their stance on the looming strike. "Duane was run out of town because he was an individual," Hill said. "Supposedly, his individuality had been bad for the team. Now management is encouraging players to be individuals and report to camp. It's hardly consistent."

Tex Schramm wished he could stop the transformation of sports sections into the *Wall Street Journal*. "If we continue to utilize the sports pages with monetary and non-competitive news, we'll jeopardize the popularity of our sport," he griped to Blackie Sherrod. "I think fans are just tired of hearing about our money hassles." Tex certainly was. Money matters were best discussed behind closed doors among family. If outsiders regarded the team's pay scale as low, they weren't factoring in the bonus money that came with advancing in the playoffs, Tex believed. That's where Dallas Cowboys football players earned their rewards.

The bargaining agreement being hammered out between the NFL's management council and the NFL Players Association would further eliminate family from the proposition. Agents had already become part and parcel of contract negotiations. But as long as the Rozelle rule prevailed, management continued to maintain an upper hand over labor.

The Rozelle rule stipulated that any team signing a player from another team had to pay compensation to that team, even if the player had fulfilled all existing contract obligations, with the commissioner determining the amount of compensation owed. This effectively rendered meaningless the concept of free agency, which was supposed to allow a player to shop for the best contract with the team of the player's choosing. John Mackey, the player representative from the Baltimore Colts and the first president of the NFL Players Association, filed a lawsuit claiming the Rozelle rule stifled competition, violated antitrust laws, and limited players' bargaining power.

Which made Tex Schramm's claims that players were like family sound like so much blather. Players playing out the last year of their contracts without being in the process of renegotiating new ones were often dropped from the roster overnight.

"The elimination of 'family' from the formula was Tex Schramm's version of 'It's a little more challenging for me to try to manipulate and control without any opposition,'" said Bob Stein, a linebacker for the Kansas City Chiefs who later became an agent. "His translation was all bullshit. Loyalty was a one-way deal. The Cowboys were pretty famous for being close to abusive to their players and for taking the attitude it's an honor to play for the Cowboys and you ought to like it and we'll pay you what we want. Other teams got playoff shares too, except they would pay their players more in the regular season."

The latest example was Lee Roy Jordan, the glue who held the defense together as middle linebacker and the defensive captain. Like Bob Lilly, the other rock of Doomsday, Lee Roy knew he was being shortchanged. He would be playing out the last year of his contract without renegotiating it in advance, he announced, taking the mandatory 10 percent cut for playing it out.

Schramm had made it his policy to sign Staubach first because his quarterback didn't care what he made; he just wanted to play football. So with another year left on his contract, Staubach was more than happy to sit down with Schramm and work out a multi-year deal. He had earned $90,000 the previous season. What did he want for this season? asked Schramm.

"I don't know. What do you think?"

"How about a hundred thousand?"

Deal done.

Having to follow Staubach to the negotiating table put Jordan at a disadvantage from the start. He opened his first sit-down with Tex in the winter by pointing out that Dick Butkus, the standout line-backer for the Chicago Bears, was now making $120,000. He wanted just as much.

"I can't pay you any more than I'm paying Roger," Schramm said conveniently. The MO usually worked. But not this time.

"I was like Bob Lilly and a number of people," Jordan later admitted. "We were just not brought up to beat our own drum. We'd go into Schramm's office and were intimidated by his power. He was so blunt. And we weren't used to hearing that. He'd say things like, 'Well, you're twenty-nine, thirty, and we've got to start looking for somebody to replace you.' Hell, we were afraid to be very blunt, because we thought it might make us an outcast in Dallas and that people would look down on us. It wasn't true, but that's what we thought. One time in the late 1960s I asked for a raise, and Tex said what I wanted was more than Landry was making. It was about $50,000 a year. I asked Tom and he said it was true. So I just told Tom he was underpaid.

"I gave Roger a hard time about the situation too," Jordan said. "Roger and Lilly were highest paid. Roger didn't worry about the extra money because he was getting a lot outside football. We got one hundred to two hundred fifty for a speaking engagement and Roger might be getting three to four hundred. But things were in proportion and that kept the rest of us down."

Jordan had been on Schramm's case since the end of the previous season about getting a contract done. He didn't want to go into training camp without one. They met in late February. "I had gathered my information and gotten all the contracts of Green Bay linebackers," Jordan said. "They talked to me and told me what they were making. I told Tex I don't think I deserve to make more than Ray Nitschke but I need to be within light years of him."

Schramm made a counteroffer in late spring that was not even half what Jordan was asking for. "He always liked to get you at training camp where you'd start worrying about getting injured without a contract and if you got worried he'd pressure you into signing," Jordan said. During camp, Tex promised small bumps in salary, nothing more.

Jordan complained louder. When Schramm sent four dollars to Alabama University for two media brochures, the check was returned with a note: *to be applied towards signing Jordan.*

Clint Murchison tried to make a joke out of it by issuing a press release: "I will not report to training camp at Thousand Oaks and the reason is strictly monetary." But no one laughed.

Lee Roy Jordan went on to have his best training camp ever. His loyalty to the team wasn't questioned. "I was taught once you make a commitment, there's no quitting, there's no turning back," Jordan said. "That was my dad's philosophy before I learned it from some other people, like Coach Bryant."

But on the Monday before the Cowboys' opening game against Chicago, Lee Roy Jordan decided to make a stand. He didn't show up at practice. Linebackers coach Jerry Tubbs called Jordan at home. Lee Roy was never late to practice. "Are you sick?" he asked.

"I'm going to hold out until I get a contract," Jordan told him.

Five minutes later, Landry called.

"Coach, I'm not going to play without a contract, I'm going to finish my career in Dallas and I'm not going to do it unless Tex gets me a contract that I can sign," Jordan informed him.

Four hours later, Lee Roy Jordan signed his contract.

"I can't believe you're doing this," Schramm complained. "To me, one of the worst things an athlete can do is deserting his team on the eve of a game when everybody is counting on him." Schramm negotiated a three-year contract that paid Jordan $75,000 his final year but he held on to a grudge against Jordan. "He didn't like my ass for that forever," Jordan said.

AFTER A SURPRISINGLY BRIEF preseason of indecision, the coach made up his mind in mid-September that Roger Staubach would start. Staubach had gotten knocked around long enough to refine his penchant for scrambling and learn to hit the deck when being pursued. "I've encouraged him to do that for five years," the coach said. "I guess he finally got to where he can slide well after he got the shoulder, rib, and various other injuries."

Morton's demotion to backup one more time and an unsettled contract beef with Schramm prompted Morton to ask to be traded to a team he could lead.

"I made a point of renegotiating my contract in camp," he said. "I did it because I had great belief in myself. But my contract's still not resolved. I think it should have been resolved long ago." The year before, Morton had left camp for ten days and thought he had a verbal agreement with Schramm. "I went through ten agonizing days and it seems to be to no avail." Tex played dodgeball, saying, "I am positive in my mind what the agreement was. I'm not going to debate it in the newspaper. There is no question in my mind. I'm not going to get into an argument with him. He may think what he wants."

Schramm, knowing the deed was already done, mildly protested that his word and his honor had been questioned. "I was very surprised when his version [of the contract dispute] surfaced," he said. "I had thought until then that we had a good chance to resolve everything."

Morton's departure and Jordan's signing resolved enough for the Cowboys to focus on football, opening at Atlanta against the Falcons with a convincing 24–0 shutout in which rookie Ed "Too Tall" Jones was awarded the game ball. But the team proceeded to dispel all the talk about a dynasty as just that—talk—by dropping four in a row to Philadelphia, New York, Minnesota, and St. Louis. *Monday Night Football* showcased the Dallas-Philly game, which was decided by a 48-yard field goal by the Eagles' Tom Dempsey, who held the league record for the longest field goal kicked, a 63-yarder, when he was with New Orleans, despite his being born with a deformed foot that required a special kicking shoe. Tex Schramm tried unsuccessfully to get Dempsey's customized shoe banned, but to no avail. The home opener 14–6 loss to the New York Giants was in front of 46,353, the smallest home crowd in nine years. For the first time ever, Staubach was booed by the home folks. "Only Bob Lilly and Helen Hayes remain unscathed," Blackie Sherrod wrote.

Ticket manager Kay Lang blamed the low crowd count on the players: "I think it started in preseason when the players were demanding this or that while the guy going to the grocery store was having a hard time feeding his kids," she said. "Then you wonder how you can justify an explanation like that when Buffalo is drawing 80,000."

The four-game losing streak was snapped at home against Philadelphia in front of an even lousier house of 43,586.

But the ground game was back to full speed with Walt Garrison's return from the injured list and the World Football League–bound Calvin Hill leading the NFL in rushing.

The Cowboys waltzed to their third consecutive win at the Yale Bowl in New Haven, Connecticut, the New York Giants' temporary home while Yankee Stadium was being renovated and a new football stadium was being constructed for the team in New Jersey's Meadowlands. The Giants quarterback was Craig Morton, whose trade had been finalized a week earlier. The 21–7 win was punctuated by wide receiver Drew Pearson's 46-yard touchdown pass to Golden Richards. Staubach was 10-19 with a TD pass and an interception. Morton went 11-22, but no TDs and three interceptions.

The Cowboys evened their record at 4-4 by edging St. Louis, 17–14, on Efren Herrera's 20-yard field goal, then took the 49ers, 20–14, with Calvin Hill gaining 153 yards and scoring two TDs and two Herrera field goals providing the difference.

The streak ended in DC with the Redskins up by a touchdown, 28–21, when time ran out. A week later, the D reappeared and Dallas blanked the Houston Oilers 10–0.

A tiny ray of hope remained going into the Thanksgiving Day game against the Redskins, who were a cinch for the playoffs with their 8-3 record, compared to the Cowboys' 7-5. The 'Skins jumped out to a quick lead and were ahead 16–3 when Captain Comeback, as Roger Staubach was becoming known, got decked by Washington linebacker Dave Robinson in the third quarter and left the game with a concussion. Since Craig Morton had been traded away, the team had no choice but to put in third-string rookie Clint Longley, an unheralded quarterback from Abilene Christian University, west of Fort Worth.

Longley acted like an experienced veteran when he took the field, chunking two touchdown passes, including a 50-yard-long bomb to

Drew Pearson to win the game in the last minute, 24–23, which earned him the nickname the Mad Bomber.

Duane Thomas had returned to Texas Stadium as a running back for the Redskins and caught a nine-yard TD pass from Billy Kilmer, ran another in from 19 yards out, and churned out 55 yards rushing.

But it wasn't enough, and George Allen, who hadn't lost to the Cowboys at RFK Stadium yet, called the Redskins loss at Texas Stadium the worst he had ever endured.

Tex Schramm had been describing the Cowboys as "the team of tomorrow" to a sportswriter before Staubach got knocked out. He quickly amended his statement to "We'll have to be the team of tomorrow today."

With Staubach back as starter, the Cowboys blew out Cleveland in Dallas the following week, 41–17, but dropped the finale to the Oakland Raiders, 27–23, in Oakland, to finish 8-6. For the first time since 1965, the Cowboys did not make the playoffs. The *Morning News*'s Bob St. John called it "the year that wasn't." Home attendance had been the lowest since 1964.

Schramm put a positive spin on his postseason analysis. "I just know I feel more like I did in the 1960s," he said. "I'm very optimistic about the future and believe our organization is ready for the challenge."

NFL Films titled the Cowboys' 1974 highlight reel *A Champion in Waiting*. The perception was that the team and the organization had all the tools. All they had to do was put it together for a full season. In the eyes of locals, the Cowboys themselves were winners, period. At least they wouldn't quite be going away during the offseason, because Roger Staubach did a national TV spot for McDonald's fast-food hamburgers; Lee Roy Jordan appeared in print ads for Volkswagen autos and opened a Ford tractor dealership; and Walt Garrison, the leading steer wrestler at the Mesquite Championship Rodeo just east of the Dallas city limits, became the national spokesman and television face for Skoal tobacco snuff, the preferred dip of cowboys everywhere.

Faith in Another Super Bowl

IF YOU WANTED TO sell something in Dallas, there was no better salesman than a Dallas Cowboy. Coach Tom Landry endorsed hats and men's business clothes. Assistant coach Ernie Stautner endorsed beer. Harvey Martin, the South Dallas product, hosted the *Beautiful Harvey Martin Radio Show* on KRLD; he was one of twenty-one Cowboys who had their own programs on the DFW radio airwaves. John Niland sold cars and joined a sports management company with Bob Lilly and Craig Morton that raised their speaking engagement fees to $500 and above. Niland also led a cast of pro players, including Abner Haynes from the old Dallas Texans and about-to-be-ex-Cowboy Billy Truax, in a locally filmed B movie, *Horror High*, with DD Lewis, Calvin Hill, the departed Craig Morton, and Pittsburgh's Joe Greene appearing as extras.

While Morton played a policeman in the first episode of *The Magician*, an NBC television series starring Bill Bixby, Bob Lilly and baseball great Mickey Mantle opened a new joint called the Other Place, across the street from Morton's Wellington's. Pat Toomay, DD Lewis, and Dave Edwards partnered in Dave Edwards's Handlebar restaurant and club at Preston Road and the LBJ Expressway, and Mike Ditka's Sportspage Club near Love Field consistently packed in crowds, a tribute to Ditka's hands-on management skills.

Down on Lemmon Avenue, Harvey Martin, Rayfield "Big Cat"

Wright, and Mean Joe Greene from the Pittsburgh Steelers got into the action with the Balls, described in the *Cowboys Insiders* as a "swanky, off-beat type place with plenty of loud music on the juke box and a live jazz group every Sunday. It is a real trip."

Dave Edwards's Handlebar didn't last long. "We each put five thousand into it and ate there all the time," Pat Toomay said. "But the management stole us blind. I learned if you're going to do something, somebody had to be there, learn the business and the controls, and manage it."

The presence of a Cowboy or Cowboys at a function guaranteed publicity. Darla Chapman's debutante ball at the Dallas Country Club was big news mainly because of attendees Don Meredith, Ralph Neely, Roger Staubach, and Clint Murchison with his date, Anne Brandt, who was recently divorced from Gil Brandt.

Mayor Wes Wise heard about the Cowboys wherever he traveled. "At conventions, fellow mayors from other cities including major NFL cities would come to me and ask, 'How in the world did you all get yourself in this position?'" he said. "You'd go to another NFL venue in some other city and the Cowboys would have almost as many fans as the home team," which Wise attributed to winning and two personalities — Don Meredith and Roger Staubach. "They captured people's imaginations," the mayor said. "It was pretty obvious that people were forgetting about the quote unquote 'city of hate' because of the Cowboys."

IN THIS LAND OF bigger and better, where the old saw "It ain't bragging if it's true" was put to the test every day, it was little surprise that hubris sometimes crept into the picture, and confidence became arrogance.

One example was the end of Salam Qureishi, the Indian who introduced computers to the Cowboys and ran Optimum Systems Incorporated. The company had grown considerably and benefited from the Murchison Brothers lobbyists and fixers, such as the former FBI agent Tom Webb, whose ties led to a lucrative contract with the Environmental Protection Agency in 1971. Clint's investments in a company called Computer Applications allowed Optimum Systems to purchase a profitable division called EBS. But Clint also pushed acquisition of a Louisiana company owned by his friend Ramon Jarrel that was bleeding money. So when Qureishi asked for capital to buy computers rather than lease them, Murchison said no.

Qureishi, an observant Muslim, had tried his best to bond with Murchison, visiting him in Dallas and in his New York penthouse and attending parties Clint threw, where the Indian was often the lone sober person in the room. Running with the high rollers took some adjustment for Qureishi. When doing business in Washington, he stayed at the Sheraton-Carlton or the Embassy Row Hotel in spacious five-hundred-dollar-a-night VIP suites, a perk of being part of the Murchison team.

For the opening of OSI's New Orleans office, a bevy of senators, congressmen, aides, lobbyists, and federal officials were flown in for a reception at the Murchison residence in the French Quarter, where they were greeted by pretty female hostesses and plied with booze, food, and whatever else they wanted.

"People drank like fish," Qureishi later said of functions involving Murchison. "There were hookers everywhere. A lavish hotel suite seemed culturally appropriate."

When Qureishi was urged to bid on the data processing contract for another Murchison Brothers investment, the Teamsters Union employee pension fund, he found their demands unrealistic and ultimately unprofitable for OSI and the project never got off the ground. Four months later, Qureishi got a call from Murchison asking him to come to Dallas to discuss the financial condition of the computing company. Qureishi went. Murchison told him OSI needed a good financial man. Qureishi pointed out they already had someone, but Murchison said he didn't know that person and escorted

Qureishi to his anteroom to introduce him to Norm Kaupp, handing Qureishi his résumé. "Get him to Palo Alto," Murchison said. "Interview him and hire him as your CFO." Two weeks later, Kaupp was hired.

Within a month, Murchison ordered a restructuring of the company. Qureishi got the runaround from two ambitious vice presidents and the new CFO while a business plan was developed. Qureishi went to New York, worked with an attorney on a rebuttal, flew to Dallas, and presented it to Clint.

After a cordial greeting, Murchison got down to brass tacks. "You should resign from the board and the company," Murchison told him. "OSI needs a corporate reorganization. I need your resignation because you can't run the company anymore."

"How can I resign from my own company?" Qureishi asked incredulously.

"Optimum is not your company," Murchison replied. "The 49ers and the Rams gave me their proxy votes. I control the board. I control the company."

Qureishi telephoned the other two football clubs who had originally invested in OSI. When Murchison's claim was confirmed, Qureishi resigned and was replaced by the CFO and a vice president.

A few hours after Qureishi arrived back at his Palo Alto home after flying from Dallas, Qureishi's driver delivered boxes of personal belongings that had been cleared out of his office. Two days later, a company representative showed up asking for company credit cards and property.

Three days later, Murchison called Qureishi. A prospective OSI client wanted him on hand to sign a contract they had been working on together. Would he fly to Chicago and seal the deal? Qureishi complied.

OSI was just another pin on the map to Clint Murchison, another deal to be made, another margin to beat, another company to be built up or run into the ground, depending on mood and loan availability. The Murchison Brothers empire was so huge and spread out, they didn't know what they had. Shortly before a Cowboys game in St. Louis, Clint Murchison called Joe Bailey, Tex Schramm's protégé, and asked him to get him a hotel room. Bailey replied he would try but that rooms were hard to come by since there was a bowlers' convention in town. A few minutes later, Murchison called Bailey back. He'd just remembered something that might help. "I think I own the hotel," he said.

Most people outside the Cowboys organization didn't know who Clint Murchison was. One associate wisecracked that you could miss Murchison in a crowd of two. Although Murchison had an office on the fifteenth floor of the building at 6116 North Central Expressway, four floors above the Cowboys, he was such an infrequent visitor there that when he showed up one day and said to the receptionist, "Tell Tex Schramm I'm here to see him," the receptionist innocently asked, "Who may I say is calling?"

Tex was probably busy anyway, because Tex Schramm did not like losing. And Dallas had not won the Super Bowl in the last two years. At home games, Tex watched the game from his private suite. Friends and family invited into the box knew not to sit near him toward the end of the game if the Cowboys were behind and a coffee cup or glass was nearby. Tex would fume and fuss and let loose a "Motherfucker!" at the final gun as he swept the table in front of him clean, knocking off every object. It was his team. And as an intimate of his later said, "He was scared to death of not winning."

Joe Bailey understood Schramm's behavior too well. "The reason he was so upset about the losses was that the losses were getting in the way of creating this legacy. The notion was not to be successful one year. It was to have sustained success over a long period of time. That's what separates you from everyone else. In sports, you have to recognize that you cannot always win, that you are going to lose from time to time. You want to create institutional value so that win or lose you will always have a loyal customer base and be well regarded. That's the insurance you need in order to have sustained success over a period of time."

Schramm's good friend Pete Rozelle, the commissioner, brought his new wife, Carrie, the daughter-in-law of Los Angeles Rams owner Jack Kent Cooke, to sit with Tex in his suite during what turned out to be a loss at Texas Stadium. Afterward, they went to dinner. Tex was still so pissed off over the defeat he put his fist through the nacho bowl. The new Mrs. Rozelle turned to her husband to ask, "If he's your best friend, who's your enemy?"

Tex was just as competitive as the team on the field. In staff meetings, he was notorious for blurting out, "Jesus Christ, doesn't anybody ever fucking *think* around here?" Innovation and creativity were qualities to be treasured and promoted within the organization. If you weren't forward-thinking, your job was in jeopardy. Tex Schramm demanded it.

He protected the owner who gave him free rein and protected the coach whose success on the field translated to the success of the entire organization. The chemistry of three very different individuals, each with his own skill set but all sharing the same goals, worked almost perfectly. Tex Schramm was an easy man to fear, but only to a point, those who knew him understood. They had seen the pussycat deep within.

After his personal secretary, Eileen Gish, a petite woman with a squeaky voice that drove Tex crazy, messed up a contract for the fourth time one day, Tex emerged from his office and threw the contract on her desk.

"Goddamn it, Eileen, you're fired," he fumed. "Get your ass out of here and I don't want to see you again."

He strode back to his office, pushed the door shut, and called Al Ward, assistant general manager, two doors down. "Keep checking on Eileen, tell me when she's gone, because I'm not leaving until she does," Tex said in a low voice. He stayed in his office until Gish left. The next morning, Tex arrived at work to find Gish sitting at her desk.

"What are you doing here?" Tex said with a furrowed brow. "I fired you."

"Oh, Mr. Schramm," Gish said. "I knew you were just teasing me." Tex went in his office and slammed the door.

He had bigger demons to battle. The 1972 suit challenging the Rozelle rule that the NFL Players Association had filed against the league finally went to court. At the trial, John Mackey said Schramm wanted to raise the pay cut for players playing out their final year option, from 10 percent to 25 percent.

Schramm wasn't just the league's bad guy. He also had a team to promote. Too much razzle-dazzle was never enough, as far as Schramm was concerned. He approached William Lively, the director of university bands at SMU, to start the Dallas Cowboys band. Lively put together spirit tunes, long fight songs, familiar orchestral transcriptions, and pop and country favorites. Tanya Tucker's country hit "Texas (When I Die)" became a standard after game-changing touchdowns.

Even though the networks had abandoned televising halftime performances in favor of reporting on other games, the midgame break got plenty of attention at the stadium. Joining the familiar 130 high-kicking legs of the Kilgore Rangerettes and their counterpart Tyler Apache Belles were gymnasts, Frisbee-catching dogs, college and high school bands, and the Dallas Cowboys Cheerleaders, who performed their own special halftime show and during other breaks in the game.

On and off the field, Tex's organizational bookend, head coach Tom Landry, loomed larger than ever to someone looking at him in the rearview mirror. "Tom Landry was tall and aloof, a born-again Christian who had an almost prissy aversion to anything of the earth.... Landry valued intellect over instinct, thought over feeling, science over the chaos of Lombardi's emotional alchemy." Those were the words of Pat Toomay as he looked back at the coach of his former team, long after Pat had been traded to Buffalo, suffered on the winless Tampa Bay Buccaneers, and finished his career with the Oakland Raiders; he wrote about his experiences along the way in a diary, in magazines, and in books. His old coach was fascinating, a subject like no other.

"As far as coach Landry was concerned, players were responsible for their own motivation," Toomay wrote. "His job was to put them in position to make plays. The schemes he devised to accomplish this task were labyrinthine. The Flex defense required recognition of offensive patterns, internalization of the probable outcomes of those patterns, and a corresponding reaction. Locating the football came only after following the branches of his logic tree, a counterintuitive approach that could take years to master.

"On offense, you have patterns, and you're trying to do something," Toomay wrote.

"Defense, you have to be totally present, you're trying to disrupt patterns and create chaos. The offense is trying to create order, the defense is trying to create chaos."

The Flex mandated that a defensive end like Toomay needn't take on a huge offensive tackle head-on if the DE was in the off-set but rather slide off the tackle. The object was to fill the gap, not to try to crush the opposing lineman. That made uneven matchups on the front line easier to withstand. It was one reason why, when gauging a player, the team put as much emphasis on intelligence as on physical prowess; the complete Cowboy utilized spiritual and intellectual training as well as martial training to carry out his assignment and beat his man.

Landry was clearly the highest-profile jock in what *Sports Illustrated* writer Frank Deford called Sportianity.

Landry liked promoting Jesus as the antidrug. "The only successful cure for drug addicts to date has been spiritual experience," he said of what he believed was a culture of decadence. "If it can solve the problem of addicts, think what young people could do if they discover Christ before getting involved in such problems as drugs. I grew up during the Depression when success and money became the most important goals for life. But beginning with the late '50s young people began to show the first influence of a more affluent society. They became more independent—a different breed. Coaches began to deal with players on a more personal level. Money and success were no longer the most important things in life."

Landry's words failed to resonate among those users of prescription drugs and abusers of socially accepted drugs, like alcohol, who played for him. Nor did they appear to reach the team owner, who was adding cocaine to his mix of pleasures with his mistresses.

Pat Toomay thought he understood men of faith. His grandfather had been a Congregational minister and a graduate of Yale Divinity School. But religion left him conflicted, especially on Sunday mornings, when he was presented with a choice between literal food and spiritual food. "On game day, you'd go from your hotel room downstairs to breakfast. Next to the breakfast room was another room where Tom was at the door," Toomay said. "There would be a devotional in there. So you would be confronted with your smiling coach at the door of the devotional and by the food. Until I found my own inner strength, I would go into the devotional, just because he's my coach, even though I really wanted the food. The born-again piety at the time was so strong and so certain."

Prayer meetings had become part of the pregame ritual for a significant number of the team, usually led by Landry's favorite mod preacher, the Reverend Billy Zeoli, a hip evangelist who understood the power and influence of his flock. "At any moment I can reach more people around the world than any other minister alive, well, except maybe for Graham," he told *Sports Illustrated*. Zeoli, a prodigious hugger known simply as Z, utilized beat lingo and referred to athletes as cats when preaching God's Game Plan, a franchised religious concept which detractors compared to McDonald's.

OF ALL THE TEAMS Billy Z hung with, he liked the Cowboys the best, largely because of Landry, who was the subject of a film Zeoli made titled *A Man and His Men*.

Zeoli and a Christian singer named Dave Boyer showed up at training camp in 1970 when 120 rookies were trying to make the team. "We walked in for this meeting, and there are these professional speakers set up and a sound board with tapes," Pat Toomay recalled. "They've got music on tape and this Boyer steps out and he sings 'If Happiness Is a Mountain Called Calvary, Then Do You Know My Jesus?' The black guys in the room were saying, 'What the fuck is this bullshit?' Boyer closed with 'America the Beautiful.' We had this kicker, Jerry DePoyster, sitting in the front row and he just sat there motionless. He'd been in the Army in Vietnam. Curt Mosher, the publicist, cornered him afterward. 'Why didn't you clap?' Mosher asked DePoyster. He said, 'I just got back from 'Nam and I don't think this place is so fuckin' beautiful.'"

Pastors such as Zeoli and organizations such as the Fellowship of Christian Athletes were responses to promiscuity, drug addiction, and the do-your-own-thing ethic, Landry believed. "Hardin Jones scared me at a drug seminar recently when he said we will lose 50 percent of the young people in the next ten years to drugs," Landry testified. So he took every opportunity to speak out and helped promote a film titled *Two a Penny*, produced by the Billy Graham Ministries.

At the same time, Landry avoided directly injecting his religious beliefs into coaching. "He showed his faith through his actions," Roger Staubach said. "But he didn't preach it to us. He cut some of the strongest Christians on the team."

Toomay's long hair and socializing with musicians was seen by the front office as a public declaration he was a hippie, even though smoking marijuana made him ill and he didn't drink anything stronger than beer. When he became a starter, after Larry Cole broke his arm during the 1971 season, assistant coach Ernie Stautner took Toomay aside and advised, "Marijuana leaves a residue in your brain, so word to the wise." The player found sanctuary stumbling into a folk music club in Dallas called the Rubaiyat, where he first heard the music of Michael Murphey and Bob Livingston. "No one was there but these two blond guys who were really interesting," Toomay said. "The takeaway lyric was 'cabful of driver, truckful of load.' I walked out of there thinking that it was funny, coming from some-place real."

When he returned, he heard Ray Wylie Hubbard, the composer of "Up Against the Wall, Redneck Mother," which would become one of the unofficial anthems of the Dallas Cowboys, and the leader of a band called the Cowboy Twinkies. "I laughed my ass off," Toomay said. Hubbard and Toomay immediately bonded despite the singer-songwriter's wild-ass ways and the hulking football player's gentle nature. More Cowboys started showing up at the club to hear folk music. "That's where culture was, something that you could get your teeth into," Toomay said.

His love of music and easygoing sociability snagged Toomay an offseason job promoting country music to radio stations from the Dallas offices of Warner-Elektra-Atlantic records. The job gave him an inside leg up on getting Ray Wylie Hubbard signed to a record contract. Before long, he was hanging out in Charlie Waters's living room listening to Willie Nelson perform for a handful of friends.

Tom Landry was using media too, remaining high-profile among the secular world through his weekly television show on Channel 4, which changed its call letters to KDFW to reflect the regional nature of the market. Landry still arrived at the television station down-town at seven on Thursday evenings to videotape the *Tom Landry Show*, which had been airing every week since the team was founded in 1960.

His host, the announcer Frank Glieber, would be ready with questions to throw at Landry and game film for him to analyze. The first three minutes of airtime reviewed the previous week's game, and then Landry took control of a Telestrator to diagram a play or formation, which he did with ease, providing viewers a hint of the coach at work. Landry then reviewed game film, like he did with the team, along with highlights of outstanding players. A guest from the team sometimes appeared. The last segment was devoted to the upcoming game as well as the coach's predictions for other NFL games.

On Friday mornings, Landry showed up at the KRLD radio studio inside Expressway Towers at eight thirty to tape his fifteen-minute radio show, which aired just before the Sunday game.

On Monday mornings at eight thirty he returned to the studio in the Cowboys building to tape his fifteen-minute postgame radio show, which aired on Monday nights at six, preceding *Ask Tex Schramm*, in which the president and general manager went on the air live to field phone-in questions from fans for forty-five minutes.

As talent, Landry projected a very different image to Dallas–Fort Worth listeners and viewers than he did at press conferences and games. He was relaxed, at ease, smiled frequently, and he seemed to actually enjoy interviewing his players.

Even when he wasn't doing radio or TV, Landry was a creature of habit. "He'd come to work at ten minutes until eight in the morning, get his cup of tea, go to the bathroom," said Gil Brandt. "At ten thirty the coaches would take a break. No stories or idle chitchat. The only reason Tom took a break was to get a Dr Pepper."

The Monday-night lineup on KRLD-AM — Landry, then Tex and Frank Glieber taking calls from listeners, and then Brad Sham's *Football Writers Roundtable*, featuring the beat writers from the *Morning News*, *Times Herald*, *Star-Telegram*, and *Cowboys Weekly* — dominated ratings.

Glieber promoted the radio game broadcasts on air, saying, "Turn down the TV and turn up the Cowboys on KRLD." The station positioned KRLD 1080 signs in the stadiums so cameras could pick them up. Three times during every game, announcers would say, "Let's check out that play on the Magnavox monitor," plugging a game sponsor and introducing the concept of the gratuitous product mention, adding to the revenue stream of televised sports.

The Cowboys' media juggernaut was bolstered by the return of Verne Lundquist as the voice of the Cowboys on the radio, replacing former Channel 8 newsman Murphy Martin, who'd lasted a season.

The media figures had plenty to talk about. Just as the Cowboys were being written off for having lost their draft edge, Gil Brandt, Tom Landry, and Tex Schramm experienced a draft like none since the early years. Their first pick, and the second overall, in the 1975 draft was defensive lineman Randy White from Maryland. Their second first-round pick, Thomas Henderson, was a linebacker from Langston, a historically black college with nine hundred students.

Henderson was a compact, feisty linebacker. His arrival at training camp was highlighted by a new gold star inlaid on his front tooth that flashed whenever he smiled. Henderson carried a sense of self-assuredness bordering on cockiness that no one on the team had ever witnessed.

Dallas was the biggest city Henderson had lived in, having grown up in Austin, two hundred miles south, and finishing high school one hundred fifty miles north in Oklahoma City. It was a great time to be a Dallas Cowboy and part of the fun for Henderson was not knowing his place. Several veterans took him aside to tell him how it was in Dallas. But it didn't register for Henderson. Segregated East Austin had had its own grocery, barbershops, drugstores, pawnshops, pool halls, clubs, and beauty shops. "I never experienced any racism being in that protected environment," Henderson said. "I was never contaminated. I never saw my parents embarrassed. I never heard anybody call my stepfather 'boy.' I was never called the N word without consequence. Somebody called me that, I'd whip their ass."

Cornell Green, Bob Hayes, and Mel Renfro would have conversations with Henderson, but he responded to a higher power. "The star on the helmet eased all that," he said. "Fathers let me date their white daughters because I was a Cowboy." Big D was Henderson's for the asking. Whatever he wanted, he could have.

———

THE TWELVE ROOKIES who came to camp and stuck were dubbed the Dirty Dozen, the biggest infusion of new blood into the franchise since the original expansion draft in 1960, and their arrival coincided with the retirements and departures of Calvin Hill; Dave Manders; Cornell Green; Bob Lilly, who had landed a Coors distributorship; and Walt Garrison, who had suffered a career-ending injury rodeoing in the offseason. John Niland was traded to the Philadelphia Eagles ("It's where God wants me to go"). Bob Hayes was bound for the San Francisco 49ers now that Golden Richards had matured into a starter, his departure coming on the heels of his testimony in the NFL Players Association lawsuit against the league. Pat Toomay was traded to Buffalo.

On his way out, Toomay had a book of his writings published called *The Crunch*. In it, he said, "Duane Thomas has become for the Cowboys what Russia was for Winston Churchill; the proverbial enigma, wrapped in a riddle, doused with Tabasco, and stuffed into a cheese enchilada... who seems to have cracked the arrogance that has encased the Cowboy front office for years." Of John Niland, he noted that after "a remarkable religious experience which involved eight policemen and Parkland Hospital, John has become a fundamentalist Christian.... 'The Bible gives me strength,' John said. 'What do you mean, it gives you "strength"?' Blaine [Nye] asked.... 'Well, take nasal spray, for instance. I was hooked on nasal spray for seven years, and now I don't need it.'"

Toomay could not help but respect Roger Staubach, who entered his eighth season of professional football with nary a rival in sight. Coach Landry was calling the plays again, but Staubach had matured into the kind of quarterback Landry envisioned to the point that he was toying with adding the Spread formation, in which the quarterback took the snap several yards from the center with the receivers spread out wide on both ends. It was a variation of the Shotgun formation that had been developed by former Cowboys assistant (and current scout) Red Hickey when he was head coach of San Francisco in 1960, to allow the QB more time to read the defense on passing downs.

Staubach and the Cowboys opened the season on a cool September afternoon in Texas by beating the Los Angeles Rams 18–7 on solid defensive play and four Toni Fritsch field goals, and then they knocked off the St. Louis Cardinals at Texas Stadium in overtime, 37–31, in a game highlighted by rookie linebacker Thomas Henderson's 96-yard kickoff return, embellished by Henderson spiking the ball *over* the goalpost after he crossed the goal line. Then they broke their *Monday Night Football* losing streak and ruined the christening of the new Silverdome indoor stadium in the Detroit suburb of Pontiac by besting the Lions 36–10 on two Drew Pearson touchdown catches—one from running back Robert Newhouse—and three Toni Fritsch field goals.

By the end of October, Cowboys sat pretty at 5-1, with one close loss to Green Bay, 19–17.

During the regular season, the routine was the same: a light Saturday-morning practice where family members often showed up. Then, it was check-in at the Hilton or Marriott for in-town games, or meeting at the airport for a noon flight for out-of-town games.

Captain Wally Nicholson piloted the Braniff 727 charter for away games. Stewardesses Jackie Moseley, Maria Root, Todie Lewis, Mary Patterson, and Carolyn Wrightsill faced the same seating arrangement every flight: Tex and Marty Schramm in 2A and B behind Joe Bailey and Doug Todd in 1A and B. Assorted coaches would be in rows 3, 4, and 5. On the right side, Clint Murchison and wife were in 3C and D. Tom and Alicia Landry sat behind them, and behind the Landrys were Gil Brandt and Ernie Stautner, the hard-core 24-7 football guys.

In the back of the plane, Chuck Howley held down the first aisle seat on the left side of coach, with Bob Lilly behind him. The radio, television, and newspaper reporters were in the back too.

Once the plane landed, two buses moved the group of eighty or so to the hotel for check-in, followed by an early-evening team meeting and an eleven o'clock curfew. Veterans chose their roommates. Bob Lilly and George Andrie had been roomies the longest. Rookies were paired off alphabetically. Hotel-room phone service was shut off at curfew and turned on again at seven in the morning.

The night before away games, members of the media gravitated to the hospitality suite the Cowboys had open at their hotel; they plied the press with a spread of free eats and booze that was without rival in the league

Game mornings began with Catholic services in a hotel conference room, Protestant devotional services in another, taping by trainers in yet another, and breakfast. By eleven a.m., the entourage checked out of the hotel and boarded buses to the stadium.

At the game, the flight crew did double duty, working for Verne Lundquist in the radio booth during away games. "Verne came to me and said, 'Look, you guys are here every week. I need a spotter and someone to do stats,'" Wally Nicholson said. First officer Richie Pettibone became the statistician. Nicholson spotted players. Flight engineer Gene Shaw ran stat sheets and other info between the main press box and the radio booth.

After the game, the team headed straight for the airport. On the flight home, Tex liked going to the back and seeing every major writer from the Dallas and Fort Worth newspapers and every sports anchor from the network affiliates. "That's when he knew he was going to be the lead story in the sports pages on Monday morning and the broadcasts on Sunday night," Verne Lundquist observed. "It's one reason he didn't want a retired player sitting next to me or to Bill Mercer [in the broadcast booth]. He wanted a media guy. He was a media guy himself. You'd think he was buying us off. But it wasn't that. There was never ever anything overt. But they did do a hospitality room the likes of which I don't think any other team has ever done."

Before the Cowboys' first game against Philadelphia on the road, a 20–17 win, the Eagles' Roman Gabriel admitted, "I have never liked Dallas. They are the most arrogant team in football. When they win, they walk all over you and rub your nose in the dirt. When they lose, they make excuses. They never give the other teams any credit and that shows me nothing...no class at all."

Gabriel should have saved his criticism for Eagles fans, a few of whom unrolled a banner that pleaded BRING BACK PRO FOOTBALL TO PHILADELPHIA before the sorry game ended.

Consecutive losses to division rival Washington and to historic rivals the Kansas City Chiefs on *Monday Night Football* at Texas Stadium put the Cowboys on the cusp with a 5-3 record. That *Monday Night Football* game was far more memorable for the camera shots called up by ABC's Andy Sidaris. A onetime director for WFAA Channel 8, Sidaris was filling in for the regular director, and as he did with the college games he covered for ABC, he called for the cameramen to get honey shots—camera close-ups of pretty women in the stands, and in the case of the colleges, the cheerleaders. The cameras found the cheerleaders representing Dallas worthy material, and throughout the three-hour game, the Dallas Cowboys Cheerleaders shone like they never had before, working the camera with personality and then some: waving their pom-poms and flirting and sashaying as only Texas girls can. The telecast would later be regarded as one of the cheerleaders' big breaks.

The team peeled off three straight wins, including the November 23 home game against Philadelphia, during which Mr. Cowboy, Bob Lilly, had his number 74 retired and became the first player inducted into the Cowboys Ring of Honor, a creation of the fertile imagination of Texas E. Schramm. All that the finest football facility ever built needed was some tradition—print a great player's name and number on the blue divider above the Circle Suites and below the press box, and voilà! Lilly was given a car, a gun, and a hunting dog during the halftime ceremony.

Two weeks later, the team fell to division leader St. Louis, 31–17, on the road as Staubach threw three interceptions and nary a touchdown and the running game was shut down. Wins against Washington and the New York Jets, where backup QB Clint Longley played the entire game so a beat-up Staubach could rest, made for a 10-4 record, good enough to get into the playoffs as a wild card.

The team's return to the playoffs gave Cowboys haters plenty to gripe about. Among the more articulate members of the growing cadre of critics was Leigh Montville of the *Boston Globe*, who was being sized up by the *Dallas Morning News* as a potential high-profile hire. Montville wrote that the Cowboys were so evocative of this golden age of professional football, they deserved immortalization: "They have been a bigger-than-life team, a team almost drawn from Central Casting, a team of people named 'Lance' and 'Billy Joe' and 'Dandy,' a team of efficiency and controversy and rhinestone glitter. They have been the best characterization of the pro football team imaginable....

"Their stadium, with its hole in the roof and with its special circle suites filled with oil money and French provincial furniture, has been the gaudiest in the game.... Their people who have loved God seemingly have loved Him more publicly than anyone else. Their people who haven't cared about God have written books about other types of lifestyles. Even their cheerleaders have been extreme. They've showed the most cleavage.... Their uniform is probably the best uniform in sports with the light blue pants and the silver helmet with the one star on the side."

Anticipation of the divisional playoff against the Vikings at Metropolitan Stadium in the Twin Cities suburb of Bloomington included memories of the '67 Ice Bowl in Green Bay and thoughts that the Sunbelt Cowboys would fold in the frigid climes of the upper Midwest. It was a relatively mild 25 degrees at kickoff with light winds, tolerable enough to play without excuses. Minnesota's quarterback Fran Tarkenton, who had been voted the league's most valuable player, and the vaunted Purple People Eater defensive line were the main concerns. Both teams were vying for a return trip to the Super Bowl, and both teams were playing at the top of their game.

It started close and ended closer. The Vikings led 14–10 with 47 seconds on the clock, Cowboys' ball on their own 15-yard line, fourth down, 16 yards to go. Staubach hit Drew Pearson on the 50-yard line for a 35-yard gain as Pearson fell out-of-bounds. The atmosphere had become so heated that a security guard kicked Pearson in the head before he got up without anyone's noticing.

Two plays later, with the clock reading :32, Staubach took the snap in the Shotgun formation, pumped a fake to Golden Richards to draw Vikings defender Paul Krause, then launched a desperation pass deep towards Pearson. The wobbly long bomb was slightly underthrown, but it allowed Pearson to shake off defender Nate Wright, who either was pushed off or slipped as both came back toward the ball, and grab the pass at his hip on the five-yard line, stutter-stepping into the end zone for a 17–14 lead. Pearson chunked the ball into the stands after scoring.

Minnesota officials and fans howled that Pearson should have been called for offensive pass interference. Objects began to rain on the field. Armen Terzian, the official who hadn't thrown a flag on Pearson, was conked with a Seagram's whiskey bottle and knocked out. He was revived, examined, and escorted to the locker room with a bandage wrapped around his head.

"It came out of the south stands and hit Terzian, the back judge, right in the back of the head at Minnesota's ten-yard line," Verne Lundquist said. "It was really ugly. It hit him and laid him out."

Viking Alan Page, who had been arguing with officials after the play and was called for unsportsmanlike conduct, stood uncomfortably close to Lundquist as the Vikings offense returned to the field and the clock ran out. Rayfield Wright, standing to the right of Lundquist, looked down at the sportscaster and said, "Little buddy, it's about to get ugly. Why don't you let Big Cat take care of you as we walk off the field?" Wright placed his cold-weather sideline cape around Lundquist's head and escorted him safely across the field, through the crowd, and down the steps to the locker room.

Billy Joe Dupree made a confession after the game that resonated. "Our Fathers and Hail Marys will get you anything." The comment would lead to the play's place in infamy as the Hail Mary pass. Roger Staubach's open expression of his Catholic faith and his admission that he had said a Hail Mary as he chunked the ball before being hit helped build the myth.

It was an especially tough loss for Fran Tarkenton, whose father, Dallas Tarkenton, died of a heart attack during the third quarter while he was watching the game on TV in Georgia.

Back in Texas, world champion bull rider Donnie Gay wrecked his feed truck listening to the Hail Mary play. "I got so excited I drove smack into a hay manger," he said.

Among the six thousand screaming fans welcoming home the Cowboys at the Braniff International terminal was a smiling Duane Thomas, camera in hand.

The Cowboys went to Los Angeles and trashed the Rams 37–7 for the NFC title. Staubach scrambled flawlessly, running for 54 yards, and threw four TD passes, going 16-26 for the day. Toward the end of the game, a Cowboys fan ran onto the field at the Los Angeles Coliseum waving a Texas flag. An estimated ten thousand fans greeted the home team upon their return to Texas.

The Cowboys were peaking at the right time. The regulars stepped up their game and unsung heroes materialized out of nowhere. One of the year's unexpected surprises was running back Preston Pearson, who had been cut by the Pittsburgh Steelers at the start of the season and who ended up racking up 1,253 combined yards for the Cowboys. Those same Steelers would provide the opposition at Super Bowl X in Miami.

Classes at Trinity Christian Academy were canceled so students, including eighteen-year-old Lisa Landry, could send off the Dallas

Cowboys at Love Field. Three hours later, the team landed in Miami in the red, white, and blue Braniff 727 bicentennial flagship designed by sculptor Alexander Calder and piloted by Captain Wally Nicholson. Three hundred fans were there to greet them, along with the Dillard High School band, which played Earth, Wind, and Fire's "Shining Star" ("Nobody gave us the music to 'Deep in the Heart of Texas,'" the band director said), and the mayor of Fort Lauderdale, E. Clay Shaw, who gave Landry the key to the city. Roger Staubach wore a snazzy plaid jacket and an open-collared shirt, as loose as he could be.

For the first time, wives of Cowboys players were allowed to stay with their husbands over the weekend prior to kickoff, at the request of Coach Landry. Landry had allowed players to stay at home on Saturday nights before Sunday games at Texas Stadium all season.

The Super Bowl, the first big national event to kick off America's two hundredth birthday, had blossomed into a full-blown major happening and the most watched sports program on television. Some of the pageantry bordered on silly, particularly on media day, when twelve hundred journalists showed up to ask players stupid questions. "This really freaks me out," admitted Drew Pearson. "At least they know who we are."

All of them knew the Dallas Cowboys, even if they didn't really know them. A reporter from the Associated Press asked Landry when he'd last smiled. He did not get an answer. Tackle Bruce Walton had to field numerous queries about his brother Bill, the UCLA basketball star who was leading the Portland Trailblazers through a Cinderella season. Toni Fritsch was asked to recommend good restaurants in Vienna.

Landry accolades flowed from the mouths of his players. Rookie Thomas Henderson said, "I've been playing football as long as I can remember and I've learned more football these seven months than I had learned in my entire career before I got here."

Landry recognized Henderson's exceptional abilities and knew when to give him some slack, calling him a pro in front of the team and then admitting, "Complimenting Thomas is like pouring gasoline on a fire." In a defensive meeting with Randy White, Too Tall Jones, Larry Cole, and Ernie Stautner, Landry had been breaking down the Flex on film with a laser pointer in the darkened room, telling Henderson, the strong side linebacker, "Thomas, you're not supposed to do this, but with your talent I see why you did it. I'm not going to change you from doing this, if it works. With your talent, you can do this."

"Tom Landry's middle name is discipline," veteran player and now coach Jerry Tubbs added for the media. "In every endeavor, whether he is going to church or whether he's getting things right on the mental aspect of football or the physical aspect of football."

Tight end Jean Fugett dropped a fly into Coach's ointment, telling reporters, "Everything is not cool." It wasn't a matter of race or favoritism; it was pay. "I made $21,000 this season in Dallas," Fugett said. "It's not so much that I want to get out. I want to get paid." He had a degree from Amherst. His wife was going to law school. And he was getting lowballed by his employer. "You come down to Dallas and you're a football player. I say to them, 'No, man. I have a radio show [he hosted a jazz program on KERA-FM]. I'm a reporter [he interned at the *Baltimore Sun*]. I'm an amateur photographer.'" He was also the team's player rep, a voluntary position that put him in Tex's bull's-eye.

Fugett's comments irritated management, but they were a mere burr in the saddle compared to the appearance of former Cowboy Pete Gent at the Galt Ocean Mile Hotel, six years out of football but with a copy of *North Dallas Forty* in his hand—"The best book ever written about professional football," according to Dick Schaap in the *New York Times Book Review*. Gent knew the book hadn't gone down well with some veterans. "That fella just as soon kill me as look at me," he said of one player. Lee Roy Jordan confirmed it, saying, "He doesn't have any friends on this team." A team official advised, "Stay away from him." Gent could be kept at arm's length but the numbers didn't lie. Whether Gent was a team favorite or not, his book *North Dallas Forty* sold two million copies in paperback.

Asked about the book, Landry told a reporter, "I don't read books in that vein." What was he reading then? *"The Rise and Fall of Richard Nixon."*

Gent was in Miami on assignment for *Sport* magazine but unlike Don Meredith and other high-profile ex-Cowboys, he was hardly a homer. "I hope Pittsburgh kills them," Gent said when he sat down to be interviewed by a sportswriter. "The Super Bowl is getting so obscene, it's something you have to see."

Gent admitted that he had felt uncomfortable as a football player in Dallas. But the passage of time and book sales had mellowed him somewhat. He was still a wild man and a badass—"I remember watching him turn into that guy who would take your head off if you got in his way, a chilling and revealing look into the psyche of the pro athlete, indeed," said an Austin acquaintance. "Sumbitch could have killed me in about two seconds." But now Gent was a gentleman writer, charged with describing others, as he did with Coach Landry at the pre–Super Bowl press conference: "Tom looked terrific, too: His hair turning steel gray, the tan skin drawn tight over his high cheek bones and prominent jaw, he was very beautiful, almost bionic. He looked unchanged and seemed to belie the image of the New Cowboys."

The two-week buildup to the big game proved effective. Coverage was wall-to-wall, with a news angle around every corner. A number of scenes for the Robert Evans disaster movie *Black Sunday,* about an assassination attempt—via a bomb-laden Goodyear blimp—on a president attending a Super Bowl, would be shot during the game.

Tickets priced at twenty dollars were fetching well over a hundred.

Twenty-six-year-old Phyllis George, Miss America of 1971 and a native Texan, joined Irv Cross and Brent Musburger as part of CBS's Super Bowl coverage, breaking a gender line, with Tom Brookshier and Pat Summerall calling the game for the network. Six hours of network airtime were devoted to the game, captured by eighteen cameras and covered by a crew of one hundred and fifty. The television audience had grown to eighty million, with advertising time going for $230,000 a minute during the game. Viewers in twelve other nations watched the broadcast. Verne Lundquist and Al Wisk called the game over the Cowboys radio network.

Greater Dallas was all het up. Fans watched the game at T.G.I. Friday's in Old Town, the Jersey Lilly on Knox Street, and bars and restaurants across the Metroplex. Central Christian Church called the day a "Super Sunday for Christ." Wall's Catering on Preston Road prepared meals for five thousand, moving owner Ronnie Wall to exult, "It's like Christmas all over again." U.S. district judge Sarah T. Hughes issued an order so Dallas County jail inmates could watch the game on TV. And seven thousand Dallasites flew to Miami.

One man offered four seats on his Miami-bound private jet in exchange for four game tickets.

Dr. Dan Perkins, a psychologist and instructor at Richland College, said of fans, "People identify with the Cowboys as if they were on the football field themselves. Some of them live out their own fantasies. When the Cowboys win, they win. When they lose, they're depressed." SMU psychology professor W. H. Telford offered a similar analysis: "People want a winner because it's almost like some of it rubs off on you. If you're a big Cowboys supporter and the Cowboys win, it's almost like you're a winner too. People are affected by it. The kind of people who get all excited about the Cowboys, if they didn't have that to think about they'd sit around and think about how their stomach hurts."

The pageantry moved Phil Pepe of the *New York Daily News* to complain that the hype was ruining the game. Among the things he was sick and tired of: hearing about Roger Staubach's "short haircut and all-American-boy image... hearing what a genius Tom Landry is"; hearing "Vin Scully saying 'The Cowboys are loading up the Shotgun'... instant replays and isolated cameras."

Thirteen players who'd been part of the Cowboys' sole Super Bowl victory, four years earlier, remained, along with the Dirty Dozen rookies and six second-year players. Too Tall, Lee Roy, Cliff, DD, Jean, Jethro, Harvey "Too Mean" Martin from Hall and Central, and new boys Randy White and Thomas Henderson anchored the defense. Staubach captained the offense.

The big game pitted the Flex version of Doomsday against the Steel Curtain, and Captain America and company against the triple threat of Li'l Abner (Terry Bradshaw), fullback Franco Harris, and wide receiver Lynn Swann.

Coming off three straight upsets of Washington, Los Angeles, and Minnesota, the wild-card Cowboys were charged up. But so were the AFC number-one-seeded Steelers, going for their second consecutive Super Bowl victory. Despite the fact Dallas had beaten them the last seven times they'd met, Pittsburgh was armed, and ready.

Before the opening whistle, Bambi Brown, an exotic dancer from Atlanta dressed in a long white dress and cowboy hat with a *D* on it, ran out onto the field to give Rayfield Wright a silver chain with a horseshoe on it. "This will give you good luck," she said. Wright threw it down. "I don't believe in things like that," the Big Cat said after the game. "I'm not superstitious. Things that happen are going to happen."

The opening kickoff hinted at a barn burner in the making. Preston Pearson fielded the kick and handed off to linebacker Thomas Henderson in a sneak reverse, who ran 48 yards to the Steelers 44-yard line. Dallas had a 10–7 lead at the half, but Pittsburgh responded with a touchdown, a field goal, and a critical blocked punt.

When Steelers kicker Roy Gerela missed a field goal from 35 yards out, free safety Cliff Harris patted him on the helmet and told him, "Way to go." Middle linebacker Jack Lambert of Pittsburgh saw what Harris did and lifted him off his feet and threw him down, which prompted coach Chuck Noll to declare later, "Jack Lambert is a defender of what is right."

Noll could afford to make the comment because the Steelers emerged victorious, 21–17, after Roger Staubach failed to conjure another Hail Mary. Pittsburgh safety Glen Edwards intercepted a Staubach pass in the end zone intended for receiver Percy Howard as the clock ran out. Howard, a special-teams player who had been drafted out of Austin Peay College although he had played only basketball, had already snagged a TD reception with less than two minutes left in the game after replacing receiver Golden Richards, who broke a rib. Staubach went 15 for 24, throwing two touchdown passes. But he also threw three interceptions and fumbled once.

It was a Cowboys loss, but the game was the "most exciting, most competitive Super Bowl yet," according to Sam Blair of the *Morning News*.

Bedford Wynne had arranged for the postgame entertainment at the Galt Ocean Mile Hotel in Fort Lauderdale. "You're in charge," Clint had told Bedford, so he rounded up Willie Nelson, the king of country music outlaws, who brought along folk rocker Jerry Jeff Walker, country music superstar Waylon Jennings — all Texans — a new boy from Alabama named Jimmy Buffett, and a songwriter named Billy C to entertain the Dallas crowd. Willie and company didn't start until eleven thirty but roared all the way to four thirty in the morning to help the handful of folks lingering around forget the outcome of the previous evening. Coach Tom Landry did not attend. He was back in his hotel room watching game film.

Born Again on America's Two Hundredth Birthday with the Most Beautiful Girls in Texas

IF YOU DIDN'T KNOW BETTER, you'd have thought the Cowboys won the Super Bowl.

The *Dallas Morning News* editorialized that "the team has been one of the best things to happen to the community in recent years. Cowboy fans come in all colors and from all political persuasions. And with all the bad news, political and economic, Dallas has suffered in recent years, the Cowboys have provided a rallying point for community pride."

This edition of the team was especially revered because they had been given little chance to succeed. Fans greeted the team in a cold rain at Love Field on their return from Miami with Gale Manley of Mesquite singing her own composition to the tune of "God Bless America." Eighty-one-year-old Enid Justin, president of Nocona Boot Company, offered boots to every member of the team, which a busload of players took her up on.

And the owner discovered a popular North Miami restaurant called Tony Roma's. Clint Murchison enjoyed the casual, upscale eatery, especially its grilled barbecued ribs, so much that he bought the restaurant and began to expand operations throughout the United States and internationally.

Murchison was merely keeping up with the trends. Several businesspeople in Dallas had successfully embraced the concept of creating restaurants and bars and cloning them. Among them was Norman Brinker, whose Steak & Ale chain combined the franchising that fast-food eateries were articulating so well with a "nice" restaurant environment.

Over on Greenville Avenue and Meadow Road in the swinging, booming part of North Dallas north of Northwest Highway, another big-dreaming, would-be-bar-and-restaurant-empire builder named Larry Lavine converted a former postal station into Chili's Hamburger Grill and Bar. Sporting a vaguely Mexican design with bright colors, the restaurant was intended to create a casual, fun environment with a burger-heavy menu inspired by the classic Dallas hamburger joints Burger House and Goff's and with an extensive alcoholic beverage menu. The name came to Lavine after a trip to the Terlingua Chili Cookoff in the southwest Texas desert—the same event that had led to Clint Murchison's bowl-of-red restaurant concept. Chili's was an instant hit. Within a year, a second location opened, and then multiple locations were added. Lavine eventually cashed out as a millionaire many times over, and the business grew into the flagship of a group of restaurant chains operating under the Brinker International corporate banner.

A few years earlier, Mariano Martinez, the owner and operator of Mariano's Mexican Cuisine in Old Town, had taken note of Slurpee machines at 7-Eleven convenience stores. The machine oozed cool, flavored drinks that kids and adults both flocked to on hot days. Martinez wondered if a machine like that could produce a margarita, a Mexican mixed drink with tequila, lime juice, and a liqueur, served with salt around the rim of the glass, with the consistency of a Slurpee. Martinez had been making frozen margaritas in a blender since the 1950s, but the consistency was runny, they were a mess to make, and the blender was always breaking. After retrofitting a soft-serve machine and experimenting with a mix to factor in the tequila, Martinez perfected the frozen margarita, which quickly became a Mariano's staple. Other restaurants and bars noticed, including Chili's. Frozen margaritas were sweeter than margaritas on the rocks, reminded drinkers of Slurpees, and were perfect thirst quenchers for the extended Texas summers—with a kick, which all factored in the drink's rapid spread across the state and beyond.

The Dallas-based 7-Eleven convenience store chain, not content to let innovation stop with the Slurpee, ushered in the modern era of junk food with the introduction of the iconic Big Gulp, a thirty-two-ounce soda cup, twice the size of the largest soda cup that had been served to the public to date.

Tom Landry had become as iconic as 7-Eleven when it came to representing Dallas. The coach and Alicia spent their wedding anniversary at the White House at a function hosting Israeli prime minister Yitzhak Rabin. Landry also landed on the Fashion Foundation of America's best-dressed list of twelve men, alongside television host Johnny Carson, New York governor Hugh Carey, and former United Nations ambassador Daniel Moynihan. "He looks terrific in anything he puts on" his size 42 long frame, said his dresser, Alicia Landry. "He is conservative and likes to look his age when he's working. I like to include something blue in his outfit. He looks best in Cowboy colors, anyway, because of his hair and his blue eyes." His chosen hat was coordinated with his sports jacket first, and then his tie.

Larry Cole, who had been moved to defensive right tackle after Bob Lilly retired, was more critical of Landry's sartorial splendor. "He dresses five years behind the times," Cole said of his coach. "He wears a pair of white shoes...you wouldn't call them loafers, they're more like tennis shoes with a flap. They look awful." As for Landry's penchant for hats, Cole was blunt. "When you're bald-headed, you like to wear a hat."

———

PLAYERS AND COACHES showed up in the society pages of newspapers attending events such as the Diamond Jim Brady two-hundred-dollar-a-couple American Cancer Society fund-raiser and the Junior League Follies in the Regency Room of the Fairmont Hotel. Whenever Landry was involved, the Cowboys *were* high society, judging from the response to the hundred-dollar-a-plate Tribute to Tom Landry to raise funds for the Trinity Christian Academy, which had named its stadium for the coach. KRLD and WRR radio stations aired the tribute live. Lee Roy Jordan, Jerry Tubbs, and Sam Huff—who all played linebacker for Landry at one time or another—were among the thirteen hundred guests, as was Marie Lombardi, Vince's widow. Landry's high school coach Bob Martin; Dick Harris, his cocaptain with the 1948 University of Texas Longhorns; country singer Charley Pride; CBS sportscaster and onetime Miss America Phyllis George; and broadcaster and former New York Giant teammate Frank Gifford were among the notables. Phyllis George, who evidently couldn't get enough of Roger Staubach, introduced the quarterback as "Joe Namath's rival and the sex symbol of Dallas." Staubach was some kind of Dallas symbol for sure; he rode a camel to the premiere of the locally produced movie *Hawmps!*, where he was the center of attention, per usual.

Another subject of attention was Anne Ferrell Brandt, the thrice-married woman whose previous husband of record had been Gil Brandt, the vice president of player development. The bicentennial had marked Clint Murchison Jr.'s second marriage, on May 3, to Anne. She was thirty-six. He was fifty-three. Some in the organization thought the Brandt marriage had been a sham all along. Gil was married to his network of scouts and his analyzing of football players, not a woman. One cynic assumed that when Anne left Gil and married Clint "they were going to kill Clint so that she and Gil could get the team." Others said Anne had been one of Clint's girlfriends on the side and when their relationship became public knowledge, they simply tied the knot. Whatever the circumstances, eight months after they married, Anne dedicated her life to the Lord Jesus Christ at the Dallas Christian Women's Club, where she had been attending meetings. Soon enough, she was holding weekly Bible groups at the Murchison mansion.

Eventually, Anne's new husband had his own come-to-Jesus reckoning. Once he was saved, alcohol and all that came with it, including girlfriends on the side and dabbling in marijuana and cocaine, were over. The Bible became his Good Book. After a loss, Clint Murchison sent Tom Landry a passage from Romans 5:3–5, "We can rejoice, too, when we run into problems and trials, for we know they are good for us. They help us learn to be patient."

Clint was hardly alone. In the middle of a decade of exceptional decadence, many of his cronies were taking the same path of reassessment. Prominent among the bunch was his original partner in the Dallas Cowboys, Bedford Wynne, the club's founding secretary-treasurer and Clint's frequent companion locator, who finally sobered up after a creditor showed up in Dallas and demanded money owed along with the promise Bedford would stay out of Las Vegas. Once Bedford cleaned up, he began proselytizing on behalf of rehab clinics and he recruited patients with the same zeal as he once had drinking and running around.

Given the growing numbers of reformed power brokers, it was no surprise that ambitious achievers who didn't even drink attended Alcoholics Anonymous meetings. There was no better place to make business contacts.

More than ever, sales and salesmanship drove North Texas growth. The culture it spawned was bipolar. Dallas's reputation as a city of churches contradicted Dallas's other reputation as the swinging-singles capital of Texas. Fueled by the popularity of the birth control pill and evidenced by a divorce rate that equaled the marriage rate (the first city in the United States to earn that distinction), its more-than-nascent breast-augmentation industry, and the big-hair stereotype that defined Dallas women, Dallas was some kind of mecca.

The Dallas Cowboys Cheerleaders built on that image, a move orchestrated by Tex Schramm's new hire Suzanne Mitchell. Dee Brock, who had overseen the cheerleaders as a volunteer since the beginning of the franchise, turned down Schramm's offer to work full-time with the cheerleaders and left the organization in 1975, eventually becoming the director of adult learning services for the Public Broadcasting Service in Washington.

Back in December during the Cowboys' final drive to the Super Bowl, Mitchell, a slender blonde born and bred in Texas, had interviewed with Schramm. She'd worked in magazine and book publishing in New York (Joe Namath lived in her building) and in Miami, and had worked for the U.S. Ski Team in Denver and Park City, Utah. When she returned to Dallas she had put her name in the hat at the Snelling employment agency and she got a callback. She sounded like a good fit for an opening with Tex Schramm.

Most of the prospects for the position replacing Eileen Gish as Tex Schramm's secretary had been a tad overeager, and sometimes starstruck. Mitchell said she came in "dressed like a hippie and didn't particularly care whether I got the job or not." When Schramm asked her what she envisioned doing in ten years, she nodded toward him and smiled, saying, "Your chair looks really comfortable."

Tex lit up. He liked this woman. But it wasn't Mitchell's give-a-shit interview responses or her journalism degree that got her the job offer; it was her past experience with the ski team, where she'd acted like a den mother to a collection of energetic, athletic, and exceptionally gifted kids. That appealed to him.

Mitchell did not immediately jump at the offer to be Tex Schramm's secretary, and for good reason. "I was quizzing him on what else do you know, what other life do you have?" she said. "There wasn't anything. He was totally, completely consumed with the NFL and with the Cowboys. The NFL first, always, with Tex. What was good for the NFL was good for the Cowboys."

Still, she went to work for the president and general manager that December. Schramm dumped his life into her lap, putting her in charge of his personal finances, the player contracts, career contracts, correspondence with fans and with the other NFL clubs, and, in a pinch, putting out the Dallas Cowboys newsletter.

The only glamorous part of the job was getting Tex prepped for his radio and television shows and helping him write his column in *Cowboys Weekly*. "He loved talking to the fans," Mitchell said. "That was his thing. The rest of us just loved what we did. It was like family. There was no nine-to-five." Fourteen to sixteen hours a day, seven days a week, was more like it.

She worked alongside Kay Lang, the ticket czarina; Jeri Mote, Gil Brandt's eyes and ears in the office; and Tula Johnapelis.

Lang, the first female executive in the NFL, was one of the guys. She'd smoke, drink, and cuss, and until Mitchell came aboard, she was the only one who would give it back to Tex. A month after starting, Mitchell got caught up in the swirl of Super Bowl X in Miami. At the Super Bowl, Cowboy cheerleader Gwenda Swearengin winked to the CBS television camera whose operator framed her in a tight shot and evidently caught the attention of the world. Once Mitchell was back at her desk in Dallas, she noticed a groundswell building. Calls about the cheerleaders were coming from agencies, sponsors, television shows, and movie producers. The cheerleader squad had been revised and updated over the course of the previous four seasons to some fanfare, but the Super Bowl broadcast put them on the map. Mitchell told Schramm about the response and asked, "What are you going to do?"

Tex's face flushed. "You do it," he told her as he walked away from her desk.

He loved to delegate to others, just like Clint delegated to him. Here was an opportunity for Mitchell to prove herself.

Why not? Mitchell thought. She had already learned that you didn't say no to Tex Schramm. Plus, she knew she could do it.

Mitchell was introduced to Texie Waterman, the tall, lithe, brunette cheerleader choreographer. With spring auditions coming up, Waterman brought Mitchell up to speed.

"I knew with Tex and with me that image was the most important thing," Mitchell said. "So the first thing I did was set rules, what they could and could not do. Tex gave me free rein."

IN APRIL, four hundred girls and two men, Ron Traxler and Robert Richardson, showed up over the course of two days to audition for the Dallas Cowboys Cheerleaders and all the glory that went with that title. Aspirants were told to wear halter tops and shorts and be ready to dance to "Boogie Fever," "That's the Way I Like It," and "Get Down Tonight," popular hits by disco purveyors KC and the Sunshine Band.

"When you come up before the judges in groups of four, we will be looking for your smile, the way you dance, your charisma—the intangibles," one of the judges, popular radio disc jockey Ron Chapman, told them before the tryouts. The other judges included Cowboys publicity director Doug Todd, Texie Waterman, stadium officials Bert Rose and Dave Arey, and publicist Mitch Lewis, who had judged all previous competitions. Mitchell had veto power over all.

Criteria used to determine finalists were difficult to pin down, other than gender; the men were quickly eliminated. "It wasn't all about one thing," Suzanne Mitchell said. "It wasn't all about dancing, it wasn't all about looks. There was an internal thing that I was always looking for in the girls." They were prospective eye candy, but they would also have to project something extra. Tex weighed in to make the point that if a girl had the looks, she could be taught dance steps later.

The judges were tough on the talent. "She'll look good from the stands, but she's not exactly the type you'd want to take home to mother," one judge said of a contestant who wore too much makeup. "She's so perfect, I mean there should be a key in her back," another judge commented about another hopeful. "She's a Malibu Barbie doll come to life." "Yeah, but if it rained, she'd probably melt," a fellow judge commented. "She's not gonna cause any cameraman to go crazy."

A former Kilgore Rangerette whose fat jiggled as she danced didn't make the final cut. Nor did the Frederick's of Hollywood model who nervously told judges, "I graduated from TWU with my clothing," meaning her degree.

Cheerleader season started in April with preliminary tryouts, semifinals in early May, and the finals at the end of May. Summer training was two to three hours daily during June, July, and August, sometimes as long as five hours. "It depended how good they were," Mitchell said.

The thirty-two winners, ages eighteen to twenty-eight, included a hairdresser, a systems analyst, security guard, and a clerk in bankruptcy court. All would have to buy their own boots and practice six days a week at Texie Waterman's dance studio in order to be paid $15.97 a game for the privilege of being a Dallas Cowboys Cheerleader. Dating players, coaches, or management was forbidden. No names could be affixed to uniforms, appear in team pictures, or be put on the girls' luggage and carry bags. Suzanne Mitchell considered sponsor decals and corporate logos to be tacky.

Mitchell screened the routines and constantly huddled with Waterman. Many routines were set to music, which required additional rehearsals with the Cowboys band.

"Even though I didn't teach them the choreography, there were certain dance steps I would not allow them to do, including bending over from the field or from a stage orientation," Mitchell said. She would watch for mistakes in routines and keep an eye on who was flagging in the heat. "Even in the studio, I would turn off the air-conditioning," she said of the training regimen. During rehearsals with the Cowboys band at Texas Stadium, Mitchell wouldn't let the girls sit down. "Oh, they dreaded that," she said. "They would be dripping, and I'd hear, 'Suzanne, I'm going to throw up.' I'd get right in their face. If they're going to throw up, they're going to throw up on me. They got through it." She didn't apologize for the boot-camp mentality. "It gives them guts and makes them realize they're capable of far more than they ever thought they were."

A basic knowledge of football was required. "They had to know the game in order to know when to perform," Mitchell said. "There were pregame routines in the middle of the field and sideline routines. We performed during change of quarters and knew the two-minute warning. If a player was injured, the girls went down on one knee. Whenever there was a third down, they'd go motionless so all eyes would be on the field."

Her reputation as a taskmaster earned her the nickname Mitch the Bitch behind her back. She knew she demanded a lot of the girls but it was all to prepare them for the limelight. "They became instant celebrities overnight and didn't know how to handle that, so they had to be taught how to interview, how to survive, how to protect themselves," she said.

"I was their worst enemy and best friend," Mitchell said. "They knew I meant business, they knew what the rules were, and they would abide by them or they had the door. And they knew that there were three thousand nine hundred and ninety-nine girls right behind them so don't mess with us."

TRAINING CAMP WAS CRITICAL to the cheerleaders' success, and Tom Landry still actually looked forward to the ritual of the players' preseason training camp, even after sixteen seasons. It was that rare time and place he could get everyone to concentrate on nothing but football for six weeks. Most everyone connected with the team enjoyed training camp because the players all worked out and trained together and because the entire organization relaxed, talked, dined, drank, and lived together for six weeks. Thousand Oaks was a long way from home and distractions, and the Pacific-cooled breezes guaranteed splendid summer weather. A handful never adjusted, such as the newspaper reporter nicknamed Boo Radley, who never left his dorm room, and Steve Perkins, now editing the *Cowboys Weekly*, who drank alone. Some veteran players, coaches, trainers, front-office types, and reporters had California honeys on the side—girlfriends who would kick their California boyfriends out for a month and a half so they could spend time with their Cowboys.

But this particular training camp was not so harmonious. Danny White, the draft pick from Arizona State who'd played in the World Football League for a year, was beating out Clint Longley for number-two quarterback. And for reasons unknown to all but himself, Clint Longley was taking it out on Roger Staubach. It started with Staubach's objection to Longley calling Drew Pearson "a skinny-legged motherfucker" and escalated with Staubach's challenge "How'd you like one of your Easter bunny teeth knocked out?"

"You gonna do it?" Longley shot back, standing his ground.

Fists flew briefly before assistant coach Danny Reeves broke up the scuffle.

"If I hadn't got there Roger probably would have killed him," Reeves said later. "And I didn't want my starting quarterback in prison."

Days later, without warning and while Roger's back was turned, Longley took a chump swing at Staubach's head in the dressing room and then immediately left camp. The cut over Staubach's left eye required nine stitches.

Before his quick departure, Longley said of Staubach, "He's been trying to provoke me the whole training camp. He's really been on me. He thinks he's a coach. He tries to involve himself in people's business. I thought he was a player. I'm going to disappear now. I need a vacation. I'm going to New Mexico."

"I didn't do nothing," Staubach protested. "Shove chairs at him?

He's just looking for a way out. That's all it is. He hit me when I wasn't looking. I was putting on my shoulder pads. He didn't say anything to me...nothing. Not a thing. I was looking the other way and he hit me. He's an outright liar. He's looking for a way to justify being gutless."

There was some other shuffling of the deck in addition to Longley's departure. Calvin Hill, who temporarily left the Cowboys to play for Hawaii in the WFL and a high dollar contract, was traded to Washington, along with Jean Fugett. The departure of the two talented malcontents contrasted with the return of Duane Thomas, who wanted a tryout with the club. "The only thing I'd want to be sure about is that he'd make a positive contribution to our team," Tom Landry said before the news became official. "I don't see any reason at his age he couldn't return to football. That's not enough for me. He has to contribute in a positive way other than playing football."

Prodigal son Duane Thomas signed a two-year contract with the Dallas Cowboys, which Tex Schramm said was Landry's deal. The coach knew Thomas had been screwed moneywise and wanted to get that distraction out of the way before seeing if Thomas still had the right stuff, working out details with retired Cowboys end Pettis Norman, Thomas's agent.

The former bad boy was repentant. "Everything must change," he said with a lingering trace of mysticism. "I have changed. My attitude now is very good and I plan to work hard...that's what my contract calls for." Meaning if he didn't stick, he didn't get paid. "It's all in Duane's hands as to what role he can play with the Cowboys. There are no guarantees, no bonuses," Schramm confirmed.

This time around, the front office, the media, and the players cheered him on. "He looked great," Roger Staubach gushed. Thomas's social skills had improved considerably. But after pulling a hamstring on the first day of training camp and missing two-a-days, Thomas was already behind the eight ball. The best he could muster on the field, where it mattered most, was a four-yard gain on a single carry in an exhibition game. His football skills were gone.

After the last preseason game, the Cowboys made their final cut, which included Ron Johnson, who'd made All-Pro as a running back for the Giants; kicker Toni Fritsch, the colorful Austrian, who was beaten out by Mexico's Efren Herrera; and Duane Thomas.

"He did everything we asked him to," Landry said of Thomas. "He tried hard and was a solid guy. It's just unfortunate that it didn't work out for him." "We were all pulling for him to make it," Roger Staubach said, echoing the sentiments of most everyone on and around the team. "I think everybody was. You could certainly tell the fans were by the way they reacted to him this year. It had to be a tough decision. He wasn't where he might have been, I just wish he hadn't missed all the work in camp."

The Cowboys opened the 1976 campaign with a 27–7 downing of the Eagles at home, a 26–6 beat-down of New Orleans on the road, and then a 30–27 close one against the Colts at home, winning with an Efren Herrera field goal with three seconds left. It was Staubach's personal best so far—22 for 28 for 339 yards, two TD passes, and no interceptions—and Herrera was emerging as a superstar in his native Mexico, getting extensive coverage in the newspapers and appearing on the television programs *24 Horas* and *Contacto Directo*.

The team beat the Seahawks by 15 points in Seattle, then ruined the opening of Giants Stadium in New Jersey by edging out New York and Craig Morton, 24–14, as Staubach hit 13 of 15 in gusty twenty-mile-an-hour winds.

Their first loss of the year was a sloppy giveaway to St. Louis on the road. Eight sure passes from Staubach were either dropped, mishandled, or swatted away. After Staubach broke his pinkie finger against the Chicago Bears, Danny White came off the bench and threw two touchdown passes and a 56-yard long bomb to Golden Richards. Then they recorded their first win in Washington, DC, in five years.

At home in early November, the Cowboys barely prevailed against the winless New York Giants. The Cowboys won the game,

9–3, on Efren Herrera's field goals and tough defensive play. At half-time, Don Meredith and Don Perkins, the first stars of the Dallas Cowboys, were inducted into the Ring of Honor at Texas Stadium, joining Bob Lilly. Their exclusive club was becoming part of the Texas Stadium legend.

Buffalo and O. J. Simpson, the Bills' all-everything running back, went home on the short end of a 17–10 battle, leaving the Cowboys sitting pretty at 9-1, their best record ever at that point in the season, even though the jaded locals weren't necessarily impressed. The Buffalo game had been an advance sellout, thanks to the purchase of two thousand tickets by Channel 8 and Burger King, which lifted the television blackout in Dallas. With easy TV access, 13,236 seats were no-shows, the largest amount in team history. "I think the last minute purchase of a large block of tickets violates the intent of the NFL's pledge to Congress to honor the former blackout legislation. I don't think it's fair to have a game artificially sold out," Tex Schramm complained. Channel 8's manager, Mike Shapiro, disagreed. "Quite naturally, we wanted to offer the game to the audiences and when it got down to a few thousand tickets we felt the investment as a public service was worthwhile."

The Cowboys dropped the next game on the road to the Atlanta Falcons, the first for the Cowboys' new radio color man, Brad Sham. Play-by-play announcer Verne Lundquist's previous color guy, Al Wisk, had departed, and his replacement, Chris Needham from Waco, was clearly out of his comfort zone. So Sham was brought in, supported by Bob Lilly as the third man in the booth for home games.

Two straight wins followed Sham's debut, but the team dropped a home game to the Redskins largely on the spirited play of former Cowboys Jean Fugett and Calvin Hill for a still impressive 11-3 record entering the playoffs. Advertisements for package deals and flights to the Super Bowl at the Rose Bowl in Pasadena, California, began popping up in local sports sections.

But the first-round playoff game against the Los Angeles Rams may have given fans second thoughts after "six interceptions, two blocked punts [both by Charlie Waters], three fumbles, fourteen penalties, seven quarterback traps, three dropped passes, four fights and a partridge in a pear tree," wrote Blackie Sherrod, who compared the game to one played "on a vacant lot on Saturday morning, in tennis shoes and overalls with peanut butter on the bib."

With less than two minutes left and LA ahead, the Cowboys had the ball on the Rams' 17-yard line and were knocking at the door. But Captain Comeback could not deliver. Butch Johnson caught a pass that would have been a touchdown if one foot hadn't been out-of-bounds. On fourth down, Staubach threw to Billy Joe DuPree at the seven-yard line—enough for a first down—but officials marked it short of a first down, ending the game. The players and fans howled. Even Landry voiced his opinion that DuPree had made the first down and wanted an explanation. The game film Landry watched didn't lie. "It [the film] showed he made the first down," Landry said. "He caught the ball at the five and got hit on the six. They marked the ball where he came down, which cost us a first down. They just missed it."

Between Roger Staubach's broken pinkie—he threw four TDs and eight interceptions in the second half of the season—and the lack of a dependable running game in spite of Robert Newhouse racking up more than 900 yards, the team had performed admirably. But having made the playoffs for the tenth time in eleven years was no consolation.

One season-ticket holder, Martina Navratilova, a world-class professional tennis player from Czechoslovakia, couldn't help but state the obvious and even came away from the loss with a teachable moment: "Pardon my words, but the Cowboys got screwed," she said. "That Lawrence McCutcheon, he never scored. And there were several other calls that were not right. On that fourth down, they got it. I realized that even the best don't always win, and it helped me understand my losses and not get so mad."

Doubt and Deliverance

THE LOSS CUT DEEP enough for the NFL Competition Committee, chaired by Tex Schramm, to consider a double-elimination tournament of the eight playoff finalists leading to a one-game Super Bowl. The proposal came a year after the committee jettisoned tie games in favor of continuing to play into overtime to determine the winner of a game. Marty Schramm gave her husband a granite paperweight for Christmas that read NEVER LET YESTERDAY TAKE UP TOO MUCH OF TODAY.

Schramm had been humbled. After five consecutive victories by the American Football Conference champion in the Super Bowl, he was forced to swallow hard and concede. "I have to admit it now. The American Conference is stronger overall than the National Conference. Everybody in the NFC has got to pull up their stuff and get with it."

He remained biased, saying, "I've still got a hardline streak. As far as I'm concerned, the NFL is ahead in the Super Bowl, 6-5." Schramm counted Baltimore and Pittsburgh, former NFL teams that had moved to the American Conference when the rival leagues completed their merger in 1970. "I'm an admitted hard loser," Schramm went on. "But this gap, if you want to call it that, can be traced back to after the merger, particularly the late '60s and early '70s. The majority of AFC teams were inferior and as a result they

370

benefited a great deal in the draft. And those clubs which benefited are coming to fruition now." The old guard couldn't be restored soon enough, as far as he was concerned. "This losing business is like going to the dentist."

Still, even after the team was knocked out in the first round of the playoffs, the Cowboy mystique spread. Eddie LeBaron, the first quarterback the Cowboys ever had, was named general manager of the Atlanta Falcons. One of his first intended hires, he said, would be Danny Reeves as coach, allowing the native of Americus, Georgia, to return to his home state. But Reeves turned the deal down to stay with Dallas, at least for the time being. Two years earlier, the New York Jets had hired away Al Ward from the Cowboys to become the team's general manager.

No one embodied the mystique like Roger Staubach, who was voted Oak Farms Dairy's My Favorite Cowboy for the fourth time in six years; he gave his trip to Acapulco to his road-game roommate, Lee Roy Jordan, who was retiring. Staubach's secretary, Rosalind Cole, fielded twelve thousand pieces of mail over the course of the year, with three-fourths of the correspondents requesting autographed pictures. Staubach turned down most offers to do endorsements and could fit only so many speaking engagements into his schedule. But he found time to do freebies for the Fellowship of Christian Athletes, the Paul Anderson youth home in Dallas, the Salvation Army, United Way, and the American Diabetes Association (his father had died from complications of diabetes when Roger was still in high school). He privately visited children with cancer, leukemia, and other terminal diseases. Some fans had written to express their disappointment in learning that the quarterback's faith was Catholic when he had said he was Christian. In an effort to bridge the historical divide between Protestants and Catholics, Roz Cole would respond that Staubach was actually both.

Staubach learned about that divide firsthand when he was invited to speak at the First Baptist Church by Dr. W. A. Criswell.

"He got criticism for having a Catholic come down and speak at the church," Staubach said, noting that the church had no black members at the time. "Every religion has differences within their churches," he said. "But at the end of the day as a Christian it's your acceptance of Jesus Christ. It sure gets complicated when you try to judge others based on their faith."

On the ex-Cowboy front, Pettis Norman, born to sharecropper parents in Georgia, owned two Burger King franchises, an apartment complex and other real estate, and Norman Investments, a company devoted to his interests; as the former agent for Duane Thomas, he found work for the onetime running back with the Dallas County Community Action Committee after Thomas declared bankruptcy. Mike Connally, who played center from 1960 to 1967, was a broker at Eppler, Guerin, and Turner Inc., making more money than he ever did in football. Bob Hayes quit his sales job at Dallas Hat and Emblem Manufacturing and was looking for new opportunities after remarrying. Dave Manders, 1964 to 1974, was looking for work too but had a hundred-acre ranch between Canton and Grand Saline in East Texas where he ran fifty head of Grand Chianina cattle. Don Meredith returned to ABC's *Monday Night Football,* after having left in 1973 for NBC, and formed his own production company.

The Super Bowl champion Oakland Raiders were cultivating a mystique of their own, one that in most respects was the polar opposite of the Cowboys'. They were pirates, thugs, and rough-and-rowdy physical players, devoted to their boss, Al Davis, and his motto "Just win, baby," as much as they were dedicated to their coach, John Madden, who related personally to his players and wore his emotions on his sleeve.

"We are a crazy bunch," admitted Raiders quarterback Kenny "Snake" Stabler. "We have almost one of everything and no two of anything. Everybody is an individualist doing his own thing. Our practices are like the Barnum & Bailey Circus. It's always fun, never a grind. Coach Madden gives us a great deal of freedom but he does draw a line. It's just that the line is farther back than most lines, but we all know where it is." They also knew that they had thrashed Minnesota, 32–14, in the big game.

Tom Landry felt enough heat from Tex Schramm about the National Football Conference's sagging reputation to send a letter to all the players asking them to work hard and reach the Super Bowl in order to save the old league "from further embarrassment and [prevent] the Minnesota Vikings from representing us again."

Landry's best hope was the draft, which remained up in the air until the NFL Players Association and the NFL owners, led by Schramm, reached a five-year agreement allowing free agency for players, with strings attached.

Dallas traded several draft choices to Seattle to get the first pick in the overall draft, Heisman Trophy winner Tony Dorsett from the University of Pittsburgh, the 1976 national college champions. Schramm described Dorsett, a handsome, engaging personality with an animated face, as the most outstanding running back since O. J. Simpson. "When you get a chance to get that type of player, you make sacrifices," he said, backing up Gil Brandt, who had declared, "I've never in my life seen as much interest in one player as there is in Dorsett.

"We made the trade predicated on Dorsett being there, not Ricky Bell [the other sought-after talent in the draft]," Brandt said. "We had all of the back log information that said by these grades, what chance a guy has to play in the National Football League. And Dorsett was a cinch pick. Everybody said he's not very big, but nobody ever hit him square. I don't think you've ever seen a boarded-up McDonald's and the reason you've never seen a boarded-up McDonald's is because they don't go out and say, Third and Wells looks like a good place to put a store. They know how many cars go by, they know everything. That's what we do. We try to know as many things that are tie-breakers that lead to success. Every year we re-evaluate players from two years previous that fail or perform beyond expectations and we adjust the weights, up or down, depending on what took place. It's kind of like companies with profit and loss."

Tony Dorsett signed a multiyear deal, making him the Cowboys' first million-dollar player—actually, the contract was for $1.2 million over five years. The sports bookies in Las Vegas installed the Cowboys as the odds-on favorites to win the Super Bowl.

Dorsett bought a gray Lincoln Mark IV with the initials *TD* on the doors and brought with him three other Lincolns that had been given to him by grateful Pittsburgh alumni, along with some buddies from Pittsburgh. His North Dallas apartment was in the same complex as Harvey Martin's and Thomas Henderson's.

Upon his arrival, he announced a change in pronouncing his name: instead of "*Dor*sett," it would be "Dor*sett.*"

And less than two weeks after coming to town, he got into a row with a bartender at the Number Three Lift in the European Crossroads center on west Northwest Highway after being accused of not paying for a drink. The result was two charges of assault, for punching the bartender and for hitting a waitress with a thrown glass. Bartender Sammie Emerick had to get four stitches under his left eye.

If the anticipation of Dorsett wasn't enough to get fans worked up, the Dallas Cowboys hype machine gave them plenty to contemplate. A dazzling blond cheerleader named Debbie Wagener, who was a checker at counter 5 at the Tom Thumb grocery at Meadow and Central by day, pouted confidently into the camera that captured her image for the cover of *Esquire* magazine's October issue, which was bannered "The Dallas Cowgirls: The Best Thing About the Dallas Cowboys."

Wagener was only part of a flurry of publicity showered upon the cheerleaders. They rated a feature in *People*, a new magazine devoted solely to celebrity that was spun off from the People page in *Time* magazine. Young Dallas women in white short shorts, navy blue halters, white-fringed vests, and shiny white boots were the highlight of Jerry Lewis's Labor Day telethon broadcast live from Las Vegas. MGM even invited eighteen cheerleaders to audition for a TV series based on the film *Logan's Run*.

The cheerleaders' tryouts had been profiled in the *Wall Street Journal*, which related the story of a prospect who called Suzanne Mitchell from Virginia and kept her on the phone for thirty minutes, telling her she was coming to Texas to try out. Mitchell advised her to get a job first. "We don't pick up these girls at Go-Go joints," Mitchell told the *WSJ* reporter. "They are reflecting on the Dallas Cowboys organization, so we have to be careful about their image. We don't let them work cocktail parties or anywhere where there's booze."

The sex they were selling was polite sex, and though Ron Traxler and Robert Richardson showed up again for tryouts, they were immediately eliminated because neither met the standards of "looking good in a halter top." Candidates danced routines to the Swivel, the Choo-Choo, and the Penguin. On hand to watch the tryouts were a camera crew from ABC's *Wide World of Sports* and a recruiter for the new Dallas Playboy Club, who was trolling for prospects.

The *Journal* reporter was unflinching in his observations: "The hips of one prospect, for example, may be a tad on the heavy side [cheerleaders who gained weight were dropped from the squad]. Another may have no sense of rhythm. A few candidates are cut because their smiles lack 'sparkle.'"

"We're not your normal two-bit, four-bit girls," Suzanna Holub told the reporter. Texie Waterman added, "I could say we're looking for 35 Farrah Fawcetts but even that might get boring."

"We're the number-one subject in the NFL," Deborah Kepley, who was competing to stay on the squad, said unequivocally. "People react like you're some kind of movie star."

The new hopefuls took a more innocent approach introducing themselves to judges Bedford Wynne, radio disc jockey Mike Selden, stadium manager Bert Rose, and photographer Bob Shaw.

Sisters Karen and Sharen York of Fort Worth, who fashioned their own outfits for tryouts, danced the Bump, then Karen said, "We just like to be out front." Another said, "I'm a brown belt in karate and if you don't choose me, I'm going to be real upset." And another: "Hi, I'm 22, I was born and raised in Dallas and I clean teeth" and "I'm single, still looking, and that's about all I can say."

"To be a Cowboy cheerleader in Dallas is a very big thing, you're the center of attention," said another veteran cheerleader, Meg Rossi.

When Roger Staubach was asked about the girls, he said, "If you're selling sex, that's not right at all." But he didn't pay attention to the cheerleaders at games anyway. They were just a "mirage" as far as he was concerned.

Tex Schramm brushed off criticism that the cheerleaders were sexist and a distraction. "We've also had critics of the plays we call." Other teams were adding cheerleader squads, he said with a hound-dog grin, "but they don't have the raw product we do."

"The girls in Texas are prettier than the girls in other states," Chuck Milton of CBS confirmed. Receiver Drew Pearson said he wasn't jealous of the attention the girls were getting. More than once he placed the ball in a cheerleader's hands when he scored a touchdown. "When you're hot, you're hot." He shrugged.

They were hot, all right. An impostor toting a Dallas Cowboys Cheerleaders poster got a gig at the Neptune Club topless bar in Corpus Christi, earning $150 for the night even though she didn't strip, she said, "because it's against Cowboys Cheerleaders' rules." Business at the club doubled.

Sixty-seven girls made the finals. Sixteen holdovers and twenty new faces made the squad.

Expectations were higher than ever for the team, too, as the Cowboys kicked off the 1977 season. The opener in Minnesota would be watched by an estimated 842,000 fans in the Dallas–Fort Worth area and heard on the radio by another 150,000 fans. According to an article on Cowboys fan culture, they all would "vacillate

Brain trust: Cowboys general manager Tex Schramm, minority owner Bedford Wynne, majority owner Clint Murchison Jr., and head coach Tom Landry (left to right) stand outside the new Dallas Cowboys Football Club offices, 1960. (*Laughead Photographers*)

Eddie LeBaron is obtained from the Washington Redskins to be the Cowboys' first starting quarterback, 1960. (*Laughead Photographers*)

Rookie Don Meredith, the good ol' boy from Mount Vernon and Southern Methodist University, is the Cowboys' designated future quarterback. (*Laughead Photographers*)

In 1963 Meredith takes over the starting quarterback position, enduring brutal poundings weekly and emerging as the first Cowboys star. (*John Mazziotta / Dallas Times Herald, courtesy of the Dallas Morning News*)

Blackie's boys: *Fort Worth Press* gang of sportswriters, the first generation of Cowboys critics; (clockwise from top left) Jerre Todd, Blackie Sherrod, Dan Jenkins, Bud Shrake, and Andy Anderson, c. 1959. (*Blackie Sherrod papers, DeGolyer Library, Southern Methodist University, Dallas, Texas, A2004.0016*)

Dynamic duo: sports scribes Gary Cartwright (left) and Bud Shrake at the *Dallas Times Herald*, 1961. (*Courtesy of the Wittliff Collections, Texas State University–San Marcos*)

Crowd waits at Love Field Airport to welcome President John F. Kennedy and First Lady Jackie Kennedy to Dallas on November 22, 1963. (Dallas Morning News *staff photo*)

Early squad of cheerleaders: Dallas-area high school cheerleaders moonlighting as the Cowboys' CowBelles and Beaux, with director Dee Brock in black. (*Eamon Kennedy* / Dallas Morning News, *courtesy of Dee Brock*)

Stripper Bubbles Cash walks down a Cotton Bowl aisle and becomes a Cowboys sensation, influencing the future look of the Cowboys cheerleaders, 1967. (*Joe Laird* / Dallas Morning News)

Wide receiver Bob Hayes (left) and Cowboys owner Clint Murchison Jr. prepare to hop onto the Braniff team charter to the NFL championship game in Green Bay, 1967. (Dallas Morning News *staff photo*)

The Packers' Herb Adderley dives for Don Meredith's fumble in the historic championship game known as the Ice Bowl, 1967. (*Associated Press photo*)

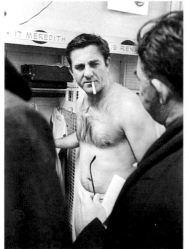

Contrite captain: a defeated Meredith meets the press postgame in the locker room after losing to Green Bay—"It wasn't a fair test of football," 1967. (*From the* Green Bay Press-Gazette, *December 31, 1967. All rights reserved. Used by permission.*)

Quarterback Craig Morton (right) with backup rookie Roger Staubach, who joined the team in 1969. (*Johnny Flynn* / Dallas Morning News)

Turning tides: former sportscaster Wes Wise (right) is elected mayor of Dallas, replacing J. Erik Jonsson (far left), 1971. (*Clint Grant* / Dallas Morning News)

Texas Stadium opens in October 1971, featuring the iconic "hole in the roof" and luxury skybox suites. (*From the collection of Dan Werner*)

"...A SPECIAL CITY..."

Life with the Dallas Cowboys magazine is given to prospective recruits to help sell the team and city, 1971. (From the collection of Dan Werner)

Defensive captain Lee Roy Jordan, the Cowboys' all-time leader in solo tackles over fourteen seasons, demonstrates his prowess for stealing the ball. (Dallas Morning News *staff photo*)

Defensive lineman Bob Lilly seethes at the conclusion of the Cowboys' Super Bowl loss to Baltimore, moments before throwing his helmet across the field in frustration, 1971. (Dallas Morning News *staff photo*)

Owner Clint Murchison Jr. in a ticker-tape parade following the Cowboys' Super Bowl loss to Baltimore, 1971. (*Courtesy,* Fort Worth Star-Telegram *Collection, Special Collections, the University of Texas at Arlington Library, Arlington, Texas*)

Walt Garrison, the Cowboys' real cowboy, crashes through the Miami line for a 14-yard gain during the Cowboys' 24–3 victory over the Dolphins in Super Bowl VI, 1972. (Dallas Morning News *staff photo*)

At last, Tom Landry coaches the Cowboys to their first Super Bowl title against the Miami Dolphins at Tulane Stadium in New Orleans in 1972. Bob Hayes, Rayfield Wright, and Mel Renfro (left to right) lead the postgame revelry. (*Gary Barnett* / Dallas Morning News)

Running back Duane Thomas is instrumental in getting the Cowboys to their first two Super Bowls, but is traded after refusing to speak to teammates, coaches, and the press for an entire season. (*Joe Laird* / Dallas Morning News)

The Cowboys goldy-throats: broadcasters Verne Lundquist, Frank Glieber, and Brad Sham (left to right). (*Kurt Wallace* / Dallas Morning News)

Roger the Dodger: determined Staubach scrambles in the "Hail Mary" playoff game against Minnesota, 1975. (*John F. Rhodes* / Dallas Morning News)

Dynasty: beaming president and general manager Tex Schramm hoists the Cowboys' second Super Bowl trophy after the team's victory parade in downtown Dallas, 1978. (*Steve Ueckert* / Dallas Morning News)

Choreographer Texie Waterman (left) and Schramm's secretary Suzanne Mitchell guide cheerleaders to the big time, 1978. (*Courtesy of the Dallas Cowboys Football Club*)

First Dallas Cowboys Cheerleaders poster, published by Pro Arts, Inc., 1978. (*From the collection of Joe Nick Patoski*)

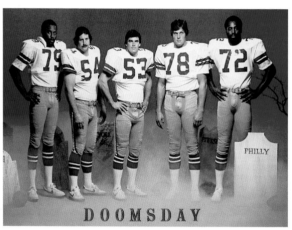

The formidable Doomsday Defense: Harvey Martin, Randy White, Bob Breunig, John Dutton, and Ed "Too Tall" Jones (left to right), commemorated with their own poster. (*From the collection of Joe Nick Patoski*)

Defensive big man Ed "Too Tall" Jones enters Texas Stadium flanked by the Dallas Cowboys Cheerleaders, whose made-for-TV movie, *The Dallas Cowboys Cheerleaders*, received a 48 percent share of the national television audience. (*Courtesy*, Fort Worth Star-Telegram *Collection, Special Collections, the University of Texas at Arlington Library, Arlington, Texas*)

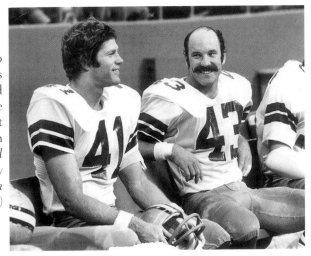

Dynamic duo: All-pro Safeties and best friends Charlie Waters (left) and Cliff Harris relax on the sidelines. (*Courtesy,* Fort Worth Star-Telegram *Collection, Special Collections, the University of Texas at Arlington Library, Arlington, Texas*)

TD 33 fly guy: Tony Dorsett makes the Pro Bowl four times during his eleven seasons with the Cowboys. (Dallas Morning News *staff photo*)

Thomas "Hollywood" Henderson's flamboyant off-the-field lifestyle contributed to his being cut in 1979. (*Jay Godwin /* Dallas Morning News)

Tom Landry's innovative, complicated, and sometimes difficult-to-follow playbook is critical in establishing the Cowboys as one of the NFL's dominant teams into the mid-1980s, posting an unprecedented winning record for twenty consecutive seasons. (*Randy Eli Grothe* / Dallas Morning News)

Danny Boy: White takes over after Staubach retires in 1979 and proceeds to lead the team to three straight NFC Championship games. But the 1982 Pro Bowler (and team punter for nine years) can't get the Cowboys back to the Super Bowl. (*John F. Rhodes* / Dallas Morning News)

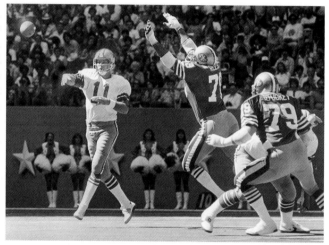

Crazy Ray, the concessions vendor turned unofficial Cowboys mascot, is a sideline fixture at home games in the Cotton Bowl and Texas Stadium for forty-six seasons. (*Juan Garcia* / Dallas Morning News)

The Big Three: Tom Landry, Tex Schramm, and player personnel director Gil Brandt (left to right) remain the organization's foundation after H. R. "Bum" Bright buys the team in 1984. (Dallas Morning News *staff photo*)

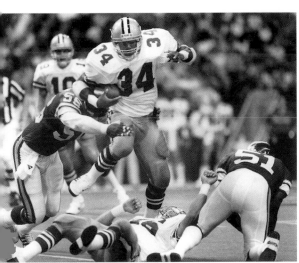

Herschel Walker joins the Cowboys in 1986 and helps build their second dynasty by being traded in October 1989, only to return seven years later. (*John F. Rhodes / Dallas Morning News*)

The Miami Hurricane known as "the Playmaker," receiver Michael Irvin, is selected by the Cowboys in the first round of the 1988 draft. (*John F. Rhodes / Dallas Morning News*)

Black Saturday: front page of the *Dallas Morning News*, February 26, 1989. (*Courtesy of the* Dallas Morning News)

The Dallas Morning News

Texas' Leading Newspaper   Dallas, Texas, Sunday, February 26, 1989   26 Sections   16¢ $1.00

Jones buys Cowboys, fires Landry

Rozelle: 'This is like Lombardi's death'

Arkansas oilman heads new group of owners

Jerry Jones (right) announces his purchase of the Cowboys at a press conference, with previous owner H. R. "Bum" Bright (middle) and soon-to-be-former president and general manager Tex Schramm in background, 1989. (*Courtesy,* Fort Worth Star-Telegram *Collection, Special Collections, the University of Texas at Arlington Library, Arlington, Texas*)

Jerry Jones's first visit to Thousand Oaks training camp creates a media storm, 1989. (*Erich Schlegel* / Dallas Morning News)

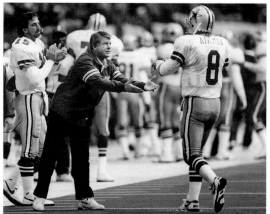

New leaders: Coach Jimmy Johnson offers encouragement to quarterback Troy Aikman. (*John F. Rhodes* / Dallas Morning News)

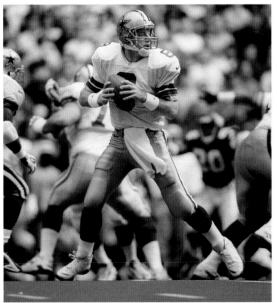

Troy at the helm: Aikman is the Cowboys' all-time leading passer. (*Louis DeLuca* / Dallas Morning News)

Unstoppable: Emmitt Smith follows tackle Larry Allen through a hole, racing toward the NFL's all-time rushing record. (*Steve Hamm* / Dallas Morning News)

The Triplets: Troy Aikman, Emmitt Smith, and Michael Irvin (left to right) dominate the '90s Cowboys' offense and lead the team to three Super Bowl wins. (*Louis DeLuca* / Dallas Morning News)

JJs triumphant: Jerry Jones and Coach Jimmy Johnson share the trophy after the Cowboys defeat Buffalo in Super Bowl XXVII, 1993. (*Erich Schlegel* / Dallas Morning News)

Sharp-dressed road warrior and free agent Deion Sanders joins the Cowboys midseason in 1995. (*Michael Ainsworth* / Dallas Morning News)

Vindication: Jerry Jones (left) and Coach Barry Switzer with the Vince Lombardi Trophy after Dallas defeats Pittsburgh for its third Super Bowl championship in four years, 1996. (Dallas Morning News *staff photo*)

The Romans and their loyal subjects: Jerry Jones (left) and Stephen Jones watch a game against the Giants from the owner's suite in Texas Stadium, 2000. (*Erich Schlegel* / Dallas Morning News)

Doubting Tuna: Coach Bill "Big Tuna" Parcells assesses young quarterback Tony Romo, 2006. (*Louis DeLuca / Dallas Morning News*)

T.O. TD: Terrell Owens spikes the ball through the goalposts after scoring the third of his four touchdowns against the Redskins at Texas Stadium, 2007. (*John F. Rhodes / Dallas Morning News*)

An injured Tony Romo yells at special teams coach Joe DeCamillis, head coach Wade Phillips, and offensive coordinator Jason Garrett (left to right) during the fourth quarter of the Cowboys' 41–35 loss to the New York Giants, 2010. (*John F. Rhodes / Dallas Morning News*)

The coach and the QB: Romo confers with his third Cowboys boss, Coach Jason Garrett. (*Michael Ainsworth / Dallas Morning News*)

America's Sweethearts: the Dallas Cowboys Cheerleaders at the first football game played in Cowboys Stadium, August 21, 2009. (*Erich Schlegel*)

Into the abyss: Jason Garrett leads the Cowboys onto the field of Cowboys Stadium. (*Tom Fox* / Dallas Morning News)

between vociferous celebration and stomach-churning rage. They will eat and drink and beam and harangue with unwonted abandon. They will argue endlessly when passion is spent, and wait anxiously for it to come again the next Sunday.

"They have become one of Texas' resources, like oil and barbecue, 'part of the mainstream of American life,' as one fan put it."

"There is nothing that can come close to the domination of the Cowboy games," said Channel 4 salesman Steve Pontius. Sunday-afternoon games captivated 84 percent of Dallas–Fort Worth television viewers.

Dallas mayor Bob Folsom, a high-profile real estate developer whose election marked the restoration of the citizens council's influence, said of the Cowboys, "They are the only representatives of the city of Dallas that many people throughout the United States get to see." And Dallas was looking good to the rest of the country.

Ann Draper, head of a party coordinating service, said, "The first thing we have to do each year is get the Cowboys schedule. Otherwise, nothing can be done. Nobody can schedule a party at the time a football game goes on." Dallas churches had certainly learned. "Yes, we know when the Cowboys are in town," said Dr. Frank Warren of the Highland Park Methodist Church, the coach's church. "We notice an increased attendance at the early services at 8:30 and 9. The 11 o'clock service is usually lighter."

Radio personality Kevin McCarthy described the Cowboys as the premier male-bonding topic. "As a man, you talk about the Cowboys at lunch [after game days]. They're the most interesting, the most diversified, and at the same time, the safest topic of conversation there is."

The marketing community had caught on to the team's purchasing power a long time before. The Oak Farms billboard on the Central Expressway featured the Cowboy of the Week. Mercantile Bank put up billboards featuring quotes from Drew Pearson, Harvey Martin, and Too Tall Jones.

Cliff Harris, who opened the Sundown Steak House and Saloon in Addison, the suburb just north of the Dallas city limits, signed autographs at Sears and Titche's. On TV, Efren Herrera hawked Pancho's Mexican Buffett; Thomas Henderson pitched Carco Auto Sales; Roger Staubach endorsed Mattel's computerized football game for kids of all ages; his coach spoke on behalf of Frey wieners; and Drew Pearson sold Toyotas and appeared dapper in print ads for the Bond clothing store. Bookings for the thirty-two-piece Dallas Cowboys band, $1,500 for three hours, were solid.

Minyard's sold the official Cowboys Press Guide for $2.50. The *Dallas Cowboys Weekly*, under the guidance of Steve Perkins and Russ Russell, saw its circulation shoot up to fifty thousand subscriptions, all prepaid. Roger Staubach's book *First Down, Lifetime to Go* was on sale everywhere.

The star power came at a price for Joe Fan. Tickets and concessions were getting pricey. A family of five attending a game and each enjoying a hot dog and a soda, ice cream, popcorn, coffee, and nachos would spend a minimum of $64.45, calculated Jim Reeves of the *Fort Worth Star-Telegram*. "The old entertainment dollar just can't stand too many bites like that," he wrote. "Take the family to a ball game, dad, but don't forget your paycheck."

But the performance on the field made it all seem worth it.

In their season opener, the Cowboys beat Minnesota with solid defense, Preston Pearson's TD catch and 63 yards rushing, and Roger Staubach sealing the deal with a four-yard run into the end zone: an overtime win, 16–10.

They stomped the New York Giants, 41–21, at home in 99-degree heat that reached 120 degrees on the artificial turf, a game highlighted by rookie Tony Dorsett's blazing 34-yard touchdown run, his second TD of the day. But the bigger home-opener story that fans at Texas Stadium were talking about was the appearance of the Dallas Cowboys Cheerleaders in modified uniforms.

Although Tex Schramm gave Suzanne Mitchell total control,

exceptions were made now and then, especially when they came from the owner's wife.

At the born-again insistence of Anne Murchison, the Dallas Cowboys Cheerleaders took to the field wearing modesty shields, triangular pieces of fabric that snapped into the fronts of their uniforms, reducing the visible cleavage their halter tops displayed so well. The response as they made their grand entrance was a shower of boos and jeers. At halftime, the cheerleaders were told to remove the shields, and they were never seen again.

Anne Murchison had a kindred soul in Alicia Landry, who weighed in with Suzanne Mitchell and Russ Russell about the cheerleaders' image in photographs.

"I'd shoot 'em in shorts, I'd shoot 'em in two-piece bikinis, I'd shoot 'em with a towel holding across their self coming out of the bathtub with a bathing suit on under it," Russ Russell recalled. "[Alicia] had Tom speak to me twice about it. In the hallway, he'd stop me, he'd say, 'Russ, Alicia is really upset with those pictures that you're doing.'

"I'd say, 'Tom, talk to Tex, he picks 'em out, Suzanne poses them, I shoot 'em, give 'em to Tex, Tex says, "Put this in, put this in,"' and Tom goes 'Grrrr.' Alicia came up to me one day and said, 'Those pictures you take are the P-E-its.' 'Alicia, go talk to Tex.'"

Tex had the last word and Tex liked what he saw. With Suzanne Mitchell as monitor, he got the desired effect: he caught male viewers' attention while the cheerleaders projected a wholesome image of America's sweethearts in hot pants.

On the field, the Cowboys were playing rough. Tampa Bay was disposed of expediently, 23–7, in a win led by linebacker Thomas Henderson, who intercepted a pass and returned it 79 yards for a touchdown, snagged a second interception, and knocked two Tampa Bay players out of the game. The team squeaked by the St. Louis Cardinals, 24–22, on a Golden Richards touchdown reception and Tony Dorsett's 77-yard touchdown run, but it wasn't as close as it looked, since a 90-yard Staubach-to-Pearson TD was nullified by a holding call. Washington was skinned, 34–16, at Irving in a game in which Tony Dorsett successfully threw a pass, Drew Pearson caught a 59-yard TD bomb from Roger Staubach, and Efren Herrera booted a 52-yard field goal.

After the Redskins game, Herrera accused Washington kicker Mark Moseley of putting lead in his shoe to boost his kicking performance, and Tex Schramm backed him up, protesting to the league and pissing off Washington coach and chief Cowboy hater George Allen even more.

"Dallas is into everybody else's business," Allen griped. "Tex and Dallas are always carrying the Holy Grail." Philadelphia Eagles coach Dick Vermeil didn't bother griping. He simply stated the obvious. "The Dallas Cowboys cannot be stopped."

Vermeil almost got away with the reverse psychology as Philly dropped a 16–10 squeaker to the Cowboys in a game closer than it needed to be. A blocked punt by Charlie Waters that was returned for a TD was the deciding difference. The Cowboys remained undefeated with a 7-0 record after annihilating the Detroit Lions at Texas Stadium on the day that number 54, Chuck Howley, was inducted into the Cowboys Ring of Honor.

Ernie Stautner's Doomsday Defense, anchored by Harvey Martin, led the league in sacks, with Mel Renfro, now in his fifteenth season; Randy White; Thomas Henderson; and Bob Breunig holding down the middle. A sense of determination settled in.

The unbeaten streak stretched to eight as the Cowboys rolled the Giants in the Meadowlands, 24–10. Following the game, Tom Landry signed another five-year contract to coach the team after going two years without a contract. He might as well make it formal since his team was executing on practically every level he could imagine.

Then the unstoppable was stopped at home in a Monday-night nationally televised game against St. Louis, which the Cardinals won by a touchdown, 24–17. Afterward, several Cards in the locker room were seen wearing black T-shirts that read *Cowboys Eat Bird Shit*.

The running back Tony Dorsett drew his first starting assignment in the next game, playing in his old hometown, Pittsburgh. The kid showed no jitters, running for 73 yards and a touchdown. Otherwise, though, the Steelers thoroughly dominated the formerly unstoppable 'Boys, holding them scoreless in the second half and sticking them with their second consecutive defeat, 28–13.

The Cowboys righted themselves and ran the table, eliminating Washington from the playoffs with a 14–7 win at RFK Stadium, followed by a 24–14 victory against Philadelphia at home, a game some fans missed so they could line up outside Texas Stadium in front of ticket booths to buy playoff game tickets. Harvey Martin added three sacks to his record twenty-three for the year while Dorsett rumbled for 208 yards, a team record, including his longest run of the season, an 84-yard dash for a touchdown.

The 49ers were dispatched in an offensive show, 42–35, before Dallas closed out, edging Denver, which had lost only one game before meeting Dallas, 14–6. Broncos quarterback Craig Morton, who was having a stellar season earning the AFC's player of the year honors, played only one series before leaving the game. Perhaps they would meet in the Super Bowl when the outcome really mattered.

"Just from observation, I guess you'd say our team is a couple years away," Tom Landry observed, downplaying what looked to be the best Cowboys team ever produced.

The first-round playoff game against the Chicago Bears pitted Tony Dorsett against veteran Walter Payton, the premier running back in the game. It was no contest. The Bears fell 37–7 on a relentless defense and two Tony Dorsett touchdown runs, earning him the cover of *Sport* magazine and the NFL's top offensive rookie honors. Tom Landry called it "our best game of the year." Harvey Martin was recognized as the NFL's Defensive Player of the Year.

The Cowboys' number-one playoff pain in the ass, the Minnesota

Vikings, endured a 23–6 thrashing on New Year's Day to earn the Cowboys the National Football Conference championship. The home game was marred only by a fire in the grandstands late in the fourth quarter. Daniel Yoder, a twenty-four-year-old Bloom Advertising employee, came to the game dressed as a snowman, the same costume he'd worn the night before for New Year's Eve. Yoder the Snowman was making his way toward the field near the end of the game to dance with the Dallas Cowboys Cheerleaders when he bumped into a vendor selling hot Dr Pepper. The canned heat the vendor was using to keep drinks warm came into contact with Yoder's costume, which went up in flames. Fans tried to put out the fire but Yoder panicked and ran until one woman chasing him knocked him down, and the fire was smothered by blankets. He suffered second-degree burns on his legs and under his chin.

Then, five days after the Sex Pistols brought their notorious punk rock circus from England to the stage of Dewey Groom's Longhorn Ballroom and generated headlines for bassist Sid Vicious's prolific bleeding after a female fan head-butted him, there was another physical confrontation, this one down in New Orleans, where the Dallas Cowboys faced off against the Denver Broncos.

Super Bowl XII at the Superdome would be the first Super Bowl played indoors, a fortunate event, since temperatures outside hovered in the thirties — frigid conditions for the Deep South.

The quarterbacks provided the main story line: This was the third Super Bowl that Roger Staubach was starting in. This was the third Super Bowl and the second Super Bowl start for Craig Morton, the ex-Cowboy who'd found happiness in Denver, where he'd led the Broncos to a league-best 12-2 record. Staubach sure felt it. "Obviously if we lose, everybody's gonna say that Craig should have stayed in Dallas," he said. "I have a lot of extra pressure on me because of that."

Craig Morton, who had married Dallas model and teacher Suzie Sirman (his second marriage) in November and had found religion (through his wife) while fending off a bill from the IRS for $34,646 (the amount owed in back taxes), would be calling his own plays.

Those details were overshadowed by the Broncomania pandemic breaking out across the Rocky Mountains. Orange and navy was the new color combo of choice, whether on powder snow or the fashion runway. More than three hundred thousand Orange Crush T-shirts and windbreakers had been sold, inspiring bootleg Orange Crush shirts with a marijuana-leaf design. Denver, the city, burnished its own glamorous image as an ascendant, midcontinental version of Dallas, only with the picturesque Rockies for a backdrop.

The Broncos organization was regarded as the American Football Conference's equivalent of the Cowboys—exciting and forward-thinking after thirteen years of losing (they had not recorded their first winning season until 1973). Rookie coach Red Miller, previously the offensive coordinator at New England, might be the next Landry. The Orange Crush, Denver's D-line, was being hailed as the new Doomsday. Morton's passing accuracy and speedy receiver corps recalled Meredith and his gang at their peak, just as the fever sweeping Broncoland was reminiscent of North Texas's in the mid-sixties, when the Cowboys had first become competitive contenders for the big prize.

Of the two teams, Denver appeared to be more blue-collar, though only slightly so. Their home, Mile High Stadium, had begun as the minor-league baseball Bears Stadium in the 1940s and lacked corporate suites. But the 71,000 season-ticket holders weren't complaining. Part of the fun of being a Denver Broncos nut was sitting in the stands in ice, snow, and cold for at least a few games every year.

Sixty thousand supporters lined downtown Denver streets before the team jetted off from Stapleton Field in an orange Braniff DC-8 jet. One thousand Dallas fans and Crazy Ray on his stick horse gathered at Love Field to bid Godspeed to the home team.

Tom Landry summed up the general attitude throughout Dallas when he said, "You know, I don't get excited about too many things." He knew precisely when that time would be, and it wasn't yet.

Thomas Henderson arrived in New Orleans wearing an orange suit, which he said he planned to burn. One reporter observed, "In contrast to the Broncos, most of whom were dressed casually, the Cowboys looked like they had stepped from the pages of a fashion magazine." Henderson was a quote machine, despite the piece of tape that had been placed above his locker after the Denver game at Texas Stadium in December with the message *Do you never shut your mouth?*

Super Bowl tickets, priced at $30, were already going for $250 on the black market. An estimated 85 million viewers would be watching the game on television across America, with a worldwide audience of 150 million. Dr. Norman Vincent Peale, the author of *The Power of Positive Thinking,* one of the bestselling books of all time, commented, "If Jesus were alive, he'd be at the Super Bowl."

Jimmy the Greek Snyder would have gladly taken Jesus's bet. He estimated $300 million was being bet on the game. Some of those bettors got an early start, setting a record handle of $2 million at the Fairgrounds racetrack on the Friday before the game.

The Cowboys kept a low profile in West Kenner, a rapidly developing suburb near the airport, closing off their practices to the public. They had reason to take the game seriously. The AFC winner had won eight of the past nine Super Bowls. The sole exception was the 1971 Dallas Cowboys, as Tex Schramm reminded everyone.

Those hardy Cowboys fans arriving early on Bourbon Street were inundated by a sea of orange. One fan, seventy-nine-year-old Ray Landry, showed up to let the press and fans know his son was a bad dresser back home. "I'll be darned if I know where he gets those hats," Ray Landry said. "Some guy keeps him in hats. His wife helps on dressing him, too. They went on a blind date when they first met. They went to a wienie roast and she said, 'I thought he was the tackiest man I ever met.'" Ray said his son lived for football. "He was a guy you couldn't punish. You could beat his hide off but he wouldn't say a word. The only thing you could do was take away a privilege, like not letting him go on a date or to the movies."

Candles were lit by fans from both teams at St. Louis Cathedral Sunday morning before the game. One priest prayed aloud, "Forgive me, Lord, for causing you so much trouble."

The Dallas Cowboys Cheerleaders flew in on game day and would hop the bus straight for the airport afterward. Suzanne Mitchell didn't like the idea of exposing her girls to the debauchery going down in the hometown of Mardi Gras. Besides, the cheerleaders needed to pace themselves after pulling five thousand fans to the opening of a savings bank in Little Rock.

The hometown Southern University Jaguars band performed before the game and played "We Shall Overcome" in honor of Dr. Martin Luther King Jr.

THE FORCE IS WITH US read the banner hung by Cowboys fans under the ceiling of the New Orleans Superdome, referencing the popular film *Star Wars*. But it didn't appear that way at the start. Butch Johnson, Tony Dorsett, and Tony Hill all fumbled on the first two possessions without turning the ball over.

Two Dallas interceptions by Randy Hughes and Bob Breunig produced a Cowboys touchdown and a field goal. Efren Herrera kicked another field goal (and missed three more attempts) for a 13–0 lead at the half, but the real story was on the D-line. Doomsday was out-crushing the Orange Crush. Jethro, Too Tall, Randy White, and Harvey Martin backed by Hollywood, DD, and Breunig, with Cliff and Charlie in back, proved impenetrable. Morton threw four picks, half what he'd thrown all year.

The Tyler Apache Belles performed their synchronized high kicks in cancan outfits in the "From Paris to the Paris of America" halftime show, featuring New Orleans musicians Pete Fountain and Al Hirt. Clifton Winston, a Fort Worth carpenter, watched on a pay TV console at the Dallas Greyhound bus station. "I've already put $1.50 in this thing," Winston said before the start of the third quarter. "But I ain't missing none of this."

The First Baptist Church in Dallas didn't cancel its evening services, like most churches had, but afterward it used its video facilities for a delayed telecast of the game. "We're having a wonderful time here," pastor Dr. W. A. Criswell reported.

Dallas's penchant for free-form improvisation and trick plays served them well in the second half. Running back Robert Newhouse even threw a touchdown pass. As time ran out, Thomas Henderson spiked the ball over the crossbar of the goalpost once again while the Cowboy band played the "Theme from Rocky."

Final score, 27–10.

It wasn't pretty, with ten fumbles, all the Morton interceptions, the muffs by Herrera, and twenty penalties between both teams. Morton, with a bad hip, played worse than he had in his first Super Bowl appearance, seven years earlier, when he quarterbacked the Cowboys to the 16–13 loss against Baltimore. This one was so bad, some sports scribes dubbed it Blunder Bowl II.

But a win was a win, and defense, which brought Tom Landry to the dance, was the difference.

Tony Dorsett celebrated in the locker room on crutches from a knee bruise, modeling an Orange Crush T-shirt. Roger Staubach suffered a fractured index finger. Thomas Henderson crushed a can of Orange Crush after the game, making a mean face for the cameras.

In accepting the Super Bowl trophy from Pete Rozelle, Clint Murchison announced, "I'm going to give this to Tom Landry, who is not only Coach of the Year but Coach of the Century."

Landry finally *and* visibly admitted the feeling was "really exciting."

"Now the AFC can chase us for a while," Tex Schramm said for all to hear.

Harvey Martin and Randy White shared MVP honors for their defensive play. Martin had been all-everything all season, recording 85 tackles and a league-leading 23 sacks over fourteen regular-season games. The team won by an average of 13 points during the season and 21 points in the playoffs, with an 87-23 aggregate. By winning three playoff games, the players earned another $32,000 each.

Cowboys World Champions T-shirts went for $10 on Bourbon Street after the game. *Broncos World Champions* T-shirts were marked down to $1.50 while bitter Denver fans cursed the "Cowgirls!" Singer John Denver hugged a little girl with an Orange Crush shirt and reassured her it wasn't the end of the world. "Hey, John," a Cowboys fan shouted to the composer of "Rocky Mountain High," "If you changed your name to John Dallas, you'd have a party to go to tonight." John Denver replied, "I'm loyal to the Broncos."

"You're a loser then," the fan bellowed.

In Dallas, fans jumped on tables and started dancing at the Filling Station on Greenville Avenue, breaking a few chairs. Filling Station waitress Sally Cutler complained, "No money! No tips!"

Back in West Kenner, Louisiana, a blue-and-white circus tent had been erected next to the team's airport motel so the whole organization could party to the country rock sounds of Willie Nelson, Waylon Jennings, and Jerry Jeff Walker. An ice sculpture of the Super Bowl trophy greeted guests. In another room, a Cowboy figure constructed of vanilla icing stood tall next to a boat piled high with oysters, shrimp, crawfish, and crab claws.

The party didn't really start until 2:30 a.m., when Waylon asked the musical question: "Are You Ready for the Country?," and it roared until close to dawn.

Bob Breunig, wielding Waylon's guitar, joined Waylon and Willie onstage to sing "Up Against the Wall, Redneck Mother." Roger Staubach turned up his collar as Breunig explained, "We had this little thing at training camp where Elvis Presley said he was going to come back if we won the Super Bowl. So here he is." Breunig proceeded to credibly sing "Jailhouse Rock" with Willie and Waylon's band, followed by "Heartbreak Hotel," "All Shook Up," and "Don't Be Cruel."

As the Ws sang "Mamas. Don't Let Your Babies Grow Up to Be Cowboys," tackle Ralph Neely waltzed with his eight-year-old daughter. DD Lewis, an old friend, hugged Willie and Waylon as country singer Charley Pride, Clint Murchison, Phyllis George, and Tom Landry looked on. When Willie Nelson crooned his signature blues "Night Life," Roger and Marianne Staubach did a slow dance.

At the victory party, a well-lit Tex Schramm said, "If anybody complains about this party, I don't care if it's Too Tall, I'll take 'em on."

Willie led the room in the gospel number "Will the Circle Be Unbroken" as the Cowboys left the stage, and Jerry Jeff closed out the celebration with "Goodnight, Irene."

ABOUT EIGHT THOUSAND FANS greeted the football team at Love Field's Braniff maintenance hangar on a blustery 35-degree Monday and watched the motorcade to city hall, where the team was feted. Thomas Henderson lost his $10,000 attaché case along with whatever was inside. The tepid welcome reflected a community secure in its backing of its team (and the cold weather). They did their job, acknowledged their greatness, and moved on. *Sport* magazine honored Harvey Martin and Randy White in New York as the most valuable players of Super Bowl XII, awarding both brand-new Thunderbird automobiles — and Harvey Martin beat out the entire Denver Broncos squad to get the lead role filming a TV commercial for Orange Crush soda. The 1977 Dallas Cowboys highlight reel was titled *The Year the Clock Struck XII*. NFL Films' Super Bowl special was titled *Doomsday in the Dome*.

Winning again and again was what it was all about. Especially with the third all-new cast of players. The system worked. The plan succeeded. For all the turnover of players and personnel, Schramm, Landry, Brandt, and Murchison remained in place. Next.

"I think there's a healthy trend in sports now," Tex Schramm philosophized in the afterglow. "What was discussed with me more than any other subject in New Orleans was the organization," he said. "I think this is the thing that allowed us to have continuity of success. Landry suffers by his own success and the success of the organization. Dammit, people keep forgetting. Look back in June. We were the unanimous choice to be in the Super Bowl. They ought to hold up these Coach of the Year things until the season's over. The bottom line is who won. If there's a consistency of success, it's taken for granted."

Schramm cited the second straight playoff loss to Cleveland in 1969 and the 1974 team as periods of doubt where they didn't let second-guessing cloud their vision. "We didn't evaluate by changing people. We went back and studied our methods, systems, and approaches."

The dean of Dallas sportswriters, Blackie Sherrod, made his own post–Super Bowl analysis, attributing the team's success to two rare possessions of Clint Murchison: a bottomless pocketbook and patience.

"When Murchison started the franchise in 1960, he was convinced (or somebody convinced him) that the organization must be built slowly, even methodically," Sherrod wrote. "None of this prefab business. It was Schramm's theory that an eventual contending team must be built through the draft...but you do not build slowly without patience. Landry is not all that patient, although his exterior looks so. Schramm certainly is not the patient type and had to keep a tight rein on his nerves. Murchison seemingly has the confident patience of the very, very rich."

"If we win a third Super Bowl, it will be important to me to win a fourth," Schramm said. "The opportunity to achieve greatness comes so seldom. Our organization has that opportunity. I want our organization to be great, like the Yankees, the Canadiens, and the Celtics. I'd like to be remembered for that kind of organization." If only Tex remembered personal details so well; he forgot his and Marty's twenty-fifth wedding anniversary.

Of the twenty-two starters on the first Super Bowl winners, only Staubach, Cliff Harris, and Jethro Pugh had started in their second championship victory (Ralph Neely was injured in '72, and Rayfield Wright was injured in '78). Six first-round draft choices started: Randy White, Too Tall Jones, Dorsett, Henderson, DuPree, and Aaron Kyle.

"Call it an era," Blackie wrote.

Some changes were afoot, mainly because Cowboys were in demand. Former player and current assistant coach Mike Ditka was interviewing with the Chicago Bears to be head coach. And offensive coordinator Dan Reeves — described as Landry Jr., only with much more warmth — was interviewing with the Rams for the head coaching position. Reeves had quit in 1973 when Landry wouldn't recommend him for the head coaching position at SMU, telling him he was "too young." But Reeves asked for his job back the next year and went from special teams, to quarterbacks and ends, to offensive coordinator. Dan Reeves turned out to be an invaluable mentor to Roger Staubach. "At first, they didn't have a quarterback coach," Staubach said. "I wish I could have had Dan Reeves my whole career. When Tom gave him a lot more responsibility, it was great. I was able to talk to him. After a game, he'd have me over to his house to watch film because he knew I was ticked off if we lost."

The way the Cowboys were playing, he was getting ticked off less and less.

D Is for *Dynasty*

TEX SCHRAMM SPENT the first half of the new year showing off the new centerpiece in his office: a sterling silver football-shaped sculpture made by Tiffany. The Vince Lombardi Trophy looked right at home next to the large glass coffee table, the sofa, and the TV that Tex liked to load with videotapes of games. "He'd ask me to polish it sometimes, or wipe it off, because he liked to have it in photographs," his assistant Betsy Berry said of the trophy that validated Schramm's career. With that kind of company, he could put his feet up on the credenza next to his desk, look out the window at Central Expressway as he talked on the phone, and fully convince himself and those around him that he owned the whole wide world.

Just in case he needed proof, he was voted the NFL Executive of the Year.

Schramm and the NFL Competition Committee were again considering adding instant replays to augment officials' calls, despite Pete Rozelle claiming it would cost $46 million to implement replay in every stadium in the league. Roger Staubach mused that over the course of the season, there were twenty controversial plays that would have benefited from instant replay but that each request for review should cost a team a time-out so the technology wouldn't be abused. The NFL Competition Committee had instituted numerous changes to the game of football for the benefit of fans. In 1970, official game time was moved from a stopwatch on the field to the scoreboard clock. Two years later, the hash marks were moved closer to the center of the field to aid offensive play. Then in 1974, the goal-post was moved from the goal line to the back of the end zone, ten yards farther away, out of safety concerns and to discourage dependence on field goals at the expense of offensive play. In 1975, the head referee was given a wireless microphone so he could explain penalties to the fans and television viewers at home. In 1977, use of the head slap by defensive linemen was made illegal.

It was a very busy winter and spring for the world champions too.

In March, while Tex was attending a Cowboys function, the Schramm residence was robbed for the fourth time, relieving the Schramms of loose change and a mink stole, following break-ins during the Cowboys' first Super Bowl victory, the first Thanksgiving-night game, and a *Monday Night Football* game. "Sooner or later they're going to learn I don't own anything," Tex said for the record.

At work, he was thinking about the four hundred pieces of mail arriving daily at Cowboys headquarters. Tex made sure it all was answered, and he hired more people specifically for that task.

"We would go out to the practice field and in everybody's locker, there were two or three pairs of shoes and a whole bunch of mail. All that mail used to piss off Tex," Gil Brandt said. Most letters were requests for autographs, T-shirts, wrist bands, or photographs. One day, it dawned on Tex there was a better way. "Why don't we just send them a little picture of the player the fans were asking about?" The answer came in the form of 4 x 6 photographs of the players, suitable for autographing or framing. Inside the envelope was a flyer informing the fan that T-shirts and other items were for sale via mail order. The money poured in.

Along with the barrage of autograph requests, speaking engagements, network appearances, endorsements, and work were extra-curricular perquisites that helped prepare players for post-Cowboys careers, including easy gigs.

Too Tall Jones and Denver's ferocious defensive lineman Lyle Alzado played assassins in the film *The Double McGuffin*, produced by Joe Camp and his Mulberry Square Productions in Dallas. Too Tall also got into concert promotion in his hometown of Jackson, Tennessee, and partnered with Thomas "Hollywood" Henderson in a Dallas disco.

Harvey Martin, Too Tall Jones's counterweight on the opposite end of the D-line, returned to his alma mater, East Texas State College, where he was given the key to the city of Commerce by the mayor and then bought a piece of Lucifer's, a shiny new disco in South Oak Cliff, where he was raised. "I grew up in Dallas," Martin said, explaining how the nightclub was a boost for the community. "I care about it. I wanted blacks to have a place to go for a good time. We have a strict dress code here, we want a class crowd. You'll never see no drugs in here either."

When he wasn't at his own place, Martin hung with Too Tall and Hollywood at the Plush Pup and the Flying Fox off Martin Luther King Boulevard in South Dallas, a place that entertainers Johnnie Taylor and Bobby Patterson frequented. Sometimes Too Tall joined Patterson onstage singing a Sam and Dave cover.

Charlie Waters went home to receive the South Carolina Pro Athlete of the Year award, recognition that along with Cliff Harris, Waters was part of football's most talented defensive back tandem.

The namesake of Larry Cole Builders opened Timberview subdivision in suburban Bedford, a job where "I get to be the coach instead of the player," the defensive lineman said. Cornerback Aaron Kyle was writing a column for the *Garland Daily News*. Roger Staubach left Henry S. Miller, one of the largest service real estate firms in the nation, to form Holloway and Staubach, hiring middle linebacker Bob Breunig as a Realtor. "Mr. Miller was really a good example for me," Staubach said of his real estate mentor. "I told Mr. Miller, 'I want to be like you. I'm not leaving to go to another firm and do the same thing I'm doing here, I'm going to leave to start my own firm.'" Staubach's understudy Danny White signed on at

Henry S. Miller, citing Dallas as "one of the leading cities in the nation as far as real estate goes."

DD Lewis, Guy Brown, and White were all getting their real estate licenses too.

Benny Barnes took a more conventional business path, joining Oak Cliff State Bank, while former kicker Mike Clark and running back Robert Newhouse worked for First Texas State Bank. Burton Lawless got into frozen seafood. Linebacker Randy White returned to his native Pennsylvania to work on his farm. Charlie Waters focused on his creative side, making metal sculpture and doing Chinese brush painting. Ralph Neely promoted *Sports Illustrated* sports clubs, John Fitzgerald sold cars for Sewell Cadillac, and Efren Herrera promoted Pamex Foods and radio's Texas State Network.

Golden Richards, who beat out Bob Hayes in 1974, hit the banquet circuit as a speaker, telling audiences at Fellowship of Christian Athletes, Big Brothers, and Boy Scouts functions about the dangers of drug and alcohol abuse.

The biggest ego on the team, Thomas "Hollywood" Henderson, contracted hepatitis and wound up in the hospital. No teammate sent him a card. Linebacker Bob Breunig said it was because "some guys resent Tom's brashness." One needed to look no further than Henderson's locker, where he posted old baby pictures "to remind myself what a beautiful baby I was," to understand why. Henderson managed an appearance in the film *Semi-Tough*, based on Dan Jenkins's novel, and dissed the movie's star afterward, saying, "Burt Reynolds is supposed to have played college ball but it had to be a long time ago. He runs as fast as my mother."

Tony Dorsett, twenty-three, voted the NFL Rookie of the Year even though he didn't start until the tenth game, was arrested for cursing two police officers who had stopped his car (which his roommate was driving at 2:00 a.m.) after the cops noticed the car was weaving. Dawn Waatti, a twenty-seven-year-old flight attendant sitting next to Dorsett in the backseat, put something down the front of her clothing, investigating officers said. She produced a bottle of Quaaludes. Dorsett was released on a $55 bond and lost endorsement deals with Fabergé and NBC due to the incident.

The fact that his date was white "didn't help any with the police," Dorsett acknowledged. "I came here from a northern city and sometimes I have to remind myself I'm in the South now. I don't want them going upside my head." Three months after an altercation at the Number Three Lift Club in which Dorsett was charged with assault, the American Civil Liberties Union filed a class action suit against the establishment, charging racial discrimination by its refusing to admit racially mixed couples.

Dorsett was clearly annoyed that the front office started bombarding him with offseason "visits" from ex-players and Dallas businessmen. "I'm not a little kid. I can take care of myself. I don't need people telling me how to act." Tex Schramm had asked ABC's *Monday Night Football* host Howard Cosell to put star Buffalo Bills running back O. J. Simpson and boxing legend Muhammad Ali in touch with Dorsett.

The star running back retreated from Action Avenue, buying a fourteen-room home in rural Wylie thirty miles north of downtown Dallas, with an $18,000 sound system, a water bed, a black marble sunken tub, and *TD* inlaid in tile at the bottom of the swimming pool. "I'm really aware now of what a fishbowl I'm living in here in Dallas, what a target I am for some people," Dorsett admitted. "I know there are some people who'd love to make a name for themselves by sticking it to me, and know now I've got to be really careful how I handle myself. It's part of the price that you have to pay, but I don't let it bother me. I really believe I can handle it. This is where I'm going to stay as long as the Cowboys make that possible. Man, I love it here. This is my kind of town and I'm happy here."

He understood that he needed to stay out of trouble, promising, "You're not going to read anything about Tony Dorsett except the news about what he's doing on the football field. Man, these are my wonder years — nobody knows that better than me. The good Lord has blessed me for some reason, and I feel an obligation to a lot of people to make the most of it."

That didn't mean he took a vow of celibacy. "I see lots of ladies," Dorsett acknowledged. "I love women and I don't like to tie myself down, you know. I'm too young for that." He busied himself learning to play tennis and ride horses and picked up endorsements for Jockey underwear and a line of Converse tennis shoes called TDs. He eyed getting into sportscasting after his football career ended.

For all his contrition, Dorsett wasn't working out in the offseason, much to the consternation of his coach. But he did some public outreach, appearing on the *Sports Challenge* TV show, going to events in Ohio and Tennessee on behalf of St. Jude Hospital charities, and appearing at the opening of Pap-Paw's Fried Chicken in Fort Worth in 105-degree heat, where a free TD photograph came with every $2.25 minimum purchase.

Meanwhile, the coach of the Dallas Cowboys went to Miami to accept the Kiwanis International Convention's Decency Award, and he condemned obscenity, pornography, homosexual rights, and the 1960s social revolution in his acceptance speech. "During the late '50s I found that I had basically little patience with people, especially people who could not excel or do their best on the football field," Landry said. "And I'd handle them all the same. Then came the great revolution of the '60s, and there were so many negative aspects to the '60s. But the kids, I think, taught us one very important lesson. They taught us to look at ourselves and recognize each person as an individual, handle each person as an individual. It helped me personally. We had to learn the humanistic approach to football and it helped me in my basic approach to life."

Anne Murchison approached her first year of marriage to Clint Murchison by sitting down for an extensive newspaper profile. The thirty-seven-year-old brunette dressed down for the occasion, wearing a shawl and a short cropped hairdo, as she talked about having found God following her marriage to her fourth husband.

"God had to give me everything to prove to me that it was worth nothing without Him and He succeeded," Anne said. "My physical life really does appear to be everything little girls dream of — marrying Prince Charming — though as an aside, Clint Murchison is better known for owning the Dallas Cowboys than for being a Prince Charming. But at the time of our marriage, I really believed that he was Prince Charming, in fact he was my God. We have our own private island in the Bahamas, a beautiful penthouse in New York, and an absolutely gorgeous home right here in Dallas in the middle of 25 acres of perfectly manicured grounds, all staffed with lots and lots of servants. There is even someone who washes my windshield every morning and makes sure I have enough gasoline in my tank. There are a number of airplanes to jump on to take me anywhere I might wish to go, exotic trips with VIP treatment wherever we go. I have a closet full of the finest clothes. If I chose to, I would never have to lift a finger."

Yet the forty-four-thousand-square-foot house, the twenty-thousand-square-foot basement, the two swimming pools, the football field, the four-car garage filled with Mercedes-Benzes, the hundred-thousand-dollar annual clothes budget, and all the other creature comforts were not enough for the new Mrs. Murchison. "Though our estate may have looked like the Garden of Eden, our lives closely resembled those of Adam and Eve after the fall," she said. "There truly was an emptiness to all of those delicious luxuries. My realized fantasies did not bring me happiness and I got more and more depressed. It wasn't that he and I were unhappy. It was that there was this unhappiness that existed in me since I was born and he couldn't possibly fill that void. There was no way he could have filled my needs, but I expected it, which was unfair to him."

Now that she had found salvation, her husband was next. "God is dealing with him," Anne said. "He has his faults and God is changing him, just as He is changing me. My husband is a quiet man, painfully shy. Because of these qualities in him that make him precious to me, he is misunderstood by a lot of people. He is brilliant, a multi-talented man — that rare combination of scientist and artist. He's a prankster, a clown and a tease, and until a few years ago these were the ways he communicated to people best. But more and more he is learning to share on a new level."

Clint Murchison could indeed afford to share. His baby, the pro football team, earned $5 million from television rights alone in 1977. With the Super Bowl victory under its belt, the football club had climbed even higher in value as fans became fanatics, scooping up anything and everything with the Cowboys star logo affixed to it.

Perhaps the most sought-after icon was a poster of the Dallas Cowboys Cheerleaders. Business manager Joe Bailey carried a group photograph of the girls that had been taken by Russ Russell to Ted Trikilis, the Medina, Ohio, printer whose Poster Arts had produced the poster of television actress Farah Fawcett in a swimsuit that had become the all-time bestselling poster in the world. And soon enough, a quarter million posters of the girls had been printed up and started flying off the shelves faster than any poster anywhere (except for Fawcett in her iconic pose). Tom Thumb grocery stores, 7-Elevens, and Skillern's drugstores in Dallas and Fort Worth were selling out of allotments as quickly as they arrived.

The '77 edition of the cheerleaders appeared on two network television specials in the spring of 1978 — the NBC *Rock-n-Roll Sports Classic* and *The Osmond Brothers Special* on ABC — before tryouts were held. The thirty-six winners for '78 took an eight-week course at the local Dale Carnegie Institute designed to teach them how to win friends and influence people.

Clint Murchison commissioned Carol Connors, who cowrote the Oscar-winning theme to the film *Rocky,* to compose a song about the cheerleaders called "We're Gonna Win."

Tex Schramm, unleashing his inner carnival barker, described them as "an international phenomenon of our time," an assessment that one aspiring cheerleader endorsed, saying, "They are the envy of everyone. It's to be a part of something people will idolize. It's like being a celebrity."

Proof of their appeal and reach was Career Day at Bellevue High School, in the suburbs of Omaha, Nebraska. The first female ever invited to the event was a Cowboys cheerleader.

The new squad was even featured in a Fabergé shampoo commercial and hosted its own one-hour special on ABC entitled *The 36 Most Beautiful Girls in Texas*, with Hal Linden, Joey Travolta, and Charles Nelson Reilly.

A pornographic film attempted to cash in on the cheerleaders and the crossover of XXX-rated movies into the mainstream, following on the heels of *Deep Throat* and *Behind the Green Door*. *Debbie Does Dallas* was about a young woman who performed a number of sexual favors in her quest to join a group called the Texas Cowgirls. Legend has it that the movie's star, Bambi Woods, had actually tried out to be a Cowboys cheerleader but had failed to make the cut—however, the actress known as Woods had never been to Texas. Still, Tex Schramm did not hesitate to file a lawsuit on behalf of the Dallas Cowboys Cheerleaders against Pussycat Cinemas Ltd. for trademark infringement. The cheerleaders successfully argued that their uniforms were mimicked by the film's producers and used in advertising. The decision did not stop the film from playing other theaters, however, and it became one of the highest-grossing porn movies of all time. The attendant publicity indirectly widened the real cheerleaders' fame.

The ascendance of the Dallas Cowboys Cheerleaders to pop stardom was neatly timed with the wealth being generated by real estate, insurance, banking, and other business sectors in Dallas. Between newly rich rednecks, liquor sold by the drink, cocaine, backgammon, single women on the make, and disco clubs like the ultraexclusive, ultrachic, and ultraexpensive Élan, where freshly minted fat cats could go and drop thousands of dollars in a night in the room and in the bathroom both, the game of conspicuous consumption was on.

Wealth creation trickled down to the underclass, signified by Dallas soul singer Johnnie Taylor and his monster hit record "Disco Lady," a platinum single that spent four weeks at number one on the *Billboard* magazine Hot 100. For two decades Taylor had ridden what was left of the Chitlin Circuit of black entertainment, which started crumbling at the end of segregation. He got into the disco trend at the right time, putting beats onto a rhythm-and-blues tune with sexually provocative lyrics about moves on the disco dance floor ("Shove it in, shove it out, Disco Lady").

Jeff Liles, a white teenager who lived down the block, mowed the lawn of the Pimp of Preston Trails, as Taylor was known in his North Dallas neighborhood. "He had a tan Stutz Bearcat and an Ice Cube Jeri-curl, and he would answer the door each week wearing a cashmere bathrobe and slippers," Liles said. "His estate was *huge*. Johnnie lived in a cul-de-sac that only had five totally massive houses. He paid me and my friend $250 a week to cut the grass and skim his pool — a *lot* of money for a teenage kid. Probably the first time I ever held a hundred dollar bill in my hand."

So much money was being exchanged that former single-location banks began expanding like 7-Elevens, once state and federal restrictions were removed. The multibank explosion came at the expense of the handshake. As banks' corporate profiles grew, so did the number of their personnel. Loans were not as easy to come by, and being on a first-name basis with the man in charge was no longer a given for the Dallas oil boys.

In April, the Sunday-night debut of a five-part dramatic miniseries airing on prime time on CBS supercharged the rampant optimism running through the city. *Dallas* was a soap opera built around a money-obsessed, morally corrupt, and not-so-fictional Texas oil family, the Ewings, headed by J. R. Ewing (played by Fort Worth native Larry Hagman). J. R. Ewing was a charming, deceitful, and determined oil baron willing to go to any lengths to win, usually at the expense of his oil rival Cliff Barnes. There was much speculation that Hagman's J.R. was rooted in Clint Murchison, both Sr. and Jr., with some H. L. Hunt thrown in for good measure.

The concept was engaging, and it corralled such a large audience that in a matter of months, the miniseries was extended into a weekly drama that went on to be the highest-rated prime-time drama ever aired in the United States; it continued to spread globally and became an international hit.

Each *Dallas* episode began with a camera zooming over the glittering downtown skyline, with Ray Hunt's swanky new blue-mirrored Hyatt Regency Hotel and the dandelion puff of the 560-foot-tall Reunion Tower catching the eye before an overhead shot of spacey Texas Stadium with the hole in the roof appeared.

The visual introduction suggested Dallas was the greatest place in the whole wide world.

The show was an extension of the Cowboys brand. Producer and creator David Jacobs had never been to Dallas when he dreamed up the idea. All he knew, he said, was the Dallas Cowboys football team and the Dallas Cowboys Cheerleaders.

The image was cartoonlike, but it was a striking image, and it dovetailed neatly with the growing popularity of the football team that inspired the show.

Clint Murchison understood the added value his team was creating even as he poor-mouthed the profitability (or lack thereof) of team ownership. "From an earnings standpoint they are small change and tough to justify," he claimed. "We did a study a few years ago [about TV blackouts]. The study showed two things. One, pro football is not a big money sport. Two, nobody will believe you when you tell them football isn't a big money sport."

The poor-mouthing could only go so far, though, when it came to Murchison's own team. "From the standpoint of value, the Cowboys are not small change. They have a value to me that other owners might not enjoy. My business takes me around the world. The Cowboys are a form of introduction everywhere. When I'm in Japan, they want to talk about Bob Hayes because he won his gold medal in Tokyo. When I'm in Saudi Arabia, people want to talk about the Super Bowl because they've seen the Cowboys play in it."

Not everyone bought into the Dallas myth. To some people, there was something about the city's certitude that made whatever Dallas represented seem repugnant; it was the same thing that made the Dallas Cowboys haters take pleasure in the team's each and every shortcoming and embarrassment.

An Australian national named Gary Duncan wrote a letter to the *Dallas Times Herald* to share his impressions of living in the city for six months. He characterized Dallas as a "totally charmless city" that "exhibits the worst of what I expected American culture to be. The buildings look like something erected fast and cheap to give maximum financial return." The food was "rubbish," the weather "hot and humid," and the symphony churned out classics "like an organ grinder." The Australian dismissed Dallasites as "uncritical in matters which don't pertain to money. I wouldn't stay in Dallas if I were offered a job for $50,000 a year."

A Texas columnist named Roddy Stinson did not wholly disagree and pinpointed some of the sources of such impressions. "While Dallas haters—and that includes most everybody east and west of the Mississippi—will delight in reading Duncan's remarks, those of us who know the city well must protest his description as unfair," Stinson wrote.

"Dallas may be short of character, soul, even morality. But charm it has aplenty. I used to visit a cousin in Dallas every summer when I was a kid, and I was always fascinated by the charming way the ground split into pieces ... I've never been in another city where that kind of entertainment was available. Except Waco.... Dallas is well known for banks that look like mortuaries, mortuaries that look like nursing homes, nursing homes that look like churches, and churches that look like banks ... and where on Sunday good Christians turn on the TV and stare at W. A. Criswell's face one minute and the bosom of a Cowboy cheerleader the next. With equal fervor.

"In short, Dallas is a place where people have learned to eat religious cake, make lots of money and have fun, too."

Some players were not among those Dallasites having fun. Kicker Efren Herrera, who speculated aloud whether the fact that he earned $32,500—well below the league average of $41,000 for kickers and despite his leading the Super Bowl champions in points scored—had something to do with the way he spoke and where he came from. "That's the way they work," Herrera said of the Cowboys' tough stance. "They want to put you in a position of losing money. They want to see a white handkerchief in the window. I've got to think about a lot of things. I'm a proud man, and I think I've made a contribution to this program. Maybe it's time I move on and see if I can contribute to someone else's program. I could see this coming two years ago. In 1976 I signed a two-year contract, and even then it came right down to the wire. It came to a point where they told me to sign or they were going to trade me to San Diego. I was $800 from being the lowest paid kicker in the league. That's hard to take. Now, when you've been playing four years and get an offer where you aren't going to be making what the medium kickers are making, that hurts."

Herrera did not report to camp because of the dispute. Tex Schramm shrugged it off. "It's a decision he had made," he said. "I'm always disappointed when someone doesn't report, someone who I like and respect. But it's not a situation we haven't been in before. Last year the big news in training camp was Blaine Nye's failure to report. He didn't come in and we still went on to win the Super Bowl." (Nye famously said, "It's not whether you win or lose but who gets the blame." Instead of going to the Super Bowl, he returned to Stanford for his PhD.)

Kickers were a dime a dozen in Tex's eyes, an assessment backed up by Gil Brandt, who said, "I guess I'll have to fly to Europe this weekend to audition kickers. It looks like we're going to need one." Instead, Brandt went back to Mexico to find Rafael Septien, a soccer player for Club America, to boot the ball for *los Vaqueros*.

Otherwise, training camp at Thousand Oaks that year was pretty much like previous camps — loose, relaxed, and swarming with college coaches, part of Gil Brandt's calculated outreach. "The Dallas Cowboys represent pro football to the American Football Coaches Association, they are the strongest link, from Gil Brandt to the scouts," said Jim Sweeney, head coach at Fresno State. College coaches were given their own playbooks, a hundred fifty reels of film each, and invitations to team meetings.

The payback was obvious. "When we are looking for prospects all over the country, it's always a plus if that player comes in knowing something about how we do things," Brandt said. "We had a coach come from Ouachita Baptist long before we knew who Cliff Harris was. When Cliff came, he already knew many of the techniques because his college coach had spent a couple training camps with us." As a North Alabama assistant coach said, "The Cowboys are simply the class of American football. That's not because they are winners, but because of the organization they have. If I can take home an ounce of their organizational philosophy, my trip has been worth it."

COACHES, PLAYERS, AND FANS alike were ready to be distracted by football again once September rolled around, ending the extended afterglow of Super Bowl supremacy. More than ten thousand fans showed up at the ticket office when sales opened for the season, with some customers waiting up to ten hours in 100-degree heat to buy ten-dollar and six-dollar tickets. Three fans trying to scalp tickets got into a fight and were arrested.

The home team played like they had beaten Denver last week instead of eight months and a million small dramas ago, opening by skunking the defending AFC East champ Baltimore Colts, 38–0. The newly resolute Tony Dorsett cut loose for 147 yards on the ground and 107 yards in pass receptions, including a touchdown. The following week he racked up 111 yards and a touchdown in a decisive 34–24 win over the New York Giants in New Jersey. Fullback Robert Newhouse complemented Dorsett's ground game with 75 yards rushing and two TDs while Roger Staubach went 18 for 28 in the air, tossing two touchdowns.

The next week's thirteen-point loss to the Los Angeles Rams in LA was a hiccup, laid largely at the feet of the Dallas quarterback, who threw four picks into enemy hands. The machine otherwise seemed to be running efficiently enough, and the execution was sufficiently free of major flaws for the team to beat the Cardinals in Irving before unexpectedly losing to Washington in a DC defensive struggle, 9–5.

A similar rhythm followed—wins against the Giants again, the Cardinals again (through the saving grace of new kicker Rafael Septien, who booted a 47-yarder in overtime to win the game), and the Eagles; then losses to Minnesota at home, 21–10, and to Miami, 23–16.

They won out against Green Bay, New Orleans, Washington, New England, Philadelphia, and the New York Jets to close at 12-4, good enough for first place in the NFC East and to be the top NFC seed going into the playoffs. Only the Pittsburgh Steelers of the AFC were better, finishing at 14-2.

Tony Dorsett had rushed for a team record 1,325 yards, and Roger Staubach passed 413 times with 231 completions for an 84.9 rating. The team was not bulletproof, as the four losses confirmed, nor was Captain America, their leader, invincible, although he played spryly for a thirty-six-year-old former sailor.

Dallas's first playoff opponent, the Falcons, gave the Cowboys a harder time than they had expected before finally going down, 27–20, on a cloudy 30-degree day at home in front of a less-than-capacity crowd. A very erratic Staubach was 7-for-17 passing before he was knocked unconscious and replaced by Danny White, who led two touchdown drives to win the game.

The battle for the NFC championship began ominously at the Los Angeles Coliseum with the Cowboys and the Rams playing to a scoreless tie in the first half. But Staubach jump-started the Cowboys in the second half, with the team racking up four unanswered touch-downs. Dorsett peeled off one 53-yard ramble. Doomsday held fast, and five interceptions were snagged, including two by Charlie Waters and one for a 63-yard touchdown return by Thomas Henderson. Henderson recovered two Rams fumbles, took running back John Cappelletti out of the game with a hard hit in the first quarter, and injured quarterback Pat Haden in the third quarter. The 28–0 shutout avenged the Cowboys' defeat in Los Angeles earlier in the season.

The trip to Miami for the two-week buildup before Super Bowl XIII was now somewhat routine. Thirty-dollar tickets were being scalped for more than two hundred dollars as the team camped out and practiced in Fort Lauderdale, sixty miles north of the Orange Bowl and the crowds. Thomas Henderson was in his element during the fortnight of hype, always quick with a quotable quip. This time around he provided considerable ammunition for the Steelers and got a load of laughs from reporters when he commented that Pittsburgh's quarterback, Terry Bradshaw, was so dumb "he couldn't spell cat if you spotted him the 'c' and the 't.'"

Staubach and Bradshaw led two very different but equally effective offenses. Regardless of his spelling ability, Terry Bradshaw completed 17 of 30 passes for 318 yards and four touchdowns in the highest-scoring and one of the closest Super Bowls ever. In the third quarter, Cowboys trailing 24–17, Staubach marched his team down the field and found Jackie Smith, the thirty-eight-year-old All-Pro tight end from the St. Louis Cardinals whom the Cowboys had talked out of retirement at the start of the season, all alone in the middle of the end zone. The throw was low but seemed to be an easy catch, prompting players to leave the sideline and run onto the field before they realized Smith had muffed the catch. In his moment of glory, Smith blew a sure touchdown and fell on his back. Announcer Verne Lundquist said all that needed to be said: "Bless his heart, he's got to be the sickest man in America!"

It wasn't over yet. Staubach hit Billy Joe DuPree for a TD pass of eight yards with 2:23 left; the Cowboys recovered the onside kick-off; and they scored again on a four-yard pass to Butch Johnson with 22 seconds on the clock, bringing the score to 35–31. But the second onside kickoff was recovered by the Steelers' Rocky Bleier, and Pittsburgh remained on top as the clock wound down to 0:00.

A pass interference call on Benny Barnes for allegedly tripping Pittsburgh receiver Lynn Swann had yielded 33 yards for the Steelers, which had proven fatal. It was clear from viewing the instant replay that field judge Fred Swearingen had blown the call; the receiver and defender had simply collided. Pat Knight, the back judge who had an unobstructed view of the play, had already deemed the play an incomplete pass before Swearingen threw his flag.

"Go and ask Henderson if I was dumb today," Terry Bradshaw, the game's most valuable player, told reporters clustered around him after the game as he spat tobacco juice into a paper cup.

Thomas Henderson was dumbfounded. "I'm a little sad," he admitted. "I didn't feel defeat until the game was over. Now I'm upset. I was working out there. Now I'm on the verge of a heart attack. I'm hurt that we lost. I'm hurt that I didn't make the big play to win the game." As for Bradshaw's smarts: "I never questioned his ability," he said.

Years later, Henderson would cop to putting a gram and a half of powdered cocaine into a nasal inhaler and mixing it with water before the game. During the second half, he said, "I pulled out my Vicks Inhaler. The Orange Bowl holds about 80,000 screaming fans, plus there were about 200 million watching worldwide on TV, and there I was on the sideline taking a couple of major snorts in front of them all. We lost that day. I lost that day. I was out of control."

Six months after the fact, the defeat still stung. "It was probably the worst loss the Cowboys have ever had," Cliff Harris said. Tex Schramm could not forget. "I still feel bitter about that call [on Benny Barnes]," he said. Pittsburgh rang up two TDs after the pass interference flag was thrown, and Schramm said, "I believe it changed the momentum of the game, which at the time was on our side."

America's Most Loved, Most Hated, Most Watched

THE DISAPPOINTMENT THAT DOGGED Roger Staubach turned to antsyness in a matter of days. "I hated to lose, and hated the pain of losing, but I wasn't a sore loser," he later said. "But then you gotta bounce back. I always had that ability to bounce back and even as painful as it can be, if we lost a game on a Sunday, by Tuesday I was back, couldn't wait for the next game." Unfortunately, the next game was eight months away.

Although the Dallas Cowboys hadn't won the Super Bowl, their winning image was some kind of consolation. The most popular commercial of the Super Bowl, starring Mean Joe Greene of the Pittsburgh Steelers accepting a Coke from eight-year-old Tommy Okon, was shot on a ramp at Texas Stadium.

The Cowboys were also an effective tool to communicate with kids. Dallas police were using Cowboys trading cards in a program initiated with the Kiwanis Club. Young people had to ask a police officer for one of fourteen special trading cards, which created one-on-one opportunities for police and kids to talk.

The exposure didn't hurt. The Dallas Cowboys had now been involved in three of the four most watched sporting events on television. The team's merchandise accounted for 28 percent of all NFL merchandise sold; they outsold the Pittsburgh Steelers two to one in pennants, T-shirts, and coffee mugs. More bootleg knockoff merchandise was manufactured for the Cowboys than for any other club.

The Cowboys' pioneering use of computers to evaluate prospects, their tendency to sign as many free agents as possible to supplement draft picks, and the vast amount of money spent on both generated resentment. The stadium, the silver-and-blue uniforms, the Dallas Cowboys Cheerleaders, the Thanksgiving Day game, the Monday-night games, the Kickers Karavan—all extremely effective promotions built on considerable hype—helped create a competitive advantage that fed on itself. Free agents were still willing to sign for less with Dallas in order to be a part of an organization that had a leg up on the rest of the league.

Brandt's expertise in evaluating players had been fed by his insatiable quest for information. Off the top of his head, he could quote a potential draft pick's height, weight, speed, IQ test results, and all kinds of information he had gleaned from everywhere he could, including from trainers and assistant coaches. No other club evaluated players as thoroughly. No other club had as many scouts—among them Bucko Kilroy, the storied mentor of scouts; Dick Mansberger, who worked the smaller and the historically black college conferences in the South that few others covered; onetime Tennessee coach Harvey Robinson, who knew everyone in the Southeast; former college star and college assistant Charlie Mackey; Dan Werner, the former quarterback draft pick from Michigan State who became the youngest scout in pro football; and the chief evaluator, Red Hickey.

"The concept is to think, be creative, be innovative, and be different," Joe Bailey, Tex Schramm's right-hand man, said. "There's the league; you know that the reason you're successful is because the league is successful, but within that context separate yourself and represent something different from everybody else. We were just much more aggressive than virtually every other team."

Validating their status was the NFL Films highlight reel that Ed and Steve Sabol put together of the Cowboys' 1978 season. The reel opened with announcer John Facenda, known as the Voice of God, proclaiming in rich, dulcet tones, "They appear on television so often that their faces are as familiar to the public as presidents' and movie stars'. They are the Dallas Cowboys, America's Team."

Tex Schramm loved it. Doug Todd, the head of Cowboys publicity, loved it. Tom Landry hated it. The team would have an even bigger target painted on its back now. But the football club didn't hesitate to use "America's Team" during pregame introductions at home.

The moniker had not been bestowed without calculation.

Bob Ryan, the producer of the Dallas reel for NFL Films, had observed Cowboys gear and merchandise worn in every other stadium the film crew visited over the season; they were easily the second most popular team in every market.

"I thought they were really an interesting team," said Ryan, who started with NFL Films in the mid-1960s, just as the Cowboys were starting to win. "They were bigger than life, bigger than the sport. It was based on fact more than fancy: they always seemed to be the second game on the Sunday double-headers on CBS. They were on *Monday Night Football* more than anyone. They had Roger Staubach, Captain America, the Doomsday Defense, and a legendary coach in Landry. From the organization to Landry to the players, they were way ahead of their time in so many areas. And they were great to deal with."

The Cowboys' Doug Todd and Joe Bailey had been talking about a title for the highlight reel on their way to New Jersey to meet with Ryan. "I had just come back from Mexico getting the *Dallas Cowboys Weekly* Spanish-language edition ready to put into three hundred fifty thousand newspapers," Bailey said. "We got the cheerleaders poster printed, our blue book translated. We wanted to dominate Mexico. One of the things I wanted to do was get Dallas Cowboys

Cheerleaders merchandise in the Sears catalog. The theme for Sears at the time was Sears, Where America Shops. Doug and I were headed up to do the film, trying to figure out what the title was going to be, and between the two of us we came up with this idea. Every time we go to all these stadiums everybody is cheering for us. Why don't we do America's Team? In 1976, we had removed the blue stripe from the middle of the helmet and replaced it with a red stripe for a red, white, and blue effect. Staubach was Captain America."

Ryan initially proposed titling the reel *Champions Die Hard,* but Doug Todd didn't like it. "We're not dead or dying," he said. They agreed on *America's Team,* which the football club put on the front of the annual team calendar. The motto quickly drew fire from sportswriters in other cities. How could they call themselves that? questioned George Solomon of the *Washington Post.* Oh, the arrogance. So Tex called a meeting and informed everyone involved in public relations that from that point on, Bob Ryan and NFL Films were to be given full credit.

Both NFL Films and NFL Properties, which was in charge of licensing and merchandising, were sustaining the history of the league and elevating the storytelling. They were also elevating the Cowboys brand, although at the time, most of the front office thought a brand was something that belonged on a cow.

Dick Bartlett of Mary Kay Cosmetics knew a bit about brands; the two brands he had helped build — Mary Kay and Tupperware — were known internationally. And Bartlett knew that when it came to the image of Dallas, "the Cowboys and the cheerleaders gave us a brand."

The brand had real resonance. In January of 1979, American Airlines, the largest airline in the United States, announced the company was moving headquarters from New York to just south of DFW Airport. As First International Bancshares president Robert H. Stewart III put it, the Cowboys factored in the move. "Next to the good, sound city government, the airport runs a strong and definite second," Stewart said. "Third, and I'm being a bit facetious," he admitted, "is the Dallas Cowboys. But I'm not sure that's really wrong. The biggest problem we have is getting Cowboy tickets for visiting executives."

It was no coincidence that the week before the Super Bowl, a made-for-television movie starring the Dallas Cowboys Cheerleaders had aired. The plot revolved around a reporter trying to dig up dirt about the cheerleaders and his girlfriend becoming a cheerleader and finding no scandal, interspersed with loads of close-ups of cheerleaders. The flick earned the highest ratings ever for a made-for-television movie. Later that year, the cheerleaders would appear in two episodes of the television series *Love Boat*, a light, wholesome comedy series, and in another made-for-TV movie.

"The Cowboys were the first rock stars in football," former cheerleader hopeful and longtime fan Judy Stone observed. "For some reason whenever they would introduce the teams when you would watch on TV, those other teams would run out, everybody looked ragtag compared to the Dallas Cowboys. Coming out of the dressing room with the white uniform and the star on the helmet made a huge impression."

Their support group on the field, the cheerleaders, were also impressive. "They were absolutely beautiful, well groomed, with killer bodies," Stone said. "They all knew how to do their makeup. Every single one of them was like that. They all had the big Dallas hair. Everybody was a perfect blond, perfect red, perfect black, or perfect brunette. There were no mousy colors. It was like having thirty-six movie stars on the field."

HITTING THE WIDE SCREENS in the spring of 1979 was the movie version of Pete Gent's *North Dallas Forty,* once again stirring up controversy within and beyond the real-life organization. The film was "gritty, bitingly honest," said a *New York Daily News* film critic. John

Wilson of the *Houston Chronicle* was more blunt, calling the movie effective satire and predicting huge box-office receipts. "The pregame scene in the dressing room really gets across something like what it is like before a football game. But to call this movie 'honest' is ridiculous. It is loaded against management." The Cowboys may be cold, Wilson wrote, but Gent was obviously trying to settle some personal scores.

Clint Murchison said he had not seen the movie or read the book, nor was he going to. But he evidently heard enough to spew, "It's insulting to everyone connected with the era—management, players, everybody. Football to me is a wonderful sport, with many inspirational qualities. These players are looked on as heroes by the young people of America. And I don't think it's rah-rah to say that's the way it should be maintained."

Tex Schramm did see the film version and initially admitted it wasn't as bad as he thought it would be, but later amended his comments, saying, "The way the professional athlete and coach are portrayed is a dishonest story of the way it really is in football. I went to the movie with four members of our organization and they were laughing at most of the scenes because they were so ludicrous."

In the Texas Hill Country hamlet of Wimberley, where Pete Gent and his wife, Jodi, had retreated to raise a family, Gent said it didn't matter who the characters were based on. "You have to create situations in fiction to make a point," he said. In his case, the point was pro ball was like all other major economic institutions. He compared managers to corporate executives. "They're supposed to increase profits, because that's the reason the corporation exists." The book was not a diatribe against the Cowboys, who were a lot cleaner than other teams, Gent insisted. "Pro football is show biz," he said. "It's like the rest of the real world; it means greed, making money, getting the edge. It's a violent show."

Lee Roy Jordan, whom Gent called "a perfect management patsy," said Gent had overplayed injuries. Gent responded by explaining management didn't want to admit player injury "because it would open up the whole area of workmen's comp. What really offended me was that Lee Roy was saying that if you stay in shape, you won't get injured. It isn't true."

Unlike *Debbie Does Dallas, North Dallas Forty* was a general release. No way could Tex sue. But that didn't stop him from feeling betrayed. "That was the player he'd most want his daughter to marry" once upon a time, Joe Bailey claimed about Gent and Schramm. Now Gent had gone over to the other side.

The other piece of bad juju threatening to disrupt the Cowboys' near-perfect world was Skip Bayless. The *Dallas Morning News* had launched a national search to bring in a name to do some hard-hitting reporting and column-izing and to solidify the *Morning News* claim that it had the most complete coverage of the Cowboys going.

John Edward Bayless II was a twenty-six-year-old writer from Oklahoma who was winning awards for applying personal Tom Wolfe–style new journalism to sports in his features and columns for the *Los Angeles Times*. The *Dallas Morning News* chose Bayless to write the lead sports column, bypassing Leigh Montville of the *Boston Globe* and a slew of other high-profile nationally known sportswriters, wooing him with a six-figure salary even bigger than Blackie's and free rein over his piece of real estate at the paper. The *DMN* announced his arrival by plastering his preppy countenance on billboards throughout the city.

Bayless made clear from the start what he thought of the town's biggest sports story by going after the biggest sacred cow, Tom Landry, dubbing the coach Saint Tom and referring to his talks as Sermons from Mount Landry. He poked holes in the team's shiny image that Tex Schramm had so thoroughly polished, constantly reminding readers how tight the Cowboys were with their pennies compared to other pro teams. "The Cowboys," Bayless wrote, "lead the league in inflation fighting." He knew his audience. In Dallas, he observed, "football is as necessary as electricity" and the franchise was "as much a cinch as a new Mexican restaurant.... Nothing is done without forethought."

Among intimates, Tex Schramm referred to Bayless as "that little cocksucker."

Skip Bayless was dishonest, Tex Schramm opined. If a writer really believed in what he wrote and Tex disagreed, Tex nonetheless respected him for being a writer. Bayless was different. He took positions in his column just to be contrarian.

"It shocks me sometimes when members of the media, such as Skip Bayless, portray us as being arrogant," Tex complained to Bob St. John, a friendly ear. "Maybe that's because our people act with self-confidence. If they confuse self-confidence with arrogance, then that's their fault. We're confident throughout the organization, because we've been winners. And we certainly have pride. From the beginning I determined everything should be first class. Everybody in our organization stays at the best hotels and flies first class. I think this helps the pride association. I also think, as many members of the media have told me, that they get a good reception with the Cowboys. They can talk to the players, coaches, me, or anybody, and they're treated with respect when they visit us, even if we don't particularly like some of them. And there's usually good copy, not always the kind we want, but good copy for them.

"Bayless has what he thinks is this trick, where he'll call you about something and pretend he agrees with your side. Oh, he'll say something like, 'Hey, what do you think of those damn players making all that money? That situation is really getting out of hand.' I'll say, 'Well, the salaries are escalating.' Then I know damn well what he's going to write. He'll pull a couple of quotes out of his hat and have me complaining about escalating salaries and write something like, by God, 'The players are the game and should be making more money.' There are some who'll sacrifice accuracy just to try to be clever and impress their contemporaries. That's a poor motivation at the expense of what's correct."

Tex was pissed. Here he was, the steward of a genuine dynasty, and this bright young sportswriter wants to psychoanalyze everything he had created. Tex enjoyed head-butting and jawboning with a prickly writer like the *Dallas Times Herald*'s Jim Dent or a cynic like the *Dallas Morning News*'s Gary Myers. Bayless, he deemed unworthy of bothering with. He was the worst of the new breed, detached from the legacies of Blackie, St. John, Shrake, Blair, Cartwright — the old guys whom Tex trusted and genuinely liked.

"Bayless came in and wrote a view of the Cowboys that was different than anyone else," observed fellow scribe Randy Galloway. "It was critical, which wasn't bad. But after a while everybody started wondering, 'Well, wait a minute, is this being done for self-promotion or is this done because there is valid reason for criticism?' The more it went on, the more Bayless became criticized as a self-promoter."

The Texas Sportswriter of the Year award, which Bayless would earn three times, and the salary with which the *Dallas Times Herald* wooed him away from the *Morning News* — supposedly higher than any other sportswriter's in America — made him seem even worse.

The dirty little secret no one talked about was the strange-bedfellows relationship between the journalists and the team. "They have a press, whether they want to admit it or not, that needs access to the teams to do their job," explained former Kansas City Chief Bob Stein. "If you are covering a team and the coach just doesn't care to meet with you or hems and haws or whatever it is, rather than talking openly to you, you're not going to have much of a career in that job. Nobody talks about that, but it's one of the reasons that the writers who do vehemently criticize a team or the league are quite courageous because what they're putting on the line is their most important tool, which is access to the facts and to the people."

"Tex really liked writers who knew their place," his assistant Betsy Berry said. "It's like, 'Look, you live in Dallas, we're the Cowboys, if you've got a problem with us, we'll work this out. You can say some things in your writing but there are other things you can't say.'"

Carlton Stowers, Bob St. John's replacement as beat writer at the *Dallas Morning News*, agreed. "You can't travel with them, live with them for six weeks out in California, go out to the damn practice every day, all of that and not feel like you're somehow at least on the fringe of this organization that is known as the Dallas Cowboys," Stowers said of the reporter-team dynamic. "At Thousand Oaks, most of your interviews were done during the lunch break. Everybody went to the dining hall, had lunch, and as soon as you were through with lunch, you sat down with whoever and did your interview."

Tex didn't like getting hornswoggled by anyone in the media. He walked out of an interview with a Channel 8 reporter after having gone over ground rules with him beforehand and then getting ambushed when the camera light went on. "We talked about this before we started," Tex growled to the reporter. "I said I wasn't going to talk about it then; why do you think I'm going to change my mind now? You're not going to embarrass me with your stupidity."

But Tex liked most of the writers, and not just because they covered the team. "I enjoy being around members of the media, because most of them are pretty well-versed in what's going on," he said. "I understand they have a job to do, because I was in journalism too. So was Pete Rozelle, which certainly helped him with the press. We're both aware of the influence the press has."

Which made Skip Bayless akin to Duane Thomas, Pete Gent, and Thomas "Hollywood" Henderson. He was not someone whom Tex Schramm could take out for a meal or cocktails and speak with casually without worrying about what he said. The days of talking on background were gone.

The team could counter bad press to a degree via the *Dallas Cowboys Weekly*. It had continued its growth spurt, especially once Schramm installed Steve Perkins, the bad boy who had told tales out of class with his 1968 book *Next Year's Champions*, as editor. "I want the best damn guy I can find to be the editor of that thing," he told Russ Russell and Joe Bailey, the designated publisher. "And I think Steve Perkins is the guy." Tex didn't mind holding grudges but when it was a matter of talent, bad feelings were shoved aside.

When the sportswriters got it wrong, players vented, which threatened to upset the delicate relationship between the team and the press, each of which needed the other. When it was Captain America of America's Team doing the venting, the risk was particularly high—students in the Dallas–Fort Worth area were polled about their heroes, and Staubach ranked first, ahead of African American newscaster Iola Johnson; the Cowboys' Hollywood Henderson; the first man on the moon, Neil Armstrong; black congresswoman Barbara Jordan; and Neiman-Marcus's Stanley Marcus.

"The only bad job on me wasn't done by a Dallas reporter," Staubach said, making clear he had no beef with the press who regularly covered the team. It was a writer from *Sport* magazine. In two hours they covered football, Vietnam, family, religion, everything. "He didn't take many notes or do much listening," Staubach related. "He spent most of his time expressing his feelings on issues. The article was titled: 'Roger Staubach: He Runs, He Passes, He Walks on Water.' The writer [Robert Ward] had an image of me. He wrote that story to fit that image."

But Staubach was nothing if not honest. "Interviewing me isn't a great story if you want controversy, unless you want to talk about my new kid or the church I spoke to last week," he said. He knew he had a persona that wasn't always interpreted correctly. "Stories often mention that I don't smoke, drink, curse or run around. Three out of four isn't bad. I've never said I don't drink. I enjoy having a beer or two after a game. I also drink wine occasionally. I just don't advocate using alcohol."

Besides taking issue with how he was portrayed, Staubach brought up another bone of contention to reporters: he wanted the ability to call his own plays. "It's the ultimate barometer of a quarterback's existence. I'll never really feel complete as a quarterback without that authority. It bugs the hell out of me, and Landry knows that. You can't argue with the man's success but the thing is, he knows I can do it, and that's what upsets me."

For Landry's part, he had mellowed a bit, to the point of his admitting he was pausing now and then to smell the roses. "The older you get, the more you enjoy life. Certain things don't seem as important as they once did. I think in recent years I've been able to understand people better. I'm more tolerant of their limitations. Maybe in earlier years I didn't understand problems people had and didn't accept them in a realistic way. Now, I don't get so hung up on perfection. Look for perfection and you'll be disappointed."

Still, he did not change his mind about who called plays. Coaches had a better perspective than quarterbacks did in that respect. But even when he had to wield the hammer, Landry did so with at least a modicum of compassion.

When Landry replaced Preston Pearson with Tony Dorsett as starter, he called Pearson directly. "When he made the change to Tony, he was man enough to call me in as a man, talk to me as a man, and tell me about it," Pearson said. "There aren't many coaches who would have done that. Sometimes a player finds out about it through the news media or through somebody on the street. So I have a lot of respect for Tom Landry."

Landry insisted it was no big deal, just common courtesy. "When I came into football, you could treat me any way you wanted," he explained. "All I cared about was being successful and getting material things. Players from my era had come up the hard way and were used to military discipline. But then came a new era of players. You had to treat them as individuals. And I don't think that's a negative at all. The way we handled players before as a mass group probably was wrong because it's wrong to handle any human being that way."

IT HAD BEEN A busy offseason. Charlie Waters, recently voted the most popular Cowboy in the Oak Farms Dairy contest, became a poster boy, posing provocatively with an open shirt. Poster proceeds would help his wife, Rosie, record a disco album with Fort Worth rock guitarist John Nitzinger. Rosie was a Kim Dawson model from Tyler who made the cover of *Playboy* magazine and became an Eileen Ford model in New York before she returned to Dallas to get a drama degree from SMU. The attention Charlie's poster ginned up made Waters want to leave town for a few weeks.

Roger Staubach led a fund-raising drive for the Dallas Symphony. Rafael Septien expanded the Cowboys fan base south of the border by filming thirty commercials in Mexico. As a Mexican national, he had had to prove to the U.S. Immigration and Naturalization Service that he wasn't taking a job away from a U.S. citizen by kicking for the Cowboys.

Three other events suggested dark forces lurking below.

Former Cowboys star Bullet Bob Hayes was arrested for delivering cocaine and Quaaludes from one undercover police informant to another—what many friends said was a setup orchestrated by a suburban police chief in search of publicity. Hayes entered a guilty plea to three counts of trafficking. A psychiatrist named John Holbrook testified that Hayes suffered from athletic withdrawal. Hayes's college coach Jake Gaither and the front office of the Cowboys showed up for his sentencing. "When I got to town last night, Bob told me, 'Legally, I'm guilty. Morally, I'm not,'" Gaither said. "Bob told me, 'I was trying to help someone, someone who is sick.'" Tex Schramm testified Hayes was easily led. Drew Pearson, Hayes's heir as the Cowboys' star receiver, called him "too gullible." Hayes agreed, telling Judge Mays at his sentencing in the 204th District Court, "I'm not the smartest guy in the world. If I was, I wouldn't be here now." He was ordered to serve two five-year sentences concurrently in the Texas Department of Corrections.

Tony Dorsett's fiancée, Gigi Clayton, a nineteen-year-old Texas-born debutante, honor student, and actress, died in early June of Guillain-Barré syndrome. Too Tall Jones, Hollywood Henderson, and Tony Hill joined their teammate as her pallbearers.

Then, days later, Clint Murchison's brother, John Dabney, the quiet, discreet other Murchison brother who owned the Dallas Cowboys, died in a car wreck after leaving the Highland Park home of new Texas governor William Clements. John had complained of feeling faint and was being driven to the hospital in a Texas Department of Public Safety vehicle that ran a red light. The fifty-seven-year-old older brother of Clint had recently been elected president of the Boy Scouts of America and headed the Investments Management Group, and he'd sat on the boards of Boys Inc., the World Wildlife Fund, and the Dallas Art Association.

And the tragedies were only part of the debris swirling around the football club.

After playing out his contract in 1978 Ed "Too Tall" Jones quit before the start of the season to enter the ring as a professional boxer. A Golden Gloves standout back in Tennessee, the twenty-eight-year-old defensive lineman couldn't find another football team willing to pay him what he thought he was worth. Thomas "Hollywood" Henderson, the only linebacker in the league who returned kickoffs, stayed out of training camp because of his own contract differences after scoring offseason endorsements of 7-Up soda with Ram QB Pat Haden and with 7-Eleven convenience stores on his own.

"Believe it or not, I made twice as much during the offseason [$220,000] as the Cowboys pay me," he complained. "Yes, Hollywood made more than Thomas Henderson. So you see, I don't need the Cowboys. I can get the publicity on my own. Now I'm Hollywood the Loudmouth and there's a bounty on my head. They'll be gunning for me all year. I ought to be paid for that. It's really depressing. Inflation is growing faster than I am."

When he finally ended his holdout, Henderson arrived at camp in a chauffeur-driven limo.

Skip Bayless was more than happy to let Henderson run his mouth for the record. "Football is too monopolized," Henderson editorialized. "The free-agent market is rigged. If no one would take

Too Tall, they won't take anybody. I'm tired of them using me. The owners get an awful lot of TV money but the players don't see any of it. CBS wants a shot of me, and I say 'Okay,' but I don't get a penny for it."

Running back Scott Laidlaw was paying attention. "The Cowboys are excellent businessmen," he said. "You just have to keep that in mind when you're dealing with them."

The players weren't the enemy, as far as Tex Schramm was concerned; it was that nasty concept called parity. He felt that having the league try to level the playing field was akin to communism, the favorite whipping boy of American politicians. Schramm derided the process to create a balanced schedule every year. That was no way to run a business or a professional football league, not in this country.

"When you step on the football field you should play the same schedule," Tex said. "Once you step on the field there should be no rules that help the weaker teams. Let the best guy win. This idea of changing the schedule is creeping socialism." Bending over backward to accommodate the have-not franchises was pandering to the welfare crowd, he felt, "people who are lazy and don't want to meet head-to-head. I don't want to say they're lazy, but some people are complacent to do things the way everybody else does things. For years, some teams have wanted to have the league [do the] scouting. How we scout is part of the competitive game. If you are more aggressive and more intelligent then you should win the football game. You should get into the playoffs and feel the benefits of doing it. This is the free enterprise system. When they start trying to affect the real competition that is when the socialism creeps in."

Controversy, conflict, personality differences, and social systems were irritants and distractions to a football team expected to dominate the professional game. The Cowboys had come too close to a second consecutive Super Bowl victory to take their eyes off the prize; at least, that's how the front office felt. Of the Dirty Dozen draftees who made the team in 1975, seven remained as starters for 1979 and two others were top-shelf substitutes.

As training camp wound down, Thomas "Hollywood" Henderson proclaimed himself a new man after a sit-down with the coach. Henderson said Landry laid down the law and told him, "'Hey, Thomas, we have put up with your shit before, but we're not going to put up with it no more.' He told me that I would have to carry my load and that I would have to do my assignments, run every sprint, play great, study, and not be late to any team meetings. He told me that I would have to join the Fellowship of Christian Athletes," Henderson said, stretching the paraphrasing of his conversation with Landry beyond belief. "The next thing you know I will be giving my testimony. Put that in your article. That's funny."

What Landry had made clear: miss practice, and you won't start.

Henderson vowed to conform. "That's what I'm striking to do. But I'm still going to take care of Thomas and Hollywood," he promised. Then he revealed he had talked to a writer and posed for *Playboy* magazine because the money he received from the publication made up for the raise he didn't get. The article would "make the hair on the back of their [the front office's] necks stand up," he promised. "The stuff they do is bull. I'm telling you it's bull. Now that he [Landry] has given me such a buildup, the cut-down could be twice as effective. They might announce my retirement after the article comes out."

Henderson then shut up. "It seems reporters are out to determine my career," he grumbled, conveniently ignoring the obvious: it takes two to make a quote.

The Cowboys' last exhibition game before the start of the regular season was a rematch of the Super Bowl nine months earlier. This time around, the Cowboys topped the Steelers, 16–14, on a 47-yard field goal by Rafael Septien just as time expired after

Staubach had marched the team down the field from the Cowboys' own 27-yard line with only 37 seconds on the clock—classic Cowboys.

Favored to win their division, the Cowboys opened their twentieth campaign at St. Louis, recording their fifteenth consecutive opening day win, 22–21, on Septien's field goal that hit one goalpost and caromed in with 1:16 left. With Tony Dorsett still healing from an injury, Robert Newhouse rushed for 108 yards while Staubach went 20 for 38. A week later, San Francisco fell to the Cowboys at windy Candlestick Park, 21–13, after which Tony Dorsett returned and ran for 108 yards, complementing Staubach's three touchdown passes to beat the Bears 24–20 in the home opener.

A crushing 26–7 defeat at the hands of the Cleveland Browns at their creaky old Municipal Stadium on *Monday Night Football* was made worse by Howard Cosell's comments to a Cleveland radio station: the Cowboys were "the most over-glamorized, most propagandized team in football. If the Cowboys were in the American Football Conference they wouldn't have been to so many Super Bowls."

Tex Schramm returned fire. "Howard's a typical New Yorker. Anything south of the Hudson is no good as far as he's concerned. These days it's hard to tell what Howard does like. I've known him for a long time. He's in show business and he's an entertainer. Sometimes, though, he isn't too entertaining."

Cosell defended his right to have an opinion, saying, "It was a statement made by a sports commentator which the commentator believes to be true," he said in his typically acerbic tone. "We still have the First Amendment."

The Cleveland loss was more directly blamed on the undefeated Browns defense, which held Tony Dorsett to 64 yards rushing and forced two Staubach interceptions and three offensive fumbles. Howard Cosell or not, it was a wake-up call.

With sharper execution, three straight wins followed—the Bengals away, 38–13, as Dorsett rushed for 113 yards; 36–20 over Minnesota in Irving as Dorsett carried the ball twenty-one times for 145 yards and three touchdowns; and the 30–6 thumping of the Rams at home, Staubach throwing for 176 yards and three touchdowns to lead the league with a 94.4 passing rating. Staubach, playing on a one-year contract, was at the top of his game.

The Cowboys beat the Cardinals at Irving 22–13, with Doomsday Jr., as the defense was being called, leading the way in front of special guest Bob Hayes, who was on furlough from the Texas Department of Corrections. Hayes received a standing ovation from fans. "It's heaven," the former Cowboys star said, choking up. "I just like all this freedom. I like wearing these clothes, and I like seeing other people wearing free world clothes. I was driving down the road yesterday, and that's all I could notice."

Revenge against the Steelers in Pittsburgh the following week turned out to be a pipe dream. In the locker room before the game, Tom Landry reminded Thomas Henderson of the deal they'd made that summer: if you don't practice, you don't start. Henderson had been in the hospital with the flu. "If I'm not starting, I'm not playing," Henderson told his coach defiantly. Ten minutes later, Landry returned. "Okay. You win this one."

The Cowboys lost to Pittsburgh, 14–3, for the second time that year; the Steelers outbullied Dallas on the line and nailed Staubach with a concussion, forcing him to leave the game. It was Pittsburgh's fourth consecutive victory over Dallas in a regular season or playoff game.

A 16–14 win against the Giants was negated by the Philadelphia Eagles earning a ten-point victory, 31–21, and the Washington Redskins spanking the Cowboys at RFK Stadium in the District, 30–24, where Staubach took numerous hits and threw three interceptions before Landry relieved him with Danny White.

Thomas "Hollywood" Henderson mugged for the television cameras on the sidelines and waved a Cowboys hankie throughout the contest, which irritated the coach, the players, and the president and general manager. Talent or no talent, when the wins weren't coming, clowning had consequences.

After the game, Henderson was unceremoniously kicked off the team and put on waivers. "I'm no longer a Cowboy," he pouted to a reporter after he got the news, his audience disappearing before his eyes. "It was an emotional thing. It hurts a lot. Right now, I'm just trying to keep my cool about it all. This is the most hollow feeling I've had in my life." Henderson was twenty-six years old, young enough to maintain his immaturity and yet old enough to know better. "[Landry] just told me that he felt his decision was the best thing for the team," Henderson said. "He felt I was manipulating the team for my own interests and he mentioned my poor performance against Washington Sunday. Mostly, though, I think it is my air, my personality."

Landry said he had warned Henderson not to mingle with gamblers or drug people. Henderson had objected to that portrayal. "There is a conspiracy against me," he said. "Right now I feel that I am victim of hearsay and rumors. I think that Coach Landry and the management thought that I had some association with some underworld figures. But there is no truth to that at all. I am clean. I think the Cowboys will miss me. They'll miss my personality and my contribution."

After his last encounter with the coach, Henderson dropped a warning: "You're not going to no more Super Bowls without me." It was Duane Thomas déjà vu. After his banishment, Thomas Henderson showed up at the Cowboys practice field one weekday. Randy White was removing his pads when he heard Henderson being Hollywood, meaning running his mouth. "Thomas, why don't you shut the fuck up?" White glared. "Get out of here. You're not on the team anymore."

Henderson mouthed off to White, who walked over to him and got in his face. Henderson threw a punch at White with zero effect. White grabbed Henderson's throat with one hand and pushed him against a wall, high enough that Henderson's feet were off the floor, and started pummeling him with the other hand until several teammates peeled him off. Hollywood quickly departed from the facilities.

Henderson getting eighty-sixed stirred up enough of a shitstorm for the nonsports media to weigh in, including *Dallas Times Herald* columnist Billy Porterfield, a witty, incisive curmudgeon from East Texas: "Tom and his button-down Dallas, Texas white man's mentality just couldn't stand a little black swashbuckling," Porterfield wrote. "I can't help but see Hollywood as one of a new breed of synthetic heroes in America. It's hard to say which came first, their own ballyhoo or our breathless expectations which they feel compelled to fill."

Peter Gent, an authority on bad-boy behavior on the Dallas Cowboys, was solicited for a comment, and Gent obliged. "You're not a person," he began, warming up to one of his favorite subjects. "You're inventory, buddy boy, and that's sad. To be a star, to be part of the magic, you give up your human rights. You're taught to learn respect for authority and be a professional and believe in the system. You believe in the system enough, and the other bull that goes along with it, you'll live calmly within the system.... If you don't believe in the system, like Henderson, you go a lot quicker. You're just an employee, that's the tragedy. You masquerade as a hero."

THE COWBOYS DROPPED a home grudge match against the Houston Oilers, 30–24; Earl Campbell, the University of Texas Heisman Trophy winner, ground out 195 yards for Houston while Staubach tossed two interceptions along with two touchdown passes. The Oilers' folksy coach, Bum Phillips, who had honed his coaching chops at Texas high schools, doffed his cowboy hat to the crowd at the end of the game. "If they're America's Team, we must be Texas's team," Phillips gushed. "I'd hell of a lot more want to be Texas's team than America's Team. Is there anything bigger than being Texas's team?"

he asked rhetorically before revealing a secret. "I know I said before today that this was just another game, but I lied."

Victories over the Giants, the Eagles, and the Redskins at home closed out the regular season with the Cowboys at 11-5, first place in the NFC East. Down 13 points against the Redskins in the fourth quarter, Staubach had conducted a comeback for the ages, tossing touchdowns to Ron Springs and Tony Hill in the final 2:20 of the game. The eight-yard desperation pass with forty-two seconds left that Hill miraculously held on to was dubbed Hail Mary 2, cementing the reputation of this edition of the Dallas franchise as the Cardiac Cowboys. It was *puro* Staubach; he completed 24 of 42 passes for 336 yards and three touchdowns, his twenty-first fourth-quarter come-from-behind win.

Charlie Waters, the injured strong safety who was in the broadcast booth with Brad Sham, couldn't restrain himself, shouting, "You gotta believe!," over and over into the microphone. The fans believed. Redskins coach Jack Pardee believed too, saying, "The Lord giveth and He can take it away in a hurry; that's the only way to understand what took place here."

Defensive end Harvey Martin rubbed salt in the wound by barging into the Redskins locker room during a team prayer afterward and tossing them a funeral wreath that had been sent to him earlier in the week, allegedly by the Redskins. Martin had placed the wreath in his locker to motivate himself all week.

Despite a few erratic performances, the Cowboys were playing with enough confidence to return to the Super Bowl, their fans concluded. The team had earned the number-one seed in the NFC, and its first playoff opponent, the hapless Los Angeles Rams, who had gotten into the playoffs as the NFL West champs despite a spotty 9-7 record, would be dispatched efficiently.

The afternoon game at Texas Stadium on the next-to-last day of 1979 veered off script from the first page. Defensive tackle Randy White put up the first points, sacking Rams quarterback Vince Ferragamo in the end zone for a safety and a two-point lead for the Cowboys. But Ferragamo hit two touchdown passes before the half ended, giving the team a 14–5 lead over Dallas. The Cowboys took control in the second half and pulled ahead, 19–14, early in the fourth quarter. But with two minutes left, Ferragamo found receiver Billy Waddy on a short crossing pattern, which he broke open for a 50-yard touchdown.

Captain Comeback had plenty of time to do his thing until the Rams defense stepped up and sacked Staubach, forcing him to throw to an illegal receiver, guard Herb Scott. On fourth down, a potential Hail Mary 3 pass to Tony Hill sailed over the receiver's head, sealing the Rams upset of the Cowboys, 21–19. After being beaten by Dallas in the playoffs in 1973, 1975, and 1978, the Rams found that the fourth time was the charm.

Where Do We Go from Here?

FAILURE WAS NOT A WORD bandied about in the Cowboys organization, but it was certainly on everyone's mind after the surprise end to the season.

"Our expectations were high," Roger Staubach said. "If we played in the NFC Championship game and lost, our season was ruined. I quarterbacked eight years really, because I had that entry year and then I was off and on a couple of those other years. So we were in four Super Bowls. We won two and lost two. I had six years of failure."

Staubach was thirty-eight and had suffered two concussions during the season. After examining Staubach's noggin, Dr. Fred Plum at the Cornell Medical School advised him to retire. "The next hit could be the one [that caused brain injury]," Staubach said of the doctor's diagnosis. Dr. Phil Williams in Dallas noted Staubach had taken some hits in the past but looked fine now. He saw nothing to suggest retirement.

Tex Schramm, sensing hesitation, offered Staubach a two-year deal for three times his current contract's salary. "Archie Manning had just signed a two-year contract for $750,000 with New Orleans and Tex said he would match that," Staubach said. "He knew I was thinking about retiring. He knew I wasn't trying to negotiate."

Just in case, Tex also got the NFL Competition Committee to implement the in-the-grasp rule, meaning the quarterback could be ruled down by referees without his actually touching a knee to the ground, a rule devised to prevent quarterbacks from getting crushed.

But the effort wasn't necessary. Danny White had been Staubach's understudy for four seasons and had performed admirably under pressure. Aware of White's capabilities, Staubach knew he wouldn't be letting the team down by retiring.

"It was a really good year physically and it was a terrible loss to the Rams," he said. "I didn't want to go out that way. But I just evaluated everything and said, 'You know I'm going to retire.'"

So he did.

Two months before ninety million television viewers were left to contemplate who shot J.R. in the cliffhanger ending of the 1979–1980 season of *Dallas,* Cowboys fans in the real Dallas pondered a far greater question: What would their beloved team be like without its fearless leader? The All-Pro, MVP, All-Everything, future Hall of Famer, greatest Dallas Cowboy of them all was leaving the game.

"Once upon a time, it cometh to pass and his name was Roger Staubach." So preached Brother Dave Gardner, the beatnik comedian and Southern storyteller newly relocated to Dallas, in his stand-up pseudo-sermon.

In reality, continuity marked the end of the Staubach era. This was bigger than any individual. This was bigger than football, bigger than Dallas. The Dallas Cowboys were a brand, an image, and a myth, as well as a football team representing the first new glamorous American city between the coasts since Chicago in the early twentieth century, still ascendant.

"Cowgirl" poster sales now surpassed those of Farrah Fawcett-Majors, an estimated five hundred thousand sold monthly. "We can beat Dallas on the field," lamented Pittsburgh Steelers president Dan Rooney. "But we can't beat them in cheerleaders. They had the first and the best."

The cheerleaders had such broad appeal that at the end of November, General John Wickham from the U.S. Department of

Defense called Tex Schramm with a request. The U.S. Army wanted the Dallas Cowboys Cheerleaders to visit the troops in Korea. Morale was low. The soldiers needed a lift.

Schramm objected. "What do you mean?" he said. "That's play-offs." But General Wickham persisted, so Schramm called Suzanne Mitchell into his office. Could she do this? Sure she could. Her daddy had been a pilot in World War II. "I thought it would be great," Mitchell said. "And it was."

On Christmas Eve 1979, twelve Dallas Cowboys Cheerleaders were in a flight shack at Camp Casey in the demilitarized zone between South Korea and North Korea, performing for the troops in temperatures colder than those at the Ice Bowl. They were escorted by Suzanne Mitchell, who had not forgotten the letters she'd received from Bible Belters accusing her of procuring and of making the girls bad examples. After Camp Casey, Mitchell had all the ammunition she would ever need to respond. "I would call after I'd get a letter and ask what the letter writer had been doing on Christmas Eve. Then I would tell them there were twelve girls who were in the DMZ in Korea performing in minus-20-degree weather serving their country.

"It wasn't just dancing, even though that was crucial, because we had ten to twelve numbers with costume changes; it was quite complicated," Suzanne Mitchell said, filled with pride. "When we'd go into a radar site or to a mess hall I would tell the girls, 'Now I want you to go and find the pimpliest, ugliest boy in this place because he's the one who needs you the most.' And they'd do it. We'd take messages home to their wives and girlfriends and mothers."

Mitchell took pleasure in "watching those girls grow and become contributors to society. They understood what it was to work hard, to become something other than their pretty little selves, which is the way they came in there. They learned what it meant to be an American, number one, and to not take for granted things, and to understand there were things more important than your lipstick and your mascara. There were cheerleaders around Dallas and Fort Worth [going to] nursing homes and orphanages every weekend. We did telethons all over the world and raised millions of dollars for kids. There were those who thought more of themselves than they should. But they didn't understand it wasn't about what was happening to them, it was what was happening through them that made a difference. That's the giving back. They were put in a position to be able to do it.

"I loved that we were able to do that."

A boatload of negativity came with the territory. "There were always people out to get you. That's just the way the media and the paparazzi are. There were huge stories about me in the *Enquirer* or the *Star* claiming I was wrapping the girls in plastic to flush out the fat. They put these pictures in there that they would construct on their own. The girls would get a big package full of butcher knives with this letter saying what they were going to do to her. I'd get them too. Then the *Playboy* mess [six ex-cheerleaders who were part of Texas Cowgirls Inc. posed salaciously for the magazine] and the pornography movie. It was a struggle for a long period of time. We fought for this image," she said. "Image was crucial to Tex. That's what it was all about."

The dream team and the dream organization happened to be located in the perfect place for doing business. The art of the deal ruled. Joe Bailey, Tex Schramm's protégé, realized he was privy to a very unique situation with a football club so closely linked to such a dynamic business environment.

"What you want in a company is this emotional, psychological contract that's going to develop between your loyalists, your customers, your patrons, your fans, and the franchise itself," said Bailey. "That's what happened. The state was passionate about football, the people of Dallas were passionate about the Dallas Cowboys, and everybody was competitive and believed in success in Dallas. The sky was limitless in terms of the potential of Texas and people had this great can-do attitude. If you wanted anything done in Dallas you just asked that group of civic leaders to get it done, and they'd get it done. It was magical.

"The people involved with the franchise thought big," Joe Bailey said. "It was not the concept of all hat, no cattle. They had the big hats and they had a lot of cattle. That sort of vibrancy carried over to the franchise. I can remember when I was a kid, being on the team plane and Meredith is singing, 'Big D, little A, double L, A, S,' going back home and everybody was cheering. People just loved being a part of that. It was bigger than the individuals."

Standing in the center ring, megaphone and whip in hand, was Texas E. Schramm Jr. "He had huge emotional intelligence," Joe Bailey said. "He understood what motivated Murchison, he understood Tom, he understood players, he understood the league, he understood the general public, he understood the culture of Texas, and he was able to sort it all out and manage it from birth, see it actually grow, and then sustain it. In business, particularly in sports, you're always looking for a peak performance organization. I saw a peak performance organization develop from ground zero to sustainable."

Beginning in the late 1960s, every year after the season had wound down, Tex Schramm, Tom Landry, and Gil Brandt would spend two or three days visiting successful companies to study their business models. Every year they would come away with new ideas; they borrowed from Delta Airlines' computerized reservation system and learned from seeing the savings that United Parcel Service realized in fuel expenses and man-hours by routing their trucks so that they took right turns only.

Proof was in the performance. Only once since 1966 had the team missed the playoffs. Landry had recognized the importance of internal leadership when he played with the New York Giants and he sought leaders throughout the twenty-year history of the Cowboys. No one had it like Staubach, he knew, although Landry saw similar qualities in Jerry Tubbs, Eddie LeBaron, Dan Reeves, Lee Roy Jordan, Bob Lilly, Chuck Howley, and Pettis Norman.

So when Captain America said Enough, it wasn't the end of the world. Roger Staubach was the greatest leader the Cowboys had ever known, the one who took the team to Super Bowls and brought home trophies twice. Tex knew that the quarterback was like no other. The face and image of the Dallas Cowboys, Staubach was the kind of player any franchise or organization would want to represent it.

"He was the greatest sports hero of his time," Tex Schramm, the most powerful man in the NFL, proudly declared when Staubach said it was over. "I can't think of another athlete in any sport in the '70s who could compare." That sentiment was shared by Jerry Rhome, one of two quarterbacks who understudied both Meredith and Staubach: "He was the best I ever shared a field with."

Tex of course couldn't stop there and had to blow up Staubach to gargantuan dimensions to make his point. "I'm certainly not going to overlook his great contribution to this football team," Schramm said. "That's well documented. But the very unique popularity of the Cowboys is based a heckuva lot on Roger Staubach. He was the hero of a nation, not just of the Cowboys, or even the league. You see, I'm still very convinced that the people want their heroes to be the all-American-boy types. He was a family man, had upstanding ideals and morals like Tom Landry, and yet had that great, gambling flair. He epitomized the adage that the game is never over."

For all his brominating, Tex was right. But there would be others to carry on the dynasty. The parts had become interchangeable. What counted was the system, not the individuals, and no one had a system like the Cowboys, created twenty years earlier by the same brain trust still running the show.

Chuck Noll and Terry Bradshaw may have bested Tom Landry and Roger Staubach, but the Cowboys would roll on. If nothing else, Tex could take some solace knowing his team was the only National Football Conference team to win a Super Bowl in the 1970s.

There were more serious things happening, anyway, and in 1979, Sam Cooke's "A Change Is Going to Come" unfortunately carried validity around Dallas. One of Dallas's few celebrities who was not a football player, Charley Pride, was refused membership to the Royal

Oaks Country Club, where he'd played golf frequently as a guest, because of his skin color. The Dallas Country Club, the Brook Hollow Golf Club, and the Northwood Country Club all barred blacks from belonging. African American golfers were expected to play at the Cedar Crest Country Club.

In ten years, the Dallas Independent School District had lost 25 percent of its students due to white flight, while Fortune 500 companies like Frito-Lay and EDS were relocating in Plano or near DFW Airport, outside the Dallas city limits.

Dallas was one very conflicted place.

"Dallas is its own confident reason for being and has been since birth," historian A. C. Greene wrote in his book *Dallas USA*. That, he observed, was "a statewide annoyance. Dallas is so smug, so pretentious, the rest of Texas hates Dallas."

One needed to look no farther than Fort Worth to glean that information. Fort Worthians liked to say the only good things to come out of Dallas were westbound highways. They saw the good citizens of Dallas as bullshitters whose bullshit got them only so far: "What has Dallas got? Ego, arrogance, extremely crooked politics and a bunch of thugs dressed in football gear that can't win the big one," one detractor noted. Another took pride in saying, "One thing I like about Dallas is there is a world-class city just thirty minutes west of here."

Until the television program *Dallas* debuted, the most popular tourist attraction in town was Dealey Plaza. Now the place to see was the ranch, called Southfork on the series, where *Dallas* was set. Fred Meyer, chairman of the Dallas County Republican Party, found its appeal offensive. "When the number one tourist attraction is a fictional location of a fictional TV show, that's a powerful argument that there is a lack of knowledge about Dallas," he said. Historian Herbert Gambrell noted that Dallas was "an example of a city that man made with a little help from nature and practically none from Providence," suggesting artifice defined the local landscape, as epitomized by Southfork.

Everyone in Dallas knew Southfork didn't define the city any more than cowboy boots and cowboy hats did. Dallas was pinstripes, wing tips, designer dresses, and "bidness." Aggressive, opportunistic, and forever promoting itself, the city embraced material wealth as the measure of success while retaining historical affection for hustlers and by-the-bootstraps salesmen in the tradition of Goss on Ross, the Tradin' Hoss, the used-car salesman whose bumper stickers read HOPE YOU MAKE IT HOME. The art-museum donor was held in higher regard in Dallas than the art or the artist. Dallas was doers and achievers, not thinkers and planners.

Devotional fervor and vocal expressions of fealty to God and Jesus were qualities worthy of admiration. But Dallas's heart, such as it was, belonged to the Cowboys. Twenty seasons after the team appeared, the blue star at the 50-yard line of Texas Stadium burned brighter than any point of light in the heavens above or the cityscape below. Football, a game anyone could believe in (as long as his team was winning), was greater than any single faith. And once the professional football club of Dallas started winning, all comparisons ceased. Finally, here was something the whole city, the whole state of Texas, and all the good people on God's green earth could grab onto.

"Dallas is our product," the Dallas Chamber of Commerce bragged in text at the front of the 1980 Dallas City Directory. "There's a certain flair about Dallas-style living... an exciting, intangible quality about this shining, modern city where the warmth of Southwestern hospitality tempers the hurry-up pace of latter-twentieth century business activity.... Dallas has long been known as the city 'where the jobs are—where the opportunities are.' This reputation has made it a mecca for the more competent and ambitious men and women, the in-migration of whom has continually enriched the Metropolitan Dallas labor force. There have been jobs and opportunities waiting for the newcomers: 320,000 new jobs created between 1970 and 1978."

Too much was not enough.

The 1.4-million-square-foot Dallas World Trade Center, already the largest building of its kind in the world, was doubling its size. The Apparel Mart, the largest wholesale apparel market in the world, was being expanded too. In fact, the six-building Market Center was the largest wholesale complex in the world, with 7.2 million square feet of space and 500 showrooms of merchandise representing 20,000 manufacturers.

Dallas was home to the third-largest concentration of national corporate headquarters in America. In 1978, Dun & Bradstreet's Million Dollar Directory listed 1,060 companies in the Dallas–Fort Worth metropolitan area with assets of $1 million or more, more companies than anywhere else except New York and Chicago. Four hundred of the Fortune 500 had division headquarters in the DFW area. Two hundred fifty-eight insurance companies were based here. Dallas ranked as one of the top five U.S. cities for conventions.

With strong population growth (904,599 residents inside the city limits, and more than two million in the metropolitan area sprawling over ten counties and 8,360 square miles), a healthy economy (median family income of $37,628), unwavering faith (over 1,200 churches and synagogues within the city), and an almost unlimited number of diversions and amusements ("a very easy city in which to have a good time," according to the Dallas Chamber of Commerce), the only limits were one's vision.

And Dallas the football franchise reflected Dallas the place. Regardless of what had happened the year before, its followers believed with certitude that the team would be next year's champions. This was the kind of team you could commit your life to. With Tom Landry at the helm, Gil Brandt flying around the world in search of new talent, and young protégés waiting in the wings, the odds remained in their favor.

For a fleeting moment, Tex Schramm was satisfied, and Clint Murchison, whose financial empire would soon come crashing down, was the happiest football fan on earth.

1980–1989

The Decline of the First Regime

THE SUMMER OF 1980 was a visitation from hell during which North Texas fried for forty-two consecutive 100-degree-or-hotter days, peaking on June 26 and 27 at 113 degrees; sixty-two heat-related deaths were reported.

During that sweltering season, Mayor Folsom could brag about the opening of the sleek, glossy eighteen-thousand-seat Reunion Arena between Union Station and the rail yards on the once-derelict western edge of downtown that would be home to the Dallas Mavericks of the National Basketball Association and the Dallas Stars of the National Hockey League—the Cowboys' new competitors for local sports fans' dollars. The optimistic future that the arena and the companion Reunion Tower represented kept bumping up against a not-so-rosy history that rose to the surface at inconvenient times. The latest incident was the discovery of lead in the soil of the poor and predominantly black neighborhood near the West Dallas Smelter.

Mayor Folsom did not brag about the Dallas Cowboys. The absence of Captain America caused every serious fan to hedge his bets. But on paper, at least, the Great White Hope looked ready to step in.

Ruggedly handsome with prominent cheekbones and tousled black hair, Wilford Daniel White had been a stellar high school quarterback at Westwood High School in Mesa, Arizona, and had excelled as a college quarterback in the adjacent suburb of Tempe, where he set seven NCAA records with the pass-happy Arizona State Sun Devils. He was second in the nation in total offense as a senior in 1973. His All-American stats were impressive enough for the Cowboys to draft him, only to lose him to the Memphis Southmen of the rival World Football League, who signed him to a contract twice Dallas's offer. After a year and a half, the struggling league folded, and White signed with Dallas in 1976 as Staubach's understudy and the team punter.

That had been his role for four years, to the point that he'd gotten frustrated being backup. Now he had a chance to show his cards. Unlike Staubach, White was a QB who stayed mostly in the pocket, which pleased his coach, though he scrambled when necessary. More important, he could read a secondary like a computer processor and possessed a sharpshooter's accuracy.

Weak-side linebacker DD Lewis and defensive lineman Larry Cole—the Cowboys' first three-decade players—led a veteran squad that included a corps of powerful running backs (Tony Dorsett, Robert Newhouse, Preston Pearson, and Timmy Newsome), a speedy fleet of receivers (Drew Pearson, Tony Hill, Butch Johnson, Doug Cosbie, Billy Joe DuPree, and Jay Saldi), a fierce O-line, an intimidating D-line (Too Tall Jones, Harvey Martin, Larry Cole, Randy White), and a very dangerous secondary. Collectively, they put the whomp on Washington, 17–3, to open the Decade of Danny White, as Tex Schramm was calling it.

Denver exacted belated revenge with a 41–20 pasting applied at Mile High Stadium, although White outgunned Broncos QB Matt Robinson, going 20-34 with two TD passes and one interception. Robinson ran in his fourteen points. From there, the opposition practically fell like dominoes: Tampa, 28–17; Green Bay, 28–7; the Giants, 24–3; the 49ers, 59–14; the Chargers, 42–31; the Cardinals, 27–24 and 31–21; the Redskins, 14–10; the Seahawks, 51–7; the Raiders, 19–13; and the Eagles, 35–27. After Denver, the only other losses blemishing the Cowboys record were to the Eagles (10–17), the Giants (35–38), and the Rams (14–38). The better-than-expected 12-4 showing was an improvement from the previous year and good enough for the Cowboys to tie Philadelphia for first place in the Eastern Division. No matter if it was Schramm's organization, Landry's genius, or Brandt's players—something was working. Staubach, watching it all from the NBC broadcast booth, could stay retired.

The Cowboys had the best offense in the league, statistically. White set a single-season record for a Cowboys quarterback with 3,287 passing yards; Tony Dorsett rushed for 1,185 yards; and Tony Hill ginned up 1,055 yards in receptions, almost twice Drew Pearson's yardage. Perhaps the greatest tribute to the team was the Cowboys presence in the Pro Bowl: O-linemen Pat Donovan and Herbert Scott, D-lineman Randy White, and middle linebacker Bob Breunig were all relatively unsung heroes who kept the front lines solid. The Cowboys entered the playoffs as a wild card but had fans believing they were destined to return to the Super Bowl even though no wild-card team had ever reached the big game before.

The Cowboys would have earned home-field advantage and the number-one seed in the NFC had they beaten Philadelphia by twenty-five points in the regular season's final game; they won by eight points instead. The Cowboys then methodically dissected the Rams 34–13 in the wild-card game. Then they put all their Staubach-era razzle-dazzle on display on a chilly 40-degree winter's day at Atlanta's Fulton County Stadium. The Falcons jumped out to a 10–0 lead and dominated all aspects of the game, leading 29–10 at the end of the third quarter. Behind 27–17 with fewer than seven minutes left, White passed the Cowboys down the field in five plays to pull within three points, with 3:24 remaining. White did it again with 1:48 on the clock, passing with precision four times and hitting Drew Pearson in the end zone the fifth time for the 30–27 win. "Roger who? Roger who?" yelled Jay Saldi after the final gun as he hugged White along with half the team.

They went against Philly for the third time that season with the feeling they had earned the right to represent the National Football Conference at the Super Bowl, in spite of the Eagles' win over the Cowboys in Philly earlier in the year. But whatever mojo the Cowboys had had the week before was left behind in Atlanta. Instead, the game played in 12-degree weather on the concrete-hard turf of Veterans Stadium was one big grind: a 7–7 standoff at the half. Then the rubber bands snapped, and the whole juggernaut fell apart— Landry's strategy, Danny White's arm, Dorsett's paltry 47 rushing yards, Doomsday. Coach Dick Vermeil's gambles, quarterback Ron Jaworski's accuracy, and the best defense in the NFL made it a 20–7 game, Eagles.

As in Atlanta, Landry wore a fur-collared coat over his jacket and tie. After the loss, the outfit moved one of the CBS crew covering the Philadelphia game to quip, "That coat told the whole story about Landry, and Dallas, too. When I think of the Cowboys, I think of Listerine." The coach was clean, sharply dressed, and wholly antiseptic, but his team lost anyway. A Pittsburgh fan piled on: "None of their fans have dirt under their fingernails. They don't even know what dirt is." "And those colors," bitched a sportswriter from Los Angeles. "They're perfect: silver and blue. They're slick, they're plastic. Pittsburgh's colors look like a steel mill. The Dallas colors look like a jewelry store."

The same Eagles would be grounded at the Louisiana Superdome by the Oakland Raiders, 27–10, giving Oakland honors as the first wild-card team from either conference to win a Super Bowl. The Raiders were coached by Tom Flores, the first Latino head coach in the NFL, and led by backup quarterback Jim Plunkett, the Super Bowl's first Mexican American MVP, marking the rise of another NFL dynasty comparable to the Steelers, the Cowboys, and the old Packers. As a model franchise, the Raiders were still Dallas's polar opposite; the biker gang of the NFL, as it were. But the trophy they took home from New Orleans validated their efforts, whatever their approach.

Climbing Back to the Mountaintop

THE 1981 SEASON AIMED TO address what was becoming a habit of coming up short of the big game, and it would be done minus the assistance of Tom Landry's heir apparent, Dan Reeves, who had finally left the Cowboys to become head coach of the Denver Broncos.

Still, the organization appeared solid. When a new sportscaster for Channel 4 named Dale Hansen showed up at a team meeting along with other media guys, he realized the Cowboys ran their business differently from other sports teams, and he came away impressed. "Schramm had all the players in a big meeting room and he brought all the reporters to the front of the room and had us introduce ourselves," Hansen said. "He looked at the team and said, 'Now, gentlemen, if I hear any complaints from these guys, it will be your ass.' Later that season, I went to the Forest Lane training facilities. I was going to do a story on Benny Barnes at the end of his career. Benny walked by me and said, 'I can't talk today.' I'd never seen that from a Cowboys player, so I grumbled I was going to have to change my focus. I didn't make a scene but my voice tends to carry. I got back to the office around two thirty and Doug Todd called. 'I understand Benny Barnes stiffed you today.' I said, 'He said he was busy.' 'No, he wasn't busy. That's not acceptable. Can you be here tomorrow? Twelve o'clock? Benny will be waiting for you.' Benny met me at the door, apologized for stiffing me, and did sit down and talk. With the Cowboys, it was 'You want Tony Dorsett? Randy White? Here's their number, call them at home,'" Dale Hansen said.

When Hansen called the Texas Rangers baseball club and asked to speak with manager Buddy Bell, a staffer informed him they could not give out Bell's phone number to anyone, including media people. Hansen cut to the chase and asked, "Would Buddy do a live shot at six p.m.?"

Hansen was told that Bell would be asked once he arrived at the ballpark. But Hansen needed to know right then in order to schedule a cameraman. "They wouldn't call him at home," he griped. "They didn't want to bother him."

That, he said, was one major difference between the Dallas Cowboys and the other organizations in DFW that sports guys dealt with on a daily basis. "It is absolute human nature that when people are just bending over backward to cooperate with you, the story's going to be a little better to your point of view," Hansen said.

The '81 Cowboys looked so much like the previous year's squad that hardly anyone knew nine rookies had been added to the roster. The 1977 second-round draft pick, Glenn Carano, Danny White's backup, had serious competition from Gary Hogeboom, the six-four QB from Central Michigan who had seen action in only two games in 1980.

The team played like NFL royalty, methodically tearing off the Redskins' heads in Washington, 26–10; shooting down the Cardinals at home, 30–17; throttling the Patriots in New England 35–21 in front of a national *Monday Night Football* audience, who witnessed designated captain Tony Dorsett exploding for a 75-yard touchdown; and racking up another win over the Giants, 18–10, in Irving.

Four in, and nothing but blue skies. That was before dropping a close 20–17 game to St. Louis at Busch Stadium and receiving a surprise 45–14 mugging at Candlestick Park at the hands of the 49ers, payback, no doubt, for the 59–14 pounding applied by the

Cowboys the year before. But the clouds of defeat parted and it was back to blue skies the rest of the way, with only a 27–24 hiccup in Detroit against the Lions and a 10–13 overtime loss to the Giants in the last game of the regular season interrupting a textbook Landry run. A come-from-behind 28–27 win over Miami decided by White throwing TDs to Doug Cosbie and to Ron Springs in the last five minutes exemplified what had become the new norm.

Danny White exceeded his predecessor again stats-wise, passing for more than 3,000 yards while exhibiting poise and leadership. Dorsett was nothing short of awesome, totaling 1,646 rushing yards to become the Cowboys all-time leading rusher. His exceptional speed combined with a magical power to cut through a traffic pileup like a hot knife through butter. His 325 yards in pass receptions were the sugar on top.

Doomsday had too many heroes to count. The front line of Harvey Martin, Randy White, John Dutton, and Too Tall was the league's most tenacious D. Dennis Thurman, rookie Michael Downs, and hometown rookie Everson Walls from Grambling State, who worked his way into the starting cornerback position and intercepted a team-high eleven passes, raised the secondary to equal status with the line.

In a season also marked by Mel Renfro's induction into the Ring of Honor and the announcement that the Cowboys would build a new deluxe office and training complex, including a sports-medicine clinic, in Irving, the 12-4 record and division championship suggested the Cowboys could not be stopped. Doomsday's dismemberment of first-round victims Tampa Bay, 38–0, returned the team to the NFC championship game for the second consecutive year.

The NFC-title opponent this time around was the San Francisco 49ers, coached by Bill Walsh, who was regarded as Landry's equal for his West Coast offense, which was designed for a running quarterback like gunslinger Joe Montana. The 'Niners had finished 13-3, one game better than the Cowboys, for the top NFC seed and were responsible for the worst of the Cowboys' four losses, the 45–14 drubbing. But the Cowboys kept pace with the 'Niners and managed a 27–21 fourth-quarter lead on Danny White's 21-yard touchdown pass to Doug Cosbie after the D recovered a fumble deep in SF territory. But as the clock wound down to the final minute, Montana marched his team 84 yards in eleven plays to Dallas's six-yard line, mainly by running the ball against the Cowboys' pass-protection defense.

On third-and-three, Walsh called a sprint right option. Montana rolled right and scrambled to elude the Doomsday line pressing down on him. He was on his heels and about to get knocked into the muddy grass when he managed to toss a high pass toward the back of the end zone. What appeared to be a throwaway turned into Montana's own Hail Mary when receiver Dwight Clark pushed off Everson Walls and made an Olympian leap at the ball high above his head, grabbed it with his fingertips, and landed with both feet squarely inside the field of play for a touchdown.

Danny White engineered a valiant comeback attempt with 51 seconds left. He hit Drew Pearson with a long bomb that would have been a touchdown if not for Eric Wright's horse-collar bring-down. Two plays later, White was sacked and lost the ball, and San Francisco recovered the fumble.

"You just beat America's Team," Too Tall Jones informed Montana after the 49ers' 28–27 win.

"Well, you can sit at home with the rest of America and watch the Super Bowl on TV," Montana snidely remarked with a defiant smile.

NFL Films described Dwight Clark's leap at the back of the end zone as the Catch, marking "the end of one dynasty and the birth of another," meaning Bill Walsh's San Francisco 49ers. Danny White would beg to differ, telling NFL Films some years later, "I've heard everybody credit the rise of the 49ers and the fall of the Cowboys [in the 1980s] to that play in that one game. And I totally disagree with that."

But Tex Schramm would eventually conclude the loss was one of the three most significant defeats his Dallas Cowboys ever suffered. "It seems like we were never the same after that," he would concede.

They weren't. But few noticed. Dallas remained great enough for others to hate. Lesley Visser, writing for the *Boston Globe*, reflected how little the public perception had changed. "Dallas, ugh. And same to all Texas...I've had it with Texas and the whole beehive hairdo of it. I'm sick of sexy waitresses and Cadillacs that make bull sounds on the horn. I've had it with Waylon and Willie, with wide open spaces and Lone Star Beer. What kind of boots are those, anyway? Made from armadillo and ostrich and dead dogs on the street."

Tex Schramm chalked up Visser's rant to the Cowboys' dominance. "Whenever a team has had as much success as the Cowboys, there are going to be disapprovers. People love you or hate you."

The machine was so slick, efficient, and above the competition that CBS publicist Beano Cook told Schramm, "You're one of the two most efficient organizations of the twentieth century."

"What's the other?" inquired Schramm.

"The Third Reich."

"IF THEY'RE AMERICA'S TEAM, what does that make the rest of us? Guatemala?" mused safety Mike Davis of the 1981 Super Bowl champion Oakland Raiders.

So when Cowboys got caught up in drug investigations, detractors cheered, dubbing them South America's Team. The coach joined in with the critics, moaning about "the incipient immorality that's all around us." Landry didn't stop there and cited the cheerleaders as part of the problem.

Schramm admitted that he and the coach were not necessarily two peas in a pod when it came to the cheerleaders. "True, Coach Landry and I don't see eye to eye on this," he said. "In effect, we have a truce. But the cheerleaders are show business, they're a success, and they're recognized as such, nationally." So was the coach, who had racked up more career wins than any National Football League coach not named George Halas or Curly Lambeau.

The Cowboys were Television's Team too. Nine of the sixteen pro football games that season that were broadcast nationally involved the Cowboys. They appeared three times on ABC, on NBC for the Thanksgiving Day game, and five times on CBS.

Those numbers were impressive, but they were reflective of a different game. According to the stats on the field, the contemporary team was good, not great, which made the natives restless, especially when they heard the president and general manager saying, "I'm never going to retire. If we could put the '80s on top of what we did in the '70s, it would be a big part of sports history. People could look and say we were one of the most unique franchises in sports. We would have been on top or near the top for 25 years and that's a long time. I figure we will have to win the Super Bowl at least three more times...so we've got to keep winning."

In response to the team's slipping stats, sportswriter Gary Myers led another media charge contending that the football club was too cheap to compete, comparing and contrasting salaries of Dallas's players with those of players on other teams. Thirty-one of the fifty-three players on the Cowboys' 1981 roster had been paid less than the league average. Drew Pearson was earning less than Tony Hill or Butch Johnson, two accomplished receivers who played in Pearson's shadow. The average salary for a Dallas Cowboy was $89,170, considerably higher than the average on Lamar Hunt's Kansas City Chiefs (which was about $64,000 annually) but well under Denver's average of $106,000. Two exceptions were defensive tackle Randy White, whose $300,000 salary and $75,000 signing bonus, along with the $14,000 in playoff bonus money, made him the league's highest-paid player at his position; and Tony Dorsett, whose $325,000 base salary ranked him as the fifth-best-paid NFL running back.

Tex had a rep for playing hardball. "If you go in and try to act forceful and threaten them, they can give you a bad time," one agent complained about management. "They always tell you about the extra playoff money." Gil Brandt had the company line down pat and used it whenever necessary: "Look, you're playing in Dallas and you go to the playoffs every year. That has to be worth something." The tight payroll afforded Brandt the luxury of taking suitcases full of dirty laundry on the road with him and including the cleaning bill with his hotel receipts.

But a changing of the guard was taking place within the team's very makeup. DD Lewis, Charlie Waters, and John Fitzgerald retired, while Too Tall and Too Mean were losing a step. Assistant coach Mike Ditka had been summoned to Chicago by George Halas, Mr. NFL and Papa Bear, to become head coach of the Bears.

Then, before the 1982 season got under way, Al Davis and his Oakland Raiders won an antitrust lawsuit that allowed the team to relocate to the Los Angeles Coliseum. Davis had failed to win the approval of three-fourths of the NFL's twenty-eight team owners to move his franchise, so he sued, although the case had taken two years to wind its way through the courts. Tex Schramm groused that Davis threatened to ruin league unity. "Share the wealth" had turned into "Every man for himself."

The Cowboys' season started with an eight-point loss to their 1970s-era Super Bowl rival the Pittsburgh Steelers, evened by a solid seventeen-point win against the St. Louis Cardinals. Two days later, the National Football League lurched to a halt as negotiations broke down between the NFL Players Association and league owners. The players wanted 55 percent of gross receipts; Cowboys players were receiving only about 35 percent of the club's gross, typical for the league. The players went on strike.

For two months there was no pro football. The absence of the nation's game was more severe than any blue law, bringing the nation literally to its knees on Sundays: church attendance rose. Television airtime was filled with repeats of the previous season's Super Bowl,

Canadian Football League games, more college games, and more major-league baseball.

Texans had other diversions, especially their second-favorite spectator sport: state politics. The November elections revealed a riptide cutting across the sea change that had been taking effect in Texas politics. Texas attorney general Mark White, a Democrat, bested sitting governor William P. Clements of Highland Park and Dallas, the first Republican governor in Texas since Reconstruction. White's election was helped along by a stalled economy and growing signs of a real estate bust. His election marked the last time every statewide office was occupied by a Democrat.

The Republican Party had been making gains throughout the South and into Texas ever since civil rights laws pushed by President Lyndon B. Johnson, a member of the Democratic Party, were passed in the early 1960s. Senator John Tower of Wichita Falls led the way with his election in 1961, followed in 1964 by the election of a congressman from Houston named George Herbert Walker Bush. Bush was an affable blue blood from New England who had moved his family to Midland, in the desolate and dull Permian Basin of West Texas, so he could increase his wealth through oil exploration and equipment supply. Bush by now was vice president of the United States under Ronald Reagan, who'd been elected in 1980.

Clements was a crusty, no-nonsense oilman, the face of the Southeast Drilling Company, or Sedco, the offshore driller he founded in 1947, and the largest offshore player in the industry. He had served as the deputy secretary of defense for Presidents Nixon and Ford, reporting directly to Donald Rumsfeld in the Ford administration.

During Clements's first year as governor, an offshore oil well in the Bay of Campeche, in the southern Gulf of Mexico, that Sedco was drilling for the Mexican national oil company Pemex blew out. IXTOC 1, as the well was named, spilled an estimated 3.5 million barrels into the Gulf for ten months—the largest single spill on record—damaging marine life throughout the Gulf and soiling Texas beaches. Clements dismissed the spill as "much ado about nothing" and consistently refused to take responsibility for the disaster. The Justice Department sued Sedco for $12.5 million to pay cleanup costs and settled for $2 million, a pittance, considering Sedco's worth.

Six months before Bill Clements went down in defeat in the governor's race, Braniff International flew its last flight. The massive debt that Harding Lawrence had accumulated while the airline expanded routes to South America, Europe, and the Pacific and flew the Concorde supersonic airliner grounded Braniff. Terminal 2W at DFW International was now silent. Although there would be efforts to resuscitate the airline, including one led by Jay Pritzer of Hyatt Hotels, Dallas's hometown airline was dead.

Limits to unbridled growth were appearing, just as the Dallas Cowboys dynasty appeared to show cracks. But even with growing indications of a recession, Big D remained a land of exceptional opportunities. After looking around the nation for a place to try their new concept of integrating a video-game arcade into a casual restaurant with full-service bar, two Little Rock, Arkansas, business partners, Dave Corriveau and Buster Corley, opened their first Dave & Buster's in Dallas in 1982, renting out a forty-thousand-square-foot warehouse at the end of Restaurant Row, just off Interstate 35. Their friends thought they were crazy. But Buster Corley said, "The business climate was good. It was a great place to start something. People were making money." Dave and Buster did too.

PRO FOOTBALL DIDN'T RESUME making money until the NFL players' strike ended in November, the week before Thanksgiving, the sixteen-game regular-season schedule downsized to nine games. By the time an agreement had been finalized awarding players a bigger piece of the pie, the Cowboys had lost $2 million. The money drain came despite $14 million the Cowboys had coming every year as their share of the $2.1 billion five-year television contracts the NFL had hammered out with ABC, NBC, and CBS before the 1982 season, up from the $650 million in TV deals the league had negotiated five years earlier. But even the fat TV contracts couldn't stop the red ink.

Playing without regard for the off-field situation, the Cowboys won five in a row. They dropped the final two games, losing to Philadelphia and Minnesota, but their 6-3 record was good enough for the number-two NFC seed in the expanded sixteen-team round-robin tournament replacing traditional playoffs; they were second only to division rival Washington. Improbably, the Cowboys worked their way to the NFC championship for the third consecutive year by eliminating Tampa Bay, 30–17, in the NFC wild-card game and then tossing former-monkey-on-the-back Green Bay by 11 points, 37–26, to face the Redskins for the NFC crown, the last stop before the Super Bowl.

It was not the battle Dallas fans had envisioned. Danny White got knocked out of the game with a concussion from a hard hit late in the first half. His replacement, Gary Hogeboom, stepped in and ran the team like an old pro in the third quarter before throwing two costly fourth-quarter interceptions, including one for a touchdown. The air went out of the Cowboys and they lost, 31–17. Coming close but not going all the way was officially a trend.

And it wasn't just football that was losing, as far as the Cowboys owner was concerned. The Murchison Brothers had lost $50 million and filed for chapter 11 bankruptcy. In order for Clint Murchison to save what remained of his empire, valued at $350 million, he was on the verge of having to make one very tough choice.

Club for Sale

BEFORE THE FIRST KICKOFF of the 1983 season, word leaked out that the Dallas Cowboys Football Club was for sale. Clint Murchison, fifty-eight years old and now in failing health owing to a little-known disease that was causing his body to waste away, needed a buyer to bail him out. The hard-to-pin-down disease, cerebellar atrophy, had affected Clint's equilibrium and speech and forced him into a wheelchair. Worse, the estate of Clint's brother John had yet to be settled four years after his death, and the fight for control by his heirs had turned nasty. Some of Clint's real estate and energy ventures had fallen through, and he was having trouble paying interest on loans that he had personally guaranteed—loans that his physical condition prompted some creditors to call in. Schramm was instructed to find a buyer willing to pay anywhere from $30 to $60 million for the Cowboys, with the caveat the buyer had to agree to keep the organization intact.

Blackie Sherrod turned wistful. "I wish I felt there was another Clint Murchison out there somewhere," he wrote. But there wasn't. There was no prospective owner lurking in the shadows who loved the game as much as Clint did and who had the same temperament as he did and who would be likely to say, as he did, "I'd rather let the people who know what they're doing run things. Besides, I'm shy."

Richard Rogers, the son of Mary Kay Ash and the CEO of the

Mary Kay corporation, was mentioned as a prospective buyer, along with Don Carter, the owner of the Dallas Mavericks National Basketball Association franchise; the billionaire Bass brothers of Fort Worth; and the now-semiretired radio magnate Gordon McLendon.

But the bidding boiled down to two Dallas groups. One was headed by H. R. "Bum" Bright, the Oklahoma-born trucking magnate who'd made his fortune in oil and gas before diversifying, and one was headed by Vance Miller, the son of commercial real estate titan Henry S. Miller, who was partnering with auto dealer W. O. Bankston, a pro football supporter in Dallas since the 1952 Texans. (In December of 1982, the Miller-Bankston group had put down $550,000 for the remaining tickets to a Cowboys game so the local TV blackout would be lifted.)

The football club continued to generate news off the field. The Cowboys took over ownership of the *Dallas Cowboys Weekly* and announced that Roger Staubach would be inducted into the Ring of Honor. Danny White, in the tradition of Don Meredith, released a single for Grand Prix Records, "You're a Part of Me," a duet with singer Linda Nail that reached number 85 on *Billboard*'s Hot Country Songs chart, and then White went solo with "Then You Can Tell Me Goodbye." But the biggest headlines were saved for the groundbreaking of the new headquarters at Valley Ranch in Irving, part of a master-planned community.

At Valley Ranch, for the first time, administrative, training, and related facilities would be consolidated in a single location; the complex would include team headquarters, three football fields, a ticket office, a retail store, a visitor center with an IMAX theater, offices for the *Cowboys Weekly*, a studio for television and radio production, and a rehearsal space for the cheerleaders. A companion office park would feature a hotel and convention center, an athletic club, and a retail area. Former scout and front-office assistant Dan Werner was put in charge of the project.

Minnesota and Baltimore had both built headquarters for their organizations, but each featured a single building with the team on the bottom floor and the front office upstairs. "We wanted the building to represent the organization," Werner explained, so it was designed with three parts, each with its own courtyard: the public domain, where the ticket office, travel office, and cheerleaders were based; the management sector, where Tex, Joe Bailey, and the business elements of the organization were clustered; and a third element, for the coaches, the scouts, and the players.

The architects were the firm of Ford, Carson, and Powell of San Antonio; its chief, O'Neil Ford, was Texas's most storied architect. Ford made the first rough drawing of Valley Ranch for the project's prospectus, which read: "In one word, class. In two words, first class. Just like the Dallas Cowboys."

The perception of the Cowboys doing everything better than the competition was a key reason there were more true believers than ever. The *Weekly* topped the one-hundred-thousand subscription mark. Two thousand women showed up for tryouts to be Dallas Cowboys Cheerleaders, who were now enshrined in a song by Homer Henderson and the Dalworthington Garden Boys titled "I Want a Date with a Cowboys Cheerleader." The Little Miss Dallas Cheerleader competition drew forty thousand starstruck fourth- to twelfth-grade girls.

Sale or no sale, Super Bowl or no Super Bowl, the football club remained in charge of its legacy and in control of its image. But only to a point.

America's Team had become South America's Team again. A New York tabloid reported that thirty-four of the drug-abuse investigations the NFL was conducting involved Dallas Cowboys players. Tex Schramm was furious about the report. "They say fifty percent of the players in the NFL use [cocaine]," he complained. "Then they follow up and say the Cowboys and the 49ers are the worst offenders. There aren't any well-placed sources who would make that statement."

Defensive end Harvey Martin, aka "the Beautiful" and "Too Mean," had been fingered by Danny Stone, a Highland Park barber and drug dealer turned government witness. After being caught up in a DEA investigation leading to the biggest drug bust in Dallas history, Stone testified he had been supplying Martin with cocaine since 1979. Martin denied everything and he was never charged.

Schramm and Landry suspected they weren't hearing the whole story.

Two weeks after the Cleveland Browns announced the creation of a director of security position, an NFL first, Tex Schramm introduced Larry Wansley to the sports media of Dallas. The formidable former FBI agent was the football club's new director of security and counseling services, a title that telegraphed his role as the team narc. Tex had found Wansley in the Dallas FBI office through Ben Nix, the NFL rep in Dallas. After a visit with Tex and Tom Landry at Tex's house, Wansley was hired, although his role wasn't completely defined. His main charge would be keeping players from getting tangled up with the law. But Wansley aimed to take an extra step.

Wansley went to Cleveland to meet with director of player relations Paul Warfield, Calvin Hill, Coach Sam Rutigliano, the Browns' new security guy, Teddy Chappelle, and a young National Football League public relations assistant named Roger Goodell. He then entered the twenty-eight-day drug-rehabilitation program at the Hazelden clinic in Center City, Minnesota, to learn about addictions and recovery programs.

"What Larry did," Schramm would later say, "was pioneer a new position that was eventually adopted by almost every team in the NFL. Not only did he see to long-overlooked security needs — from team offices to training camp to hotels we'd stay at on the road — but he became a trusted sounding board for the players who had no one else to go to with problems, professional and personal. Larry went out and found experts in everything from financial investment to home security and brought them in to talk with the players and their families. While the coaches prepared them for Sunday's games, Larry was helping them to get ready for life after football."

The presence of security directors would not stop Don Rogers of the Browns from fatally overdosing on cocaine or Harvey Martin's increasingly bizarre behavior as he began showing up late or missing appointments altogether and skirting dangerously close to being charged for trafficking. But at least it offered an option by setting rules and limits while also offering counseling, continuing education, career transition advice, and programs for wives and girlfriends.

One of Wansley's first assignments was to accompany Harvey Martin to Hazelden in May for a ten-day stay, with the encouragement of Landry and Schramm. *Sports Illustrated* cited "that little ripple of bad luck," a polite way of addressing the IRS's demand for $250,000 in back taxes accompanied by the threat of jail time, the collapse of Martin's nightclub and five restaurants, the eleven lawsuits pending against him, and his nearly $612,000 of debt. Martin declared bankruptcy, was fired from his sportscaster job at Channel 5, lost his title as defensive captain of the Cowboys, broke off his engagement to Sharon Bell, and was accused in print of snorting cocaine, with photos to back it up. Otherwise, he was still the Beautiful.

The rehab attempt was a disaster. The trip to the Minnesota clinic was supposed to be secret. Only Martin's mother knew where Martin was going and why—her and just a few of his buds, Martin confided to Wansley on the flight north. But Martin's buds couldn't stay quiet, which explained why several Twin Cities television trucks were waiting at the entrance of the clinic. Landry tried to cover for Martin, telling the press nothing was wrong with the player; he had been sent to Hazelden by management to evaluate the clinic on behalf of the club. Martin went into total denial upon his return to Dallas and his world continued spinning out of control.

Denial was a common Dallas theme, especially when someone

was caught. Rex Cauble, a quarter horse fancier famous for his chain of western-wear stores named after his favorite horse, Cutter Bill, went to trial in Dallas, accused by the Feds of running the Cowboy mafia, a loose collective of smugglers and dealers who were importing tons of high-grade marijuana from Central and South America. Cauble pleaded innocent, standing behind his well-known reputation for loud and constant railings against hippies and the youth drug culture. He got five years anyway.

The head of the Environmental Protection Agency was not so sure there was a problem with lead in the soil in West Dallas and decided, at the request of President Reagan, to wait to remove the tainted soil. The Dallas Citizens Council denied it had had a hand in helping Starke Taylor, a real estate investor, get elected mayor, beating former mayor and sometime maverick Wes Wise.

And the Cowboys were in denial for insisting they had the inside line on the Super Bowl, the reward awaiting the two best teams in the NFL at the end of the season. Dallas played like the big studs of pro ball, leading the NFC and with Danny White enjoying his best year yet, statistically, passing for 3,980 yards with 334 completions and 29 TDs. But he blew a regular-season contest against Washington when he ignored Landry's play call ("No, Danny, no!" Landry screamed from the sidelines) and was at the helm when the team self-destructed in front of football America, falling to Joe Montana and San Francisco 42–17 on ABC's *Monday Night Football* in the last week of the season.

The 12-4 record was only good enough for second place in the NFC East but it got Dallas into the playoffs again. Washington finished 14-2 and appeared unstoppable behind the deft passing of Joe Theismann, a cocky QB who backed up his cockiness with incredible skills, and the grinding, relentless power running of John Riggins.

The Cowboys were itching for a rubber match against their traditional division rival when it counted most: at the conference championship. But first there was the wild-card hosting of the Rams of

Los Angeles at Texas Stadium, a formality turned into finality as the Rams upset the Cowboys, 24–17, for Dallas's third consecutive loss, ending their year. For the first time in four years, the NFC conference championship would be played without the Dallas Cowboys. It had been five years since their last Super Bowl appearance. And bench-jockeying was turning into blood sport.

During an offseason in which another start-up rival league, the United States Football League, launched a second year of spring games, several Cowboys, led by star receiver Drew Pearson, played charity basketball games throughout the Southwest, as Cowboy players had been doing for years. The fund-raisers were extremely popular, letting fans in surrounding communities see their Sunday heroes up close on the basketball court.

After a game in Coalgate, Oklahoma, the players returned to Dallas on a team bus. Pearson later said he enjoyed two beers on the ride back. The bus arrived in Dallas around 1:00 a.m., and the players scattered. Pearson was driving his little brother home when their vehicle crashed into an eighteen-wheeler, killing his brother and leaving Pearson with severe injuries. He would spend the rest of 1984 in physical rehabilitation.

It saved Pearson from participating in a very ugly season.

On May 18, Clint Murchison Jr. sold the Dallas Cowboys Football Club and the team's interest in Texas Stadium. Murk was racked by disease, hounded by mounting debt and loans being called in, and had eight lawsuits pending, including one filed by his nephew John Dabney Murchison Jr. for raiding the trusts of the Murchison offspring to keep his businesses afloat. The creator of the Dallas Cowboys Football Club had no other choice.

Schramm had rejected a prospective buyer from Florida as a carpetbagger and eventually settled on Bum Bright, the squint-eyed sixty-three-year-old native of Muskogee, Oklahoma. Bright was the front man for an eleven-member limited partnership that Schramm helped Bright assemble (with Pete Rozelle's approval) after Bright rejected the idea of buying 51 percent of the team himself. The group paid $86 million for the football team and controlling interest in their home field. Bright's purchase was financed by Republic Bank of Dallas, where he was a major stockholder. The competing ownership group of W. O. Bankston and Vance Miller was tainted by the reputations of both men (Bankston had a history of gambling, which did not go down well with NFL security, and Miller was known for his raw ambition) and further compromised by the fact that half the money for the team would be borrowed.

Bright was cut from the same cloth as Murchison—brusque, beefy-jowled, with oversize horn-rim glasses and a crew cut. Like Murchison's, his wealth was built on oil. Bright grew up in North Dallas, where he'd belonged to the same Boy Scout troop as Murchison. He earned a petroleum engineering degree from Texas A&M and parlayed $6,500 he had saved from his hitch in the Army Corps of Engineers during World War II into a fortune by trading oil leases and becoming head of Bright and Company, an oil exploration and production company. By 1950, the thirty-one-year-old Bright had made his first million. He proceeded to diversify his investments into more than 120 companies, with a focus on trucking, real estate, and financial services.

Bright was worth $600 million, more than twice what was left of the Murchison fortune. He insisted the purchase was nothing more than a smart investment with civic benefits. He liked football, but he did not love football like Clint Murchison. He was in it for the tax shelters that came with ownership, a perquisite that had appealed to Clint Murchison when he had first pondered owning a professional football team, thirty-two years earlier.

Bright's group included James L. Huffines Jr., the chairman of the Bank of Dallas and an auto dealer; Arthur Temple, whose family's Temple-Inland lumber corporation was the largest in the East Texas Piney Woods—big enough for the family to be able to buy *Time* magazine; bankers George Underwood Sr. and Jr.; Brad Camp and Foster Yancy, who were working on a prime piece of real estate at North Central Expressway and Royal Lane; commercial developer James L. Williams; a Houston oil services businessman and savings and loan owner named Ed Smith; and the young Dallas Realtor and savings and loan owner Craig Hall, recently relocated from Michigan.

Bright agreed to be a hands-off owner and let Schramm and Landry take care of business—as if he wanted to step into what had become a mess that would soon be highlighted by yet another quarterback controversy. "If you think that Clint Murchison was an invisible owner, you will be shocked at me," Bright promised at his introductory press conference. "My group that I represent and I will be more invisible than he was," he vowed. "It is not an intent to get involved in running the football team."

Bright had plenty to occupy his time: his other businesses and his chairmanship of the Texas A&M University Board of Regents. But Texas Aggie maroon historically clashed with University of Texas burnt orange—Tex Schramm's and Tom Landry's colors—and it showed ever so subtly in the new owner/management dynamic. Bright had been part of the search committee put together by the Texas Aggies after Bear Bryant left to coach at Alabama in 1958 and he had come away unimpressed with the New York Giants defensive assistant named Landry. Time had not changed his opinion. The only coach the Cowboys ever had was expendable as far as he was concerned, and not just because Landry was a Longhorn. But Tex retained the power to make or break Landry.

Bright did exert passive influence by not opening his wallet as willingly as Murchison did. The change of ownership spurred cost-cutting measures for the team's new headquarters under construction at Valley Ranch, even though the project remained head and shoulders above what any other NFL franchise was doing. "The initial cost was $20 million but we needed to get it under $15 million," project manager Dan Werner explained. "So instead of three courtyards we had two." Tex wanted the best, including Arizona flagstone on the walls. Bright preferred his own construction people and wanted to have each and every expense justified.

As long as the team held its value, Bright felt he was better off not knowing how a football team operated. But it was hard to escape the images of out-of-control Cowboys pouring out of media outlets in Texas and beyond. The previous fall, former linebacker Thomas "Hollywood" Henderson was arrested for smoking crack with two teenage girls. Henderson was also accused of threatening the females with a gun and sexually assaulting one of them. The other girl was described as a "paraplegic minor." Henderson claimed it was a coke-and-cock deal gone bad, but nonetheless pleaded no contest and received a sentence of eight months in rehab and two years in prison.

In May of 1984 Harvey Martin announced his retirement from the game, citing a shoulder injury, bankruptcy, his star-crossed trip to Hazelden, and Larry Wansley "bird-dogging" him at training camp the year before. The Beautiful had been one of the most lovable players ever on a Cowboys roster, in part because he had grown up in Dallas, in part because of his gentle, almost-childlike disposition. Sheltered by his mama growing up, he was an easy mark, clueless about running businesses, not hard to take advantage of, and all too ready to sign for Cowboys credit whenever a piece of paper needed his signature. It had worked for seven years. Now the string had run out. Balls, Lucifer's, Smokey John's, the Rib Cage were gone. The IRS, the cops, loan officers, and the DEA were calling.

The off-field exploits of America's Team took a backseat in news coverage to the city of Dallas hosting the Republican national convention in late August, where incumbents Ronald Reagan and George H. W. Bush of Houston were nominated again as the party's candidates for president and vice president of the United States, cementing Dallas's reputation as a hub of conservatism.

Days later, true to Dallas's split personality, the first nightclub in Texas to sport a doorman and a velvet rope line in front, where only the coolest of customers were allowed inside, opened its doors. The Starck Club underscored the fact that it wasn't just Dallas Cowboys who liked to act up. Prominent Dallasite Blake Woodall (as in the Woodall-Rogers Freeway) had hired international designer Philippe Starck to create an exclusive nightclub along the lines of New York's trendy Studio 54. A clientele of semi-celebs, local socialites, plenty of Dallas Cowboys, and tabloid Euro-royals — including Prince Albert of Monaco and Princess Sarah Ferguson of England — immediately materialized, drawn to a chic environment that included unisex bathrooms; music programmed by disc jockeys imported from New York and Europe; and copious consumption of cocaine, the designer drug Ecstasy, and other illicit substances.

Meanwhile, Deep Ellum, the historically black honky-tonk district of Dallas that had fallen into ruin, underwent an occupation by hippies and alternative types intent on bringing live music and edgy theater to the moribund district, marking a creative rebirth.

THE COWBOYS WERE IN some kind of transition too, only no one could put a finger on what it was. Only two players each from the draft classes of '82 and '83 remained on the roster for the Cowboys' silver season, making the team's scouts easy targets for all the players they passed on, such as the Dolphins' dynamic passer-receiver combination of Dan Marino and Mark Clayton, who were drafted in 1983.

At Thousand Oaks, the *Morning News* polled thirty-four Cowboys about whom they wanted to lead the team into the season. Twenty players voted for Gary Hogeboom, the six-four, two-hundred-pound understudy with a rifle arm. Four players chose Danny White, the starter. Ten offered no comment. The players were also asked whom they thought Landry would select. Twenty-three opined it would be Danny White. Only five thought Hogeboom would get the nod. Six players offered no comment.

Coach Landry paid attention. When the Cowboys' season began, on September 3 at Anaheim Stadium against the Rams for the *Monday Night Football* opener, Gary Hogeboom was taking snaps from behind center. Hogeboom looked good. He played the entire game, completed 33 of 47 passes, and racked up 343 yards as the Cowboys thumped the Rams by a touchdown, 20–13. Hogeboom continued to start despite being sacked four times by Lawrence Taylor in the Cowboys' withering 28–7 loss to the New York Giants. The tall quarterback adjusted his game, the offensive line began to protect him, and the Cowboys recorded wins over Philadelphia, Green Bay, and Chicago.

Neither the starting quarterback nor the former starting quarterback could spark the offense in the October 7 home game against St. Louis, and the Cardinals went home winners, 31–20. Hogeboom played flat and was spelled by Danny White, who performed well enough in relief, going 5 for 8, to get the starting call the following week. Both quarterbacks got plenty of playing time on the road against the Redskins, but neither was effective and the Cowboys went down again, 34–14, falling to a 4-3 record. Hogeboom and White shared the field-general role again in the 30–27 overtime win against lowly New Orleans before White went all the way against the Colts in a refreshingly decisive 22–3 butt-kicking at Texas Stadium.

Hogeboom quarterbacked most of the 19–7 loss to the Giants, throwing a touchdown and two interceptions before White completed only one of six passes in relief. Hogeboom went all the way and exacted revenge on St. Louis on the road, 24–17, despite throwing two interceptions, but lost at Buffalo, 14–3, again throwing two interceptions to hand the Bills their first win of the year.

The 7-5 record put Dallas on the bubble of making the playoffs. Landry went with Danny White the next week at home against New England on Thanksgiving Day, and he was rewarded with a 21-for-41 passing performance with two touchdowns and two interceptions as the 'Boys edged the Pats, 20–17. White then threw *four* interceptions, but the Cowboys still left Philly with a decisive 27–10 win. And while White completed four touchdown passes when the Redskins came visiting the next week, he also chunked two INTs to the 'Skins' Darrell Green, this time costing the Cowboys the game as Washington edged Dallas, 30–28.

White started in the season's last *Monday Night Football* game from the Orange Bowl in Miami, featuring the Cowboys against the formidable Dolphins, whose 13-2 record was the best in the AFC. It would be the last Cowboys game that Don Meredith would cover from the ABC *Monday Night Football* broadcast booth before quietly retiring to Santa Fe. The Dolphins demonstrated why their record was close to flawless by scoring first and then responding to every Dallas score afterward (including Tony Hill's amazing fingertip grab at his shoelaces of a touchdown pass from Danny White with two minutes left in the game), limiting Dorsett to 58 yards and beating the Cowboys 28–21.

Falling short against Miami exacted a heavy price. It had been a good year on paper. Dorsett had rushed for 1,189 yards and six touchdowns on the season, and tight end Doug Cosbie led the team in receptions with sixty, for 789 yards and four TDs. But a 9-7 record was good enough only to tie the Giants and St. Louis for second place in the NFC East behind the Redskins, not good enough to make the playoffs. For the first time since 1974, the Dallas Cowboys would not participate in the NFL postseason extravaganza.

The Dolphins would earn a spot in Super Bowl XIX at Stanford University, where they would be sacrificed to what amounted to the home team, Bill Walsh's San Francisco 49ers, who were cementing their place as the NFL's team of the 1980s by finishing the season with eighteen wins and a single loss.

Ad rates for the Super Bowl had reached a million dollars a minute, and the money potential was not lost on league owners. The Baltimore Colts, the original Dallas Texans from 1952, moved once again under cover of night when owner Robert Irsay packed the team's equipment into a fleet of moving vans and relocated to Indianapolis because Irsay could realize far more profit with the incentives that Indy civic leaders were offering.

DALLAS'S TRANSFORMATION CONTINUED. The Anglos were now a minority inside the city limits, outnumbered by Hispanics and blacks. Black folks in Dallas were finally being dealt into the political system. Diane Ragsdale and Al Lipscomb were elected to the city council, and John Wiley Price, a combative personality who led with his mouth, became Dallas's first African American county commissioner.

Lenell Jeter, a young African American engineer with E-Systems who had been wrongly sentenced to life in prison (despite there being no evidence and only eyewitness accounts of the crime) by a Dallas jury for allegedly robbing a rural Greenville KFC of $645, was released from jail after doing a year's time. The DA eventually dropped the charges altogether.

The RSR Corporation, owners of the West Dallas Lead Smelter, paid out $20 million to families of 370 children living near the smelter.

Doubt became the new certainty. The freewheeling go-go business climate behind Dallas's 1970s image appeared to be flagging. The most troubling sign was federal investigators shutting down suburban Mesquite's Empire Savings and Loan, which had been tied to the I-30 condo scam, earning the institution instant notoriety as the largest savings and loan ever declared insolvent.

The bidness doldrums were balanced by research breakthroughs. North Texas's first test-tube baby, Victor Newman Barham, was born. Cholesterol researchers Michael Brown and Joseph Goldstein at UT Health Science Center in Dallas won the Nobel Prize for medicine. The tallest skyscraper in Dallas, the seventy-two-story,

921-foot-tall Dallas Main Center, debuted and would change its name seven times in the coming years as its primary tenant bank was taken over by a bigger bank.

No one was taking over the Cowboys, though. Landry and Schramm remained at the controls. Before the 1985 campaign got under way, Tex was visited at Thousand Oaks training camp by Los Angeles Raiders owner Al Davis, resplendent in the kind of white jumpsuit that Elvis Presley favored when he performed in Las Vegas. Supposed enemies, Schramm and Davis made nice for the press. The lovefest was a welcome distraction for all the on- and off-the-field fires that Schramm was trying to put out. His favorite reporter, Bob St. John, had left the beat. And the drug talk wouldn't go away. For all the focus on players using coke, everyone in the organization sidestepped discussing the use of steroids, which were bulking up linemen but leading to serious side effects.

The results on the field had been above average at best since the 49ers beat them with the Catch to end the 1981 season. But despite the Cowboys' absence from the Super Bowl, there were plenty of reasons to hope, as there always were at the start of the season, when all teams had the same 0-0 won-loss record. The Cowboys Center at Valley Ranch would open in October to rave reviews hailing the new headquarters as the finest in the land. Texas Stadium had been gussied up with two Diamond Vision video scoreboards, an NFL first, and the addition of 118 Crown Suites at the top of the stadium, which gave the club 296 private suites, more than any other franchise.

The team would be moving forward without its voice. In May, the Dallas Cowboys' longtime television announcer Frank Glieber died of a heart attack while jogging at Kenneth Cooper's aerobics center. He was fifty-one. Although the Round Mound of Sound, as he was known, often broke in new sportscasters for CBS, including former Oakland coach John Madden and, over the previous season, former Philadelphia coach Dick Vermeil, Glieber never signed a contract with the national network. He enjoyed the Dallas media market and was working for Channel 5, KXAS, at the time of his death. His booming, detached delivery had defined the Cowboys on television for three decades.

Brad Sham had moved into the play-by-play chair for Cowboys radio broadcasts a year earlier, after Verne Lundquist relinquished his radio gig to become the go-to guy in Dallas for CBS Sports NFL broadcasts. Sham's partners in the broadcast booth that season were Dale Hansen, the sports director at Channel 8; former stars Charlie Waters, Roger Staubach, Drew Pearson, and Bob Lilly; and Lundquist and Glieber. Pearson got a tryout on CBS NFL telecasts in 1984 paired up with Jim Kelly, while Lundquist worked with another ex-player, Terry Bradshaw; Jean Fugett would get a test drive in 1985 paired up with Dan Dierdorf. For 1985, Sham and Hansen would do the calls on the 162-station Dallas Cowboys radio network.

The Cowboys opened at home thoroughly pounding the Redskins, 44–14, in a game where the defensive secondary picked off five Joe Theismann passes, leading Danny White to anoint D backs Dextor Clinkscale, Michael Downs, Everson Walls, and Ron Fellows as Thurman's Thieves, in honor of their leader, Dennis Thurman. The team shook off a 44–0 shellacking at the hands of the Chicago Bears, one of the most dominating teams in NFL history under the tutelage of former Cowboy and assistant coach Mike Ditka, to rebound against the Giants, quarterback Phil Simms, and bright young coach Bill Parcells with a come-from-behind win in the next to the last game of the season, 28–21. With both Danny White and Gary Hogeboom knocked out of the game, third-stringer Steve Pelluer, a fifth-round 1984 draft selection from the University of Washington, steadily drove the team 72 yards down the field for the game-deciding touchdown, clinching the Eastern Division title, their first in four years. At the request of Dennis Thurman, Coach Landry gave him a high-five after the game.

A healed-up Hogeboom was behind center again for the final

game of the regular season, and he performed admirably, completing 29 of 39 passes, including a touchdown pass. But the big guy also threw two interceptions that led to the Cowboys' fall to San Francisco, 31–16, to close the year.

Ten and six was good enough for the playoffs this go-round, stirring hopes of a restoration. The Cowboys' return to postseason play marked their thirty-sixth appearance in a playoff game, an NFL record. Danny White started at quarterback against Los Angeles and went 29-43 with 217 passing yards. But he also tossed three interceptions and the Rams blanked the Cowboys, 20–0, largely on the legs of SMU grad and Texas high school star Eric Dickerson, who ground out 248 yards and scored two touchdowns.

It was one and done.

Tony Dorsett had had another great year, rushing for 1,307 yards and seven touchdowns, and 449 yards in pass receptions, while receiver Tony Hill led the club in pass receptions with 74 catches for 1,113 yards and seven touchdowns. But individual achievements did not hide the obvious: something was amiss in Cowboy-land.

The string of lousy draft picks were under so much scrutiny that Salam Qureishi, the Indian who had designed the Cowboys' vaunted computerized draft system and then been fired by Clint Murchison, was rehired by the football club. If you were looking at it from the outside, the core of the organization appeared the same: Landry still coached, Tex still promoted, and Gil still scouted. But the grousing grew louder when all three were rewarded with bonuses that Clint Murchison had structured into the team's sale to Bum Bright—Tom and Tex receiving $2.5 million each, and Gil getting $500,000. Exceptionally handsome rewards considering they'd had what was really just an okay year.

The Fall

IN THE YEAR OF the Texas Sesquicentennial, celebrating Texas's independence from Mexico in 1836, the arrival of the Heisman Trophy winner from Georgia and the premier player from the United States Football League was hailed as redemption.

Never before had a new player from a rival league been so welcomed in Dallas. But Herschel Walker wasn't just any player, and the USFL wasn't bush league.

The USFL formed in 1983 as a spring and summer league intended to compete against and complement the NFL. The ABC television network and the new start-up cable sports channel ESPN paid the league $13 million to air their games in 1983, and they upped the fee to $16 million in 1984, providing enough seed money for teams to raid NFL rosters for players. ESPN's head honcho, Chet Simmons, was named league commissioner. Longtime Cowboys nemesis George Allen, the former coach of the Washington Redskins, took control of the Chicago Blitz franchise, while former Denver Bronco coach Red Miller headed up the Denver Gold franchise. For the league's second season, the city of Dallas was surrounded by USFL franchises: the Houston Gamblers, the San Antonio Gunslingers, and the Oklahoma Outlaws in Tulsa.

The Gamblers' Jim Kelly, a University of Miami graduate, was the USFL's first star quarterback. Brigham Young QB Steve Young was the league's first bonus baby, signing a ten-year $40 million contract with the Los Angeles Express, the fattest deal ever in pro football to that point. But it was Herschel Walker who defined the league. He gave up his senior year at college to sign a deal with the New Jersey Generals of the USFL; at the time, the NFL forbade league franchises to sign underclassmen. Walker played three seasons for the Generals, who were purchased by real estate mogul Donald Trump shortly after Walker was signed.

When the San Antonio Gunslingers owner Clinton Manges had his franchise revoked after the 1985 season for not paying his bills, and the league announced it was moving its 1986 schedule to the fall to compete head-to-head against the NFL, the Cowboys' risky drafting of Walker in 1985 paid off; the running back bolted to join them.

Walker's presence meant two Heisman Trophy winners in the backfield, although Tony Dorsett was beginning to show his thirty-two years. Walker guaranteed more publicity for a team that already had more pub and press than any team in football. The exceptionally agile Walker even performed with the Fort Worth Ballet.

Tex Schramm tried to make other improvements by bringing in a new passing coordinator, Paul Hackett, from the hated San Francisco 49ers; there, Hackett had developed a rep as the best young quarterback and receiver coach in the business. Schramm had convinced Hackett to turn down the head coach position at the University of Southern California; he would have a much brighter future with the Cowboys, where he could be mentored by Landry (after being under Bill Walsh) while working with Danny White and Steve Pelluer. Gary Hogeboom had been traded to the Colts during the offseason.

Schramm thought Hackett could be the new Danny Reeves — Landry's successor-in-waiting, as the prospect of Landry leaving drew more imminent with each season. Schramm told intimates he thought Landry had been dropping hints about retirement. Landry sure wasn't acting like he was thinking about it, especially after he received a three-year extension on his contract (an increasingly unhappy Bum Bright thought Schramm had told him it was three one-year contracts, rather than one three-year contract). But Hackett's presence seemed to irritate Landry. Landry's traditional approach to game preparation did not mesh with Hackett's contemporary thinking, which revolved around the West Coast offense he had developed with the 49ers.

"Tex finally crossed that line when he hired Paul Hackett and [a year later, offensive line coach] Jim Erkenbeck," said Dale Hansen of Channel 8. "Landry didn't have complete autonomy anymore. Schramm saw the decline of his organization. In his efforts to fix it, he blew it up. Neither assistant had any loyalty to Landry. Landry, like so many people in sports, knew it was time, but he wanted to go out on top. Tex had been talking to Jimmy Johnson, the very successful coach of the University of Miami, a year earlier. He had him in his suite at the Super Bowl. Tex wanted to replace Landry, but that's not how they were put together."

Schramm had a lot on his plate. He was instrumental in the NFL Competition Committee's finally adopting instant replay to help officials, but only after the start-up rival USFL implemented it. He pushed the rule allowing the quarterback to stop the clock by throwing the ball to the ground after taking the snap from center, all in the name of pumping up offense and inflating scores. Pete Rozelle forwarded Schramm a letter Bum Bright had sent to him, thanking Rozelle for mentioning how helpful Tex had been and what a difference he made "to the entire defense of the litigation with the USFL."

The United States Football League had sued the NFL, and after a stretched-out period of litigation, the case went to trial in the spring of 1986. The rival league won a hollow victory by being awarded three dollars in damages, in no small part due to Schramm's efforts and the maneuverings of the NFL's legal team, headed by Paul Tagliabue.

Satellite technology arrived at Thousand Oaks, allowing television stations to do live reports from training camp. WFAA Channel 8 was the first station with a satellite transmitter truck at camp, and Tex Schramm went the extra mile to accommodate the station. "He thought this was the coolest thing ever," Channel 8 sportscaster Dale Hansen said. "We sent the signal from Thousand Oaks back to Dallas via satellite. I didn't know that people with those big satellite dishes in their backyards could pick up the live feed, and I was talking some serious stuff. I got cards, like the one from Greenwich, Connecticut, that read, 'Mr. Hansen, I love your sportscasts with the Cowboys, but I really love your sportscasts when you don't know you're on the air.'"

The Channel 8 Thousand Oaks report went live nightly at 8:30 California time. Schramm provided guests for the broadcasts by pulling players out of meetings. Coach Landry would be interrupted at about 8:20 by a producer who would say, "We need Drew Pearson. We need Bob Breunig." Pretty soon, players were flagging Hansen down asking to be on the show and showing up for their segment early to get out of meetings.

The next year, new offensive line coach Jim Erkenbeck confronted Hansen for taking Nate Newton out of a linemen meeting for a television shot. Erkenbeck grabbed Hansen and sought out Tex Schramm. When he found him, Erkenbeck pointed at Hansen and bellowed, "This son of a bitch took one of my linemen out of our meeting. Now what in the hell do you call that?"

"Public relations." Schramm smiled and walked away with Hansen by his side.

TEXAS E. SCHRAMM, who saw the world outside of the United States as untapped NFL territory, spearheaded the event that capped the 1986 preseason: the first NFL American Bowl at Wembley Stadium in London, England. The defending Super Bowl champion

Chicago Bears beat Dallas, 17–6, in front of 80,000 fans packed into Wembley, a turnout Tex envisioned as a portent of things to come.

THE REAL SEASON OPENED at Texas Stadium against the Giants on *Monday Night Football.*

The NFL debut of Herschel Walker was the draw, but the return of defensive back Everson Walls and Danny White taking snaps from center with Steve Pelluer as his backup were the difference makers. Walls held receiver Lionel Manuel to one catch for 19 yards. Walker took over the running game after Tony Dorsett sprained an ankle in the second quarter, rushing for 64 yards on 11 carries, the last touch a 10-yard touchdown with 1:14 remaining, and White went 23-39 and two TDs with no interceptions to win, 31–28.

White and Pelluer codirected the league's number-one offense to a 6-2 start and a tie for first in the NFC East by passing and handing off to Dorsett or Walker. But White's season ended on week nine when he broke his right wrist after being blindsided by New York Giants defensive linebacker Carl Banks in a 17–14 loss.

Pelluer's inexperience showed over the final eight games, during which the Cowboys managed to scratch out only a single victory. Two Heisman-bred running backs could not compensate for a flimsy O-line. The 4-3 Flex lost whatever effectiveness it had left in the defensive scheme, in no small part due to the release of defensive backs Dextor Clinkscale and Dennis Thurman before the season.

Herschel Walker may have gained more than 1,500 yards, but he did it with more than 350 carries, a grueling pace for any running back, and nowhere near enough to help the Cowboys. The 7-9 record marked the Cowboys' first losing season in twenty-one years. Danny White was one of the best quarterbacks in the NFL, but injuries kept him from rising to the level of his predecessor. Doomsday had devolved and was overshadowed by Pittsburgh's Steel Curtain and the rough-boy cornerbacks from the outlaw Raiders.

———

THE LUSTER OF THE Big D blue star was hardly tarnished, insisted Raiders owner Al Davis. "Hard as we might try, the Raiders will always be the second most hated team in the league. We'll never catch Dallas."

The biggest football story of the year had nothing to do with the Dallas Cowboys. Channel 8's Dale Hansen and producer John Sparks reported that players on the Southern Methodist University Mustangs had been receiving payments under the table from football program boosters and had one player, David Stanley, on the record admitting he had been paid $25,000 to play football. He was hardly the only one and it was hardly a new thing. Eric Dickerson, who had been the most highly recruited high school player in the nation at Sealy High School, near Houston, showed up at high school with a gold Trans-Am after he'd committed to SMU in 1978.

The payoffs were one sign of football's importance.

Another was the defeat of Governor Mark White by former governor William Clements in November 1986, partly due to the unpopularity of the no-pass, no-play rules that had been championed by H. Ross Perot and White and subsequently applied to Texas high school athletics.

Bill Clements had spent his time out of office selling his offshore drilling company, Sedco, to Schlumberger of Houston for $1 billion and conducting academic business as chairman of the board of trustees at Southern Methodist University.

Two weeks after taking the oath of office the second time around, in January of 1987, Clements admitted that in the past the SMU board had secretly approved payment to thirteen football players from a slush fund created by boosters, including Murchison Rover Boy George Owen; the board had agreed to end the practice in late 1986. Clements said he'd learned about the fund in 1984 and that the practice hearkened back to the 1970s. "We made the wrong decision," he admitted with uncharacteristic understatement.

The football program at Southern Methodist University hadn't had this much success on the field since the days of Doak Walker; they were drawing crowds and beating bigger Southwest Conference powerhouses, such as the University of Texas and Texas A&M, especially when the running game was led by Eric Dickerson and Craig James. The victories came at a considerable price—the death penalty issued by the NCAA on February 25, 1987, banning SMU from playing football for two years as punishment for cheating and paying players. The practice was not unusual for college football in Texas, but no school had done it so blatantly. The NCAA had put SMU on probation five times in the previous eleven years. This time, the governing body of college athletics made the punishment stick.

The story that Channel 8 broke was a result of aggressive investigative reporting done by both the *Dallas Times Herald* and the *Dallas Morning News,* which were engaged in the last great newspaper war in the United States. At one point, most large American cities had multiple daily newspapers, but the rise of television broadcast journalism and other options for disseminating news had forced most crosstown competitors to merge, enter into joint publishing agreements to cut costs, or fold. But in Dallas, big money was being poured into large staffs hell-bent on beating the opposition with scoops and investigative journalism. Both papers were breaking stories long before their television and radio counterparts, and they were winning awards for their work. In the case of the SMU scandal, the reporting of the *Dallas Morning News*'s David McNabb was critical in getting the Mustangs the death penalty.

If only the Cowboys could have been banned from playing in 1987. Dallas's professional team got off on the wrong foot before the season even started. On January 22 Rafael Septien, the Pro Bowl kicker who had led the Cowboys in scoring over the past nine years, was indicted by a Dallas County grand jury on the charge of mishandling of a minor. He had been accused of fondling the ten-year-old friend of his roommate's daughter. After initially pleading not guilty,

Septien changed his plea, two and a half months later, to guilty of indecency with a child, accepting a sentence of ten years' probation and a fine of $2,000. His career with the Cowboys was over.

The Cowboys' new kicker was another Mexican national named Luis Zendejas, who played at Arizona State. Zendejas's presence solidified the Cowboys' reputation as Mexico's Team as well as America's and Texas's.

That was quite a legacy to leave the world. On the last day of March in 1987, Clint Murchison Jr. passed away after a bout with pneumonia. He was sixty-three. The death of the man who had willed the Dallas Cowboys into being and who had found the best and brightest to make his football club the model for all others formalized the darkness looming all around. The son of the biggest wildcatter in Texas went out quietly, with a muted funeral service at Shady Grove Church, a fundamentalist church he and Anne had joined, with Tom Landry delivering one of the eulogies. Murchison's disease had left him speechless and immobile while his warring heirs fought for their pieces of an insolvent empire with over $500 million in liabilities. With obituaries in the national media as well as Dallas and in East Texas, Murchison's passing was duly noted, but not widely mourned.

His greatest legacy, the Dallas Cowboys, the Cadillac of NFL franchises, was getting the Chevy Impala treatment from Bum Bright. It was bad enough seeing Bright's primary businesses getting squeezed by creditors as part of a larger economic downturn that was gripping Texas, but he was nickel-and-diming his football club/ tax shelter as it was bleeding money.

The collapse of the energy and commercial real estate sectors of the Texas economy was creating a recession so severe that Governor Clements, whose restoration as governor was due to his no-new-taxes pledge, was forced to sign a $5.7 billion increase in state taxes — the highest increase ever in Texas — just to keep the state afloat.

———

MONEY WAS A POINT of contention in football too. Tex Schramm had imported Bob Ackles of the British Columbia Lions, the Grey Cup champions of the Canadian Football League, as vice president of pro personnel. Ackles's main task was monitoring the waiver wires for players other teams were releasing, so no stone would go unturned in finding talent. Schramm was pulling out all the stops, but nothing seemed to be working.

After losing to St. Louis, 24–13, when the defense collapsed and the Cardinals scored three touchdowns in the last two minutes, and barely edging out the defending Super Bowl champion New York Giants, 16–14, to open the 1987 season on the road, the Cowboys were forced to cancel their home opener when the NFL Players Association called a strike. A collective bargaining agreement with owners couldn't be settled. Both sides were dug in. Play was resumed the following week, the clubs stocking their rosters with replacement players — scabs who rejected the union — while Schramm and the NFL management council haggled with players representatives. Bizarro NFL continued until October 18, when the players voted to return to work without a collective bargaining agreement. They would fight their battle in court.

Bad blood boiled between the scabs and the players who had stuck with the union. No club epitomized that tension better than the Cowboys, who went 2-1 during the strike and had drawn a near-capacity crowd of 61,234 for the third replacement game largely on the performance of former scout squad quarterback Kevin Sweeney, who threw four TD passes the first two games. For game three, the Redskins showdown, Sweeney handed the starter's job back to Danny White, who had crossed picket lines along with Randy White, Too Tall Jones, Tony Dorsett, and seventeen other regulars to play with the replacement Cowboys. But the mixed team lost, 13–7. By the end of the game, a "We Want Sweeney" cheer echoed around the stadium.

More players crossed picket lines on the Cowboys than on any other team, partly because Tex Schramm informed his stars that they would lose their annuity payments if they went on strike. Forget solidarity with the union brothers. Texas was a right-to-work state, meaning no play, no pay. It was every man for himself. That attitude did not sit well with some teammates, among them Doug Cosbie and Everson Walls, who lost money but stayed on strike. It effectively tore the Cowboys apart, even after the strike ended.

"Tex was abandoned by the owners," said Russ Russell, his friend, associate, and occasional business partner. "He had the players association against the ropes. He had [the union] beat here in Texas. We had a full stadium. We loved the replacement players. No one wanted to see Danny White. The crowd booed when Tom sent in regular players. Bum called Tex and told him to tell Tom to put the replacement players back in the game. Tex said he couldn't do that."

"Then fire him," Bum had bellowed, according to Russell.

"What? In the middle of a game?" Tex replied, then ignored the order.

Unfortunately for Schramm, the other owners weren't getting the same reaction and wanted a settlement.

Several replacement players, including QB Kevin Sweeney, wide receiver Kelvin Edwards, and safety Tommy Haynes, managed to stick with the real Cowboys when normal play resumed, not that the real Cowboys had much going for them. They were so bad, angry-fan jokes about killing the coach began to get traction.

In one of the stranger games Dallas was involved in, the Cowboys squared off against the Rams in Anaheim for a *Monday Night Football* telecast that closed out Dallas's road schedule. Early in the second quarter, director of security and counseling services Larry Wansley received an urgent call from the NFL security representative assigned to the game. A death threat against Cowboys coach Tom Landry had just been called in. Somewhere in the stadium, Wansley was told, a sniper with a high-powered rifle was lurking.

Wansley hurried to the sidelines to make Tom Landry aware of the threat. "I've got to get you off the field," he told the stunned coach. The Cowboys coach handed his playbook to Danny White, who had been sidelined with a broken wrist and was sending in plays to quarterback Steve Pelluer. "Take over," Landry instructed White before being escorted off the field by a phalanx of security personnel and into a nearby tunnel. In the locker room, Wansley explained to Landry that stadium security was taking the threat seriously and urged him to spend the second half coaching from the press box. Landry would have none of it. "I need to be with the team," Landry told him flatly.

Wansley didn't push back. "Once I realized that he was determined to return to the sidelines for the second half, I borrowed a [bulletproof] vest from an LA police officer working security and had Tom put it on."

"Coach, what's going on?" White asked Landry when he returned.

"The police have received a threat on my life," Landry told him without emotion. "There's supposed to be a sniper in the stands. They wanted me to stay in the locker room, but I persuaded them to let me wear a bulletproof vest and come back out. Don't stand too close to me. They might miss and shoot you instead."

When Landry turned to White to give him the next play, White was standing five yards away.

"Coach, you're going to have to speak up," White shouted before walking closer with a wide grin on his face. "You don't have to tell me not to stand close to you," he said. "The way this season has gone for me, that sucker's drunk and he's gonna shoot and miss you and hit me."

Landry cracked a slight smile. For the remainder of the game, Larry Wansley shadowed Tom Landry while staying in radio contact with security officials who were furiously searching the stadium for a possible sniper. The fourth quarter ended with the Cowboys ahead 29–21 in a game noteworthy because nothing happened.

"If it had been my life that was threatened and I was standing out there in front of sixty thousand fruitcakes, knowing someone might have the crosshairs on me, I don't know what I would have done," Danny White later said. "But it didn't seem to faze him. He went right on calling plays and running the game like there was nothing to it."

Tony Dorsett had a subpar game rushing for 54 yards, but the numbers were enough to put an exclamation mark on an exceptional career as Dorsett joined Jim Brown, Franco Harris, and Walter Payton as the only players to rush for more than 12,000 yards. But neither he nor Herschel Walker broke 1,000 yards for the season, and their passing counterparts Danny White and Steve Pelluer failed to distinguish themselves.

In the final game of a year that was more down than up, the Cowboys skidded past the Cardinals, 21–16, in front of 36,788 observers, the worst home crowd of the season, replacement games included. No home game had sold out. Even the hard-core loyalists were turning their backs on the 7-8 Cowboys, who recorded their second consecutive losing season.

Despite the team sucking badly, the Cowboys could take solace in their 75-45 record for the 1980s. Only San Francisco, Miami, and Washington had more wins. But only Dallas had nothing to show for the effort.

Bum Bright, the supposedly hands-off owner, went on the record to say, "I get horrified sometimes at our play-calling. It doesn't seem like we've got anybody in charge that knows what they're doing, other than Tex."

Even Schramm had doubts. "I'm not sure it's all on the players," he admitted to reporters. "When things aren't working, and you see the same things, it shakes your confidence. There's an old saying, 'If the teacher doesn't teach, the student doesn't learn.'"

Cowboys game tickets, priced at twenty-three dollars plus 8 percent tax and a two-dollar handling fee, were no longer hard to get.

Most of the upper-level Crown Suites that Bright had added to the top of Texas Stadium remained unsold.

Dan Werner, who had been working for Joe Bailey after getting Valley Ranch built, hadn't received a raise in several years, in part because Bright wasn't paying any more than he had to. So Werner moved from the front office to arrange travel logistics for the team on road trips and sell packages to fans to increase his paycheck.

Larry Wansley also made a change, taking a leave as director of security and counseling services to run security for singing sensation Whitney Houston, the biggest pop vocalist in the world, on a three-month European tour in the spring. Tex urged him to do it. Learning the variables of security in different countries would broaden Wansley's knowledge and better prepare him for the NFL's inevitable expansion into Europe. Plus, Schramm loaded him up with Cowboys merchandise, which the band and crew, including Houston, happily wore.

Wansley's timing was good because it was the offseason. Had he had a crystal ball, he might have stayed on tour through the fall.

No Light at the End of the Tunnel

THE RECESSION SHOWED signs of abating around Dallas when the U.S. Department of Energy chose Ellis County, south of Dallas, as the site of its proposed Superconducting Super Collider, a fifty-two-mile-underground particle accelerator that would cost $5 billion and bring fourteen thousand jobs to Texas. GTE telephone relocated its corporate headquarters from Connecticut to Las Colinas in Irving, while computer maker Fujitsu opened a complex in Richardson and hired a workforce of four thousand.

That kind of good news tempered the closings of Foley's department store downtown, Dallas's historically black Bishop College, the Dallas Ballet, and the First Republic Bank.

Dynamic Dallas was not unlike the 1988 edition of the Dallas Cowboys.

Their 7-8 record helped land them the eleventh overall pick, Michael Irvin, the highly coveted University of Miami receiver who had set school records for career catches, yards, and touchdown pass receptions before deciding to turn pro after his junior year. Informed he had been chosen by the Cowboys, Irvin displayed the brash confidence that earned him the reputation as a trash talker who could back it up: he advised the sizable gathering to "go tell Danny White I'm going to put him in the Pro Bowl." Tex Schramm liked what he heard, remarking, "This will speed our return to the living."

The cocky Irvin arrived in Dallas with a golden-sun medallion on a large dooky chain around his neck, diamond stud earrings in his lobes, and his reputation as the Playmaker, the guy who could break open a game. He would wear Drew Pearson's 88.

Irvin was the fifteenth of seventeen children of the Reverend Walter and Pearl Irvin of Fort Lauderdale, Florida. His mom was a homemaker. His father was a traveling Baptist preacher and roofer whose work ethic influenced his sports-minded son, who played basketball and football with equal skill. The reverend passed away three days before Michael's first senior-year football game at St. Thomas Aquinas High School, putting more weight on the son's shoulders to provide for his large family and influencing his decision to pass up scholarships at Syracuse, Louisiana State, and Michigan State so he could stay closer to home. He decided to play for the University of Miami, which had just won its first national college championship.

After sitting out one season as a redshirt, Irvin combined forces with young quarterback Vinny Testaverde and Miami's new coach Jimmy Johnson to go up against Barry Switzer's number-three-ranked Oklahoma Sooners in Norman. Irvin caught three consecutive passes from Testaverde for touchdowns, and Johnson, who had lost to Switzer five times when he was coaching at Oklahoma State, finally got a win against him when the Hurricanes upset the Sooners, 27–14. Miami finished 10-1 and was ranked number two nationally while Irvin had scoring catches in eight straight games.

The next season, Miami went 11-0 but fell to Penn State at the Fiesta Bowl for the unofficial national championship. With Steve Walsh installed at quarterback for 1987, Miami went undefeated and took the national title by beating Oklahoma 20–14 in the Orange Bowl.

With Irvin coming to Dallas, maybe some of that Miami magic would rub off on the Cowboys. The Cowboys' scouting and draft department had picked some clunker first-rounders in recent years, among them defensive lineman Larry Bethea, who would be arrested in August and later convicted of stealing $64,000 from his own mother. Bethea would shoot himself in the head before police could arrest him for two armed robberies.

Tony Dorsett had been traded away to Denver for a draft pick who failed to make the team. Mike Renfro, the veteran who led the wide receivers with 46 catches and 662 yards for 1987, was being challenged by the rookie Irvin, who filed training-camp-diary reports for K104, the DFW urban radio station.

Steve Pelluer beat out Danny White at Thousand Oaks to start at quarterback for the Cowboys; the season opened with a close loss to the rebuilding Pittsburgh Steelers, 24–21, with Pelluer going 24 for 37 passing for 289 yards and two touchdowns and two interceptions. Catching one of those TD passes was Michael Irvin, the first Cowboys rookie receiver to start on opening day since Bob Hayes back in 1965. Even Tom Landry was learning to bend his own rules now and then.

The next week, Irvin sat on the bench with a sprained ankle, and Steve Pelluer was less impressive, going 12-24 for an anemic 162 yards, no touchdowns, and one interception. The quarterback's performance was compensated by Herschel Walker's rushing for 149 yards—enough power for a 17–14 win in Tempe, Arizona, the new home of the Cardinals, where half the crowd rooted for the team from North Texas.

By week six, Danny White got the call from Landry to spell Pelluer against Washington, a game that the Redskins had safely in hand. White lasted two games before suffering a season-ending wrist injury. The coach went with Kevin Sweeney, the little-regarded seventh-round pick from Fresno State in the 1987 draft and noted scab who got the nod for two games but failed to deliver before Steve Pelluer ultimately replaced him.

Quarterback indecision on top of injuries had made a bad situation worse, and the Dallas Cowboys finished 1988 with a 3-13 record, the poorest showing since the second year of their existence as an expansion franchise. Irvin led the NFC with 20.4 yards per catch. Starting running back Herschel Walker became the tenth player to gain 2,000 yards rushing and receiving in a single season. Collectively, though, the team was a failure.

NFL Films charitably titled the Cowboys highlight reel *That Uncertain Season.* Dallas Cowboys fans were not so ambiguous. Sixty-one percent of the fans surveyed in a phone poll taken by the *Dallas Times Herald* wanted Tom Landry fired. Cowboys safety Bill Bates, the gritty safety and special-teams standout, admitted public perception of the team was not good. "The excitement at Texas Stadium didn't exist," he observed. "Everyone came to the games and just sat on their hands. You'd score a touchdown and it'd be, 'Yeah — nice play.' No one was screaming or jumping up and down. Something had to change."

At the end of the season, moves were made. Defensive coordinator Ernie Stautner was fired and co-offensive coordinator Paul Hackett was demoted to special-projects coach, but Landry vowed to return. The only coach the Cowboys ever had just tied Curly Lambeau's record of twenty-nine consecutive years coaching one team. At sixty-four, he was good for another five or ten years, he figured.

There was an upside to the shitty record: Dallas got the first overall pick in the upcoming draft. Their primary target (and every other franchise's target) was Troy Aikman, the talented quarterback for the UCLA Bruins. Aikman was born in West Covina in Southern California but grew up following the Cowboys in Henryetta, Oklahoma, a farming town on Interstate 40 halfway between Oklahoma City and the Arkansas state line. After two years at Oklahoma University, Aikman transferred to UCLA, where he developed into a pro-style quarterback and won the Davey O'Brien Award as the nation's top college quarterback. The Bruins were 20-4 over the two years Aikman led the offense. He finished his college career beating Arkansas, 17–3, at the Cotton Bowl in Dallas, where Tom Landry,

Tex Schramm, and an Arkansas-ex named Jerry Jones all watched from the grandstands. All three touted him as the Cowboys' next great quarterback if the Cowboys got first overall pick.

The organization was willing to bet Valley Ranch that Aikman could cure whatever ailed the Cowboys. The team was 36-44 so far during the Bum Bright era, with no playoff wins. The combination of Aikman, Irvin, and Herschel Walker offered hope, as did the planned shift to a 3-4 defense, now the preferred formation of NFL defenses.

The impact of the bad record wasn't just the alienation of fans but the devaluation of the franchise itself. The Cowboys lost as much as $9 million in 1988. Ninety of the 118 Crown Suites at the top of the stadium were for lease. Sellouts had become rare as hen's teeth. And like the diversified empire builder/football club owner who had preceded him, Bright had gotten caught up in the wave of fast money bets gone bad on real estate and banking. Bum Bright's worth, pegged at $600 million when he bought the team, declined by half, forcing him to liquidate. He could no longer afford to own the Dallas Cowboys.

Federal and state banking regulators had relaxed rules through the early 1980s (despite the warnings of Representative Wright Patman of the First Congressional District in East Texas, who headed the House Banking Committee), and by 1985, the number of savings and loan institutions had tripled, owing to oilmen flush with cash looking to make their capital grow by underwriting the new unregulated institutions that were making risky commercial and construction loans in a booming real estate market. The game worked as long as land flips paid off with increasingly higher values. But when the price of oil plummeted below twenty dollars a barrel beginning in 1986 and stayed there for three years, the house of cards collapsed and plunged the Texas economy into a recession. Commercial foreclosures in Dallas topped $1 billion. Several S & L operators went to jail, as did stockbroker Billy Bob Harris, Craig

Morton's former business partner and roommate, although most violators skated, leaving the American public holding the bag. In 1989, Congress would pass a taxpayer-financed bailout of $50 billion.

If there was any silver lining to Texas's spectacular fall from financial grace, it was, for some, the election of Texas resident and Republican Party stalwart George H. W. Bush as president of the United States; Bush succeeded his former boss Ronald Reagan by besting former Massachusetts governor Michael Dukakis.

Once it became public that the Cowboys were for sale, rumors flew around Dallas and the league throughout the 1988 season. Bright was asking $180 million for the football team and control of stadium rights for the next twenty years. Jerry Buss, the owner of the Los Angeles Lakers National Basketball Association franchise; the Dallas NBA Mavericks' owner Don Carter (again); movie magnate Marvin Davis; real estate mogul Donald Trump, and Bob Tisch of the Loews Corporation were prospective suitors. An oil and gas wildcatter from Arkansas named Jerry Jones was also in the mix.

Bum Bright considered more than seventy-five different ownership groups in all before he settled on a buyer, a man who would pay him what he wanted, on his terms.

1989–2011

Regime Change

ONE HUNDRED AND FIFTY YEARS after John Neely Bryan envisioned setting up a trading post by the Trinity River ford where three forks of the river converged, another Arkansan fidgeted in a plush leather chair while the pilot of his Learjet traced the trail Bryan had blazed on foot and horseback.

The mind of the man in back was racing as fast as his jet; he was lost in thought, oblivious to the chatter of the folks sitting next to him: his business partner Mike McCoy; his minority partner Ed Smith of Houston; his sons, Jerry Jr. and Stephen; his daughter, Charlotte; and his wife, Gene.

Smith, a Houston businessman who had been a minority owner during Bright's tenure, had tried to buy the Cowboys outright but couldn't rustle up the money, so he retained 27 percent ownership as part of Jerry Jones's group. Jones held 63 percent. Other investors included the Wyly brothers, Charles and Sam, and Sam's son Evan—Dallasites with Louisiana roots whose grubstake, the University Computing Company, founded in the early 1960s, led to their buying the Bonanza Steakhouse restaurant chain, Michael's arts and crafts retailers, and the Frost Brothers department stores.

Jerry Jones was about to pull off the impossible. He had lived and breathed football, achieved success in life beyond the imagination of most mortals, and was about to realize what he had been able only to

489

dream about—owning his own professional football club. And not just any club, but the Dallas Cowboys, the pro team of his youth, the only NFL team that mattered in Arkansas, and the classiest franchise in professional sports. He was betting everything on the buy. It was the greatest risk he had ever taken in a career defined by huge risks and educated bets. If Tex Schramm was right about what he told Jones six months before when they briefly met—"You can't make any money buying this team"—he was doomed to failure. But Jones had already thought that through. He would go out in a blaze of glory, if that was to be his fate. But he knew better. Believing in himself was half the game, and if anyone believed in himself, it was Jerral Wayne Jones.

The jet broke through overcast skies to touch down at Love Field. The group was shuttled directly to the Mansion on Turtle Creek, the finest luxury hotel in all of Texas, where Jones met his partner in crime Jimmy Johnson. Johnson and Jones were Razorback football buddies who had achieved considerable success in their respective fields—Jones as an oil and gas capitalist, Johnson as a college football coach, most recently with the defending national champion University of Miami Hurricanes.

Jones paced nervously back and forth in his suite, jumped on the telephone whenever it rang, and did what he could do to contain himself, knowing he was about to make a big splash in Big D.

Never mind the hundreds of millions of dollars he'd ginned up from out of the ground in the forms of oil and natural gas. Never mind he was one of Arkansas's great success stories, right up there with Sam Walton, who took retail to a whole 'nother level, and his friend Don Tyson, the chicken king, who through the consolidation of local farmers grew his business into the biggest conglomerate of chicken producers on earth.

Jerry Jones wasn't the boy from North Little Rock made good anymore. He was about to become the biggest shit between Atlanta and Vegas and beyond: the owner of the Dallas Cowboys.

Jerry Jones had commanded Bum Bright's attention since the previous September. "The more I got to know him, the more I knew he was the right man to own the Cowboys," Bright said. Jones insisted no other football franchise would do. "The Dallas Cowboys are the only team I would want to own."

Jones and Bright agreed on terms written on a napkin, and shook hands. The contract and other particulars would be worked out later. The deal was done.

Word was Jones was ready to do what Bright had not and clean house. Tex Schramm had been trying to assemble an ownership group that would meet Bright's price and keep management in place, and Roger Staubach tested the waters on Tex's behalf but found no takers. Those kinds of folks had been hard to find during the economic downturn. Schramm asked Bright to hold off because he was putting together a "salvation team" that would maintain local ownership and keep the ship of state sailing ahead. One outside group offered to top Jones's offer by $10 million, according to Bright; Bright demurred but informed Jones he could make a quick $10 million if he flipped the team.

"I wouldn't do it for twice that," Jones replied. He had the fever.

"Then why didn't you pay me more?" Bright asked.

"Because I didn't have to." Jones smiled.

JERRY JONES WAS A born salesman, a charismatic figure who had been smiling and selling since he was nine, when he dressed up in a black suit and bow tie, slicked his hair back, pasted a solicitous grin on his face, and stood at the entrance of Pat Jones's Supermarket in Rose City, Arkansas, helping his daddy and his family sell their goods.

His was a familiar journey.

The migration from Arkansas to North Central Texas had been constant since the 1860s. Arkansas was poor, rural, and Southern. A place like Dallas meant opportunity beyond the farm. Dallas was a real city, practically made for someone like Jerry Jones.

Jerry's daddy, J. W. "Pat" Jones, grew up in England, Arkansas, twenty-eight miles outside of Little Rock toward the Mississippi Delta, a small community famous for its food riot: the state of Arkansas went broke in 1931 in the wake of the Great Depression and a hard drought resulted in major crop failures, leading the residents of England to demand merchants give them food, which the merchants did.

The wiry, self-assured Pat Jones was a bantam rooster, five feet six inches tall, who distinguished himself around town as a salesman, a respectable calling in the southern United States. Like almost everyone else, Jones sold beans, because that's what was grown around England. His beans were no different than other beans. He just sold his more effectively. Buyers who bought from him may not have been any better off than buyers who bought from a stand just down the road, but they went away pleased that they had been persuaded and entertained by Mr. Jones, who made each and every transaction seem special.

Jerral Wayne was born to Arminta Jones in Los Angeles on October 13, 1942. Pat Jones had taken a job in an aircraft manufacturing plant in Los Angeles during World War II; he stayed long enough to check out Hollywood and find it lacking. The family, including Jerry's sister Jacque, returned to Arkansas in 1945 at the end of the war and got back to selling, opening up a fruit stand in an area of North Little Rock known as Rose City, right by the train tracks and next to the feed store. It was a busy spot, since the roads from St. Louis and Memphis converged there before leading into Little Rock, across the Arkansas River, or heading west to Oklahoma and Texas.

North Little Rock was the rough side of the river, flood prone and industrial, with the nickname of Dogtown because it was where the good people of Little Rock dumped their unwanted pets. The working-class community had one tavern for every six citizens.

Pat Jones's fruit stand proved so successful he borrowed money to open the area's first grocery store, Pat's Supermarket, complete with a meat market and a bakery. The family lived upstairs above the store until business improved, at which point they moved to a house next door.

Pat Jones didn't just sell food and other staples. He made retail memorable, transforming his store into a dance and entertainment center. The grand opening of Pat's Supermarket attracted so many customers and onlookers, the North Little Rock Fire Department had to be called out to manage the crush. Jones brought in musicians to play at the store, among them the storied western swing band the Light Crust Doughboys. He performed with his own band too, Pat's Supermarketeers. Brother Hal Webber and his hillbilly show broadcast weekly live on KLRA from the back of the store. People came from fifteen counties to shop at Pat's, its owner liked to brag.

On weekends, Pat dressed in a white cowboy suit to welcome shoppers and was soon joined by his son, Jerry, who learned every aspect of the business, from stocking shelves to managing employees.

When he wasn't at the grocery, the affable Pat would be working on a barbecue beef or pork sandwich and drinking beers at the White Pig Inn, a small white-frame building covered with Permastone and owned by Vance Seaton. The White Pig was an all-comers kind of joint, serving cops and hoodlums both and taking bets from all for the horse races at Oaklawn, for which the radio was turned up loud.

After the Pig closed for the night, if Pat had more roaring in him, he retreated to the Broadway Motel coffee shop. One night he stayed out late enough that Arminta had to track him down; she brought along Jerry so she could tell their boy, "Son, I don't want you to grow up to be this way."

Pat imparted a belief in the value of hard work to his son, along with a willingness to take on risk. The elder Jones built more supermarkets with bank loans before cashing out to buy the Modern

Security Life Insurance Company of Springfield, Missouri. Selling insurance was the best kind of selling there was. All the customers wanted it once they were informed how much they needed it, and it didn't spoil or suffer from theft like the groceries did.

Pat Jones told his son, "I knew I was never going to be a millionaire, so I just decided to try to borrow a million."

When Jerry wasn't working for his father honing his sales skills, he was falling in love with the game of football. He quarterbacked the Fourth Street Junior High team to an undefeated season in ninth grade and started piling on carbs to bulk up enough to play fullback for North Little Rock High School. He liked the camaraderie and the hitting. He and his best friend, Jerry Sisk, enjoyed "knocking the shit out of each other," as he later put it, as a form of practice. In his senior year at North Little Rock, the Charging Wildcats beat Little Rock Central, their traditional rival, who usually dominated, but they lost to Conway High, a defeat so crushing, Sisk and Jones led the entire team to the First Baptist Church on a Sunday morning to apologize directly to Coach Albright, who was sitting in his pew.

Jerry Jones arrived at the University of Arkansas in the deep hills of Fayetteville with a sculpted flattop and a fixed, friendly smile. A diamond pinkie ring adorned the little finger of the hand steering his Cadillac Eldorado. Fellow students recognized his salesmanship, since he sold them shoes, insurance, and tickets to football games and peddled student tickets on their behalf. He was that rare soul who broadcast the fact that he was *somebody* when he walked into a room.

Jerry Jones's freshman coach, Barry Switzer, sized him up as a player with a whole lot of "hustle and try-hard...who could look you in the eye and talk right through you." Switzer moved Jones from running back to guard.

At six feet and 185 pounds, Jones was a fine physical specimen, although slightly undersized for a lineman. With racial segregation still keeping blacks out of the Southwest Conference in 1960, scrappy and determined white boys like himself could not only earn full scholarships but also shine on the field.

His freshman year, Jerry met Eugenia "Gene" Chambers, the 1960 Miss Arkansas USA and onetime Arkansas Poultry Princess from Danville. It was a blur of a romance. The gorgeous small-town banker's daughter fell for the charismatic moon-eyed son of the grocery-and-insurance empire builder. Raven-haired with riveting eyes and a wide smile, Gene was the most beautiful woman Jerry had ever known. They dated, he proposed, she said yes, and they married at the end of their sophomore year.

As a junior, Jones roomed for road games with Jimmy Johnson, a rough-and-tumble kid from Port Arthur, Texas. As seniors, Jones at offensive guard and Johnson at defensive tackle were key players on the national champion Razorbacks, along with Ronnie Caveness, Jim Lindsey, Loyd Phillips, Harry Jones, Jim Williams, and Dick and Ken Hatfield. The Frank Broyles–coached team went undefeated, beating the Nebraska Cornhuskers 10–7 in the Cotton Bowl on New Year's Day 1965. The Alabama Crimson Tide, the only other major college team that had gone undefeated that season, under the guidance of Coach Bear Bryant and All-American quarterback Joe Namath, lost 17–13 to Arkansas's nemesis, the Texas Longhorns, in the Orange Bowl on the same day.

After graduation, Jerry Jones pursued a master's degree in business, sold insurance, and recruited salesmen for Modern Security Life, where he was executive vice president.

Learning from his father, he took on as much debt as he could, borrowing $50,000 from John Ed Chambers, his father-in-law, to invest in Shakey's pizza parlor franchises around Springfield, Missouri, and buy into Tyson Foods of Springdale, Arkansas. He was so overextended that he almost went broke before his calculated bets began to pay off.

But Jones's eye was on a bigger prize. A year out of college, Jones met with Joe Robbie of the new Miami expansion franchise in the start-up American Football League. He wanted to buy a small piece of the Dolphins franchise. Robbie didn't extend an offer to Jones, but he did answer enough of the young man's questions for Jones to make a run at the San Diego Chargers of the AFL, who were put up for sale by owner Barron Hilton in early 1966. Jones rounded up a motley crew of investors and offered $5.8 million for 85 percent of the franchise. Pat Jones intervened and convinced his son to put the brakes on the deal. The financials Jerry had put together were shaky. Six months later, the Chargers sold for almost twice the price. Jerry's skills may have needed polishing, and his ability to put together an investor group needed vetting, but his instincts were on target.

While Jones expanded his business interests, his wife, Gene, raised Stephen, born in 1964; Charlotte, born in 1966; and Jerry Jr., born in 1969. The year that Jerry Jr. arrived, Pat Jones sold his insurance company, and Jerry Sr. moved his family to Little Rock, establishing residence in Pleasant Valley, an exclusive country-club golf-course subdivision. He later located his office where he could watch his son Stephen practice as quarterback for Catholic High School. Stephen gave up a chance to go to Princeton so he could play linebacker at Arkansas, his parents' alma mater, under the tutelage of Ken Hatfield, who got the Arkansas head coach job over Jimmy Johnson, who was now the head coach at Oklahoma State.

Jones eventually shifted his business focus to oil and gas, starting as an independent operator by leasing land from major oil companies in the Red Fork Sand northwest of Oklahoma City and east of the Texas Panhandle and drilling between existing wells in fields no longer being explored. He struck oil on twelve of his first thirteen plays, with the first well yielding $4 million in oil. His Oklahoma connections allowed him to party with his old freshman coach, Barry Switzer—who had become head coach at the University of Oklahoma and was overseeing one of the most successful college football programs anywhere—and with Switzer's defensive coordinator Larry Lacewell, another Arkansas native.

Jones also sponsored his old friend Jimmy Johnson's coach's show, which aired on television across Oklahoma, even though Jones didn't have anything to sell as an advertiser except himself.

In less than ten years, Jones made $50 million from the Red Fork Sand. Life was good. But he was never quite satisfied. "I've never gone to sleep a night yet without wanting something more to drink," Jones liked to say, explaining his unquenchable thirst for the next deal.

In 1980, he entered into a business partnership with Mike McCoy, the smart, energetic head of another independent, Texas Oil and Gas. They immediately bonded. "Jerry has never met a high-risk deal that he didn't like," McCoy said. "He's a risk taker, and the riskier, the better." They founded Arkoma Production Company in Fort Smith, the hub city of western Arkansas.

Their first drilling venture lost big-time, but the next play, in Latimer County in southeast Oklahoma, brought $40 million in revenues. Gas plays in the San Joaquin Valley of central California brought in another $40 million in the first two years of their partnership. By the end of the 1980s, Jones's net worth headed north toward $300 million.

Some of that wealth came at the expense of Arkansas utility customers. In 1983, the state utility that delivered gas to Arkansas residents, Arkansas-Louisiana Gas Inc., agreed to purchase all the gas Arkoma could produce at a set rate higher than ArkLa was paying other producers. The head of ArkLa, Sheffield Nelson, had partnered with Jerry Jones in various business ventures, including a TV station, racehorses, farms, and condominiums.

Arkoma made major discoveries in the Cecil and Aetna fields in the Arkoma Basin. In 1985, the gas industry was deregulated and prices dropped, but ArkLa was still committed to pay $4.50 per thousand cubic feet for all the gas Arkoma could bring, compared to 50 cents per thousand being paid to other producers.

Mack McLarty, who replaced Sheffield Nelson as president and CEO of ArkLa when Nelson resigned, in 1984, noted that ArkLa was paying Arkoma $40 million a year for gas it didn't need. The only way out for ArkLa was to buy Arkoma for what would total close to $174 million.

Sheffield Nelson ran for governor of Arkansas in 1990 as a Republican. A lawsuit filed earlier that year accusing ArkLa of fraud, favoritism, and self-dealing with Arkoma turned into a campaign issue. The Arkansas Public Service Commission investigated and concluded ArkLa unnecessarily spent between $59 million and $97 million to buy Arkoma and had to refund ratepayers $21.4 million. The controversy was arguably the deciding factor in Nelson's loss to the Democratic Party nominee, Bill Clinton.

The gas business gave Jerry a growing familiarity with Dallas, because that's where the banks were, and where the Dallas Cowboys reigned as America's Team, regardless of their recent record. As an unreconstructed football nut, Jerry Jones couldn't help but notice. The NFL was bigger than the Arkansas Razorbacks, the Texas Longhorns, the Texas Aggies, the old Southwest Conference, and the Southeastern Conference even.

Before completing the purchase of the team, Jones sought advice from several owners, general managers, and coaches, including San Francisco head coach Bill Walsh and general manager John McVay. He also consulted Dan Burke, then the president of ABC. "Burke told me you have 2,000 producers in Hollywood working on the perfect script, but there is no way to capture the soap opera effect of what goes on around the NFL game during the week," Jones would later relate.

He knew what he was buying. He just didn't know what he was getting into. Reporters from both Dallas papers, as well as the Fort Worth daily, already watched the Cowboys like hawks. If something was up, each paper wanted to break the story. Which explained the intrepid reporter clandestinely watching the lobby of the Mansion on Turtle Creek on a Friday afternoon in late February of 1989.

The reporter had been tipped off to look for Jerry Jones or Jimmy

Johnson. The men had arrived separately, both with their wives, who had been sorority sisters and roommates. Johnson had been 52-9 in his five years at Miami, where his teams developed a rep as the Bad Boys of College Football—mean, nasty fellows who fought, spit, kicked, and did whatever it took while displaying big chips on their shoulders. For all their thuggishness, inattention to academics, and tendency to showboat, the Hurricanes won, which was what counted most. And Johnson was ready to test his mettle in the pros.

As for Schramm, Jones wasn't impressed by the general manager and president, no matter how powerful he was. If he was that good, the Cowboys wouldn't be in the dumpster. Hell, Jerry could do what Tex was doing and do it better. He knew how to sell. Tex had gotten lazy and fat and had lost his edge.

Schramm learned about the sale two nights before it happened, when Channel 5's sports director, Scott Murray, announced on KXAS TV's Texas News program that Jones was acquiring the club.

Dale Hansen had been called back to Channel 8 while emceeing a banquet after their news director heard the Channel 5 teasers to tune in at 10:00 p.m. for an exclusive report on the Cowboys' new owners. When Hansen arrived, his producers showed him the Scott Murray Channel 5 promo: "The Cowboys have been sold, details at 10."

Hansen immediately called Schramm and asked, "What's going on?"

"Nothing," Schramm said.

"C'mon, Tex, I'm your guy, I'm the Cowboys color analyst."

"There's no story there, Dale. There's nothing to it."

"I'll call you back after the report," Hansen told him.

"I'll wait for your call."

Murray's extensive report at ten o'clock detailed that Jerry Jones was buying the team and that Landry was going to be fired.

Hansen called Schramm back.

"Our young boy in Fort Worth has just fucked up his entire

499

career," Schramm said when he answered the phone. "That stupid fucker is dead."

"The report sounded credible," Hansen allowed.

Schramm shot back: "Do you really think they'd sell the Cowboys and I wouldn't fuckin' know about it?"

But Bum Bright had done exactly that. Keeping Schramm and Landry out of the loop until all the i's were dotted and the t's were crossed had been Bright's plan.

"Bright wanted Schramm and Landry to be stuck just like they were," Hansen said. "He reveled in it. He called me bragging about it—'Schramm spent more of my money buying goddamn houses for his girlfriends, and that sonofabitch Landry treated me like shit. To hell with both of them.'"

Schramm spent Murchison's money like it wasn't his own. If it *were* his own money, he wouldn't have spent so much. Clint Murchison never cared. He made a $600,000 investment that he sold for $81 million and had enjoyed twenty-five years of owning the Dallas Cowboys. He didn't care that Schramm donkeyed off $300,000 for media parties. Bum Bright cared, but Schramm still viewed owners as money guys who didn't meddle and he continued to have enough stroke to tell Bright to stay over in the corner. For the most part, Bum had. Until now.

Scott Murray's information turned out to be solid. A nephew of Jones had tipped off a television station executive in Arkansas about the pending sale, and the exec leaked to Murray.

On Friday morning, Schramm heard the rumor repeated by his friend Don Shula, the coach of the Miami Dolphins. Jimmy Johnson had called Shula's son David to gauge his interest in coaching the Cowboys offense. Schramm finally realized what was about to happen, and it happened quickly.

Jerry Rhome, who was an assistant for San Diego, was watching film with Landry at Valley Ranch that afternoon when Tex Schramm walked in the door and told the coach he needed to talk to him outside. Landry returned in a few minutes, said nothing, and Rhome turned on the film again. A couple minutes later, Rhome looked over at Tom and saw tears in his eyes. "I've been fired," Landry told him. He wished Rhome well in his coaching career and exited Valley Ranch.

On Friday night, Jerry Jones and Jimmy Johnson left the Mansion on Turtle Creek, where they had been holed up for the afternoon with their spouses, preparing to close the deal with Bright the next day. Linda Kay Johnson was hungry. Jones said there was a little Mexican place on Lemmon that hardly anyone knew about. So the four of them trotted over to Mia's on Lemmon Avenue, a storefront in a strip mall that also happened to be Tom and Alicia Landry's favorite Tex-Mex restaurant. No sooner had the party sat down and ordered beers than Ivan Maisel, a sportswriter who covered college football for the *Morning News*, tapped Johnson on the shoulder. Maisel and his fiancée lived a block from Mia's. They had headed there after Maisel had spent the afternoon staking out the Mansion, looking for Jones or Johnson.

"Oh shit, what are you doing here?" Johnson said once he recognized Maisel.

A photographer had already been summoned. Fifteen minutes later, he stood before the table at Mia's with Jimmy Johnson begging him not to take their picture. Jerry Jones told the shooter to go ahead and take all the shots he wanted. He was ready for the spotlight.

Seven years earlier, when Jimmy Johnson coached at Oklahoma State and Jerry Jones was doing gas plays throughout the Arkoma basin, Jones had told Johnson they would be together running an NFL franchise soon enough. Here they were.

Jones and Johnson showed up at Bright's office in the Bright Banc building on Stemmons Expressway at six on Saturday morning accompanied by a team of lawyers, secretaries, and accountants. The price they had agreed on was $140 million for the football club and the stadium lease—more than had ever been paid for an NFL franchise. Jones pledged more than $80 million to banks and his limited partners. A Texas bank held one $40 million note.

A $300,000 difference in the price was settled by a coin toss. Jones flipped the coin, which hit the ceiling and a wall before landing in an ashtray in Bright's office. Jones, who had called tails, rushed to see the coin, Bright remained at his desk. Heads was up.

"As far as I'm concerned, Jerry is as square as a graham cracker," Bum Bright declared after the purchase. "He did exactly what he said he would do. He paid the money, and he paid in cash. I have nothing but the highest regard for how he handled the transaction."

Bright would later buy a two-headed quarter from a magic shop and send it to Jones with a note that read: *You'll never know.*

Bright was happy to be relieved of ownership. He had effectively doubled his money in five years by owning the Cowboys, blunting his other losses.

Jones was on the flip side. By buying the Dallas Cowboys, he had gone all in, risking his accumulated wealth while inheriting a $30 million debt.

Once the ink was dry, Texas Earnest Schramm came face to face with Jerral Wayne Jones, the new owner of the Dallas Cowboys, at Bright's office. Walking into Bright's inner sanctum, a visibly irritated Schramm spied Johnson and said, "You need to get your ass out of town. You people have embarrassed Tom Landry enough already."

Bright reintroduced Jones to Schramm. When they had met the previous fall, Jones hadn't left much of an impression besides the fact he was a young Arkansas oil and gas multimillionaire with a whole lot of swagger. This time was different. The forty-six-year-old Jones did not beat around the bush when he made clear his intentions. "To tell you the truth, you've got my job," Jones informed Schramm. "But based on what Bum has told me, I want you to stay on as an adviser to me."

Brash meets brasher. Tex Schramm had gotten used to being the commanding presence in a room. Jerry Jones, the purchaser of the Dallas Cowboys Football Club, made a point of showing him up. He was the new big, swinging dick. If being a successful, self-made man of means made him come off as arrogant, so be it. Arkansas Big Rich was about to become Dallas Big Rich by taking the reins of the biggest show in town.

Bum Bright suggested to Jones that Schramm should be the one to tell Landry what was going on. (The coach had seen the full-color photograph of Jones and Johnson leering at him from the front page of Saturday's *Morning News* and had split, piloting his family in their Cessna 210 from Love Field to their golf-course home near the Lakeway resort west of Austin, two hundred miles south.)

Jones disagreed. "I have to face him," he said firmly. "I can't do this unless I face him personally." A man couldn't do business without manning up. Anyway, the public relations firms in Dallas and Washington, DC, that he had consulted recommended he do the deed.

That afternoon, Jones and Schramm flew in Jones's Lear 35A to Robert Mueller Airport in Austin, where they rented a car and drove to Lakeway. Schramm had called ahead to give Landry a heads-up: they needed to talk about the future. They found coach and son practicing their putts on the Hidden Hills golf course's putting green in the waning light. The group retreated to an empty sales office.

Jones introduced himself to Landry, informing him, "I'm here and so is Jimmy." It was Jones's clumsy way of saying Jimmy Johnson was part of the new ownership group and that Landry was fired. Landry knew what was coming; he had choked up talking with Gil Brandt in a phone call the day before.

"You could have saved yourself a trip," Landry replied flatly. "You could have handled this whole thing a lot better. This is just grandstanding. You could have saved your gas.

"You've taken my team away from me." Landry's blue eyes burned holes into the Arkansan's skull.

Landry and Schramm shook hands, both with tears streaming

down their cheeks. It was over. No recourse, no appeal, no *nada*. Their dynasty was done.

Jones would later acknowledge the meeting had not gone the way he had imagined. "I was basically just trying to say something you just can't say," he admitted. And he hadn't said anything very well. He claimed it was the first time he'd ever fired an employee face to face. Before, he'd let others do it for him.

"I wanted to be a stand-up guy, do it myself," he said. "I felt I was not a man if I did not go down there and do it myself. And my gut was telling me I needed to have a personal dialogue with Coach Landry."

Before the press conference that Saturday evening back at Valley Ranch, publicist Doug Todd spoke to Jones while he was shaving and putting on a fresh shirt in Tex's private restroom. Schramm suggested that Todd let Jones know what to expect. Todd offered some talking points, but Jones waved him off. "I can handle it," he replied confidently.

The three major local news stations, Channels 4, 5, and 8, interrupted regular network programming to carry the press conference live. Minority owner Ed Smith took Tex's chair at the press conference, leaving Tex standing as he fought tears. "It was a very difficult meeting," Schramm told the gathering of reporters, speaking of the Jones-Landry encounter. "It's very, very sad. It's tough when you break a relationship you've had for twenty-nine years. That's an awful long time."

Landry took it hard, Schramm said. "For Tom, he was emotional."

"I just met him today," Jerry Jones said of Tom Landry at the press conference, following Schramm's remarks. Then he practically crowed, "It feels like Christmas." Jones rambled for several minutes and praised Landry. "He was magnificent to me for what he had been through. He's special. Tom Landry is the Cowboys."

Or was. Jones liked his new guy better. "I have so much respect for Jimmy Johnson," Jones told the reporters. "He doesn't fish much, and he doesn't play golf much. He footballs. Coaching is so fortunate to have him. Doctoring, the medical profession, could have a Jimmy Johnson, a surgeon or an engineer."

Jones made plain he was committed. "I will sell my house in Little Rock and move to Dallas," he vowed. "My entire office and my entire business will be at [the Cowboys] complex. This will be a hands-on operation. I want to know everything there is to know, from player contracts to socks and jocks and television contracts. This is my company, and I will be making all the decisions. The Cowboys will be my life!"

After he was asked where Tex stood, Jones used the press conference to further put Tex Schramm in his place. "Tex is used to standing out front, but he's a little behind me here tonight. He's still going to be an important part of the Cowboys, but it's my vote. I'm the owner."

Jones's eyes were bloodshot. It had been a long day. Schramm looked like all the air had gone out of him. After the press conference, he invited reporters into his office for a scotch wake. "I have a lot of work to do with this son-of-a-bitch," the general manager said determinedly. "Goddammit, I can't believe he'd say those things."

Down the hall, Jones and his posse watched a replay of the ten o'clock newscasts, the posse cheering Jones's name every time it was mentioned, as they had at the press conference. But when the reporters started analyzing what had just transpired, the cheering stopped and the Jones gang left Valley Ranch to continue partying elsewhere.

Tom Landry returned to Dallas on Sunday and emptied his office that afternoon. "It hurts, but I don't feel bitterness right now," he told a reporter before voicing his reliance on faith. "I try not to feel bad when things happen that I have no control over. I always accept things as they are, so I don't worry. Besides, Jones and Johnson were buddies and this was going to happen."

"Shock. Disbelief. Anger" shouted the headline of the *Morning*

News lead editorial on Sunday. Frank Luksa railed about "the undignified, thoughtless manner [Landry] was fired Saturday." The *Morning News*'s David Casstevens called Jones "dumber than a box of rocks, public relations–wise."

Commissioner Pete Rozelle eulogized. "This is like Lombardi's death," he said. "There are relatively few coaches whose careers compare with Tom. No question he's a Hall of Famer in my opinion. He's not only been an outstanding coach but a tremendous role model for kids and our fans. He has contributed a tremendous amount to the league."

Bob Lilly weighed in, admitting, "A lot of old Cowboys are crying tonight."

A few people, including some NFL franchise owners, were not sad to see Landry go. "The other owners respected and admired him but they also resented him because he was so successful," observed Russ Russell, the *Cowboys Weekly* publisher. "The Rooneys and Maras worked so hard to build what they had and here comes Tex and in fifteen years he's built America's Team. That grated on them. Drafting, free agents, all this was brand-new. But the rest of the league had caught up with the Cowboys. Our drafts weren't spectacular anymore because everyone had the same information. Tom had diminished capacities coaching. People that were brought in to help like Hackett, he shoved aside. He still did everything himself. He still had three assistants. He's still calling goal line plays. Danny White said he sent in the wrong team on a goal line play."

The Greek chorus concurred. Landry had been like "a bankrupt baron sitting in a castle," wrote David Casstevens. "The electricity was off, the furniture covered, the servants gone. But he still dressed for dinner every night."

While Landry cleaned out his office, he told a reporter, "I was looking forward to this year. I thought it was going to be a tremendous challenge. But that's over with. It's a chapter closed. This is the worst scenario, I guess, but I'm not bitter."

On Monday, he spoke for the last time to his team, who had gathered at Valley Ranch for an offseason training session. He began his address in the auditorium saying, "I never thought the hardest thing I'd ever do was tell you goodbye. You're a great bunch of football players. This is a pretty tough moment for me." He got through half of his prepared remarks before he broke down sobbing. His players gave him a standing ovation as he departed.

The calls for Landry's head, heard throughout three decades of the team's existence, had finally been heeded. But suddenly he was missed. Landry was a family man, churchgoing and honest. People didn't like the way the new owner sounded or how he came off on television. Jerry Jones didn't care. He wanted more. Jack Dixon, Jones's treasurer, suggested to publicist Doug Todd that Jones go on all the local television talk shows "since the iron's so hot." Todd said he'd have to talk to Tex. Dixon cut him off. There would no longer be a need to talk to Tex, Dixon said, walking out of the room.

On Monday, shortly after Tom Landry had said good-bye to his team, Jerry Jones found a friendlier audience: the Arkansas General Assembly, which officially recognized him for buying the Cowboys. He told the gathering of lawmakers in Little Rock that two death threats against him had already been reported back in Dallas but that they were "an emotional reaction to Coach Landry," not him. As if.

Johnson backed him up. At a dinner in Little Rock a few months later, Jimmy testified. "Everybody says that Jerry Jones is lucky. Well, let me tell you how to get lucky. Become the hardest-working son of a bitch in America, then you'll get lucky, too."

Jones was a hero in Arkansas. His former football coach and University of Arkansas athletic director Frank Broyles spoke for the entire state in praising Jones. "When Jerry bought the Cowboys, he put Arkansas back on the map. People didn't have much to cheer about around here."

Jimmy Johnson got his own baptism by fire at his first press conference, held on Tuesday, February 29, in front of a hive of two hundred angry inquisitors, the largest turnout ever at a Cowboys press conference, according to longtime Associated Press reporter Denne Freeman. The *Houston Post*'s Dale Robertson compared the atmosphere to that of a "lynch mob." One reporter even asked if Johnson had failed a polygraph test involving a recruit when he was an assistant at Arkansas. "I'm sure there have been more hostile press conferences, but I've never seen one," Blackie Sherrod told Bob West from Johnson's hometown *Port Arthur News.* "The funny thing is, most of the hostility came from people who wanted to string up Tom Landry two years ago."

Johnson kept his game face on, explaining that he flew to Dallas Friday thinking Jones wanted to talk face to face about the Cowboys job, although at one point, he did remark, "This has been a grind." Repeatedly, he stressed he meant no disrespect to Coach Landry.

"This is the most incredibly negative situation I've ever seen in this town," remarked columnist Randy Galloway, who became a Johnson admirer during the process. "If Jimmy thinks the press was tough on him, he should be thankful the fans weren't in there. But I sure like the way he handled himself."

The Arkansas connections provided the DFW media with plenty of ammo. Jerry Jones became known as Jethro, the name of the unpolished, crass lead character in the 1960s-era television comedy *The Beverly Hillbillies.*

Six months before he was cut from the roster at training camp, outside linebacker Jeff Rohrer was videotaped singing the theme from *The Beverly Hillbillies* with his own improvised lyrics:

> *The first thing you know ol' Jer's a millionaire.*
> *The kinfolks said, Jer, move away from here.*
> *They said, Dallas, Texas, is the place you wanna be,*
> *So he hopped in his Lear and bought America's Team.*

Jones tried to deflect the criticisms good-naturedly. He knew any kind of publicity was good publicity. "It is not all bad for the NFL," he said. "It's certainly not bad for the Cowboys. I think there are people who haven't watched NFL football much in Missouri or Ohio and are aware something is going on with the Dallas Cowboys."

For the first forty days, Jerry and his wife, Gene, lived at the DFW Airport Marriott while he scrambled to fix the organization he'd just purchased. Jimmy Johnson and his wife, Linda Kay, moved into a condo three blocks from Cowboys headquarters, but Jimmy wasn't there much. His full-time residence was Valley Ranch, where he rejiggered the coaching staff: he brought in six of his assistants from the University of Miami, keeping four Cowboy holdovers, and hired offensive coordinator David Shula from the Miami Dolphins and quarterback coach Jerry Rhome from the San Diego Chargers. A refrigerator was stocked with green bottles of Heineken beer, Jimmy's favorite drink.

On the presentability front, Greg Aiello, the Cowboys marketing director, got a call from Republican Party politico Jim Francis, Bum Bright's former aide. Francis suggested that Jones get some media training from Fairchild and LeMaster, a media consulting firm that showed clients how to deal with television cameras and reporters' questions. Jerry recognized he needed guidance and listened closely, learning among other things that every comment he made to the media people should actually be directed to fans.

He had perfected a stump speech he enjoyed delivering to Rotary Clubs and other civic groups in Arkansas and surrounding states, and it explained his viewpoint as well as anything: "Business is a contact sport. If you're not moving forward, you'll get run over." But now he needed to do outreach in Texas.

On the Thursday after Black Saturday, Jones called department heads together at Valley Ranch to offer reassurance. There wasn't a finer management team in the NFL than the one standing in front of him. "The key thing is that I need you more than you need me," he told them. "There will not be any more changes in this office. I really don't know how to run a football team. I need all of you."

Afterward, he told reporters, "There shouldn't be any worries here."

Then Jones moved into Tex Schramm's office, the biggest executive space at Valley Ranch, and cleared the decks. Over the next few weeks, every day, Jones was shown a slip from his accountant detailing how much money was being saved by cutting overhead. That's because every day, Jones slashed and burned. Treasurer Don Wilson was fired. Tex's number-two man, Joe Bailey, left before he could be fired. Bob Friedman, director of photographic services, retired. Pat Miller in payroll and Ann Lloyd, a twenty-two-year veteran in the ticket office, were dismissed. Doug Todd, the publicist with eighteen years of experience, was called into Jack Dixon's office and told "This is not going to be a good meeting" before he was whacked; it would take a call from Pete Rozelle to get Todd his severance pay. Despite the fact that Jimmy Johnson had brought along Rich Dalrymple, the director of sports information at the University of Miami, making Todd dispensable, Jerry Jones had previously told Todd, "Everything in your department is number one." That was then. This was now. Band director Bill Lively was retained but the band was axed; the sixty seats they occupied in the end zone could be sold to customers.

Tommy Loy, whose solo rendition of the national anthem had been a constant since the opening of Texas Stadium, was let go. *Four* trumpet players would replace him. Travel agency head Dan Werner, who oversaw construction of Valley Ranch, got the Ted Mack hook. Carlton Stowers resigned as editor of the *Dallas Cowboys Weekly*. His replacement, Jarrett Bell, would be canned shortly thereafter.

Suzanne Mitchell quit as director of the Dallas Cowboys Cheerleaders. Her replacement, Debbie Bond, lasted six weeks. In June, fourteen cheerleaders resigned after Jones tried to do away with Suzanne Mitchell's rules forbidding club employees to fraternize with cheerleaders and preventing the Dallas Cowboys Cheerleaders from appearing at events where beer, wine, or liquor was served. Thirteen returned when Jones insisted the proposal was a misunderstanding. "They're the pick of the litter," he said, defending their virtue.

New management did not waste time; they continued to clean house, throwing out all the extras that Jones thought made the organization too fat. Training camp was reconsidered because Thousand Oaks was costing the team $500,000 a year. The scouting budget was slashed from $3 million to $1 million.

Jones saw Texas Stadium as an underutilized cash cow. Only six of the 188 luxury suites added to the top of Texas Stadium by Bum Bright had been purchased or leased. His sales people went out and leased twenty-eight new boxes, adding $18 million to the positive cash flow, revenues that belonged solely to the Cowboys and were not shared with the league the way ticket sales were.

Texas Stadium was devoid of corporate logos, advertising being a potential revenue stream that Tex Schramm considered beneath the dignity of the franchise. Jones, however, welcomed advertising inside and outside the stadium. He added seats wherever he could, including behind obstructions. He took Clint Murchison's personal-seat-license concept up a notch with ProSeat, a company he created to compel season-ticket holders to spend $1,000 to $15,000 to dib prime seats; the price of the seat depended on its location, and that premium was on top of the actual cost of a ticket. To provide more attractive seating to potential buyers, he recalled complimentary season tickets provided to former players, personnel, and friends of the football club.

Though he pissed off ex-players, who could no longer get free tickets, and saw lawsuits from angry ticket holders who didn't like being moved, having to pay ProSeat extra money for what they already had, and paying for playoff tickets even when the game was played in another city, Jones created at least five thousand new seats, bringing in another $10 million annually.

Jones pushed the Irving City Council to grant the stadium a license to sell beer and wine, persuading the council that individual sales on-site would cut down on drunk driving. That added another $1 million in annual revenues. He opened a blue-and-white party tent on the parking lot outside the stadium, named it the Corral, charged admission, and sold six-dollar frozen margaritas to fans.

Then he threatened to move the Cowboys' headquarters from Valley Ranch to Texas Stadium until the mortgage company holding the note agreed to discount Jones's monthly payments by 40 percent.

Jimmy Johnson joined the wrecking crew, tracking down former employees who were still tooling around Big D in company cars, sending out letters reminding ex-staffers that only current employees could use the Brookhaven Country Club golf course, and reducing his scouting staff to four, relying instead on his assistants, who had recruited in college and would scout the pros.

Tex Schramm hated what he was seeing. "You could tell right from the beginning that he didn't give a damn about history," Schramm said of Jones. "You can tell this man has absolutely no feeling for the past. You almost expected him to take the stars off the helmets."

Schramm had run the football club like a family. Jones wanted to run it like a business.

Russ Russell saw the sharp contrast in philosophies up close. "When Jerry came in, he didn't know shit about anything, obviously, but he's very imaginative and he's a good businessman," Russell said. "He looks around and says, 'I don't understand. Why do we have empty suites? Somebody should be selling those suites. They're worth a fortune.'

"Before Jerry, the Cowboys didn't sponsor beer, and the cheerleaders didn't sponsor anything. Tex would not promote the Cowboys for money, would not use them to endorse beer or sponsor grocery stores or brick companies. That was beneath it all. That wasn't the league he saw. He wouldn't let the cheerleaders appear anywhere liquor was sold. It's like he wanted me to fly first class. I told him I could save hundreds of dollars flying coach. He'd say, 'No, no we don't do that. Everyone goes first class.' That's why they took the writers to the Velvet Turtle or Bookbinders.

"Jerry wanted everyone to get business cards from the same printer. He said, 'We need to be watching the paper clips.' What? That's not the Cowboy way. They wanted everything run through their sponsorship. That's good business, but it's a different way of doing business.

"You could throw an idea at Jerry and he'd throw it back with a twist, instantaneously. I understood Jerry. If I went and bought a grocery store, I wouldn't want anyone telling me how to run my store. If I want to stock cans or be a butcher, I can. It's my store."

Long before Jones's arrival, Joe Bailey had taken away Russell's title and salary as publisher of the *Cowboys Weekly*, but Russell had continued taking photographs for the publication because he liked hanging around the team. A few weeks after Jerry Jones took control, Jack Dixon called Russell into his office to find out how the weekly newspaper was run and why it was losing money.

"You work for us?" Dixon asked Russell.

"I don't know," Russell told him, mentioning he'd received the form letter from Jimmy Johnson that former employees' golf privileges at Brookhaven Country Club had been eliminated.

"Jerry wants to know what he should do with the weekly," Dixon told Russell. "It lost sixty-five thousand dollars last year."

"I'd sell it," Russell advised.

"Who would buy it?" Dixon asked.

"I would," Russell said. "If I could get a seat on the plane [to away games and training camp], I'd pay you a hundred and fifty thousand for it." Russell thought the weekly was losing money because Joe Bailey didn't know how to run it.

Dixon offered a salary of $50,000 a year. Russell said he'd prefer $40,000 and 10 percent of the net profit.

Dixon asked how profitable the paper could be. Russell reckoned $1 million annually.

Russell got the job.

Russell immediately changed printers to save $120,000. He generated $65,000 for the club by marketing a Cowboys calendar that utilized stock photos.

When Russell got face time with the big boss, he convinced Jerry Jones to spend $60,000 for a Cowboys Are Reloading ad campaign for the weekly.

"How much money would we make?" Jones asked Russell.

"We'd be lucky to break even."

"Why would we want to do that then?"

"Because next year, for the cost of a nine-cent stamp, I can double that because ninety percent will renew."

"Do it," Jones said, walking away.

Russell took over the game-day programs, too, which were losing money. His pay for that was 10 percent of the net, no salary. The weekly would realize a $100,000 profit for 1989.

Making the Cowboys money got Russell on Jones's good side. When Jerry Jones Jr., his brother, Stephen, and his sister, Charlotte, were brought into the front office, Jerry Jr. was put in charge of the Internet. The Cowboys were farseeing enough to want to integrate its use into the organization but wary enough to let Junior handle what appeared to be a low-risk investment. Then, when Junior wanted to put articles about the Cowboys from the weekly on the Internet for free, Russell blanched. He found an ally in Junior's father, who kept his son on a short leash.

When Russell proposed giving away subscriptions to ticket holders to improve circulation in Dallas–Fort Worth, Jerry suggested including the subscription in the price of a ticket. That way, he wouldn't have to share with the other owners under the league's revenue guidelines, which Jerry Jones was bent on changing.

Jack Dixon continued looking to add value. So when he was

informed that a group from Austin wanted the Cowboys to move training camp from Thousand Oaks, California, to the capital city of Texas, Dixon sat down with Chuck Taylor, the front man for the Austin Chamber of Commerce's sports commission.

"If you want to carry these discussions forward, a check for the amount of $1,000,000 deposited in our account would demonstrate your sincerity," Dixon bluntly informed Taylor. Taylor emptied out his wallet and threw a couple of hundred in bills on the table.

"That's all I've got." He smiled. Taylor knew who he was talking to. The former Oklahoma Sooner player's sister worked for Arkoma, the oil and gas exploration company owned by Mike McCoy and Jerry Jones and where Jack Dixon had been the chief financial officer.

Taylor and a secret committee that included Lee Cooke, Austin's mayor; Pat Hayes, the president of St. Edward's University; *Austin American-Statesman* sportswriter Kirk Bohls; and KXAN Channel 36 sportscaster Drew Speier had done their homework. They had been meeting for months and on the sly prepared a video presentation that showed the facilities at St. Ed's and featured the mayor issuing a personal request to Jerry Jones to consider moving training camp to Austin.

Taylor's trump card was Coach Mike Parker, the University of Texas assistant coach who had played at Arkansas and who knew Jones and Jimmy Johnson personally. Coach Parker spoke Coach Johnson's language and used his part of the video pitch to show off St. Ed's training facilities and the other amenities he knew a coach would look for.

As far as Jimmy Johnson was concerned, Austin's heat and humidity were positives. Thousand Oaks, California, and its salubrious summer climate and convenient proximity to LA was for pussies (and for pussy, for those players, coaches, and front-office types with West Coast girlfriends). Johnson had built national college championship teams by training his men in the swampy atmosphere of southern Florida. Austin would be a fine place to prepare his players—those good and strong enough to make the roster.

After several more meetings with Jack Dixon and sit-downs with Stephen Jones, Chuck Taylor and company finally got an audience with Jerry Jones. There remained a historic wariness toward Austin on Jones's part; Jerry and Jimmy had traveled to Austin to play the University of Texas Longhorns when they were Razorbacks, and there was still a lingering soreness over Arkansas's loss to Texas in the 1969 Big Shootout, one of the best regular-season college match-ups ever, in which number-one-ranked Texas scored all of their points in the fourth quarter for a come-from-behind victory over number-two-ranked Arkansas, winning 15–14.

But the endorsement of fellow Razorback Mike Parker went a long way toward tamping down misgivings about doing business in what once was regarded as enemy territory. So did Jones's real estate investment on the booming northwestern fringe of Austin in a mixed-use project called Riata.

But the owner was blunt about the Cowboys' fan base, gathering the Austin delegation around a map of Texas and drawing a line across the state through Waco. "Everything south of here is Oilers' territory," Jones said. "We've lost the Hispanic fans and we've lost San Antonio and all of South Texas. We need to get them back."

Holding training camp in Austin looked like a pretty good way to do that.

Jones told Austin's Mayor Cooke, "You pay us and we'll come."

Cooke did not flinch. "No, you come. We'll build it for you." Cooke pointed out Austin was the only star on the map that matched the star on the Cowboy helmet.

That didn't prevent the owner from seeking the best deal possi-ble. Jones brought up the recent interest expressed by business lead-ers in Tyler, one hundred miles east of Dallas, to stage training camp there. Tyler would not tap into the demographic and region Jones craved most, but it did provide a bargaining chip. As with all his ventures, Jerry Jones was always looking for an edge.

As word leaked out about Austin's wooing, Thousand Oaks; Wichita Falls, Texas; and San Antonio also offered bids. But by then Austin had become a lock, especially after financial incentives were added to sweeten the arrangement.

The move would be formally announced in December of 1989 at dual press conferences at Valley Ranch and St. Edward's University in Austin. The city, the chamber of commerce, and the university were all thrilled about camp bringing crowds to town during what were traditionally the slowest weeks on the tourist calendar. To anyone remotely interested in the Dallas Cowboys, the campus would be showcased on television along with its spectacular view of the downtown Austin skyline.

Not everyone dealing with the Cowboys recognized the genius of Jones's money-first philosophy. But to Jones, tradition meant nothing. When in doubt, knock it all down, pave it over, and start anew. In that respect, Jones was no different than any Dallas leader before him. The only measure by which success could be judged was the dollar.

Jones had his own doubts to contend with; he endured sleepless nights, tossing and turning over what had to be done, staving off paranoid nightmares that Tex Schramm would somehow persuade the NFL owners to rescind the deal. He had come to Dallas to save the Cowboys, but the fans did not appreciate what he knew he had to do in order to win.

Jones's fears about Schramm vanished once the sale of the Dallas Cowboys Football Club received official approval from NFL owners two months after Jones and Johnson stormed into Dallas. Tampa Bay's Hugh Culverhouse gave Jones a fair amount of grief for firing Landry before the sale was official; Jones contended Schramm did the firing for him.

The day the owners validated the sale, Tex Schramm quietly resigned as president and general manager.

The Cowboys did use the first overall pick in the draft to select Troy Aikman, and they took Steve Walsh, the quarterback of 1987 national college champion University of Miami, in the supplemental draft to create competition between the two rookies at training camp. Walsh would be reunited with his college coach Jimmy Johnson. Johnson would later insist he had no intention of starting another Cowboys quarterback controversy and had taken Walsh as potential trade bait to exchange for more draft picks.

Jimmy Johnson did the picking and came up with some gems — running back Daryl Johnston from Syracuse as the Cowboys' second pick, along with University of Pittsburgh center Mark Stepnoski and defensive end Tony Tolbert from Texas–El Paso. The owner advised, but he let his coach make the decisions.

On May 2, eight days after the NFL draft was over, Gil Brandt was shown the door, completing the purge. Brandt left a few months ahead of Pete Rozelle, who retired as the commissioner of the National Football League. Jim Finks, who had worked as the general manager for the Minnesota Vikings, the Chicago Bears, the Chicago Cubs baseball team, and the New Orleans Saints, was considered a shoo-in to succeed Rozelle. But when the owners met again to vote for a new leader, Jerry Jones sided with ten other younger owners to put a hold on Finks. The league needed a leader who would fully capitalize on the NFL's potential and market it accordingly, Jones believed. He threw his lot in with Paul Tagliabue, the league's attorney, who was the eventual choice.

Later that year, Tex Schramm would sign a three-year contract to become president and CEO of the World League of American Football, an offseason developmental league centered in Europe that was meant to broaden the NFL's international presence. "He's the only guy in the world who could lead the World League," Steelers president Dan Rooney said, endorsing Schramm. Joe Bailey, Tex's protégé, would become the World League's vice president. At least the league owners appreciated Schramm's talents.

Tex Schramm quietly simmered while he worked to spread the gospel of America's Game globally. "When a man buys a team, certainly that man has a right to surround himself with the people he wants," he would later admit. "I don't begrudge him that at all." But he did begrudge the way it was done. Instead of leaving everyone with a good feeling, Jones "was very, very cold.

"I felt very strongly about creating a heritage, tradition, style, and class," Schramm said. "We were very conscious that our team was a team, not only in Texas but everywhere, that people could relate to."

Gil Brandt just shrugged it off. "I compare it to going through a bad divorce," he said. "You divorce your wife, but you still have a little feeling for her." After three wives, he would know.

DESPITE HOW POORLY LANDRY had coached the past few seasons, his abrupt dismissal led to his beatification. Suddenly, he was no longer the coach who forgot how to win. He was an icon worthy of veneration. On April 22, a farewell Hats Off to Tom Landry Day parade drew a hundred thousand well-wishers into the streets of downtown Dallas. The honored coach shed a few more tears at the ceremony, which he described as the "most exciting and meaningful" day of his life.

A year later, Landry would be inducted into the Pro Football Hall of Fame.

The television sportscasters, the newspaper sportswriters, and the sports-radio talk shows did their part by dog-piling on Jones, the interloper, the hillbilly, the cheap dime-store antithesis of Clint Murchison Jr., a man who did not or could not appreciate the Cowboys' legacy and who did not understand Dallas. He was ham-handed and lacked basic manners. He was such an oaf that all the promise the young rookie quarterback Troy Aikman brought to the once-proud franchise wasn't even being talked about. The football team sucked. The drama upstairs was the better show.

It got so bad that Bum Bright went public with the revelation that he had wanted to fire Landry himself. The crusty old Aggie was trying to defend Jones but came off as a wuss instead. Saying so after the fact didn't quite resonate with the fans. Bum didn't do it when it counted, and now here he was trying to kiss the ring of the guy he'd sold the Cowboys to.

"If I'd have known there would have been this much heat over Tom, I'd have taken it myself," Bum swore. "I know that Jerry doesn't deserve all this stuff. It wouldn't have been as hard for me as it has been for Jerry because he was the one continuing. I just didn't realize."

If *ifs* and *ands* were pots and pans, there'd be lots of them.

Bum Bright continued to own a suite at Texas Stadium, but once the sale of the Cowboys was complete, he never again attended a game. He was circumspect about the transaction in a Dallas wheeler-dealer kind of way. "This is a new generation of coaches and ownership. This must evolve. It happens in every business."

The arrival of Jones and Johnson dominated all other Dallas news, including the opening of the Sixth Floor Museum in the former Texas School Book Depository.

Living up to the caricature created by the media seemed to come naturally to Jerry Jones. He insisted that he hadn't done anything offensive. If he was provocative, that was okay as long as it ginned up publicity that was good for business.

"I've done most of my business and most of my speaking outside the state of Arkansas," he told the *New York Times,* seeming more like a hick with each sound bite. "I wish I had a dollar for every time I've spoken in Kansas City and St. Louis." Jones was oblivious to the insults he was hurling. Kansas City and St. Louis were pissant cities. Dallas was on a whole other level, or so its boosters liked to think.

But the media couldn't see that Jones was really the fun-house-mirror image of Clint Murchison. The Murchisons were Big Rich whose stupendous wealth was tied to early plays in the East Texas field in the 1930s. Jones represented the latest generation of wildcatters working ahead, behind, and around the major oil and gas producers and doing it smartly and aggressively enough to build up a considerable pile of money.

Clint Murchison played football at prep school and club ball at MIT—effete, sissy schools as far as football went. Jerry Jones played real football for North Little Rock High and for the national champion Arkansas Razorbacks, the team that could move an entire state to yell *"Pig—sooey"* in unison, about as hard core as football got.

Murchison owned a team out of an honest passion for the game. Jones owned a team because of his passion for football and also because he sincerely believed that with his experiences as a football player and as a wildcatter, he could make money while also getting the satisfaction of having his very own professional football franchise.

Murchison was notorious for catting around on the sly, and he liked to troll for sweet young things with his buddy Bedford Wynne and his Rover Boys. Jones didn't hide his appreciation of a good-looking woman and protested he couldn't help it if women enjoyed his flirtations and come-ons.

The Cowboys were one of the few institutions that a broad cross-section of Dallas followed faithfully. The idea of this Arkie blowing into town and tearing apart one of the only organizations that all of the natives were proud of did not sit well with them. Jones seemed like an idiot, utterly clueless about his latest purchase.

But what the newly reborn Landryites failed to recognize was that Dallas *never* revered tradition. Dallas was all about tearing down the past and whatever else stood in the way of the next big new. Dallas was all about opportunity. History mattered not a whit.

Besides, the man really responsible for Tom Landry's dismissal was another native Texan. Jimmy Johnson had grown up in Port Arthur, in the heart of a strip of petrochemical refineries cynically referred to as Cancer Alley near the Louisiana state line. Johnson's parents, C.W. and Allene, came from Arkansas for jobs.

As a teenager, Jimmy was a hyperactive, badass lineman with a slick flattop at Thomas Jefferson High School in Port Arthur. His coach, Clarence "Buckshot" Underwood, was a motivator from the Bear Bryant school of coaching. Johnson couldn't get enough of football and claimed he grew his hair out and started styling it to cover the scars on his noggin from playing street football on the grassy median of DeQueen Boulevard.

He drank beer and honky-tonked but otherwise kept his nose clean, although he did admit to teasing a classmate named Janis Joplin—nicknamed Beat Weeds by Johnson and his buds—for wearing a black leotard to class years before she became a famous rock singer in San Francisco.

Johnson majored in industrial psychology at Arkansas and played defensive noseguard for the Razorbacks ahead of Jerry Jones until Jones was moved to offensive guard. The two JJs weren't "Bobos" who were "play pretty" tight but rather casual friends brought together by the fraternal bond of pigskin.

After college, Johnson worked his way up the coaching ladder, first as an assistant at Louisiana Tech and then as head coach at Picayune High School in Mississippi. He jumped back on the college assistant merry-go-round at Wichita State, moved on to Iowa State under former Razorback teammate Johnny Majors, then landed at Oklahoma working for his old freshman coach Barry Switzer before moving on to defensive coordinator back at Arkansas. In 1976 Johnson was a candidate for Frank Broyles's head coaching job at Arkansas. Passed over, he went to work with Jackie Sherrill at the University of Pittsburgh before stepping up into the head coach position at Oklahoma State for five years.

Johnson applied for the Arkansas head coach's job again when Lou Holtz departed, and Jerry Jones recommended him to Frank Broyles, who had moved up to athletic director. Johnson interviewed with Broyles. The athletic director had already chosen Johnson's old Razorback teammate Ken Hatfield, but he didn't tell Johnson it was a done deal, which Jimmy Johnson never forgot.

In 1983, Johnson was named head coach at the University of Miami, where he quickly developed a rep for aggressive defenses that went after quarterbacks; he didn't wait and look for keys, which was Tom Landry's style. Johnson encouraged his players to taunt and strut and be cocky like he was, admitting, "I like to gloat." He held grudges, exacting revenge on his alma mater for hiring Hatfield by putting the worst defeat ever on the Razorbacks, 51–7. He fidgeted and chafed at fund-raisers, alumni dinners, and other ceremonial duties college coaches were expected to endure, and he fumed and fussed in front of his team effectively enough to earn their fear and respect. Win, and he didn't give a shit what they did after the game, he told them. They took him at his word and won.

Johnson considered the bad-boys rap put on his teams to be racist, since many of the Hurricanes players were black and came from poor backgrounds and they played against historically white schools. When Miami arrived in Phoenix to play coaching legend Joe Paterno's Penn State for the national championship at the Fiesta Bowl, Johnson's team stepped off the jet dressed in combat fatigues, underscoring Johnson's message that football was war. But quarterback Vinny Testaverde threw five interceptions to give Penn State a 14–10 win despite Johnson's belief that Miami was the better team.

The following year, Miami won the big prize, beating Barry Switzer's Oklahoma Sooners — three-time national champions — 20–14.

Johnson succeeded by utilizing a lot of what he'd learned in pursuit of his degree at Arkansas. "My decision to major in psychology made the difference between a good, solid, Xs-and-Os college coach and a national championship coach," he stated. He understood why pro teams and even colleges were hiring sports psychologists as consultants, even though he didn't believe in hiring one for his teams. "They're doing part of the job which, in my opinion, any coach or manager should be doing, which is to make the player feel as good about himself as he can possibly feel, all the time."

Critics considered Johnson's style a willful abrogation of the good sportsmanship and character building that was supposed to be part of the amateur athletic experience. Johnson saw college ball for what it had become—prep school for the pros.

He was a no-nonsense workaholic, at his desk to watch film before first light, staying until close to midnight. He was a stranger in his own house. "When my mom got mad at me and my brother, she'd shake her finger and say, 'Wait till your father gets home!'" Johnson's eldest son, Brent, said. "But we figured out he wasn't coming home, so it wasn't much of a threat." Winning football was his identity. No matter what transpired—injuries, blown assignments— Johnson took it personally. His tightly wound persona was embodied in what appeared to be a spray-painted hairdo, each strand swirled and sculpted to perfection, a testament to his arrogance as much as a willful avoidance of what Tom Landry was.

Johnson had enjoyed his time in Miami and brought seven aquariums with him to remind him of Florida's water and the home he had purchased in the Florida Keys. He also brought the same demanding but tolerant attitude he was known for at Miami. Win, and the Cowboys could party in Dallas all they cared to. Screw up, and they'd be gone.

Righting the Ship

THE RUN-UP TO JIMMY JOHNSON'S and Jerry Jones's debut with the Dallas Cowboys was marked by public relations disasters and public relations damage repair. Before the start of the 1989 season, Jerry Jones was featured on ABC's new newsmagazine *Primetime Live*, interviewed by political reporter Sam Donaldson. Donaldson asked Jones about a comment he'd made about wanting athletes who do more than "look good in the shower" and to which he'd added, "Aikman looks good in the shower."

Did Jones make a habit of checking showers? Donaldson inquired. Jones smiled and said, "I've been in a lot of showers and played on a lot of football teams." The interview shifted the public's perception ever so slightly. Jones had been regarded as an oaf, but Donaldson's line of questioning elicited a bit of sympathy.

Only thirty of the forty-eight Cowboys who'd hit the showers at the start of the 1988 season remained after Thousand Oaks a year later. Danny White and Randy White had retired. Steve DeOssie, Timmy Newsome, and Doug Cosbie were moved or let go. Quarterback Steve Pelluer, who was holding out for a bigger contract, was put on the trading block; Jimmy Johnson said, "Pelluer's got balls the size of raisins and I'm getting rid of that sonofabitch," and made good on his promise. He hoped to start the rookie Troy Aikman at quarterback, something Tom Landry would never have done.

Of sixteen players drafted, seven survived camp and roster cuts. Bobby Ackles, who had been hired by Schramm to keep tabs on waiver wires, compared and contrasted the old coach with the new coach: "Tom really didn't like to claim veteran free-agents. He wanted to bring in his draft choices and college free-agents and that was it. I think it's a difference in philosophy. It's the difference in a team that is rebuilding as opposed to a team that feels it is not rebuilding."

Still, the Cowboys went 3-1 during the exhibition season as Troy Aikman emerged triumphant over Steve Walsh and got the nod to be starting quarterback.

The 1989 season began auspiciously. City council members Al Lipscomb and Glenn Box issued official proclamations welcoming Jerry Jones to Dallas, which was more than a tad ironic, considering Lipscomb came into the public eye in the mid-1960s for organizing Fair Park neighborhood protests against plans to expand parking lots around the Cotton Bowl.

Jimmy Johnson had come to Dallas without a contract, but he was too busy evaluating the team he'd inherited to bother with the details. He lived and breathed football and nothing else (and not always in a good way). By the time the team finally started playing for keeps, he had worked out a ten-year, ten-million-dollar deal with Jones.

But the Cowboys entered the week three home opener against the Washington Redskins winless, after dropping road games to New Orleans, 28–0, and Atlanta, 27–21.

The new owner introduced himself to the Texas Stadium crowd by escorting the movie star Elizabeth Taylor onto the field. Jones asked referee Pat Haggerty if his guest could call the coin toss. Haggerty flipped, Taylor called heads, and the Redskins' Dexter Manley complained. "Visitors get to make the call. I want a do-over." Haggerty flipped again. The 'Skins lost the call again. Liz and Jerry retreated to Jones's suite above the 50-yard line to watch the game while Manley bitched about Hollywood intruding on football.

Dexter Manley just didn't understand where Jerry Jones was

coming from. This was a cross-promotion opportunity. The fuzzy-hatted Taylor had been in Dallas promoting her cosmetics line. She got extra pub for the walk-on; Jerry got extra pub for the walk-on. They both came away more famous than before.

Most spectators at the stadium were focused on the football team, which was wiped out by Washington, 30–7. Backup Steve Walsh spelled quarterback Troy Aikman in the third quarter after the rookie delivered an admirable performance as Washington's personal piñata. Walsh did no better. Running back Herschel Walker gained a measly 33 yards.

The Cowboys's helmet-haired coach fumed in the aftermath. "I don't want them to put it behind them," Jimmy Johnson said as tiny plumes of smoke practically wafted from his ears and nostrils. "I don't want them to forget how awful they looked. We are not a good football team, as anybody who saw us play can tell. And it's not a good feeling. The only thing we'll not accept is being a poor football team. We'll work and do whatever it takes. We'll find those players who want to work. It's the only way to get better."

Privately, Johnson was freaked. These babies were lazier and more useless than his college teams. The Hurricanes could come right in and whip their asses.

The Giants, coached by Bill Parcells, nailed Dallas to the wall the next week, 30–13, sending Aikman to the injured reserve list for six weeks with a broken left index finger.

Losses to the Packers, 'Niners, and Chiefs followed. Jones got so outraged over a referee's call in the 49ers game that he ran onto the field to yell at the field judge. His outburst earned him more criticism for being arrogant, clueless, and disrespectful, leading fans to wonder who was really running the team, the coach or the owner.

The October 29 home game was highlighted by the induction of Lee Roy Jordan into the Cowboys Ring of Honor, an accolade that likely wouldn't have happened if Tex Schramm was still in charge, given his grudge against Jordan for holding out for a new contract.

Even Jordan's presence could not inspire the home team to rise out of their funk. The visiting Cardinals poked the Cowboys, 19–10.

The one victory of the JJs' debut season couldn't have happened at a better place: Washington's RFK Stadium, where the Redskins were dumped, 13–3. Steve Walsh had stepped in for Troy Aikman and he performed effectively with few mistakes. The unsung hero, though, was running back Paul Palmer, who had grown up in nearby Potomac, Maryland. Palmer cut loose for 110 yards rushing and scored two touchdowns. The rest of the team performed decently enough. The defense held Washington to 50 rushing yards, and the offense committed zero turnovers with neither the offense nor defense penalized yardage for infractions. Redskins fans showered the home team with boos throughout the game. Afterward, a giddy Bill Bates, thrilled about his coach's first win in the pros, ran over and mussed up Jimmy Johnson's heavily sprayed hair.

It was back to normal the next week in Phoenix, where the Cardinals put the hurt on the Cowboys once again, 24–20, followed by a 17–14 loss at home against Miami. Next up came division rivals Philadelphia Eagles, at home. The Eagles' coach Buddy Ryan had already established himself as a vocal leader who enjoyed stirring up controversy even before he put a bounty on the heads of Cowboys kicker Luis Zendejas and quarterback Troy Aikman. This was according to Zendejas, who had been cut by Philadelphia earlier in the season after being traded to the Eagles from the Cowboys the year before. Zendejas said he'd heard about Ryan's bounty from an Eagle insider. According to the challenge, a Philly defensive player who knocked Aikman out of the game would get five hundred dollars, with Zendejas's head worth two hundred dollars.

The Eagles rolled, 27–0, in the Thanksgiving TV game that would become known as Bounty Bowl I. After one kickoff, Zendejas was hit hard enough to suffer a concussion and was helped off the field. Jimmy Johnson attempted to chew out Ryan after the game but said that Ryan "put his fat ass into the dressing room" before Johnson could get to him. Ryan shot back that he resented Johnson's comment and had actually lost two pounds. "I thought I was looking good," he said.

The two teams met again two weeks later in frozen, snowy Philadelphia for Bounty Bowl II. Eagles fans polished their reputations as being the nastiest fans in the NFL by chunking snowballs at Johnson; Cowboys punter Mike Saxon; broadcasters Verne Lundquist and Terry Bradshaw, who were calling the game for television from the press box; and even Eagles players as Philadelphia downed the Cowboys, 20–10.

Troy Aikman, the eleven-million-dollar rookie with the hundred-million-dollar smile and a charismatic presence not seen since Staubach, finished the season with the worst rating of all starting NFL quarterbacks. But for all the hits he took and mistakes he made, he was beginning to fit the mold. Aikman was made for the Cowboys. His deep baby-blue eyes, thick mane of blond hair, full lips, soft-spoken manner, and overall studliness gave him the look of a matinee idol. The drawl came naturally. Now, if only he could play.

Aikman was at home in North Texas, no adjustments necessary. But he was also a product of Southern California, where his father worked pipeline construction. He had played all kinds of sports and fantasized with the neighborhood kids about playing baseball for the University of Southern California Trojans or the Los Angeles Dodgers. The vision was real enough that young Troy spent hours practicing signing his autograph.

When Troy was twelve, his father, Kenneth, moved the family to a 172-acre ranch seven miles from the town of Henryetta, Oklahoma, population 6,000. The boy lost his friends and felt alone in Oklahoma. But he adjusted to the ranching lifestyle and learned to slop hogs, and he made a lifelong friend in Daren Lesley. He also discovered that while baseball and basketball were fun sports to play, football was a whole other deal in Oklahoma.

As a sophomore, he started at quarterback for the Henryetta Fighting Hens, who went 4-6. The next year the Hens won two games and lost eight but still made it to the state playoffs for the first time in twenty-five years. His senior year's team went 6-4. In spite of the 50-50 records, the kid from California stood out. He ignored overtures from baseball's New York Mets and almost committed to Oklahoma State University, where he was being recruited by Jimmy Johnson, but in the end he opted for the University of Oklahoma, where he was coached by Barry Switzer.

As the first freshman starting quarterback for the number-two-ranked Sooners in nearly forty years, Aikman went 2 for 14 and had three passes intercepted by the Kansas Jayhawks, who upset OU (as the University of Oklahoma is known), 28–11, in Aikman's debut game. But he adjusted, and the following year he led the Sooners to a 3-0 start and a number-one national ranking going into the game against the University of Miami Hurricanes, coached by Jimmy Johnson, who had left Oklahoma State. Aikman completed six of his first seven passes for the Sooners before he was tackled so hard, his ankle was broken. The Hurricanes went on to beat Oklahoma.

Coach Switzer adopted the run-intensive Wishbone formation for Aikman's replacement, the speedy Jamelle Holieway. The Sooners responded by winning every game and becoming the national champions, according to the Associated Press, after beating Penn State 25–10 in the Orange Bowl.

Seeking to avoid a quarterback controversy, Switzer encouraged Aikman to transfer when his ankle finally healed. Once again, Jimmy Johnson tried to persuade Aikman to play for him—now at the University of Miami. Instead, Aikman headed west to UCLA, where he blossomed with the pass-intensive offense designed by Coach Terry Donahue. Over two seasons, Aikman became the third-highest-rated passer in NCAA history.

After Aikman was drafted, Jerry Jones knew he had a winner when he met with Aikman and his agent at a Dallas steakhouse to talk about his contract. A crowd had quickly gathered outside the restaurant when they heard who was inside. Jones offered to sneak

Aikman out the back when they were finished with their meal. Aikman said he preferred meeting the public. He hadn't been practicing signing his autograph all those years for nothing.

The Cowboys might have reached .500 in 1989 if the new management had left well enough alone. Those players who managed to shine had ties to Tex Schramm, Tom Landry, and Gil Brandt, the men who drafted Michael Irvin and put Aikman at the top of the draft list before they were ousted.

But Jones and Johnson were executing a plan that involved reducing overhead and rebuilding with new talent simultaneously. Everson Walls, the Cowboys' all-time interception leader and one of the most feared cornerbacks in the league, would be let go at the end of the season. In October, Johnson and Jones made clear their intentions when they traded away the team's biggest star, Herschel Walker, and four future draft picks to the Minnesota Vikings in exchange for five players and eight future draft picks. Tom Landry would never have let go of Walker. The new boys thought different.

Money had been so tight around Valley Ranch that before the Walker trade, Los Angeles Raiders owner Al Davis actually talked Jimmy Johnson out of trading away his young receiver Michael Irvin. Offensive coordinator David Shula thought Irvin was expendable after he had suffered a torn anterior cruciate ligament in a game against San Francisco that took him out of action for the year. Perhaps he could be trade bait, Shula thought.

The coach and the owner were that desperate. It had been thirteen years since the Cowboys had won a Super Bowl. Fans' anxiousness suggested that that was far too long, especially with Landry and Schramm gone. Johnson and Jones felt the pressure. Oil and gas was a game and a hustle that, like the insurance business, started with the con. College football was a big deal. But NFL football was serious bidness.

Jimmy Johnson was so focused that he separated from his wife of twenty-six years, Linda Kay, almost as soon as they arrived in Dallas. Their sons were grown up and Jimmy wanted to live alone so he could concentrate on football. By the time the season ended, the couple had filed for divorce. Jerry Jones paid the $1 million divorce settlement in exchange for Johnson's giving all his radio and television income to the Cowboys and promising to wear Cowboys apparel. Johnson began to be seen squiring Rhonda Rookmaaker, a hairdresser who lived near Johnson's apartment, around town.

Whenever C.W. and Allene Johnson came to Texas Stadium to watch their son's team, Jimmy had them pay for their seats. Finally, he asked them to stop coming until the team starting winning. The Cowboys sucked so royally he was embarrassed his parents were hearing all the booing and cussing directed his way.

Pat Jones's boy kept his eyes riveted on the bottom line. The finances needed stabilizing if he was going to build a better football team, but he was also dealing with the $80 million class action lawsuit filed on Arkoma by shareholders of ArkLa Gas, charging that McCoy and Jones had excessively profited from their gas sales to ArkLa. That was old news, as far as Jones was concerned, since he had already plowed the profits into the football club he now owned.

Tom Landry, still sore from his booting, went on ESPN to express his reaction to the new regime's first season, saying with a tinge of admonishment, "It's really a disappointment they didn't rely on us."

About the only thing worth bragging about was the Herschel Walker trade. Twelve trades had been made by new management, but Walker's dramatically reduced Jones's player payroll and added a bounty of additional draft picks. As the only real available trade bait despite his $5 million paycheck, Walker had been considered expendable to the new coach and new owner. Johnson wanted draft picks, not used furniture. Jones wanted to cut the fat. The Browns had expressed interest in Walker, but it was the Vikings' Mike Lynn who agreed to give up three first-round draft choices, three second-round picks, and a third-round pick, along with Minnesota's first- and second-round draft picks for 1990, in exchange for Walker and four late-round future draft picks.

The conditional terms were creative: for every Minnesota player that the Cowboys kept on the roster going into the 1990 season, a draft pick would be returned to the Vikings. But Johnson cut or traded away every player who came from the Vikings before the deadline, preserving those future draft picks for the Cowboys.

To consummate the trade, Jerry Jones paid Herschel Walker an extra $1.2 million, gave him a car and a rent-free home in Minneapolis, and provided twenty round-trip airline tickets between Texas and Minnesota.

Personnel director Bobby Ackles called it "the biggest theft in the history of the NFL." Ackles, one of the few holdovers from the Schramm regime, had proven useful by spotting diamonds in the rough such as tight end Jay Novacek, who had been left in the plan B free-agent pool by the Cardinals.

The club used the Minnesota draft picks to trade up and pick University of Florida running back Emmitt Smith in the first round of the 1990 draft. Dallas was in sore need of a quality running back once Walker was gone. Jimmy Johnson wasn't sold on Smith's speed or size, but his staff was. Smith thought coming to Dallas was preordained. He was a native of the Florida Panhandle town of Pensacola, where Roger Staubach had played football while he was in the Navy. Smith's mother, Mary, was a homemaker. His father, Emmitt Sr., was a city bus driver who had been a talented high school football player but whose bad knees had kept him from a college scholarship. The Smiths were a humble family who lived in housing projects and sometimes survived on powdered milk and government-supplied cheese. Despite those hurdles, they raised their son to be a solid citizen.

As a toddler, Smith informed his parents that when he grew up, he was going to be a Dallas Cowboy. He wasn't kidding. As a teenager, young Emmitt led Escambia High School to two state titles, and he was recognized as *Parade* magazine's national high school player of the year in 1986, which earned him a scholarship to the University of Florida. He set single-game and season rushing records for the Gators and was voted the Southeastern Conference player of the year as a junior. But after Steve Spurrier was hired as Florida's head coach in the offseason, Smith entered the NFL draft, where he anticipated being a first-round pick despite the shared belief of many scouts that he was too small, at five foot nine, and too slow to make it in the pros.

The reality of Big D fairly blew Smith away when he finally arrived at his dream destination. Dallas was fairly blown away too. The personable, likable Smith showed up for his introductory press conference wearing black linen shorts with yellow polka dots.

"My first few weeks in Dallas were quite an adjustment," Smith later admitted. "The biggest thing that struck me was all the cowboys. I'd never seen so many of them in one city, and I'd never seen any black cowboys at all. I was also shocked seeing all the Dallas highways. To a young man coming from Pensacola and Gainesville, they seemed to stretch from here to forever."

The city and the state showered love and adoration on him once the young Florida stud got their attention. He wasn't just a great football player. He was a good human being who set an example without making a fuss over himself.

DESPITE THE COWBOYS' SUFFERING the shittiest season they had had since their debut in 1960, four hundred media credentials were requested to cover Cowboys training camp at their new summer home in Austin. More than one hundred thousand fans showed up at St. Edward's University to watch the new coach and owner guide their once-beloved 'Boys back to prominence, the largest attendance at any NFL camp. Austin's nightlife—from swanky restaurants to titty bars such as Expose to the team's unofficial after-practice head-quarters, the Copper Tank brew pub, right off Austin's honky-tonk Sixth Street strip—welcomed the influx of players, coaches, front-office personnel, media, and fans. So did Jerry Jones, who negoti-ated exclusive rights to all Cowboys merchandise sold at Austin training camp. Additional money generated from corporate sponsorship of a Cowboys golf tournament and other events made summer camp in Austin a profitable venture.

And that mattered even more than ever, since Jones had bought out Ed Smith and other minority owners within a year of arriving in Dallas, giving him 95 percent control of the team. The Cowboys really were his baby.

Emmitt Smith was one of several competing to be Moose Johnston's complement in the backfield as the 1990 season got under way. Smith shared playing time with Alonzo Highsmith, Alexander Wright, and Tommy Agee. But midway through the campaign, Smith complained to a reporter that he wasn't getting enough snaps to make a difference.

The loud reaction to the comment was Smith's first real taste of Cowboys media frenzy. More important, his complaint got results. He enjoyed his first standout game in week five, rushing for 121 yards and a touchdown against the Tampa Bay Buccaneers. Seven weeks later, he rushed for 132 yards and two TDs in a win over the Redskins. Once Smith started getting more than 20 touches per game, the pressure on Troy Aikman abated, allowing the second-year quarterback to develop his passing game, at least until he was injured and replaced by backup Babe Laufenberg.

Neither Aikman nor Laufenberg had their number-one target on call. Michael Irvin started the season on the injured reserve list and stayed there through the first four games. When he came back, it appeared he had lost a step. He no longer looked like the impact player he was purported to be. Irvin closed out 1990 with a total of 20 catches for 413 yards.

The Cowboys' 7-9 finish was quite an improvement over 1989's 1-15 record, and good enough for Jimmy Johnson to be voted the Associated Press's NFL coach of the year. But it was not good enough for Johnson. Even though the team's fortunes had improved with Emmitt Smith in the backfield, Johnson was still looking for deadwood to clear out.

A Turnaround for the Ages

THE WINDS OF CHANGE blew through Dallas, the city, and Texas, the state, as well as the Cowboys, the football team.

Ann Richards, an Austin liberal Democrat, was elected governor of Texas; she edged by Clayton Williams Jr., the multimillionaire Republican conservative from Midland, to become Texas's first female leader in sixty years. Williams had been considered a shoo-in in an increasingly Republican-leaning state until he made the off-hand remark that rainy weather was like rape—"You might as well lay back and enjoy it." Richards pushed back. She already had a feisty, no-quarter-given reputation. In 1988, she gave an acerbic speech at the National Democratic Convention zinging eventual president George H. W. Bush, saying, "Poor George, he can't help it. He was born with a silver foot in his mouth," and "He was born on third base and thought he hit a triple."

On the sports front, the hoped-for recovery of the Cowboys was almost overshadowed by the exploits of native Texan Nolan Ryan, the baseball pitcher who threw his sixth no-hitter and won his three hundredth game during the summer of 1990, stirring up more excitement than at any other time in the brief history of the Texas Rangers American League franchise. *Almost.* By the time football season started, the Rangers had been forgotten all over again. Even a 7-9 Cowboys team trumped all other local sports.

In late January of 1991 Tex Schramm got a bit of press when he was voted into the Pro Football Hall of Fame, along with Texas-born running back Earl Campbell, Jan Stenerud, John Hannah, and Stan Jones. The timing was convenient, since Tex's election more than balanced his disappointment at the ending of his brief reign over the World League of American Football; his tenure had been cut short by NFL owners in October, who replaced him with Mike Lynn, the Minnesota Vikings general manager who made possible the Herschel Walker trade.

The five NFL owners who made up the WLAF's board of directors had wanted a development league to feed the NFL. Schramm envisioned a high-dollar global league of its own that was underwritten by big television contracts in multiple nations; after Schramm proposed a franchise for Hawaii—in addition to franchises in Europe and in San Antonio, Texas—which skyrocketed travel expenses, the owners pulled the plug.

"Tex felt there should be total separation from the NFL and he would run the whole show," explained Pittsburgh Steelers owner Dan Rooney, who sat on the WLAF board alongside Kansas City's Lamar Hunt and New England's Victor Kiam, all allegedly friends of Schramm. Schramm didn't hide his disappointment. "I think I deserve more than that kind of treatment," he said bluntly. He had been run off from the Cowboys and now he was being chased away by the whole league. With Rozelle gone as commissioner and Murchison dead, Schramm's influence withered.

Before he left the WLAF, Schramm made an encore as the "old sportswriter" with Doug Todd's assistance, writing an article for the *Dallas Morning News*'s SportsDay section that speculated about pro football in the twenty-first century.

Schramm offered these predictions:

By the year 2,000 [*sic*], what you're going to be able to see when it comes to football on television will be incredible. You will be watching the games on high-definition TV which almost gives you a 3-D look. Someday, it *will* be 3-D. You will be able to decide which part of the game you want to watch. Today, in Canada and in a small city on the East Coast of the U.S., they are experimenting with TV which allows you to decide which camera view you want to see. You'll be able to follow individual players. You will have your own instant replay from different angles. That technology exists today. Millions of dollars are being poured into this 'new' television, and it's coming. Obviously, you'll be able to watch any game at any time, anywhere.

"But, they're still going to be fighting the problem of whether to televise home games," Schramm wrote.

Football cannot survive as a studio game. The crowd is what makes the game exciting. In the next ten years, the war that is going to be fought is the tremendous advantage of staying home and watching the new TV vs. getting up and going to the game. Stadiums are being forced to change their facilities and their thinking to make attending a game a very pleasurable experience. No more being hot, no more being cold, no more getting wet, no uncomfortable seats, no out-of-control spectators. The first people who have really come to grips with this are the horse race people. In their new facilities, you have it all. You're going to have to be able to go to a football game in comfort and see all the facets of the game you see at home. That's the big question facing football: Will the stadiums be able to keep pace with television?

Schramm got some things plumb wrong, starting with his take on the drug culture.

In the 21st century, and I mean early in the 21st century if not before, sports somehow is going to have to become drug-free. It's going to take a lot of sacrifice and a much stricter, non-compromising approach. Since the World League is going to be just that, an international league with all the attendant legal implications, we can't have drug problems. So, it's going to be one strike and you're out. Whereas, back in the '50s, the use of alcohol was almost part of the folklore of sports, drug abuse in sports today is offensive to the public. Real sports success can't exist with that image.

Schramm's biggest stretch was advocating for legalized betting, acknowledging gambling as the true national pastime, not football. "Gambling is never going to go away," he wrote. "Unfortunately, it may grow to the point where the spread is more important than winning and losing. Football must take a hard look at the whole question. What you could see by 2,000 is a scoreboard that doesn't start at 0–0. It starts with the national line already figured in. In a handicap horse race, you put more pounds on the better horses. Club golfers register their handicaps. Maybe that's the way all sports will be in the 21st century."

Schramm touted better equipment, which would reduce injuries. He bragged on the World League's Operation Discovery, in which forty-eight young athletes unfamiliar with American football learn the game and spread its global appeal. "Sports historically has led the way in race relations in this country," Tex reasoned. "We're still not where we should be, but we are trying and we are making progress. I can foresee that same spirit spreading throughout the world."

He was ever the visionary, even as he faded into the sunset. Schramm was gone long before the WLAF began play, in 1991. But before the league folded a year later, several Schramm-inspired innovations were tested, including the introduction of radio helmets and the two-point conversion after touchdown, a standard feature of the old American Football League that the NFL finally embraced in 1994. Schramm continued to keep his box at Texas Stadium. He held court at a monthly lunch with his old sportswriter friends Frank Luksa, Blackie Sherrod, Carlton Stowers, and Bob St. John, along with Pat Summerall and Bert Rose. He launched a consulting firm, the Schramm Group, which included protégé Joe Bailey, promotions ace Russ Potts, and television producer Lee Martin. But the business failed to draw many interested parties.

In truth, it was "the beginning of the Great Void," as Schramm would describe it, a period of time spent increasingly in Key West, where he fished, hung out with Pat Summerall and other friends, dabbled in real estate, and promoted the World Cup Blue Marlin Championship, a one-day contest spanning the globe. Tex had won the inaugural tournament in 1985 with a 537-pound marlin caught off the coast of San Salvador. Now he had all the time in the world to catch all the marlins he cared to. At seventy-one, he was too old to rebuild anyone's football club and too Tex for most organizations to put up with. "It appears that people in top management roles are fearful of people who are aggressive, innovative, persistent, and stubborn," he harrumphed.

Schramm's induction into the Hall of Fame certainly put a period on the end of an era. As if on cue, *Dallas*, the prime-time television soap opera, went off the air. Nobody much cared anymore about the made-up program about mythical Dallas. The reality show known as the Dallas Cowboys Football Club was far more entertaining anyway.

The other big Cowboys news off the field revolved around America's Sweethearts—the Dallas Cowboys Cheerleaders. The new regime's ouster of Suzanne Mitchell as director had not been fully resolved until Kelli McGonagill, a cheerleader from 1984 through 1989 and the assistant director for two years before spending a year in sales and promotions for the football club, was promoted to director. McGonagill replaced Leslie Haynes (who succeeded Debbie Bond) and was the stabilizing force the DCCs needed.

Joining McGonagill was the new head choreographer, Judy Trammell, who had danced with the cheerleaders from 1980 to 1984.
Trammell succeeded Shannon Baker Werthmann, another four-year
veteran of the cheerleaders, who had become head choreographer
after the 1982 retirement of Texie Waterman, the woman who
taught the cheerleaders how to dance. Trammell had spent six years
as Werthmann's assistant.

McGonagill and Trammell would take the cheerleaders to a whole
other level of popularity by transforming operations into a self-sustaining
business. McGonagill proved herself an astute disciple of Jerry Jones,
making branding deals, entering into corporate sponsorship agreements, and aggressively marketing the Dallas Cowboys Cheerleaders.

The football team gave the girls something to cheer about when
they hit pay dirt again in the draft. Still possessing extra picks from
the Herschel Walker trade two seasons before, the Cowboys selected
defensive tackle Russell Maryland from the University of Miami as
the number-one overall pick, along with sixteen other picks in the
twelve-round draft. The unprecedented haul included lineman Erik
Williams, receiver Alvin Harper (a track star who summoned visions
of Bullet Bob Hayes), defensive tackle Leon Lett, and cornerback
Larry Brown.

Emmitt Smith demonstrated his juking prowess with three consecutive 100-yards-plus games to start the regular season, even
though his mad skills were shadowed by the team's tepid 1-2 record.
Troy Aikman was beginning to show poise, maturity, and precision
in his third season, in no small part due to the influence of Norv
Turner, who came from the Rams to replace David Shula as offensive coordinator. Turner developed a close relationship with Aikman, which was not the case with Shula, while Michael Irvin was
finally nurtured back to full operating strength as the Playmaker.
But Smith's performance was clearly the most potent weapon.
Whenever Emmitt ran, he got the defense's attention, which allowed
the other components in Turner's offensive scheme to fall into place.

According to the scoreboard, when the Cowboys faced the Redskins at RFK Stadium in late November, they were only marginally better than they'd been the year before. Washington had beaten Dallas by two points in the season opener at Texas Stadium and hadn't looked back, going undefeated. The Cowboys were another story. A promising 6-3 record had devolved into a bleh 6-5 record after a 26–23 overtime loss to Warren Moon and the Houston Oilers in the Astrodome, and a poorly executed 22–9 defeat at the hands of the Giants at the Meadowlands, in which the Dallas offense could produce only field goals.

Which made the 14–7 lead over the 'Skins at the half all the more surprising. Dallas appeared primed to pull off a major upset until Aikman reinjured his right knee and left the game in the third quarter. His replacement, Steve Beuerlein, obtained from the Los Angeles Raiders specifically for occasions like this, executed several outrageous gambles by Jimmy Johnson including an onside kick and a Hail Mary pass, while Emmitt Smith took 34 handoffs, and Michael Irvin grabbed a crucial 26-yard TD pass — he was 9 for 130 yards on the day — to hold off the Redskins. The 24–21 win snapped Washington's twelve-game winning streak and had Dallas teammates high-fiving one another at midfield.

Steve Beuerlein's job from that point on was simple: hand the ball to Smith or Johnston or throw it to tight end Jay Novacek or wide receiver Alvin Harper or Michael Irvin, who was fearless running pass patterns over the middle. The line and the Dave Wannstedt–coached defense would hopefully take care of everything else.

The Washington game triggered a run of five consecutive wins to close out the regular season at 11-5. Irvin torched defenses with 93 receptions for 1,523 yards to lead the league while Smith led the league in rushing with 1,563 yards. The Cowboys' best showing in eight years was good enough to enter the postseason as a wild card.

Troy Aikman's questionable status could not stop the entire state of Texas from coming down with a bad case of playoff fever. It had been awhile since the words *Super Bowl* were uttered by the faithful. Then the Cowboys trapped the Bears at Soldier Field, 17–13, for the team's first postseason victory since 1982. Steve Beuerlein passed for 180 yards and a touchdown with no interceptions.

Next up was a trip north to do battle with the Detroit Lions, who hadn't lost a game in the Silverdome all year.

The run-up to the divisional game was highlighted by the two top dogs of the Cowboys organization engaging in a very public ankle-biting episode over quarterbacks. Jerry Jones said Troy Aikman deserved to start. He was fully healed and looked fine. Besides, he was the franchise's future. Jimmy Johnson blew up over Jones's comments.

"Who is running this football team?" Johnson fulminated. As head coach, *he* would determine who would start at quarterback, and it would be the best player available at opening kickoff. The amount of coverage newspapers, radio, and television devoted to the question confirmed the renewed interest in the Cowboys. Attendance at home games had shot back up to more than 60,000. Several home games sold out. But this road game with everything on the line would reveal what kind of team the fans were supporting.

Steve Beuerlein got Johnson's starting nod against the Lions. He underperformed, ending his day 7 for 13 with a measly 91 passing yards, yielding no touchdowns and an interception before he was relieved. Aikman mustered 114 passing yards going 11 for 16 in relief with the outcome of the game all but assured. Neither Dallas quarterback came close to matching Detroit's Erik Kramer, who went 29 for 38 as he torched the Dallas D for three touchdowns and 341 passing yards, including a 47-yarder to Detroit's star running back Barry Sanders. The Lions scored first and never looked back, systematically slicing and dicing the Cowboys, 38–6, for Detroit's first playoff win ever.

The *Dallas Morning News*'s Randy Galloway did not enjoy bearing witness. He had seen this movie too many times: "They had come this far, this fast, but then they lose like that," Galloway wrote. "Every defensive wart exposed. Every coaching move trumped. Every angle covered by the other guys. They had come this far, this fast, but then they depart the playoffs looking Sunday like a ringer that had slipped past NFL security."

The Detroit game revealed too many flaws to declare the ship of state righted, but Johnson and his team could take solace knowing that the eventual Super Bowl champion Redskins had beaten them by only two points early in the season and lost at home to the Cowboys by three points in week thirteen. These Cowboys could run with the big dogs. It was getting ahead of the pack that was the hard part.

Aikman went into the offseason ticked off. He thought he should have been starting games as soon as possible instead of warming the bench for Beuerlein. "We are guaranteed only 16 days a year at the office. I'm paid well. I don't want to miss any days unless it's absolutely necessary." He thought Coach Johnson didn't treat him like he deserved. "That was a situation that wasn't handled right," Aikman said. "I was constantly in the dark about my status. Week to week, I learned more on where I stood from the reporters than I did from Jimmy."

As the Cowboys were rolling into the playoffs, another hard-fought battle that Dallas fans were in the middle of came to an end. On December 8, 1991, the Belo Corporation, the owner of the *Dallas Morning News* and WFAA TV, among other media holdings, announced the purchase of the *Dallas Times Herald* for $55 million. The next day, the *Times Herald* ceased publication. The Great Dallas Newspaper War was settled.

Coverage of the Cowboys would not be going away; there just wouldn't be as many print choices or perspectives as before. The *Fort Worth Star-Telegram* would become the *Dallas Morning News*'s primary rival, joined by an explosion of cable television channels such as

ESPN and Fox Sports Southwest, which devoted twenty-four hours a day to sports, and local radio stations that were doing the same.

Jerry Jones joined the media scrum by becoming the first league owner to have his own weekly television program and his own newspaper column. In 1991, he doubled the franchise's broadcast revenues by dumping KRLD-AM as the team's flagship radio station in favor of KVIL, the FM station whose cheery music format and equally cheery morning man Ron Chapman consistently ranked it near the top of Dallas radio ratings.

Then commissioner Paul Tagliabue named Jones to the NFL Competition Committee, the prestigious group of decision makers once dominated by Tex Schramm. Jones was feeling sufficiently full of piss and vinegar to fire Bobby Ackles, the director of player personnel, in May. Ackles had dared to ask Jones if assistant coaches and front-office personnel would be getting playoff checks for their wild-card win over Chicago five months previous, as was customary around the NFL. "Life isn't fair, I don't want to hear it anymore," Jones bitched sourly. He'd heard enough about playoff checks. Everyone should be glad he had a job. It was at that point that Jones stood up and yelled at Ackles, "You're out of here. Have your office cleaned out by the end of the day."

Ackles's responsibilities would be handled by twenty-seven-year-old Stephen Jones, who took over players' contracts, and by Larry Lacewell, the new scouting director, who had Arkansas ties to Jones and Johnson.

Jimmy Johnson had claimed old man Jones had bullied Stephen Jones so much that he brought him to tears. Maybe the new position was his way of making up for it.

Jones demanded fealty from his people and acknowledgment that he, and no one else, was the top dog, but Jimmy wasn't paying tribute like he should have.

Johnson could ignore stuff like Jones being accused during training camp of trying to persuade the girlfriend of KRLD reporter Rob

Geiger to "give me five minutes and I'll take you to heaven" while inquiring if the woman was wearing panties under her skirt.

Johnson chalked up that kind of behavior to Jones being a celebrity-crazed megalomaniac. But too often, Jones confused being owner with being a head coach. Jerry's insistence on being involved with the draft and trades was bad enough. His habit of showing up on the sidelines was downright irritating.

Jerry enjoyed cultivating ambitious, success-oriented people like himself as acquaintances. The owner's suite was populated largely with local bigwigs and B-list national celebrities famous for being famous, such as New York developer Donald Trump and his wife, Marla Maples, right-wing political radio pundit Rush Limbaugh, civil rights activist Reverend Jesse Jackson, and country music singer Reba McEntire. Occasionally, authentic giants came to watch the Cowboys as Jerry's guests, as was the case when Nelson Mandela, the South African leader who broke the grip of apartheid, came to Dallas, and with the president of Mexico Vicente Fox.

It was when Jones brought those famous people with him onto the field and into the locker room that Jimmy Johnson got his dander up. His silence spoke volumes when the league fined Jones $10,000 for allowing Charlton Heston and Marla Maples onto the sidelines.

Jones was nowhere near as accommodating to Cowboys players.

On the heels of two outstanding seasons, including leading the league in yards and carries in 1991, Emmitt Smith asked Jones to renegotiate his contract despite having one year left on his original three-year deal. Jones stalled, eventually offering Smith the same amount as the Detroit Lions' Barry Sanders, the NFL's top rusher. But that did not appease Smith, who decided to play out the final year of his contract before testing the unrestricted free-agent market. Loyalty only went so far in this version of the NFL.

After a decent training camp in Austin and an exhibition schedule that included playing the Houston Oilers at the Tokyo Dome on

August 1, a game the Cowboys lost, 34–23, the team raised its sights higher.

It was a heady period for Texas as the 1992 season geared up. Dallasite H. Ross Perot was ginning up interest as a third-party candidate for president of the United States; he would spend $72 million of his own money to challenge sitting president George H. W. Bush and the Democratic Party candidate, Arkansas governor Bill Clinton.

But like everything else, politics played second fiddle to the Dallas Cowboys as soon as season play began, with the home team slamming the defending Super Bowl champion Washington Redskins 23–10 behind Emmitt Smith's 140 rushing yards on 27 carries on *Monday Night Football*. The Dallas D set the tone when cornerback Issiac Holt blocked the Redskins' punt after their first series of plays.

The Cowboys made it two in a row by charging ahead of the New York Giants in New Jersey, 34–0, only to have the Giants close the gap and trail by six points in the fourth quarter. Aikman put the game out of reach by hitting Michael Irvin for 12 yards on third-and-seven on the Dallas 36 to seal the 34–28 win. Before starting against the Cardinals the next week, Irvin was so jacked up, he told receivers coach Hubbard Alexander, "Ax, I feel it. I need the ball. These guys can't hold me."

The arrival of defensive end Charles Haley from San Francisco in a trade for draft futures had been heralded as the last piece in the big puzzle that would return the Cowboys to greatness. But for all his promise, Haley wasn't delivering. In a hard-fought December contest at Mile High Stadium played in 15-degree weather against Dan Reeves's Broncos, the Cowboys held on to a 17–13 lead at halftime. Still, the defense's sloppy play threw Jimmy Johnson into a rage. As the team filed into the locker room, Johnson grabbed Haley by his shoulder pads and dragged him into the shower.

"Get in here!" Johnson screamed. "You can't dog it on my team, you big son of a bitch. If I let you go, nobody in the fuckin' league will pick you up again. You better get some quarterback sacks or you're out of here. You understand that shit?"

Haley understood. He was credited with two sacks in the Cowboys' 31–27 win. Troy Aikman did his part, completing seven of eight passes to march the team 80 yards before Emmitt Smith scored on a draw from two yards out, putting the Cowboys in front for good.

A 20–17 road loss to Washington that included Troy Aikman fumbling the ball in his own end zone caused Johnson to blow up again. On the flight home to Texas, he had sharp words for everyone around him, including the pilot. He ordered flight attendants to withhold food from the players. But he was selective about whom he showed his red ass to. He broke up a card game on the flight by picking on rookie middle linebacker Robert Jones and not anyone else. "He never messed with his bread-and-butter guys, because he was a bully," Jones would later say of Johnson. "Bullies only pick on the guys they can mess with." Robert Jones got tongue-lashings. Michael Irvin didn't.

Johnson took pleasure ragging on running back Curvin Richards, a native of the Caribbean island of Trinidad who had played at La Porte High School near Houston, then for the University of Pittsburgh. When Richards couldn't run sprints in practice due to an asthma attack, Johnson ordered him to "get your ass over to the asthma field."

In the final game of the season, Richards was taken out and then cut from the roster after fumbling twice, even though the outcome was already safely in hand as the Cowboys caged the Chicago Bears, 27–14.

Richards's transgression was nothing compared to the faux pas committed by Jerry Jones. At the start of the fourth quarter, Jones left his box to stand on the sidelines, as he often did. This time, he brought Prince Bandar bin Sultan, the Saudi Arabian ambassador to the United States, along with the prince's six bodyguards.

"What the fuck are these guys doing here in the middle of a game that we're blowing?" Johnson asked Jones.

When the entourage showed up in the locker room while Johnson was reaming out the players, Johnson went ballistic. The visitors and the bodyguards accompanying the prince had disrupted his rant and he wasn't having it.

Jerry Jones did not approve of Johnson's behavior. "Where I sit, I cannot tell people to kiss my ass," he calmly remarked. "Where Jimmy sits, he feels he can." Jones pointed out that Johnson had no alumni that he had to butter up and no stupid fund-raising dinners to attend. But the coach clearly did not seem to appreciate all the good the owner had done. Johnson wanted control of his team. So did Jones.

Jimmy felt the same way about Jerry, calling him "the most egotistical man who ever walked the face of the earth. It's scary." Maybe they weren't as tight as everyone thought.

Emmitt Smith, still embroiled in contract negotiations, joined his coach in taking issue with Jones's game-day habits. "Jerry seemed to be basking in front of our crowd," Smith observed. "He treats our football team like some kind of show. And Jerry Jones is the star— at least in his own eyes."

Jones crossed the lines of division between front office and the team because he could and because he was a football guy who understood the game. He thought he was Clint, Tex, and Tom all in one body: "I laid every dime on the line, now Jimmy is making it an 'us-against-Jones' situation with his players and coaches." Jimmy Johnson wanted autonomy in all football matters, and Jones had said he might "just fire his ass" more than once. "I hate the son-of-a-bitch," Jones confided to his longtime friend Don Tyson.

That was off the field. On the field, the thirteen wins during the regular season were the most ever for a Cowboys team. They were the youngest team in the league and had the number-one defense and an offense that could score ten different ways.

Twenty thousand fans showed up at safety Bill Bates's ranch in

McKinney for a pep rally before the Cowboys headed off to the playoffs in Philadelphia, where they taxidermied the Eagles and quarterback Randall Cunningham in the first round, 34–10.

The next Thursday, sixty-nine thousand fans jammed Texas Stadium for a send-off pep rally before the team traveled to Candlestick Park by the San Francisco Bay to renew the Catch rivalry in the NFC championship.

The 49ers had beaten the Cowboys six consecutive times over the previous twelve years, surpassing the Redskins and the Eagles as most reviled rivals. But Dallas was determined to snap the skein and this time around had the goods to do so.

The score was tied at the half, 10–10, as both teams hunkered down and applied defensive pressure that neither team's offense managed to break. Then Daryl "Moose" Johnston crashed into the end zone from the four-yard line for a 17–10 lead and Dallas put the pedal to the metal. Aikman threw a rope to speedster Alvin Harper on a post route, and Harper left a trail of torn-up soggy turf on his 70-yard touchdown dash, his second TD reception of the day. Harper's catches were the critical difference in the 30–20 Cowboys victory.

Beating the 49ers in their house put the cherry on top of the first season in which Aikman hadn't missed a game. The youngest team in pro ball had kept hearing how they were a year away, but this game suggested their time was now.

After the game, the tightly wound coach found the owner and they broke with their recent behavior and embraced with an honest hug. The coach then tried to get his troops' attention in the locker room, climbing on a bench to talk to the team. "Hey! Hey! Hold it," Johnson hollered. "I don't mean to put a damper on any of this, but you understand, we do have one game left to play." Waving his arms all around, he went on, "Hey! Fantastic, fantastic, fantastic. Every single one of you. And I'm not just talking about these last sixty minutes. I'm talking about the quarterback school, the mini-camp, the offseason, training camp, down in Austin when it was hot and you were tired, and all that. Everybody, you did one hell of a job. And the only thing else I've got to say is, How 'bout them Cowboys?"

The room erupted. Nothing could stand in the way of this team.

Sports Illustrated's Rick Reilly had declared the *Morning News*'s SportsDay "the *Encyclopedia Britannica* of sports sections," and when the Cowboys returned to the big dance and suited up for Super Bowl XXVII on the last day of January, the *Morning News* demonstrated why: the paper sent thirty-five staffers to cover the big game against Buffalo in the Rose Bowl in Pasadena, California.

It was a homecoming for Troy Aikman. He spent the day before media day of Super Bowl week driving *Fort Worth Star-Telegram* reporter Richie Whitt around the UCLA campus after telling Whitt, "I need to get away."

Aikman had a hard time moving around North Texas in public and anywhere football fans congregated. It was only natural. The Cowboys were the one thing about Dallas that was truly great. Dallasites who didn't like the Cowboys were about as common as year-round residents of South Padre Island who hated the beach.

The Cowboys were personal. No matter where you went in Dallas — First Baptist Church, the Salesmanship Club, the Greenville Avenue Bar and Grill, Henderson's Fried Chicken, the Neiman-Marcus tea room, Love Field, the Greyhound bus station, NorthPark Center, the Stoneleigh P, the Yello Belly Drag Strip, R. L. Griffin's Blues Palace, Herrera's, the Tradewinds Social Club — everyone talked the Cowboys. Men argued the merits of players' stats. Women compared the physical attributes of the hunks on the team. Every bar in town that opened on Sundays was packed for Cowboys games. Once again, after way too long a break, they were the city's biggest celebrities. They represented, Jerry Jones included. For the first time in a Super Bowl, the owner had his own microphone and name placard at media day. He was still talking thirty minutes after the team bus left to return the players to their hotel.

It was going to be a huge show. Michael Corcoran, the country music columnist for the *Morning News*, was assigned to review the halftime show, which featured pop star Michael Jackson.

A day before the game in the bar of Loews Santa Monica, where the team was headquartered, Corcoran bought drinks for Cowboy great Lee Roy Jordan and current star Charles Haley. "Lee Roy Jordan and his wife were drinking grapefruit juice and vodka," Corcoran said. "Charles Haley came over. He was drinking a beer."

Visiting with Cowboys past and present revealed a generational shift. "Fans were bringing balls and jerseys asking for [Haley's] autograph," Corcoran observed. "Haley told them, 'I don't do autographs.' But he was entertaining them, talking to them for ten, fifteen minutes, joking around, throwing a ball with a kid."

Lee Roy Jordan did not approve. "That's terrible," he said. "You've got to sign autographs. Back in our day, we'd sign everything. Those people pay your salaries. You got to show them some respect."

Corcoran had a different take: "Charles Haley gave fans something more than an autograph. He gave them a memory."

Tex Schramm was on hand with 94,374 others for the first Dallas Cowboys appearance in a Super Bowl in fourteen years. He was invited as a guest of the Atlanta Falcons founding owner Rankin Smith. Jerry Jones still preferred to ignore his predecessor. Whatever Tex's feelings actually were toward the Cowboys owner and coach, he voiced support of the team he'd helped build, remarking from the press box, "That Cowboy logo in the end zone looks good."

Schramm hadn't spoken to Jones since his firing, he told reporter Frank Luksa. He admitted "seeing another person living in your house gives you mixed emotions. At first, I believed it would be a problem, the whole thing...playoffs and the Super Bowl."

A quintuple-bypass heart surgery the previous spring had tempered Tex's old bluster, but being back at the Super Bowl reenergized him.

The Super Bowl itself had changed since Tex and the Cowboys' last appearance. The selection of Pasadena had been made a few years earlier when the original choice, Phoenix, was disinvited, due to the state of Arizona's refusal to recognize civil rights leader Martin Luther King's birthday as a holiday. Tickets were now priced at $175 each. Residents in nearby neighborhoods charged up to $40 to let ticket holders park on their lawns. NBC positioned fifteen cameras around the field, with fourteen video recorders ready to rewind every play. Five blimps, four F-16 U.S. Air Force jets, five airplanes, six helicopters, and a hot-air balloon filled the sunny Southern California skies above the stadium.

Country singer Garth Brooks sang and Academy Award–winning actress Marlee Matlin signed the national anthem. NFL star running back O. J. Simpson, now an NBC broadcaster, conducted the coin toss.

The Buffalo Bills' path to Pasadena had been no less difficult than the Cowboys', even though the game marked Buffalo's third consecutive Super Bowl appearance. They had come back from a 28–3 deficit at halftime to shock the favored Houston Oilers in overtime in the first round of the playoffs, thus denying the nation an all-Texas Super Bowl. They vanquished the Pittsburgh Steelers 24–3 in the divisional round, then turned the Miami Dolphins into sushi in the AFC championship game, 29–10.

The Bills and their talented quarterback Jim Kelly appeared to be riding that momentum, jumping out to a 7–0 lead after Buffalo blocked the punt following Dallas's first offensive series. Aikman completed three of his first six passes but looked out of sync; the Bills' two-deep zone defense was keeping Michael Irvin and Alvin Harper from breaking a long play. But Aikman found his groove once Emmitt Smith's relentless ground game wore down the Bills' zone.

Smith bulled 38 yards to the Buffalo 19-yard line before Aikman hit a wide-open Irvin for a touchdown on a slant route after the receiver faked out cornerback Nate Odomes. Dallas then kicked off to Buffalo and on the first play from scrimmage, Bills running back Thurman Thomas had the ball stripped by Leon Lett on the Bills'

18-yard line and Jimmie Jones fell on it for Dallas. On the next play, Irvin caught Aikman's pass on a post corner route and took it in from the three, making Irvin's second touchdown in eighteen seconds. Offensive coordinator Norv Turner's perceptive play-calling, Aikman's sharpshooting accuracy, Irvin's gymnastic leaps and fancy footwork, and Smith's punishing running game pushed the Cowboys to a 28–10 lead at the half.

Michael Jackson, the king of pop and the most popular entertainer in the world, starred in the twelve-minute halftime show, which featured two of Jackson's biggest hits, "Billie Jean" and "Black or White," the latter his duet with former Beatle Paul McCartney. Ever since the first Super Bowl, the halftime show had been a bland affair featuring safe entertainers such as clarinetist Pete Fountain and the Up with People revue. But NFL bigwigs had paid attention to the historical drop-off in viewers at halftime. Jackson, still a high-powered superstar despite a career on the decline, changed the way Super Bowl halftime shows were presented. In front of a worldwide audience of nearly one billion watching in seventy countries, he performed an electrifying tour de force on the pyramid-shaped stage, accompanied by thirty-five hundred singing children; a choreographed phalanx of dancers; a munitions dump's worth of fireworks; smoke machines; extensive special effects; and a "Heal the World" finale color-card display involving everyone in the whole stadium. Viewership actually rose during halftime, even though Jackson himself had no clue what was going on in the game before and after his performance, being unfamiliar with football.

After the halftime show, the Bills might have been better off if they'd stayed in the locker room and watched replays of Michael Jackson. Buffalo was blitzed, sacked, and run out of town over the course of the second half, ending the game with nine turnovers (five fumbles and four interceptions—two from Jim Kelly, two from Frank Reich) to Dallas's two.

Although the Bills closed to within 14 points in the fourth quarter, an Aikman-to-Harper bomb for a 45-yard touchdown dashed any chance of Buffalo's redemption. Harper dunked the ball over the crossbar to make it clear this one was over. The 52–17 score would have been worse had not Leon Lett clowned around on his way to the end zone with a recovered fumble. Lett had the ball stripped by Don Beebe, and the ball skittered into the end zone for a touchback instead of another Cowboys touchdown.

Emmitt Smith finished with 108 rushing yards. Irvin snagged six passes for 114 yards. Troy Aikman, America's boy next door, was awarded the Pete Rozelle trophy and a Buick Park Avenue as the game's most valuable player for completing 22 of 30 passes for 273 yards, four touchdowns, and no interceptions, and rushing for 28 yards. Aikman said getting praise from his father, Ken, was the best part of the win. "He's tough to please to say the least. When he told me how proud he was of me, that made it all worthwhile."

Jimmy Johnson's perfectly coiffed hair was soaked and flattened by a cooler full of ice water before being ruffled by Michael Irvin's hands. "He messed up my hair pretty good," the coach said, beaming. Johnson and Irvin had won a national college championship together in 1987. Five years later, they were sharing an even bigger title. Irvin declared, "I've already told them I want diamonds in my ring bigger than headlights."

Jimmy Johnson and Jerry Jones hugged, signifying that for all their differences, they had finally reached the goal they had both set out to reach. Jones had a comb on hand to give to Johnson after his ice-water shower.

Emmitt Smith was blown away. "The greatest day of my life was being born," he said. "This is the second greatest day." He had been in awe of all the celebrities he met during Super Bowl week, among them basketball great Magic Johnson, comedians Arsenio Hall and Martin Lawrence, actor Wesley Snipes, and filmmaker John Singleton. Now they were all in awe of him.

Nate "the Kitchen" Newton, three hundred and twenty-five

pounds of Cowboy bulk, was almost speechless. "It is unbelievable, I am so filled with joy," he said. "I can't even express it. If I could explode, I would. But I can't, because my insurance ain't paid up."

The Cowboys win was one of the most watched TV events in history. After the game, Jones threw a party at the Santa Monica Civic Center for the team, his associates, and his friends, including the group of a hundred and sixty people he'd flown in from Arkansas. Don Tyson, the chicken king, paid tribute to his friend Jerry Jones, proclaiming, "Here is a guy who, by God, made it by himself. He planted his own crop and he harvested the damn thing." President of the United States Bill Clinton called Jones to tell him the people of Arkansas were prouder of Jones's accomplishment than of Clinton's getting elected.

Jones took the stage at the party to urge the gathering to roar, shouting, "Come on, everybody, let's show them how we party in Dallas."

Back home, a Fort Worth mortgage executive, Bob Havran, winked and celebrated the instant amnesia that seized Cowboys fans by saying "Tom who?" and acknowledging what the victory meant to a fan base still simmering over the dismissal of the last and first coach of the Cowboys. "This is great for Texas," said Havran. "When people feel better, they do things and make deals. Everybody in the office gets along better."

Despite plenty of criticism about how Jerry Jones and Jimmy Johnson had gone about it, no one could argue with the results. Wellington Mara observed that the JJs "pretty well turned the league on its ear."

Numbers 8, 22, and 88 were the three main reasons why.

SUCCESS ON THE FIELD did not distract Jerry Jones from keeping an eagle eye on the bottom line. Bonuses were limited to players, coaches, and upper-level management. Scouts, trainers, front-office employees, and other personnel were left out. Super Bowl rings awarded to lesser staff members were studded with zircons, not diamonds, which led columnist Randy Galloway to conclude that Jones "treats his people like shit" even when they win.

Jones begged to differ. "I grew up with a philosophy that I still use," he said. "Have a big front door and a small back door." He proved it with the Cowboys. The football club generated $36.2 million in total revenue his first year of ownership. In four years, he pumped up that figure to $65 million through ticket sales, corporate sponsorships, broadcast rights, merchandise, beer sales, and anything else he could put a price on.

He had sold more than ninety luxury suites in the past four years, good for an additional $50 million, and had leased the remaining inventory. During preseason games, Jones even sold logo space on the field to a bank and a grocery chain.

"They're the best promotion machine I've ever seen," marveled Ron Chapman, program manager at radio station KVIL, who had seen a few promotions in his thirty-year broadcasting career. "They'll sell anything to anybody."

Jones's coach was one of the few nuts that Jerry Jones's salesmanship could not crack.

Jimmy and Jerry had worked in tandem since arriving in Dallas, but they no longer liked each other much. Jones was a meddler. Johnson was a control freak who overworked players and gave his assistants grief for spending more time with their families than with the team. Neither could resolve his feelings toward the other. Neither thought the other understood the pressure he was under. Jimmy didn't respect Jerry like he should. Jerry forgot someone else was the coach.

Why Not Another?

THE CONQUERING SUPER BOWL XXVII heroes' February 9 victory parade through downtown Dallas was supposed to be the crowning moment of the remarkable four-year turnaround that Jimmy Johnson and Jerry Jones had engineered. Fifteen tons of confetti fluttered from the skies over downtown Dallas as Mayor Steve Bartlett, who had pledged to make Dallas America's City, said, "This is one of the greatest things that's happened to this city." Michael Irvin guaranteed more, advising the officials and dignitaries gathered around city hall to "save your spot. We'll see you at the same place and same time next year." But that brief moment to savor was drowned in a sea of ugly.

Four hundred thousand people turned out, twice what had been anticipated. A tight, twenty-block parade route with only 235 police officers on hand, a police chief who was out of town, and poor planning by Jerry Jones's right-hand gal pal Susan Skaggs were cited as factors after the crowd turned into a mob. Decorum, rules, and barricades were ignored. Fights broke out, mostly blacks assaulting whites and Hispanics. Girl gangs went at it in front of television cameras. Looting, car fires, and random incidents of violence, including a Channel 8 cameraman's getting knocked out by a wine bottle thrown at him during a fight, upstaged the celebration. Twenty-four young men and women were arrested.

The disaster was blamed on everything from kids skipping school and free bus service to cutbacks in defense spending, a real estate slump, oil industry stagnation, the 40 percent office vacancy in downtown Dallas, and continued corruption in banking and S & Ls. Robert Camuto of the *Fort Worth Star-Telegram* put a segregated city divided by the Trinity River at the top of his list of culprits, noting that the city consistently failed to address that festering sore. Ed Sims, a multicultural sociologist at Northlake Community College, said, "The only thing that surprises me is that it didn't develop into a full-scale riot—that it reached a point and stopped. Why would they have a parade in the midst of high racial tensions that would draw people from all these segregated areas? There's a free-floating anger and resentment that can explode at any time.

"When you have rage, it is unpredictable and it is deadly," Sims said. "In the African American community you have that anger going on every day, but the cameras and the microphones aren't there."

Later in the year, Congress voted to cancel the $10 billion Super-conducting Super Collider project south of Dallas, the biggest and most expensive scientific experiment ever launched in the United States, putting a huge hit on the entire North Texas economy.

Those dark realities were forgotten in the wake of other news: the big American Bowl exhibition game against the Detroit Lions at London's Wembley Stadium on August 8 ended in a 13–13 tie, and Emmitt Smith went missing from training camp. The NFL Players Association had won a court battle that effectively ushered in the era of free agency for players in 1993, and Smith responded by holding out for sixty-four days for a new contract; if he didn't get one, he too would become a free agent. That did not stop him from starring in a commercial for Reebok shoes, where he uttered the tagline "All men are created equal—some just work harder in the preseason."

The American Bowl game had not sold out despite the Cowboys' rep as Great Britain's Team, reflecting the absences of Smith and Troy Aikman, who was recovering from an operation on a herniated disk. And Emmitt Smith did not suit up for the first two games of the 1993 season for the Super Bowl champion Cowboys. The owner had offered Smith $9 million for five years, insisting his running back was "a luxury, not a necessity." Smith stood pat amid charges and countercharges that he was disloyal and that Jones was racist because he wouldn't pay Smith what he was paying Aikman.

The Cowboys lost those two opening games to Washington and to Buffalo, putting the Cowboys' Super Bowl aspirations in the doubtful category. No 0-2 team had won a Super Bowl. Jones finally broke down and signed Smith to a four-year contract worth $13.6 million, making him the highest-paid running back in NFL history, passing the Buffalo Bills' Thurman Thomas, who had negotiated a deal for $100,000 less.

And once the Cowboys' power runner was backing up the quarterback and his receivers, the team rolled, winning seven straight games. On a rainy Halloween afternoon in Philadelphia, Smith surpassed all expectations by rushing for 237 yards on 30 carries, breaking Tony Dorsett's previous single-game team record. "It was not a day to throw the ball," Alvin Harper observed. "It was a day to sit back and let Emmitt do the job."

One week later, a ghost from the past materialized to watch the Cowboys at Texas Stadium. Tom Landry, for twenty-nine years the only coach the Cowboys ever had, was back. Landry had kept a high profile, running his own investment group, chairing the Dallas International Sports Commission, testifying on Sundays from the pulpit, speaking for the Fellowship of Christian Athletes and other groups, and embracing the creationist philosophy of David Barton, who preached that the United States was founded as a Christian nation and was on the road to ruin thanks to secularists, the Supreme Court, and an apathetic clergy. Landry thought Barton's beliefs should be taught in public schools.

After three years of saying no, Tom Landry gave in to the requests of Roger Staubach and other former players and was inducted into the Ring of Honor during halftime of the November 7 game against the Giants, the team that Landry had played and been an assistant coach for. Landry pushed for Clint Murchison and Tex Schramm to be inducted as well, but to no avail.

With Don Meredith, Don Perkins, Bob Lilly, Roger Staubach, Chuck Howley, Lee Roy Jordan, Mel Renfro, Jerry Jones, and a Cowboys cheerleader looking on, Landry stood tall in his trademark fedora and coat and tie, wearing tinted aviator glasses, his hands folded in front of him. He somberly listened to Jones praise him, then donned his Ring of Honor sports jacket as the stadium erupted in cheers. Breaking into a small smile, he said, "Well, I want to say this is an outstanding day for me personally. I don't know how I can thank all the people that are responsible for putting this thing on here. I do think this is a great time. I'm honored to be in the Ring of Honor."

Landry would return to Texas Stadium a year later to attend the inductions of Randy White and Tony Dorsett; these were his only two appearances at Texas Stadium after his firing. But Landry never really got over it. "Jerry and those people are just different than me," he candidly told writer Jim Dent. "I don't know why they do some of the things they do. All the same, there is nothing that says that I have to be around for them. You can't hate them for what they are. It is hard for me to hate a person. But it just seems that he took over the team and kicked a lot of good people out and then he locked the doors. Of course, he is winning. So he just feels that he can do whatever he wants to do.

"I still don't agree with it. But again, he bought the Cowboys and paid a pretty good price for them. So he had the right to do whatever he wanted to do. I still don't understand why he wanted to do it himself. He could have done it in a better way than he did. His treatment of Tex and everybody else was bad. I didn't feel so bad about myself. But I felt extremely bad about Tex. The way he handled Tex in the press conference just wasn't right. He could have done a better job with everything."

Landry's ultimate assessment of Jones to Dent was harsh: "He seems to only measure himself when it comes to money. That is not right. Of course, he is not the only person in our country who does that. But at the same time, all you hear from him is the amount of money he's trying to make. Yes, I pray for Jerry, and people like Jerry, because I believe that we all need a spiritual approach. Whether he has one or not, I don't know."

Another less heralded event cemented Landry's legacy. Thomas "Hollywood" Henderson celebrated ten years of sobriety at a dinner at the Radisson Hotel in downtown Austin; it had been ten years since he'd drunk alcohol, smoked a joint, or snorted a line of cocaine. Wanting to make amends, Henderson had reached out to his coach.

"I sent him an invitation, called his office, called his office, called his office," Henderson related. But he never heard back. One thousand friends and family members showed up for the event. "I take my seat and I hear a rumbling," Henderson recounted. "I turn and look and I see the fedora and I see a tan leather jacket, and I just welled up. I cried. He showed up. I got a chance to talk in front of him. I got a chance to tell him some things that he didn't know. He sent me a note saying about the same thing he said about me on stage—'If I knew then what I know now, I would have handled you a lot differently but I'm really proud of you.' He said, 'It takes a man of great character to go through what you've been through and come out of the other side of it.' It was huge to me."

THE ANNUAL THANKSGIVING DAY game was played against the Miami Dolphins on a slippery home field coated with snow and ice. The Florida team performed like they had grown up in Green Bay. Late in the fourth quarter, the Cowboys blocked a last-minute field-goal attempt by kicker Pete Stoyanovich, which prevented Miami from taking the lead. Unfortunately, Leon Lett did not realize the ball was still alive when he ran toward it and kicked it to the seven-yard line, where a scrum ensued. The Dolphins recovered the ball at the one with three seconds left, giving Stoyanovich a much easier second chance, which he did not blow. The Dolphins won 16–14, and Leon Lett bawled in the locker room.

It was the Cowboys' last loss. Even after missing the first two games of the season, Emmitt Smith rushed for 1,713 yards to lead the league for the second consecutive year, grabbing 57 pass receptions along the way. Receivers Michael Irvin and Alvin Harper and tight end Jay Novacek were unstoppable. Aikman was simply at the top of his game in spite of injuries that took him out of service several times over the season, completing 271 out of 392 passes for 3,100 yards. The Cowboys finished 12-4, the best record in the NFC, closing out with a 16–13 overtime win against the New York Giants in chilly, blustery New Jersey on the second day of the new year. Despite separating his shoulder in the first half, Emmitt Smith banged out 132 yards on 30 carries and picked up 61 yards in pass receptions, saving his best for last by grinding 41 yards in the overtime drive that settled the game, earning the Cowboys a bye in the first round of playoffs.

The playoffs were practically over before they started.

Michael Irvin led the Cowboys with nine catches as the Green Bay Packers were methodically taken apart and their quarterback Brett Favre disarmed, 27–17.

Next came the January 23 NFC championship game against San Francisco at Texas Stadium. The 49ers had dominated Dallas in crucial playoff contests until the year before, and the Cowboys were pining to make it two in a row. While both teams approached the game cautiously, three days before the game and out of nowhere, Jimmy Johnson phoned Randy Galloway on his WBAP sports-talk radio show to announce to one and all, "We will win the ballgame. And you can put it in three-inch headlines. We will win the ballgame. We're going to beat their rear ends, and then we're going to the Super Bowl."

Johnson made good on his promise as Aikman led the team to 251 yards in the first half and a 28–7 lead. Aikman was taken out of the game with a concussion in the third quarter when three-hundred-pound defensive lineman Dennis Brown crashed into him, ramming his knee into the side of Aikman's helmet in the process. But Aikman's backup Bernie Kosar, who had been released by Cleveland earlier in the season, maintained the flow by going 5 of 9 passing for 83 yards and two scores, including a TD toss to Alvin Harper, with no interceptions. Emmitt Smith enjoyed one of his best days ever as a receiver, catching seven passes for 85 yards and a touchdown. But it was the supporting cast (Newton, Lett, Haley, et al.) that sealed the 38–21 win, which concluded with the ceremonial dumping of the watercooler over Johnson's heavily sprayed hair.

Aikman didn't remember much about the game. He was still out of it when the final gun sounded. Checking his mental state, a team trainer asked him where the Super Bowl was going to be played.

"Henryetta?" Aikman guessed.

And who was the previous year's Super Bowl MVP?

Aikman was clueless. He'd forgotten he had won the award.

He spent the night at Baylor University Medical Center for observation.

The good people of Aikman's hometown seized the moment and printed bogus tickets for Troy Aikman's Super Bowl at Henryetta to raise money for local youth.

SUPER BOWL XXVIII would be a rematch with the Buffalo Bills, the first time the same conference champions had squared off in a Super Bowl in consecutive years. It was Buffalo's fourth Super Bowl appearance in a row, and the 0-for-3 AFC champs were itching to win.

Tickets for the showdown at Atlanta's Georgia Dome were priced at $175; scalpers were getting up to $1,000 per.

Opening kickoff had the Bills ripe for revenge and in full control. Quarterback Jim Kelly's accuracy, the footwork of running back Thurman Thomas (a Texas high school football star from Houston's Willowridge High School), and kicker Steve Christie's two field goals, the second one for a Super Bowl–record 54 yards, powered the Bills to a 13–6 lead at the half.

The halftime show exuded a distinct Southern flavor. The Rockin' Country Sunday showcase of Nashville entertainers Clint Black, Travis Tritt, and the reunited Judds mother-daughter duo was capped by Naomi and Wynonna leading everybody in "Love Can Build a Bridge."

The Bills could not bridge the gap between their determination and their execution. In the second half Hotlanta turned out to be Dallas's kind of town. The momentum shifted in the third quarter when Leon Lett made up for his brain fart in the Thanksgiving Day snow-bowl game by forcing a Thurman Thomas fumble that was picked up by James Washington and run in for a touchdown. On the next series Dallas had the ball, Emmitt Smith slammed it into the end zone. The Cowboys didn't quit until the clock did, with Dallas ahead 30–13.

Alvin Harper recorded three catches for 75 yards. Emmitt Smith took MVP honors for rushing 132 yards on 30 carries, scoring two touchdowns and catching four passes. For a five-nine, two-hundred-pound guy considered too small and too slow to be a premier NFL running back, he sure had a way of avoiding tackles and frustrating defenses. Blackie Sherrod compared his running style to "frantic hopscotching, barefoot, on a blistering sidewalk."

Troy Aikman would go into the offseason still shaking out the cobwebs from the sixth concussion of his career and admitting he found himself forgetting things. Roger Staubach had quit after his fifth concussion in his final season—his twentieth overall—and Troy was catching up.

Memories of the wilding at the previous year's victory parade, a beefed-up presence of fourteen hundred policemen, and a fan base that had quickly become jaded limited the turnout to sixty-five thousand fans for the Cowboy's Super Bowl party and parade through downtown Dallas. The parade was newsworthy mainly for the absence of violence and its relative joylessness despite the fact the hometown Cowboys had joined Pittsburgh and San Francisco as the only franchises to win four Super Bowls. Buffalo joined Minnesota and Denver as the only teams to lose four Super Bowls; the Bills were the only ones who could claim four consecutive defeats.

Breaking Up Is Hard to Do

Almost two months after the Dallas Cowboys repeated as Super Bowl champions, Jimmy Johnson and Jerry Jones finally had it out. Troy Aikman, the easygoing, tobacco-chewing, yet intense leader of the team, used to view his coach as something of a crazed militant. But once the team started winning, Johnson appeared to loosen up and grew closer to his players, especially Aikman. The wild mood swings became less and less frequent. What didn't change was the tension between the lip-smacking coach (lip-smacking was a habit of his, something he did whenever he was excited or under the gun) with the sculpted hair, and the relentless, obsessive owner.

After the second Super Bowl win, in Atlanta, Jerry Jones sat down with Frank Luksa of the *Morning News* and discussed the strained relationship with his coach, admitting the two partners were not getting along and suggesting changes would be made, while Jimmy Johnson allowed to another reporter that he might be interested in coaching the new expansion franchise in Jacksonville.

Also on the heels of the Super Bowl came the debut of the first radio station in the Dallas media market to program sports around the clock. KTCK-AM went on the air in February, ready to upset the status quo. The Ticket, as the new station called itself, aimed to fill a niche with smart, opinionated sports talk, despite its weak signal.

Within a few weeks of going on air, the guys on the Ticket had plenty to talk about.

The coach and owner–general manager of the Dallas Cowboys, along with delegations from every other National Football League franchise, converged in Orlando in March for the NFL owners' meetings. At the March 21 bash at Disney World's Pleasure Island bar mall, hosted by the ABC television network for the twenty-fifth anniversary of *Monday Night Football,* Jerry Jones worked the room, shaking hands, chatting up familiars, and accepting congratulations. His team had won the Super Bowl for the second consecutive year and he had been instrumental in the $4.4 billion deal the NFL had worked out with the networks, advocating especially for the Fox network, which ponied up $1.6 billion to wrest from CBS the rights to NFC Sunday games.

Jones's Cheshire cat grin was on full display as he approached the table where Jimmy Johnson sat talking with assorted current and former Cowboys assistants and employees and their wives and girlfriends, including former director of personnel Bobby Ackles, whom Jones had fired the year before, and Ackles's wife, Kay.

Jones banged the table and proposed a toast, raising his cup of scotch: "Here's to the Dallas Cowboys, and here's to the people who made it possible to win two Super Bowls."

Johnson did not join in the toast. Neither did Ackles nor the recently fired TV coordinator Brenda Bushell, who was restrained from lifting her glass by Jan Wannstedt, the wife of former defensive coordinator and new Chicago Bears head coach Dave Wannstedt. Johnson's girlfriend, Rhonda Rookmaaker; former offensive coordinator Norv Turner, who had just become head coach of the Washington Redskins, and his wife, Nancy; and publicity director Rich Dalrymple and his wife, Roz, all sat silent.

Jones was taken aback by the silence at first, then he slammed his cup on the table. "Fuck you. Have your own party," he said, storming off.

Jimmy Johnson let out a belly laugh. Others laughed along nervously. The glassy-eyed Johnson, who had been popping Heinekens one after the other for at least an hour, had been in the middle of an anecdote about butting heads with Jones during the draft when the owner had walked up, ruining his punch line.

Jones found a more receptive audience in the *Morning News*'s Rick Gosselin and Ed Werder, the *Tampa Tribune*'s Joe Fisaro, and Cincinnati writer Geoff Hobson, especially after he advised them, "Don't run off to bed, boys. Stick around and have a drink. You don't want to miss the biggest story of the year. I'm thinking about firing Jimmy."

Jones was more than a little loaded when he put his swagger on full display in front of the writers, boasting, "I could step out tomorrow and hire Barry Switzer as coach of the Dallas Cowboys tomorrow and he could do a better job than Jimmy." Do tell. Lou Holtz could coach the Cowboys. Holtz, the former Arkansas coach who had moved on to Notre Dame, had met with Jones on the sly a month earlier to discuss joining the Cowboys. He and Jerry went back a ways, and Lou was always ready to listen.

Jerry's point — five hundred others could do it. "Shit, *I* could have coached the hell out of this team." Jones cackled. But he wasn't kidding. He meant it.

The next morning, Jimmy Johnson decided to leave Orlando early and go to his vacation home in the Florida Keys. He knew he had hit a nerve with Jerry the night before. Larry Lacewell, his scouting director and go-between with Jones, confirmed it: the *Morning News* had broken the story about Jones's thinking about a change of coaches. Before he left, Johnson sought out Jones. Jones told Johnson he was still the coach of the Cowboys, no matter what he heard. That hot talk happened the night before. Sans alcohol, cooler heads were prevailing, it appeared.

A week later, on March 28, Jones and Johnson had a serious sit-down at Valley Ranch. Johnson wanted to coach one more year without restrictions and without Jerry's veto on coaching and player-personnel decisions. Jones wasn't having it. He had been insulted one too many times. He was sick of it. No matter how good a coach Johnson might be, he had disrespected Jerry. This thing wasn't going to work. It was, for real, time for a change.

ON TUESDAY, MARCH 29, 1994, Jerry Jones and Jimmy Johnson squinted before the glare of camera lights and a gaggle of reporters at Valley Ranch. "We have mutually decided that I would no longer be the head coach of the Dallas Cowboys," Johnson somberly informed the gathering. "I feel better about Jerry Jones right now for understanding me as I've ever felt," he said. The two men hugged at the end of what columnist Randy Galloway described as a "lickfest." Jones paid Johnson a $2 million bonus to go away quietly. The coach went home and cried.

Their parting would be the story of the year in Dallas.

On Wednesday, March 30, some twenty-four hours after Johnson had cleaned out his office and nine days after Jones and Johnson had gotten into their beer-and-booze-fueled dick-swinging contest, Jerry Jones called another press conference at Valley Ranch to introduce the new head coach of the Dallas Cowboys: Barry Switzer.

"I was so fortunate to be lying on the couch last week when I had a phone call," the new hire told the gathering. Switzer had been doped up following a colonoscopy when Jerry Jones had called with two questions: "Do you still want to coach?" and "Would you like possibly to think about coaching the Cowboys?"

Jerry had spoken to Switzer while he was in Orlando, even though he supposedly also had his eye on Holtz, as well as Butch Davis, Johnson's defensive coordinator, and some other big names in the coaching profession. But Jones had a point to make—anyone could coach these Cowboys—and he sought to prove it by hiring the University of Oklahoma Sooners coach, who had resigned under fire in 1989 and was all but retired.

"We had met about a year ago in Oklahoma City and had briefly talked," Jones admitted. "It was very apparent to me then that his enthusiasm, and that charisma and charm and that drive, was very special."

At his introductory press conference, Switzer gleefully whispered to a friendly sportswriter, "I feel like I've won the lottery!"

He may have been run out of the college game but the gift that fell into Barry Switzer's lap was a whole other thing, tailor-made for his tastes and proclivities. He could be whoever he wanted to be with the Cowboys, as long as they won. The team brimmed with so much talent, Switzer really wouldn't have to do much other than not fuck up. The roster that had won two consecutive Super Bowls was his. Just let the players and assistant coaches do what they were supposed to do, and everything would be fine.

The fifty-six-year-old Switzer had grown up barefoot, dirt-poor, and without running water in the wrong part of Arkansas. His mother was strung out on pills and alcohol. Just before his senior year at the University of Arkansas in 1959, Barry confronted her and asked her to get help for her addictions; she walked onto the back porch and blew her brains out.

His daddy was a bootlegger who had done time and who was shot by his black girlfriend for fooling around with another woman. The girlfriend then killed him and herself both in a one-vehicle car crash on their way to the hospital.

Barry was something of an untamed wildcat too. He worked hard to enjoy life to the fullest and did not apologize for his frailties. As head coach at Oklahoma for sixteen years, he had blazed a path for Jimmy Johnson to follow when he took over as head coach at Miami. Switzer ran OU like a pro team. He had zero interest in academics and allowed his players to do whatever they wanted off the field as long as they won the battle between the goal lines. He learned a lot about black folks from his father, the bootlegger, who sold his goods to African Americans living in and around the Switzers' hometown of Crossett, and he became the first major college coach to recruit black players from the inner city and give them leadership positions on his teams. The Sooners went on to win three national college championships.

OU was continually cited for recruiting violations and for letting boosters "take care" of players, implying pay for play. When the school was placed on three years' probation by the NCAA in 1989 for a number of infractions, including the quarterback's arrest for offering to sell cocaine to an undercover police officer, Switzer resigned, saying NCAA rules were "too uptight," and adding, "I don't care that much what people think anymore."

Switzer had been set for life in Norman, but he was willing to get back in the game when Jerry Jones called, fully aware that football fans in Dallas were predisposed to dislike him. Switzer was the guy who led the OU teams that put it to Coach Darrell K Royal and the University of Texas Longhorns almost every October at the Cotton Bowl's Red River Shootout. Now the fortunes of the one football team that mattered to all of Texas were in the hands of an Okie and an Arkie—a setup that was difficult for a diehard fan in the Lone Star State to accept. Unless, of course, the Cowboys won.

The hire reunited Barry Switzer with Larry Lacewell, the Cowboys scouting director who had been Switzer's defensive coordinator at OU until he resigned, in 1978, after he discovered that Switzer was having an affair with his wife. But that was then, they both insisted. Switzer and Lacewell's personal bond went deeper; they were native Arkansans who had played football together in junior high before going their separate ways.

A female reporter asked Switzer if he was prepared for the pressure that came with being the Cowboys' coach.

"Read my book, darlin'." Switzer winked.

His 1990 book, *Bootlegger's Boy,* ghosted by Bud Shrake, had earned hundreds of thousands of dollars in royalties and a thirty-million-dollar lawsuit from Jack Taylor, a *Dallas Times Herald* reporter who claimed Switzer had implicated him in a scheme to have an OU player carry cocaine back to Oklahoma following the 1988 Orange Bowl. After a six-week jury trial in Austin, each side was judged guilty of invading the other's privacy and of acting with malice but not guilty of libel. Switzer declared victory.

As the Valley Ranch press conference wound down, Switzer slapped Jones on the back and smiled. "Jerry, you're the bad guy here, right? I read the poll in the paper." He proceeded to make clear that he was not going to be a problem to Jones like his predecessor was. "The people who know Barry Switzer know I don't have an ego that allows me to put myself in a position that would injure that relationship. I just hope I can do as good a job as Jimmy Johnson... that's damn sure what you're hoping," he said to Jones, grabbing him and shaking him playfully. "That's why I'm here. We've got a job to do and we gonna do it, bay-bee!"

Win or lose, Switzer, the local media quickly realized, was going to be a whole lot more fun to cover than Johnson had been.

For his part, Jones said he felt relieved, telling reporters, "I looked at myself in the mirror this morning and this is the best that I have felt about myself in a long, long time."

Vinnie Paul of Pantera, the Metroplex metal band whose album *Far Beyond Driven* was number one in the nation, knocking Bonnie Raitt out of the top position, reflected the mind-set of most Cowboys fans. He didn't get it, asking everyone around him, "That son of a bitch Jerry Jones, what the hell is he doing? Why mess with success?"

The JJs may have come to Dallas as a pair, but Jones would later tell writer Jim Dent that he didn't have a good grip when he arrived in Dallas. "These were very, very tough times," he said. "Here I was coming into a league that I didn't know anything about, taking on a management position that I had no experience in. And, at the same time, taking huge risks with huge amounts of money, more risks than I had ever taken in my life. Here was a person who hadn't lived a public life, and all of the sudden I was thrown in there and getting the public criticism. You have to understand that after I bought this football team that I had some doomsday-type thoughts. Whether it was real or imagined, I still felt that it was there."

Which might have explained Jones's insomnia, chest pains, and irregular heartbeat.

Gary Cartwright, Cowboys critic emeritus, observed in *Texas Monthly* magazine that as the owner, Jones could do whatever he wanted, and in this case what he wanted more than anything was to win without Jimmy Johnson.

The departure of Jimmy and the arrival of Barry turned an already-vicious media pack rabid. No way would Switzer or Jones be getting a free pass.

A bigger question was what it all meant for Troy Aikman, the Cowboys' franchise quarterback. Aikman had left Oklahoma and transferred to UCLA because he didn't fit in with Switzer's offense. It had taken a couple years for Aikman to flourish under Jimmy Johnson's tough but tolerant regimen, and despite Aikman's initial response to the news, when he said that Switzer was a proven winner, Switzer's laissez-faire style presented a challenge. Michael Irvin was pissed that his old college coach Jimmy Johnson had been sent packing over "ego, personality, whatever the hell it was."

The Cowboys' 1993 highlight reel was reedited by NFL Films after Johnson's departure to feature Emmitt Smith, the MVP of the Super Bowl, and Jerry Jones, who told the Cowboys' kickoff luncheon crowd, "I guess I should apologize for being the most valuable player in the highlight film."

Jones had other reasons to have a swollen ego besides the performance of his team. He had led the league owners in working out a collective bargaining agreement with the players that opened up free agency but also guaranteed owners the first $1 billion in revenues before splitting proceeds with players. The deal would hold through 2010. He had also been instrumental in swinging the $1.6 billion deal with Fox Television for rights to National Football Conference games beginning in 1994, part of the league's $4 billion in contracts with three television networks. The deal effectively doubled each NFL franchise's TV revenue. For the first time since 1956, CBS would not be televising NFL football games.

Jimmy Johnson landed at Fox Sports as a commentator, the refuge of choice for former coaches and players who wanted to get into broadcasting. Johnson worked with former pro players Terry Bradshaw and Howie Long. He would get his digs in with his commentary, even mocking his former partner's facelift on the air by comparing him to the much-enhanced singer Michael Jackson.

Before training camp opened in Austin, Barry Switzer got a personal lift when OU athletic director Donnie Duncan suggested Switzer be checked for attention deficit disorder, which made a person seem manic and flighty. Switzer saw a doctor, got a positive diagnosis, and started taking Ritalin. He arrived at summer training camp in Austin feeling laid-back and relaxed, a mood that spread throughout the locker room. The loose atmosphere was a marked departure from Jimmy Johnson's tightly wound ways. Forced swims in the 68-degree waters of Barton Springs would no longer be part of summer initiation.

Barry Switzer insisted he had as much power as Jerry Jones. "You [can] underline it: I am the number two man with the Dallas Cowboys," he said as camp opened. "Those guys [assistant coaches] know who the boss is. They know they work for me. I make the call on the coaches. Jerry and I discussed that. They know that. They know how I work, how the system works."

If he wasn't a disciplinarian, Switzer brought other less tangible attributes into the locker room. He had gained the trust of the team's African American players, as Michael Irvin acknowledged during training camp. "He grew up with the brothers, he got street cred," Irvin said. That was before Irvin walked out of a team meeting at which the coach was telling players that his predecessor had poisoned the well and had made the owner out to be a bad actor. "You don't know the bullshit some of these guys have been through with this owner," Irvin said as he left the room.

Irvin clearly had mixed feelings. He had suffered through 3-13 and 1-15 seasons and had no desire to relive those years. "We were used to winning with Jimmy," he admitted after the fact. "It wasn't that I had a problem with Barry. I was upset with the situation.

"We had a car that was running perfectly. Why do you take it to the shop? That was my problem."

Switzer told Steve Sabol of NFL Films his own history was intertwined with the African American experience. "My world was surrounded by the black community," Switzer said. "My dad—a black woman shot him and murdered him because she caught him in bed with another black woman. I was raised knowing there wasn't any difference in any of us." Switzer had started black quarterbacks in 1971 and 1972 when no other top-shelf college football program was doing so, and his teams won more games during the 1970s than any other college program's. Yet when he left OU, in 1989, *Sports Illustrated* described the football program as "an ethical wasteland."

Switzer had the attention of the team's black players, but he still needed to do some fence-mending with at least one white star. Troy Aikman did not dig what he was seeing. "Jimmy had such presence on the football field, whether it be at the practice field or the games. That is not there," Troy said in early August at camp. "Whereas Barry blends in and lets the guys go about their business."

"I don't know what's going on around here," Switzer said on the same day while taking a bite out of a frozen fruit bar. "I guess I'm getting tired of this shit." He took a few more bites and asked, "We got any more around here? I tell you what. The damn situation's gotten to where it gets too much damn attention answering the same damned ol' questions and it's pissed me off. Then one thing happened this morning. But anyway..."

The perception of Switzer as Jerry's butt boy had been fueled by Jerry's constant presence at Switzer's side, something Jimmy would never have tolerated. Jerry even ran pass patterns for the TV cameras. Jones enjoyed being involved in coaching decisions, and since it was his team, he had entrée.

Still, Jerry Jones was right about one aspect: with the talent this team possessed, just about anyone could coach it.

The preseason played out well enough. Eighty-four thousand fans attended training camp in Austin despite the absence of Jimmy Johnson. The Cowboys South of the Border fan base turned out in record numbers at Aztec Stadium in Mexico City for an exhibition game against the Houston Oilers; it was witnessed by 112,376 fans, the largest crowd ever to watch an NFL game.

Then, on a Thursday morning during the last week of Cowboys training camp, the first dustup of the Switzer era occurred. Channel 8 sports director and Cowboys radio color man Dale Hansen was on Norm Hitzges's radio show on KLIF talking about the Cowboys. Hitzges asked how Hansen thought the Cowboys were going to do in the coming season. Hansen said he saw no reason they shouldn't win the Super Bowl.

Were there any concerns that would keep Dallas from doing that? Hitzges asked in his screwed-down, in-all-sincerity inquisitive manner.

"Nothing beyond a bunch of assistant coaches stabbing [Switzer] in the back," Hansen mused.

Joe Avezzano, the special-teams coach, thought he should have been made head coach after Johnson left. Butch Davis, the defensive coordinator who'd been with Jimmy Johnson since Oklahoma State, thought *he* should be head coach. "That could be a problem," Hansen said.

Hitzges asked for an example. Hansen described seeing Switzer walk into the locker room and argue with trainer Kevin O'Neal, who had come from Miami with Jimmy Johnson, and then hearing O'Neal tell Switzer to fuck off, which made Mark Tuinei and other players nearby laugh. Hansen thought that was bad juju.

When the head coach was asked about what Hansen said, Switzer accused the sportscaster of "fabricating stories." A much-publicized head-butting ensued.

During training camp, Switzer had three minutes at the end of Hansen's Thursday-night sportscasts. But after the charges of internal dissension were leveled, Switzer went longer than that, accusing Hansen of, among other transgressions, claiming ex–defensive tackle Tony Casillas had a brain tumor, and he punched Hansen on the arm during the live broadcast.

Even after the cameras were turned off, Switzer kept going: Hansen was betraying his employer. "Hey, we're on the same team," Switzer told him. "We both work for the Dallas Cowboys." Switzer asked Hansen who his sources were about the rumors of assistant coaches in revolt. No way would he spill the beans, Hansen told him.

"Yeah, I'm mad," Hansen said a day later. "He attacked my integrity. I expected him to go on the attack. The only thing that surprised me was Tony Casillas. That was a ridiculously cheap shot. I was only doing my job, asking questions."

"I thought it was great TV," Switzer told Barry Horn, the sports media columnist for the *Morning News*. "I play the game and he plays the game. The rumors in the media aren't going to run this football team. I run the football team. I had fun with that tonight. But Hansen needs to work out with weights. He's a little soft."

Hansen was unbowed. "There are better reporters in this town than I am," he said. "He is going to be asked a lot of tough questions. He's not in Oklahoma anymore." Hansen did agree with Switzer on one point. "I think that was good television," he said. "I think people will talk about it."

Switzer made clear he didn't want Hansen's head. "Hell, no. We were just having some fun last night. . . . I just expect him to do his job and be fair, don't manufacture things, and be up front."

Brad Sham tried to intervene three days later, on August 21, by defending Hansen on the pregame show before the Broncos-Cowboys exhibition game at Texas Stadium. "I have commandeered the microphone for this segment because it is my first chance to be in front of one since my partner of ten years had a little TV ho-ha-ha with Barry Switzer the other night," Sham began, making clear whose side he was on in a moment that would never have happened when the team was Tex Schramm's. "Barry Switzer crossed the line in my judgment," he said, speaking directly to Hansen in the broadcast booth. "I think Barry owes you an apology."

Sham didn't stop there, saying, "Bulletin: What Jerry Jones and Barry Switzer say is going on isn't always what's going on."

The owner did not appreciate Sham's impromptu commentary. Jerry Jones said he believed Sham was calling Switzer and him liars. Sham's comments and Hansen's comments were "not positive." Sham tried to clarify his remarks. "What I was saying is that sometimes they only tell part of a story. They just give the company line."

Hansen was not quite as delicate, saying, "I'm not interested in satisfying Jerry Jones. I'm interested in satisfying the audience." He added, "That's not right. Jerry would be fourth on my list after the audience, the management of KVIL-FM, and the management of Channel 8. I've learned in the broadcast business that if the audience is satisfied, then management becomes satisfied."

Sham had been doing play-by-play since 1976, Hansen had been the color guy since 1985, and the broadcasters may have been employed by KVIL—but Jones had the final say. As a result of Sham's comments, he was fired from Jones's Monday-night TV special edition and would no longer interview Switzer before games on the Cowboys radio network.

"This in no way was an attempt to hurt Brad or his relationship with this organization," Jones said after ordering the change. "I did, however, feel it was necessary to emphasize the importance of the editorial control of our program. I can tolerate criticism on a newscast. But he was doing it on my time. It doesn't embarrass me. But by doing nothing, I would be condoning it. That would not be very smart."

Ron Chapman, KVIL's program manager, remained staunchly in Jones's corner. "All of it [the broadcasters' comments] is wonderful and noble," he said. "I'm not sure it belongs in a broadcast."

Hansen got his, too, when his Bennigan's show on KRLD radio was suddenly bumped from Tuesday to Wednesday to accommodate Switzer's show. Switzer hadn't sat with Hansen for a one-on-one interview since they had had their blowup, but he did take time to visit with Skip Bayless on his radio show on KTCK, where he criticized the way Sham defended Hansen "in a pompous, arrogant attitude. He wears two hats. When he sits in that booth, his hat has two stars on the side."

By THE TIME training camp wrapped, it was clear that control and discipline, the cornerstones of Jimmy Johnson's coaching style, were not priorities with Barry Switzer, and the fans were eating up the drama. Every home game since the start of the 1992 season had been a sellout, and 1994 would be no different.

Before the regular season got under way, Michael Irvin would complain that his $1.25 million–plus annual salary wasn't enough to take care of his sixteen siblings, since he'd bought his mother, Pearl, a new house in Fort Lauderdale. He needed an adjustment in pay or he would be forced to test the free-agent market when the season ended. Jerry Jones was inclined to offer a salary bump to placate the Playmaker. Keeping his biggest stars happy was sound business now, especially with all the movement free agency had brought to the game. The San Francisco 49ers had enticed Cowboys linebacker Ken Norton Jr. and Atlanta Falcons cornerback Deion Sanders to leave their teams and come out west to play, with money as the incentive. Jones would have to play the same game, and it was best that he start at home with Irvin.

The Barry Switzer era debuted at Three Rivers Stadium in Pittsburgh, where the Cowboys crushed the Steelers, 29–6. The new coach was a sight to behold, wrote Stanley Marcus, Mr. Neiman-Marcus, who was now an opinion columnist for the *Morning News*. Marcus exhibited fine observation skills and a gentle biting wit in his new role. Tom Landry had been stoic, Mr. Stanley wrote, and refused to show joy or gloom, "suggesting that he might have undergone a course in facial muscle control." Jimmy Johnson was "a bundle of nervous energy." Barry Switzer was harder to fathom: "It's a kinetic face, activated by constant gum-chewing."

Switzer had a kinetic mind too. Four days after coaching his team to an opening-day victory, the coach was delivering flu medicine to an ailing Charles Haley at home. Jimmy Johnson would have never done that. In an early-October game against the Redskins, Switzer left the sidelines at RFK Stadium in the final three minutes to use the restroom. Jimmy Johnson wouldn't ever have done that, although the outcome of that game was already certain, with the Cowboys leading 34–7. After the game, Switzer proudly referred to his defensive players as "Mandingo Warriors." Surely, Jimmy wouldn't have called them that.

But Switzer was no less relentless than Johnson in pursuing wins. A week after the Cowboys destroyed the Cardinals 38–3 in a game where Randy White and Tony Dorsett joined the Ring of Honor during halftime, they squeaked past winless Cincinnati, 23–20. The Bengals head coach, David Shula, refused to shake Switzer's hand at midfield following the contest because Switzer had compared the Bengals to winless Iowa State before the game and in front of reporters. "You can stick Iowa State up your ass," Shula informed Switzer.

The scrutiny of Coach Switzer intensified after offensive tackle Erik Williams rammed his Mercedes into a freeway wall in late October while speeding and talking on his cell phone; he suffered injuries that ended his season. That same October night, their number-one draft pick, defensive end Shante Carver, rolled his pickup truck on North Central Expressway and abandoned it; he claimed the truck had been stolen, but he eventually fessed up. A week later, defensive lineman Leon Lett and cornerback Clayton Holmes tested positive for illicit drugs and were suspended for four games by the NFL.

The head coach's loose style included his leaving the team on some Saturday nights to fly in Jerry's jet to watch his son Doug quarterback the University of Arkansas–Pine Bluff Golden Lions, a historically black school.

The coach was unapologetic to the second-guessers who thought he should be spending Saturday nights preparing for Sunday afternoons. "My dad never saw me play high school football because he was in the state penitentiary," Switzer bluntly explained. "The idea of a guy in there running a projector until midnight on a Saturday, looking for an edge to win, that's Hollywood. Those things don't happen. In college, I was always at a high school stadium the night before [a game]."

Switzer still knew how to turn on the fire when he wanted to, threatening to "cut any of you fuckers who think Jerry is coaching the team," and yelling in the locker room after a game, "Fuck Jimmy Johnson! We played with a lot of emotion today. We've got a job to do and we're gonna do it, bay-bee!"

Two weeks after Texas governor Ann Richards was defeated by George W. Bush (son of the former president of the United States and the titular owner of the Texas Rangers baseball club), ushering in the modern era of Republican-majority Texas, the Dallas Cowboys were leading the Redskins at halftime at home, 24–7, when Charles Haley confided to his teammates that they needed the old coach to motivate them.

Switzer heard Haley and went off: "This ain't Jimmy's team! This is our team! We don't need Jimmy!"

The Cowboys won, 31–7, and media talk about the team needing motivation subsided.

Jerry Jones grabbed the spotlight back from Switzer by unveiling plans for the greatest show in sports, a Disneyland-inspired entertainment-and-office complex built around Texas Stadium with virtual-reality theaters, restaurants, a retractable roof over the stadium, and expanded seating to accommodate 100,000 fans. Jones badly wanted a Super Bowl to be played at the Dallas Cowboys' home, but league officials regarded Texas Stadium as undersized and unprotected from winter weather. The $350 million redo that Jones envisioned would address those shortcomings.

Jones put himself front and center again when the Cowboys unveiled a new double-star jersey for the Thanksgiving Day game, an event announced at a press conference that drew more than thirty television, radio, and newspaper reporters, demonstrating the Cowboys' star power and Jones's instinctive ability to gin up publicity. Jones modeled the jersey while being interviewed before the Turkey Day game. More than a hundred thousand jerseys were sold over the following week, earning Jones a $1 million bonus from the apparel manufacturer for introducing the new line.

Fans at Texas Stadium were more focused on the football game than the merchandise. Troy Aikman had sprained his left knee, and for the sixteenth time in six seasons, he would miss a game due to injuries, making his league-record $50 million contract worth second-guessing. Aikman's backup Rodney Peete was hurt too, leaving the job of facing off against the Green Bay Packers and their franchise quarterback Brett Favre to third-string QB Jason Garrett, a second-year player from Princeton who was making his first start.

Garrett got off on the wrong foot, giving away an interception on his first pass attempt, and at the half, the Cowboys trailed 17–6. But over the course of nineteen minutes in the second half, Garrett found his groove, and the Cowboys rang up five touchdowns to upset Green Bay, 42–31. Garrett was 15-26-1 with 311 passing yards and two TDs, while Emmitt Smith ran for 133 yards and made six catches for 95 yards. Michael Irvin escorted Garrett off the field at the end of the game, his right arm wrapped around the redheaded quarterback like a protective big brother. Garrett didn't get much more playing time once Aikman and Peete returned, but his Thanksgiving Day performance coming off the bench to shine in front of a full house was the stuff of legend. The kid was Clint Longley to the tenth power.

By December, Barry Switzer had vindicated himself in the eyes of Cowboys fans if not in the eyes of all his players. Troy Aikman was having a stellar year despite the bad knee, and his injury gave backup Rodney Peete enough playing time to stay sharp. And Jones hovered far enough in the background for Switzer to assert on numerous occasions that the head coach was in charge, not the owner. If the owner meddled, the head coach was quitting, he insisted.

The coaching drama was one element addressed in the forty-five-page spread on the Cowboys in the December 12, 1994, issue of *Sports Illustrated*. Jones had banned Jimmy Johnson from attending Cowboys practices when Johnson was part of an HBO crew, but the snub did not keep Johnson from coming around and confessing, "I went through a period where I had negative feelings about everything involving the Cowboys. I admit that. I didn't want them to win, or have success. But in the last month or so, when the players have gone through this little struggle, I found myself being pulled back into it on an emotional basis. The Cleveland game was a turning point. I didn't like what I was seeing. I wanted them to win that game there at the end. There are too many players here in Dallas who are important to me, and to have that outweighed by a handful of people in this organization I care absolutely nothing about...well, that wasn't right."

The lucrative three-year contract he'd signed with Fox made any lingering wounds easier to forget.

Switzer's Cowboys appeared to be as good as the teams Jimmy Johnson had overseen, despite the well-publicized discord, the wilding, and other negatives, such as Troy Aikman's throwing twelve interceptions, Emmitt Smith's pulled hamstring, Alvin Harper's losing a step, and Ernie Zampese overreaching to prove he was better than Norv Turner as the offensive coordinator. The first three losses blemishing their 12-4 regular-season record turned on a ref's bad call, an errant pass, and an extra inch. They were that good.

The Cowboys again trampled the once mighty Packers, 35–9, in the divisional playoffs, setting up another grudge match at Candlestick Park against the 13-3 San Francisco 49ers, who earned home-field advantage by beating Dallas during the regular season, 21–14. Jerry was itching for this showdown as much as Barry was. Following the playoff win over Green Bay at Texas Stadium, Jones held court in the Corral party tent outside the stadium. Fueled by frozen margaritas, he declared, "To hell with Jimmy Johnson!," to the celebratory gathering surrounding him.

Jones was still pushing Johnson away, and the quarterback still felt differently. Troy Aikman missed Jimmy Johnson's ability to breathe fire and intimidate players into stepping up their game. When he yelled, Johnson scared people. Switzer was more like the players' buddy and dorm counselor. When he yelled, he just came off as crazy.

Aikman, who had continued talking to Johnson on the phone, was no fan of Switzer's coaching. But Aikman knew well enough that those thoughts were best kept to himself. His conflicted feelings took a backseat to his competitive fire; he said only "I guess a lot of the players want to prove we can win without Jimmy." No matter who was at the helm, this edition of the Cowboys shouldn't be stopped by petty jealousy; they were too good.

But on this winter's day, they weren't too good for the 49ers, at least at first. San Francisco leaped to a 21–0 lead early in the game at a very muddy Candlestick Park after Troy Aikman tossed off a 44-yard interception, and the SF offense, led by Steve Young, converted two Cowboys fumbles into touchdowns.

"It's a horror movie I'm watching," Switzer yelled, gathering his offense together to offer hope. "You know what's great about being down twenty-one to nothing in the first five minutes?" he screamed on the sidelines. "We've got fifty-five minutes to get back into the son of a bitch!"

"Hey, we're fine," Aikman replied, offering a calmer version of the same sentiment. "We're going to win this thing."

The Cowboys clawed back, led by Aikman and Irvin, with the quarterback converting third downs almost flawlessly. Late in the fourth quarter, Aikman threw a third-down pass toward Michael Irvin, who was being closely shadowed by Deion Sanders. Irvin couldn't reach the throw because Sanders blocked his path. The pass was ruled incomplete. Switzer got so ticked that the officials had refused to throw a flag on Sanders for interference, he rushed out onto the field and bumped back judge Ken Baker with his chest, drawing a 15-yard penalty for unsportsmanlike conduct.

Still, the Cowboys had a chance. On third-and-25 from his own 42, Aikman hit Alvin Harper for a 14-yard catch. But he couldn't find an open receiver on fourth-and-11 and was sacked by the 'Niners' Tim Harris. The Cowboys lost, 38–28. Emmitt Smith had entered the game with a tender left hamstring and he gritted it out, managing to rush for 74 yards and two touchdowns before leaving with a pulled right hamstring. Michael Irvin caught 12 passes for almost 200 yards, a franchise record, while making the other two touchdowns. But Emmitt knew the score, telling a reporter after the game that once the 49ers were up 21–0, "it was like spotting Carl Lewis 20 yards in a 100-yard dash."

As the game ended, Irvin and Smith hugged each other, acting like the Cowboys had won, with Smith telling Irvin, "Mike, don't go. Don't leave me here. We're going to be all right." It had been a roller-coaster ride; at several points during the season Irvin was ready to bail on the Cowboys and sell his services to the highest bidder who was most likely to reach the championship game. He now realized the Cowboys were that team.

Another factor in the loss was the yellow flag thrown on the coach. "Sure, it's a mistake and I gave them 15 yards," Switzer admitted afterward. "I contributed to us getting beat."

Jerry Jones spoke cautiously about Switzer's chest bump with the zebra. "I'm not going to second guess the decision I made to hire Barry Switzer," the owner said, before pointing out he was on the coach's side. "I know that I will get a lot of criticism. But you have to remember there was a helluva lot of finger pointing going all the way back to 1989 when we went 1-15."

Troy Aikman still wasn't convinced. "The way Jimmy wanted to get things done was very consistent with the way I wanted to get things done," he said a few days later. "When Jimmy was here, things were very easy for me. I saw eye to eye with the football coach." Aikman did not like having to be the one to bring the fire to the team, a responsibility formerly handled by Jimmy Johnson. Switzer wasn't about to push the envelope. Aikman insisted he loved Switzer as a person; he just wasn't getting the job done as coach. No one was policing the team.

Michael Irvin defended Switzer. "Any other rookie coach comes in and takes a team to the championship game, he gets all kinds of praise," he said. "But what they're saying here is, we should have been there anyway. The truth is, Barry did a great job of just keeping things together."

The San Francisco 49ers would go on to sink the San Diego Chargers, 49–26, in the Super Bowl. Quarterback Steve Young was named the game's MVP and the league's most valuable player of the year, while the 'Niners' Deion Sanders snagged most valuable defensive player honors.

Dallas fans could have been proud that their team had lost to the better team. Instead, most were pissed the Cowboys didn't go all the way, knowing they should have been the best.

The Smell of Success

LESS THAN TWO MONTHS after his team lost to San Francisco, Jerry Jones signed Michael Irvin to a five-year, $15 million contract, making him the highest-paid receiver in NFL history; Irvin also got a $5 million bonus. Loyalty with benefits beat free agency. But Jones couldn't reward everyone. Wide receiver Alvin Harper, center Mark Stepnoski, and defensive tackle Jim Jeffcoat departed for other teams that were willing to pay them their asking price.

Adding to the escalating salary game were three new competitors for DFW sports fans' dollars. NASCAR stock-car racing, a largely Southern pastime that was aggressively expanding, entered the market in the form of a $75 million racetrack under construction north of Fort Worth that would be the largest spectator venue in the state, seating 150,000. The National Hockey League had arrived two years before when the Minnesota North Stars moved into Reunion Arena and became the Dallas Stars. And a new horse-racing track in Grand Prairie, the Lone Star Park, was also under construction.

That wasn't all that was on Jerry Jones's mind. Circumstances just wouldn't let him forget about his breakup with Jimmy Johnson. At the 1995 spring NFL owners' meeting at the Arizona Biltmore outside of Phoenix, Bobby Ackles, Dave Wannstedt, Norv Turner, and others who had been in Orlando the year before as Jimmy Johnson's tablemates sat together once again in a banquet room at a Fox TV party, laughing and listening to Jimmy Johnson, Fox commentator, regale them with stories. Jerry Jones held court at a nearby table. Carmen Policy, the general manager of the San Francisco 49ers, walked into the room three sheets to the wind but still able to recognize the situation and see who was sitting where. He walked up to Johnson's table and repeated what Jerry Jones had said a year earlier in his unrequited toast: "Here's to the Dallas Cowboys!" This time, the table joined him in the toast. The entire room erupted in laughter.

Lamar Hunt said he admired Jerry Jones as "a very creative person and a wonderful selling person." To some of his employees, though, Jones could be insufferable. After eighteen years as part of the Dallas Cowboys radio broadcast crew, Brad Sham bailed as the play-by-play voice of the Cowboys to go to work for baseball's Texas Rangers. Sham diplomatically explained that there were more games to call with the baseball team. What he didn't say was that the ownership group Sham would have to please did not include Jerry Jones. Dale Hansen reluctantly stayed to provide color for Dave Garrett, the new play-by-play announcer imported from Oklahoma City at the recommendation of Barry Switzer.

Meanwhile, NFL franchises were playing musical chairs, spurred on by cities willing to pay hundreds of millions of dollars to secure a franchise, beginning with the expansion Carolina Panthers in Charlotte and the Jaguars of Jacksonville, Florida. The Raiders returned to Oakland in 1995, a year after the Rams moved from Los Angeles to St. Louis, leaving the second-largest population center in the United States without an NFL team. At the end of the 1995 season, Bud Adams would announce the Houston Oilers were moving to Tennessee since Adams had not been able to persuade city or county officials to build a new stadium. Baltimore, which had been without a franchise since the Colts left, in 1984, enticed Art Modell to move the Browns from Cleveland to Baltimore, where they became the Ravens; two days later, the voters of Cleveland approved construction of a new stadium for their now-relocated franchise. A new version of the Browns would be born as an expansion franchise in 1999, with Houston due for another team too.

In the midst of the franchise shuffles came a bold move engineered by Jerry Jones. His target was revenue-sharing. Long ago, the NFL had adopted this policy to enable smaller-market teams such as the Green Bay Packers to be competitive with larger-market teams like the Giants, Jets, and Bears. The NFL negotiated television contracts for the entire league and controlled revenue from merchandising and licensing.

Seventy-seven percent of all television, merchandise, and ticket sales were shared equally by the thirty clubs. Jerry Jones thought he deserved a bigger slice. The Cowboys were the most popular team in American sports, responsible for 35 percent of all NFL merchandise sold, but they received only one-thirtieth of the revenues from NFL Properties; $3 million was disbursed to each team from the deals the league made with manufacturers and retailers. The Cowboys' merch was worth much more than that, Jones contended. For that matter, why did the Cowboys have to pay visiting teams 40 percent of the gate to a full house and get only 40 percent when they filled up their opponents' stadiums?

Jones questioned the league's ability to prevent individual clubs from cutting their own deals, particularly the Cowboys, since the franchise didn't rent Texas Stadium but operated the facility. When Jones made his own sponsorship agreement with JCPenney, the NFL had put the kibosh on the deal, citing the league's revenue-sharing agreement. But the Dallas owner was hardly intimidated.

On August 3, 1995, Jerry Jones held a press conference at training camp in Austin. Outfitted in white boots with the Pepsi logo emblazoned on the sides, he kicked a plastic bottle of Coca-Cola to dramatize his announcement that Pepsi-Cola and Dr Pepper were replacing Coca-Cola as the official soft drink of Texas Stadium. Although Coke was the official drink of the NFL, "they have been given the boot" at Texas Stadium, Jones declared. He promised he would be "drinking Pepsi, selling Pepsi, and promoting Pepsi" from here on out. The ten-year, $20 million PepsiCo pouring-rights deal was with the stadium, not the football club, so Jones claimed he could deposit the revenues in his own pocket rather than sharing them with the league.

"This is a direct hit on the Coca-Cola deal with the league," Jones emphasized. "Ultimately, all logos, the helmet and star associated with the Cowboys will be handled by the Dallas Cowboys and not the marketing arm of the NFL," Jones said while acknowledging, "That is not a popular stance to take with other members of the NFL." Pepsi products, along with Texas favorite Dr Pepper, would be sold inside the stadium and would get broadcast, signage, and special-events-advertising rights.

The *Morning News's* Ed Werder wrote that Jones's message was explicit: "Corporations wanting to form partnerships with the Cowboys should proceed directly to One Cowboys Parkway rather than the NFL offices in New York." Werder accurately predicted the deal would increase the rancor and discord between Jones and other owners and the league home office. The initial reaction of the NFL's director of communications, Greg Aiello, formerly the head of marketing for the Dallas Cowboys, was "The commissioner is in Tokyo having a Coke." Upon his return, Commissioner Tagliabue went on the record to call Jones's move "unfair and destructive" and "short-sighted and self-serving." Art Modell, the owner of the new Baltimore Ravens, complained, "We can't have owners going out and cutting their separate deals. It would ruin the league."

In fact Coca-Cola was becoming more scrupulous with its sports-marketing budget, which didn't escape the notice of the Kraft family, owners of the New England Patriots, who were talking to Pepsi too.

Randy Galloway wrote that the move officially made Jones "an NFL outlaw" who was "sending word to the Cincinnatis, the Green Bays, the Seattles, etc. they would no longer be living out of the Dallas Cowboys' back pocket.... For you patriots, Jones is fighting communism, NFL style."

Jones saw it differently. "I believe in the concept that if you're aggressive, and all of the other teams can do the same thing, then we can make the pie bigger," he told ESPN. "What I'm doing is in the best interest of the league," Jones affirmed to Ed Werder. "Frankly, I think people in this league need to get off their butt and go to work instead of sitting around waiting for the communal check to arrive. It's called the incentive plan."

Jones did the deed to benefit the Dallas Cowboys and himself. The boost in revenue would help the team pay for free agents and signing bonuses. As a peace offering, Jones said the league should withhold the Cowboys' share of Coca-Cola revenue.

A $58 million gap had been created between the profitability of the Cowboys, the wealthiest team in the league, and the poorest franchise, and that gap was growing wider. But no way was Jones about to toe the line. Fuck socialism. This was America.

A $2.5 million deal with Nike for Texas Stadium rights followed, along with exclusive deals with American Express and Acme Brick.

The league would respond by filing a $300 million suit against Jones for plotting to destroy NFL Properties. Jones hit back with a $700 million suit claiming antitrust laws were being broken. The suits and countersuits eventually led to a settlement that allowed the Cowboys and all NFL teams to control team-specific licensing.

Carmen Policy, the president of the San Francisco 49ers, admitted that his club could learn a few tricks from Jones but that "we don't operate on that quick-buck mentality." Jones was a different breed of cat. Policy said, "When I think of Jerry Jones, I think of a snake-oil salesman. I also think of a gunslinger. I also think of a wildcatter from the oil fields."

Which was just about right. Despite the animosity, Jones sat on the NFL's two most powerful committees—competition and broadcast—because he knew how to make a buck.

THE ELECTION OF RON KIRK, the first African American mayor of Dallas, in May of 1995 was a sign of improved race relations, even if change had come to Dallas more slowly than it had elsewhere in the formerly segregated South. Kirk would later point out that Tom Bradley, the former mayor of Los Angeles; Willie Brown, the mayor of San Francisco; and Maynard Jackson, the first black mayor of Atlanta, were all Texas natives who had had to leave to become leaders.

Race did not top the list of Barry Switzer's and Jerry Jones's concerns. They were more obsessed with the newly implemented National Football League salary cap that had forced Jones to trade away or release key players the franchise could no longer afford—center Mark Stepnoski, receiver Alvin Harper, defensive end Jim Jeffcoat, and safety James Washington. Those departures and an injury to starting cornerback Kevin Smith that would keep him out for the entire season created the panicked motive, and the means, to sign free agent Deion Sanders.

Sanders, the NFL's defensive player of the year and the NFL's first two-way player since Chuck Bednarik of Philadelphia in the 1950s, had been a thorn in Dallas's side in the previous year's final loss to San Francisco. He was truly the complete athlete, able to run, catch, block, and intercept—everything except tackle, one of his primary responsibilities as a cornerback—and sell himself like few other players had ever done.

His winning smile and outgoing personality that mixed faith (he was a born-again Christian) and his prowess as a ladies' man were made for Dallas. Sanders grew up in Fort Myers, Florida; played football, baseball, and ran track for Florida State; and spent four years with the Atlanta Falcons before selling his services to the

49ers while also playing major-league baseball for the Yankees, Braves, and Reds. He was the only athlete to play in both a Super Bowl and a World Series.

The week two signing of Neon Deion, aka Prime Time, cost Jerry Jones $35 million for seven years plus a $13 million signing bonus. Stephen Jones had strongly advised against the deal; he didn't think the club could afford the tab. But if the greatest cornerback in NFL history could help Dallas win the big one, it was worth it, reasoned Stephen's father.

After the contract was finalized with Sanders's agent, Jerry detoured his Lear to Little Rock and went to the house in North Little Rock where he had grown up to do some soul-searching. He needed to convince himself he had made the right call.

Despite Jones's signing Sanders and doling out $40 million in bonuses in 1995, his marketing deals and corporate partnerships, along with his raising ticket prices at Texas Stadium and adding more seats, had helped the football club realize $30 million in profits over the past three years, with even higher revenues projected. In that respect, Deion Sanders was a steal. The bling-flashing extrovert was worth several million in publicity just for being Deion, even if he didn't start playing for the Cowboys until week nine of the 1995 season due to injuries.

The Cowboys had charged out of the chute with nostrils flaring, shutting out the New York Giants at the Meadowlands, 35–0, on ABC's *Monday Night Football* season opener; knocking off the Denver Broncos at home, 31–21; edging the Minnesota Vikings in Minneapolis in overtime, 23–17; and then defeathering the Cardinals, 34–20. The game against Minnesota was Michael Irvin's twenty-seventh with 100 yards or more in receptions, another franchise record.

Troy Aikman got knocked out early in the fifth game against the Redskins at RFK Stadium. Backup Wade Wilson performed admirably, going 21 for 29 passing for 224 yards with a touchdown while giving up an interception, but the Cowboys still came up short, 27–23. Coach Switzer chewed out Charles Haley, Tony Tolbert, and Leon Lett for dragging ass on defense after the game, then apologized. "I made a mistake and I'm man enough to admit it," he said. "When we lose, we'll lose as a team. I think that it's wrong for me to cite individual players. There is no need to criticize and I'm not going to do it anymore. It doesn't help them emotionally to prepare to play and focus the next week."

Aikman returned the next week and outdueled Brett Favre as the Cowboys rolled Green Bay, 34–24. San Diego, Atlanta, and Philadelphia fell like dominoes.

The Cowboys were prepared to rout their currently most hated rivals, the defending Super Bowl champion San Francisco 49ers, who were clearly diminished with a 5-4 record. But the 'Niners came into Texas Stadium and pulled off an upset, knocking Troy Aikman out of the game at 6:39 in the first quarter with a Dana Stubblefield sack that left Aikman's left knee severely bruised, and then knocking his replacement, Wade Wilson, out of the game too. SF QB Elvis Grbac, substituting for an injured Steve Young, hit Jerry Rice with an 81-yard touchdown pass, and Merton Hanks picked up a Michael Irvin fumble on a completed pass and ran it in for a 38-yard touchdown. After scoring the first 24 points of the game, San Francisco let up enough for the Cowboys to fight back, but only so much. The 'Niners pinned Dallas with their second loss of the season, 38–20. SF president and general manager Carmen Policy couldn't contain himself, blurting out to his team in the locker room, "How 'bout them 49ers?" San Francisco linebacker Rickey Jackson was defiant, saying, "They got Deion from us. They can spend all the money they want. But they can't mess with the heart. Jerry Jones can't buy that."

Jerry Jones had purchased the loyalty of the best receiver in the game, Michael Irvin, who broke Tony Hill's team record of 7,988 career receiving yards against San Francisco.

But Jerry Jones couldn't buy good sense to put in his coach's head. In 23-degree December weather at Philadelphia's Veterans Stadium, Barry Switzer and the Cowboys choked. The owner had been on Switzer's ass the whole game, running up to him to complain about Switzer's strategy. Change it now, Jones demanded within earshot of all. Aikman needed a blocker in the backfield to protect him.

Late in the fourth quarter with the score tied and the Cowboys' ball on their own 29-yard line facing fourth-and-one ("Fourth-and-three-inches," the coach would later insist), Switzer called for Emmitt Smith to run the ball to the left and go for a first down rather than kick into a stiff wind. Smith was stopped short. But officials ruled that the clock had already wound down to the two-minute warning. After the official time-out, the Cowboys opted not to punt and went for the first down one more time. Again, Smith didn't make it. Philadelphia got the ball, and the Eagles' Gary Anderson kicked the game-winning goal for a 20–17 win. Remorseful, Switzer told his players afterward about his father's being shot by his mistress and his mother's committing suicide as a way of showing resilience in tough times.

NBC's Mike Ditka described Switzer's brain freeze as "the sequel to *Dumb and Dumber*." Fox television analyst Jimmy Johnson remarked, "When you have fourth down on your own 29, I don't care how short it is, you punt the ball." Newspaper scribes would compare Switzer's call to the Edsel, the leisure suit, and Adam biting the apple. Randy Galloway said the coach "made a national fool of himself."

For all the criticism, no one actually playing second-guessed Switzer's call. To them, running the same play again was a show of confidence in what the team could do, even if they hadn't pulled it off.

Within a week, the loss to the Eagles was old news. Fortified by the addition of Sanders at cornerback, the Cowboys finished at 12-4 again. Emmitt Smith led the league in rushing for the fourth consecutive year with a personal-best 1,773 yards. Michael Irvin recorded

111 receptions during the season—88 for first downs and 27 on third or fourth downs—earning Pro Bowl honors for the fifth year in a row.

They went into the divisional round of the playoffs against Philadelphia determined to go all the way. "I want to win for selfish reasons," Michael Irvin said beforehand. "We don't have anything to prove to anybody. We've got goals we set, and we'd like to go out and accomplish those goals. That's just it. I'm not going out saying, 'Hey, we did this to show the world.'" The Cowboys didn't bother making it close, sending the Eagles back to Philadelphia with a 30–11 spanking.

Next came Green Bay, who had the upper hand for most of the NFC championship game at Irving on a chamber of commerce's dream of a winter day: a game-time temperature of 78 degrees. The Packers' defensive tackle Reggie White and the Cowboys' offensive tackle Erik Williams engaged in a vicious battle in the trenches. "It was as nasty a football game as you ever want to see," Williams said afterward. "This was a mean, violent war, and we made up our minds that we were going to win the war at all costs."

After three quarters, the Packers led the Cowboys 27–24. Then Emmitt Smith pounded his way into the end zone twice in the fourth quarter—two of 35 carries for 150 yards, and the second and third touchdowns he scored that day—and the defense stopped Favre cold for a 38–27 Cowboys victory. Aikman played at peak performance, going 21 of 33 for 255 yards in the air and two touchdown passes to Michael Irvin, who made mincemeat of the Packers' coverage.

Michael Irvin defended his coach on national television during the postgame wrap, shouting, "He takes all the shit, all the maligning. Give him his due!" Irvin's mother, Pearl, reacted by promising, "I will be talking with my boy. I don't need to tell you he didn't learn to speak that way in this house. I almost fell through the floor the first time he said it. I have never in my life heard Michael talk that way."

Irvin couldn't help himself. He was going to the Super Bowl again. "We let somebody borrow it home last year," he said. "We've got to check the lease and see if they left it dirty. But it's home, period. Where we belong."

PITTSBURGH AND a new-generation Steel Curtain defense would provide the opposition for Super Bowl XXX in Tempe, Arizona.

Barry Switzer apparently thought the roman numerals meant an XXX-rated Super Bowl. When he stepped off the team bus and checked into his suite at the Buttes resort, the team headquarters in Scottsdale, the party started. Friends; relatives; his ex-wife, Kay; and his girlfriend, Becky Buwick, all crowded into the suite, and they commenced to roar for the next two weeks.

The party was well covered, along with every other detail relating to the big game, but by midweek, a bigger story had developed: accusations of racism leveled at Troy Aikman. The charges were based on something departed assistant coach John Blake, an African American, had told Barry Switzer before Blake resigned to take over Switzer's old job at the University of Oklahoma. On December 3, the Cowboys had lost to Washington in a game where the coach thought his quarterback was dogging it out of deference to the 'Skins coach Norv Turner, who had been Aikman's mentor when Turner was with the Cowboys. The next day, Blake informed Switzer there was a perception that the QB chewed out only the black players and specifically cited an incident involving wide receiver Kevin Williams.

Switzer summoned Aikman to his office at 9:00 a.m. on December 5 and asked him to apologize to the black players that afternoon; if he didn't Switzer would apologize on Aikman's behalf. Aikman walked out and did not speak another word to Switzer. Neither would discuss what was said.

Aikman was the biggest star on a team with many stars. Unlike the others, he wasn't flash and bling but old-school and down-home—introverted, even—in how he dealt with the attention that came with being a public figure. He appreciated a good chaw of tobacco and country music. He wasn't Don Meredith country, but he was a Nashville cat nonetheless, a man whose tastes ran to the milder form of the style. (After meeting the band Shenandoah backstage at Billy Bob's in Fort Worth during his rookie season, Aikman had appeared as Cowboy Joe in the video for their song "Leavin's Been a Long Time Comin'," and he had dated country singer Lorrie Morgan, who was seven years older than he was.)

Switzer acknowledged that the relationship with his quarterback was strained, admitting, "I'm not going to drink RC Colas or double-date with him, but that's not important."

Of the twenty-two Cowboys starters, four were white, including Aikman. But Irvin, Haley, Sanders, and Darren Woodson had Aikman's back. "I know the relationship I have with Troy," Michael Irvin said. "I am as black as anybody you could ever see. I am as black as they come. And I know this man loves me."

Haley stated the obvious: "You have to remember 90 percent of this team is black, and therefore if he's going to yell at somebody it's probably going to be a black guy who made the mistake. If I thought he was a racist, I would have told the man. But I went up to him and told him if he stopped being Troy Aikman, then he would be a punk. I told him to be himself and not worry about what people say. I like what he brings to the team. I think it is unjust for people to think he is some kind of racist or something."

Aikman had no choice but to respond during Super Bowl week, and he took the high road. "The players on this football team know it has been discussed, it's been resolved and that is all that matters," he said. "There are a number of things being written about this week regarding my relationship with Barry. I don't think anybody pays a whole lot of attention to it within our organization or locker room."

But Aikman also made clear that as important as the Super Bowl clash was, it would not solve what he saw as problems, as he related to Jim Reeves of the *Fort Worth Star-Telegram*: "The idea that one game, one victory, would change the way I feel about this season — no, that's not going to happen."

The Cowboys were shuttled around Phoenix in stretch limos. Nate Newton was in hog heaven, telling the press, "The Tempe police gave us a list of places not to go, and there's where I went. I like wicked, dude." Meanwhile, the team owner tooled around the Valley of the Sun in singer Whitney Houston's tour bus.

"What message does this send to your players who can't afford a limo?" Barry Switzer was asked.

"Well," Switzer said, pondering, "play better and get paid more."

As for the game, Joe Montana, the former quarterback of the San Francisco 49ers, conducted the coin toss before the start of the contest at Arizona State University's Sun Devil Stadium. Dallas was heavily favored. Troy Aikman looked good from the get-go, completing 11 of his first 13 passes and at one point throwing ten consecutive completions. Deion Sanders grabbed a 47-yard pass reception playing wide receiver in the first quarter that set up Dallas's first touchdown, giving the Cowboys a 10–0 lead. But the Cowboys had only a thin 13–7 edge going into the halftime show, which starred Diana Ross, who was promoting her latest single, "Take Me Higher." And in many respects, the Steelers were outplaying them.

The Steel Curtain kept Dallas's offense at bay through most of the second half, and Pittsburgh trailed the Cowboys by a field goal, 20–17, after a successful onside kick with 4:13 on the clock. But for the second time in the second half, the Steelers' quarterback Neil O'Donnell threw the ball to the Cowboys' Larry Brown, Deion Sanders's counterpart at cornerback, instead of to his intended receiver, effectively handing Dallas a 27–17 victory.

The Steelers had more total yards (310-254) and more first downs (25-15) and were able to limit the Cowboys to 56 yards rushing, with Emmitt Smith gaining only 49 yards on 18 carries. But it was the score on the board that counted. Aikman would have won MVP honors again if not for Larry Brown's two interceptions.

Emmitt Smith might have had an off day with his ground game, but the two TDs he scored gave him an NFL-best five Super Bowl touchdowns. Charles Haley, who had recorded eleven sacks in post-season play, now had five Super Bowl rings to put on his fingers, more than any other NFL player.

Afterward, a relieved Troy Aikman looked like the weight of the world had been lifted from his shoulders. "The first Super Bowl was the most fun," he said, looking back. "The second one, we went through a lot. But this one, we had the most adversity of all. If we would have lost, being favored by all those points, there would have been enough blame to go around for everybody." Aikman was stating the obvious. The Cowboys were the richest, most talented team in football, sporting a $62 million payroll that creatively circumvented the NFL's $37.2 million salary cap.

On the field at the end of the game, Michael Irvin offered the stadium crowd and television viewers his own analysis. "Bottom line, we got it done, no matter how rocky the waters were at times," Irvin said. "If you don't want to give it to us by choice, don't write about it by force, because you know your editors are going to make you do it. That is their job." He once again showered praise on his coach, who he said had been undeservedly ragged by local media since he was hired.

Switzer returned the favor when he addressed his players along with the gathered press in the locker room. "I really appreciate all the things some of you guys said to me personally, some of you players in the ball game. It really means a lot to me. It really does," he said, choking up. "And I want to thank our coaching staff. I want to thank these guys for all the bullshit we have to put up with and all the people outside. They're loyal. They stuck with me. They fought their rear ends off and I believe in them and they believe in me."

Switzer understood that some of the media grousers would say he'd won with Jimmy's guys. "But I could have lost with them, too," he later pointed out.

Handed the trophy in the postgame ceremony, an ebullient Switzer addressed the Cowboys owner. "I want to say to Jerry Jones something that's very important that he said to me all year: Are you having a good time, Jerry?" Switzer shouted, as Jones reached over to grab the Lombardi Trophy. "I wanna tell you. We did it our way, bay-bee! We did it! We did it! We did it!"

Jerry Jones was humble, for Jerry. "I want to thank Coach Landry, I want to thank Jimmy, I want to thank Barry."

The party roared till dawn in suite 4000 at the Buttes, the tail end of a two-week bender. Before the game, Switzer had sung along with son Greg, who was playing Ray Charles's "What I Say" on the piano in his suite, improvising lines that made fun of his critics and Jimmy Johnson. Win or lose, Barry made sure he was going to have a memorable week in Arizona. As he stepped off the team bus following the game, Switzer declared he needed some Jack Daniel's whiskey and Percodan to kill the pain, then shouted to Leon Lett, "Let's win the party!" Michael Irvin showed up at Switzer's suite shortly thereafter, resplendent in sunglasses, black derby, and a checkered suit. Upon his arrival, he yelled above the din, "Hey, let me ask you something. Is there anyone who deserves this more than Barry Switzer?" The crowd in the room responded with a hearty "Hell, no!"

Switzer's $22,000 room tab was picked up by the owner.

Jones threw his own party after the game, and his cost $400,000. A party tent in the back of the resort had been gussied up into a silver-and-white ballroom with blue twinkling lights. Country singer Reba McEntire performed for twenty-five hundred special guests. Troy Aikman told the gathering, "Thank God we won. I can't imagine what it would be like at one of these parties if I had to come out and talk to you if we had lost." Sirloin and roast pork were served. Informed that drinks would no longer be served after 1:00 a.m., per

Arizona law, Jones said he'd pitch a tent and serve his own liquor. That party roared until 4:00 a.m.

One hundred twenty-five thousand fans attended the victory parade in downtown Dallas a week later. The third Super Bowl parade in four years hit the sweet spot; it was neither violent nor security-conscious sterile. Bands, six floats with players, and clowns filled the streets. A small plane towed a banner that read YEA COWBOYS! MICHAEL, NEIMAN MARCUS HAS YOUR SPRING CHIFFON. Michael Irvin had told society columnist Maryln Schwartz that his wife had brought home some chiffon items from Neiman's, and the word had spread. Jerry and Barry continued partying at Joey Vallone's restaurant in Dallas, where a very soused Jones threw a napkin in a man's face, the man's wife told columnist Helen Bryant.

A week later, only eighteen Cowboys showed up at the White House to be feted by President Clinton, whom Jerry Jones had bet against in the 1990 gubernatorial election in Arkansas; Aikman, Irvin, and MVP Larry Brown were no-shows. Clinton found a kindred spirit in Switzer, whom the president complimented by saying, "He's been second-guessed so much, for a while I thought people had mistaken him for me."

Inhaling While High

ONCE THE FAIRY DUST settled and the euphoria subsided, Barry Switzer confided to Larry Lacewell that he was thinking of hanging it up. He and Jimmy Johnson were the only coaches who had won both a national college championship and a Super Bowl. He had no goals left.

"You can't do that," Lacewell insisted.

If nothing else, Switzer needed to alter the perception that he had become paranoid about Troy Aikman since the racism blowup. If he left, everyone would think Aikman had run him off.

No one in mid-1990s Dallas was better known or more popular than Troy Aikman. Almost everything he touched turned to gold. He signed on as spokesman for Chief Auto Parts, and the chain's sales rocketed. He dabbled as a country music singer, in 1993 releasing a much-maligned single, "Oklahoma Nights," which enjoyed strong DFW sales. His children's book, *Things Change* (Taylor Trade Publishing), was the bestselling children's sports book of 1995, and he recorded two country music duets. One was with Waylon Jennings, assisted by Bill Bates, the rousing "The Good Old Dallas Cowboys," on which his voice was thin and reedy compared to Waylon's booming baritone; the other was with country star Toby Keith, "Two Pair of Levis and a Pair of Justin Boots," for the album *NFL Country*.

Aikman resided in Hackberry Creek, a gated community of new McMansions just across the LBJ Freeway from Valley Ranch; he lived there mainly for privacy, because wherever he went, girls followed. He was filling up his Yukon at a gas station one afternoon near Valley Ranch headquarters with *Star-Telegram* beat writer Richie Whitt riding shotgun when two women drove up, recognized the man pumping gas, and asked for autographs.

"Happens all the time." Aikman smiled to Whitt after obliging.

The two gals drove off, then wheeled back around and stopped. The woman on the driver's side fidgeted around, opened the door, got out, and placed her panties under Aikman's wiper blade, cooing, "I love you, Troy," before walking back to her vehicle.

"Wish that happened all the time." Aikman laughed.

It was a prophetic understatement.

The publication of the third book in Skip Bayless's Cowboys trilogy, *Hell-Bent: The Crazy Truth About the "Win or Else" Dallas Cowboys*, written after the third Super Bowl win, stirred up a shitstorm around a question Bayless posed: Was Troy Aikman gay?

Aikman was hunky and handsome but hardly the womanizer that Jerry Jones was. When he was paired with Lorrie Morgan after the first Super Bowl, some gossips wondered whether Morgan was a beard. So when the most prominent Cowboys critic (Bayless) raised the question, the chattering class went nuts.

Radio pundit Norm Hitzges trashed Bayless, but he hadn't read the book, Dale Hansen pointed out. Hansen, who was quoted extensively, did read the book and defended it as honest, citing Bayless's debunking of his own question. No, Troy Aikman *wasn't* gay. But the rumors didn't go away. Bayless later said, "Switzer asked me at one point if it was true. I told him I didn't know."

The public directed its anger at Bayless and Hansen. Troy Aikman's father, Ken, threatened to go down to Channel 8 and beat the shit out of Hansen if not kill him. "And he could have," Hansen admitted. Aikman allegedly queried his attorney about the implications of his beating the shit out of Bayless himself.

Years later, Bayless would talk about the book with sports blogger

Michael Tillery. "Troy would call me at home saying I can't write this and I can't write that," Bayless said. "It really wasn't about the gay stuff. It was about the n-word and game throwing. Barry would say he's just afraid you are gonna write the gay stuff. I told Barry I had no idea and nor do I care if he's gay or not. It definitely became part of the clash and mudslinging between the two of them. My only regret about the book is that it does not say that Aikman is gay. I had no idea and nor do I care to this day. A number of the black players—they didn't like him to start with because he was distant, knee-jerk emotional, quick-tempered. His friends on the team loved him for one reason and that was because he could play. When it was time to play, he performed. Deep down...trust me...the stars on that team...the black players...and you know who they are...they didn't like the guy."

Hansen initially tried to tamp down the Troy-is-gay tempest with the observation that he'd never seen Emmitt Smith with a girlfriend either, that he always showed up at public events with his mother or alone. That comment royally pissed off Smith.

What Hansen and Bayless didn't know at the time was that Aikman had issued an edict to his teammates not to read the book. He wasn't going to and no one else should.

The defending Super Bowl champions had more pressing challenges to grapple with anyway, starting with money. Fifteen of the highest-paid Cowboys were due more than thirty million, and the club's salary cap was forty million. Ten million would have to be divvied up among the other thirty-eight players. Instead of spending big money in the draft, Larry Lacewell opted to go for second-stringers and special-teams prospects while starters Russell Maryland, Dixon Edwards, and Super Bowl MVP Larry Brown left for better offers elsewhere.

In the era of free agency, it seemed, what Jerry Jones and Jimmy Johnson had rapidly constructed could fall apart just as quickly.

The business profile of Dallas had shifted dramatically too, symbolized by the newest darling of the video-game industry, Ion Storm, opening its offices on the fifty-fourth floor of the JP Morgan Chase Tower in downtown Dallas. Game developers having the top floor of one of the Dallas skyline's tallest perches left the coat-and-tie crowd flummoxed.

Trailing behind the Ion Storm boys were two Indiana University business graduates working in Dallas. Todd Wagner and Mark Cuban had started a company called AudioNet, which became Broadcast.com in 1995. They were motivated by the simple desire to use the Internet to listen to radio broadcasts of Indiana Hoosiers basketball games. In less than four years, Broadcast.com would become the largest aggregator of radio stations on the Internet, leading Cuban and Wagner to sell to Internet giant Yahoo for $5.7 billion in stocks. A half a year later, Cuban would use $285 million of his share of the profits to buy majority ownership of the NBA's Dallas Mavericks from H. Ross Perot Jr.

A FEW OF THE Cowboys were getting busy too. In early March of 1996, a little more than a month after the Dallas Cowboys' third Super Bowl win in four years, Michael Irvin celebrated his thirtieth birthday in a room at the Residence Inn by Marriott in Irving. Joining him were former Cowboy lineman Alfredo Roberts and two dancers from the Men's Club, an upscale topless bar frequented by Cowboys players, their head coach ("They have great food," Barry Switzer once said), and their owner—sometimes between practices, at least until Erik Williams wrecked his car after spending quality time and money at the club.

Irvin happened to be inhaling lines of cocaine off the breast of one of the dancers when police walked in; they had been summoned by the hotel's desk clerk. Four grams of cocaine—what remained of ten and a half grams of party favors—some marijuana, a tubular snorting device, razor blades, and sex toys were confiscated. One of the dancers, Angela Beck, insisted the drugs and paraphernalia were hers; Irvin had promised Beck that he'd treat her like a princess if she took responsibility. As he was being handcuffed, Irvin tried another tack, asking the arresting police officer, "Can I tell you who I am?"

Irvin's arrest for possession of weed and coke was national news. The married father of two lawyered up with four attorneys and pleaded not guilty to possession of cocaine, a felony charge that could get him as much as twenty years in prison, and not guilty to possession of marijuana, a misdemeanor.

Between arraignment and trial, Dallas policeman Johnnie Hernandez was arrested and charged with soliciting the murder of Irvin. Hernandez gave an informant from the Drug Enforcement Administration $2,960 as a down payment on the $30,000 he was willing to pay to have Irvin taken out. Rachelle Smith, Hernandez's common-law wife and the other dancer in Irvin's room at the Residence Inn, had been threatened by Irvin after she had testified in front of a grand jury that the drugs found at the Residence Inn belonged to Irvin, not Beck. "He told me that if I didn't change my testimony, he would put everybody against me and everybody would hate me," Smith later told Judge Manny Alvarez. "He said that he'd make a touchdown and everyone would love him again." Smith also said she had partied with Irvin to have sex with Beck, not with Irvin.

Irvin showed up for his trial accompanied by a substantial posse of attorneys, friends, and supporters, looking dapper in a tailored suit, red-and-lavender alligator shoes, and sunglasses, a muted contrast to the full-length mink coat he wore to testify in front of a grand jury, where he autographed a Bible for one adoring fan. One of his attorneys, state senator Royce West, suggested the DA was going after Irvin to put celebrity blacks in their place "at the back of the bus."

Troy Aikman attended one day of the trial, to support his friend and teammate, he told reporters. On the day testimony ended, Irvin changed his plea to no contest and walked with a $10,000 fine, eight hundred hours of community service, and four years' probation for the cocaine possession. The marijuana and witness-tampering charges were dropped.

The NFL suspended Irvin for the first five games of the season, but his troubles didn't stop there. A sales manager for an auto dealer filed suit against Irvin in May for allegedly assaulting him at the Cowboys Sports Café. That same month, a videotape surfaced showing Irvin scoring cocaine from a woman while he chatted up her young son:

"Little man knows something. What you know, little champ?" Irvin asked the boy.

"I want to be like you," the boy said.

"So, see? You know I'm a good man, huh?"

They were only the latest in a long series of incidents. At Miami, Irvin was the most vocal on a team notorious for trash-talking, but he backed up his boasts with his performance on the field. As a Dallas Cowboy, Irvin allegedly punched out a referee at a charity basketball game in 1991. Two years later, he was charged with disorderly conduct in Florida for his public display of outrage when a liquor-store clerk wouldn't sell him a bottle of wine. In 1995, a woman from Plano accused him of assaulting her in the parking lot of a nightclub. Two paternity suits had also been filed against him.

"You have a very visible team leader who has shown one face to the community, and it fell in love with it," Dr. Don Beck, director of the National Values Center, in Denton, told Kevin Sherrington of the *Morning News*. "The other side of Michael Irvin is equally powerful, but in a subterranean way. He seems to be operating in an area absent of any moral code with the same enthusiasm he exhibits on the other side. I personally think it has crossed the line with some fans." Others, however, were already prepared to forgive, he said. "They'll fawn all over him."

Skip Bayless paid Irvin a backhanded compliment by calling him "the consummate con artist."

In fact, Irvin's outrageous behavior combined with his considerable talent and showboat tendencies took the heat off the still-steaming resentment some Cowboys fans harbored over the Jones-Johnson family feud.

Irvin's birthday bust eventually led to the revelation of the White House, a five-bedroom, two-story brown-and-beige-brick home at the end of a cul-de-sac at 113 Dorsett Drive, across a canal from the Dallas Cowboys Valley Ranch headquarters. Alvin Harper had rented out the place in 1994 on behalf of Michael Irvin, Nate Newton, Charles Haley, and several other Cowboys players who wanted a safe place to party.

Its nickname came from the implication that only white chicks were allowed to come over and screw the star players. Haley was the White House's designated governor. Harper was nicknamed Freaky and was the mayor, a title also bestowed upon Irvin and Newton. The leaseholder, Dennis Pedini, a hanger-on and confidant, had turned informant after Irvin was indicted for possession of illegal drugs. In addition to 113 Dorsett Drive, an apartment in Valley Ranch and a house in the adjacent suburb of Coppell were safe houses for partying Cowboys, Pedini claimed.

"It's amazing what goes on, but when you have that kind of money and access to whatever you want, anything is possible," Pedini told KXAS TV in an exclusive story.

Although the players had stopped using the White House in the summer of 1995, confirmation of its existence—by Dan Le Batard of the *Miami Herald*; no local reporter was willing to risk future access to the team by recognizing the open secret in print—affirmed the perception that the Cowboys had become mirror images of their coach and the owner: out-of-control wild men who could do anything they pleased as long as they won.

Nate Newton confirmed it when he tried to defend the existence of the White House, reasoning, "We've got a little place over here where we're running some whores in and out, trying to be responsible, and we're criticized for that too."

Jerry Jones's response was to hire extra security.

The argument that bad behavior was part of the Cowboys legacy was bolstered in August, when former defensive end Harvey Martin, the South Oak Cliff local-boy-made-good before money troubles got him, was arrested for domestic violence after a crack-smoking binge. It was his third arrest in five months for physically beating women.

Not everyone bought into the behavior. Fourteen-year veteran Bill Bates, that rare Cowboy recognized in the community for his character and leadership instead of his party-boy tendencies, admitted, "For a guy who his whole life wanted to play for the Dallas Cowboys, you know at times it really makes you sick to your stomach."

IN A SEASON MARKED by Jimmy Johnson's return to the NFL coaching ranks—he took the reins of the Miami Dolphins from a retiring (and increasingly ineffective) Don Shula—Michael Irvin's suspension for the first five games made quite an impact, as did tight end Jay Novacek's season-ending back injury and an injury to Emmitt Smith in the first game of the season that left him temporarily paralyzed.

The Cowboys stood at 2-3 going into their week-six bye. On Irvin's October 13 return, he snagged five passes for 51 yards. Earlier that week, his lawyers reached an out-of-court settlement with the North Texas Toyota Dealers Association, which had sued Irvin for $1.2 million in damages for the bad publicity his drug-possession trial generated, effectively destroying Irvin's Toyota endorsement deal. Two weeks later, Irvin caught 12 passes for 186 yards as the Cowboys dunked the Jimmy Johnson–coached Dolphins, 29–10.

The unexpected reacquisition of Herschel Walker by the Cowboys as a backup wide receiver to Irvin and company, kickoff return specialist alongside Kevin Williams, and backup to running backs Emmitt Smith, Daryl "Moose" Johnston, and Sherman Williams added just enough offensive power to make the Cowboys dangerous in spite of their 5-4 record. A team effort carried the Cowboys to a 20–17 overtime win against a very solid 7-2 San Francisco 49ers team for Barry Switzer's first win against the NFC West rivals, and the Cowboys finished 10-6, a step down from the previous four years but still good enough to repeat as NFC East champions.

And just in time for their playoff run came the accusation by a twenty-three-year-old Mesquite woman named Nina Shahravan: Michael Irvin had held a gun to her head while Erik Williams and another unidentified man raped her, Shahravan claimed. Irvin responded cautiously and suggested he not be judged too quickly, despite his string of troubles. He swore he hadn't been at Williams's house the day the incident allegedly occurred.

What turned out to be a bogus controversy proved to be a fatal distraction. The Cowboys had trounced Minnesota in the wild-card game, 40–15, before the rape charges became public. But the run-up to the game with the NFC West champion Carolina Panthers, a franchise in its second year of existence, was dominated by the rape charge, despite Irvin and Williams's protestations. After Michael Irvin sprained his shoulder on the second play of the game, Troy Aikman committed three costly turnovers that effectively handed the Panthers a 27–16 win, ending the Cowboys' year short of the level of achievement they had grown accustomed to. Shahravan eventually copped to perjury and filing a false police report and spent ninety days in jail.

Being famous and infamous moved Michael Irvin to request a trade in May of 1997. In June, he sued the Dallas Police Department and KXAS TV for airing the rape allegations. Also in June, he denied reports that he had assaulted a man in a San Francisco nightclub, although he did find time to make a prison visit to former Dallas cop Johnnie Hernandez, who had tried to put the hit on Irvin after his coke bust. By the time football season started, Irvin changed his mind about being traded or retiring, and he settled out of court with KXAS TV, Irvin and Erik Williams each receiving $1 million.

Jerry Jones felt he understood Irvin as few other owners could. Jones liked to party too and embraced the Dallas nightlife and its darker underside as a wild, unregulated hub of gambling, booze, and babes.

Jones enjoyed entertaining the customers in the restaurants and clubs he frequented. There were many: the Memphis and Broadway Grill, in the northern suburb of Addison; Drew Pearson's 88 in North Dallas; uptown joints along McKinney Avenue; the Library bar at the Melrose Hotel; celebrity chef Stephan Pyles's Star Canyon restaurant; the hip 8.0 Club; and his original home away from home, the Mansion on Turtle Creek, where another celebrity chef, Dean Fearing, oversaw the restaurant.

Reporter Skip Bayless left Dallas after the 1996 season to go to work for the *Chicago Tribune*, where he won awards as the lead sports columnist before moving to the *San Jose Mercury-News*. Bayless had seen the writing on the wall. Newspapers, once the leading medium for sports, were yielding influence to cable television and radio, both of which Bayless had tapped into. He had been a regular on ESPN radio's first nationally syndicated program *The Fabulous Sports Babe* and was featured on ESPN television's *Prime Monday* and *The Sports Reporters.*

Troy Aikman and Emmitt Smith wouldn't talk to Dale Hansen for a year due to what they regarded as his complicity in the Troy-is-gay rumors that Skip Bayless had raised. Less than a season later, Hansen resigned his color announcer position for the Cowboys. Life in the broadcast booth without Brad Sham was no fun.

Jerry Jones and Barry Switzer were still together; Switzer was back as head coach, but without the customary contract extension. Jones also brought in ex-Cowboy Calvin Hill to counsel players and hopefully clean up the Cowboys' tarnished image. The failings once overlooked had become more obvious after the team had fallen short of the Super Bowl.

Before the year was done, Jones would lose his best friend: his father, Pat, who passed away two years after he had open-heart surgery. Pat Jones's life was the blueprint upon which everything his son did was built. Sell, and sell with a smile, and your customers will pay you and thank you. Pat Jones's relentless drive, his oversize personality that suggested he had never met a stranger, and his appreciation for both the upright and holy and the honky-tonk bright lights were traits embraced by his son Jerral Wayne. Pat lived long enough to see his son succeed, which was what it was all about as far as they were both concerned.

During the 1997 preseason, Coach Switzer got himself into some legal trouble. He was arrested for carrying a loaded .38-caliber handgun onto the team plane at Dallas–Fort Worth International Airport. "I'm embarrassed for Jerry Jones and the Cowboys organization for an innocent, honest mistake that I made," he said after the incident. Owner Jones fined him $75,000 anyway, the biggest fine in league history. Switzer wasn't alone in making mistakes. Lineman Nate Newton was charged and later acquitted of sexual assault, and some players trashed the dormitory at St. Edward's University, where they stayed for training camp, peeing in the hallways.

The Cowboys kicked off the real season at the end of August at Three Rivers Stadium in Pittsburgh, putting the hurt on the eventual AFC Central champion Steelers, 37–7. Aikman threw four touchdown passes—two to Michael Irvin—without getting picked off. By week five, the Cowboys sat atop the NFC East with a 3-1 record. But the road ahead was about to get as rough as the offseason had been.

In the subsequent four weeks, the team lost to the Giants by three points, lost to the Redskins by five points, beat Jacksonville by four points, and lost to Philadelphia by a point. After a 17–10 loss to 8-1 San Francisco at 3Com Park (the old Candlestick) that left Dallas hanging with a 4-5 record, Switzer and Aikman exchanged words, and rumors started flying that Jerry Jones was talking to retired 49ers coach George Seifert about taking over the Cowboys at the end of the season.

Two wins put the brakes on the slide before the Cowboys dropped their final five games of the season. Barry Switzer reckoned as how he might "want to travel to Europe, get on my Harley and go to Portobello, Portofino, or wherever. This is all I've done for 40 years. I'll do things with my family and kids. They're more important anyway."

In December, Switzer was sentenced to a year's probation and eighty hours of community service and fined $3,500 by Tarrant County Criminal Court judge Daryl Coffey for showing up at DFW with the gun. Coffey reported getting lots of calls. "People either like him or really hate him. Some thought his case should be dismissed and he get an apology. Others wanted him to go to the penitentiary, and that's not even in the law."

The Cowboys closed at a sad 6-10. For the first time since 1990, there were no playoffs to look forward to. Neon Deion, the Triplets, and Herschel could only do so much. The team had clearly lost its bearings. Barry Sanders of the Detroit Lions sold more NFL gear in Dallas than Deion Sanders did, more than Troy, Michael, and Emmitt too, moving Deion Sanders to renounce fornication and declare his dedication to Jesus, inspired by Bishop T. D. Jakes of Potter's House. The Super Bowl champion Green Bay Packers passed the Dallas Cowboys as the team with the hottest pro football merchandise.

The head coach, who had skipped the final walk-through practice of the season because he said he wasn't feeling well, stared at the ruins of a dynasty. The party was over.

The city of Dallas was stuck in something of a rut too. A Dallas city councilman, Paul Fielding, was convicted on federal charges of fraud and extortion, and race remained such a contentious topic in Dallas that President Clinton moved a forum on race relations to another city. "Our wonderful image throughout the nation seems to be taking a beating," wrote Dallas's preeminent historian, Darwin Payne.

The Decline of the Second Regime

ON JANUARY 9, 1998, Jerry Jones announced that Barry Switzer was northbound on I-35, headed back to Norman. Switzer was ready to return to the comfort of his couch. His departure handed full control back to Jerry Jones, an almost ideal circumstance in the forever-whirling mind of the owner–general manager.

But even a mega-ego like Jerry's had brief moments of humility. Jerry Jones admitted to reporters that as much as he was inclined to step in and take over as head coach, he knew better. His other duties running the business would not allow him to operate at the peak performance level he expected from everyone who worked for him. Experienced coaches could do the job better, he had reluctantly concluded, and several million residents of the Dallas–Fort Worth Metroplex breathed a collective sigh of relief.

They shouldn't have exhaled so quickly.

Jerry Jones had plenty of options for Barry Switzer's successor, the fourth head coach of the Dallas Cowboys. Troy Aikman, sportswriters, and sports-radio announcers all suggested candidates: former Cowboys assistant Norv Turner, Green Bay Packers offensive coordinator Sherman Lewis (an African American who was considered the best assistant coach in the NFL), and former San Francisco head coach George Seifert. They were all ignored. Jones did his own vetting and concluded the best choice was Chan Gailey, the soft-spoken offensive coordinator for the Pittsburgh Steelers. The peanut gallery emitted a collective "Wha—?" There was little buzz or support for Gailey. Aikman was heard muttering "They're screwing this team up" when he got the news. But Gailey had overseen the run-oriented offenses of the Super Bowl champion Broncos and Steelers and, just as important, had coached for Ken Hatfield when the former Razorback headed the Air Force Academy Falcons, a circumstance that carried considerable weight in Jerry Jones's world. Hatfield spoke highly of Gailey, and Jones trusted Hatfield, which mattered more than what anyone else thought.

Once again, Jones went with what he regarded as the familiar.

Gailey appeared to be cut from the same cloth as Tom Landry: he was laid-back and quiet, a smart strategist and technocrat. The Georgia native had grown up in the same town as Cowboys legend Dan Reeves—Reeves had coached him in Little League—and he was no fire-breather like Johnson; he wasn't even as hot-tempered as Switzer. Sloe-eyed and dour-faced with a receding hairline, he looked more like a funeral-insurance salesman than a pro football coach. Gailey conveniently melted into the background as soon as he arrived; he focused on building a better roster and let his boss do the talking.

After eight summers in Austin, training camp relocated to the campus of Midwestern University in Wichita Falls, 140 miles northwest of Dallas. The Cowboys' run in Austin had been a good one, but crowds had declined, and after players trashed the St. Edward's University dorms, St. Ed's was ready for the arrangement to end. Austin was hot and humid, but Wichita Falls was hotter and even more miserable, with average August high temperatures in the 100s and without Austin's party-town distractions.

The conditions got to Michael Irvin early. His teammate Everett McIver suffered a deep laceration to his neck in a dormitory incident over a haircut, Irvin, and a pair of scissors. Irvin was not held liable, nor was he sanctioned for breaking the terms of his probation for the cocaine-possession conviction. McIver's silence was bought with an under-the-table payment to keep it all on the QT.

Even without Irvin getting into trouble, it was a brutal summer. Robert Wilonsky, the Balls columnist for the *Dallas Observer*, attended camp accompanied by music writer Michael Corcoran from the *Dallas Morning News*. "It was 108 degrees," Wilonsky said. "You were hoping the stories about the one-armed stripper were true because at least it would give you something to do."

Wilonsky snagged an interview with Michael Irvin, who impressed his inquisitor. "Michael Irvin was very public about his missteps," he said. "He wore them as a badge of honor. It made him a better man, he said. I had interviewed him several times after the White House, after getting busted with the roach and all that other stuff, and every time, he used them [to his benefit]. He presented himself as a precautionary tale. He didn't want people to forget about him, either. 'You want to talk about the bad shit I did? Okay. That's fine.' He owned it. He took charge of it. That was the smartest thing he's ever done because you can't dog a guy who dogs himself."

Other than the Irvin sit-down, there wasn't much to be said for training camp as far as Wilonsky was concerned. "Corcoran and I stayed at the Holiday Inn, the fanciest hotel in all of Wichita Falls. It had a giant sauna/Jacuzzi in the room. It was disgusting. Yet Michael insisted we go out and get a bunch of beer, roll a couple joints, and sit together in the hot tub. So we did. All there was to do was watch practice, go look for one-armed hookers, sit in the Jacuzzi, drink beer, and try to pretend it wasn't weird."

What was weird was watching Chan Gailey manage to keep Aikman, Irvin, and Smith healthy and in sync, projecting authority to the players and deference to the owner simultaneously. With the Triplets on offense; Leon Lett, Greg Ellis, Darren Woodson, and Deion Sanders leading the defense; and their biggest distraction, Barry Switzer, removed, the team had the potential to go all the way.

Coach Gailey turned out to be quite the accomplished juggler.

The Cowboys' running game was revitalized despite losing Aikman for five games two weeks into the season in a 42–23 loss to Denver — a week before a federal grand jury indicted an Arlington resident, Wadih el Hage, the former personal secretary of Muslim extremist Osama bin Laden, on charges that he lied about his ties to bin Laden's terrorist organization.

Aikman's backup Jason Garrett guided the Cowboys to a 3-2 record during Aikman's absence. Once Aikman was back in the saddle, the Cowboys peeled off four straight wins against the Eagles, the Giants, the Cardinals, and the Seahawks before dropping a 46–36 home game to an 11-1 Vikings team led by receiver Randy Moss, who caught three Randall Cunningham touchdown passes; losing a 22–3 road game to New Orleans; and suffering a 20–17 letdown to Kansas City. The team closed out with victories over Philadelphia and Washington, and Gailey became the first coach ever in the NFC East to sweep his division rivals. The Cowboys finished 10-6 atop the division, good enough to put the sizable contingent of Gailey critics at bay, if only for a week or so.

Their first-round playoff opponent was the NFC East runner-up, the Arizona Cardinals, a wild card. Fans could be forgiven for looking beyond the low-regarded Cardinals, since the 'Boys had beat them decisively twice during the regular season.

But the Cards' fierce secondary intercepted Aikman three times, the critical difference in a 20–7 upset. The Cowboys were jerked to a halt. Fans were getting wary. Were the Cowboys back? Or was this a brief hiccup in the midst of a long, slow fall?

Given the season's ending, the biggest success story out of Dallas in 1998 had nothing to do with the Dallas Cowboys and everything to do with musically inclined cowgirls. The Dallas girl group the Dixie Chicks, who had played every charity ball in Dallas over the previous five years, made their national debut with an album, *Wide Open Spaces,* that went triple platinum, signifying sales of more than three million units — about six times the number of people who had gone to Texas Stadium that season to watch America's Team.

Darkness Falls

PRETTY GIRL SINGERS, the draft, Michael Irvin's vow to retire again, and prospects for the coming season were briefly forgotten in the spring of 1999. Former tackle Mark Tuinei, only one season removed from the game of pro football, was found unconscious in his car in suburban Plano and later pronounced dead in a nearby hospital. Tuinei had accepted an offer to return to Punahou High School in Hawaii as an offensive-line coach. An autopsy revealed a fatal mix of heroin and Ecstasy in his system. Tuinei was one of three Cowboys to have played fifteen seasons or more (Ed "Too Tall" Jones and Bill Bates were the others). His death brought attention to the adjustments players faced once they were through with football.

Training camp returned to Wichita Falls, where the Cowboys' three-week residency was such a big deal, their team photograph adorned the cover of the phone book. Even Hank Hill, the lead character in the satirical television cartoon series *King of the Hill*, set in modern suburban Texas, visited Wichita Falls training camp with his son, Bobby, in an episode about Hank and his buddies trying to persuade the Cowboys to return their training camp to their mythical hometown of Arlen. No one liked Wichita Falls except the residents.

On the last Sunday in August, on the verge of the annual fresh start, Dallas Cowboys owner Jerry Jones popped up in the news for being arrested after driving away with his family in tow before a

Highland Park police officer could finish writing a speeding ticket. Jones was on his way to church for the christening of a grandson; he was driving in one car with his family, and other family members were following behind in a Suburban driven by an employee. When the Suburban was stopped by a police officer for going forty-five in a thirty-mile-an-hour zone, Jones stopped on his own and went over to the officer, who was questioning the other driver, and told him they were in a rush and late for the christening. Jones asked if he could go ahead to the church, but the officer demurred, telling him he would be as quick as he could. Jones drove away anyway and did not stop for another police vehicle that went after him.

Jones drove up to the church, dropped off the passengers, and drove off, then pulled his vehicle into a driveway a block away, where he was handcuffed, taken into custody, and arraigned on the class B misdemeanor charge of fleeing, punishable by a fine of up to $2,000 and 180 days in jail. The charge didn't stick.

Besides, Jones's defiance of the law had been done in the name of faith and family. He wanted to get to church. He may have been a ruthless cutthroat, but he was a man of the Bible.

Chan Gailey's second edition of the Cowboys charged out in front of the pack, knocking off Washington, 41–35, in overtime at the Redskins' new Landover, Maryland, home field, Jack Kent Cooke Stadium, powered by five Aikman TD passes. That was followed by Texas Stadium routs of Atlanta, 24–7, and Arizona, 35–7. But two consecutive 13–10 road losses, to the Eagles and then the Giants, doused the optimism, as did the sight of Michael Irvin being carried off the field on a stretcher during the October 10 division matchup at Philadelphia. At the rate he'd been playing the first three games of the year, Irvin was looking at his first sub-1,000-yard-receptions season in nine years. Then in the first quarter, his head was slammed onto the Vet's concrete-hard playing surface after he snared a pass from Aikman. He lay motionless for twenty minutes, and the nasty hometown Eagles crowd, who had even booed Santa Claus, cheered

Irvin's downfall and exit as he was wheeled to an ambulance. He suffered temporary paralysis due to spinal cord swelling.

In late October, Irvin was found to have a narrowed spinal column, and in December, two weeks after twelve people were killed and twenty-seven injured when a bonfire built by Texas A&M students collapsed before the Aggies' annual game against the University of Texas Longhorns, Michael Irvin was placed on the Cowboys injured reserve list.

Aikman had endured hits from the Philly D that same game that were almost as bad and almost as frequent as during his rookie year. His two interceptions factored in the Cowboys' 13–10 loss, which pretty much summarized the entire 1999 season. Emmitt kept running, gaining 1,387 yards for the year; free-agent acquisition Rocket Ismail performed admirably in Irvin's stead, with 1,097 receiving yards and five TD catches; and undersized middle linebacker Dat Nguyen, the first Vietnamese American in the NFL, became a crowd favorite.

But Chan Gailey never could really get the various parts of the Cowboys in sync. The 8-8 record was a tribute to underachievement, but it was enough to get the Cowboys into the playoffs again, even if they didn't deserve it. Their fall to the Vikings, 27–10, was so effortless that the team's first-round exit was almost a foregone conclusion. The Aikman-Irvin-Smith juggernaut appeared done. So was Chan Gailey's tenure, which Jones abruptly ended. The owner finally accepted the sports scribes' long-running analysis: Gailey was in over his head. He couldn't handle the Cowboys' big stage.

Jerry Jones's quick answer was Dave Campo, the Cowboys' defensive coordinator, who had come to Dallas from the University of Miami as Jimmy Johnson's assistant in 1989. Campo was considered a solid coach whose defenses mostly remained sound while the Cowboys offense was falling apart. His personality was similar to Chan Gailey's, though he had a more excitable manner of speaking. The internal hire meant the dynamic between owner–general manager and head coach was understood in advance. Campo knew what he was getting into and dove in enthusiastically.

In mid-January of 2000, Campo's former boss Jimmy Johnson announced his retirement as coach of the Miami Dolphins. The Jacksonville Jaguars had decimated his team, 62–7, in the divisional playoffs after the Dolphins had beaten the Seattle Seahawks 20–17 in the wild-card round. Johnson claimed he was burned out (again). He had almost quit the year before but was talked out of it by his quarterback Dan Marino, with whom he had developed a contentious relationship. This time around, Marino hung up his cleats when Johnson called it quits. Johnson's lack of success in Miami tempered some Dallas fans' anger toward Jerry Jones. Maybe it wasn't all the fault of the owner and general manager that the Cowboys' 1990s dynasty had been unnecessarily destroyed.

Johnson once again retreated to the Florida Keys with his girlfriend, Rhonda Rookmaaker, his thirty-one-foot Contender boat *JJ*, and his icebox full of Heinekens. He would return to the broadcasting booth to analyze NFL games for Fox, but his coaching career was over.

A few weeks later, on February 12, Tom Landry, the first and longest-tenured coach of the Dallas Cowboys, passed away at Baylor University Medical Center in Dallas. He was seventy-five. He had been undergoing treatment for acute myelogenous leukemia since the previous May.

The team gathered around one last time — Schramm and Brandt, Ditka, Reeves, Tubbs, Gene Stallings, Staubach, Eddie LeBaron, running back Claxton Welch, tackle Rayfield Wright, guard Jim Arneson, cornerback Mark Washington, receivers Bobby Hayes and Drew Pearson, Cliff and Charlie, Garrison, and dozens more. They came for the viewing at Sparkman-Hillcrest Funeral Home, a private dinner at the Landrys', a family memorial service at Highland Park Methodist Church, and a televised memorial public service at the Meyerson Symphony Hall, as thousands mourned Landry's passing.

———

THE LAST ACTIVE COWBOY that Tom Landry had coached, Michael Irvin, made his retirement from football official a few months later. Although he was only thirty-three, Irvin acknowledged his neck injury could prove permanently damaging if he continued to play.

He would be joined by Daryl "Moose" Johnston, who also hung it up.

Irvin's and Johnston's retirements coincided with Deion Sanders's release from the club. Jerry Jones drafted three cornerbacks to fill Sanders's shoes while he traded away his number-one and number-two draft picks to obtain receiver Joey Galloway from the Seattle Seahawks to fill Irvin's spot on the roster.

The changes attempted to shore up the foundation of a structure that appeared increasingly unstable.

Aught for the Aughties

THE INSTALLATION OF Dave Campo as head coach signaled a positive change at the top—he was the one constant remaining from the Jimmy Johnson era—and the draft suggested the front office was addressing weak spots. But the Cowboys' core had been so hollowed out, it was close to impossible for the 2000 edition of the Cowboys to do much more than underperform. Making it feel worse than it really was were opponents who still viewed the team as the three-time Super Bowl champions of the 1990s and tended to step up their respective games whenever Dallas showed up on the schedule.

The season opened on September 3 at Texas Stadium against the Philadelphia Eagles in 109-degree heat—an NFL record. Philly kicked off the game with an onside squib that they recovered, letting Donovan McNabb march his team down the field for a touchdown. Things quickly deteriorated. Troy Aikman was 0-5 passing, including an interception for a touchdown, and was sacked four times before he left the game toward the end of the first half with a concussion, the victim of a crushing hit applied by James Darling and Hugh Douglas.

Aikman's replacement, former Eagle Randall Cunningham, was competent in relief, completing 13 of 26 passes, one for a touchdown, although he also threw an interception. Whatever chance the Cowboys had vanished in the fourth quarter when receiver Joey

Galloway—the new Irvin, according to Jones—was injured, ending his season. Emmitt Smith gained all of 29 yards. The 41–14 final score said all that needed to be said.

The Cowboys proceeded to lose to perennial patsy Arizona in Phoenix before finally picking up their first win by surprising the Redskins in Landover.

The next game set the tone for the rest of the season. Terrell Owens, the other standout receiver for the San Francisco 49ers besides Jerry Rice, symbolized that extra-special effort ginned up by teams whenever they played the Cowboys. In a September 24 showdown at Texas Stadium, Owens caught two touchdown passes for the 49ers. Each time after scoring he ran to midfield to stand astride the giant blue star at the 50-yard line with his arms raised in triumph. Emmitt Smith responded by spiking the ball at the star on the 50 after he scored a touchdown. But after Owens's second victory dance, Cowboys safety George Teague could not restrain himself: he walked up to Owens and knocked him on his ass. Teague managed to deftly dodge an angry 49er who came at him after he hit Owens. Teague's retaliation made the 49ers' 41–24 blowout a little easier to accept. Teague was thrown out of the game by officials. San Francisco coach Steve Mariucci suspended Owens for being a hot dog.

The Cowboys' miserable 5-11 season concluded at the end of December, a few weeks after the contested election of Texas governor George W. Bush as president of the United States was upheld by the Supreme Court. Troy Aikman's second concussion of the season, applied by Washington's LaVar Arrington, was the tenth of his career.

In the new NFL, free agency and big money had made even veteran superstars expendable once they hit thirty. The Cowboys waived Troy Aikman on March 7, 2001, citing his back issues and the string of concussions. More significantly, a $7 million bonus was due him if Aikman was on the roster the next day. Aikman reached out to several other teams, but two concussions in one year were enough for every team to shy away from offering him a contract. He retired a month later, delivering a long, rambling good-bye at Valley Ranch.

Aikman had guided his team to more wins in the 1990s—ninety—than any NFL quarterback in any decade. He earned most valuable player recognition in Super Bowl XXVII for throwing a record four touchdown passes. But Aikman had also set a record by being sacked eleven times in one game in 1991 against the Eagles. He was ready for retirement.

At least Aikman exited with more hope than defensive end Dimitrius Underwood, who had already tried to kill himself once before the Cowboys picked him up from the Dolphins in 2000. In September of 1999, Underwood had slashed his own neck before repeatedly yelling, "I'm not worthy of God." During the 2000 season, playing for the Cowboys, Underwood had four sacks and twenty-four tackles. In January of 2001, he tried to kill himself again, by running into traffic, twice, on a busy suburban highway in Coral Springs, Florida, kicking and denting a car, asking passersby for a gun, and telling police he wanted to "go to Jesus." Underwood was taken into custody and hospitalized. The Cowboys released him later that month. Underwood would go on to serve stints in the Dallas County Jail for aggravated robbery (of a paraplegic), assault on a public servant, and evading arrest. He was later diagnosed with bipolar disorder.

Underwood's crimes made Michael Irvin look almost angelic. The Playmaker had been arrested again in 2000; he was found with marijuana and cocaine, as well as a woman who was not his wife. This time around Irvin was not charged and the case was dropped after the district attorney determined the police had conducted an illegal search.

It was life after football that so many athletes had a tough time adjusting to. On November 4, 2001, former offensive lineman Nate "the Kitchen" Newton was arrested for possession of marijuana—he had 213 pounds of it in his automobile. Newton posted bond and was awaiting trial when he was arrested again, five weeks later, while attempting to transport 175 pounds of marijuana. Following a brief stretch in jail, Newton repented and became a radio sports-talk host.

THE 2001 EDITION OF the Cowboys featured an open casting call for Troy Aikman's job. Quarterbacks coach Wade Wilson and a very large committee would do the culling. Tony Banks had been picked up from the Baltimore Ravens, last season's Super Bowl champions, but Banks didn't make it out of training camp. Quincy Carter, the University of Georgia quarterback who was Jerry Jones's personal second-round draft pick, despite low ratings from many draft analysts, emerged as the starter. Jones liked Carter because he thought the speedy back came from the same mold as Michael Vick, the number-one overall draft pick, who would start for the Atlanta Falcons. "Jerry wanted to have a fast passing and running quarterback. That was Quincy," a team insider said. "The scouts made sure everyone knew he was Jerry's pick because at the first practice, he couldn't hit his receivers on a curlback."

It was a season to remember, then forget. Two days after a listless opening loss at home to the Tampa Bay Buccaneers, in which Quincy Carter left the game and was replaced by Anthony Wright, twenty-eight terrorists from Saudi Arabia and other Middle Eastern nations hijacked four commercial airliners and crashed them into the two towers of the World Trade Center in New York; the Pentagon in Washington, DC; and a field in Pennsylvania, killing over three thousand people. The day of infamy that would become known as 9/11 cast a shadow across the world. When league play resumed two weeks later, safety George Teague led the team onto the field carrying a large American flag. That same game, Bullet Bob Hayes became the eleventh Cowboy to be inducted into the Ring of Honor, with the recognition that Hayes's speed had forced NFL defenses to adopt zone coverage. Quincy Carter sat on the bench nursing a sprained thumb injured in practice when he'd hit Troy Hambrick's helmet. His replacement, Anthony Wright, went 12 for 25 with 193 yards passing, but he could not ignite the rest of the offense and Dallas fell to San Diego and their twenty-five-year-veteran quarterback Doug Flutie, 32–21. Another loss to the Eagles followed before Carter returned from the injury list.

Carter went one-for-five against the Oakland Raiders at the Coliseum before he was spelled again by Anthony Wright. Once again, Wright was effective but unable to fire up the offense, leaving the Cowboys on the short end of a 28–21 score that marked their fourth consecutive loss.

The Washington Redskins, quarterbacked by the freshly traded Tony Banks, provided the opposition the next week and Wright went 15-28 playing the whole game, which was just enough for a 9–7 Cowboys win. After the bye week, the third quarterback to start a game for the Cowboys that season, Clint Stoerner, went all the way in the 17–3 win over Arizona. Stoerner started against the Giants the following week but was pulled in the fourth quarter after throwing his fourth interception, despite the game being tied. His replacement, Ryan Leaf—the troubled former-number-two overall draft pick released by San Diego in March and by Tampa Bay in early September—ran some series but couldn't pull off a win as the Giants won in overtime, 27–24.

Leaf started the next week against the Falcons in Atlanta, facing off against rookie sensation Michael Vick, but the Cowboys came up short again, 20–13. Leaf started again against the Eagles in another crushing loss, 35–3, but came closer against Denver in a 26–24 loss before Quincy Carter returned. Carter led the Cowboys to a 20–14 win over Washington and started the final five games, of which Dallas lost three.

The next-to-last game, against the 12-4 San Francisco 49ers, finally gave fans reason to celebrate. Emmitt Smith joined Walter Payton as the only running backs to rush for more than 16,000 yards, and Carter threw two touchdown passes in the 27–21 upset. The respite from mediocrity was brief. The Cowboys dropped the final game of the season to Detroit, 15–10, the Lions' first win that year.

The second consecutive 5-11 season was better forgotten. Dave Campo had no choice but to fire offensive coordinator Jack Reilly. There was no quarterback. Maybe the release of Aikman came too soon, but the Cowboys had also lost their fire. The only stars left were Emmitt Smith, who was looking as lonely as Herschel Walker back in the day, on offense, and Dexter Coakley and Dat Nguyen on defense.

Darkening an already gloomy scenario was the passing of former defensive end Harvey Martin on Christmas Eve of 2001; his teammate Drew Pearson was at his side. Martin was felled by pancreatic cancer, but a post-Cowboys life of drug and alcohol abuse, spousal abuse, and a string of arrests had preceded his passing. At least Martin had pulled himself up and gotten straight enough to take a job selling chemical products for former teammate John Niland.

THE 2002 SEASON BEGAN with a new flagship radio station, KLUV-FM, and a new training camp location; the horrid heat and small town dullness of Wichita Falls was abandoned for tourist-friendly San Antonio and the climate-controlled Alamodome. The team would go through summer training shadowed by a film crew from HBO, which was making a pilot for a show called *Hard Knocks*. The program tracked several story lines, including the arrival of Chad Hutchinson to challenge Quincy Carter at starting quarterback, rookie Roy Williams's indoctrination at safety, and Emmitt Smith preparing to break the biggest rushing record of all, along with vignettes with Jerry Jones and Dave Campo. But the scrutinizing eye of the camera over the course of four episodes could not change what appeared to be another below-average edition of the Cowboys.

Cementing that impression was the passing of Bob Hayes, who

died at the age of fifty-nine in his hometown of Jacksonville, Florida, on September 21 due to kidney failure after extended battles with prostate cancer and liver ailments.

The one bright spot was Emmitt Smith's breaking Walter Payton's record of 16,726 yards as the all-time NFL rushing leader with an 11-yard gain against the Seattle Seahawks at Texas Stadium on October 27. With Irvin and Aikman absent, the accomplishment of the last Triplet standing demonstrated how remarkable their early 1990s play had been. No three Cowboys had achieved so much in so short a time. Looking back was the salve that took the pain away from the once and future true believers who were having a hard time reconciling the Cowboys' third consecutive 5-11 year.

Fans were reminded of past and better days too when Tex and Marty Schramm's sixty-one-year marriage was ended by the death of the former Martha Anne Snowden, on December 8, 2002.

In April of 2003, Tex sat beside Jerry Jones at a Valley Ranch press conference looking like a clearly diminished man. His jowls sagged, his facial wrinkles were deeply pronounced, and the sparkle had disappeared from his pale blue eyes. He wasn't P. T. Barnum anymore. That would be the man Schramm was sitting next to.

The press conference marked the first time Jerry Jones and Tex Schramm had been seen together in public since Schramm's unceremonious dumping fourteen years earlier. It was Tex's first trip back to Valley Ranch. Jones and Schramm had met for lunch in March, and Jones had asked Schramm about his initial vision of the Ring of Honor and how it helped build the image of what Jones called "the most special franchise that's ever been."

Judging from Jerry's stiff body language, he still didn't think that much of Tex. He was simply doing what had to be done. With Tex on his last legs, a few old hands such as Russ Russell and Larry Wansley had quietly counseled Jones on the wisdom of taking the initiative (Wansley had left the Cowboys to head up security for the

World League and Tex before becoming security chief at American Airlines). It was time that the man who created the Ring of Honor was inducted into it.

"I reminded Jerry every chance I had," Russ Russell said. "I told him if he was ever going to be put in the Ring, this was the time. Jerry let me have the honor of taking Tex to lunch with Rich Dalrymple at Mother's Daughter's Diner to tell him he was being inducted into the Ring of Honor. He wanted that. He was in the national hall of fame and wondered if they would remember him in his hometown."

Tex Schramm looked tired and weak in the days leading up to the press conference announcing his pending induction. But when the camera lights came on, the attention was a tonic. The one, the only, the original architect of the Dallas Cowboys, Mr. Texas Earnest Schramm Jr. his own self, was back. "He was articulate. He was attentive. He was bright," Russ Russell said. "He was Tex Schramm that day. He was onstage again and he was himself. It was his last bright public moment."

The gathering included Roger Staubach; various club officials, including secretary Jerri Mote; broadcaster Pat Summerall; and several media friends from the Schramm era. Schramm took the opportunity to talk about his departed partner. "My wife, Marty, would have enjoyed this moment," he said. "She was a great Cowboys fan and a great Tex Schramm fan. Wherever she is right now—I know she's up there—she's a happy wife."

Numerous Schramm achievements were cited: two Super Bowls, five conference championships, and thirteen division crowns. The multiple innovations instituted during Schramm's twenty-three-year reign as head of the NFL Competition Committee were listed: playing the second Thanksgiving Day game, creating the in-the-grasp rule to protect quarterbacks, making defensive head slaps illegal, tightening pass interference rules (all to encourage offense), wiring the referee with a microphone to explain penalties to the crowd and television audience, using sudden-death overtimes to break ties, and spearheading the merger between the AFL and the NFL.

He had been as hard-nosed a negotiator as the Teamsters' Jimmy Hoffa and tighter than a tick with the club's money, at least when it came to contract negotiations. All that was water under the bridge.

Twenty-eight years after Tex initiated the tradition by inducting Bob Lilly into the Ring of Honor on November 23, 1975, the originator's name in silver letters was to be added to the wall behind the Cowboys' bench.

Recognition of Schramm brought back a rosy glow but also underscored the Cowboys' shitty record of late, which had become a matter of serious concern, and provided fuel for the media furnace. That deficit was at least partially tempered by the fact that Jerry Jones and, through him, the Cowboys organization were making more money than ever. That was the score that mattered most to sports economists and sports business academics, part of a rising field of interest predicated on profit, not points, in sports.

By that gauge, the Cowboys were kicking ass and taking names. Merchandise was bringing in $50 million instead of the $3 million that the team had received from NFL Properties before Jones challenged the league. But sales were beginning to flatten. It wasn't easy moving swag when the team wasn't winning, no matter how good a showman and promoter Jones was. Dave Campo came off as another dull yes-man in the tradition of Chan Gailey, meaning Jones's calls were not as smart as he thought. No players were lighting up the marquee, and the scrutiny was getting ever more intense.

Trolling for Tuna

THE THIRD 5-11 SEASON in a row was enough for Jerry Jones to ax Dave Campo when the year was done. Finally, Jerry would break stereotype and come up with a new coach who wasn't a rising assistant or someone with Arkansas connections.

Bill Parcells, the former head coach of the New York Giants, the New York Jets, and the New England Patriots, was Jerry Jones's big catch. With two Super Bowl rings on his fingers, Parcells had been cooling his heels the past four seasons by working on television as an analyst. When he allowed to a colleague that the Dallas opening would be a challenge he'd be willing to take on, word traveled fast.

Jones coaxed Parcells out of retirement with so many promises of absolute control that the running joke around Valley Ranch became "every day is Jerry's day to wash Bill's car." The owner couldn't have been more solicitous. He was so desperate to win again, he was willing to do *anything,* including cede some of his authority.

Parcells was an imposing presence, with close-cropped blond hair and beefy jowls, as well as a physique that had earned him his Big Tuna sobriquet. His passive-aggressive nature made him come across as "a grumpy ol' sumbitch," as one longtime Dallas sports observer put it. His successes were in the East, not in Arkansas, Texas, Oklahoma, or the South, although he had been the linebackers coach at Texas Tech in Lubbock years ago, where he had developed a longtime friendship with Brownwood high school football coaching legend Gordon Wood. Parcells was a take-charge guy, insisting on total control as head coach and keeping players, assistants, and the front office on short leashes when it came to executing orders. Parcells projected a no-quarter-given toughness not seen around Valley Ranch since Heinekens were stocked in the refrigerators.

Coach Parcells's disdain for the media showed. A scowl was semipermanently pasted on his face. He kept his remarks as brief as possible and was sufficiently glib and flip when he did say something to discourage probing follow-up questions. His strong personality suggested he and Jones were not destined to get along. Both insisted otherwise. Jones claimed their arrangement allowed him to control draft picks and trades. Parcells's agreement was secured by the $17 million, four-year contract he had signed.

Parcells cleaned house; he released Emmitt Smith before the start of the season. Emmitt could continue playing and receive the same money he was making at Dallas and stretch out his rushing records somewhere else. The winning bidder was the Arizona Cardinals, where he would finish as the all-time National Football League rushing leader with 18,355 yards on 4,409 carries, a record that has not yet been surpassed.

Some of the money formerly spent on Smith was invested in two key draft picks, tight end Jason Witten and cornerback Terence Newman, while quarterbacks coach Sean Payton signed an undrafted small-college prospect from Eastern Illinois, Tony Romo, for a $10,000 bonus — less than what Emmitt Smith had earned playing a single quarter.

Under Parcells's top-sergeant leadership, the Cowboys had a great training camp in San Antonio. The personnel he inherited were better than the record indicated, and most were hunkering down to save their jobs. Parcells issued orders, the team responded, and the fans came back. After the Cowboys dropped the opener at home to a not-very-good Falcons team, 27–13, a game during which

Quincy Carter threw for 268 yards, a touchdown, and an interception, Carter delivered the next week at the Meadowlands for Parcells's *Monday Night Football* homecoming against the Giants, passing for 321 yards and one interception in the 35–32 overtime win. Carter could only muster an anemic 165 passing yards in the next game against the Jets, but the Cowboys still won, 17–6. He bounced back with a two-touchdown, 277-yard passing game to lead the Cowboys over Arizona, 24–7, only to slump again in the meet-up with Philadelphia, with a mere 146 passing yards, which only slightly improved to 190 yards the next week playing the Lions. And yet, the Cowboys were rocking along at 5-1. The team finished in second place in the NFC East with a 10-6 record, and they could have been 11-5 if they weren't so mistake-prone.

With a ticket to ride on the postseason merry-go-round, Dallas fell off its high horse surprisingly fast, getting tripped up and soundly beaten on both offense and defense to lose the wild-card game to the NFC South champion Carolina Panthers, 29–10. Still, the team packed away their gear thinking that with Parcells around, and one big change on the field, "wait until next year" was no idle threat.

Quincy Carter had remained sufficiently erratic with interceptions, fumbles, and bad running decisions to prevent unconditional approval from fans and coaches alike, but he had showed poise, nerve, and potential at quarterback. It didn't matter. Before the 2004 season got under way, Jerry Jones's dream quarterback was dropped from the roster. He had failed a drug test, allegedly turning up dirty for marijuana, at training camp in Oxnard, California, where the Cowboys had moved after two camps in San Antonio. The swiftness of Carter's dismissal gave weight to the perception that Parcells had wanted to dump Carter as soon as he became head coach. Peeing in a cup made it formal.

Parcells brought in an old familiar face, Vinny Testaverde, the journeyman quarterback who played for Parcells on the Jets. Despite his forty-one-year-old body, Testaverde would compete against Drew

Henson, the former University of Michigan quarterback who had been playing baseball for three years in the New York Yankees farm system before the Cowboys traded for him. Quincy Carter's spot on the roster was filled by second-year free-agent signee Tony Romo, who became the number-three QB on the depth chart.

In the draft, Parcells and Jones passed up running back Steven Jackson from Oregon State and took Notre Dame power back Julius Jones to step up the Cowboys' running game, which had turned anemic since Emmitt Smith's departure.

As much as the owner wanted to be involved, Jerry Jones tried to observe the ground rules agreed upon. Parcells discouraged hot dogs, showboats, and meddling owners and did not necessarily agree with Jerry's assessment that "football is show business. You can't forget it is entertainment." Parcells just wanted to win. He brought in more former players that he was comfortable with, among them former Jets receiver Keyshawn Johnson. He had enough control not to bitch about other shortcomings within the organization or about the man constantly peering over his shoulder.

The Big Tuna in Big D did shift some of the spotlight from Jones and his management style. With a big-name coach sewed up for at least four years, Jones could focus more on the next new for the football club: a new home.

Texas Stadium, the home of the Dallas Cowboys since 1971, was showing its age. Clint Murchison's futuristic football stadium was now ratty, decrepit, and duct-taped. The Cotton Bowl still retained a venerable look, despite its age and spartan amenities. Texas Stadium looked like a thirty-year-old modular strip mall gone raggedy-assed. No women wore furs to games anymore, not even in December and January. The land around the stadium had never been developed as envisioned; the stadium remained the centerpiece of a freeway interchange. So the Irving City Council did not sound too interested in plowing several hundred million into Jones's proposed upgrade to transform it into a hundred-thousand-seat pleasure dome.

They were none too interested in plowing hundreds of millions more into a whole new venue, either. The council had ordered a study that concluded the Dallas Cowboys brought $51 million a year in economic benefits to Irving. That was not enough for the leadership of the suburban city to justify such a huge expenditure.

So Jones announced he was looking inward—to downtown Dallas and to Fair Park, where the Cotton Bowl was located. If Dallas kicked in $425 million from increased hotel and car rental taxes, like Phoenix had done in a recent stadium-building frenzy, Jones promised a state-of-the-art facility that Dallas and all of Texas could be proud of. But first he had to woo Dallas mayor Laura Miller, the former muckraking city columnist for the *Dallas Observer*, and the Dallas County commissioners.

Miller was a particularly tough nut to crack. She had made her name as a columnist by going after previous mayor Ron Kirk for his insider cronyism and won the election to replace Kirk as a reform candidate. The city's shelling out hundreds of millions for a new stadium when Dallas schools were in crisis and getting worse and city infrastructure was in dire need of upgrading would not please the voters who elected her. But Miller also understood the much-touted multiplier effect and the positives that the football team brought to Dallas.

She was reluctantly ready to work out a deal when the Dallas County commissioners voted Fair Park and, indirectly, Dallas out of the picture. At least, that's how it appeared. The Cowboys had not delivered the documents requested by the commissioners in time for a bond election to be scheduled for the initiative. County judge Margaret Kelleher, a Republican, and commissioner John Wiley Price, the Democratic Party leader on the court, concluded the Cowboys' paperwork was incomplete and had not provided the court the information it needed. The numbers didn't make sense, anyway, and displacing existing residences and businesses was too politically risky.

The failure to build Cowboys Stadium inside the Dallas city limits had less to do with Miller and lots to do with the football club. Jones expressed interest in a second location south of downtown Dallas on Industrial Boulevard, but that too may have been a smoke screen, since by that point, talks were already well under way with officials from the suburb of Arlington.

Jerry Jones liked to tell audiences about Laura Miller's kiss-off once Dallas County commissioners ruled out Fair Park. According to Jones's telling, when Jones informed Miller, "We're going to Arlington," she put her hand on his knee, looked into his eyes, and, smiling, said, "You go on and do that."

Jones had targeted the bedroom suburb fifteen miles west of downtown Dallas and fifteen miles east of Fort Worth for good reasons. Arlington was an entertainment hub where the Six Flags Over Texas amusement park, the Wet n' Wild water park, and the Texas Rangers ballpark were clustered. Clint Murchison and Tex Schramm had dismissed Arlington out of hand when they were looking for a location to build what became Texas Stadium because they considered Arlington too far from Dallas. Forty years later, Arlington was a prime central location in a metropolitan area that sprawled more than sixty miles east to west and seventy miles north to south.

The Texas Rangers ballpark, which opened in 1994, had been financed by a half-cent sales tax increase that Arlington voters overwhelmingly approved in 1991 after rejecting bond issues for a mass-transit system, a Smithsonian Institution museum, and a river-walk development. Lobbying for the baseball stadium were Rangers president Tom Schieffer, a former state legislator from Fort Worth, and the face of its ownership group, George W. Bush, son of the president of the United States. Bush and Schieffer worked churches, civic groups, and anyone in Arlington willing to host a meeting to demonstrate the good a baseball park could bring to the community. With public support, they built a neoclassical brick ballyard, designed by David M. Schwarz, that was plopped in the middle of a massive asphalt parking lot. Upon the stadium's completion, Schwarz touted the multiple revenue streams that had been built into the facility, increasing the club's potential profitability.

The bonds to pay for the stadium would be retired in ten years, ten years ahead of schedule.

The Cowboys and the City of Arlington launched a study in 2004 that calculated $238 million in additional economic benefits would flow into the community annually if a new football stadium was constructed—more than four times the estimated revenue of the City of Irving's study, a testimony to the inexact science of economic impact.

A vote was scheduled to see if Arlington voters were again willing to raise their sales tax by a half-cent, to hike up the local hotel-motel tax by 2 percent, and allow a 5 percent increase in rental car taxes. Cumulatively, those increases would generate $325 million over twenty years, Arlington's share of building a new home for the Cowboys. The Cowboys would kick in a similar amount, pay $60 million in rent over thirty years, donate at least half a million a year to youth sports projects in Arlington, and guarantee taking care of any additional costs. The NFL would guarantee an additional $150 million.

The Jones family invested $5 million to tell its story before the election and explain how America's Team would make Arlington America's City, in the words of PR consultant Rob Allyn. The face of the organization, Jerry Jones, was advised to keep a low profile, an acknowledgment of Jones's lightning-rod-for-controversy persona. Stephen Jones would do the talking for the organization, backed by Roger Staubach, Troy Aikman, and the Arizona Cardinals' Emmitt Smith.

Opponents tried to make it personal anyway, organizing the No Jones Tax Coalition, which raised $45,000 to publicize what they considered the hidden costs of corporate welfare. But the "aginners" could not muster more than 45 percent of the vote.

Gene and Jerry Jones traveled the world to inspect other venues for stadium ideas. Channeling the spirit of Clint Murchison, Jerry wanted to create a venue that had the same effect the Astrodome in Houston had had when it opened in 1965: "It sucked the air right out of you," he recalled. The new facility *had* to be better than anything else. Otherwise, it wouldn't be fit for the Dallas Cowboys.

Bryan Trubey of HKS Architects Sports and Entertainment Group of Dallas worked up designs with creature comforts and bells and whistles that had never before been envisioned. Gene Jones decorated the building with contemporary art, tooling around its skeleton in a golf cart to make spur-of-the-moment decisions that had implications of hundreds of thousands of dollars. Mrs. Jones and her daughter, Charlotte, sought out the finest contemporary artists, especially in North Texas, but they neither micromanaged nor put their egos first.

The estimated cost of the new stadium ultimately doubled to north of a billion dollars, with additional expenses borne by Jones, who took on as much debt as banks would allow. He kicked in another $75 million in collateral for an additional $475 million in financing, raising his stake to close to a half a billion in debt. His cushion was having twice the number of luxury suites to sell.

Another plus: the planned stadium took the focus off the Cowboys' performance on the field. After returning to California for training camp at Oxnard, just down the road from Thousand Oaks, the 2004 squad minus Quincy Carter muddled to a 6-10 record. Installing Vinny Testaverde at QB backed by a very hesitant Drew Henson, reconfiguring the defense to a 3-4 scheme (Parcells's preference), compensating for the loss of safety and team leader Darren Woodson to injury, and trading away cornerback Mario Edwards were one adjustment too many in the Big Tuna's makeover.

The 2005 squad looked more like a Parcells team after training camp in Oxnard again, and it wasn't just the appearance of Drew Bledsoe, another quarterback Parcells had a history with. The one-time Pro Bowler had been discarded by the New England Patriots in favor of new quarterback Tom Brady, so Parcells brought Bledsoe in to compete against Vinny Testaverde, and by the end of preseason, Bledsoe earned the right to start, while assistant coach Sean Payton nurtured along third-stringer Tony Romo.

The Cowboys opened in San Diego and brought home a 28–24 win with Bledsoe in charge, connecting on three touchdown passes, two to Keyshawn Johnson.

On September 19, Troy Aikman, Michael Irvin, and Emmitt Smith were inducted into the Ring of Honor during the halftime of a hard-fought game against the Washington Redskins on *Monday Night Football*. The 'Skins took the game, 14–13, despite an impressive 21-for-36 for 261 yards passing game for Bledsoe.

Bledsoe got into a decent groove and the Cowboys cruised, although the quarterback lost his best protection when tackle Flozell Adams was injured and out for the season in the week six 16–13 win over the New York Giants. After week eleven, the 'Boys were riding high at 7-3, but an overtime loss to Denver started a rough skid that left the Cowboys on the playoff bubble going into the last game of the season against the St. Louis Rams. Bledsoe had 242 passing yards and one TD. But two interceptions figured in the Cowboys' 20–10 defeat. The 9-7 season record was only good enough for third place in the NFC East.

All fans could do was wait. Parcells had the players he wanted. Rookie outside linebacker DeMarcus Ware, the Alabama kid from tiny Troy University who was Dallas's top draft pick for 2005, led the defense in sacks for the year. Drew Bledsoe threw for more than 3,000 yards and conducted five late-game-winning drives, a performance any NFL quarterback could be proud of, despite also dogging it in several critical games. Jones liked what he saw overall. All the team had to do was win more.

The Cowboys radio network changed flagships once again in 2006, as Jones worked out a five-year deal with KTCK-AM, the Ticket, whose hosts had become notorious critics of the Cowboys. Switzer, Bailey, Campo, and Parcells had been torn up and scrutinized with equal harshness, with the staff's best zings aimed at the owner, often through host Gordon Keith's Fake Jerry character. Perhaps being the official station of the Dallas Cowboys would tone down the vitriol. Brad Sham returned to the fold to call the play-by-play on the radio again, joined by Charlie Waters, with Kristi Scales adding sideline reports.

There were changes at the top of the league too. Commissioner Paul Tagliabue retired. His replacement, Roger Goodell, was elected on the fifth ballot by the owners. The son of U.S. senator Charles Goodell of New York, he had started as an intern at the NFL's home office in 1982, under Pete Rozelle, and worked his way through public relations positions as Lamar Hunt's assistant before stepping into the dual roles as chief operating officer and executive vice president for the league in 2001.

But the change that got Cowboys fans talking was Jerry Jones's brash offseason move. The owner–general manager went out and signed Terrell Owens, the wideout who had gotten under the Cowboys' skin as a receiver for San Francisco. Owens had helped get Philadelphia to the Super Bowl in 2004. But over the next season, he had created so much locker room dissension, the Eagles suspended him without pay for four games, then deactivated him altogether.

On March 18, 2006, four days after he was given his unconditional release from the Eagles, Terrell Owens sat alongside Jerry Jones at Valley Ranch, where the two men were having a shit-eating-grin contest. Jones announced he'd signed Owens to a three-year, $25 million contract, including a $5 million signing bonus. Jones saw Terrell Owens as cut from the same cloth as Michael Irvin and Deion Sanders, a larger-than-life personality who may have created dissension but was a winner. Jones contended that T.O., as he liked to be called, was an easy choice. His single-game reception record and multiple Pro Bowl appearances were not aberrations. "I wouldn't call this a high-risk move," Jones confidently told the press. "We understand that this signing will open the door for scrutiny. I know and Terrell knows that much is expected of our players on and off the field. I have always believed in taking advantage of opportunity. Terrell is well known for what he can do. This may really work and work great for the Dallas Cowboys."

Head coach Bill Parcells was unhappy. The coach didn't like how Owens had managed to rip apart the Eagles internally. This was not his idea, Parcells made plain. He went the extra mile to disrespect Owens, referring to him as "the receiver" and "the player," avoiding mentioning him by name. Columnist Randy Galloway of the *Fort Worth Star-Telegram* followed suit and started calling Owens by his middle name, Eldorado.

The Player known as Eldorado did well enough in his first official game in a Cowboys uniform, snagging six passes and scoring a touchdown on the road, although the Cowboys wound up blowing a 10–0 lead to give away the game to the Jacksonville Jaguars, 24–17. Drew Bledsoe's three interceptions ruined an otherwise impressive opening-day performance with 246 passing yards.

Week two marked a turnaround against the Redskins in Irving. Bledsoe looked like the quarterback who had led the Patriots to the Super Bowl, going 19 for 38 with 237 passing yards, two touchdowns, and zero interceptions. Terry Glenn, another ex-Pat who once frustrated Coach Parcells to the point he referred to Glenn as "she," caught six passes for 94 yards to lead Cowboy receivers as Dallas soundly thumped Washington 27–10, although all the coach could focus on were missed plays and unnecessary penalties. The star of the T.O. Show dropped three passes, one for a sure touchdown, and caught three for 19 yards, all in the first quarter; he left the game in the fourth quarter with a broken ring finger that would require surgery and two to four weeks of rehab. Owens vowed to return before the October 8 game at Philadelphia against his old teammates.

Coach Parcells was underwhelmed. Mistakes by his players ate him up, and this squad was making plenty of them. "It's hard on me. I'm telling you, it really is," he said after the game. "I feel ill right now."

The illness must have been contagious. On September 26, an ambulance was rushed to Terrell Owens's residence after a 911 call from his publicist Kim Etheridge, who calmly told the operator, "I think he took too many pills." Etheridge did not identify Owens by name. She had found him passed out with an empty bottle of pain pills and managed to pry two pills out of his mouth before she called.

After T.O.'s trip to the hospital, the stories changed. Initially, it was said that T.O. was depressed and had tried to kill himself by downing a handful of hydrocodone pills, the equivalent of an extra-heavy dose of heroin. At a press conference Kim Etheridge insisted T.O. didn't try to kill himself; he had a reaction to the drugs he was taking for his broken finger and to a dietary supplement. He had twenty-five million reasons (as in dollars) to stay alive, she contended. Visibly angered, she accused police of lying. Etheridge's comments were generally dismissed by Cowboys fans as publicist spin. They weren't buying T.O.'s belated contention that he wasn't depressed and that his stomach hadn't been pumped out at the hospital.

Senior corporal Glenn White, publicist for the Dallas Police Association, responded to the accusations by saying Owens owed police an apology. "The officers reacted because they were called to this location to do this job," he said. "Now they're being put under a microscope by some fancy little football person. Give me a break. Those officers are ten times better than this man."

Dallas media played the Owens incident like the car wreck it was, proving true the well-known news director's credo: If it bleeds, it leads. Intentionally or not, Owens was pushing the right buttons to keep people talking. The Freak Show was no longer an image problem for the Dallas Cowboys. It *was* the Dallas Cowboys' image.

When the Cowboys traveled to Philadelphia on October 8, Terrell Owens suited up with the rest of the team, and Philly fans were ready to give him his due, erupting into a roar when he dropped a ball warming up before the game. It was not his day. He caught three passes for 45 yards. Several throws by Bledsoe were plain out of reach. Lito Sheppard swiped a Bledsoe pass that was under-thrown to a wide-open Owens and ran it back 102 yards for a touch-down late in the fourth quarter that sealed the 38–24 win for the Eagles. T.O.'s former partner D. McNabb of the Eagles had a fine day with two touchdown passes.

The Player threw a hissy fit on his way to the locker room, rant-ing that the Cowboys really never wanted him and that he was being misused. Jerry Jones calmed Owens down. At the postgame press conference, Owens said he wouldn't take the bait and point his fin-ger at Bledsoe or anyone for the loss. Coach Parcells had nothing to say.

Then there was the Falcons-Cowboys head-butting in Atlanta in December. Cornerback DeAngelo Hall had been bumping and pushing Owens early in the game until Owens spit in his face, and later admitted it, insisting Hall had it coming. T.O. was fined $35,000 by the league office for his transgression. Deion Sanders, who had played for both the Falcons and the Cowboys, got Hall and Owens together afterward to make peace.

The antics of Terrell Owens almost obscured the story of the year involving the Dallas Cowboys — but not quite.

Midway through the week-five game against the New York Giants, Parcells pulled the increasingly inconsistent Drew Bledsoe and handed the reins to Tony Romo. Over the course of the next two games, Romo stirred up more excitement than any Cowboys quar-terback since Troy Aikman. Even better, he scrambled like Roger Staubach and played it loose like Don Meredith.

BORN IN SAN DIEGO while his father was in the Navy, Romo had grown up in Burlington, Wisconsin, where he quarterbacked the high school team and competed in basketball, tennis, and golf. At Eastern Illinois University, a Division 1-AA school that played in the

Ohio Valley Conference, he set passing records and earned the Ohio Valley Conference Player of the Year Award as a sophomore, and the Walter Payton Award his senior year as the NCAA 1-AA small-college player of the year. Romo attracted the attention of scouts, although not enough to merit being drafted in 2003. Denver Broncos coach Mike Shanahan had his eyes on Romo, but Sean Payton, the quarterbacks coach of the Cowboys, beat him to it, adding the $10,000 bonus to sign him.

Tony Romo understood why he wasn't considered draft material. He wasn't an outstanding physical specimen, and he had played at a small college. But he believed he could compete in the NFL. "I probably got away with a lot of stuff because of my instincts," he said of his college experience. "If you put me up against the guys at the combine, they're 6-5 and throw nice, tight spirals. But what they can't predict is, can he throw off his back foot? Can he roll to his left, throw it with a guy in his face? Can he not see over a defender but know where the receiver is and hit him in stride? Does he have the instincts to see things quickly and get the ball out?"

Romo was third on the Cowboys' depth chart in 2003, behind Quincy Carter and Chad Hutchison, and third behind Vinny Testaverde and Drew Henson in 2004 after Quincy Carter's release. He had worked his way up to number two behind Bledsoe in 2005 but saw little playing time. In the offseason, Sean Payton, who had become head coach of the New Orleans Saints, offered a third-round draft pick for Romo, but Jerry Jones didn't take the bait.

Romo had taken a few snaps during the 34–6 trashing of the Houston Texans, throwing a short touchdown pass to Terrell Owens. The next week, during the October 26 home game against the Giants, he got the call to take over in the second half with the Cowboys trailing, 12–7. Romo's first pass was intercepted, but he steadied himself and went 14 for 25 with two TDs, throwing two more interceptions along the way including one run back for a touchdown. Those mistakes factored in the Cowboys' 36–22 defeat.

But Romo showed enough skills that Parcells gambled and started him against the Carolina Panthers the following week in a nationally televised game. The Cowboys soundly thrashed the defending NFC South division champions, 35–14. Three weeks later, Romo led the Cowboys to a 21–14 upset of the Indianapolis Colts, the NFL's only undefeated team and the eventual Super Bowl champion.

On Thanksgiving Day, he orchestrated the 38–10 sinking of the Tampa Bay Buccaneers. Romo was behind center through the 5-1 streak that elevated the team to the top of the NFC East. But Romo was error-prone and the team stalled to go 1-3 in December, losing their final game at home to a lousy 2-13 Detroit Lions team, 39–31, denying the Cowboys the division championship they once had in hand. Still, the team's 9-7 was good enough to enter the playoffs as a wild card, fronted by a fearless young quarterback with an exceptional 95.1 passer rating.

Fans found a new hero to worship in number 9. Romo was handsome, irreverent, beyond loose, and acted like a kid, wearing baseball caps backward and sporting a goofy grin. America's Team was Mexico's Team more than ever. Antonio Ramiro Romo was the grandson of Mexican immigrants who settled in Wisconsin after emigrating from Coahuila, the Mexican state that shared the Rio Grande as a border with Texas, to San Antonio. His good-guy sweetness was a marked contrast to the team's over-the-hill quarterbacks and to Terrell Owens's naked craving for attention.

"Do not anoint this kid," Bill Parcells warned an overeager press corps.

Romo was certainly not Quincy Carter. The most recent best hope to lead the Cowboys had dropped out of pro football and was so down and out that he couldn't post bond when he was arrested on December 15 for possession of marijuana. Columnist Randy Galloway of the *Fort Worth Star-Telegram* paid his $500 bail. "I've had a lot of fun with Quincy over the years, his problems and everything else," Galloway said. "But it's Christmas and Quincy Carter is in jail and I hate to see that happen. For him to be in the position today where he can't post a $500 bond, there's unfortunate problems in his life."

The January 6, 2007, game at Qwest Field in Seattle was practically a gimme, despite the Seahawks' identical 9-7 record. Dallas had the Big Mo. The Cowboys led 10–6 at halftime but trailed by a point when the clock wound down to 1:19 remaining in the game on a chilly 40-degree early evening. Tony Romo crouched down on one knee at the nine-yard line, eight yards behind the line of scrimmage at the Seahawks one-yard line, waiting to take the snap from L. P. Ladouceur on fourth-and-goal. All Romo had to do was set the ball on the ground, as he had been doing all season long in his original role as backup quarterback, and hold it for the kicker on the field-goal attempt.

Once the ball was positioned, Martín Gramática would swoop in, swing his leg, and boot it through the goalposts for a 23–21 Dallas win, which would advance the Cowboys to the second round, a level of success they hadn't reached in eleven years. The kick would mark the culmination of the Parcells era, justify the biggest player-acquisition gamble Jerry Jones had ever made, and validate Tony Romo as the Cowboys' franchise quarterback.

The nine-yard chip shot was a no-brainer. The Seattle crowd was muted, resigned to accept their team's fate.

Ladouceur's snap was flawless, but Romo couldn't handle it. He fumbled the ball long enough to upset Gramática's timing. Romo paused, gathered his wits and the football, and took off toward the left corner of the end zone, lumbering his way toward the goal until he was dragged down at the two-yard line by Jordan Babineaux. Television play-by-play announcer Al Michaels was awestruck, yelling, "Amazing! Unbelievable! How crazy is this?" Michaels's color guy, John Madden, had a more measured reaction, observing, "There is nothing automatic in football."

After the game, Tony Romo sobbed in the locker room. He had let his team down.

Coach Bill Parcells certainly felt the weight of the muffed snap and took it personally.

At the postgame press conference, the coach seemed semicatatonic as he said, "I did the best I could, but it wasn't quite good enough." Parcells had a fear of flying and often rode in the cockpit on team charters. On the long flight back to Texas, he told the crew, "This is probably going to be my last trip."

In the back of the plane, Jason Witten tried to console Tony Romo by asking him, "So, what's up?" Before Romo could respond, Witten offered this advice: "Look, you're going to be a better player for this, and we're going to be a better team."

Fifteen days later, via e-mail, Bill Parcells resigned as head coach of the Dallas Cowboys. Another year was left on the sixty-five-year-old head coach's five-year contract, but enough was enough. His bright young quarterback couldn't handle a snap or set the ball for a field goal. The Player known as Terrell Owens was a walking, talking head case who could never be coached. With his 34-32 record and no playoff wins for the Cowboys, Parcells could not stomach the idea of going back for more.

For his part, Owens told the *Star-Telegram*, "[Parcells] is like my grandmother. You love the person, but they are stuck in their old school ways."

Troubled Men

JANUARY'S LINGERING disappointment had not yet given in to the usual expressions of optimism by the time summer smothered North Central Texas. Jerry Jones stepped up his pitch. "To our fans, I would like them to know that it is still all about winning," Jones said after Parcells quit. "We have made progress on that front in the recent past, and we will continue to build on that progress with the belief that we have to do better."

The Cowboys had rebuilt to the point that a return to the playoffs seemed almost inevitable. The big hurdle was advancing deeper into the playoffs. If the Cowboys could do that, nobody cared who was coaching.

Before hiring a new head coach, Jones signed Jason Garrett as offensive coordinator. Garrett had been a backup to Troy Aikman at the peak of his career and his coaching skills were well known. He had been the quarterbacks coach for the Miami Dolphins, whose owner, Wayne Huizenga, told Jones he could interview Garrett for a position in Dallas only if Garrett could call plays, which he wasn't doing at Miami. At forty-one, Garrett was too young and untested to get the call as head coach, at least as far as Jones was concerned, but Jones knew other clubs were chasing Garrett too.

Once Garrett was set at offensive coordinator, the head coach search intensified. Nick Saban, Norv Turner, Mike Singletary, Gary

Gibbs, and Wade Phillips were among the NFL and college names thrown into the hat. Jones settled on Phillips, the soft-spoken Texas-born son of Houston and New Orleans coaching legend Bum Phillips and the defensive coordinator at San Diego after head coaching stints at New Orleans, Denver, Buffalo, and, briefly, Atlanta. Wade Phillips was an effective strategist with a passive personality that wouldn't clash with Jones's ego. He would not be competing for television face time. Power-sharing was not an issue. And the $3 million annual salary for three years suited him just fine. He'd be working with a cabinet Parcells had left well stocked; the roster brimmed with talent, including the exciting young quarterback.

Off the field, Jones went to the NFL owners' annual meeting to pitch Arlington as the site for the 2011 Super Bowl, bringing along Roger Staubach to make the sell. The owners favored Arlington over Indianapolis by two votes.

On the field, twenty-one of the twenty-two starters from 2006 returned. For all his clowning, Terrell Owens had led the NFL in scoring catches, and wild-maned running back Marion Barber tallied more touchdowns than any conference player. The offensive line anchored by Flozell Adams and Leonard Davis, acquired from the Arizona Cardinals, was one of the best, if not the very best, in the NFL. Properly protected, Tony Romo had all the potential to rise to the stature of the storied Cowboys quarterbacks. Old backup Drew Bledsoe had been released. The Minnesota Vikings' Brad Johnson was the new backup.

Tom Leppert was elected mayor of Dallas, besting Ed Oakley, Dallas's first openly gay mayoral candidate, in a runoff in which 11 percent of eligible voters participated. Two months later, training camp, er, that is, the Dallas Cowboys Ford Tough Training Camp opened in San Antonio. The introductory press conference was an infomercial: Jerry Jones unveiled the Ford F-150 pickup as the official vehicle of Cowboys training camp and introduced the southwestern market general manager for Ford, Dave Mondragon, before he moved on to football matters, such as reminding the gathering he was still very much in control. "I bought this team to run it," Jones informed the assembly.

With the pudgy Wade Phillips coaching, the imaginative Jerry Jones orchestrating, and a very good football team on the field, the Dallas Cowboys picked up where they had left off seven months before. Everyone associated with the team seemed confident this team was going deeper, maybe all the way.

The opener at home against the New York Giants was the featured *Sunday Night Football* game on NBC. Viewers were treated to a back-and-forth offensive contest that ended with the Cowboys ahead, 45–35. Although the vaunted one-gap 3-4 defense mixed with the 46 defense Phillips learned from Buddy Ryan didn't contain the Giants' Eli Manning and his receivers Plaxico Burress and Amani Toomer, both of whom had eight receptions (the Giants piled up 438 yards on offense), Tony Romo matched up well enough to win, generating a career high 345 passing yards going 15 of 24 and hitting tight end Jason Witten and wideouts Terrell Owens (twice) and Sam Hurd for touchdowns, while Marion Barber ran in the first six points for Dallas from 18 yards out. Jason Garrett's debut as offensive coordinator was an unqualified success.

The next three opponents, Miami, Chicago, and St. Louis, affirmed the Cowboys' offensive juggernaut and an improved defense. Wade Phillips's D forced five turnovers, and Terrell Owens caught the go-ahead touchdown pass on fourth down with four minutes left to lead the Cowboys to a 37–20 win over the Dolphins. Owens was penalized for using the goalpost as a prop after the touchdown for his dramatic re-creation of a New England Patriots assistant coach clandestinely filming a closed Jets practice, an incident that had been revealed a week earlier. The Bears were embarrassed in Chicago, 34–10, as Romo's QB rating improved, making him second only to New England's Tom Brady. Romo spearheaded the 35–7 rout of the Rams by throwing three touchdowns, running another one in, and scrambling like Staubach when he had to. In those three games the Cowboys scored 106 points to their opponents' 37 points. The away game at Buffalo was not so flawless, with the Cowboys having to score 12 points in the fourth quarter in order to come from behind and edge the Bills, 25–24, on Nick Folk's last-second field goal, winning in spite of Romo's unraveling and tossing five interceptions (along with two TDs) and losing a fumble.

The unbeaten New England Patriots, perhaps motivated by Terrell Owens making fun of their Spygate scandal, were a cold splash of reality, ruining fan fantasies of a perfect season and the Cowboys' best start since 1983: Tom Brady outgunned Romo, going 31 for 46 with five touchdown passes, shredding Dallas's secondary for a decisive 48–27 win in Irving.

But the New England game was an aberration. The team had jelled to the point they could dominate Minnesota 24–14 with Chris Canty's blocked field-goal attempt run back 68 yards by Patrick Watkins for a touchdown; reward Romo with a six-year, $67.5 million contract extension; cage the Eagles in Philly, 38–17, with Terrell Owens grabbing ten passes, one for a touchdown; beat the Giants 31–20 on Romo's four TD passes, two to Terrell Owens; best Washington, 28–23, on four Romo-Owens TDs; shoot down the Jets on Thanksgiving, 34–3, with Romo and Owens connecting for another passing TD; and bully the Packers and the Lions without much pushback.

The mighty Cowboys clinched the NFC East at the end of November for the first time since 1998, sitting pretty with a 12-1 record, their best in franchise history at this point in the season, after once-beaten Green Bay came to town to match Romo against his boyhood idol Brett Favre. Romo rang up 309 passing yards and four touchdowns for a 37–27 Cowboys victory; Favre left the game with an injured shoulder and departed Irving never having won a game at Texas Stadium.

Romo and the team as a whole slacked off after clinching, dropping games to Philadelphia and Washington while beating Carolina. The QB was punchless in the 10–6 loss to Philadelphia, throwing three picks. The Philly D kept the Cowboys out of the end zone for the first time in fifty-four games. The offense couldn't put the ball past the goal line again in the final game against the Redskins and had to settle for two field goals in the 27–6 loss. Romo was 7 for 16 with no touchdowns. Despite running out of gas, the Cowboys tied their best record ever, 13–3, and entered the playoffs as the NFC's top seed.

Jason Witten, Terrell Owens, Terry Glenn, and Patrick Crayton had been catching practically everything Romo threw their way— when Romo was firing on all pistons. Marion Barber and Julius Jones were an effective rushing duo—most of the time. The defense led by outside linebacker DeMarcus Ware and cornerback Terence Newman brutalized the opposition once Coach Phillips's 3-4 and 46 schemes took hold, it seemed. Jerry Jones had made all the right adjustments to create a very good Dallas Cowboys team, which was beginning to be compared to the dynasty teams of the 1990s. All that was missing were three Super Bowl rings.

Tony Romo appeared to have the right stuff. "He processes and sees things faster than anybody I've ever played with," said Steve Tenhagen, Romo's tight end at Burlington High School in Wisconsin who set pass reception records at the University of Wisconsin–Whitewater. "There were passes thrown into spots you wouldn't think were open and he'd find a way to get the ball there. He has the ability to see it before it happens. That instinct, you just can't teach that."

Romo's rising stock as a player was matched by his celebrity. Being the starting QB of the Dallas Cowboys bought a certain cachet. But Romo brought something extra to the table. He was easily the best golfer to ever wear a Cowboys uniform, and being skilled at that recreational activity enjoyed by jocks and business titans alike was no small thing; it had helped that his mother, Joan, worked the counter at Brown's Lake golf course in Burlington and brought her son to work with her when he was growing up.

He was telegenic and came off like a normal guy. Dating *American Idol* winner Carrie Underwood from Checotah, Oklahoma, put him on the national-celeb radar. When he hooked up with singer/actress Jessica Simpson, the TV tabloids and Internet gossip sites went bonkers. Simpson, the Richardson-raised pop-teen confection with a radiant smile who showed more teeth than any blonde since Farrah Fawcett, was already a veteran of her own reality TV series with her ex Nick Lachey and was considerably more grown up than when she first burst onto the scene in 1999 with the worldwide pop hit record "I Wanna Love You Forever." She qualified as top babe material.

But sports fans did not take to Jessica like 'tweeners and reality-TV addicts did, and worse, they started calling her Yoko, a reference to Yoko Ono, the lover, confidante, and, many believed, puppeteer of John Lennon. Yoko, they said, broke up the Beatles. Simpson would do the same to the Cowboys if Romo didn't look out for himself.

The sniping rose to a fever pitch as the playoffs loomed. Dallas had a bye for the first round of playoffs due to its sparkling record, and the quarterback took advantage of the free week in early January and took off in a private jet accompanied by his girlfriend; his favorite passing target and road roomie, Jason Witten; and the Simpson family on a getaway vacay to Cabo San Lucas, Baja California, Mexico.

With not much else for the press to talk or write about during the bye week, Dallas's star couple on vacation became Topic A.

When the Cowboys resumed their quest, they hosted the New York Giants, the NFC East runner-up and wild card whom they had handily dispatched twice already. The Giants' Eli Manning drew first blood, hitting wide receiver Amani Toomer in the first quarter on a 52-yard pass. Romo responded by hitting Owens for a five-yard touchdown pass, and Barber ran in from the one-yard line for the

Cowboys' second score before Manning and Toomer combined for another touchdown pass, ending the first half with the teams tied 14–14.

The Dallas offense could only muster a 34-yard Nick Folk field goal in the third quarter, but it was good enough for a 17–14 lead that held until there was 2:24 left in the fourth quarter, when Brandon Jacobs scored again for the Giants from the one-yard line. In the waning moments, Romo hurled a pass into the end zone intended for receiver Terry Glenn, but the Giants' cornerback R. W. McQuarters picked it off to end Dallas's season. The Giants' Michael Strahan had eight tackles and was instrumental in shutting down Romo's passing game in the second half while limiting Marion Barber to 34 yards in the final two quarters. Eleven penalties for 84 yards assessed against the Cowboys were the critical difference in the 21–17 defeat.

Jessica got the blame, from the fans and from the media. It did not matter that it was the Giants' ninth consecutive win on the road, or that Eli Manning had finally found his touch, or that the Giants were good enough to go on to win the Super Bowl. Jessica Simpson was worse than Yoko because she made the Cowboys lose.

Terrell Owens was in tears after the game ended. "You can point the finger at him, you can talk about the vacation, and if you do that, it's really unfair," he said in defense of his quarterback. "That's my teammate. We lost as a team."

The following June, Jessica Simpson was seen with Tony Romo and paparazzi photographed her in a T-shirt that read *Real Girls Eat Meat.* The gossips said it was a diss of Romo's previous flame Carrie Underwood, who was a vegetarian. It didn't make a dime's worth of difference to the object of her affections. Soon enough, the real-girl carnivore and the star quarterback parted ways.

Jerry Jones went on a spending spree that offseason to keep talent and find new blood. He bumped Jason Garrett up to assistant head coach with a $3 million salary—the same as Wade Phillips—after Baltimore and Atlanta both offered him the head coach position.

Dave Campo, the Cowboys' former head coach, was brought back as defensive secondary coach after a five-year absence during which he had been the defensive coordinator at Cleveland and the secondary coach at Jacksonville.

Jones also pursued another well-known NFL troublemaker, Adam "Pacman" Jones, a cornerback out of West Virginia who had been the Tennessee Titans' number-one draft pick in 2005. Pacman Jones excelled as a return specialist and in the defensive backfield, but he sat out the 2007 season thanks to a yearlong suspension ordered by league commissioner Roger Goodell, who cited Jones's off-the-field behavior. He had been tied to a shooting inside a Las Vegas gentlemen's club, Minxx, where Jones had partied after the National Basketball Association's all-star game. At 2:00 a.m., Jones arrived with his posse at the glorified titty bar with $100,000 in his pocket, some of which he converted into singles so he could shower the dancers with bills in a ritual known as "making it rain." Some of the dancers tried to scoop money off the floor. Jones reacted by pulling one dancer's hair and punching her, and bouncers ejected him from the club. On his way out, Jones threatened to kill one security guard. Shortly afterward, an unidentified gunman entered the club and fired several shots into the crowd, paralyzing one of the club's bouncers from the waist down. Jones was not convicted of any crimes relating to the incident.

However, the Pacman Jones Vegas incident was one of several that prompted Roger Goodell to institute a personal-conduct code. The commissioner had been spending a considerable amount of his time policing players, including Jones, the Bengals' Chris Henry, and the Bears' Tank Johnson, who were the first to be suspended under the new policy. Joining them was Wade Wilson, the Cowboys' quarterbacks coach, who was suspended for five games and fined $100,000 after he admitted using a banned substance for medical purposes. New England Patriots coach Bill Belichick would also be fined $500,000 and the Patriots would be fined $250,000 and lose their first-round draft pick for illegally videotaping New York Jets' practices. None of the incidents matched Michael Vick's, the Atlanta Falcons' star quarterback, who was thrown out of football altogether after his criminal conviction for running a dogfighting ring. Vick would serve twenty-one months in prison.

The Vegas dustup was only the latest of several involving Pacman, strippers, and the law. He had faced assault and felony vandalism charges in Nashville before he started playing for the Titans and was arrested at least three other times, leading Tennessee to trade him early in 2008.

The transaction between the Titans and the Cowboys pulled off in late April was loaded with stipulations. The Titans received the Cowboys' fourth-round pick in the 2008 NFL draft. If the league reinstated Jones, the Cowboys would also give up their sixth-round pick in the 2009 draft. If he remained suspended, the Titans would give up their fourth-round draft pick in the 2009 draft. It was the first NFL trade involving a suspended player.

Jerry Jones considered Pacman worth the risk. He stipulated that the player would have a full-time bodyguard as part of the four-year, incentive-loaded contract he signed. *Morning News* columnist Tim Cowlishaw did Jerry one better, suggesting Pacman be allowed no more than ten dollars of walking-around money; "Pretty hard to make it rain in a club with two fives," Cowlishaw noted. Deion Sanders, Michael Irvin, and Jim Brown all offered to advise the young player. His arrival at summer training camp at the River Ridge Sports Complex in Oxnard, California, gave notice that Terrell Owens was no longer the most outrageous Cowboy on the roster.

The Formerly Most Flamboyant Player was placated when Jerry Jones re-signed Owens to a three-year contract for $34 million ("$1 million for every year I've lived," Owens noted), with $13 million guaranteed. A giant-size bowl of popcorn that required two men to carry was hauled into the signing ceremony to symbolize Owens's intent to keep fans entertained and Jones's intent to reward him. "There's your signing bonus," Jones told Owens when the popcorn arrived. Jim Reeves of the *Fort Worth Star-Telegram* thought Jones was crazy for giving Owens such a fat contract. Thirty-four large ones was "absurd for a 34-year-old (35 in December) receiver who will only get slower and more susceptible to injury the deeper he gets into the deal," Reeves wrote.

It was easy for Jones to ignore Reeves's insult. T.O. led the NFL with thirteen touchdown receptions in 2006 and recorded fifteen more TD catches in 2007.

Just in time for the arrival of the newest bad boy at Valley Ranch came *Boys Will Be Boys*, written by former *Sports Illustrated* writer Jeff Pearlman and arguably the most salacious book written about the Cowboys. The opening scene portrayed Michael Irvin holding the bloody shears that he had used to stab Everett McIver in the neck over an argument about who was first in line to get a haircut at training camp. Pearlman proceeded to detail Irvin's ladies fixation, Charles Haley's fixation with his own large penis, the upscale strip clubs that members of the team and coaching staff frequented, the club's policy of vetting American Airlines flight attendants for their charter flights in the tradition of Clint Murchison and Bedford Wynne, and Jerry Jones's involvement with women other than his wife.

Pearlman also delivered a serious analysis of the Jones-era Cowboys, recognizing the early- and mid-1990s team as one of the greatest NFL dynasties ever.

Elsewhere on the popcorn front, eighty young ladies out of a thousand applicants were invited to Texas Stadium for the cheerleader-training-camp competition, where twenty-one newcomers and twenty-one veterans were selected after a talent presentation, two dances, a kick-line routine, and written tests on football knowledge, current events, and football team and cheerleaders history.

The CMT cable channel documented it all on the third season of *Making the Team,* a reality series about trying out for the Dallas Cowboys Cheerleaders. Director Kelli McGonagill Finglass (she acquired the new last name after marrying Cowboys director of sales, marketing, and advertising Joel Finglass in 1996), fitness trainer Jay Johnson, and team choreographer Judy Trammell would all reprise their roles in the program, which followed *My Big Fat Redneck Wedding* on the CMT reality-TV schedule.

Finglass had made the best of her one-year stint in sales and promotion to oversee production of the DCCs' first swimsuit calendar video, which aired on the NFL Network, and to establish DCC dance and drill team competitions, Camp DCC, Cheers for Years, and Cheers for Fitness. Finglass also sought out corporate sponsorships for the cheerleaders, signing up Planet Tan, Jay Johnson's Boot Camp Fitness, Adventure Tours USA, and Capezio footwear. The cheerleaders brought $1 million a year in profits to the football club.

For the ultimate reality check, HBO sent a film crew in for another up-close-and-personal and relatively unvarnished behind-the-scenes look at training camp. Dallas was the focus for the second time in four seasons of *Hard Knocks*. This time, the arrival of Pacman alongside T.O. and owner Jones was all the reason they needed.

All that popcorn added gallons of extra butter flavoring to the already tasty tub of great expectations. The Cowboys-Patriots preseason exhibition drew more than 100,000 spectators to Aztec Stadium in Mexico City, where the vast majority of the crowd rooted for Dallas. Then the front office had the pleasure of announcing that all home games had been sold out before the start of the Dallas Cowboys Football Club's final season at Texas Stadium.

Pacman Jones wasn't part of the stories emanating from Valley Ranch as the team jumped to a 3-0 record after beating Cleveland on the road, 28–10, and opening in Irving for the last time by outscoring the Eagles, 41–37. Romo, Barber, and Owens were summoning visions of a previous Cowboys threesome. But against the Green Bay Packers, Jones rang up eight tackles, stripped the ball from a Packers running back and ran it back to set up a field goal, and generally played well enough to suggest the other Jones knew what he was doing by signing him. The game also marked the introduction of another receiver weapon for the Cowboys in Miles Austin, a special-teams player with seven career receptions before he burned the Packers on a 52-yard touchdown catch.

The Redskins upset the Cowboys in Irving, 26–24, limiting the running game to 44 yards despite Romo throwing touchdown passes to Witten, Owens, and Austin, but Dallas recovered to tame the Bengals, 31–22, on Romo TDs to Witten, Owens, and Patrick Crayton — and Pacman leading the D with six tackles.

That was before a call reporting a disturbance was made to Dallas police from downtown Dallas's posh Joule Hotel early on Wednesday, October 8. Pacman Jones had gotten into a fight with his bodyguard. No arrests were made and no charges or police reports were filed. NFL commissioner Goodell nonetheless stepped in, and on October 14 suspended Jones indefinitely without pay for violating the league's personal-conduct code (again). It was the twelfth off-the-field altercation involving Jones in four years. Pacman immediately entered a rehabilitation facility for alcohol abuse.

Before he was suspended, he had racked up five tackles in the Cowboys' game against the Cardinals in Glendale, Arizona; the Cowboys fell, 30–24, in overtime on a blocked kick after Nick Folk barely cleared the crossbars on a 52-yard field goal at the end of the fourth quarter to tie the game. Pacman chilled and Dallas lost to St. Louis, 34–14, as Romo sat with a broken pinkie, and Brad Johnson took over, and lost to the Giants, 35–14, the losses interrupted by a 13–9 win over Tampa Bay. After an off week, Romo returned, as did corner Terence Newman, and the Cowboys rattled off wins over Washington (14–10), San Francisco (35–22), and Seattle (34–9), to more closely resemble the start-of-season Super Bowl favorites.

Jerry Jones tried bolstering the receiving corps by acquiring Roy Williams from the Detroit Lions for three future draft picks, signing Williams to a five-year, $45 million contract, effectively designating him as the Cowboys' number-one receiver.

Pacman Jones's indefinite suspension ended when he was reinstated for the December 7 game against the Steelers at Pittsburgh's Heinz Field, during which he ran back punts and kickoffs for 51 yards, made a solo tackle, and fumbled once before severely injuring his neck, suggesting his career might be over. Pittsburgh made up a ten-point deficit with 7:30 left on the clock to win by a touchdown, 20–13, allowing the Giants to clinch the NFC East. But Dallas's 8-5 mark still looked good enough for entry into the playoffs as a wild card, if they won their final three games. The Giants were methodically dispatched, 20–8, the following week at Texas Stadium. But in the last game ever played in Irving, the offense stalled and Dallas trailed 20–7 after three quarters before they finally showed some of their vaunted weaponry. Nick Folk kicked a field goal, and Romo targeted Terrell Owens and Jason Witten for touchdowns in the final 3:50 of the game to add 17 points to their total, but the comeback was too little, too late, and the Ravens flew out of DFW with a 33–24 win.

Pacman Jones suited up to play in the Cowboys' last game of the season, a critical division matchup with Philadelphia at Lincoln Financial Field, with a berth in the playoffs still on the line for both teams. His presence made not one whit of difference. The Eagles pasted the Cowboys with a 44–6 defeat that eliminated Dallas from postseason action. It was one of the worst losses in the team's history. Romo, T.O., Witten, running backs Marion Barber and Tashard Choice, Pacman, DeMarcus Ware, Flozell Adams, Patrick Crayton, Miles Austin, Terence Newman, Roy Williams — the whole team — stunk it up. The individuals were all stars in their own right. But as a team, they couldn't get it together. Their performance convinced some fans that masterminds Wade Phillips and Jason Garrett had their heads so far up their asses, they couldn't wiggle their ears.

"There's not enough Maker's Mark in the world to take the sting out of this one," Brad Sham, the official radio voice of the Cowboys, concluded after the final seconds ticked down to end another season.

Restoration in a New House

IN OTHER YEARS, a 9-7 record could have gotten the Cowboys into the playoffs. But in 2008, it was good enough for only third place in the NFC East. The surprise letdown led to two even more surprising moves.

In early January of 2009, the Cowboys announced the release of Adam Jones. Police identified him as the main suspect who had ordered the Las Vegas shooting in 2007. Even Jerry Jones could recognize the seriousness of these charges.

Then, on March 5, the Cowboys announced the release of Terrell Owens. The Player had been assured by Jerry Jones that his job was secure a week earlier, but Jones finally caved to the wishes of most of his players and coaches and advisers, not the least of whom was COO/executive vice president/director of player personnel Stephen Jones, who had been privately pushing his father to release Owens and Jones and excise any other troublemakers from the roster. As the season had been winding down in December, T.O. had gotten into a dustup with tight end Jason Witten, Tony Romo's roommate and favorite receiver. Owens accused Witten of conspiring against him in collusion with Romo and assistant head coach Jason Garrett.

Regardless of his stats, Owens had lived up to Skip Bayless's assertion that T.O. stood for "team obliterator." He may have been a kindred soul and like a son to owner Jones when it came to promo. But when it came to Romo, enough was enough. Owens had destroyed the 49ers when he accused quarterback Jeff Garcia of favoring other receivers, and he did the same with Donovan McNabb and the Philadelphia Eagles. In announcing his release, Jones contended that Bill Parcells had approved the acquisition of Owens three years before, but at the same time he admitted that the coach and the Player had never spoken. That was no way to run a professional football franchise. T.O. had made too many enemies and had not won enough advocates around Valley Ranch. He could be some other team's headache now.

"It's not because he doesn't mean well," Stephen Jones, head of player personnel for the Cowboys, would later say with charity. "I just don't think he can help himself."

One sign that the whole organization needed shaking up was the brief return of Dan Reeves, Tom Landry's original head-coach-in-waiting and former head coach of the Atlanta Falcons and Denver Broncos. Reeves arrived at Valley Ranch in early February as part of a makeover Jones was trying to orchestrate. Two days later, he departed Valley Ranch, citing his and Jones's inability to agree on a job title and responsibilities.

THEN THERE WAS MORE than a sign. On May 2, twenty-seven rookies were going through afternoon drills at a minicamp inside the field house at Valley Ranch when the lights hanging from the top of the modified tent began to sway. A severe thunderstorm rolling in from the southwest produced a microburst with winds exceeding fifty-five miles an hour that pounded the steel-framed fabric-covered facility. The gusts were so severe, the fabric walls started to flap and sag, and the western wall fell onto the field, followed by the collapse of the roof and the eastern wall.

Fifty-eight people inside the eighty-foot-tall tent managed to escape, warned by the eerie sounds of steel frames buckling from the force of straight-line winds. Twelve rookie players and several members of the coaching staff and media were not so fortunate.

Nick Eatman and Josh Ellis of DallasCowboys.com heard someone screaming and recognized the voice of Todd Archer of the *Dallas Morning News*, who was pinned down by a tangle of steel. With the help of safety DeAngelo Smith and linebacker Brandon Williams, they were able to raise the steel bars high enough for Archer to squirm out.

Three people were severely hurt. Thirty-three-year-old Cowboys scouting assistant Rich Behm was permanently paralyzed from the waist down when his thoracic spine was fractured. Special-teams coach Joe DeCamillis, forty-three, the son-in-law of Dan Reeves, suffered fractured cervical vertebrae—a broken neck—but no paralysis. Assistant athletic trainer Greg Gaither, thirty-five, fractured the tibia and fibula of his right leg.

The 406-foot-long field house had been erected over the practice field in 2003 at the request of Coach Parcells and at a cost of $4 million. In 2008, the company that had installed it, Summit Structures, reinforced the tent with additional bracing and a new exterior fabric, at the request of the Cowboys after four similar tent facilities had collapsed over the previous four years.

A trust fund was set up for Behm, his wife, and three children, and Behm and DeCamillis eventually reached an out-of-court settlement for $34 million with several Jones family companies and the company that built the structure. Both remained employees of the Dallas Cowboys Football Club.

THE COLLAPSED PRACTICE-FIELD TENT was a distant memory by the time the fiftieth season of the Dallas Cowboys began. A plethora of fanfare, pomp, and circumstance, accompanied by searchlights and an eerie white glow emanating from within, datelined Arlington, Texas, heralded the official opening of the spanking-new Cowboys Stadium.

A new theme song was composed for the rollout, "Cowboys Stomp," a country-rock-pop-metal marching anthem featuring Cowboy Troy, the black rapper from Victoria, Texas, who was part of the Big and Rich country crew that took over country music in Nashville in the 1990s. Cowboy Troy's collaborators were pop-country guitarist Keith Burns, country singer Michelle Poe, and the "world-famous" Dallas Cowboys Cheerleaders shaking their pom-poms and booties in the background.

The official song replaced the old "Dallas Cowboys Pride" fight song featuring country crooner and Dallas resident Charley Pride, a number backed by a disco orchestra that had sounded more commercial jingle than fight song. But these were hardly the only songs being sung about the Cowboys. A slew of independent hip-hop street productions popped up on YouTube and all over the Internet boasting about the superiority of the team from D.

On "How Bout Them 'Boys?," Dru 24/7 Hustla bragged about the five championship rings and the Cowboys' new crib in Arlington while giving shout-outs to DeMarcus Ware, Felix Jones, Marion Barber, Jon Kitna, Roy Williams, Leonard Davis, and Tony Romo. C Smoke's "Do Da Shotgun (Part 2)" cited Dallas's Dirty D, Jason Witten, and Miles Austin while recalling Terrell Owens (who "was a can-cer"). Elyon Entertainment's 2009 freestyle version "How 'Bout Them Cowboys?" challenged each opponent with the refrain "You don't want to see us."

Classics such as "My Heroes Have Always Been Cowboys," made famous by Texas music icon Willie Nelson, lingered. But like the old Texas Stadium favorite "Up Against the Wall, Redneck Mother" and Texas Stadium itself, these were faded memories from another era.

Whatever fan base had been lost with regime change or attrition had been replaced by a younger, more energetic following, whose numbers had grown considerably in the mid-1990s when the Cowboys played for the NFC championship four years in a row and won three Super Bowls under two coaches and a most unusual owner.

Now those fans were getting antsy. It had been fourteen seasons since the Cowboys' last trip to the Super Bowl. They wanted their reward. Now. The new stadium was eye candy, but sooner or later, the focus would shift to the team playing in the stadium.

Those players included a dozen Pro Bowlers headed up by Tony Romo and his best receivers, suggesting everything was go for the NFL's Go Team.

AFTER TAKING CARE OF Tampa Bay on the road, 34–21, the football team took to their new home against the Giants in front of 105,121 ticket holders and a national television audience looking on. It was a close-fought game to the very end, when New York kicker Lawrence Tynes nailed a 37-yard field goal as time ran out. Four turnovers by the Cowboys factored in the Giants' 33–31 win, taking the shine off the Cowboys' debut in their new house. But not for long.

A slightly smaller turnout of 90,588, still far more than either the Cotton Bowl or Texas Stadium could hold, showed up for the week two *Monday Night Football* national telecast on ESPN, where their 'Boys looked close to indestructible as they methodically tore apart the Carolina Panthers, 21–7, holding them to a single touchdown and only 63 rushing yards. Jones's economy of scale proved prescient. Build it big enough and outrageous enough, and the crowds would come.

Five games in, Dallas sat at 3-2 after sneaking past their former crosstown rivals, the winless Kansas City Chiefs, in overtime, 26–20, in a throwback game at Arrowhead Stadium for which the Chiefs wore their old Dallas Texans uniforms and the Cowboys reminded older fans how ugly-ass their original big-stars-on-the-shoulders garb had been. The game marked the first start for receiver Miles Austin, standing in for the injured Roy Williams. Austin caught ten passes for 250 yards — breaking the Cowboys' single-game receiving-yards record set by Bob Hayes — with two catches for touchdowns.

Miles Austin made fans forget T.O. and Roy Williams in his second start for the Cowboys against Atlanta, grabbing six passes, including two for long touchdowns, in the 37–21 win. Austin led the receiver corps again with five receptions, including one for a touchdown, in the 38–17 victory over the Seahawks. After beating the Eagles 20–16; losing to Green Bay 17–7; edging the Redskins by a point, 7–6; and rolling the Raiders 34–7, the Cowboys entered their week-thirteen away game against the Giants in New Jersey looking good at 8-3. But they dropped that game by a touchdown, 31–24, then lost at home to San Diego by a field goal, 20–17. What had once appeared to be a Super Bowl–worthy crew inspired a little doubt, but the 24–17 upset of the undefeated New Orleans Saints (the eventual Super Bowl champs) in the New Orleans Superdome, led by DeMarcus Ware, who sacked quarterback Drew Brees twice, restored hopes of Cowboys greatness. This team could be one of those. The defense was relentless. The offense was potent enough to score from any part of the field.

After two shutouts — against Washington on the road, 17–0, and Philadelphia at home, 24–0 — the Cowboys closed out at 11-5. Other than the 13-3 season two years previous, when Phillips took over as coach, it was Dallas's best record since the season they'd won Super Bowl XXX. Tony Romo broke Danny White's single-season club record for passing, set in 1983.

The Eagles, who ended the regular season tied with Dallas atop the NFC East, were the Cowboys' first-round playoff opponent. The Cowboys whipped them for the third time that season, 34–14, in Arlington, marking the Cowboys' first playoff win in 13 years.

The Minnesota Vikings provided the opposition in the divisional round. In spite of the climate-controlled environment of the Metrodome in downtown Minneapolis, the Cowboys offense executed like they were playing outdoors in the Minnesota winter and freezing their asses off. The only score Dallas could muster was a 33-yard Shaun Suisham field goal in the second quarter. Tony Romo threw one interception and no touchdowns and fumbled three times facing a punishing Minnesota pass rush that sacked him six times and pummeled him with ten more hard hits. He was thoroughly outgunned by forty-year-old Brett Favre, who tossed four touchdowns for the 34–3 Vikes victory.

Making the playoffs but falling short of the big game appeared to be the MO of the post-1995 Cowboys. Four teams — Cleveland, Detroit, Jacksonville, and the Houston Texans — had never made it to the big game. San Francisco, Washington, Miami, Buffalo, Kansas City, the New York Jets, San Diego, and Denver had not returned since the Cowboys' last Super Bowl appearance. But nineteen other franchises had.

That didn't deter Jerry Jones from bragging while loaded, as captured on a cell-phone video camera broadcast to the world over the sports-gossip Web site Deadspin. He was hanging at Ocean Prime, one of his favorite restaurants, and he told a friendly fan armed with a cell-phone camera that former coach Bill Parcells was "not worth a shit" but was a necessary evil. "They were on my ass so bad — 'Jerry's got to have a yes-man,'" Jones slurred. "So to get this fuckin' stadium, I needed to bring his ass in."

When the video went viral, Jones spoke to local reporters to clarify his remarks. He meant no disrespect toward Bill Parcells and told the press that he had called the former Cowboys coach to explain his comments.

The same night Jones was captured on video dissing Parcells, a former U.S. Air Force captain named Patricia Gavin claimed Jones sexually assaulted her in the ladies' room of Ocean Prime; this was according to the lawsuit she filed on September 30, 2010, seeking $500 million in damages. Gavin also accused Jones of taking her to his home in his limo and stealing her purse, which contained a check for $2 million in British sterling, giving her two hundred dollars under the assumption she was a prostitute, and instructing his advisers to dose her with date-rape drugs.

It was not the first suit filed by Gavin charging a celebrity had done her wrong. Jones responded by obtaining a restraining order to keep her away from his family and him. The woman's lawsuit did nothing but cement Jerry Jones's reputation as a high-profile celebrity, at least as big as Michael Irvin once was in Dallas.

THE SHENANIGANS INVOLVING the owner did little to quell perennially heightened expectations. The 11-5 record, Jerry Jones's boundless optimism, and the club's adept promotion machine already had Dallas fans believing theirs would be the first team in NFL history to play in a Super Bowl in their home stadium.

They weren't necessarily deluded. On paper, the Cowboys were loaded. Twenty of twenty-two starters returned. The defensive line performed like a wall of stampeding bulls, and linebacker DeMarcus Ware was as resilient and agile as the cornerbacks and safeties. Tony Romo was almost on the same level as the league's premier QBs — Peyton Manning, Tom Brady, Ben Roethlisberger, Phillip Rivers, Aaron Rogers, Eli Manning, and Drew Brees. The team's offensive stats were second only to those of Super Bowl champion New Orleans. Number 9 jerseys were showing up everywhere.

Keeping fan interest high was the very public obliteration of the team's former home. At 7:00 on Sunday morning, April 11, under streaky gray skies, twenty thousand onlookers gathered around the highway junction in Irving while thousands more watched from skyscrapers all the way downtown, and hundreds of thousands turned on their television sets. They were all preparing to watch Texas Stadium get blown up. On cue, a ton's worth of strategically placed TNT would ignite in near-perfect timing to buckle the girders and bring down Clint Murchison's dream palace.

It had been thirty-eight years, long enough for Texas Stadium to become an institution and Dallas's most recognized symbol, no matter where it happened to be located. Parents brought children. Tailgate parties started getting fired up the night before. Offices in high-rises with a view of the stadium opened up for employees.

The city of Irving hyped the event for weeks with a live webcam of the stadium site and later sold video and film interior shots of the implosion to several television and film production companies in need of explosion and destruction footage.

ESPN's Chris Berman hosted the event broadcast live locally. The honor of pressing the button to implode the stadium belonged to eleven-year-old Casey Rogers, from nearby Terrell, who had earned the right by winning a national essay contest. The freckle-faced Rogers wrote about the charity he had started for Dallas's homeless people three years earlier.

The crowd joined the countdown, and fireworks went off. On cue, Rogers pushed the button, triggering a series of flashes accompanied by sharp booms as the dynamite charges detonated inside the stadium, followed by a loud rumble. A cloud of smoke rose. The walls and the roof imploded, gently crumpling down to the ground in a pile of dust and rubble. The crowd cheered. All in less than a minute.

"Awesome!" Rogers declared. "It was better than I thought it would be."

Three girders did not fall but remained erect as archaeological remnants among the ruins.

Pam Seal, a Dallas Cowboys Cheerleader from the class of '75, decided the night before to drive in from Mesquite with her husband and kids. "It was much more emotional than I expected," she said. "I'm so glad that I had my family out there to hold my hand through it. I didn't think I would be that much of a basket case about it. It was like saying goodbye to an old friend."

The event itself was sponsored by Kraft Foods, which also put together the essay contest as part of Kraft's Cheddar Explosion promotion. It was the first demolition with a corporate sponsor. The creative mind of Jerry Jones had struck again.

During a farewell event two days earlier, Alicia Landry paid reverent tribute, saying, "Texas Stadium will never become tarnished, neglected, or dishonored, but always remembered, revered, and respected, a memory that will be cherished, a place forever honored by all of us who were there."

ONCE HISTORY WAS DISPATCHED, all eyes reverted to the present. Rookie wide receiver Dez Bryant out of Oklahoma State looked so talented at training camp that no one blinked when he took number 88, Michael Irvin's and Drew Pearson's old number, and rendered Patrick Crayton expendable trade bait. Number-one receiver Miles Austin, whose public profile was elevated by his new girlfriend, Kim Kardashian, a woman famous for being famous, had someone to give him a run for his money.

Bryant was criticized for ignoring a rookie hazing tradition by refusing to carry Roy Williams's pads at camp, but he made up for the faux pas by treating the team's offense (along with some uninvited defensive players) to dinner at Pappas Brothers Steakhouse and picking up the $54,896 tab.

The professional prognosticators were not as certain as the fans about the Cowboys' prospects. The O-line looked good on paper but was porous as cheesecloth. There were problems at safety. The team's titular head, Wade Phillips, was the most passive coach in the NFC East, dubbed Coach Cupcake by the *Fort Worth Star-Telegram*'s Jennifer Floyd-Engel for his quiet, deferential manner. But with the ultimate game headed to North Texas for the first time, the homers believed.

The Cowboys opened at FedEx Field in Landover, Maryland, against the Redskins in a mistake-prone defensive grind that almost ended magically: Tony Romo finding receiver Roy Williams in a crowd for a 13-yard touchdown and the win as time expired. But a yellow flag was thrown on six-year offensive tackle Alex Barron for holding, negating the play, and the game ended with the Redskins in front, 13–7. It had been the Cowboys' to lose. The 'Skins never scored an offensive touchdown. Their seven points came at the end of the first half when, with four seconds left, Dallas offensive coordinator Jason Garrett called for a risky shovel pass that was stripped away from running back/receiver Tashard Choice by defensive cornerback DeAngelo Hall, who ran the ball from 32 yards out for a Washington TD. After the game, Garrett and head coach Phillips both said Romo should have taken a knee instead of trying to run the play. Sloppy play dominated both sides of the ball for Dallas, which led ESPNDallas.com blogger Calvin Watkins to note that twelve penalties for 91 yards do not a Super Bowl champion make.

Dez Bryant ran back a punt for a 62-yard touchdown in the week two home opener against Lovie Smith's Chicago Bears to put the Cowboys ahead 7–3 in the first quarter, but the Bears' gutsy QB Jay Cutler kept coming back, with the lead changing five times. The Bears controlled most of the second half, but Dallas pulled within three points with 7:14 remaining in the game before the Cowboys' David Buehler's 44-yard field-goal attempt went wide, handing Chicago a 27–20 win. The 0-2 start was Dallas's worst in nine years. The deciding difference was Jay Cutler's three touchdown passes to Tony Romo's single TD pass and two fatal interceptions. The homers tried to soothe their souls by pointing out the 1993 Super Bowl champion Cowboys started their season the same way. Back then, however, those first two losses were recorded while Emmitt Smith held out for a new contract. This time around, there was no Emmitt waiting in the wings.

A 27–13 win at Houston over the hapless Texans in front of a Houston crowd of more than 71,000, including a sizable contingent of Cowboys supporters, was a course correction. Three sacks of Texans QB Matt Schaub, three takeaways by the defense, and Tony Romo's two touchdown passes to Roy Williams keyed the victory.

Following the week three bye, the Cowboys dropped what should have been an easy home game to a lousy Tennessee Titans club, 34–27. Lineman Marc Columbo was penalized for excessively celebrating a touchdown that tied the game 27–27 after Romo gave him the ball and bumped chests, causing Columbo to fall to the turf. Lineman Leonard Davis forgot how to block, leaving Romo vulnerable to six sacks. Two sure passes were tipped and intercepted. The Cowboys team left the field as puzzled as anyone about how they had gotten into a 1-3 hole.

All aspirations were filed away for next season following consecutive losses to Minnesota (by a field goal in a game where the Cowboys beat themselves), the Giants (by six points), Jacksonville (by eighteen points), and Green Bay (by thirty-eight points). In the *Monday Night Football* home game against the New York Giants, Tony Romo broke his left clavicle when he was slammed to the carpet by linebacker Michael Boley, who blew in untouched in the second quarter with the Cowboys ahead, 10–7. Jon Kitna, the thirty-eight-year-old veteran who hadn't played in a game since 2008, when he was with the hapless Detroit Lions, took over and did a serviceable job in relief, although the Giants came out on top, 41–35. Romo was done for the year.

At the halfway mark, the 1-7 Cowboys made clear to fans and haters alike that Super Bowl XLV would be played at Cowboys Stadium by two other teams, and Jerry Jones fired Wade Phillips.

Randy Galloway was thoroughly disgusted, not with Phillips and Jones, but with everyone. "In the 51-year history of the Cowboys, I cannot remember a team that totally quit on a head coach like this one did on Wade Phillips," Galloway wrote. "No matter what any of us think about Wade as a head coach, the players disgraced themselves and their mommas."

For once, Galloway did not finger Jones as the villain. Somewhere along the way, the owner had earned Galloway's grudging respect. "No matter how many times we continue to stick the man, he counterpunches strong with a good yet friendly stick-and-jab," he wrote.

Wade Phillips's replacement was head-coach-in-waiting Jason Garrett, who took the job with an "interim" qualifier. Everything would be reevaluated at the end of the season, Jones assured all parties concerned. After he canned Phillips, Jerry Jones resurfaced in Las Vegas, where he was photographed with his left hand resting on the shoulder of a hot little chicklet young enough to be his granddaughter.

Quarterback Jon Kitna threw three touchdown passes in Garrett's first game as head coach and Dallas upset the Giants and the league's top defense at the Meadowlands, 33–20. They beat Detroit at home the following week before the New Orleans Saints came to town. The Saints jumped to a 17–0 lead on their first three possessions and led 20–7 at the half. The Cowboys chipped away and edged ahead 27–23 when Tashard Choice ran the ball in with 5:51 left. On the next offensive series for the Cowboys, receiver Roy Williams was chugging toward the end zone when defender Malcolm Jenkins stripped the ball away at the Saints' 11-yard line. The takeaway opened the door for Drew Brees and the Saints to go marching down the field and win the contest, 30–27, for Jason Garrett's first loss as head coach.

The Cowboys traveled to Indianapolis's new Lucas Oil indoor stadium, where the secondary picked off the NFL's best all-around quarterback, Peyton Manning, four times, twice for touchdowns, to earn a gritty 38–35 upset in overtime. It was the third win in four games for the Garrett-coached Cowboys. But Philadelphia spoiled any fantasies that Garrett was the definitive difference when they swooped into Arlington to beat the Cowboys 30–27 and perch atop the NFC East. DeSean Jackson caught four passes from reformed QB Michael Vick for 210 yards to put the hurt on Dallas.

After a win over the Redskins and an unnecessary 27–26 loss to the Cardinals following a valiant comeback, the final game of one of the most disappointing seasons ever for the Dallas Cowboys was played at the Philadelphia Eagles' Lincoln Financial Field. The game marked the debut of Stephen McGee, the Cowboys' number-three quarterback. McGee had been a high school star for the Burnet (Texas) Eagles, where he'd played alongside receiver Jordan Shipley, and then had excelled at Texas A&M. He stepped in for an injured Kitna to go up against Philly's second-stringers, who were substituting for the starters in anticipation of the playoffs. McGee played tough and threw a four-yard touchdown pass in the last minute to Jason Witten for a 14–13 Pyrrhic win. The Eagles would lose to eventual Super Bowl champion Green Bay.

The Cowboys closed the 2010 season at 6-10, a complete letdown considering where they had been predicted to be. The last half of the year wasn't a total wash, though, given how much the team improved their 1-7 record once Garrett took over as coach.

Anyone who gave a damn about the Dallas Cowboys believed a full year with the redheaded head coach would make a crucial difference, based on Garrett's experience as a quarterback at Princeton and as the Cowboys' number-two and number-three quarterback at the peak of Troy Aikman's reign, and on his skills as an assistant head coach and offensive coordinator and as the quarterbacks coach who had polished Romo.

The intangible beyond those qualifications was Garrett's longer history with the Jones-era Cowboys. His father, Jim, a well-traveled NFL assistant coach for forty years, had scouted for the Cowboys since 1987. Brother John was the tight ends coach, and brother Judd was director of pro scouting. The Garretts knew the Joneses about as well as any family could, certainly well enough for Jason to know his dancing partner.

The sports commentators couldn't help but speculate on what kind of strings Jerry would be pulling. "Jason Garrett is . . . The Man," Randy Galloway wrote. "Jerry Jones says so. Jerry, of course, has the only vote....A real head coach who is respected by the owner-GM will be able to hire his own assistants."

If Garrett wasn't hiring his support staff, the 2011 draft picks certainly had his fingerprints all over them — several offensive linemen to protect Tony Romo.

How much difference Garrett could make, how much influence Stephen Jones exerted as COO/director of player personnel, and to what degree the talent would continue to underachieve — those were the wild cards.

And Jerry Jones was the house dealer.

D and Mr. Jones

HE WAS A PURE entrepreneur with the heart of a corporate raider who put the dollar above all. He needed no outside advice or wise men of experience to whisper in his ear. His way was the only way. "I made the decision to run this football team without NFL football experience," Jerry Jones had said, attempting to mythologize his past. "I didn't know that some of the things we would try couldn't be done. No one sat down with me and told me, 'There's no way you can have this organization put together the way you want it if you don't get some longtime NFL experience.' I thought the way we were doing it was the only way we could do it. When I came in here, there was absolutely no handbook on how to run an NFL team. If you had tried to do things in a traditional way, you could make a case that it just wouldn't have worked out. I came in here with the purpose of rolling the dice. And to be honest, I really don't care how people around the league feel about that. That is just my way of doing business. I didn't see any other way of doing business and making money."

What Jones didn't seem to see then, or now, was how much the franchise and legacy he had purchased meant to so many.

Living rooms across Texas were still decorated with store-bought signs posted near the televisions reading QUIET, COWBOYS GAME IN PROGRESS. But to paraphrase Don Meredith channeling Willie Nelson, the party was over. The earnest effort by Dallas people who saw the future of pro football and brought it to Dallas had ended long ago. A bigger story replaced it. NFL football was an entertainment brand, and as a business, it generated more profits than its founders could ever have imagined. That was the real game being played. With contracts climbing above $100 million for valued studs, a club's profit mattered as much if not more than their won-loss record.

Jerry Jones was made for these times. Like him or not, the NFL owed him a debt of gratitude for showing other owners how to pay fat salaries and still thrive, bringing the business world to sports.

The league's annual gross for 2010 was around $9 billion. The first billion off the top went to the owners, to handle expenses. The remaining $8 billion was split, with 60 percent ($4.8 billion) going to the players and 40 percent (another $3.2 billion, for a total of $4.2 billion) going to owners.

Jones had monetized *everything*. Training camp in San Antonio for 2011 realized a $400,000 profit, while the football club signed a licensing agreement with Marvel's Super Heroes for co-branded merchandise featuring Captain America, Spider-Man, Iron Man, Thor, and other superheroes decked out in the Cowboys' team colors, logos, and jerseys.

By doing so, the Cowboys owner–general manager had become a star in his own right and the best-known Dallas Cowboy. He bantered with former Cowboy Deion Sanders in Pizza Hut commercials and made television pitches for Pepsi, Burger King, American Express, and Nike. He even did a break dance endorsing Papa John's Pizza and cameoed in the HBO series *Entourage*.

Cowboys Stadium was the centerpiece of these new values: three million square feet of sporting pleasure with the biggest video screen (well, the biggest for four months, at least, until a Middle Eastern oil sheikh had Mitsubishi Diamond Vision build a bigger one for the Meydan Racecourse horse-racing track in Dubai), and the biggest, most expensive corporate suites, selling for $5 million a pop. Single-game club seats were priced at $340. Personal seat licenses went for anywhere between $16,000 and $150,000, depending on location.

While the building was a showcase of technological wonders, it was also an energy hog in the tradition of a 1961 gas-guzzling Cadillac, racking up monthly electricity bills ranging from $200,000 to $500,000. Renewable energy was not part of the design, suggesting the edifice was not a futuristic model but rather a last-gasp symbol of excess.

Despite the numerous gaffes, hiring mistakes, and a fifteen-year absence from the title game (now the longest stretch in franchise history), Jones's Dallas Cowboys were the premier team in the nation's number-one sport, the biggest draw at home and on the road, and the most watched pro team on television. One out of every four items of NFL merchandise sold since 1975 had the Cowboys logo affixed to it. The Dallas Cowboys star adorned charcoal, antibacterial wipes, ecofriendly water bottles, toasters, vinyl car mats, pet-charity calendars, special lottery tickets, and official Texas Department of Transportation license plates. Season-ticket holders came from every state in the nation, as well as Canada, Mexico, Saudi Arabia, and the United Kingdom. *Forbes* magazine pegged their worth at $1.8 billion, making the Dallas football club the most valuable franchise in all of American sports. Jerry Jones's business was worth ten times his initial investment.

The sole unbranded element remaining in 2012 was Cowboys Stadium itself, which Jones wisely kept for the football club before he sought a sponsor who would pay hundreds of millions for the stadium's naming rights.

Credit for these achievements belonged not to the football team, which consistently performed below people's high expectations, but to the owner. "Jerry Jones is one of the great marketers sports has ever seen," said Marc Ganis of Sports Corps Ltd. consultants. "He finds ways to keep the Cowboys relevant, part of the national conversation."

"In my mind, if you keep working, good things will happen," Jones told the Associated Press. "Even though [fans] could be critical of how I do it, how we're structured, I know they believe that we're one of the top teams. I want that interest, not apathy. I do think the reason that's there is because they know that I'll do whatever I can do [to win]."

Jerry Jones had turned the Cowboys into the Cow*buys,* but he had one glaring weakness, and his insistence that he be identified as the owner *and* general manager revealed it. As GM, he had paid top dollar for Deion Sanders, Terrell Owens, Adam Jones, Roy Williams, Barry Switzer, Bill Parcells, and Jason Garrett without necessarily getting the return he desired so badly.

The *Dallas Morning News*'s Tim Cowlishaw laid the blame squarely at Jones's feet. Good owners knew how to hire great people, delegate power, and let them do their own thing. No other club would consider hiring Jerry Jones as general manager if he didn't bring along his fat wallet.

Still, Jerry wanted to be more involved than ever. He started working out an hour and a half every day, developing a fitness regimen not unlike Tom Landry's, while orchestrating an imperceptible changing of the guard that would eventually put his children in charge. The Cowboys were a family business now. Jerry Jones raised Stephen, Jerry Jr., and Charlotte to succeed him, adding the Joneses to the Maras, Rooneys, Krafts, and Steinbrenners as prominent sports-team-owning families.

Charlotte Jones Anderson, the valedictorian of her Little Rock High School class and a graduate of Stanford, where she learned organizational management, had matured into a dynamic woman in charge of brand management and special events for the Cowboys. She was regarded as the Jones sibling most like her father: charismatic, driven, determined, and unstoppable.

Jerry Jr. was chief sales and marketing officer, while Stephen was the heir apparent, responsible for day-to-day operations and personnel decisions. As the pragmatic counterweight to his father's passion, Stephen Jones was the best hope to restore the Cowboys to greatness—but that wouldn't happen until the old man stepped aside.

The media landscape had undergone a seismic shift since Jerry Jones came to Dallas. Pro football had kept pace with the explosion of information technology as fax machines gave way to cellular telephones and the Internet, e-mails, smartphones, blogs, Twitter, and Facebook. Each tool provided more detailed and expansive coverage of NFL football, as much as a consumer could absorb. Dallas fans were early adapters.

So were Dallas Cowboys players, ex-players, and coaches, who all took control of their media messaging through Twitter, the social-networking tool that gained popularity in 2007 at the South by Southwest interactive conference in Austin. Twitter allowed a person of interest to blast out brief messages of 140 characters or less to followers who signed up to receive messages from that person. With Twitter and other social media, high-profile folks had an effective means of communicating without having third parties filter their comments.

The Cowboys had their own technology department, headed by chief information officer Pete Walsh, who started planning for Cowboys Stadium in 2004 and was in the process of replacing playbooks with iPads, saving more than five thousand pages of printouts per game. Walsh's presence marked considerable progress since the days when Jerry Jones had put Jerry Jones Jr. in charge of Internet operations.

Larry Wansley discovered technology's impact on communications the hard way. Wansley had returned to head up security for the Cowboys after retiring in 2004 from American Airlines, where he developed policies that became the template for the Transportation Security Administration in the United States after 9/11. Wansley was frustrated that players weren't answering his calls or returning his messages, and his son Bryan, who also worked for the Cowboys organization, in quality control, proceeded to educate him about text messages and Twitter tweets.

Web sites such as the silverandbluereport.com, knowyourcow boys.com, thelandryhat.com, cowboyslocker.com, and bloggingthe boys.com complemented the official dallascowboys.com Web sites, which, true to form, were notches above the competition in presentation, original content, and ease of access. One of the Cowboys' official Web sites, CowboyFan4Life.com, featured the Blue Star Arcade with Cowboys-themed computer games.

The *Dallas Cowboys Official Weekly* had evolved into the *Dallas Cowboys Star*, published weekly from summer camp to Super Bowl in hard copy and online with state-of-the-art graphics, solid reporting from Mickey Spagnola, Josh Ellis, and Jeff Sullivan, a monthly column from the great Sam Blair, and cheerleader features and photo spreads.

No professional or fan Web site measured up to the reporting of the *Dallas Morning News* SportsDay section, in spite of layoffs that had eliminated close to a thousand positions at the newspaper over the past ten years. SportsDay's staff was anchored by columnists Tim Cowlishaw, Kevin Sherrington, and Jean-Jacques Taylor (until he jumped to ESPNDallas in 2011), NFL beat writer Rick Gosselin, reporters Gerry Fraley, Rainer Sabin, and David Moore, and sports-media writer Barry Horn, all of whom cranked out content for the newspaper and dallasnews.com's online Cowboys coverage.

The *Fort Worth Star-Telegram* provided formidable, if under-manned, competition on a daily basis with lead columnists Randy Galloway and Gil LeBreton, along with Mike Jones, Mac Engel, and writer/bloggers Charean Williams and Clarence E. Hill Jr.

Television remained the eight-hundred-pound gorilla. The NFL Network, launched on November 23, 2003, eight months after the owners voted unanimously to approve it, and NFL.com drove an unprecedented number of eyeballs to the sport online. NFL football was the nation's most popular TV show. Games on CBS, Fox, and NBC averaged 20 million viewers, more than twice the average 8.2

million viewers of prime-time programs on the networks. Twenty-three of the twenty-five most watched television programs of 2011 were NFL games. No wonder the NFL was able to hammer out nine-year contracts with NBC, CBS, Fox, and ESPN in 2011 worth $4 billion annually to the league. The NFL was no longer just a sports league. It was the golden goose of show biz.

Following in the footsteps of the NFL Network was the Dallas Cowboys Network, developed in conjunction with Comcast cable television in 2004 to give DFW fans even more of the home team to watch.

Dallas–Fort Worth print and electronic media had ceded power and influence to national media with a Dallas presence, such as ESPN. The Worldwide Leader in Sports plucked writers Calvin Watkins, Jean-Jacques Taylor, Ed Werder, Todd Archer, Tim McMahon, Richard Durrett, and Matt Mosley, and editor Barry Vigoda from the *Morning News* and writers Jeff Caplan and Jim Reeves from the *Fort Worth Star-Telegram*, raising their profiles considerably. Fox Sports Southwest also added staff from both newspapers. The futures of sports guys on the 6:00 p.m. and 10:00 p.m. newscasts on local TV stations and of the star sports columnists in the daily newspapers were no longer assured.

As mutually crucial to each other's success as the media and the Cowboys were, the tight relationship between the football team and Dallas–Fort Worth media that Tex Schramm had so famously cultivated since the franchise's birth had disappeared, replaced by an invisible wall that protected players and personnel from their public. Football players no longer lived among the community they represented on the field. Astronomical salaries and soaring celebrity made each individual a business enterprise. Savvy players arrived in the NFL accompanied by their own agents, accountants, managers, attorneys, financial advisers, and publicists.

"I never met Bill Parcells," complained Channel 8's Dale Hansen. "I've interviewed Tony Romo once."

Frank Luksa observed that in lieu of one-on-one time with players at Valley Ranch, access had devolved to media hour, when players were available for interviews daily. "For fifty-five minutes, it's the taxi squad. The regulars time it to show up in the last five minutes, if at all."

No one saw anything the management didn't want seen. No one intentionally said anything outrageous either.

Football players had become objectified as the game they played live made them TV stars. Television made it easier to keep track of a game whose participants were faster, physically larger, and stronger. On an HDTV screen, players looked like interchangeable pieces to be moved around and manipulated, just like characters in a John Madden video game. The NFL Network's Sunday-afternoon *Red-Zone* show similarly changed how fans watched the NFL on television, online, and on their smartphones, covering every touchdown score from every game in real time, making watching a single game almost beside the point.

TV had changed the spectator experience for fans in the stadium as well. "Official time-outs"—that is, mandated breaks for television commercials—had destroyed teams' momentum during a game, forcing both sides to stand around for a couple of minutes so viewers at home could be sold more products.

The actual fan experience at the stadium was a multimedia extravaganza of bloat, corporate sponsorships, and promotions, such as a free extra topping at Papa John's with each Cowboys home-game touchdown, a Cowboys-oven-mitt giveaway, and pregame and postgame concerts outside the stadium brought to you by Miller Lite, the only official beer of the Cowboys.

The star of the stadium experience was the giant video board, which spat out a steady stream of high-volume dance and hip-hop music with some mainstream country and classic rock (for example, Thin Lizzy's "The Boys Are Back," Quiet Riot's version of "Cum on Feel the Noize") thrown in, overwhelming conversation and directing all attention to the big screen hovering above the field. Why squint through binoculars when the video board showed tight HDTV close-ups of players smiling and scowling?

The stream of wall-to-wall commercials and corporate-sponsored fan games was interspersed with video images of Cowboys players admonishing fans to "be loud," "stand up," and "make noise," with cutaways to the faux spirit groups like the drum-line leader dancing and drumming with the Miller Lite Rhythm & Blue dancers; Rowdy, the cartoon-headed mascot; and the rah-rah cowboys in black hats who danced, carried big flags, and did push-ups after touchdowns, emulating high school and college spirit groups. The visual blitz effectively destroyed what little spontaneity remained in the team-fan relationship.

The cheerleaders, shaking their shiny silver-and-blue pom-poms and dancing their perfectly sculpted asses off, radiating smiles and Texas wholesome sexy all the way, were the big screen's biggest stars, getting close-ups and the attention of the majority-male audience as they went through their high-energy disco-beat routines. (Offscreen, their relevance was affirmed in the spring of 2012 by Sharon Simmons, a fifty-five-year-old grandmother and personal trainer/nutritionist who announced her intention to try out for the squad. "It says something about women and their success stories," cheerleader director Kelli Finglass said. "I'd give her accolades for her preparation and look forward to her audition.")

America's Sweethearts' only rivals were the fans themselves, many of whom worked up dance routines, donned costumes, or made signs to pander to the stadium camera and get on the big screen.

The Way We Were

BEFORE SUPER BOWL XLV was played in Arlington on February 6, 2011, a familiar cast of characters from the Cowboys' 1990s glory days met on a Fox Sports studio set outside the stadium. Troy Aikman, Daryl "Moose" Johnston, and Coach Jimmy Johnson worked for Fox as broadcasters, and Johnson had become almost as legendary a broadcaster as former Oakland Raiders coach John Madden. Michael Irvin did commentary for the NFL Network, and Jerry Jones was a constant on every network covering the Cowboys.

The talk between them about what might have been turned into a JJs-plus-players lickfest. Daryl Johnston said that Jimmy and Jerry visualized early on that they'd win three Super Bowls in a row. "It took us [the players] a little bit longer to buy into and understand how good this team could be," he admitted, making the point that teammates from the glory days have remained friends. If only free agency, coaches and players being recruited by other teams, and petty disagreements hadn't pulled the team apart, they would have won even more than that.

"I don't know that we would have won more," Troy Aikman said, offering a dollop of levity. "But what I do know is we would have been really good and really competitive for a long time."

Jimmy Johnson reminded his old quarterback how cocky they all were. "Remember that first Super Bowl? You were standing on the sideline next to me. You'd thrown four touchdown passes and I kinda took you aside and said, 'Hey, you want to set a record and go in and throw another one?'"

"That was some of that Miami coming out of you," Aikman replied with a grin. Aikman meant the University of Miami, not the Miami Dolphins, a team that Johnson had coached for four years winning only one playoff game.

"Michael, you were there when we came in," Coach Johnson said, turning to Irvin. "When we were 1-and-15, did you look at Jerry and I and say, 'Do these guys know what they're doing?'"

Irvin said he had a pretty good clue. The Playmaker related, "When Jerry first bought the team and made the change and made the announcement, I called Coach and said, 'I'm not a snitch. But I've got a few people on a piece of paper that need to get out of there.' They were all the guys that when we were losing would walk by me and say, 'Don't worry, we pick up the check on Tuesday.' I wrote their names down, just like Santa, and I gave their names to Coach and I said, 'These guys are not nice, they've been naughty.' Coach says, 'They got to go.'"

"We got rid of all of them." Johnson laughed.

"We got rid of the riffraff," Irvin agreed, cracking up.

"When we first walked in, Jimmy introduced me to Michael," Jerry said, joining the conversation. "He said, 'Now he's a wide receiver, but before he left Miami, he'd whipped everybody on the team. He's going to be good for us.'"

Johnson reminded Jones of his tendency to double-down on a bet wherever and whenever he could. "Before the second Super Bowl, remember, you called me in and said, 'Jimmy, we're going to change uniforms for the game this weekend. We're going to have different helmets, different jerseys.' I said, 'You're going to change the uniforms? Troy is accustomed to throwing to a certain color of helmet. If we win, everything's fine. But if we lose, they're gonna laugh us out of town.'" The uniforms stayed the same.

"We had the youngest team in the league," Johnson crowed. "We had a rookie owner and a rookie head coach—nobody knew any different." Aikman closed the segment pushing for Jimmy Johnson's inclusion in the Ring of Honor. "If we deserve to be in it, Jimmy Johnson certainly does."

"That's very persuasive, guys," admitted Jones. "When I introduced Jimmy right after I bought the team, 'course I'm arm waving, I said, 'He's worth five Super Bowls, he's worth five Heisman Trophy winners, we've got us a coach.'" Jones then paid Johnson the ultimate compliment. "When he was at Oklahoma State, I didn't have anything to sell. I still would sponsor his coach's show [on television]."

Jerry then reached over and put his arm around Jimmy. Later that year, Jones announced the overdue induction of Drew Pearson into the Ring of Honor, along with Charles Haley and Larry Allen, but not Jimmy Johnson, or Ed Jones or Harvey Martin, for that matter.

In an earlier interview with Channel 8's Dale Hansen on location at his Florida home, Jimmy Johnson had praised his former collaborator, saying, "Jerry gave us the tools to win," while charitably acknowledging, "Sometimes he gets distracted because he wants to be in the middle of everything."

Despite the team's uneven performance on the field, Johnson said without hesitation, "The number one team in the NFL today is the Dallas Cowboys." Bygones really were bygones.

A FOOTBALL GAME FOLLOWED the reunion of the Cowboys' core.

As the playoffs progressed, local businesses had started rooting for a Chicago Bears–New York Jets matchup that would bring in big-spender fans in private jets. Instead, they got the Pittsburgh Steelers and the Green Bay Packers, storied NFL franchises with solidly blue-collar fan bases.

During the two-week run-up to the main event, a revolution

erupted in Egypt and what would have been former president Ronald Reagan's one hundredth birthday was celebrated. But the only subjects to rival the manufactured hype about the big game were the ice storm that blasted into the Metroplex five days before Super Bowl Sunday, closing DFW airport and plunging the region into a deep freeze, and the second ice storm and the snowstorm that followed three days later, paralyzing transportation and putting a major damper on corporate events and private and public parties scheduled throughout the area.

It was so cold and nasty, the Green Bay Packers, who were headquartered in Dallas, moved their practices to the $4 million, 80-yard-long indoor football field at Highland Park High School, the richest public school district in the region. The Packers' official team blog reported the reactions of the players to the facility. Receiver Jordy Nelson from Riley County, Kansas, said Highland Park's facility was unlike anything he'd seen on the high school level. "We don't have that for a game field," Nelson said. "There's none of that in Kansas. The Washington Redskins don't even have an indoor facility. . . . It's Texas football for you, I guess. They always talk about it, now we get to see it." The Packers should have seen the $60 million high school stadium under construction in the suburb of Allen, north of Dallas, which would have given them more to talk about.

Two days before the game, melting chunks of ice slid off the roof of Cowboys Stadium, injuring six workers on the ground below. The storms and accompanying cold wave moved *Sports Illustrated*'s Peter King to tweet, "I-30 between Dallas + Fort Worth is a plow-less snow-windswept moonscape. This is officially a debacle."

The weather did not affect the amount of money being spent on the Super Bowl. One local who bought tickets at face value sold his six $1,000 seats for $45,000, paid for in crisp hundred-dollar bills. Four U.S. Navy F-18 jets flew over the stadium during the playing of the national anthem at an expense of $450,000 to American taxpayers, even though fans inside the stadium could witness the flyover only by watching the giant video screen. The retractable roof was shut. The state of Texas, facing a $27 billion deficit and severe cuts to its public schools budgets, contributed $31 million in the name of economic development.

THE GREEN BAY PACKERS jumped to an eighteen-point lead by the second quarter, only to have the Pittsburgh Steelers slowly erode the margin and pull within four points in the third quarter. But the Packers' quarterback Aaron Rogers kept pushing ahead every time Pittsburgh's Ben Roethlisberger brought the Steelers close enough to make a game of it. The 31–25 win was more decisive than the six-point margin indicated, although the game wasn't out of the Steelers' reach until a little more than a minute was left on the clock.

It was somehow poetic that the very first nemesis of the Dallas Cowboys won the first Super Bowl in the Cowboys' house. There was also some twisted irony in watching Jerry Jones, paragon of free-market capitalism and corporate welfare, pay tribute to the only franchise in major professional sports owned by the community that supported the team.

The socialists won in Jones's monument to sports as entrepreneurial enterprise. But in the games of media coverage, gross receipts, and sales, Jerry Jones won bigger. His stadium was clearly the finest football facility ever built. Most of the 111 million viewers across America and 167 million viewers worldwide could recognize that.

Who didn't get to see the game became even bigger news. Four hundred ticket holders who paid at least eight hundred dollars each for their seats were denied entry because the temporary seats being installed for the game had not been inspected by the Arlington fire marshal. Several displaced Steelers and Packers supporters outside united in a "Jer-ree sucks" chant before the game got under way.

Even though the NFL offered refunds triple the face value of the tickets and later upped the ante to include a ticket to next year's Super Bowl, some ticket holders were not placated. Gerry Grillo from New Jersey said he'd paid a ticket broker three thousand dollars for his seat, meaning he'd still lose money on the offer. "We were put in a holding pen for two hours," he complained. Glen Long, a Steelers fan who flew in from Baltimore, said stadium personnel "treated us like prisoners." Long laid the blame at the feet of the owner. "Jerry sold tickets he didn't own," he charged. "They call that fraud anywhere in the world. This is ridiculous. They sold tickets to an event that they knew they didn't have. That's just wrong."

Fans who had tickets elsewhere in the stadium were subjected to security waits to gain entry that were so long and slow-moving, a few male fans unzipped and urinated on the sidewalks rather than lose their places in line.

The disappearing four hundred seats was one of the greatest customer-service disasters in NFL history. And yet, several hundred other fans who had willingly paid two hundred dollars each to stand outside the stadium on a concrete patio surrounded by outdoor heaters and watch the game on a big screen were not complaining.

"For an organization that thinks it's God, the NFL sure couldn't handle an act of God," wrote the *Houston Chronicle*'s Ken Hoffman the day after, bringing an old Texas rivalry back into focus. "It was almost enough to make one feel sorry for Dallas or Dallas/Fort Worth or North Texas...or wherever the NFL insisted the Super Bowl was played."

Jones remained uncharacteristically incommunicado for days following the event as the lawsuits started coming in. His personal secretary, Marilyn Love, already a vigilant gatekeeper, stepped up her scrutiny and made it even harder for folks to get to the boss.

When Jones did reemerge it was to get involved with negotiations between the NFL owners and the NFL Players Association; the players were threatening to strike if a suitable collective bargaining agreement could not be hammered out. Jones played the same role

Tex Schramm once did, the hard-nosed negotiator who gave no quarter.

He also saw money where no one else did. Take the radio network. The Fan, 105.3 (KRLD-FM), was its new Dallas flagship and it had one of the most storied broadcasters anywhere, Brad Sham, who returned for his thirtieth year as the Cowboys' radio play-by-play voice, along with Babe Laufenberg and Kristi Scales. The sixty-eight-station regional network, and the seventeen-station Spanish-language Cadena de Plata hosted by Victor Villalba, Andres Arce, and Luis Perez, were joined by the Compass Media syndicated network of seventy-nine terrestrial radio stations, extending as far as Alaska.

AFTER THE HOTTEST SUMMER ever recorded in a single state, accompanied by the most severe drought since record-keeping had begun in the mid-1800s; an NBA championship won by the hometown Dallas Mavericks and celebrated with a parade attended by two hundred thousand people; and baseball's Texas Rangers reaching the World Series, Dallas was jonesing for Cowboys football again. Everyone was ready to see if Coach Garrett and a healed Tony Romo had the right stuff.

Even when the Rangers returned to the World Series for a consecutive second year in October of 2011, Michael Young, the Texas Rangers star and veteran, admitted his team would never replace the Cowboys in local fans' hearts. "They are the Dallas Cowboys. I don't care what we do." Sportscaster Brad Sham agreed, telling the *Star-Telegram*, "Football is our most popular sport and it's always going to be. Any way we measure that—TV ratings; jerseys sold; vociferous callers to talk radio stations—when you cut to the bone, most of the blood that will be spilled will be football."

There was no finer drama than Cowboys football. The last six games of 2010 had been decided by three points or fewer. The first three games of 2011 were just as close. The Cowboys totally dominated the New York Jets in the opener at the Meadowlands on NBC's featured *Sunday Night Football* game but managed to lose anyway, 27–24, thanks to two Romo flubs that had fans and scribes howling for his head and wondering if it was time for a new quarterback search.

True to form, it was the most watched Sunday-night national telecast in fourteen years.

The Cowboys traveled to Candlestick Park in San Francisco for the week two match against the 49ers, who hadn't chalked up a winning season in nine years. But at the half, SF appeared fully in control, with a 14–7 lead. Romo had suffered a broken rib taking a hit on the third play of the game and valiantly tried to lead. But he was watching from the sidelines at the start of the second half as the veteran Jon Kitna took over and immediately threw two interceptions. Toward the end of the third quarter, Romo tapped his coach on the shoulder and said he was ready to go. Romo proceeded to toss a 77-yard pass that was caught by Jessie Holley (who had gotten a position on the roster three years before by winning Michael Irvin's *Fourth and Long* reality-television show), carrying Dallas to a thrilling 27–24 overtime comeback victory, sealed by walk-on rookie Dan Bailey's field goal.

It was Romo's twentieth consecutive game throwing at least two touchdown passes. After the game, it was learned that Romo had played with a punctured lung as well as a broken rib. His gutsy play under duress earned him recognition; he was voted the FedEx Air NFL Player of the Week, and the winning pass was voted the GMC Never Say Never Moment of the Week.

Week three's home opener against Washington was the *Monday Night Football* feature. A week earlier ESPN had renewed its contract for *Monday Night Football,* paying $15.2 billion for ten years. The $1.5 billion–a–year figure was quite a bump from the annual $1.1 billion the sports network had previously been paying for rights to the highest-rated program on cable television. The Cowboys and Redskins did not disappoint. Romo, clearly jacked up on pain medication, controlled a very sloppy offense marked by five muffed snaps by new center Phil Costa and a diminished receiver corps (Miles Austin and Dez Bryant were injured), and he kept the team close enough for new kicker Dan Bailey to boot six field goals for all of Dallas's points. But it was the defense, coached by new D coordinator Rob Ryan, the lion-maned twin brother of Jets coach Rex Ryan and son of Cowboy nemesis Buddy Ryan, that won the game. The relentless D attack was spearheaded by outside linebacker DeMarcus Ware, who had led the NFL in sacks for two of the past three seasons, and emerging linebacker Sean Lee. The Cowboys really didn't deserve to win the 18–16 squeaker. But Romo's warriorlike resolve and leadership, his chewing out his line and receivers when necessary, was finally a given.

For the first half of the next game against the resurgent 3-0 Lions, the Cowboys played like Super Bowl contenders, owning Detroit's defense with a flawless line and three Romo TD passes, two to Dez Bryant, for a 27–3 lead. Then two and a half minutes into the second half, the demons reappeared. Romo tossed an interception to former teammate (and a groomsman at his wedding) Bobby Carpenter, who ran for a TD. Detroit rang up a second pick-six on the following series, while Lions QB Matthew Stafford, a high school star at Dallas's Highland Park, played Rob Ryan's defense like puppets. Romo and the offense ended their last drive with a third interception, and Dallas suffered their biggest blown lead ever, losing 34–30. On the postgame wrap on the NFL Network, Deion Sanders ranted, sputtering, "I live in the Metroplex. Dallas fans are sick of it!" The headline on dallasnews.com immediately after the game screamed "Romo Is Lions' MVP."

Fans who once proclaimed themselves Romosexuals wanted to get off the Romo-Coaster but couldn't. Which begged the bigger question: Who were these Cowboys?

Winless St. Louis provided the first easy opposition of the season, rolling over as expected, 34–7. Rookie running back DeMarco Murray, coming off the bench to fill in for the injured Felix Jones, took his first handoff from Tony Romo and ran for 91 yards, the second-longest run in team history, and ended the day with 253 yards, besting the NFL's all-time rusher Emmitt Smith's and Hall of Famer Tony Dorsett's highest single-game totals. Still, the 3-3 Cowboys rated no higher than eighteen on the NFL's power rankings.

The reasons for the low rank were revealed at the Linc in Philly, where Michael Vick picked apart the Cowboys' number-one defense while the offense never got in gear, leading to the Eagles' 34–7 de-pantsing of Dallas. D coordinator Rob Ryan, who had trash-talked Philly's offense for weeks, calling the Eagles "all-hype," took full blame, but it was a team loss. The burly Ryan, whose swept-back hairstyle was compared to country singer Emmylou Harris's, quoted Shakespeare later in the week to explain he wasn't backing down: "You jest at scars [that] never felt a wound."

During halftime of the eventual 23–13 home win against Seattle, Drew Pearson, Larry Allen, and Charles Haley were inducted into the Ring of Honor, a club more exclusive than the Pro Football Hall of Fame. Pearson's induction was overdue, and the inclusion of Allen was justified by Jerry Jones's desire to have someone from his dynasty representing. Haley was a more controversial pick, since he was the first inductee to have been traded to the Cowboys rather than brought up through their system. For all his stats and critical contributions to the Super Bowl trifecta, Haley was neither a leader nor a popular figure among the fans or the press, making his selection another reason to question Jones's judgment.

Romo went 19-31 for 279 yards and two TDs and no picks, while DeMarco Murray showed more signs he was the Cowboys' best running back since Emmitt Smith, ginning up 139 yards on 22 carries.

By the time Washington came up on the schedule again, it was obvious this team possessed weapons no Cowboys team had since the dynasty days. Murray's rookie start surpassed the start of every Cowboys running back, including Perkins, Hill, Thomas, Dorsett, and Smith, which gave Tony Romo the luxury of picking his spots for a few milliseconds longer and hitting nine different receivers against the Redskins, including Jason Witten, Laurent Robinson, and Martellus Bennett, Jessie Holley, and Dez Bryant, whose OT catch clinched the Cowboys win. Over three games, Romo threw eight touchdowns and no interceptions for an off-the-charts 125.4 quarterback rating.

Despite two picks quick against a newly rejuvenated Miami and being outplayed by the Dolphins on both sides of the line, Romo led a final drive that ended with Dan Bailey kicking the winning field goal as time ran out. Then the winningest active quarterback in the NFL November games reprised his role as king of the December dogs, as Romo threw no interceptions, yet they still lost to Arizona in overtime and to the Giants at home on missed last-second second-chance field goals. Dan Bailey was iced by coaches' time-outs in both games, the first one by his own coach in a blown call that Garrett couldn't explain. With Dallas up by twelve and 5:41 left in the Giants game, Rob Ryan's defense proceeded to give up two touchdowns to New York in the final 3:15, with the Giants sealing the collapse by blocking Dan Bailey's second field-goal attempt at the end of the game, while DeMarco Murray ended his sensational debut season by breaking his ankle. The win in Arlington broke the Giants' four-game losing streak.

For seven of the past eight seasons, the Cowboys had entered December with seven wins and a shot at the playoffs, only to falter. But this time around, a 21–15 win against Tampa left them still in control of their destiny. Beat the Giants and Eagles, and the division crown and entry into the playoffs was theirs.

The 20–7 gimme loss to the Eagles didn't matter, actually. It would come down to the last game against the Giants, the winner taking the NFC East and going to the playoffs, the loser going home.

The December 2011 swoon concluded on January 1, 2012, against the Giants at MetLife Stadium in the Meadowlands. Rob Ryan's complex schemes left the defense looking at one another when they weren't being pushed around and picked off by Eli Manning backed by a solid running game. Tony Romo couldn't find his receivers in the Giants' blanket coverage. At halftime, after a missed field goal, the Cowboys trailed 21–0. Their season was effectively over despite a third-quarter rally that brought them within seven points of the Giants before Manning torched the D again with game-killing passes to Victor Cruz for a 31–14 win.

It happened again. No matter how much tweaking, how much analyzing, how much want-to there was, the Big Fold was now officially tradition. Despite a two-game division lead going into December, the club's losing four of the last five games proved it didn't have the right stuff for Super Bowl consideration. The Cowboys were 8-8 for 2011, on par with their overall 120-120 record, with one playoff win since 1997. Was this the curse of Landry? Tex Schramm's revenge? Was it something inherent in the organization or the people running it? On paper, at least, the players, the coaches, and the personnel were all regarded as top-shelf.

A *SportsNation* poll taken the day after the season ended had 51 percent of fans blaming Jerry Jones, 18 percent holding Jason Garrett responsible, 27 percent saying it was Rob Ryan's fault, and only 4 percent saying Tony Romo was the culprit. Columnist Randy Galloway called owner Jones "a football idiot." Others cited Jones's coming down to the sidelines to talk one-on-one to Coach Jason Garrett after Tony Romo injured his hand during the next-to-the-last game of the year, effectively usurping the coach's authority in front of a national television audience and illustrating Jones's inability to keep himself from meddling. Punking the coach during the game was no way for an owner *or* a general manager to act. Still, two days after the season ended, Jones made it clear on his radio show that he would not give up being general manager.

"The facts are that I've spent twenty-two years doing this exactly the same way," Jones said on his show on KRLD-FM. "I've made a lot of changes from year to year as time goes along, but frankly, I know that when we do not have the kind of success, when we don't have expectations lived up to, the one that should get the most heat is the one that ultimately makes the decisions, period, with the Dallas Cowboys. And that's me. The thing you've got to realize is that when you have an owner that is full-time as the owner, then you create a situation where you have as much turnover at GM as you do at the coaching level. And I think that just deters from the mix."

The Cowboys were Jerry-rigged. There had been only one general manager in the fifteen-year stretch that had produced a single playoff victory. And the club was bringing in more money than ever, a tribute to the effectiveness of Jones's con. Like it or not, fans continued buying in, even though they all knew that the solipsistic ego of the owner, unlike the football team, could not be stopped. The organization reflected the man at the top. The storied star may have been tarnished, but all a true fan could do was what he had done since the beginning: forgive and forget and let the sting fade with the passage of time, hope replacing his disgust by the following September as he again entertained the notion that this was the team, and this was the time when it would all come together, like it once had so effortlessly.

ON PAPER, THE 2012 season was an average one, the new normal for the Dallas Cowboys. In reality, the year was anything but average, at times suggesting a return to respectability, if not greatness, and at other times suggesting a descent to the muddy bottom of mediocrity. There were plenty of reasons to be optimistic. Defensive coordinator Rob Ryan would have a full training camp to implement his version of the 3-4 defense. And there were plenty of reasons to be wary, including a preseason 911 call from Dez Bryant's mother, sixteen years his elder, saying her son was trying to kill her (she ultimately refused to press charges), as well as the usual bloviating from owner and general manager Jerry Jones.

The Good Cowboys formally kicked off the NFL season in New Jersey in a Wednesday-night nationally televised game against the New York Giants. Tony Romo looked like the best QB in the league, chunking two TD passes to third-string wide receiver Kevin Ogletree, while Rob Ryan's D recorded three sacks on Giants QB Eli Manning. The 24–17 win suggested the Cowboys could mix it up with any NFL team, including the defending champions.

One week later, the Bad Cowboys took over. Felix Jones fumbled the opening kickoff, and Seattle ran back a blocked punt for a 10–0 lead less than five minutes into the game. DeMarco Murray was limited to 44 yards rushing while the Seahawks' rookie QB Russell Wilson finished with a 112.7 passing rating as Seattle administered a physical beating of the emotionless visitors, 27–7.

The team barely survived the week-three home opener against Tampa, edging the Bucs 16–10 in a contest highlighted by Dez Bryant's 44-yard punt return, DeMarcus Ware's critical fourth-quarter sack, and three Dan Bailey field goals. The 'Boys were flagged for six false-start penalties, three against lineman Doug Free and two against tight end Jason Witten. The game worked its way into infamy when Jerry Jones's son-in-law, Shy Anderson, was seen on NBC cameras solicitously wiping Jones's glasses with a cleaning cloth. A week later, Anderson announced the rollout of a new eyeglass cleaning product, Jerry Wipes. That dovetailed neatly into the *Monday Night Football* game at Cowboys Stadium, which marked the opening of the first Victoria's Secret lingerie store in an NFL stadium. "We've got some beautiful places out at that stadium, some gorgeous surroundings, and nothing would be nicer than to have the showing of pretty clothes," Jones said on his weekly radio show on 105.3 The Fan. The actual game, against the Chicago Bears, was horrid. Romo threw *five* interceptions — two for TDs (his second five-interception game, tying Eddie LeBaron for the team record)—and the Bears' offense and defense collectively kicked Dallas every which way for a 34–18 triumph in front of an Arlington crowd that included at least 30,000 Chicago fans, underscoring the absence of a home-field advantage in the luxurious stadium. The Ravens match in Baltimore marked a third consecutive loss. Dan Bailey couldn't thread a 51-yard field goal for a last-second Cowboys victory in a game that Dallas had dominated in stats, but not in the score, a 31–29 Ravens victory. But four Dan Bailey field goals in the week-six game against Cam Newton and the Carolina Panthers got the Cowboys back into the hunt with a 19–14 win.

The next week was a bumpy ride on the Romocoaster. Four interceptions by number 9 and Eli Manning on fire translated into a 23–0 New York lead before an unprecedented comeback was orchestrated by the Dallas QB to take a 24–23 Cowboys lead in the third quarter. Dez Bryant made a heroic end-zone leap to seal the win as the clock ran out, but an official review determined one hand landed out-of-bounds, giving the Giants a 29–24 win, keeping the Giants unbeaten at Cowboys Stadium. The drama was over-the-top; the team record was horrible.

Another loss, to the unbeaten Falcons at the Georgia Dome, despite a 6–6 tie going into the fourth quarter, pretty much wrote off 2012 playoff hopes, despite Jason Witten snagging seven catches to pass Michael Irvin (750) in Cowboys career receptions. Before the game, on *Football Night in America,* the lead-in program to NBC's *Sunday Night Football,* Bob Costas asked owner Jones if he would have fired another general manager besides himself by now. "Well, I think so, because he was there to dismiss. I have always worked for myself and you can't do that. You basically have to straighten that guy out in the mirror when you work for yourself. But certainly, if I'd had the discretion, I've done it with coaches and certainly I would have changed a general manager."

Ex-partner Jimmy Johnson called Jones a liar for trying to rewrite their Super Bowl history again, and derided the Cowboys' "country-club atmosphere" at Valley Ranch.

A win against a reeling Eagles squad, 38–23—in a game that was achingly close until Dwayne Harris returned a punt for a 78-yard touchdown to start a fourth-quarter run that also included Brandon Carr's 47-yard interception touchdown and Jason Hatcher's recovery of a fumble in the Eagles end zone—and a 23–20 overtime defeat of the Cleveland Browns, arguably the worst team in the NFL in 2012, kept the Cowboys in contention. Then rookie QB Robert Griffin III came to Arlington for Thanksgiving Day to lead the Redskins to a 38–31 win, after the Cowboys once again fell behind at the start of the game. The grounded Eagles provided another win as Tony Romo threw three second-half touchdown passes—breaking Troy Aikman's franchise record for career touchdown passes—and Dez Bryant continued to show flashes of being a playmaker, marking his fourth consecutive game with a touchdown catch.

The Cincinnati Bengals matchup marked the third consecutive game the Cowboys faced a Texas-bred quarterback—Austin's Westlake High QB Nick Foles, who replaced Michael Vick after Vick suffered a concussion; Robert Griffin III, a graduate of Killeen High who won the Heisman at Baylor; and now Andy Dalton, of Katy and Texas Christian, who was having a very good second year in the league. But that story line vanished very early Saturday morning when starting lineman Josh Brent was driving his Mercedes away from Privea, a private upscale club that attracted several Cowboys, with his college bud Jerry Brown, a standby on the practice squad, riding shotgun. Brent was rolling at a high speed on a frontage road in Irving when a wheel grabbed the curb and flipped the vehicle. Brown was pronounced dead at the scene and Brent was arrested for intoxication manslaughter. Despite that shadow, the Cowboys gutted out a win over the Bengals, with Dez Bryant ignoring a broken finger to catch another touchdown and Dan Bailey kicking the game-winning field goal as time ran out in a 20–19 nail-biter. Bryant

and Bailey reprised their roles the following week against the Steelers, Dez catching another touchdown despite the broken finger, and
Dan kicking the overtime winner, making it 27–24. With division
leader New York folding and facing weak competition, the 8-6 Cowboys appeared playoff bound. They once again went into OT, this
time against the Saints, in Dallas's last home game of the year, but
only after two Romo TD passes in the last five minutes in his third
400-yard game of the season. But a lucky fumble bounce after a
hard Morris Claiborne hit put New Orleans in position for an easy
field goal to end the extra period, 34–31.

Despite the 8-7 record, the Cowboys were still in the hunt before
the final game of the season. Tony Romo had overcome his historical
late-season swoon to have a December to remember with a 101.2
NFL passing rating. Engineer a Cowboys win against the Redskins
at Landover and it would be playoff time as the NFC East
champ—the Redskins would play for the same stakes. The drama
quotient was high enough for the league to schedule the game for
NBC's national *Sunday Night Football* telecast, literally the last
game of the 2012 NFL season.

Sadly, the Bad Tony Romo showed up to chunk three interceptions. The injury-plagued Cowboys were outplayed in every aspect
of the game. The Redskins' hobbled QB Robert Griffin put the
weight on fellow rookie running back Alfred Morris, who ran over a
tattered Dallas D for 200 yards in the 28–18 'Skins win.

Once again, Tony Romo entered the postseason saddled with the
reputation that he couldn't win the big game. It didn't matter that he
was almost single-handedly responsible for at least five wins earlier
in the season to lift an average team into playoff contention; he just
couldn't win the one game that would validate the team, the franchise, and Jerry Jones. For the third time in five seasons, the Cowboys had a chance to win the NFC East crown, and for the third
time, they lost.

Head bowed, the Cowboys' field general shuffled off the field like a tragic figure straight out of Shakespeare. "Your legacy will be written when you're done playing the game," Romo said. "And when it's over with, you'll look back…It's disappointing not being able to get over that hump."

The aftermath wasn't pretty. Defensive coordinator Rob Ryan and running-backs coach Skip Peete were fired. John Garrett, Jason's brother, left to coach at Tampa Bay, and Joe DeCamillis took his special-teams skills to Chicago. Replacing Rob Ryan was seventy-two-year-old Monte Kiffin, the architect of the Tampa 2 defense, which mightily influenced the modern game. It was classic Jones, going for another known entity rather than seeking and finding the new hot hand in coaching. And that's where the shakeup ended. Nothing changed at the top, where change was needed most. Nothing would. Catch-22. The biggest fan base in the NFL was being held hostage by the megalomaniacal owner of the franchise. The big change fans clamored for—a new general manager, at the very least—was one wish the team owner would not grant. The owner wouldn't fire the general manager because he was the same person, Jerry Jones.

The Way We Are

JERRY JONES WAS the face of a Dallas that was very different from the place where Clint Murchison Jr. grew up and where Tom Landry, Tex Schramm, and Gil Brandt created the finest football franchise on earth. Dallas and its surrounding communities had continued to prosper and expand in scale. But different dreamers were at the wheel. The independent entrepreneur, much like the independent oilman (or wildcatter), had given way to the waste-dump tycoon, the private investment banker, and the hedge-fund manager.

The official population of Dallas, Texas, in 2010 was 1,197,816, but Dallas the region had sprawled into a broad mass of 5.2 million residents, the fifth-largest concentration of humanity in the United States, surpassed only by New York, Los Angeles, Chicago, and San Francisco. The home of the Dallas Cowboys being two suburbs removed from the city limits of the real Dallas was a mere technicality.

Growth and money were in the 'burbs. Between 2000 and 2010, the population of the city of Dallas increased by less than 1 percent while the rest of the region grew by 20 percent or more. DFW International Airport functioned as an aerotropolis, the regional equivalent of a downtown hub only on a larger scale, directly linked with two thousand companies based in nearby Las Colinas, the corporate-planned community designed for airport accessibility.

The whole region diversified. According to 1990 census figures,

Dallas was turning increasingly Latino—with 42 percent of the population identifying themselves as Hispanic—and poorer per capita. And where suburbs were once the refuge of whites fleeing blacks and browns and the perceived dangers of the inner city, the suburbs of Dallas were almost as multicultural as the city they were attached to. Valley Ranch, the planned community in Irving with the Cowboys' headquarters as the anchor tenant, was fully developed and had transformed into a global community, with small strip malls catering to Indian, Asian, Mexican, and Central American clienteles.

Downtown Dallas could be proud of the $300 million makeover of the seventeen-block Arts District, with its new opera house, performing arts center, theater, museum facilities, and a park built over Woodall-Rogers Expressway, even though publicity about its build-out was lost in the wave of hype devoted to Cowboys Stadium.

Dallas remained a place of infinite possibility.

Mike Rawlings, whose election as mayor of Dallas in 2011 was touted by prominent billboard endorsements from ex–Dallas Cowboys Roger Staubach and Pettis Norman, had arrived in town in 1976 driving a Volkswagen Beetle and with two hundred dollars in his pocket. "Dallas was a bit more like the Wild West was in the sense that there was so much new out there," he said. "If you could fog up a mirror, you were able to get a job. People stuck their nose in the ground in every place and made money. The key was knowing how to make money and not lose it because everybody assumed everything was going to go in a rocket ship to the moon."

Rawlings was a classic Dallas success story, finding his niche in advertising, rising up the ranks to run the TracyLocke agency, becoming the CEO of Pizza Hut, then forming the CIC Partners investment firm and making enough of a fortune to give back, first as Dallas's homeless czar under Mayor Laura Miller and then as director of parks and recreation.

CIC Partners was a principal in the Legends concession partnership between Jerry Jones, the New York Yankees' Steinbrenner family, and Goldman Sachs investment bankers. Concessions at Texas Stadium had been controlled by the Jones family. "But they saw that by combining with the New York Yankees, they could take a smaller piece of a bigger pie," Rawlings explained. "That was big news for the Cowboys organization because they were always 100 percent folks. Taking only a third of this company, they saw a much bigger play. Financially, it's been a wonderful deal for the Cowboys."

Contemporary Dallas was a different place than the one Rawlings had arrived in. "There's much more vibrant diversity in this town," he said. "When I moved here, it was white bread. It was like a gallon of whole milk — and I love milk. There were pockets of diversity, but you just didn't see it. The Latino community makes up forty percent of the population. We've had two black mayors. We're much more urban. There is big money that's not simple money."

A racial divide remained, with South Dallas's old-guard black leadership most closely allied with Highland Park's white leadership, a continuation of the unholy alliance forged by the Dallas Citizens Council in the 1950s and 1960s to tamp down violence while accommodating integration of public places and eventually of schools.

If there was racial progress being made, the Dallas Cowboys were the most visible evidence. The National Football League, where stacking according to race was once the unspoken rule, had reversed course, and the playing field now tilted in the other direction. African Americans made up 70 percent of NFL rosters, including the Cowboys'.

Dallas's next-generation optimism was kept in check by movers and shakers in high-dollar enclaves such as Highland Park, where it was illegal for groups to jog on the street, and University Park and Old Preston Hollow. Old and New Dallas people such as the Joneses, the Hickses, the Bushes, the Cubans, the Perots, the Simmonses, the Wylys, the Pickenses, and the Wolenses quietly exerted influence, making possible projects such as the $182 million Margaret

Hunt Hill suspension bridge over the Trinity River, the first of three modern bridges that were part of turning the neglected Trinity River floodplain into the world's largest urban park.

Such ambitious projects came at the expense of fixing aging roads, sewers, and other infrastructure; reopening previously closed libraries, pools, and schools; and addressing an underperforming public school system. The lack of attention to these basic amenities were factors in convincing the Boeing Corporation to choose Chicago over Dallas and Denver when the company relocated its headquarters from Seattle in 2001, despite Dallas's promoters offering considerably more money than the other cities did.

But Dallas had other things going for it. Dallas was the City of Self-Help Motivational Speakers, as it was home to Zig Ziglar, Dr. Phil, and a cast of other high-profile motivators. Dallas was the City of Televangelism, represented by local-preachers-made-good such as James Robison; outsiders such as Israeli import Benny Hinn and talk-show evangelical Glenn Beck; and the pastor of the First Baptist Church, Robert Jeffress, who made national news by calling Mormonism a cult in his endorsement of Texas governor Rick Perry to be the Republican Party candidate for president in 2012. Dallas was the City Where Faith Meets Commerce, a recognition of Dallas's dual functions as the Hollywood and Nashville of Christian media, with dozens of businesses creating, marketing, and distributing Christian music, Christian film, and Christian publishing.

Dallas was also a great location to make a movie or television series. Instead of the caricatures promoted by the television series *Dallas*, which was being recycled and updated for the TNT cable channel, and by the ABC series *GCB* (short for Good Christian Bitches), the city supplied less obvious backdrops for TV's Matt Nix, the creator of the drama-comedy *Good Guys*, which aired on the Fox network in 2010. Nix had been planning to shoot the show on location in Los Angeles until he saw Dallas. "I looked around, and thought this looks like a 1970s cops show set—the entire city," Nix said. "It is crumbling infrastructure, it is shitty streets, it is crap power lines. It is an ugly fuckin' city when you're just driving around the neighborhoods."

Landlocked, flat, covered with concrete, Dallas was no beauty. But as the rest of the country dipped into a recession, she looked pretty good, leading the nation in new job creation in 2011.

If there was a Jones metaphor to glean from this new D, it was continuation of the ability to get things done. "When I headed up the homeless effort, nobody thought that we could get a $23 million bond package passed," Mayor Rawlings said. "I raised over $13 million outside of city hall to help fund this. That's the thing that Dallas does. The Cowboys epitomize that. Jerry epitomizes that. What Jerry did with that stadium in Arlington is like nothing else. It's off the charts. Nothing's going to be built like this for thirty years. It just can't be, from a financial standpoint, and the size and the quality, it is epic in proportion."

As the owner of the Dallas Cowboys Football Club, Jerry Jones continued to draw more attention than any of his players or coaches, signing autographs in the stands, pacing the sidelines with the coaches, getting camera close-ups at every turn. He was praised for his business smarts and for increasing the value of his investment, and at the same time he was easily the most hated personality associated with the Dallas Cowboys. Nationally, only the Oakland Raiders' eighty-one-year-old owner, Al Davis, and quarterback Michael Vick, who had enjoyed a stellar comeback season after two years in prison for running a dogfighting ring and for animal abuse, stood between Jerry and the title of Most Disliked Person in American Sports, according to a 2011 E-Poll Market Research survey of fans. Then Davis died and Vick started winning.

The criticism did not appear to bother Jones. At least people were talking. When the CBS television network's 60 Minutes newsmagazine profiled him in late 2010, the program garnered its highest ratings of the year. The segment began with a JerryWorld version of a come-to-Jesus moment as host Scott Pelley introduced him: "This may be the lowest year of his life. Losing reveals more of a man's character. Especially when he's the most innovative, controversial, and bombastic owner in the NFL. He's the only owner in the league who is the general manager, and the only owner who is a celebrity. Number one offense in the league, number four defense in the league, worst record halfway through the season."

"Stats are for losers," Jones answered to the camera. "They relish in them. The stat is the score. And when you don't win that score, nothing good happens. Have we gotten too full of ourselves? Possibly." But he was unrepentant.

"What I know is I've been through it before, and if I was going to be in the foxhole with somebody, I'd be there with me," he said.

The Cowboys and Dallas

THE SWAGGER HAD NEVER LEFT, even if their record no longer justified the confident arrogance that defined Dallas the team and Dallas the people. In fans' minds, Deion was still intercepting passes; Troy, Roger, and Dandy Don were passing with pinpoint accuracy to Michael and Drew and Bullet Bob; and Emmitt and Dorsett were forever running free.

Players from the past remained heroes, which explained the presence of Michael Irvin as a costar in the remake of the film *The Longest Yard* starring comedians Adam Sandler and Chris Rock, and Irvin's appearance in another Adam Sandler film, *Jack and Jill*. After his playing days, Irvin had joined ESPN's *Sunday NFL Countdown*, but trouble still seemed to follow as he fended off a rape accusation from a woman in Florida in 2007 and then countersued, seeking $100 million in damages. He was stopped for speeding, and a smoking pipe and plastic bag with marijuana residue were found on his person. He told authorities he had taken the pipe and baggie from a friend trying to quit drugs. His penalty was suspension for two shows by ESPN.

Irvin hired on as an analyst at the NFL Network in 2009, where his wide-knot neckties always gave viewers something to talk about. He hosted *Fourth and Long*, a reality-TV series for the Spike TV cable network starring twelve football players competing for the last spot on the training-camp roster of the real Dallas Cowboys. Emmitt, Deion, Troy, and Jerry all made cameos.

He also competed in season nine of *Dancing with the Stars,* the celebrity dance-off television series. Irvin's compadre Emmitt Smith had famously won season three of *Dancing with the Stars,* in 2006, excelling with smooth moves where Jerry Rice of the 49ers, Warren Sapp of the Raiders and Buccaneers, Jason Taylor of the Dolphins and Jets, and Irvin could not.

Irvin also took the bold move to talk publicly about his older brother, Vaughn, now deceased, admitting to *Out* magazine that he had had a hard time accepting his brother was a gay man. Working with Dallas pastor T. D. Jakes, Irvin looked back and said, "We realized maybe some of the issues I've had with so many women, just bringing women around so everybody can see, maybe that's the residual of the fear I had that if my brother is wearing ladies' clothes, am I going to be doing that? Is it genetic?"

Irvin credited his father, Walter, with teaching him tolerance through Christianity and encouraging him to love his brother unconditionally. Irvin now believed the African American community should support marriage equality. "I don't see how any African-American, with any inkling of history, can say that you don't have the right to live your life how you want to live your life," he told the magazine. "No one should be telling you who you should love, no one should be telling you who you should be spending the rest of your life with. When we start talking about equality, and everybody being treated equally, I don't want to know an African American who will say everybody doesn't deserve equality."

As for that *Dancing with the Stars* winner, Emmitt Smith eschewed film, television, and sports punditry to run his real estate, construction, and financial planning businesses and oversee the Pat and Emmitt Smith Charities, all under the Emmitt Smith Enterprises umbrella, making the occasional endorsement and otherwise just being himself.

———

THE SOLE FORMER EXECUTIVE from the first dynasty who remained in the public eye was Gil Brandt. The man who modernized scouting was a senior personnel analyst on the NFL.com Web site, helped select *Playboy* magazine's annual All-American Football Team, and appeared weekly on Sirius satellite radio on the NFL's *Late Hits, RedZone,* and *NFL Tailgate Show* programs.

The best of the ex-Cowboys "goldy throats," as Blackie Sherrod used to call sports broadcasters, was the third Triplet, Troy Aikman.

The team of Aikman and Joe Buck was the number-one crew calling games for the NFL on Fox, with Pam Oliver adding field reports. Buck spat out the details like a machine gun, and his statements were tempered by Aikman's knowledgeable insights and observations, which were delivered in a warm, human voice.

Aikman played himself in the movie *Jerry Maguire* and did cameos on several television series, such as *Coach,* as himself. He had moonlighted as a country music singer, owned Troy Aikman Ford, and was half owner of the Hall of Fame NASCAR team with Roger Staubach. And he was the best-known, most popular ex-Cowboy.

In early 2011, Aikman sent a Tweet that he and his wife of ten years, Rhonda Worthey, a former Cowboys publicist, were divorcing. The couple had two daughters together and another daughter from Worthey's previous marriage.

Their 10,520-square-foot Mediterranean-style home on two lots on Highland Drive in tony Highland Park went on the market for $24 million, the most expensive home listed in Dallas.

The 29,122-square-foot suburban home in Prosper belonging to Deion Sanders remained on the market with an asking price of $21 million two years after it was first listed. Sanders's high-rise penthouse at the Azure uptown was going at $7 million until it was taken off the market. Terrell Owens had a condo at the Azure, and a second property in Deep Ellum that were being hit with foreclosure by the banks that held the note.

Owens returned to the local sports scene as a receiver for the Allen Wranglers, an Indoor Football League team, but was dropped from the roster before the end of the season. Wearing his old number 81, the thirty-eight-year-old Owens scored three touchdown receptions in his 2012 debut. Owens was broke and couldn't catch on with any NFL teams, so he returned to Dallas to play what amounted to minor-league pinball football and was given one-half ownership of the franchise. Most of the $80 million he had been paid over fifteen seasons was gone. He owed over $535,000 annually in child support to four women raising his children, although Owens married none of them.

Unlike Owens, Deion Sanders had put down roots, such as they were. A month after being inducted into the Pro Football Hall of Fame in Canton, the Prime Prep Academy that Sanders backed was approved as a charter school in the state of Texas with campuses in Dallas and Fort Worth. Three of Sanders's five children would be among its 650 students. Two weeks after that announcement, he filed for divorce from his wife of eleven years, Pilar, his costar in *Deion & Pilar: Prime Time Love*, a reality show on the Oxygen network. He said, "Enough is enough. If I wanted a model or a television star I would have married one a long time ago. All I wanted was a housewife." Through much of the summer and fall, Sanders, attired in a generic white football uniform with wings, appeared as a fairy in commercials for DirecTV's NFL Sunday Ticket package.

Other former Cowboys remained in the public eye. Nate Newton went to prison for smuggling marijuana twice, did his time, got lap-band surgery, got down to 180 pounds, and endorsed Dr. Kim's bariatric surgery on Dallas–Fort Worth television and on billboards throughout North Texas. After spending time in a spiritual commune, Frank Clarke became a live-in nanny in Durham, North Carolina.

Danny White served as head coach and part owner of the Arizona Rattlers of the Arena League from 1992 to 2004, winning the Arena Bowl in 1992 and 1997 and then coaching the Utah Blaze indoor football team from 2006 to 2008. Mark Stepnoski, one of the star linemen of the Aikman era, advocated on behalf of NORML, the National Association for Reform of Marijuana Laws.

Roger Staubach netted $750 million from the sale of his commercial real estate company to Jones Lang LaSalle and remained active on the JLL board as well as on the board of directors of American Airlines. His civic profile grew larger when he was asked to head up the committee that brought the Super Bowl to Dallas.

Herschel Walker, the running back whose trade from Dallas provided the building blocks for the team of the 1990s, took up mixed-martial-arts fighting and voiced interest in returning to the NFL at age fifty, saying he was primed to become the George Foreman of pro football.

The first star running back for the Cowboys, Don Perkins, left Dallas for Albuquerque as soon as he was done with football. He took daily walks from his home near the campus of the University of New Mexico to hang out at the Frontier restaurant, where his jersey was displayed and where Perkins enjoyed telling stories to visitors who recognized him. He also admitted to memory lapses, explaining, "I took a lot of hits from Butkus and Nitschke."

Pat Toomay lived in the same city after spending most of his post-football life in Dallas. He had been drawn to native American cultures and the tranquillity New Mexico offered.

Don Perkins's backfield colleague Dandy Don Meredith found happiness up the road in Santa Fe, where he retreated from the public eye, played golf, and enjoyed the company of his family and friends; he passed away on December 5, 2010, from a brain hemorrhage, at the age of seventy-two. Eleven months later, in northern Michigan, his old running buddy Peter Gent died of pulmonary disease. He'd found some kind of peace of mind hanging with his teammates from the Bangor High School Vikings team that had taken state in basketball their senior year.

Trouble hounded some, while others left trouble in their rear-view mirrors. Eugene Lockhart Jr. was jailed in 2009 by the FBI for an alleged $20 million mortgage fraud scam. Rafael Septien pleaded guilty to indecency with a minor after being charged with aggravated sexual abuse of a ten-year-old girl. He wound up in his native Mexico in the popular resort of Cancún, where he sold timeshares for Krystal Hotels. Dextor Clinkscale survived being arrested in 1998 (he was never charged) for molesting an eighteen-year-old boy to become the director of sports for Jesse Jackson's Rainbow/PUSH Coalition in Atlanta.

The large contingent of former Cowboys staying in and around Dallas included Chuck Howley, whose cleaning business earned him ten times what his football career had, landing him in tony Preston Hollow with a large ranch in East Texas on the side. Charlie Waters and Cliff Harris continued working together, sponsoring a charity golf tournament and sharing a Web site, cliffandcharlie.com, to work the motivational-speaker circuit as a duo, like they did so well on the field ("Let Cliff and Charlie fire up your corporate team"). Bill Bates, perhaps the hardest-playing Cowboy of all, and a slew of other ex-Cowboys also did motivational speaking. Margene Adkins was a security guard at Lockheed Martin defense contractors in Fort Worth.

Lance Rentzel returned to the Dallas area and kept a low profile. Pettis Norman ran a trucking company and remained a political player in South Dallas. Lee Roy Jordan ran a successful lumber business near Love Field. Jethro Pugh owned gift shops at DFW International Airport. Jay Novacek joined Walt Garrison as a real cowboy, with a private hunting ranch called Jay Novacek's Upper 84 Ranch in Nebraska. Garrison continued to whittle, making "pissants," among other objects, for his friends.

When he wasn't general managing the Allen Wranglers minor-league team in the spring, Drew Pearson was a regular during the football season with Channel 5's sports director Newy Scruggs on *Out of Bounds*, a thirty-minute program that followed NBC's *Sunday Night Football*. (Scruggs was another example of the Cowboys' appeal; he left a cushy sportscaster's job in Los Angeles in 2000 to break into the Dallas market.)

Bob Lilly, Mr. Cowboy, retired to Sun City, Texas, a retirement community near Georgetown, and continued pursuing his love of photography while cutting back on public appearances. "Sometimes I get tired of being Bob Lilly," he admitted to a friend.

Abner Haynes, Dallas's first homegrown black football star for Lincoln High, North Texas State, and the rival Dallas Texans of the old American Football League, was still fighting for the rights and pensions of former pro football players. Individual franchises and the league in general were still deficient in helping players understand "how you have to deal with yourself because you're good at violence," Haynes contended. There was a price paid by those playing for the amusement of others. "Y'all are playing games with our lives," he said. "You don't see the suffering. You don't know pain, so it's all fun from where you sit. No one comes up and knocks the shit out of you and tells you to get up and do it again and if you can't, you're no good."

Echoing Haynes was TD, Tony Dorsett. The Frisco resident joined a class action filed by over three hundred ex-players who sued the NFL, its teams, and, in some cases, helmet maker Riddell for head and other debilitating injuries, claiming the league pressured them to play when they were hurt and then failed to help them pay for health care in retirement to deal with the problems that had resulted. "I'm suffering for it," Dorsett told the Associated Press, "and the NFL is trying to deny it." He said he had played willingly but accused owners and the league of forgetting players once their careers were done. "Yeah, I understand you paid me to do this, but still yet, I put my life on the line for you, I put my health on the line," Dorsett said. "And yet when the time comes, you turn your back on me? That's not right. That's not the American way.... They use you up."

Weeks later, Randy White, Bob Lilly, Rayfield Wright, Charlie Waters, Chuck Howley, Lee Roy Jordan, John Fitzgerald, Walt Garrison, Ralph Neely, Jerry Norton, Jerry Tubbs, the Talbert brothers, Preston Pearson, and Harold Hays were among the ex-Cowboys joining another class action lawsuit against the NFL over concussions.

Older players who had competed without the cushions of million-dollar contracts had a hard time getting by. In 2007, Hall of Fame defensive back Herb Adderley, a twelve-year veteran who'd spent three of those years with the Cowboys, had his pension increased from $126.85 to $176.85 per month.

Adderley's plight did not distract from the fact that no matter what their eventual stations in life, players formed a bond between brothers each and every season that would never be broken. Proof was the friendship of Everson Walls, the cornerback from 1981 to 1989, and running back Ron Springs, who played from 1979 to 1984. Walls donated a kidney to Springs in 2006 to save his life after his long battle with type 2 diabetes, and when Springs passed away, in 2011, Walls eulogized him for his impact on organ donation, diabetes, and kidney disease in the African American community. "I have had people call and text me and say they donated organs because of what we went through," Walls told the *Fort Worth Star-Telegram*. "It's amazing to be able to leave that kind of legacy. What a mark he made on society as a whole. Forget sports. This is a real life situation and he was the face of that. He is the face of the sacrifice and the strength of people who deal with kidney disease and diabetes."

Even Duane Thomas and Thomas Henderson, bad boys from the deep past, came around to realize the Dallas Cowboys had defined their lives—but only to a degree in Henderson's case, since winning the $28 million Lotto Texas jackpot in 2000 was a pretty big deal too. Thomas, who painted fine art in Arizona, and Henderson, who counseled at-risk youth and ran his own foundation in Austin, both professed loyalty to the Cowboys and were fans of the current team.

New stars continued to make news just because they were

Cowboys. Wide receiver Dez Bryant, an African American who had grown up poor behind the Pine Curtain of East Texas and who dropped out of Oklahoma State following his junior year after the NCAA sanctioned him for illegal contact with professional sports agents (that is, talking to Deion Sanders), signed a five-year deal with the Cowboys in 2010 for $12 million, with $8.4 million of that amount guaranteed. Flush with cash, Bryant went on a jewelry-buying binge for himself, his family, and his friends. A parade of advisers, including Deion Sanders and Calvin Hill, materialized to explain life under the microscope as a Dallas Cowboy.

Like most young black ballers on the team, Bryant was taken to Potter's House, the West Dallas main house of worship for the thirty-thousand-member congregation following Dallas's highest-profile African American pastor, Bishop T. D. Jakes. The hope was that church, along with the help, assistance, and direction of his advisers, would lead Bryant to choose the right path in life as well as on the field, and that Bishop Jakes would be able to influence him in the same way he had influenced Michael Irvin and helped to turn his life around.

But on March 19, 2011, off-duty policemen working as security guards at NorthPark Center issued Bryant a criminal-trespass warning after one guard asked him to pull up his pants, which were low enough to expose his boxer underwear. Bryant had refused the request. "What the fuck are you stopping me, like I stole something?" he challenged the security guards, then told them he wasn't leaving until his attorney and his representative arrived. The off-duty officers escorted Bryant to his car and issued the criminal-trespass warning that banished him from the mall for sixty to one hundred eighty days.

The dustup was settled with apologies but led to three lawsuits filed against him for a total of $861,350, including one for close to half a million in unpaid bling, back rent owed, and legal fees. Deion Sanders said he no longer wanted to speak with him. No matter how many advisers he had or how much Jesus was in his heart, Bryant appeared as if he might wind up among the 78 percent of NFL players who declared bankruptcy or found themselves in dire financial straits within two years of retirement from the game.

The truth was, most current players were no longer the larger-than-the-game personalities that the franchise once bred. Two linemen, Leonard Davis and Marc Columbo, had been part of a heavy metal band called Free Reign that also included former Cowboy and current Dolphin Cory Procter. But the band was famous because they were Dallas Cowboys, not because they were outstanding headbangers.

Tony Romo came closest to transcending his role as a football player. His May 2011 wedding to Candice Crawford was Dallas's social event of the season. Crawford, a Lubbock native, was the high school football reporter for KDAF TV in Dallas and a former Miss Missouri USA whose brother, Chace, was a featured actor on the CW network series *Gossip Girl* and was *People* magazine's 2009 Summer's Hottest Bachelor. Candice met Tony as a college intern working for the Cowboys in 2008 on the football club's offseason television show *The Blitz*. They started dating a year later.

Romo organized more than forty of his teammates in players-only practices during a league-wide lockout over a collective bargaining agreement while the soon-to-be Mrs. Romo planned the wedding. Romo's groomsmen were mostly high school and college football buddies, with one exception: his current teammate Jason Witten.

Moët champagne, short ribs, and Papa John's pizza, the brand endorsed by Jerry Jones, were on the menu at the million-dollar-plus wedding, put together by Todd Fiscus and his Todd Event Design Creative Services, the go-to Dallas party planners.

The wedding underscored the Cowboys' high profile in the community, as did the Gene and Jerry Jones Foundation, a major source of charity funding in the Dallas–Fort Worth area; the annual Thanksgiving Day game had become the National Kettle Kickoff for the Salvation Army's Christmas drive. A side benefit of the construction of Cowboys Stadium was the creation of the Gene and

Jerry Jones Family Arlington Youth Foundation, which would contribute $500,000 a year for thirty-three years to benefit local youth.

Local hipsters complained the omnipotence of the Dallas Cowboys caused Dallas's cooler attributes to be ignored. "Between Leeann Rimes, Jessica Simpson, Edie Brickell, Erykah Badu, and Norah Jones, over fifty million albums have been sold by Dallas women," said music promoter Jeff Liles.

"Female pop stars are our greatest asset and no one knows about it," Liles griped. "Instead, we're known for perennial fuckin' losers. Eighty-five thousand people will drive to Arlington, pay $75 to park, walk a mile to pay another $200 to sit and watch their team lose on a big-screen TV when we can barely get 350 people to pay $25 to watch a living legend sing."

Liles ranted, but like the true believer he was, toward the end of every summer, he felt the tug too. "Even if it continues to let you down, you're still committed," he said. "The tribe is committed to who they are and what they are. It's as natural as eating or going to the bathroom. It is our church. Even if I've been out until four in the morning after Saturday night, my body knows when it's 11:45 Sunday morning."

The football team represented. The team symbolized the wide-open Dallas when J.R. was America's favorite villain; money flowed like water from the S & Ls; and loose ethics, loose money, and loose men and women came together to reimagine how business was done and how life was lived; and it continued to symbolize Dallas in the here and now, where the faithful knew that no matter what the win-loss record was, the Cowboys would be out front with whatever the new-new happened to be in the National Football League, reimagining the sport before anyone else did and raking in more money than any other team because of it. Those qualities continued to retain old fans and attract new ones as much as, if not more than, the actual fortunes of the football team.

With eighteen of twenty-one pro shops located outside the Metroplex, the Cowboys are Texas's team as well as America's. It is the Cowboys star that is affixed to every pickup truck in a row outside a sports bar in the Rio Grande Valley, six hundred miles south of Dallas, where everyone inside speaks Spanish, not English. It is the Cowboys star that is hand-painted on an aluminum-sided mobile home on the outskirts of Lubbock on the South Plains of West Texas. Even though it is a time zone away, the Cowboys are El Paso's home team. The big-screen televisions in juke joints that cater to rural African American customers throughout the Piney Woods of East Texas feature the Cowboys, first and foremost, as do the bars and restaurants along Sixth Street in Austin and on the Riverwalk in San Antonio. Lowbrow, highbrow, working class, upper class, born again, mainstream, and alternative — they are all Cowboys fans.

What began as an idea and is now the premier franchise in American sports could have flourished only in the fertile blackland prairie of North Central Texas. The half century between 1960 and the present was a period of remarkable growth and transcendence, spurred on by some unique and larger-than-life individuals who saw opportunity and seized the moment. The city made the team possible. In exchange, the team gave the city its identity and a sense of pride and glory.

Times have changed, values have changed, the game of pro football has changed, the cast has changed, and Dallas has changed. But through it all, one thing remains clear.

It couldn't have happened anywhere else.

Acknowledgments

Thanks to:

John Parsley, my editor, for the guidance, advice, and wisdom; Michael Pietsch, my publisher, for believing; and to Jim Fitzgerald, my agent, for watching my back.

Kris, Jake, Andy, and Margaret, Chippy, and Lindy for being the family you are.

Rich Dalrymple, Joe Trahan, and the Dallas Cowboys Football Club for graciously opening their archives.

Carol Roark and the staff of the Texas/Dallas History and Archives Division of the Dallas Public Library, for their help and knowledge, and to the staffs of the DeGoyer Library at Southern Methodist University, the Special Collections of the University of Texas at Arlington, and the Witliff Collections and Southwestern Writers Collection at Texas State University.

John Morthland for the research and reading.

And very special thanks to Christina Patoski for transcriptions and photograph research, and to Jerome Sims of the *Dallas Morning News* for leading us through the photo archives.

Additional thanks to the following for interviews: Gary Cartwright, Bill Mercer, Suzanne Mitchell, Christi Schramm Wilkinson, Judy Hubbard, Carol Hermanovski, Brad Sham, Verne Lundquist, Russ Russell, Roger Staubach, Jerry Norton, Tony Liscio, Annette Liscio,

Acknowledgments

David Foster, Betty Manders, Mark David Manders, Lee Roy Jordan, Patrick Toomay, Don Perkins, Dale Hansen, Rusty Warren, Carlton Stowers, Dan Werner, Bob Ryan, Bob Stein, Joe Bailey, Alex Burton, Hank Tatum, Betsy Berry, Bobby Patterson, Bubbles Cash, Chuck Curtis, Duane Thomas, Claude Albritton, Jimmy Heldt, Thomas Henderson, Dan Reeves, Eddie Stone, Gil Brandt, Frank Luksa, Jay Randolph, David Wynne, Angus Wynne III, Brent Stein, Jo Ellen Walton, John Wesley Tackett, Larry Wansley, Buzz Kemble, Jerry Tubbs, Jerry Rhome, Lawrence Herkimer Jr., Mike Rawlings, Mike Rhyner, Michael Corcoran, Robert Wilonsky, Darwin Payne, Joe Gracey, Bobby Earl Smith, Randy Galloway, Sam Blair, Stan Richards, Dick Bartlett, Walt Garrison, Wes Wise, Jim Ferguson, Jeffrey Liles, Abner Haynes, Jean Fugett, Norm Hitzges, Jerry Wancho, Wally Nicholson, Jim Schutze, Gary A. Morris, and Christian-Charles dePligue.

Sources

ARTICLES

Various issues: *Dallas Express*, 1952–1953

"Criswell Rips Integration: Minister Delivers Fiery Talk," *Dallas Morning News*, February 23, 1956

"Criswell Talk Stirs Comment," *Dallas Morning News*, February 24, 1956

"Dallas NFL Pro Grid Club Names Tex Schramm as GM," *Dallas Morning News*, November 25, 1959

"Rangers Hire Tom Landry," Charles Burton, *Dallas Morning News*, December 29, 1959

"NFL House Hunting," *Dallas Times Herald*, December 29, 1959

"Rickey, Continental Loop Gain Twin Cities Support," Associated Press, January 8, 1960

"NFL May Expand into Court," *Dallas Morning News*, January 8, 1960

"The Infighting Was Vicious," Tex Maule, *Sports Illustrated*, February 8, 1960

"The Fuss Budget," *Dallas Times Herald*, March 6, 1960

"Cotton Bowl Dates Flame into Battle," Bud Shrake, *Dallas Times Herald*, March 6, 1960

"Game Could Move," Louis Cox, *Dallas Times Herald*, March 7, 1960

"Colts, Bears to Play Here," Bud Shrake, *Dallas Times Herald*, March 8, 1960

"Free-for-All: SWC Hits Pros...US Looks at NFL vs. AFL," Charles Burton, Sam Blair, *Dallas Morning News*, March 10, 1960

"Dallas Rangers Pledged Salesmanship Club Support," *Dallas Morning News*, March 11, 1960

"NFL Sends Cards to St. Louis," Bob Oates, *Los Angeles Examiner*, March 14, 1960

"AFL's Artillery Pops Three Heavy Salvos," *Oak Cliff Tribune*, March 14, 1960

"NFL Rangers Add 6 Players, Including Tubbs," Charles Burton, *Dallas Morning News*, March 14, 1960

"Defense Left to the Coach," Bud Shrake, *Dallas Times Herald*, March 17, 1960

"Bell Says One, One Too Many," Gary Cartwright, *Dallas Times Herald*, April 1, 1960

"Rozelle Did Neat Job on Schedule," Charles Burton, *Dallas Morning News*, April 8, 1960

"It Figures: A Cowgirl to Handle Cowboy Sales," *Dallas Morning News*, April 23, 1960

"Gifford Applies the Appraisal," Blackie Sherrod, *Dallas Times Herald*, May 18, 1960

Some Hither, Others Yon column, Blackie Sherrod, *Dallas Times Herald*, May 23, 1960

"AFL Seeks Cowboy Scalp," Gary Cartwright, *Dallas Times Herald*, June 19, 1960

"Suit Decision a Year Off?," Louis Cox, *Dallas Times Herald*, June 18, 1960

"Rozelle Sees Battle Clouds," Bud Shrake, *Dallas Times Herald*, June 8, 1960

"Cowboys' Ownership Expanded," Charles Burton, *Dallas Morning News*, June 9, 1960

"SMU Lets Pros Go, Go, Go," Louis Cox, *Dallas Times Herald,* July 9, 1960

"Cowboys Pass Up Scenery," Bud Shrake, *Dallas Times Herald,* July 24, 1960

"Clarke Sets Record in Landry Mile," Charles Burton, *Dallas Morning News,* July 25, 1960

"Landry, Dallas Coach, Has Big Job," Mike Donohoe, *Seattle Post-Intelligencer,* July 22, 1960

"Northwest News," Don Fair, *Oregonian,* July 28, 1960

"TV, Radio Broadcasters Named for Dallas Pro Teams," Bob Brock, *Dallas Times Herald,* August 5, 1960

"First Game: Cook's Tour," Dan Cook, *San Antonio Express,* August 10, 1960

"Colts Just Like TCU, Says Meredith," Bill Rives, *Dallas Morning News,* August 13, 1960

"About the Hunt for a Hunt," Bill Rives, *Dallas Morning News,* August 13, 1960

"Cowboys Cheer Texans," Bud Shrake, *Dallas Times Herald,* September 6, 1960

"It May Take Time But Don's on Way," Bud Shrake, *Dallas Times Herald,* September 7, 1960

"Cowboys Bounce Giants," Bud Shrake, *Dallas Times Herald,* August 29, 1960

"Dallas Tries Pro Football Again," Charles Burton, *Dallas Morning News,* September 19, 1960

"Layne's Magic Tops Cowboys," Blackie Sherrod, *Dallas Times Herald,* September 25, 1960

"A Bullseye? Box Office War," *Dallas Morning News,* September 29, 1960

"AFL Asks Court to Throw Dallas Out of the NFL," Associated Press, October 15, 1960

"A Black Sunday on the Bayou; It Was a Case of Murder: Cleveland Thrashes Cowboys," Bud Shrake, *Dallas Times Herald,* October 17, 1960

"New Pro Teams Absorb Heavy Losses, Step Up Promotion to Woo Fans; Dallas Texans, Cowboys War with Balloons, TV Stars; Players' Salaries Climb," Roger W. Benedict, *Wall Street Journal*, October 24, 1960

"Meredith Fans Are Impatient," Charles Burton, *Dallas Morning News*, October 28, 1960

"Pokes Call in Meredith," Bud Shrake, *Dallas Times Herald*, November 4, 1960

"Cowboys Will Stay—Wynne," Bud Shrake, *Dallas Times Herald*, November 10, 1960

"Cowboys Run on Schedule," Bud Shrake, *Dallas Times Herald*, November 21, 1960

"The Plot Seems Familiar," Bud Shrake, *Dallas Times Herald*, November 22, 1960

"Landry Still Sees Hope; Last Stop: Chicago," Charles Burton, *Dallas Morning News*, November 23, 1960

"Wait Til Other Years," Bill Rives, *Dallas Morning News*, November 27, 1960

"Lying by the Clock," Blackie Sherrod, *Dallas Times Herald*, December 5, 1960

"Cowboys' Rally Ties Giants," Bud Shrake, *Dallas Times Herald*, December 5, 1960

"Hunt Denies Merger Talk," *Dallas Morning News*, December 11, 1960

"Rumors Say Pro Leagues Will Merge in '61, But...AFL's Bosses Say 'Ridiculous,'" Bud Shrake and Gary Cartwright, *Dallas Times Herald*, December 11, 1960

"Anyone for Texan-Cowboy Duel? Loser Leave Town," *Dallas Morning News*, December 25, 1960

"Cowboys, Texans Grab Tops; AFL Lock Up Seven of Top 15," Gary Cartwright; "NFL's Signing Big Haul," Bud Shrake, *Dallas Times Herald*, January 5, 1961

"Texans May Challenge Cowboys to Exhibition," Gary Cartwright, *Dallas Times Herald*, January 16, 1961

Sources

"Challenge Talk Stirs Comment," Gary Cartwright, *Dallas Times Herald*, January 17, 1961

"Eastern Division Due for Cowboys," Charles Burton, *Dallas Morning News*, January 22, 1961

"Growing Whiskers the Hard Way," Blackie Sherrod, *Dallas Times Herald*, January 26, 1961

"Science at Work; 'Poke Year Is Captured,'" Bud Shrake, *Dallas Times Herald*, February 19, 1961

"NFL Signs TV Contract," Associated Press, April 27, 1961

"LeBaron Speaker at Lincoln Fete," *Wall Post-Star*, May 13, 1961

"Cowboys, Texans in Bucket Battle," *Dallas Morning News*, May 21, 1961

Some Hither, Others Yon column, Blackie Sherrod, *Dallas Times Herald*, May 21, 1961

"The Joker Is Wild; Laughs Parade for Murchison," Bud Shrake, *Dallas Times Herald*, June 4, 1961

"Brawn Patrol," Jimmie Woodward, *Dallas Times Herald*, June 8, 1961

"High Finance: Texas on Wall Street," *Time* magazine, June 16, 1961

Dallas at the Crossroads, film produced by Sam Bloom, Dallas Citizens Council, 1961

"Jungle Jamie's 'Cut from Squad,'" Dan Jenkins, *Fort Worth Press*, August 6, 1961

"Lone Gone Here to Stay," Blackie Sherrod, *Dallas Times Herald*, August 8, 1961

"He Worked Out His Own System," Dan Jenkins, *Fort Worth Press*, August 11, 1961

"The Happy Strife of G. P. Marshall," Blackie Sherrod, *Dallas Times Herald*, November 17, 1961

"Richer and Richer," Dan Jenkins, *Dallas Times Herald*, December 19, 1961

"Chicken Feed Feud; Cowboys vs. Indians; Prank Failed," United Press International, December 19, 1961

"Rozelle Gets 5-Year Pact," Charles Burton, *Dallas Morning News*, January 9, 1962

"Allen Inspects the Fire Escape," Charles Burton, *Dallas Morning News*, October 1, 1962

"Looks Like a Real Take-Charge Guy," Sam Blair, *Dallas Morning News*, October 1, 1962

"Other Voices, Other Rooms," Bud Shrake, *Dallas Morning News*, October 17, 1962

"A Change of Attitude," Bud Shrake, *Dallas Morning News*, October 19, 1962

"CCC Scores Again," Bud Shrake, *Dallas Morning News*, November 5, 1962

"Any Boos for Halas?," Bud Shrake, *Dallas Morning News*, November 18, 1962

"The Paying Fan Speaks," Bud Shrake, *Dallas Morning News*, November 19, 1962

"The Status Quo Is Quo Status," Blackie Sherrod, *Dallas Times Herald*, November 19, 1962

"It Say So—Here," Dan Jenkins, *Dallas Times Herald*, December 18, 1962

"Texans by a Field Goal?," Gary Cartwright, *Dallas Times Herald*, December 19, 1962

"Lamar: 'No Test Yet'; Clint: 'We Are Staying,'" Gary Cartwright and Frank Boggs, *Dallas Times Herald*, December 19, 1962

"Big Man Even in Big D," Joe David Brown, *Sports Illustrated*, January 21, 1963

"The Shadows of the Image," Gary Cartwright, *Dallas Morning News*, January 20, 1963

"A Look at the Best," Bud Shrake, *Dallas Morning News*, January 11, 1963

"Texans Form Battle Plans," *Dallas Times Herald*, February 13, 1963

"Diehard Fans Plan to Plea for Texans," *Dallas Morning News*, February 13, 1963

"Texan Owner Says K-City Move 'Sure,'" Associated Press, February 10, 1963

"Texan Move Depending on 25,000 Ticket Sale," United Press International, February 10, 1963

"The K.C. Goal Indeed Golden," Blackie Sherrod, *Dallas Times Herald*, February 11, 1963

"Promises Must Be Met, Hunt Says," *Dallas Morning News*, February 10, 1963

"Texans to Head for Kansas City—If," Gary Cartwright, *Dallas Morning News*, February 9, 1963

"Time to Win," Frank Boggs, *Dallas Times Herald*, February 11, 1963

"Everything's in the Book," Sam Blair, *Dallas Morning News*, March 27, 1963

"Dallas and K.C. Even the Score," Gary Cartwright, *Dallas Morning News*, April 4, 1963

"Now Comes Recovery," Blackie Sherrod, *Dallas Times Herald*, May 23, 1963

"Texans Say Official 'Adios,'" *Dallas Morning News*, May 23, 1963

"The Pro Griddle: Andy Is Handy Grabbing Fumble," Dave Anderson, *New York Daily News*, August 20, 1963

"Some Athletes Who Puff Don't Huff; Cowboy Doc's Survey Reveals the Truth," Gary Cartwright, *Dallas Morning News*, August 22, 1963

"Cowboy Coaches Seek Reel Truth," Gary Cartwright, *Dallas Morning News*, August 27, 1963

"36,432 See NFL Opener," Sam Blair, *Dallas Morning News*, September 16, 1963

"It's That Time Again," Sam Blair, *Dallas Morning News*, September 18, 1963

"The Inscrutable Mr. Landry," Gary Cartwright, *Dallas Morning News*, October 31, 1963

"JFK News Dulls Pros," Bill Hendricks, *Fort Worth Press*, November 25, 1963

"Browns Smother Cowboys," Gary Cartwright, *Dallas Morning News,* November 25, 1963

"The Amazing Mel Renfro," Bud Shrake, *Dallas Morning News,* December 4, 1963

"Changing Costumes," Sam Blair, *Dallas Morning News,* January 22, 1964

"Growing Old with Cowboys," Bud Shrake, *Dallas Morning News,* February 6, 1964

"11-Year Cowboy: Landry Signs Contract to Coach Through 1976," Gary Cartwright, *Dallas Morning News,* February 6, 1964

"True Stories: Scout's Honor," Gary Cartwright, *Dallas Morning News,* April 28, 1964

"Still Thinking," Frank Boggs, *Dallas Times Herald,* April 30, 1964

"The McDonald," Steve Perkins, *Dallas Times Herald,* May 29, 1964

"Strange Surroundings: Cowboys Rookie Keeps Looking for Hoops," Gary Cartwright, *Dallas Morning News,* August 2, 1964

"The Good Mirth," Sam Blair, *Dallas Morning News,* August 11, 1964

Some Hither, Others Yon column, Blackie Sherrod, *Dallas Times Herald,* August 16, 1964

"Cowboys Edge Washington, 24–18," Gary Cartwright, *Dallas Morning News,* September 21, 1964

"Five Years, Cloud of Dust," Gary Cartwright, *Dallas Morning News,* October 15, 1964

"Strength in Silence," Gary Cartwright, *Dallas Morning News,* November 14, 1964

"Meredith Signs New Pact," Gary Cartwright, *Dallas Morning News,* January 28, 1965

"'65 Cowboys in New Look," Gary Cartwright, *Dallas Morning News,* August 25, 1965

"Aussie Ridgway Get His Kicks," Steve Perkins, *Dallas Times Herald,* August 27, 1965

"Cheers for the Cowboys!," B. B. Bishop, *Dallas Times Herald Sunday Magazine,* November 14, 1965

"Kay Still Unshaken," Gary Cartwright, *Dallas Morning News,* September 12, 1966

"Dallas' Pro Football: A New Face: Those Bruisin' Confusin' Cowboys," Paul Rosenfield, *Dallas Times Herald Sunday Magazine,* December 4, 1966

"The Smiles of Texas Are upon Clint's Cowboys," John R. McDermott, *Life,* December 16, 1966

"Fans Welcome Champs in Love Field Hysteria," Kent Biffle, *Dallas Morning News,* December 19, 1966

"Football Fanatics Jam Fairgrounds After Night Vigil," Bill Morgan, *Dallas Times Herald,* December 21, 1966

"Sherman Will Provide TV for Cowboy Fans; Aid to Blackout Victims," *Dallas Morning News,* December 28, 1966

"Best Cowboy Year 2 Yards Too Short," Bob St. John, *Dallas Morning News,* January 2, 1967

"Site in Irving Reported Eyed for Stadium," Jim Brannan, *Dallas Times Herald,* January 27, 1967

"Clint Tosses Stadium Pass; Cowboys Call $13,000,000 Audible, Flip Ball to Irving," Gary Cartwright, *Dallas Morning News,* January 29, 1967

"Young Designers Gave Décor Zing," Bill Morgan, *Dallas Times Herald Sunday Magazine,* July 2, 1967

"K-Day Nears for Danny V," Sam Blair, *Dallas Morning News,* July 12, 1967

"Cowboys Trim Kickers Down," Associated Press, *Dallas Times Herald,* June 17, 1967

"Reminiscences of a Cowboy Fan," Clint Murchison Jr., *Dallas Times Herald,* July 9, 1967

"Well, It's Home," Bill Morgan, *Dallas Times Herald Sunday Magazine,* August 27, 1967

"Year of the Cowboys: The Cowboys Come Home," Steve Perkins, *Dallas Times Herald Sunday Magazine*, August 27, 1967

"More Police Promised for Future Ball Games," James Ewell, *Dallas Morning News*, August 30, 1967

"Official Says Crowd Too Big," Don Smith, *Dallas Morning News*, August 30, 1967

"Support Your Local Stripper," Dick Hitt, *Dallas Times Herald*, November 10, 1967

"Poke Ducat Sale Gets Long Line," Bill Sloan, *Dallas Times Herald*, December 13, 1967

"Councilwoman Critical of Irving Stadium Deal," David Morgan, *Dallas Morning News*, December 25, 1967

"Dallas Businessmen Face Problem on Stadium Bonds," Al Altwegg, *Dallas Morning News*, December 31, 1967

"Ramsay 'Hopeful' Cowboys to Stay," Gene Ormsby, *Dallas Morning News*, December 30, 1967

"Paradise Lost Once Again for Cowboys in Final Seconds; Packers Win, 21–17," Bob St. John; "W-w-what a D-d-day!," Sam Blair, *Dallas Morning News*, January 1, 1968

"C-C-Cowboys F-F-Frozen Out: Chilled in Icebox Bowl," Kent Biffle, *Dallas Morning News*, January 1, 1968

"Make No Mistake About It," Tex Maule, *Sports Illustrated*, January 29, 1968

"Fans Oppose Plan of Stadium Bonds, Don Griffin Says," *Dallas Times Herald*, February 11, 1968

"A Divorce from Nature," Blackie Sherrod, *Dallas Times Herald*, February 13, 1968

"Cowboy Woes Minor: Negroes Feel Part of Team," Steve Perkins, *Dallas Times Herald*, July 21, 1968

Cowboys Insider Newsletter, vol. 1, no. 1, August 9, 1968

"Thinking Man's Duel," Bob St. John, *Dallas Morning News*, August 11, 1968

"Time Is Now for Cowboys," Steve Perkins, *Dallas Times Herald*, August 16, 1968

"Cowboys Left Holding Bag, 31–27," Bob St. John, *Dallas Morning News*, August 25, 1968

"Off Meredith's Chest; Injury Could Shelve Dandy for Colt Game," Bob St. John, *Dallas Morning News*, September 5, 1968

"Cowboys Silence Boobirds with Scoring Record," Dick Hitt, *Dallas Times Herald*, September 24, 1968

"Pokes Play Oddball, Too; Wackiest Play of the Year," Steve Perkins, *Dallas Times Herald*, September 30, 1968

"Dallas Puts No Vacancy Sign Out," Maryln Schwartz, *Dallas Morning News*, October 26, 1968

"The Fading Art of Manslaughter," Blackie Sherrod, *Dallas Times Herald*, November 13, 1968

"Signs Point to Cowboy Win," Steve Perkins, *Dallas Times Herald*, December 20, 1968

"Browns Set Pokes' Sun in East," Steve Perkins; "A Dandy Day—It Wasn't!," Blackie Sherrod, *Dallas Times Herald*, December 22, 1968

"Cowboys' Worst Hour," staff; "Scream's on Them," Sam Blair; "Cowboys Blow Their Thing, 31–20," Bob St. John, *Dallas Morning News*, December 22, 1968

"Brown Wait Ends," United Press International, December 22, 1968

"Cowboys Cheered in Defeat," Dave Montgomery, *Dallas Times Herald*, December 22, 1968

"Season Leaves a Dark Brown Taste," Sam Blair, *Dallas Morning News*, December 23, 1968

"Hamburgers for Cowboys," Bob St. John, *Dallas Morning News*, December 23, 1968

"Cowboys' Norman Says Set Goals," *Dallas Times Herald*, December 25, 1968

"Ramsay 'Hopeful' Cowboys to Stay," Gene Ormsby, *Dallas Morning News*, December 30, 1968

"Rose to Head Stadium," *Dallas Times Herald*, June 29, 1969

"Feeling Turns Out Mutual," Steve Perkins, *Dallas Times Herald,* June 29, 1969

"Feeling Mixed About Cowboys," Steve Perkins, *Dallas Times Herald,* June 29, 1969

"Mind Over Matter for Pokes?," Steve Perkins, *Dallas Times Herald,* June 30, 1969

"Staubach Is on the Move for Cowboys," *Dallas Times Herald,* July 6, 1969

"Mr. Number One," Steve Perkins, *Dallas Times Herald,* July 7, 1969

"Pokes Wives Model," Val Imm, *Dallas Times Herald,* September 2, 1969

"...And Then There Were None," Randy Galloway, *Dallas Morning News,* September 6, 1969

"The Quarterback Quandary: Have They Solved It?," Steve Perkins, *Dallas Times Herald,* September 14, 1969

"The Cowboys' Bandwagon Rolls," Steve Perkins, *Dallas Times Herald Sunday Magazine,* September 15, 1969

"They Make Football Fun," Frank A. Muth, *Dallas Times Herald,* September 30, 1969

"Background in Foreground," Bob St. John, *Dallas Morning News,* October 30, 1969

"Cowgirls Score, Too; YWCA Puts Together a Winning Combination," Vivian Castleberry, *Dallas Times Herald,* November 30, 1969

"Frozen in Time," Sam Blair, *Dallas Morning News,* December 31, 1987

"Cowboys at Work," Steve Perkins, *Dallas Times Herald,* February 10, 1968

"Texas Stadium: Activity Heavy as Vote Nears," Jim Featherston, *Dallas Times Herald,* January 13, 1969

"Coach Landry's Conversion; Passage in Bible 'Grabbed My Attention Early,'" Helen Parmley, *Dallas Morning News,* May 2, 1970

"Landry to Head Graham Crusade," *Dallas Morning News,* July 3, 1970

"Cowboy Camp Opens Friday: Landry Optimistic, Pleased with Craig," Bob St. John, *Dallas Morning News,* July 5, 1970

"Dandy Advised Tom to Quit After Loss," *Dallas Morning News,* July 5, 1970

"At Last, City Title's on the Line," Bob St. John, *Dallas Morning News,* September 5, 1970

"On Playing Football for Money," Richard Curry, *Dallas Times Herald,* September 6, 1970

"The Big Daddy of Sport," Edwin Shrake, *Sports Illustrated,* September 7, 1970

"Mechanical Man Drills with Dallas Cowboys," Frank X. Tolbert, *Dallas Morning News,* November 30, 1970

"Whew! Fans Limp After 5–0 Thriller," Richard Hill, *Dallas Times Herald,* December 27, 1970

"No Flowers, Just Money," Jim Trinkle, *Fort Worth Star-Telegram,* January 21, 1971

"Staubach Eagerly Awaits His Big Chance," Associated Press, January 21, 1971

"Tip Spurs Super Dispute," Associated Press, January 20, 1971

"Thomas' Fumble: Who Covered It?," Frank Luksa, *Fort Worth Star-Telegram,* January 23, 1971

"The Sighs Had It," Sam Blair, *Dallas Morning News,* January 25, 1971

"Other Voices, Other Lands," Blackie Sherrod, *Dallas Times Herald,* January 25, 1971

"Bubba Admits Refs Made Super Blunder," *Dallas Morning News,* February 10, 1970

"Morton: The Best Is Yet to Come," Craig Morton, *Dallas Times Herald,* February 21, 1971

"No Pact for Bullet Bob," *Fort Worth Star-Telegram,* March 2, 1971

"Craig Has Had Enough of Landry Calls," Associated Press, March 4, 1971

"Short Order," Steve Perkins, *Dallas Times Herald*, March 10, 1971

"Cowboys' Landry Learned to Bring God into His Life Each Day: Lenten Guideposts," Tom Landry, *Fort Worth Star-Telegram*, March 15, 1971

"Super Pitch Is Lost 'Cause Pokes Win," Steve Perkins, *Dallas Times Herald*, March 24, 1971

"Murchisons Make Money—Quietly," Richard Curry, *Dallas Times Herald*, March 28, 1971

"Mrs. Hayes: I Want to Stay," Drenda Williams, *Fort Worth Press*, May 2, 1971

"Cowboy Staubach Says 'God Center of His Life,'" *Irving Daily News*, May 9, 1971

"Graham, Landry Discuss Crusade," *Dallas Times Herald*, May 5, 1971

"250 Protest Allen's Defeat," Douglas Domeier, *Dallas Morning News*, May 10, 1971

"Pokes' Thomas Out, Paper Says," United Press International, May 11, 1971

"A Short Shot," Blackie Sherrod, *Dallas Times Herald*, May 12, 1971

"'Pokes Refute Pay Charge," Frank Luksa, *Fort Worth Star-Telegram*, May 12, 1971

"Dallas Wins NFL Tightwad Title," Melvin Durslag, *Los Angeles Examiner*, May 16, 1971

"They'll Get a Picture," Steve Perkins, *Dallas Times Herald*, May 16, 1971

"Hayes Given 5-Year Pact," *Dallas Morning News*, June 25, 1971

"Howley Joins Thomas in Absence," Bob St. John, *Dallas Morning News*, July 17, 1971

"Morton Played Under Hypnosis," Steve Perkins and Frank Taggart, *Dallas Times Herald*, July 18, 1971

"Hypnotist Looking to Alworth, Hayes," Steve Perkins, *Dallas Times Herald,* July 19, 1971

"Talk Show," Blackie Sherrod, *Dallas Times Herald,* July 22, 1971

"The Strange One," Sam Blair, *Dallas Morning News,* July 22, 1971

"Maybe Duane Has Outrun His Blockers," Bob St. John, *Dallas Morning News,* July 22, 1971

"From a Camp Follower," Bob St. John, *Dallas Morning News,* July 29, 1971

"Duane Thomas to Rejoin Cowboys," United Press International, July 30, 1971

"Resolved! It's Over for Duane," Bob St. John, *Dallas Morning News,* July 31, 1971

"42,000 Pour in to Hear Billy Graham," Helen Parmley, *Dallas Morning News,* September 18, 1971

"Best Cowboy Team Ever," Steve Perkins, *Dallas Times Herald,* September 19, 1971

"Cowboys Bomb Eagles 42–17," Frank Luksa, *Fort Worth Star-Telegram,* September 27, 1971

"Cowboys Get All Skinned Up," Steve Perkins, *Dallas Times Herald,* October 4, 1971

"Morton Rallies Pokes to Victory Over Giants," Phil Stephens, *Irving Daily News,* October 12, 1971

"Pokes Give, Saints Keep," Steve Perkins, *Dallas Times Herald,* October 18, 1971

"What Else Is Reasonably New," Dick Hitt, *Dallas Times Herald,* October 22, 1971

"Texas Stadium: Way Was Stormy," Bob St. John, *Dallas Morning News,* October 24, 1971

"New Jewel for a Sparkling City," *Dallas Morning News,* October 24, 1971

"Just Like Old Times in New House," Bob St. John, *Dallas Morning News,* October, 25, 1971

"Staubach No. 1—Right Now," Bob St. John, *Pro Football Weekly*, November 6, 1971

"'Perk' Speaks Out," Bill Livingston, *Dallas Morning News*, October 29, 1971

"Cowboys De-Feeted by Old Kicker," Bob St. John, *Dallas Morning News*, November 1, 1971

"Roger No. 1 Rest of Year," Steve Perkins, *Dallas Times Herald*, November 3, 1971

"Cowboys Kick Skid with 16–13 Win," Frank Luksa, *Fort Worth Star-Telegram*, November 8, 1971

"Thomas: Cowboys' Quiet Man," Steve Perkins, *Dallas Times Herald*, November 10, 1971

"Doomsday Knell Tolls for Philly," Bob St. John, *Dallas Morning News*, November 15, 1971

"Look Ahead," Blackie Sherrod, *Dallas Times Herald*, November 15, 1971

"Pokes Push 'Skins 'Over the Hill,'" Frank Luksa, *Fort Worth Star-Telegram*, November 22, 1971

"Cowboy Fans Voice Complaints," Maryln Schwartz, *Dallas Morning News*, November 21, 1971

"Schramm Says Jim Brown Convinced Duane to Return," Steve Perkins, *Dallas Times Herald*, November 24, 1971

"A Bit of Opulence," Dorothy Fagg, *Dallas Times Herald*, November 24, 1971

"Cowboys Talk Turkey to LA, 28–21," Bob St. John, *Dallas Morning News*, November 26, 1971

"Family Man Meets Broadway Bachelor," Frank Luksa, *Fort Worth Star-Telegram*, December 4, 1971

"Lights Out for Broadway, 52–10," Bob St. John, *Dallas Morning News*, December 5, 1971

"Lilly Sports," Roger Kahn, *Esquire*, December 1971

"All's Well, Pokes Take Giant Step," Steve Perkins, *Dallas Times Herald*, December 12, 1971

SOURCES

"Cowboys Lasso Playoff Spot, 42–14," Bob St. John, *Dallas Morning News*, December 13, 1971

"Thomas, Dallas Romp by Cards, 31–12," Frank Luksa, *Fort Worth Star-Telegram*, December 19, 1971

"It's On to Minnesota After Cards Fall in Place," Steve Perkins, *Dallas Times Herald*, December 19, 1971

"Doomsday Defense Freezes Vikings, 20–12," Bob St. John, *Dallas Morning News*, December 26, 1971

"Hill Understands the Silence," Denne Freeman, *Dallas Times Herald*, December 30, 1971

"Cowboys Were Super, Baby!," Andy Anderson, *Fort Worth Press*, January 3, 1972

"Super Cowboys Bowl 'Em Over," Bob St. John, *Dallas Morning News*, January 1, 1972

"Cowboys Got the World on a String," Blackie Sherrod, *Dallas Times Herald*, January 17, 1972

"Talk Show by Thomas," Milton Richman, United Press International, January 17, 1972

"Thomas Speaks!," Randy Galloway, *Dallas Morning News*, January 17, 1972

"Tex Schramm Residence Burglarized," *Dallas Times Herald*, January 18, 1972

"Spirit Strong for 'Square' Staubach," Dave Anderson, *New York Times*, January 19, 1972

"Will to Win," Ross Newhan, Times Post News Service, January 30, 1972

"Thomas' Pot Case Clouds Trade Talk," Steve Perkins, *Dallas Times Herald*, January 31, 1972

"Staubach Projects Image of Good Scout in Talk Here," *St. Louis Post-Dispatch*, January 27, 1972

"Golly Gee, Duane Thomas Can Talk (with Assistance)," Milton Richman, United Press International, January 27, 1972

"The Moment for Adios," Steve Perkins, *Dallas Times Herald*, April 16, 1972

"Thomas Is San Diego's Problem Now," Roger Kaye, *Fort Worth Star-Telegram*, August 1, 1972

"New Look," Blackie Sherrod, *Dallas Times Herald*, August 16, 1972

"Some Home on the Range, 'The Day of Indignity Is Past,'" Edwin Shrake, *Sports Illustrated*, August 14, 1972

"Pokes Snap Out," Frank Luksa, *Dallas Times Herald*, September 18, 1972

"Cowboys Give, Packers Take, 16–13," Bob St. John, *Dallas Morning News*, October 2, 1972

"Pokes Survive Scare, 17–13," Roger Kaye, *Fort Worth Star-Telegram*, October 9, 1972

"Double 'D' Corrals Colts 21–0," Roger Kaye, *Fort Worth Star-Telegram*, October 16, 1972

"Jurgensen Registers 'Most Gratifying' Performance," William Gildea, *Washington Post*, October 23, 1972

"Pokes Rule Lions' Den," Frank Luksa, *Dallas Times Herald*, October 31, 1972

"Cowboys Hold Off Chargers, 34–28," Roger Kaye, *Fort Worth Star-Telegram*, November 6, 1972

"Fritsch Boots Cowboys Past Cards," Associated Press, November 13, 1972

"Cowboys Blitz Eagles," Frank Luksa, *Dallas Times Herald*, November 20, 1972

"49ers Mine 'Pokes' Hopes," Andy Anderson, *Fort Worth Press*, November 24, 1972

"Laird Swears in Cowboy Company," Tom Stephenson, *Dallas Morning News*, November 24, 1972

"Cowboys See a Light," Frank Luksa, *Dallas Times Herald*, December 4, 1972

"Baugh's TD Pass to Hutson Beats Cowboys, 34–32," *Oak Cliff Tribune*, November 30, 1972

"Cowboys Skin the Skins, 34–24," Frank Luksa, *Dallas Times Herald*, December 10, 1972

"Roger No. 1, Again," Bob St. John, *Dallas Morning News,* December 14, 1972

"Giants Whip Pokes," Jon Harrison, *Irving Daily News,* December 18, 1972

"Coal for 'Frisco Stockings," Andy Anderson, *Fort Worth Press,* December 24, 1972

"'Pokes, Staubach Perform Miracle," Roger Kaye, *Fort Worth Star-Telegram,* December 24, 1972

"Fans See Red as Pokes Lose," Doug Domeier, *Dallas Morning News,* January 1, 1973

"Things 'Shaky' with Cowboys," Roger Kaye, *Fort Worth Star-Telegram,* March 24, 1973

"Wild-Throwing Ranger, and Other Pitches," Galyn Wilkins, *Fort Worth Star-Telegram,* March 26, 1971

"The Lock-Out," Frank Luksa, *Dallas Times Herald,* March 28, 1973

"Parks Never Cared to Play in Texas," Roger Kaye, *Fort Worth Star-Telegram,* April 1, 1973

"No Big Deal," Frank Luksa, *Dallas Times Herald,* April 1, 1973

"Garrison Tops Entry List for Mesquite Rodeo," *Dallas Morning News,* April 16, 1973

"Craig Wants to Call His Own Plays in '73," Roger Kaye, *Fort Worth Star-Telegram,* April 7, 1973

"Terror Tech," Frank Luksa, *Dallas Times Herald,* April 22, 1973

"Cowboy Crisis Brewing Over Contracts," Frank Luksa, *Dallas Times Herald,* May 13, 1973

"More to 'Poke Player Dispute Than Money," Roger Kaye, *Fort Worth Star-Telegram,* May 19, 1973

"Staubach-Morton Battle to Highlight Cowboys' Camp," Roger Kaye, *Fort Worth Star-Telegram,* July 1, 1973

"Dave, Cowboys in Waiting Game," Andy Anderson, *Fort Worth Press,* July 12, 1973

"Craig's Gone, But Not Far," Frank Luksa, *Dallas Times Herald*, July 14, 1973

"Toomay Joins Angry Bunch," Frank Luksa, *Dallas Times Herald*, July 16, 1973

"Morton Rejoins Cowboys," Roger Kaye, *Fort Worth Star-Telegram*, July 22, 1973

Some Hither, Others Yon column, Blackie Sherrod, *Dallas Times Herald*, July 22, 1973

"A Big Operation," Dick Hitt, *Dallas Times Herald*, July 24, 1973

"Of Morton, QB Muddle," Bob St. John, *Dallas Morning News*, August 31, 1973

"Bids Open on Disgruntled Morton," Andy Anderson, *Fort Worth Press*, September 12, 1973

"Morton Takes Shot at Tex," Frank Luksa, *Dallas Times Herald*, September 12, 1973

"Cowboys Dig Bear Act," Frank Luksa, *Dallas Times Herald*, September 17, 1973

"Manders, Howley Rejoin Old Friends," Frank Luksa, *Dallas Times Herald*, September 19, 1973

"Pokes Mangle Saints 40–3," Roger Kaye, *Fort Worth Star-Telegram*, September 25, 1973

"Cowboys' Aerial Blitz Demolishes Cards (45–10)," Roger Kaye, *Fort Worth Star-Telegram*, October 1, 1973

"Pokes Can't Hold Fort," Frank Luksa, *Dallas Times Herald*, October 9, 1973

"Theme Tower Ad Ruckus Roars," Larry Payton, *Irving News*, October 11, 1973

"Jackson Sparkles in Rams' Victory," Bob St. John, *Dallas Morning News*, October 15, 1973

"Cole's Theft Fires Pokes," Roger Kaye, *Fort Worth Star-Telegram*, October 23, 1973

Sources

"Cowboys Stunned by Eagles," Roger Kaye, *Fort Worth Star-Telegram*, October 29, 1973

"Doomsday Cuts Loose on Bengals," Bob St. John, *Dallas Morning News*, November 5, 1973

"Sound Off on Poke Fans," Frank Luksa, *Dallas Times Herald*, November 6, 1973

"Cowboys Survive with Defense, 23–10," Bob St. John, *Dallas Morning News*, November 12, 1973

"Gabe-less Eagles Grounded," Andy Anderson, *Fort Worth Press*, November 18, 1973

"14–7 Demotes Cowboys," Roger Kaye, *Fort Worth Star-Telegram*, November 23, 1973

"Landry to Call Poke Plays Again," Frank Luksa, *Dallas Times Herald*, December 2, 1973

"And Now, Bring On Washington," Bob St. John, *Dallas Morning News*, December 3, 1973

"Roger, Pokes Stagger Redskins, 27–7," Roger Kaye, *Fort Worth Star-Telegram*, December 10, 1973

"Cowboys Deck Cards, Reclaim East Title," Frank Luksa, *Dallas Times Herald*, December 17, 1973

"Long Bomb Wrecks Rams 27–16," Roger Kaye, *Fort Worth Star-Telegram*, December 24, 1973

"Vikings Outshoot Pokes," Frank Luksa, *Dallas Times Herald*, December 31, 1973

"Morton Regrets Past Poke Soft Approach," Frank Luksa, *Dallas Times Herald*, February 11, 1974

"Cowboys Turn Tables on WFL," Frank Luksa, *Dallas Times Herald*, April 2, 1974

"Hill Moves to New World," Frank Luksa, *Dallas Times Herald*, April 10, 1974

"Cowboys' Morton Signs with Texans, Will Play in 1975," Dale Robertson, *Houston Post*, April 11, 1974

"Cattle Barons Brand Cancer Fight," Maggie Kennedy and Wanda McDaniel, *Dallas Times Herald*, June 17, 1974

"Schramm Returns Fire at Garvey," Andy Anderson, *Fort Worth Press*, July 11, 1974

"Hill in the Middle," Randy Harvey, *Dallas Times Herald*, August 6, 1974

"Garvey Angers Staubach," Bob St. John, *Dallas Morning News*, August 6, 1974

"Niland Heads West for Poke Camp," *Dallas Times Herald*, August 6, 1974

"Other Rooms," Bob St. John, *Dallas Morning News*, September 19, 1974

"Book Fever," Blackie Sherrod, *Dallas Times Herald*, September 12, 1974

"Cowboys' Defense Tames Falcons, 20–0," Bob St. John, *Dallas Morning News*, September 16, 1974

"Eagles Shock Cowboys (13–10)," Roger Kaye, *Fort Worth Star-Telegram*, September 27, 1974

"The Unique Point of View," Randy Galloway, *Dallas Morning News*, September 25, 1974

"'Pokes Pitiful in Loss to NY," Roger Kaye, *Fort Worth Star-Telegram*, September 30, 1974

"Strike, Economics Help Empty Poke Seats," Randy Harvey, *Dallas Times Herald*, September 30, 1974

"Cowboys Die at Finish Again, 23–21," Bob St. John, *Dallas Morning News*, October 7, 1974

"Cardinals Sing Cowboy Swan Song (31–28)," Bob St. John, *Dallas Morning News*, October 14, 1974

"Cowboys Win by Knockout," Frank Luksa, *Dallas Times Herald*, October 21, 1974

"Morton Takes a Giant Step," Frank Luksa, *Dallas Times Herald*, October 23, 1974

"Pokes Drew from Trick Bag," Frank Luksa, *Dallas Times Herald*, October 28, 1974

"Pokes Thinking Playoff After Winning Close One," Andy Anderson, *Fort Worth Press*, November 9, 1974

"Cowboys Hold Off 49ers," Frank Luksa, *Dallas Times Herald*, November 11, 1974

"'Pokes Bite the Dust 28–21," Roger Kaye, *Fort Worth Star-Telegram*, November 18, 1974

"Cowboys Put the Plug to Oilers," Bob St. John, *Dallas Morning News*, November 25, 1974

"Teacher Learns with His Students," Doug Domeier, *Dallas Morning News*, November 26, 1974

"Cinderella Clint Zaps 'Skins," Andy Anderson, *Fort Worth Press*, November 29, 1974

"'Mad Bomber' Keeps Alive 'Pokes Hope," Bob St. John, *Dallas Morning News*, November 29, 1974

"The Cowboys Call on the Mad Bomber," Edwin Shrake, *Sports Illustrated*, December 9, 1974

"From Chandeliers to Velvet, Cowboy Boxes Only Way to Go," Maryln Schwartz, *Dallas Morning News*, December 8, 1974

"Cowboys Keep Hopes Alive, 41–17," Bob St. John, *Dallas Morning News*, December 8, 1974

"Curtains for Cowboys," Bob St. John, *Dallas Morning News*, December 11, 1974

"Cowboys End It with 27–23 Loss," Bob St. John, *Dallas Morning News*, December 15, 1974

"Ask Tex Schramm," Bob St. John, *Dallas Morning News*, December 15, 1974

"Coach," Herbert Warren Wind, *New Yorker*, December 16, 1974

"Morton Looks at 'Pokes," Andy Anderson, *Fort Worth Press*, February 2, 1975

"Mackey Charges Schramm Favored a 25 Per Cent Cut," Associated Press, February 5, 1975

"Hunt Had Option for Poke Interest," Frank Luksa, *Dallas Times Herald*, March 23, 1975

"Seein's Believin' in Cowboys' Film," Andy Anderson, *Fort Worth Press*, March 26, 1975

"Garrison Injures Knee in Rodeo Competition," *Dallas Times Herald*, June 20, 1975

"Hayes 'Doesn't Fit,' Placed on Trading Block," Roger Kaye, *Fort Worth Star-Telegram*, July 9, 1975

"Cowboys Trade Hayes to 49ers," Roger Kaye, *Fort Worth Star-Telegram*, July 17, 1975

"Toomay Leaves a Keepsake," Blackie Sherrod, *Dallas Times Herald*, July 30, 1975

"Cowboys Put It Together," Frank Luksa, *Dallas Times Herald*, September 22, 1975

"Suddenly, Cowboys Win It," Frank Luksa, *Dallas Times Herald*, September 29, 1975

"Cowboys, Steelers Accept NFL Owners' Contract Offer," Associated Press, September 27, 1975

"Cowboys Wallop Detroit, 36 to 10," Bob St. John, *Dallas Morning News*, October 7, 1975

"Pokes Plod Past Giants, 13–7," Associated Press, October 13, 1975

"Cowboys Frustrate Craig Again, 13–7," Bob St. John, *Dallas Morning News*, October 13, 1975

"Young Pack Haunts Dallas with 19–17 Win," Bob St. John, *Dallas Morning News*, October 20, 1975

"Hill Expected WFL Fold," Frank Luksa, *Dallas Times Herald*, October 23, 1975

"Fritsch, Cowboys Get Kicks, 20–17," Bob St. John, *Dallas Morning News*, October 27, 1975

"Redskins Frustrate Cowboys in Overtime (30–24)," Andy Anderson, *Fort Worth Press*, November 3, 1975

"Cowboys Lose, Chiefly on Fumbles," Bob St. John, *Dallas Morning News*, November 11, 1975

SOURCES

"Posterity Needs the Cowboys," Leigh Montville, *Boston Globe*, November 16, 1975

"Cowboys Hold Off Plunkett," Frank Luksa, *Dallas Times Herald*, November 17, 1975

"Cowboys Ground Eagles, 27 to 17," Bob St. John, *Dallas Morning News*, November 24, 1975

"Roger Dodges Media's Saint Staubach Image," Gus Clemens, *San Antonio News*, November 28, 1975

"Cowboys Get Job Done," Frank Luksa, *Dallas Times Herald*, November 30, 1975

"Cardinals Ambush Lackluster Cowboys 31–17," Roger Kaye, *Fort Worth Star-Telegram*, December 8, 1975

"Cowboys Go Wild with 31–10 Win," Frank Luksa, *Dallas Times Herald*, December 14, 1975

"Cowboys 'Warm Up' with Cold 31–21 Win," Roger Kaye, *Fort Worth Star-Telegram*, December 22, 1975

"Cowboys Need Miracle and Get It," Frank Luksa, *Dallas Times Herald*, December 29, 1975

"Cowboys Make It Look Super Easy in Rout of LA," Blackie Sherrod, *Dallas Times Herald*, January 5, 1976

"'New' Cowboys in Old Spot," William Wallace, *New York Times*, January 14, 1976

"Super Bowl Buildup Is Going Too Far," Phil Pepe, *New York Daily News*, January 12, 1976

"Landry Termed 'Best' by UPI," *Irving Daily News*, January 12, 1976

"Niland: The Cowboys Use a Computer Attack," George Usher, *New York Newsday*, January 12, 1976

"Wives Allowed with Cowboys," *Dallas Times Herald*, January 13, 1976

"This One Really Could Be Super," Bob Collins, *Rocky Mountain News*, January 13, 1976

"Cowboymania: Why Texas Will Identify with Dallas Team," United Press International, January 13, 1976

"Well-Wishers See Cowboys Off," Bill Sloan, *Dallas Times Herald*, January 13, 1976

"Cowboys Have a Super Touchdown," Jim Sarni, *Fort Lauderdale News*, January 13, 1976

"Phyllis George," Louis Montgomery, *Miami Herald*, January 15, 1976

"Staubach Takes Calls by Landry," Associated Press, January 15, 1976

"Super Notebook," Sam Blair, *Dallas Morning News*, January 15, 1976

"Everything Is Not Cool... Just Cooler," Bill Nack, *New York Newsday*, January 15, 1976

"The Old Cowboy Who Found He'd Rather Write Than Switch," Dick Schaap, *Washington Star*, January 16, 1976

"Super Bowl Can't Please 'Em All," Randy Harvey, *Dallas Times Herald*, January 18, 1976

"Steelers Defeat Cowboys, 21–17, and Take Super Bowl Again," William N. Wallace, *New York Times*, January 19, 1976

"Landry Laments Five Costly Points," Murray Chass, *New York Times*, January 19, 1976

"Steel Curtain Crashes on Cowboys 21–17," Roger Kaye, *Fort Worth Star-Telegram*, January 19, 1975

"Winning Isn't the Only Thing," editorial, *Dallas Morning News*, January 20, 1976

"Fans Warm Up Cowboys," Charles Jackson and Jan Hamill, *Dallas Times Herald*, January 20, 1976

"Landry Drafted for Best Dressed," Yvonne Saliba, *Dallas Times Herald*, February 3, 1976

"Landry Is First String," Ann Atterberry, *Dallas Morning News*, February 3, 1976

"Here and There," Sam Blair, *Dallas Morning News*, February 18, 1976

"Couple Dazed by Cupid," Jeanne Prejean, *Dallas Morning News*, February 20, 1976

"The Dallas Forty at Super Bowl X," Pete Gent, *Sport*, March 1976

"Great Night for Landry," Frank Luksa, *Dallas Times Herald*, March 12, 1976

"Hill and Thomas: Pro and Con for Cowboys," Frank Luksa, *Dallas Times Herald*, March 28, 1976

"Duane's Back with Cowboys," Bob St. John, *Dallas Morning News*, May 1, 1976

"Reaching for the Stars," Frank Deford, *Sports Illustrated*, May 3, 1976

"400 Gals, 2 Guys Vie to Lead Cowboy Cheers," Paul West, *Dallas Times Herald*, July 10, 1976

"Cowboy Cheerleaders Call for Jane Q. Public," Yvonne Saliba, *Dallas Times Herald*, July 19, 1976

"Round 2: Longley Wins—or Does He?," Roger Kaye, *Fort Worth Star-Telegram*, August 13, 1976

"Cowboys Cut Ron, Duane," Bob St. John, *Dallas Morning News*, September 7, 1976

"Cowboys Humble Eagles in Opener 27–7," Roger Kaye, *Fort Worth Star-Telegram*, September 13, 1976

"Cowboys March In on Saints, 24–6," Bob St. John, *Dallas Morning News*, September 20, 1976

"Bottom-Line Winning Important to Cowboys, Too," Steve Mott, *Dallas Times Herald*, September 26, 1976

"Cowboys Claim Thriller over Colts 30–27," Roger Kaye, *Fort Worth Star-Telegram*, September 27, 1976

"Cowboys Wake Up; Beat Seattle, 28–13," Bob St. John, *Dallas Morning News*, October 4, 1976

"No Letup: Cowboys Thumb Giants, 24–14," Bob St. John, *Dallas Morning News*, October 11, 1976

"Cards Flatten Cowboys 21–17," Roger Kaye, *Fort Worth Star-Telegram*, October 18, 1976

"Cowboys Throttle Bears; Roger Hurt," Bob St. John, *Dallas Morning News*, October 25, 1976

Sources

"Relentless Pokes Crush 'Skins 20–7," Roger Kaye, *Fort Worth Star-Telegram,* November 1, 1976

"Pokes Slay Giant—Sort of—by 9-3 Count," Roger Kaye, *Fort Worth Star-Telegram,* November 8, 1976

"Ray Jones: Cowboys' Court Jester," Sean Mitchell, *Dallas Times Herald,* November 14, 1976

"Cowboys Slide Past Redskins, 17–10," Bob St. John, *Dallas Morning News,* November 16, 1976

"Cowboys' Schramm Hits 'Artificial' Sellout of Bills Game," Michael Rabun, United Press International, November 17, 1976

"Falcons Fly Past Cowboys, 17–10," Bob St. John, *Dallas Morning News,* November 22, 1976

"Cowboys Escape by Fingertips, 19–14," Bob St. John, *Dallas Morning News,* November 26, 1976

"Cowboys Nail Down NFC East Title," Bob St. John, *Dallas Morning News,* December 6, 1976

"'Skins Do What They Have to—Rope 'Pokes (27–14)," Roger Kaye, *Fort Worth Star-Telegram,* December 13, 1976

"Cowboys Rammed Out of Playoffs," Bob St. John, *Dallas Morning News,* December 20, 1976

"It Was a Playoff Game?," Blackie Sherrod, *Dallas Times Herald,* December 20, 1976

"Staubach, Eight Enter Prep Hall of Fame," Joe Quinn, *Cincinnati Post,* December 25, 1976

"Customers Always Write," *Dallas Times Herald,* December 26, 1976

"Dallas Fan Learns Lesson," United Press International, January 19, 1977

"NFL Draft in Limbo," Roger Kaye, *Fort Worth Star-Telegram,* January 9, 1977

"Schramm's Solace Gift," Denne Freeman, Associated Press, January 13, 1977

"Duane Thomas: From Super Bowl to Bankruptcy," Bob St. John, *Dallas Morning News,* January 14, 1977

"Spittin' Image," Skip Bayless, *Los Angeles Times,* February 12, 1977

"New Agreement Keeps Air in Pro's Football," Bob St. John, *Dallas Morning News,* February 27, 1977

"They're Not Down in Dallas," Dave Brady, *Pro Football Weekly,* March 1, 1977

"Fans Still Want Staubach," Frank Luksa, *Dallas Times Herald,* March 13, 1977

"The Cowboy Name Game," Sam Blair, *Dallas Morning News,* March 16, 1977

"Football Fever," Jan Hubbard, *Beaumont Enterprise,* April 15, 1977

"Two Bits, Four Bits...," John Anders, *Dallas Morning News,* April 17, 1977

"Cowboys Draft Dorsett," Joe Carnicelli, United Press International, May 3, 1977

"Dallas Cheerleaders Don't Really Cheer But Cheered," Douglas Martin, *Wall Street Journal,* May 12, 1977

"Cowboys' Dorsett: Living with Fame, Comfortably," Mary Elson, *Dallas Times Herald,* July 10, 1977

"Cowboys Hope Promise Becomes NFL Reality," Frank Luksa, *Dallas Times Herald,* September 16, 1977

"Cowboys: The Sweet Madness Begins Anew," Mary Elson, *Dallas Times Herald,* September 17, 1977

"Field Goal or No, Cowboys Win, 16–10," Bob St. John, *Dallas Morning News,* September 19, 1977

"Cowboys Put Giants Back in Place," Bob St. John, *Dallas Morning News,* September 26, 1977

"Cowboys Outclass Tampa Bay 23–7," Roger Kaye, *Fort Worth Star-Telegram,* October 3, 1977

"Cowboys Win Bitter Struggle, 30–24," Bob St. John, *Dallas Morning News,* October 10, 1977

"Cowboys Skin Blitz for 34–16 Victory," Bob St. John, *Dallas Morning News*, October 17, 1977

"Cowboys' Remarks Make Allen Angry," *Fort Worth Star-Telegram*, October 22, 1977

"Special Teams Seal Cowboys' Triumph," Roger Kaye, *Fort Worth Star-Telegram*, October 24, 1977

"Harvey Martin Is After Your Money," Carlton Stowers, *Dallas Morning News*, November 4, 1977

"Cowboys Stretch Win Streak to Eight," Roger Kaye, *Fort Worth Star-Telegram*, November 7, 1977

"Hart's TD Passes Beat Cowboys, 24–17," Roger Kaye, *Fort Worth Star-Telegram*, November 15, 1977

"Harris, Steel Curtain Cast Cowboy Doubts," Roger Kaye, *Fort Worth Star-Telegram*, November 22, 1977

"Dallas Finds 14–7 Cure at Washington," Bob St. John, *Dallas Morning News*, November 28, 1977

"Cheer Ruse Draws Jeers," Barry Boesch, *Dallas Morning News*, December 2, 1977

"Records Fall as Cowboys Clip Eagles," Roger Kaye, *Fort Worth Star-Telegram*, December 5, 1977

"Cowboy Fans Miss Game to Grab Playoff Tickets," Steve Magagnini, *Dallas Times Herald*, December 5, 1977

"Dallas Outlasts 49ers in Slugfest, 42–35," Frank Luksa, *Dallas Times Herald*, December 13, 1977

"Cowboys Whip Broncos But Miss Out on Morton," Frank Luksa, *Dallas Times Herald*, December 19, 1977

"Fan's Party Costume Wraps Him in Flames," Ann McDaniel and Paul Hagan, *Dallas Times Herald*, January 2, 1978

"The Orange Crush," Mark Whicker, *Dallas Times Herald*, January 7, 1978

"'Pokes Just Not Dudes This Time," Gil LeBreton, *New Orleans Times-Picayune*, January 10, 1978

"Denver Hardly 'Blasé' About Super Bowl," Mark Whicker, *Dallas Times Herald*, January 10, 1978

"Henderson Dons Orange for Trip," Aaron Kyle, *Dallas Times Herald*, January 10, 1978

"Landry's Dad Still Remembers," *Dallas Times Herald*, January 11, 1978

"Rozelle to Explore Instant TV Replays," Gary Long, *Miami Herald*, January 14, 1978

"A Super (27–10) Cowboy Sunday," Donna Darovich, *Fort Worth Star-Telegram*, January 16, 1978

"Dallas Still the Biggest 'D' Doomsday Leaves Orange Crushed," Bob St. John, *Dallas Morning News*, January 16, 1978

"For Dallas, Super Victory No. II," Frank Luksa, *Dallas Times Herald*, January 16, 1978

"Cowboys, Followers Jazz It Up," Paul West, *Dallas Times Herald*, January 16, 1978

"Schramm vs. Rosenbloom," Frank Luksa, *Dallas Times Herald*, January 19, 1978

"A Calm in the Storm," Blackie Sherrod, *Dallas Times Herald*, January 27, 1978

Some Hither, Others Yon column, Blackie Sherrod, *Dallas Times Herald*, February 12, 1978

"Staubach Says Instant Replays Could Be Used," Associated Press, February 18, 1978

"Tex Schramm 0, Burglars 4," *Dallas Morning News*, March 2, 1978

"Anne Murchison's Wealth 'Worth Nothing Without God,'" Gwen Bushart, *Dallas Times Herald*, March 15, 1978

"Dallas' Dorsett Charged with Disorderly Conduct," *Dallas Morning News*, March 18, 1978

"Newsmen Also Have Responsibility to Athletes," Roger Staubach, *Houston Chronicle*, March 27, 1978

"Texas E. Schramm: Cowboy GM Wants to Be Remembered for Organizational Greatness," Hal Lundgren, *Houston Chronicle*, March 27, 1978

"'Learned My Lesson,' Dorsett Says," Lynn Callison, *Dallas Times Herald*, April 2, 1978

"Variety Spices Cowboys' Lives During Offseason," Roger Kaye, *Fort Worth Star-Telegram*, May 20, 1978

"More Need Staubach Image," Frank Boggs, *Colorado Springs Sun*, June 7, 1978

"Estate Bought by Murchison," *Dallas Morning News*, June 8, 1978

"Now About That Time You Beat the Vikings," Sheila Samples, *Lawton Cannoneer*, June 8, 1978

"NFL Call Letters Changed to S-E-X," Knight News Service, June 14, 1978

"Cracks Showing in 'Stone Face' Image," Roger Kaye, *Fort Worth Star-Telegram*, June 18, 1978

"Ask Tex Schramm," Steve Perkins, *Tulia Herald*, April 22, 1978

"Don't Try to Tell Me Dallas Has No Charm," Roddy Stinson, *San Antonio Express-News*, June 23, 1978

"Landry Given Super Bowl of Awards by Kiwanis," Michael Janofsky, *Miami Herald*, June 28, 1978

"Clint Murchison," Hal Lundgren, *Houston Chronicle*, July 17, 1978

"Meredith on Landry: 'Never Really Got to Know Him,'" Frank Luksa, *Dallas Times Herald*, July 17, 1978

"Herrera Talks But Still Balks," Carlton Stowers, *Dallas Morning News*, July 21, 1978

"Red Carpet Welcome for College Coaches," Tom Turbiville, *Irving Daily News*, July 27, 1978

"Cowboys' 'Party' Difference," Ronald Weathers, *Birmingham News*, July 30, 1978

"Herrera's, Cowboys' Offers $30,000 Apart, He Asks for Trade," Frank Luksa, *Dallas Times Herald*, August 3, 1978

"Texans Prime for Big Future," Cheryl Hall, *Dallas Morning News*, August 31, 1978

"Everybody Wants to See the Cowboys," Doug Bedell, *Dallas Times Herald*, August 31, 1978

"Bradshaw Shows Cowboys Who's Super," Frank Luksa, *Dallas Times Herald*, January 22, 1979

"Behind the Cowboy Struggle to Reach Super Bowl XIII," Mark Ribowsky, *Sport*, January 1979

"Times When Even Friends Can't Help," Sam Blair, *Dallas Morning News*, March 18, 1979

"Hayes 'No Criminal,'" *Dallas Morning News*, March 18, 1979

"Trying Times for Bob Hayes," Carlton Stowers, *Dallas Morning News*, March 26, 1979

"It Is All in Your Mind," Skip Bayless, *Dallas Morning News*, April 21, 1979

"Charlie Waters Tries Cashing In," *Dallas Times Herald*, May 27, 1979

"John Murchison Stricken, Dies After Collision," *Dallas Times Herald*, June 15, 1979

"Nurse Takes Last 'Fling,' Joins Crowd at Cheerleader Tryouts," Patti Kilday, *Dallas Times Herald*, April 24, 1979

"Charlie Waters: Teen-Age American's Reluctant Sex Symbol?," Skip Hollandsworth, *Dallas Morning News*, June 10, 1979

"Dorsett's Fiancée Dies Mysteriously," Doug Bedell, *Dallas Times Herald*, June 15, 1979

"Can the Cowboys Live Without Hollywood's Hooray?," Skip Bayless, *Dallas Morning News*, July 10, 1979

"New Commandments from Mount Landry," Skip Bayless, *Dallas Morning News*, August 2, 1979

"Roger Dodges Dandy's Doubts," Frank Luksa, *Dallas Times Herald*, August 1, 1979

"A Little Matter of Organization," Skip Bayless, *Dallas Morning News*, August 8, 1979

"Still Thinking About Pittsburgh," Galyn Wilkins, *Fort Worth Star-Telegram*, August 10, 1979

"Pat Toomay: Is He Washed Up or Bottled Up in the NFL?," Sam Blair, *Dallas Morning News*, August 12, 1979

"'America's Team' Isn't Just an Image," Sam Blair, *Dallas Morning News*, August 14, 1979

"Moralists Revel in Staubach's Success," Jim Murray, *Los Angeles Times*, August 19, 1979

"Brandt Picture Perfect for Cowboys Job," Jim Murray, *Dallas Times Herald*, August 19, 1979

"German Writer Finds Football 'Real War Game,'" Frank Luksa, *Dallas Times Herald*, August 19, 1979

"Entertaining, But Not Honest," John Wilson, *Houston Chronicle*, August 19, 1979

"'Dirty Dozen' Still a Cowboy Draft Legend," Blackie Sherrod, *Dallas Times Herald*, August 22, 1979

"Dallas Takes Two, Tangos," Carlton Stowers, *Dallas Morning News*, August 26, 1979

"In Dallas, the Cops Use Cowboys to Reach the Kids," Marcia Smith-Durk, *Dallas Times Herald*, August 28, 1979

"Clint Murchison: The Cowboys' Invisible Owner," John Meyer, *Dallas Times Herald*, August 31, 1979

"Dallas," Rich Koster, *St. Louis Globe Dispatch*, August 27, 1979

"Cowboys Busch-Whack Cards with Kick, 22–21," Carlton Stowers, *Dallas Morning News*, September 3, 1979

"How Much Longer for Ageless Staubach?," Jim Dent, *Fort Worth Star-Telegram*, September 2, 1979

"Mouth of the South Suddenly Has Grown Quiet," Frank Luksa, *Dallas Times Herald*, September 2, 1979

"'Awards Make Me Uneasy,' Admits Oft-Cited Staubach," Carlton Stowers, *Sporting News*, September 1, 1979

"World's 'Knock Off' Capital," Carlton Stowers, *Dallas Morning News*, September 5, 1979

"Hollywood Apologizes to Landry," Frank Luksa, *Dallas Times Herald*, September 8, 1979

"For Some, the Glitter of Hollywood Begins to Fade," Carlton Stowers, *Dallas Morning News*, September 9, 1979

"Cowboys Escape 49ers with 21–13 Victory," Frank Luksa, *Dallas Times Herald*, September 10, 1979

"The Celluloid Heroes of Pain," Joan Ryan, *SportSpectrum*, September 8, 1979

"Cowboys Sued by Norman," John Meyer, *Dallas Times Herald*, September 12, 1979

"Opponents Gain Ground on Dallas," Jim Dent, *Fort Worth Star-Telegram*, September 14, 1979

"Saint Roger: Something Amiss with the Myth," John Schulian, *Chicago Sun Times*, September 14, 1979

"Paying Homage to the Cowboys," Jim Dent, *Fort Worth Star-Telegram*, September 15, 1979

"Who's Who Isn't the Point of 'ND40,'" C. W. Smith, *Dallas Times Herald*, September 16, 1979

"Dallas' Win Comes to Pass Late, 24–20," Carlton Stowers, *Dallas Morning News*, September 17, 1979

"Browns Ruin Cowboys' Perfect Mark," Carlton Stowers, *Dallas Morning News*, September 25, 1979

"Why Do They Make It Look So Hard?," Carlton Stowers, *Dallas Morning News*, September 26, 1979

"Conspiracy?," Tony Kornheiser and Jane Leavy, *Washington Post*, September 28, 1979

"Cowboys Rush to Glory Over Bengals, 38–13," Frank Luksa, *Dallas Times Herald*, October 1, 1979

"Chief Landry Has Reservations for Cowboys," Carlton Stowers, *Dallas Morning News*, October 3, 1979

"Schramm Raps 'Socialistic' Scheduling," Jim Dent, *Fort Worth Star-Telegram*, October 4, 1979

"Dallas/Fort Worth Students Rank the Heroes," Julia Sweeney, *Dallas Times Herald*, October 8, 1979

"Dorsett, Big Plays Win for Dallas, 36–20," Frank Luksa, *Dallas Times Herald*, October 8, 1979

"Bob Hayes: Behind Bars But Not Bitter and Not Forgotten," Jim Dent, *Fort Worth Star-Telegram*, October 13, 1979

"Cowboys Embarrass LA, 30–6," Frank Luksa, *Dallas Times Herald*, October 15, 1979

"Cowboys the NFL's Classiest, Even Offices Imaginative," Michael Graham, *Cincinnati Post*, September 26, 1979

"'Pope Roger' an Indispensable Cowboy," Jim Dent, *Fort Worth Star-Telegram*, October 21, 1979

"Cowboys Mix, Master Cards, 22–13," Carlton Stowers, *Dallas Morning News*, October 22, 1979

"Steelers Have It Their Way All Day, 14–3," Frank Luksa, *Dallas Times Herald*, October 29, 1979

"Anne Murchison Found Clint, Oil Money and the Cowboys Weren't Enough—Without God," Connie Hershorn, *People*, October 29, 1979

"Cowboys Ruin Giant Effort at :03, 16–14," Frank Luksa, *Dallas Times Herald*, November 5, 1979

Some Hither, Others Yon column, Blackie Sherrod, *Dallas Times Herald*, November 11, 1979

"Eagles Erupt Early, Stave Off Cowboys," Jim Dent, *Fort Worth Star-Telegram*, November 13, 1979

"Redskins Hadn't Been Aware They Were So Good," Skip Hollandsworth, *Dallas Times Herald*, November 19, 1979

"Hollywood's Star Fades So Landry Waves Bye-Bye," Carlton Stowers, *Dallas Morning News*, November 20, 1979

"Hollywood's Image Proved His Undoing," Frank Luksa, *Dallas Times Herald*, November 21, 1979

"Gent: Henderson Wasn't a Corporation Man," Richard Justice, *Dallas Times Herald*, November 21, 1979

"In the American Grandstand with Hollywood," Bill Porterfield, *Dallas Times Herald*, November 21, 1979

"Oilers Keep Cowboys on the Skid," Jim Dent, *Fort Worth Star-Telegram*, November 23, 1979

"Cowboys Perk Up to Thrash Giants, 28–7," Frank Luksa, *Dallas Times Herald*, December 3, 1979

"Cowboys Fight Way into Playoffs, 24–17," Carlton Stowers, *Dallas Morning News*, December 9, 1979

"With Money on Line, Pearson Was There," Galyn Wilkins, *Fort Worth Star-Telegram*, December 17, 1979

"Texas NFL Teams Keep Women Reporters on the Outside," Dan Shaughnessy, *Washington Star*, December 16, 1979

"Gone, Yes, But What a Way to Go!," Dave Kindred, *Washington Post*, December 18, 1979

"'America's Team' Dies Hard," Dave Anderson, *New York Times*, December 18, 1979

"Rams' Big Plays Finish Cowboys, Dallas on Sidelines After 21–19 Defeat," Frank Luksa, *Dallas Times Herald*, December 31, 1979

"How Gauche, They're Serious About All This," Skip Bayless, *Dallas Morning News*, September 5, 1980

"Those Lot Points Don't Compute," Skip Bayless, *Dallas Morning News*, September 7, 1980

"Cowboys Ride Herd on 'Skins, 17–3," Carlton Stowers; "Joe, Washington Drown in Deep Waters of Dallas," Sam Blair, *Dallas Morning News*, September 9, 1980

"Cowboys Still Looking for Answers," Carlton Stowers, *Dallas Morning News*, September 14, 1980

"Denver Puts Orange Crush on Cowboys," Carlton Stowers, *Dallas Morning News*, September 15, 1980

"Cowboys String Up Buccaneers, 28–17," Carlton Stowers; "The Ghost of No. 12 Scrambles Out of Texas Stadium," Skip Bayless, *Dallas Morning News*, September 22, 1980

"White Saves Cowboys from Weak Defense," Carlton Stowers, *Dallas Morning News*, September 29, 1980

"Cowboys Take a 24–3 Victory Over Giants in 3-Ring Circus," Carlton Stowers, *Dallas Morning News*, October 6, 1980

"Fumbling 'Frisco Victim of Dallas' 59ers," Carlton Stowers, *Dallas Morning News*, October 13, 1980

"A Roundup of the Week Oct. 6–12," compiled by Craig Neff, *Sports Illustrated*, October 20, 1980

"Philly Fans Belly Up for a Double," Carlton Stowers, *Dallas Morning News*, October 20, 1980

"Schramm Pure Cowboy Blue Blood," Skip Bayless, *Dallas Morning News*, October 26, 1980

"Turnovers Key Dallas' Comeback," Carlton Stowers, *Dallas Morning News*, October 27, 1980

"White Rages Over Delay Calls," Carlton Stowers, *Dallas Morning News*, October 28, 1980

"White's Magic Turns Trick in 27–24 Victory," "Landry Believed Winning Pass Was Longshot Gamble," Carlton Stowers, *Dallas Morning News*, November 3, 1980

"Self-Inflicted Loss Wounds Cowboys," Carlton Stowers, *Dallas Morning News*, November 10, 1980

"A Roundup of the Week Oct. 27–Nov. 2," compiled by Craig Neff, *Sports Illustrated*, November 10, 1980

"Defense Born Again; Dallas Stings Cards," Carlton Stowers, "Pearson Passes Hayes as All-Time Cowboys Receiver," David Casstevens, *Dallas Morning News*, November 17, 1980

"A Roundup of the Week Nov. 3–9," compiled by Craig Neff, *Sports Illustrated*, November 17, 1980

"Cole Fuels Dallas in 14–10 Victory," Carlton Stowers, *Dallas Morning News*, November 24, 1980

"Cowboy Steamroller Buries 'Hawks, 51–7," Carlton Stowers, *Dallas Morning News*, November 28, 1980

"Cowboys Win Knots NFC East Race," Carlton Stowers, *Dallas Morning News*, December 8, 1980

SOURCES

"A Roundup of the Week Nov. 24–30," compiled by Craig Neff, *Sports Illustrated*, December 8, 1980

"It's Always Too Early to Count Out the Cowboys," Carlton Stowers, *Dallas Morning News*, December 14, 1980

"A Roundup of the Week Dec. 1–7," compiled by Craig Neff, *Sports Illustrated*, December 15, 1980

"Rams Better Cowboys in 38–14 Blitzkrieg," Carlton Stowers, *Dallas Morning News*, December 16, 1980

"A Roundup of the Week Dec. 8–14," compiled by Craig Neff, *Sports Illustrated*, December 22, 1980

"Cowboys' Victory Missed 'Spread,'" Carlton Stowers, *Dallas Morning News*, December 22, 1980

"Dallas Grabs Rams by Horns, 34–13," Carlton Stowers, *Dallas Morning News*, December 29, 1980

Coming of Age: The Story of the Dallas Cowboys 1970–74, written and edited by Bob Ryan, NFL Films Video, Mt. Laurel, NJ

America's Team: The Dallas Cowboys 1975–79, written and edited by Bob Ryan, NFL Films Video, Mt. Laurel, NJ

"Cowboys Drew Inside Straight, 30–27," Carlton Stowers; "Just Call It the 'Cowboy Mystique,'" Skip Bayless, *Dallas Morning News*, January 5, 1981

"A Roundup of the Weeks Dec. 15–28," compiled by Craig Neff, *Sports Illustrated*, January 5, 1981

"Tony D and Big D Laughed Last," Pat Putnam, *Sports Illustrated*, January 5, 1981

"Y-A-W-N, It's Just SO-O-O-O Hard to Be Humble, Y'all," John Crittenden, *Miami News*, January 10, 1981

"Where There's Wilber There's a Way; Eagle Defense Freezes Dallas Assets, 20–7," Carlton Stowers; "A Chill Settles over Tony D., Blue Cowboys," David Casstevens, *Dallas Morning News*, January 12, 1981

"And Now for the Rest of the Story," Frank Luksa, *Dallas Times Herald*, June 7, 1981

"'Air Age' Has Cowboy Defense Up in Arms; Secondary Problems Could Haunt Landry," Carlton Stowers, *Dallas Morning News*, September 3, 1981

"2-Way Battle Expected in NFC East" and "Prosperous NFL Faces New Problems," Bob St. John, *Dallas Morning News*, September 3, 1981

"Cowboys Clobber Redskins, 26–10," Carlton Stowers; "This Routine Was No Joke," Skip Bayless, *Dallas Morning News*, September 7, 1981

"Dallas Holds All the Cards," Carlton Stowers; "Signs of Cards' Downfall Clear to White," Don Greenberg; and "These Birds Couldn't Fly," Skip Bayless, *Dallas Morning News*, September 14, 1981

"Cowboys on a Roll, Stop Patriots," Carlton Stowers; "Dorsett Now No. 2 Cowboys Rusher," Dan Barreiro, *Dallas Morning News*, September 22, 1981

"Dallas Defense Slays the Giants," Carlton Stowers; "Cowboy Defense: Almost Great," David Casstevens, *Dallas Morning News*, September 28, 1981

"Looking for a Ringleader," Skip Bayless, *Dallas Morning News*, October 3, 1981

"Athletes and Writers Have Tenuous Working Setup," Skip Bayless, *Dallas Morning News*, October 4, 1981

"White Knight Has Dark Day," Skip Bayless; "Cardinals Give Dallas a Swift Kick, 20–17," Carlton Stowers, *Dallas Morning News*, October 5, 1981

"Dallas Blown Out, 45–14," Carlton Stowers; "Calling Dr. Freud," Skip Bayless, *Dallas Morning News*, October 12, 1981

"Loons Hate the Villains," Skip Bayless, *Dallas Morning News*, October 21, 1981

"Dallas Wins Shootout, 28–27," Carlton Stowers; "White Remained Confident Cowboys Would Pull It Out," Sam Blair; "Walls Is Out of This World," Skip Bayless, *Dallas Morning News*, October 26, 1981

"Cowboys Get Share of East Lead," Carlton Stowers, *Dallas Morning News*, November 2, 1981

"Swift Kick; Lions' FG at the Gun Drops Cowboys into Second," Carlton Stowers, *Dallas Morning News*, November 16, 1981

"Counting Blessings," Skip Bayless, *Dallas Morning News*, November 27, 1981

"It's Official: Cowboys Playoff Bound," Steve Pate, *Dallas Morning News*, December 1, 1981

"Cowboys Jolt Colts, 37–13"; "Pearson's Throw to Hill Sealed Fate," Gary Myers, *Dallas Morning News*, December 7, 1981

"An 'Expert' Admits It: Cowboys Are the Best Around," Skip Bayless; "Cowboys Capture NFC East Title," Gary Myers, *Dallas Morning News*, December 14, 1981

"Cowboys Fall in OT to Giants," Gary Myers, *Dallas Morning News*, December 20, 1981

"Jones' Pressure Grounds Bucs," David Casstevens; "Cowboys Storm into NFC Final," Gary Myers, *Dallas Morning News*, January 3, 1982

"Cowboys Shooting for a Super Future," Gary Myers, *Dallas Morning News*, January 10, 1982

"Cowboys Out, 28–27," Gary Myers; "Clark's TD Catch Designed for Solomon," Dan Barreiro; "Mystique Strikes Out," Skip Bayless, *Dallas Morning News*, January 11, 1982

"How Quickly the Fans Turn," Skip Bayless, *Dallas Morning News*, January 14, 1982

"Highs, Lows of Cowboy Salaries," Gary Myers, *Dallas Morning News*, February 23, 1982

"Tex Still Bleeding Blue for His Cowboy Heart," Frank Luksa, *Dallas Times Herald*, February 24, 1982

"The Davis Aftermath," Barry Boesch, *Dallas Morning News*, May 9, 1982

"War and Peace with Randy White," Dan Barreiro, *Dallas Morning News*, September 2, 1982

"Steel Curtain Closes on Cowboys," Gary Myers; "Steelers Smash the Mystique One More Time," Randy Galloway, *Dallas Morning News*, September 14, 1982

"Strike-Clouded Games Can't Stir Same Spirit," David Casstevens, *Dallas Morning News*, September 19, 1982

"Cowboys Make Light of Strike," Gary Myers; "NFL Issue Is Control, Not Money," Hal Bock, Associated Press, *Dallas Morning News*, September 21, 1982

"Ed Garvey, Tex Schramm Address Key Issues in Players' Strike," Gary Myers, *Dallas Morning News*, September 26, 1982

"Cowboys Strike Up with Victory; Dallas Trips Bucs, 14–9," Gary Myers; "Football Played Under a Cloud," Randy Galloway, *Dallas Morning News*, November 22, 1982

"Motivation: Is Money, Fear or Both Fueling Cowboys' Run at Super Bowl?," Gary Myers, *Dallas Morning News*, January 12, 1983

"The Football Dorsett Can't Forget," David Casstevens, *Dallas Morning News*, January 16, 1983

"Cowboys Hope to Keep Edge," Gary Myers, *Dallas Morning News*, January 18, 1983

"Redskins Superior to Cowboys," Gary Myers; "Day of Contrasts for Dallas QBs," David Casstevens; "Momentum Lost Along with White," Sam Blair; "Mistakes Crush Cowboys' Plan," Randy Galloway, *Dallas Morning News*, January 23, 1983

"America's Team Is Troubled," Randy Harvey, *Los Angeles Times*, July 28, 1983

Schramm Upset by Story Linking Cowboys to Drugs," Gordon Forbes, *USA Today*, August 23, 1983

"A Shining Knight No More," Gary Smith, *Sports Illustrated*, September 12, 1983

"Cowboys Would Miss Murchison," David Casstevens, *Dallas Morning News*, November 15, 1983

"Winds of Change Bound to Come," Blackie Sherrod, *Dallas Times Herald*, November 16, 1983

"Murchison Has Let Experts Do Their Jobs," Gary Myers, *Dallas Morning News*, November 20, 1983

"Heroes for Sale," Kent Demaret, *People* magazine, December 12, 1983

"Redskins to Cowboys: Hit the Road," Mark Blaudschun, *Dallas Morning News*, December 12, 1983

"The 'Boys Lost Poise," Paul Zimmerman, *Sports Illustrated*, December 19, 1983

"Cowboys Lose, to Face Rams in Playoffs," Gary Myers; "No Way to Get Ready for Playoffs," Randy Galloway, *Dallas Morning News*, December 20, 1983

"The Redskins Went on a Rampage," Ralph Wiley, *Sports Illustrated*, January 9, 1984

"NFL Clears Cowboys Sale," Jim Dent, *Dallas Times Herald*, March 20, 1984

"The Cowboys Owners," Gary Myers, *Dallas Morning News*, March 20, 1984

"New Owners Can Replace Schramm," Gary Myers, *Dallas Morning News*, March 21, 1984

"The Troubled Empire of Clint Murchison," David Zurawik and Warren Vieth, *Dallas Times Herald*, July 1, 1984

"Showing Off for the G.O.P.," David S. Jackson and Gregory Jaynes, *Time*, Monday, August 20, 1984

"Cowboys Hope Fast Start Will Erase Memories of '83" and "Bright Nervous About Opener," Gary Myers, *Dallas Morning News*, September 1, 1984

"Switching Signals," Sam Blair, *Dallas Morning News*, September 2, 1984

"Hogeboom's Hour," Gary Myers, *Dallas Morning News*, September 3, 1984

"Boomer Shows Why He's No. 1," Randy Galloway, *Dallas Morning News*, September 4, 1984

"Murchison Fights $100 Million in Creditor Dues," Bill Lodge, *Dallas Morning News*, September 9, 1984

"Redskins Dim Cowboys' Chances," Sam Blair, *Dallas Morning News*, December 10, 1984

"Cowboys KO'd in a Wild Finish," Gary Myers; "In the End, Dallas Is Just a 9-7 Team," Randy Galloway, *Dallas Morning News*, December 18, 1984

"Doomsday for Cowboys," Gary Myers; "Next Year Should Be Hogeboom's Turn," Randy Galloway; "A Talented Bunch Needs to Show Heart," David Casstevens, *Dallas Morning News*, December 27, 1984

"Cowboys' Bosses Split $5 Million," Gary Myers, *Dallas Morning News*, May 30, 1985

"America's Team Has Moved Westward," Art Rosenbaum, *San Francisco Chronicle*, September 3, 1985

"44–0: Bears Flatten Cowboys, Hand Them Worst Defeat," Gary Myers; "Wilson, Bears Expose Dallas' Lack of Attack," Randy Galloway, *Dallas Morning News*, November 18, 1985

"50–24: 'We Embarrassed Ourselves,'" Dan Barreiro; "Even Shrinks May Have Trouble Explaining Five-0," Randy Galloway, *Dallas Morning News*, December 9, 1985

"BIG ZERO: Cowboys Eliminated by Rams, 20–0," Gary Myers; "Disgraced and Angry Cowboys Need a Lot of Repair—and Fast," Randy Galloway, *Dallas Morning News*, January 5, 1986

"Cowboys' Soft Spots? Everywhere," Blackie Sherrod; "Cowboys Seek Help After Strange Season," Gary Myers, *Dallas Morning News*, January 6, 1986

"Cowboys Play Stiff Penalty, 17–14," Tim Cowlishaw; "Cowboys' Torch Passes in Silence as Thoughts Turn Toward Pelluer," Blackie Sherrod; "Pozderac's Jump Start Put on Hold," Randy Galloway; "White May Be Out for Season," *Dallas Morning News*, November 3, 1986

"Cowboys Planning No Overhaul for '87," Tim Cowlishaw, *Dallas Morning News*, December 21, 1986

"Bears Finish What They Started," Tim Cowlishaw; "Perfect End to

Dismal Year," Randy Galloway, *Dallas Morning News*, December 22, 1986

"The Cowboys, the Indian, and the Computer That Fumbled," Aaron Latham, *Texas Monthly*, September 1986

"The Cowboys: Still Not Loveable," *Detroit News*, September 14, 1986

"C. W. Murchison, Jr., Dies in Texas at 63," Peter H. Frank, *New York Times*, April 1, 1987

"'All I Could See Was a Blue Flame': 60-Yard Walker Run Stuns New England in OT, 23–17," Tim Cowlishaw; "Odds Are Fourth-and-Long on Landry Updating at QB," Randy Galloway, *Dallas Morning News*, November 16, 1987

"Cowboys' Losses Pile Up," Tim Cowlishaw; "Cowboys' Play Only Half Bad," Blackie Sherrod, *Dallas Morning News*, December 14, 1987

"Sports, Inc.," Richard Rosenblatt, Associated Press, July 25, 1988

"Cowboys Band Going 'Bigger' Time," Ladye Sparks, *Dallas Cowboys Official Weekly*, July 30, 1988

"Cowboys' Schramm Rips Cocaine Story," *Dallas Times Herald*, October 3, 1988

"Cowboys: Hard Not to Draft Aikman," Bernie Miklasz; "No Light at End of Tunnel," Blackie Sherrod; "Pelluer's Low Day Heightens QB Dilemma," Tracy Ringolsby; "Cowboys Lose Battle, Win Draft War," Bernie Miklasz, *Dallas Morning News*, December 18, 1988

"Jones Buys Cowboys, Fires Landry," Gary Myers, *Dallas Morning News*, February 26, 1989

"Jimmy Johnson Ideal Replacement for Landry," Bob West, *Port Arthur News*, February 26, 1989

"Metroplex Media in Attack Mode on Jimmy Johnson," Bob West, *Port Arthur News*, March 1, 1989

"A Chapter Closed," William Oscar Johnson, *Sports Illustrated*, March 6, 1989

"Big Changes in Big D: New Coach Jimmy Johnson's Game Plan Calls for a Different Brand of Cowboy Football," Paul Zimmerman, *Sports Illustrated*, March 20, 1989

"Cowboys: America's Team to Wonder About; New Owner His Own Man," Thomas C. Hayes, *New York Times*, July 23, 1989

"0 for September," Jarrett Bell, *Dallas Cowboys Official Weekly*, September 30, 1989

"Picks in Walker Deal Better Defined," Tim Cowlishaw, *Dallas Morning News*, October 14, 1989

"For Cowboys, 0-8 Was Enough," Marjorie Herrera Lewis, *Dallas Morning News*, November 6, 1989

"Cowboys Thwart Williams, Shock Redskins, 13–3," Tom Friend, *Washington Post*, November 6, 1989

"The Decade for Dallas," *Dallas Morning News*, December 9, 1989

"Cowboys Self-Destruct in Finale," Jim Souhan; "Finally, This Clunker of a Season Is Over," Blackie Sherrod, *Dallas Morning News*, December 25, 1989

"Jones' Broom Scored Close to Clean Sweep," David Casstevens, *Dallas Morning News*, February 5, 1990

"Ex-Owner Ready to Fire Landry Long Before Jones Did Deed," Randy Galloway, *Dallas Morning News*, February 26, 1990

"Cowboys a House of Cards," Mike Downey, *Los Angeles Times*, July 27, 1990

"Arkla's Day in Court (Arkla Inc.; Arkoma)," *Arkansas Business*, September 10, 1990

"Cowboys Step Out in Style, 17–14," Rick Gosselin; "Cowboys' Win Helps Put '89 Ghosts to Rest," Randy Galloway, *Dallas Morning News*, September 10, 1990

"Call It the WLAF or We LAF," Steve Hubbard, Scripps-Howard News Service, October 22, 1990

"Schramm: Personality Conflicts Led to Firing," Jim Dent, *Dallas Times Herald*, November 25, 1990

"Cowboys Hold the Cards," Rick Gosselin; "One Bump Removed from Wild-Card Road," Randy Galloway; "Sham, Hansen Hide Emotions in Probable Home Finale," Cathy Harasta; "Edge on

Contenders Boosts Dallas' Hopes," Tim Cowlishaw, *Dallas Morning News*, December 17, 1990

"Rookie Award a Bonus for Smith," Tom Shatel, *Dallas Morning News*, January 11, 1991

"Cowboys Rock Around Clock, 26–14," Rick Gosselin; "Grand Opening for Cowboys," Cathy Harasta; "Cowboys' Smith Shoulders the Load," Dan Noxon; "Turner Flies with Caution, Lands a Victory," Randy Galloway, *Dallas Morning News*, September 2, 1991

"Cowboys Streak into Playoffs, 31–27," Rick Gosselin, *Dallas Morning News*, December 23, 1991

"Mowed Down in Motown," Rick Gosselin; "Aikman's Comeback Has Disappointing Ending," Don Noxon, *Dallas Morning News*, January 6, 1992

"Deep Into His Job," Ed Hinton, *Sports Illustrated*, September 7, 1992

"The D Is Back in Dallas," *Sports Illustrated*, November 16, 1992

"Cowboys Win Pot in Low-Stakes Game; Smith Earns Rushing Title in 27–14 Win," Tim Cowlishaw, *Dallas Morning News*, December 28, 1992

"'How 'Bout Them Cowboys!' Cowboys Stand atop NFC, 30–20," Tim Cowlishaw; "Aikman, Johnson, Cowboys: All the Way Back from 1-15," Randy Galloway; "These Unflappable Upstarts Seem Older Than Their Peers," Blackie Sherrod, *Dallas Morning News*, January 18, 1993

"Schramm Recalls the Day the Bottom Fell Out," Kevin O'Keefe, *San Antonio Express-News*, January 17, 1993

"Oldest Cowboy Sails Alone into the Sunset," Sean Kirst, *Syracuse Post-Standard,* January 20, 1993

"Lean, Mean Money Machine—Jerry Jones Has Put the Silver and Blue Cowboys Back in the Black with an Amazing Financial Turnabout," Mitchell Schnurman, *Fort Worth Star-Telegram*, January 24, 1993

"Jones and New Coach Johnson Had Dinner at Landry's Favorite

Restaurant Mia's the Night Before Sale Was Finalized," *Los Angeles Times*, January 28, 1993

"Big D's Big Victory Brings Back Bragging Rights," Bud Kennedy, *Fort Worth Star-Telegram*, February 1, 1993

"Schramm Discovers He's Still a Cowboy at Heart," Frank Luksa, *Dallas Morning News*, February 1, 1993

"In 22 Seconds, the Rout Was On," Jimmy Burch, *Fort Worth Star-Telegram*, February 1, 1993

"Any Questions," Tim Cowlishaw, *Dallas Morning News*, February 1, 1993

"Looking Back—and Ahead—for Troy Aikman, His Four-Touchdown Super Bowl MVP Performance Was a Perfect Ending for the Season," Richie Whitt, *Fort Worth Star-Telegram*, February 7, 1993

"For Dallas, Violence Was a Reminder," Robert Camuto, *Fort Worth Star-Telegram*, February 14, 1993

"On the Road Again," Steve Rushin, *Sports Illustrated*, August 16, 1993

"Buffalo Swipes Victory from Cowboys, 13–10," Tim Cowlishaw; "With Smith, This One's a Runaway," Randy Galloway, *Dallas Morning News*, September 13, 1993

"Lett's Mistake Ices Cowboys," Ed Werder; "A Quick Slip Out of First Place," Blackie Sherrod, *Dallas Morning News*, November 26, 1993

"Running in the Rain," Tim Cowlishaw, *Dallas Morning News*, December 25, 1993

"Bring It All Home; Emmitt Plays Hurt, Leads Dallas to Title," Tim Cowlishaw, *Dallas Morning News*, January 3, 1994

"Sweet Georgia-Bound," Tim Cowlishaw; "'Niners Choke on Jimmy's Words," Randy Galloway; "Aikman Has Concussion, Should Be OK for Game," Ed Werder, *Dallas Morning News*, January 24, 1994

"IT'S OVER: Jones, Johnson Reach 'Mutual Decision' to Part," Tim Cowlishaw, *Dallas Morning News*, March 30, 1994

"OU Supporters Swell with Pride at Switzer's Return to Coaching,"
Ken Stephens; "Switzer Named Cowboys Coach," Tim Cowlishaw;
"Switzer Named Cowboys Coach—Complex Persona Has Ruled
Career," Doug Bedell; "Jones Makes His Role Clear—Switzer
Says He Won't Interfere," Ed Werder; "This Time, Switzer Must
Learn the Rules," Randy Galloway; "Whoever Is Coaching This
Team, Jones Will Spell Success with an 'I,'" Frank Luksa, *Dallas
Morning News*, March 31, 1994

"Hansen, Switzer Have Argument During Live Interview on Ch. 8,"
Barry Horn, Tim Cowlishaw, and staff writers, *Dallas Morning
News*, August 19, 1994

"Cowboys to Review Broadcasts—Sham, Hansen's Tone Bothersome
to Jones," Barry Horn, *Dallas Morning News*, August 25, 1994

"Cowboys Get Easy Win, Tough Loss," Tim Cowlishaw; "Switzer
Picks Wrong Time to Roll Dice," Randy Galloway; "What's Going
On with Brad Sham?," Barry Horn, *Dallas Morning News*,
November 8, 1994

"Reading the Troy Scale: QB Spots Silver Linings," Randy Galloway,
Dallas Morning News, November 27, 1994

"Lackluster Cowboys Lose Finale, 15–10," Tim Cowlishaw; "Hard
to Tell If Giants Won or Cowboys Lost," Frank Luksa, *Dallas
Morning News*, December 25, 1994

"The Enigmatic Coach," Stanley Marcus, *Dallas Morning News*,
December 20, 1994

"Cowboys Need a Dose of Jimmy," Randy Galloway, *Dallas Morning
News*, December 29, 1994

"Turnover at the Top; 49ers Take Title from Cowboys," Tim Cowlishaw,
Dallas Morning News, January 16, 1995

"COMMENTARY: Switzer, Cowboys Backed into Next Season,"
Mike Lupica, *Newsday*, January 22, 1995

"Oral History: Tom Landry," interviewed by Wes Wise and Bob Por-
ter, Sixth Floor Museum, Dallas, Texas, April 16, 1995

"Jerry Jones and Pepsi," ESPN *SportsCenter*, August 3, 1995

"Pepsi Challenge: Cowboys' Jones Signs Pact with Rival of Official NFL Sponsor Coca-Cola," Ed Werder, *Dallas Morning News*, August 4, 1995

"'Outlaw' Jerry Jones Offers Pepsi Plan for Welfare Reform," Randy Galloway, *Dallas Morning News*, August 4, 1995

"Dallas Cowboys' Stadium Ousts Coke, Despite N.F.L. Deal, and Gives Pepsi 'Pouring Rights,'" David Barboza, *New York Times*, August 7, 1995

"Fired-Up 49ers Leave Stunned Cowboys Gasping for Air at Texas Stadium," Thomas George, *New York Times*, November 13, 1995

"Ambushed—49ers KO Cowboys Early, 38–20," Ed Werder; "Jones Reaps What He Sows," Randy Galloway, *Dallas Morning News*, November 13, 1995

"Field Goal Is Giants-Killer; Cowboys Edge NY, 21–20," Dave Caldwell, *Dallas Morning News*, December 18, 1995

"Rising Above the Pack Cowboys Rule Green Bay, NFC Again," Ed Werder, *Dallas Morning News*, January 15, 1996

"These Cowboys Not Even Worthy of America's Envy," Thomas Boswell, *Washington Post*, January 21, 1996

"Switzer: Blake Told of Rumors About Aikman, Racial Tensions," Ed Werder, *Dallas Morning News*, January 26, 1996

"Aikman and Switzer—It's a Mess," Scott Ostler, *San Francisco Chronicle*, January 26, 1996

"Hansen Apologizes for On-Air Remarks," Barry Horn, *Dallas Morning News*, January 29, 1996

"Jones Successfully Buys NFL Crown," Dave Anderson, *New York Times*, January 29, 1996

"XXX-CELLENT!," Rick Gosselin; "Jones Magnanimous Following Victory," Dave Caldwell; "Irvin Surpasses Mark," Bill Nichols; "Return to Glory," Jean-Jacques Taylor, *Dallas Morning News*, January 29, 1996

"Jerry's Super Tent Is Celebration Station," Maryln Schwartz, *Dallas Morning News*, January 30, 1996

"Special Delivery: The Steelers Handed the Cowboys Two Ugly Interceptions and a 27–17 Victory," Michael Silver, *Sports Illustrated*, February 5, 1996

"Cowboys Cavalcade — 125,000 at Parade Hail Players As Conquering Heroes," Sherry Jacobson, *Dallas Morning News*, February 8, 1996

"White House Trip All Too Familiar for Cowboys," David Jackson, *Dallas Morning News*, February 14, 1996

"The NFL," Peter King, *Sports Illustrated*, February 19, 1996

"Cowboys Used Informant's Residence for Wild Sex, Drug Parties, He Says," Melissa Williams, Associated Press, May 9, 1996

"The Fallen Stars: Cowboys Used to Be Untouchable, but Offseason Troubles May Mean the Party's Over in Dallas," Bill Plaschke, *Los Angeles Times*, May 17, 1996

"Ethics, Fan Loyalty Tested as Michael Irvin Scandal Grows Darker," Kevin Sherrington, *Dallas Morning News*, July 1, 1996

"The Party's Over," Richard Hoffer, *Sports Illustrated*, July 8, 1996

"The Ringmaster of the Media Circus: Michael Irvin; the Dallas Cowboys Star Fumbles His Private Life, and the World Piles On," Skip Hollandsworth, *Texas Monthly*, September 1996

"Finally, Cowboys Show Some Signs of Life," Randy Galloway, *Dallas Morning News*, October 1, 1996

"Cowboys Try to Refocus on Playoffs," Timothy W. Smith, *New York Times*, January 2, 1997

"End of the Trail: Upstart Panthers Finish Cowboys' Season, 26–17," Dave Caldwell, *Dallas Morning News*, January 6, 1997

"Cowboys Do Provide a Super Ride," Scott Ostler, *San Francisco Chronicle*, January 10, 1997

"Result Positive, But Offense Gets Negative Marks," Frank Luksa; "Bears' Blitzes Stifle Emmitt, Run Game," David Moore, *Dallas Morning News*, September 29, 1997

"Final Daze: Switzer Says He Has Discussed Stepping Down for

New Role," Bart Hubbuch, *Dallas Morning News,* December 22, 1997

"Dallas Year in Review," Aline McKenzie, *Dallas Morning News,* December 28, 1997

"Cowboys' Fall Putting Hit on Retailers," Stacy Ann Thomas, *Dallas Morning News,* December 28, 1997

"The Man Who Gave Us America's Team," Greg Mazzola, *Coach and Athletic Director,* January 1998

"Switzer and the Cowboys: A Chronology," Barry Horn, *Dallas Morning News,* January 10, 1998

"Deadbeat," Thomas Korosec, *Dallas Observer,* January 15, 1998

"Gailey Cleaning 6-10 Wreckage," Randy Galloway, *Dallas Morning News,* July 23, 1998

"Standing at the Crossroads Aikman Knows This Season Will Mark Turning Point for Cowboys," David Moore, *Dallas Morning News,* September 1, 1998

"A Smashing Debut: Cowboys 38, Cardinals 10," David Moore, *Dallas Morning News,* September 7, 1998

"Losing Ground: Chiefs 20, Cowboys 17, Dallas Drops 3rd Straight," David Moore; "Cowboys Stuck in Reverse," Tim Cowlishaw, *Dallas Morning News,* December 14, 1998

"Cowboys Fall Flat in Playoffs"; "Sanders Can't Provide Cowboys Needed Shot in Arm," Jean-Jacques Taylor, *Dallas Morning News,* January 3, 1999

"The Five Years with Jimmy Were Stormy," *Dallas Morning News,* February 25, 1999

"Unable to Lead, Schramm Left Behind," David Moore, *Dallas Morning News,* February 25, 1999

"Landry's Image Is Solid Gold," David Moore, *Dallas Morning News,* February 25, 1999

"Cowboys Owner Jerry Jones Arrested," Associated Press, August 29, 1999

SOURCES

"'There's No Excuse for What We Did': Philadelphia Fans Criticized for Reaction to Irvin Injury," Associated Press, October 14, 1999

"The Ghost of Tom Landry," Pat Toomay, *Dallas Observer*, October 21–27, 1999

"Thrown for a Win: Cowboys 20, Eagles 10," David Moore, *Dallas Morning News*, December 13, 1999

"Cowboys Drop Ball in Playoffs, Defeat Sends Franchise into Off-Season of Uncertainty," Jean-Jacques Taylor, *Dallas Morning News*, January 10, 2000

"Relatives, Friends Bid Landry Farewell," Brooks Egerton and Selwyn Crawford, *Dallas Morning News*, February 17, 2000

"How H. L. Hunt Viewed Utopia," Rusty Cawley, *Dallas Business Journal*, September 22, 2000

"The King's Corner: My Two Cents," Peter King, *Sports Illustrated*, October 2, 2000

"Underwood Runs into Traffic," Sallie James, *South Florida Sun-Sentinel*, January 6, 2001

"The NFL: My Two Cents—Bob Stoops to Dallas? Forget It," Peter King, *Sports Illustrated*, October 22, 2001

"Quick Study," Richard Deitsch, *Sports Illustrated*, October 29, 2001

"1,000 Attend Service for Martin," Mike Jackson, *Dallas Morning News*, December 30, 2001

"The NFL: Dallas' Bright Spot," Peter King, *Sports Illustrated*, January 14, 2002

"Ex-Olympic Star, Cowboy Hayes Dies," Associated Press, September 19, 2002

"Cowboys Stun Rams with Last-Second Field Goal," Associated Press, September 29, 2002

"The Old Coach and the Sea," Linda Robertson, *Miami Herald*, 2002

"Rough Skies," Carlton Stowers, *Dallas Observer*, November 21, 2002

"Garcia, Owens Get It Done Against the Cowboys," Associated Press, December 8, 2002

"Spurrier Wins Finale Against Campo's Cowboys," Associated Press, December 29, 2002

"Jones Invites Schramm to Join Ring of Honor," Ken Sins; "Tex Schramm: Master Innovator," Bob St. John; "Press Box Never the Same Without Tex," Mike Rabun, *Dallas Cowboys Official Weekly* (May 2003)

"North Texas' Luxury Home Market Has Plenty of Room; Sales of High-Priced Properties Have Fallen During Tight Economy," Steve Brown, *Dallas Morning News*, June 22, 2003

"Cowboys Outfox Eagles to Move to 5-1," Associated Press, October 19, 2003

"Ride 'Em, Cowboy," Jeffri Chadiha, *Sports Illustrated*, October 27, 2003

"Passion's Been Hallmark of Hansen's 20-Year Stay — Channel 8 Tenure a Surprise, Even to the Veteran Sportscaster," Barry Horn, *Dallas Morning News*, November 2, 2003

"Eagles Pound Cowboys, Take NFC East Control," Associated Press, December 7, 2003

"Stallworth's TD Romp Beats 'Boys," Associated Press, December 28, 2003

"Host Panthers End Parcells' Turnaround Job," Associated Press, January 3, 2004

"Montana Hits Clark to Win NFC Championship," Rick Weinberg, ESPN.com, January 2004

"Bright Hasn't Attended a Game Since Team's Sale," Matt Mosley, *Dallas Morning News*, February 25, 2004

"Brandt Isn't Bitter, Still Remains Close to the Game," Matt Mosley, *Dallas Morning News*, February 25, 2004

"Trick Is Treat: Parcells' 'Boys Edge Gibbs' 'Skins," Associated Press, September 27, 2004

"Parcells Embarrassed After Bengals Bust 'Boys," Associated Press, November 7, 2004

"McNabb, Owens Help Eagles Soar in Big D," Associated Press, November 14, 2004

"Gone and Forgotten: The Dallas Texans of 1952," Thomas H. Smith in *Legacies: A History Journal for Dallas and North Central Texas*, Dallas Historical Society 17, no. 1 (Spring 2005)

"Barber's Record Night Helps Eli to First Win," Associated Press, January 2, 2005

"Redskins Dominate Cowboys, Keep Playoff Hopes Alive," Associated Press, December 18, 2005

"Cowboys Drop Season's Final Game to Rams," Associated Press, January 1, 2006

"Terrell Owens, Jerry Jones, Bill Parcells—the Odd Trio," Eric Williams, Yahoo! News, April 9, 2006

"SportsDay's Founder Didn't Use a Script," Barry Horn, *Dallas Morning News*, July 1, 2006

"Laying Down the Law," Michael Silver, SI.com, August 17, 2006

"Police: Owens Accidentally Overdosed; Cowboys WR May Play vs. Titans," Jaime Aron, Associated Press, September 28, 2006

"Giants Devour 'Boys' QBs, Take Over First in NFC East," Associated Press, October 23, 2006

"What Keeps Bill Parcells Awake at Night," Michael Lewis, *New York Times*, October 29, 2006

"Romo Off and Running, Rallies Cowboys Past Panthers," Associated Press, October 29, 2006

"Novak's Second Chance FG Caps Redskins' Comeback," Associated Press, November 5, 2006

"Romo, Cowboys Hand Cardinals Eighth Straight Defeat," Associated Press, November 12, 2006

"Burlington's Boy, Dallas' Hero," Gary D'Amato, *Milwaukee Journal Sentinel*, December 10, 2006

"Former QB Carter Arrested for Marijuana Possession," Jaime Aron, Associated Press, December 15, 2006

"Cowboys Lose to Lowly Lions," Associated Press, December 31, 2006

"Romo's Botched Hold Grounds Cowboys, Lifts Seahawks," Associated Press, January 6, 2007

"'Never Had I Been So Blind,' W. A. Criswell's 'Change' on Racial Segregation," Curtis W. Freeman, *Journal of Southern Religion* 10, 2007

"Terrell Owens on Bill Parcells," Memphis Bengal, *Sports Frog*, January 23, 2007

Herb Adderley E-mail to Abner Haynes, January 24, 2007

"Michael Vick—Time to Pay the Piper," Sportsdoc, *Sports Business News*, July 18, 2007

"Cowboys Open Phillips Era with Win Over Banged-Up Giants," Associated Press, September 9, 2007

"Cowboys Win in Phillips' Debut, Top Ailing Giants," Associated Press, September 9, 2007

"Dolphins Have Trouble Controlling the Ball as Cowboys Start 2-0," Associated Press, September 16, 2007

"Brady Lights Up Cowboys for Career-High 5 TDs in the Duel," Associated Press, October 14, 2007

"The Best of the Rest: Romo Not in Brady-Manning Class, But He's Doing Fine," Tim Layden, SI.com, October 18, 2007

"Watkins' TD Off Blocked Kick Delivers Boost for Cowboys," Associated Press, October 21, 2007

"Owens, Romo Highlight Cowboys' Punishing Win vs. Eagles," Associated Press, November 4, 2007

"Owens Pulls in Four TDs as Cowboys Heat Up After Half, Top 'Skins," Associated Press, November 18, 2007

"Cowboys Beat the Stuffing Out of Jets for Best 11-Game Start in Team History," Associated Press, November 22, 2007

"Romo, Witten Hook Up as Cowboys Clinch NFC East," Associated Press, December 8, 2007

"Skins Clinch Playoff Berth with Blowout of Cowboys," Associated Press, December 30, 2007

"Romo's INT Sends Eli, Giants to NFC Title Game," Associated Press, January 13, 2008

"Two Tales of One City: How Cultural Perspective Influenced the Framing of a Pre-Civil Rights Story in Dallas," Camille Kraeplin, *American Journalism*, Winter 2008

"Cowboys Fall Short on Last Effort as Giants Move On to Face Packers," Associated Press, January 13, 2008

"A Ch-Ch-Chilling Recollection of the Classic 'Ice Bowl,'" Frank Luksa, ESPN.com, January 15, 2008

"A Social History of the Dallas Blonde," Joe Bob Briggs, *D*, May 2008

"Danny Villanueva's Greatest Kicks...Then and Now," Ray Buck, *Fort Worth Star-Telegram*, June 6, 2008

"Cowboys' Jerry Jones Hopes Terrell Owens Can Keep the Popcorn Popping Next Three Seasons," Jim Reeves, *Fort Worth Star-Telegram*, June 6, 2008

"Dallas Cowboys WR Frank Clarke Went from NFL to Nanny," Albert Breer and Barry Horn, *Dallas Morning News*, June 29, 2008

"100 Greatest—Number 2 Player, Tom Landry," Jason McDaniel, *Valley Morning Star*, August 22, 2008

"Cowboys' Pacman Gets into Fight with Bodyguard at Dallas Hotel," Ed Werder and Matt Mosley, ESPN.com, October 8, 2008

"Best Local Daily Sports Columnist—Tim Cowlishaw," *Dallas Observer*, December 2008

"T.O., Cowboys, All Smiles After Defeating Giants," Associated Press, December 14, 2008

"Romo, Cowboys Hand Wild-Card Spot to Eagles; Sources: Romo Collapses in Shower After Eagles Clinch," Associated Press, December 28, 2008

"The Skip Bayless Interview Part I: Colorful, Conscious and Of Course, Controversial," Michael Tillery, Thestartingfive.net, February 23, 2009

"The Skip Bayless Interview Part II: Colorful, Conscious and Of Course, Controversial," Michael Tillery, Thestartingfive.net, March 10, 2009

"Valley Ranch Collapse: What Happened?," Cynthia Vega and Arnold Payne, WFAA TV, May 4, 2009

"For $1.15 Billion, Cowboys Get Braggin' Rights," David Barron, *Houston Chronicle*, August 22, 2009

"For Cowboys, the Regal Has Landed," Cedric Golden, *Austin American-Statesman*, August 22, 2009

"Double Dazzle: Lots of Flash in Stadium's Debut, Felix's Return," Tim Cowlishaw, *Dallas Morning News*, August 22, 2009

"A Winning Beginning: Cowboys Fans, Players Rave About New Stadium," Jeff Mosier, *Dallas Morning News*, August 22, 2009

"A 'Mind-Blowing' Stadium, 2 Tears of Joy, Cowboyritas and Very Happy Fans," Gordon Dickson and Susan Schrock, *Fort Worth Star-Telegram*, August 22, 2009

"Jerry Jones's Billion Dollar Blunder?," Toni Monkovic, *New York Times*, August 22, 2009

"On Football: Video Board Looms as 'Jerry's Folly' of 'Boys' Field," David Climer, *Nashville Tennessean*, August 23, 2009

"Football Fans at Cowboys Stadium's First Game Rave About Views," Scott Farwell, *Dallas Morning News*, August 23, 2009

"2 Dallas Cowboys: You-Know-Who Has Left Town, and Now Big D Looks to Homegrown Wideout Roy Williams to Make Some Noise," Andrew Lawrence, *Sports Illustrated*, September 7, 2009

"Clash of the Texans; Dallas' AFL Team Battled to Gain Fans, Respect; Cowboys, Texans Had a Civil War," Bill Nichols, *Dallas Morning News*, October 11, 2009

"Romo, Austin Hook Up for 2 Scores in Cowboys' Win," Associated Press, October 25, 2009

"Fine and Dandy: Half-Century After Signing Up for Pro Football, Don Meredith Still Has a Song in His Heart," Brad Townsend, *Dallas Morning News*, November 26, 2009

SOURCES

"Giants Beat Cowboys, Tighten East on Big Plays," Associated Press, December 6, 2009

"Cowboys Blank Eagles to Claim NFC East Title," Associated Press, January 3, 2010

"Cowboys Top Eagles for 1st Playoff Win Since '96," Associated Press, January 9, 2010

"Favre Throws 4 TDs as Vikings Trample Cowboys," Associated Press, January 17, 2010

"The 35 Biggest Pop Culture Moments in Modern Dallas History," D, January 2010

"Game Change: SMU Set New Course by Playing Against Black Athletes," Jeff Miller, *Dallas Morning News*, March 1, 2010

"Billy Graham Opens Texas Stadium," Brandon Formby, Irvingblog, *Dallas Morning News*, April 9, 2010

"Jerry Jones Reacts to Video: Comments Were 'Social Moment'; 'Kidding' About Parcells," Todd Archer, *Dallas Morning News*, April 16, 2010

"Mike Shanahan, Donovan McNabb Debut as Redskins Capitalize on Cowboys' Mistakes," Associated Press, September 12, 2010

"Cowboys Mistaken for Contenders," Calvin Watkins, ESPNDallas.com, September 13, 2010

"Jay Cutler, Bears Hand Cowboys First 0-2 Start Since 2001," Associated Press, September 19, 2010

"Rodgers, Packers Humiliate Rudderless Cowboys," Associated Press, November 7, 2010

"What Went Wrong: How the Dallas Cowboys' Field House Collapsed," Joe P. Hasler, *Popular Mechanics*, November 15, 2010

"Colts Drop Third Straight on Cowboys FG in OT," Associated Press, December 5, 2010

"Love 'Em or Hate 'Em, Cowboys Still America's Team," Jaime Aron, Associated Press, December 23, 2010

"Cowboys Edge Eagles to Finish 5-3 Under Garrett," Associated Press, January 2, 2011

"Only Real Negative for Garrett Is the GM Who Picked Him," Randy Galloway, *Fort Worth Star-Telegram*, January 4, 2011

"The Packers and the Steelers Broke the Hearts of the Cowboys," Judy Battista, *New York Times*, January 26, 2011

"Game Follows Season of NFL TV Ratings Success," Rachel Cohen, Associated Press, January 30, 2011

"Davis, Vick Top List of Most Disliked in Sports," Tom Van Riper, Forbes.com, January 31, 2011

"Pony Excess," Thaddeus D. Matula, *30 Films for 30 Years,* ESPN Television, February 2011

"Attention Incoming Sports Fans: If You're Going to Embrace Our City During Super Bowl Week, the First Step Is Recognizing Our Super Heroes," Richie Whitt, *Dallas Observer,* February 3, 2011

"The Dallas Cowboys: A Family Business," Gloria Campos, WFAA TV, February 3, 2011

"Guest List for Jerry Jones' Super Bowl Suite," Alan Peppard, *Dallas Morning News,* February 5, 2011

"This Super Bowl Earns a Grade of Big D," Ken Hoffman, *Houston Chronicle,* February 7, 2011

"A Super Mess: Seating Fiasco Leaves Ticket-Holders Angry," *Austin American-Statesman*, February 7, 2011

"1,250 Fans Displaced After Cowboys Stadium Failed to Have Seats Ready," Scott Farwell, *Dallas Morning News,* February 7, 2011

"Larger-Than-Life Dallas Is Barely Growing," Matt Stiles and Emily Ramshaw, *New York Times*, February 27, 2011

"Dallas Real Estate News: Terrell Owens Shedding Not One But TWO Azure Condos!," Candy Evans, SecondShelters.com, March 9, 2011

"Jerry Jones Plays the Role of Villain in the NFL Showdown," Randy Galloway, *Fort Worth Star-Telegram,* March 16, 2011

"Dez Bryant Warned After NorthPark Disturbance," Rebecca Lopez, Wfaa.com, March 22, 2011

"Ex-Cowboy Ron Springs Dies at Age 54," Clarence E. Hill Jr., *Fort Worth Star-Telegram,* May 13, 2011

"The Price Is Now Right: Troy Aikman Home Listed for $24 Million, Not $27.5," Candy Evans, Secondshelters.com, May 23, 2011

"Aikman's House for Sale for $24 Million," Natalie Solis, Myfoxdfw. com, May 23, 2011

"Aikman Changes Play at Property Line," Bruce Felps, NBCDFW. com, May 23, 2011

"Now Jean-Jacques Taylor; Is Dallas' Only Daily Being Wadded Up Before Our Very Eyes?," Richie Whitt, *Dallas Observer,* July 21, 2011

"Dallas Weighs Training at Home," Tom Orsborn, *San Antonio Express-News,* July 28, 2011

"NFL Notes," *Austin American-Statesman,* September 9, 2011

"New Pro Football Season Lifts NBC in TV Ratings," Associated Press, September 13, 2011

"Why Romo Isn't a Hopeless Case," Randy Galloway, *Fort Worth Star-Telegram,* September 15, 2011

"Romo's Heroics Earn Rave Reviews," Clarence E. Hill Jr., *Fort Worth Star-Telegram,* September 20, 2011

"Rangers Don't Mind Carving Own Niche in Football Town," Tim Madigan, *Fort Worth Star-Telegram,* October 8, 2011

"Al Davis: A Walking Controversy," Benjamin Hoffman, *New York Times,* October 9, 2011

"Austin Has 250 Receiving Yards, Two TDs in Victory," Associated Press, October 11, 2011

"2nd Place in the Division, and in the Heart of Texas," Jason Cohen, *New York Times,* October 23, 2011

"Can Stadium Sports Really Be Green?," Ian Gordon, Motherjones. com, October 24, 2011

"Even Against Series, Viewers Flock to the N.F.L.," Bill Carter, NYTimes.com, October 25, 2011

"Rob Ryan Lose Swagger? 'Uh, Hell, No,'" Tim MacMahon, ESPNDallas.com, November 4, 2011

"Can Professional Sports Do More Than Politics to Save the Planet?," Amanda Little, Forbes.com, November 15, 2010

"Romo Playing Best Football of His Career," Clarence E. Hill Jr., *Fort Worth Star-Telegram*, November 23, 2011

"December Demons Haunt Cowboys," Jean-Jacques Taylor; "Dallas Cowboys Still Control Own Destiny," Calvin Watkins; "Cowboys' Defense Crumbles vs. Giants," Todd Archer, ESPNDallas.com, December 12, 2011

"After Rough Start, Romo Finally Seems to Get It," David Moore, *Dallas Morning News*, December 19, 2011

"Cowboys Are What They Are, a Pretender," Gil LeBreton, *Fort Worth Star-Telegram*, January 2, 2012

"Cowboys Fold Again with Playoff on the Line, Fall to Giants," Clarence Hill Jr., *Fort Worth Star-Telegram*, January 2, 2012

"No Surprise: Cowboys' Swoon Is Complete," Jean-Jacques Taylor, ESPNDallas.com, January 2, 2012

"Garrett Whiffed on First Try to Bash Jones Curse," Randy Galloway, *Fort Worth Star-Telegram*, January 3, 2012

"Jerry Jones: GM Would Clutter Process," Tim MacMahon, ESPNDallas.com, January 3, 2012

"Terrell Owens, Wideout for the Allen Wranglers Tells GQ He's Nearly Broke," Bruce Tomaso, *Dallas Morning News*, January 23, 2012

"Cowboy Hall of Famer Tony Dorsett Suing NFL: 'They Use You Up,'" Associated Press, February 2, 2012

"Former Cowboys WR Terrell Owens Hit with Dallas Foreclosure Filings," Steve Brown, *Dallas Morning News*, February 27, 2012

"Grandmother, 55, to Audition for Dallas Cowboys Cheerleaders," Marisa Taylor, ABCNews.com, March 2, 2012

"Transcription of Dez Bryant's Mother's 911 Call," Jon Machota, *Dallas Morning News,* July 17, 2012

"Tony Romo Throws 2 TDs to Kevin Ogletree in Cowboys' Win over Giants," Associated Press, September 5, 2012

"Cowboys to Introduce 'Jerry Wipes' for Eyeglasses," Chris Chase, *USA Today,* September 13, 2012

"Seahawks Use Defense, Special Teams to Roll Past Cowboys," Associated Press, September 16, 2012

"Rapid Reaction: Cowboys 16, Bucs 10," Calvin Watkins, ESPNDallas.com, September 23, 2012

"Victoria's Secret Opening Shop in Dallas Cowboys Stadium," Lance Madden, *Forbes,* September 28, 2012

"Bears Return 2 of Tony Romo's 5 picks for TDs to Rumble to Victory," Associated Press, October 1, 2012

"Jones' Kick Return Lifts Ravens over Cowboys, 31–29," Associated Press, October 14, 2012

"Cowboys Stymie Cam Newton, Rally Past Panthers on Dan Bailey's FGs," Associated Press, October 21, 2012

"Home Loss to Giants Leaves Cowboys Dispirited and Fans Disgusted," Tom Spousta, *New York Times,* October 28, 2012

"Falcons Hold Off Cowboys, Remain Perfect," Associated Press, November 4, 2012

"Jerry Jones the Owner Says He Would Have Fired Jerry Jones the GM," Barry Horn, *Dallas Morning News,* November 4, 2012

"Vick Concussed in Eagles' Loss to Cowboys," Associated Press, November 11, 2012

"Dez Bryant Reaches Plea Deal on Mom Assault Charges," Rebecca Lopez, WFAA.com, November 15, 2012

"Browns Lose to Cowboys, 23–20," John Kuntz, *Cleveland Plain Dealer,* November 18, 2012

"Robert Griffin III's Triumphant Return to Texas," Dave Sheinin, *Washington Post,* November 25, 2012

"Cowboys Beat Eagles, Stay Alive in Playoff Race," Associated Press, December 2, 2012

"Grieving Cowboys Beat Bengals 20–19 on FG," Associated Press, December 9, 2012

"Cowboys Rally to Beat Steelers in Overtime," Associated Press, December 16, 2012

"Cowboys Fall in OT, but Still Control Playoff Fate," ESPN news services, December 23, 2012

"Alfred Morris-led Redskins Take NFC East, Eliminate Cowboys," Associated Press, December 30, 2012

"Romo, Cowboys Do What They Do Best...Fail," Randy Galloway, *Fort Worth Star-Telegram*, December 30, 2012

"Cowboys Season: Game-by-Game Recap," staff, *Fort Worth Star-Telegram*, January 5, 2013

BOOKS

The Lusty Texans of Dallas. John William Rogers. New York: Dutton, 1951.

The Super-Americans. John Bainbridge. New York: Doubleday, 1961.

The Key to Dallas. Lon Tinkle. Philadelphia: J. B. Lippincott Company, 1965.

The Hundred Yard War: A Novel of Professional Football. Gary Cartwright. Garden City, NY: Doubleday, 1968.

Next Year's Champions: The Story of the Dallas Cowboys. Steve Perkins. Cleveland: World Publishing Company, 1969.

Dallas Cowboys: Pro or Con? Sam Blair. Garden City, NY: Doubleday, 1970.

The Dallas Cowboys and the NFL. Donald Chipman, Randolph Campbell, and Robert Calvert. Norman: University of Oklahoma Press, 1970.

The Dallas Texans' Saga—or At the Time the New York Yanks Became the Baltimore Colts. Giles E. Miller. Dallas: Gemco Press, 1972.

Sources

The Dallas Cowboys' Super Wives. Bobbi Field. Austin: Shoal Creek Publishers, 1972.

The Dallas Cowboys: Winning the Big One. Steve Perkins. New York: Grosset and Dunlap, 1972.

North Dallas Forty. Peter Gent. New York: Morrow, 1973.

The Crunch. Patrick Toomay. New York: Norton, 1975.

Dallas Yesterday. Sam Hanna Acheson. Dallas: Southern Methodist University Press, 1977.

Staubach: First Down, Lifetime to Go. Roger Staubach with Sam Blair and Bob St. John. Waco: Word Books, 1978.

Wheeling and Dealing: Confessions of a Capitol Hill Operator. Robert "Bobby" Gene with Larry L. King. New York: W. W. Norton and Company, 1978.

Dallas Rediscovered: A Photographic Chronicle of Urban Expansion, 1870–1925. William McDonald. Dallas: Dallas County Historical Society, 1978.

1979 Greater Dallas City Directory, volumes 1 and 2. Southfield, MI: R. L. Polk and Company, 1978.

The Man Inside Landry. Bob St. John. New York: Avon Books, 1979.

Dallas Cowboys Wives' Cookbook and Family Album. Compiled by Mary Breunig. Fort Worth: Higgins Printing Company, 1979.

The Dallas Cowboys Wives' Family Fitness Guide and Nutritional Cookbook. Compiled by Mary Breunig. Fort Worth: Higgins Printing Company, 1981.

Dallas: An Illustrated History. Darwin Payne. Woodland Hills, CA: Windsor, 1982.

Journey to Triumph: 110 Dallas Cowboys Tell Their Stories. Carlton Stowers. Dallas: Taylor Publishing Company, 1982.

Bob Lilly: Reflections. Bob Lilly and Sam Blair. Dallas: Taylor Publishing Company, 1983.

Dallas USA. A. C. Greene. Austin: Texas Monthly Press, 1984.

The Cowboy Chronicles: A Sportswriter's View of America's Most Celebrated Team. Carlton Stowers. Austin: Eakin Press, 1984.

The Dallas Cowboys: The First Twenty-Five Years. Carlton Stowers. Dallas: Taylor Publishing, 1984.

The Semi-Official Dallas Cowboys Haters' Handbook. Mark Nelson and Miller Bonner. New York: Collier Books, 1984.

Any Given Sunday. Patrick Toomay. New York: Donald I. Fine, 1984.

The Accommodation: The Politics of Race in an American City. Jim Schutze. Secaucus, NJ: Citadel Press, 1986.

Tex! The Man Who Built the Dallas Cowboys. Bob St. John. Englewood Cliffs, NJ: Prentice Hall, 1988.

Once a Cowboy. Walt Garrison with John Tullius. New York: Random House, 1988.

The Landry Legend: Grace Under Pressure. Bob St. John. Dallas: Word Publishing, 1989.

The Murchisons: The Rise and Fall of a Texas Dynasty. Jane Wolfe. New York: St. Martin's Press, 1990.

God's Coach: The Hymns, Hype, and Hypocrisy of Tom Landry's Cowboys. Skip Bayless. New York: Simon and Schuster, 1990.

Texas Big Rich. Sandy Sheehy. New York: William Morrow and Company, 1990.

The Dallas Cowboys Wives' Cookbook. Compiled by the Dallas Cowboys' Wives. Fort Worth: Branch-Smith, 1991.

Gordon McLendon: The Maverick of Radio. Ronald Garay. Santa Barbara, CA: Greenwood Publishing Group, 1992.

The WPA Dallas Guide and History. Edited by Maxine Holmes and Gerald D. Saxon. Denton: University of North Texas Press, 1992.

Classic Clint: The Laughs and Times of Clint Murchison, Jr. Dick Hitt. Plano: WordWare Publishing, 1992.

The Boys. Skip Bayless. New York: Simon and Schuster, 1993.

Turning the Thing Around: Pulling America's Team Out of the Dumps—And Myself Out of the Doghouse. Jimmy Johnson as told to Ed Hinton. New York: Hyperion, 1993.

Stars and Strife: Inside the Dallas Cowboys' Reemergence as America's Team. Mike Fisher. Fort Worth: Summit Group, 1993.

Shoot for the Star: An Inspiring Story of Beating the Odds to Fulfill a Lifelong Dream. Bill Bates with Bill Butterworth. Dallas: Word Publishing, 1994.

King of the Cowboys: The Life and Times of Jerry Jones. Jim Dent. Holbrook, MA: Adams, 1995.

Hell-Bent: The Crazy Truth About the "Win or Else" Dallas Cowboys. Skip Bayless. New York: HarperCollins, 1996.

Things Change. Troy Aikman with Greg Brown. Dallas: Taylor, 1996.

The Dallas Cowboys Encyclopedia: The Ultimate Guide to America's Team. Jim Donovan, Ken Sins, and Frank Coffey. Secaucus, NJ: Citadel Press, 1996.

Cowboys Have Always Been My Heroes: 1960–1989. Peter Golenbock. New York: Warner Books, 1997.

Cotton Bowl Days: Growing Up with Dallas and the Cowboys in the 1960s. John Eisenberg. New York: Simon and Schuster, 1997.

All the Rage: The Life of an NFL Renegade. Charles Haley with Joe Layden. Kansas City: Andrews McMeel Publishing, 1997.

Michael Irvin. Richard Rosenblatt. Philadelphia: Chelsea House Publishers, 1997.

I Hate the Dallas Cowboys: And Who Elected Them America's Team, Anyway? Edited by Bert Sugar. New York: St. Martin's Griffin, 1997.

Drew Pearson Tells His Own Story. Audio book. Waco: Athletic Achievement Corporation, 1998.

Mamas, Don't Let Your Cowboys Grow Up to Be Babies. Michael Holmes. Toronto, Canada: ECW Press, 1998.

Landry: The Legend and Legacy. Bob St. John. Nashville: Word Publishing, 2000.

I Remember Tom. Denne Freeman and Jamie Aron. Champaign, IL: Sports Publishing, 2001.

SOURCES

Hello, Darlin'. Larry Hagman. New York: Simon and Schuster, 2001.

Texas Sports Writers: The Wild and Wacky Years. Bob St. John. Plano: Republic of Texas Press, 2002.

Blood, Money and Power: How LBJ Killed JFK. Barr McClellen. Springdale, AR: Hannover House, 2003.

Dallas Cowboys Stadium Stories: Colorful Tales of America's Team. Brad Sham. Guilford, CT: Globe Pequot, 2003.

Texas Literary Outlaws. Steven L. Davis. Fort Worth: TCU Press, 2004.

The Island Remembers Great Foods and Good Times at Spanish Cay, a Private Bahamas Paradise. Burk Murchison and Beryl Hutchinson. Plano: Five Points Press, 2004.

Ladies and Gentlemen, the Bronx Is Burning: 1977, Baseball, Politics, and the Battle for the Soul of a City. Jonathan Mahler. New York: Farrar, Straus and Giroux, 2005.

White Metropolis: Race, Ethnicity, and Religion in Dallas, 1841–2001. Michael Phillips. Austin: University of Texas Press, 2006.

Cowboys Essential: Everything You Need to Know to Be a Real Fan. Frank Luksa. Chicago: Triumph Books, 2006.

Never Just a Game: Tex Schramm. Bob St. John. Denton: AWOC Publishing, 2006.

The Man Who Would Not Shut Up: The Rise of Bill O'Reilly. Marvin Kitman. New York: St. Martin's Press, 2007.

Playing to Win: Jerry Jones and the Dallas Cowboys. David Magee. Chicago: Triumph Books, 2008.

Land of the Permanent Wave: An Edwin "Bud" Shrake Reader. Steven L. Davis. Austin: University of Texas Press, 2008.

Spare Time in Texas: Recreation and History in the Lone Star State. David G. McComb. Austin: University of Texas Press, 2008.

Juanita Dale Slusher aka Candy Barr. George A. Day. Austin: ERBE Publishing, 2009.

The Big Rich: The Rise and Fall of the Greatest Texas Oil Fortunes. Bryan Burrough. New York: Penguin Press, 2009.

SOURCES

The Water Boy: From the Sidelines to the Owner's Box; Inside the CFL, the XFL, and the NFL. Bobby Ackles with Ian Mulgrew. Hoboken, NJ: Wiley, 2008.

Greater Dallas Directory, 63rd edition, volumes 1 and 2. Cole Cross Reference Dictionary. Omaha, NE: Cole, 2010.

America's Team: The Official History of the Dallas Cowboys. Jeff Sullivan; foreword by Jerry Jones. Dallas: Insight Editions, 2010.

Index

795